W9-DFD-687

PATTERNS IN
AMERICAN
HISTORY

Volume 2

Volume 2

PATTERNS IN
AMERICAN
HISTORY

ALEXANDER DE CONDE
University of California, Santa Barbara

ARMIN RAPPAPORT
University of California, Berkeley

WILLIAM R. STECKEL
The University of Wyoming

WADSWORTH PUBLISHING COMPANY, INC.
Belmont, California

Fifth printing: August 1968

L.C. Cat. Card No.: 65–14831

Printed in the United States of America

S ince these two volumes, which combine extensive editorial commentary with selected readings, differ noticeably from most anthologies of American history, an explanation of their structure and what we have sought to do may be helpful. Our structure is basically thematic. We have tried to show that American history can be analyzed and understood by means of patterns, or topics, that have a measure of order and unity. We believe that there are significant themes which the college student should encounter on more intimate terms than is possible in the textbook, that these themes can provide a sound basis for teaching and for class discussion, and that they should be studied in depth through both interpretive and narrative literature—though we usually prefer the interpretive over the descriptive. With these ideas in mind, we have organized each chapter around a significant theme. Since there are thirty chapters and the usual course in American history covers an academic year of about thirty weeks, each chapter or topic offers material that can fit into one week's work in such a course.

PREFACE

Our introductions in each chapter, which are considerably longer than those found in most anthologies, constitute a unique feature of the book. These introductions show the unity in the topic; they help the reader by explaining significant themes, or by guiding him to a discovery of themes, of pervasive points of view, or of clashing interpretations; and they offer some insight on historical method and analysis. In the editorial commentaries preceding each selection, we have been guided by similar principles. In addition, we have stressed points that may serve as a departure for class discussion; and we have often included significant biographical data on the author of a selection, believing that this data will help the reader see historical writing in a context of scholarship.

We have sought to provide authoritative, stimulating, and enlightening selections, always with the view of introducing the reader to some of the best thinking in American historical literature. Although the main thread or unifying theme is the usual political one, we have tried to create variety and balance with readings that stress other aspects of American history, such as the economic, the diplomatic, the social, and the intellectual. We think our treatment of such themes as the nation's geographical foundations, war as a social institution, and the intellectual problems in agrarianism and urbanism point up elements or connections in the mainstream of American development that have frequently been neglected in books of readings.

Since our purpose is to stimulate ideas and interpretations rather than to be concerned with the mechanics of scholarship, we have omitted the footnotes that frequently appear in the original selections. We do not consider the footnotes unimportant, however; we believe they are valuable, and hope that some readers will have their intellectual appetites whetted enough to go to the larger works from which many of the selections come.

In Volume 1, Professor Steckel assumed the major responsibility for Chapters 1–10 and Professor DeConde for 11–16; in Volume 2, Professor DeConde for Chapters 1–4 and Professor Rappaport for 5–14.

A.D.
A.R.
W.R.S.

CONTENTS

5   THE NEW MANIFEST DESTINY, 179

6   PRAGMATISM, 215

7   THE PROGRESSIVE ERA, 247

8   THE FIRST WORLD WAR, 289

9   THE 1920s IN LITERATURE, 343

10   THE GREAT DEPRESSION, 385

11 THE NEW DEAL, 439

12 THE SECOND WORLD WAR, 501

13 THE COLD WAR, 551

14 MIDCENTURY, 589

PATTERNS IN
AMERICAN
HISTORY

Volume 2

Historians generally agree that from the end of the Civil War to the beginning of the twentieth century, the business leader—extolled as a symbol of individualistic capitalism—emerged as the dominant figure in American society. He, rather than the politician, the man of letters, or the theologian, came to occupy the highest rung on the ladder of status. To many, at that time and since, he was the essence of the Gilded Age. Almost all segments of society paid obeisance to his ideals, and in the highest circles of government there were men eager to offer him homage.

This prominence of the businessman in the Gilded Age grew from pre-Civil War roots. Since colonial days he had held an important place in American society, but the primitive state of technology had limited his opportunities to amass wealth. With the coming of the industrial revolution and its stimuli, the business leaders gained access to vastly expanded sources of profit. Although the pre-industrial entrepreneur was experienced mainly in commerce, he was willing, even eager, to expand his activities to take advantage of the new money-making opportunities.

1

INDUSTRIAL AMERICA AND THE BUSINESSMAN

The new opportunities came in the 1830's with the advent of railroads and the diffused use of factory machinery. This decade witnessed broad economic expansion and an increase in profits. Fortunes in business pyramided, and as they did so the political and social influence of the business leader began to rise. By 1850, bankers, manufacturers, and railroad men were gaining control over the politics, as well as the economy, of states on the Atlantic seaboard such as Massachusetts, New York, and Pennsylvania. By 1860 the United States was already a maturing industrial state. By 1890, for the first time, the value of manufactured goods exceeded that of agricultural products, even though farm output was at a record high and increasing yearly. During this latter period of accelerated industrial revolution, the wealth of the entrepreneurial leaders increased with stunning rapidity, and their political and economic power spread over the nation.

This pervasive influence of the industrial leader, which replaced that of the planter and farmer, reflected the deep change that transformed not only the surface of America but also its social structure. Massive and rapid industrialization created an empire of great cities linked by railroads and telegraphic communication. Within these cities grew a new materialistic middle class, which glorified success in business and wedded itself to the uniformities and abundance of mass production. The essence of industrial America became success expressed in money and physical

1

possessions; such success was the measure of human achievement. Even religious leaders preached that material success provided outward evidence of an inward moral character. Success and the business leader, in effect, became synonymous, and the business of America, apparently, was business.

The new materialism had a deeper social significance. The aggressive, hard-driving entrepreneurs contributed to the building of a confident America, one with a glowing faith in perpetual growth. This worship of success, this striving for wealth and position—at least to the extent that it was based on the idea that all men could succeed—enhanced the American belief in social equality and actually assisted in maintaining an open society.

On the other hand, many historians have considered the moral code of material success extremely shallow and therefore devoid of merit. The cost of industrialization in America, they have insisted, was unnecessarily high in wasted lives and resources. There is truth in this view, but we should also remember that the cost in America was no higher, and was probably lower, than in other emerging industrial nations, such as Japan and Russia in the nineteenth and twentieth centuries, where people lacked the abundance produced by capitalistic industries controlled by the businessman.

As for the business leader of the Gilded Age, historians as well as contemporaries have both condemned and praised him. Critics have held him responsible for concentrated wealth and mass poverty, for class cleavages and conflicts, for urban slums and rural depression, and for wide and frightening fluctuations of the business cycle. Many have questioned his business and political tactics, his social ethics, and the means he used to achieve his dominant position. Even by the standard of his own day, it has been argued, the most successful businessman has seemed the most ruthless.

The concept of the robber baron sprang from this viewpoint. Critics held that no great fortune could be accumulated by wholly honest means. The entrepreneurs of the Gilded Age made their fortunes, it was said, by robbing and cheating investors and consumers, by manipulating securities, by appropriating the capital entrusted to their care to their own use, by accumulating capital through fraud, and by corrupting government. They were, in other words, predators, moneyed barbarians, robber barons cast in a medieval mold who acquired wealth not by producing goods and services for profit but by plundering society and brawling among themselves.

Early defenders of the entrepreneurs rejected this analysis. They called businessmen the captains of industry. In recent years, students of entrepreneurial history have re-evaluated business leadership, and their scholarship also has challenged the robber-baron interpretation. They have conceded that the businessman rose to dominance in an age of corruption, but they have stressed his material contributions to the building of the nation. These giant entrepreneurs, it is argued, were not merely capitalists who supplied money; they were men who possessed a genius for industrial production. By bringing together in a working relationship the resources of a nation, the labor of millions, and the capital of the Western world, they built American industry. They helped transform America from an agrarian land to the world's greatest industrial nation; they were the ones who brought Americans an economy of abundance.

In defense of the morality of the barons, it has been pointed out that they were men of their time and culture. Their ethics, their tactics, and their objectives were no different, no more materialistic than those of ordinary men. They differed only in their ambition, energy, vision, and zeal for profit. They were not alone in their lust for wealth. The desire to pile up riches possessed all Americans. The entrepreneurs were not the only ones who exploited resources or speculated in property. If the industrial leader, therefore, truly embodied the ideals of his time, to villify him is to condemn the society that nurtured him.

Two aspects of the role of the businessman in the Gilded Age are thus clear: he had a vital part in shaping modern America, and his historical image is a controversial one. It is important, therefore, to take a close look at him; to try at least to understand him and his place in history. The selections in this chapter explain the circumstances that raised the businessman to pre-eminence; they show what kind of a person he was and they analyze his ideas and ideals.

Thomas C. Cochran and William Miller

The Triumph of Industrial Enterprise

The following selection, written by two leading students of entrepreneurial history, describes the industrial order that emerged from the Gilded Age. It analyzes business practices and institutions in this period of vast economic growth and rapid technological innovation without glossing over accompanying waste of precious resources and inefficiency in the use of the new technology. It explains how tooth-and-claw competition gave way to cooperation in business enterprise and how entrepreneurial individualism was succeeded by industrial combination. In other words, the selection provides a broad social analysis of the America that bred the giant entrepreneurs. It tells us how the industrial businessman gained success and why that success brought him leadership in American society. [Reprinted with permission of the publisher from The Age of

Enterprise: A Social History of Industrial America *by Thomas C. Cochran and William Miller. Copyright 1942 by The Macmillan Company.*]

For half a century before 1860, American industrialists had been altering the course of American history. Their corporations had affected property relations, their machines had revolutionized conditions of labor, their locomotives and telegraphs had speeded the pace of American life, their railroads had begun to draw outlying rural areas into the orbits of great cities. At every stage these changes had been resisted by sovereign planters and their commercial allies, until, at last, on the battlefield, their ranks were broken, their influence destroyed. Times had changed in America and in the world since 1800, mainly because of the impact of *industrial enterprise.* It was not strange, therefore, when the revolution came that industrialists should carry the mace of authority.

Traditional language had no words to describe the business activities of the new leaders after the Civil War, no words to define the functions of their institutions. Traditional politics could not cope with their demands, nor could traditional law harness them to social welfare. In place of the old canons, they imposed the rule of the jungle upon a willing people who worshiped at the altar of "Progress." Remorselessly they exploited precious resources, stripping incomparable forests, leaving gaping holes in mountain sides to mark exhausted mines, dotting with abandoned derricks oil fields drained of petroleum and natural gas. In reckless haste they constructed railroads through the wilderness and immense factories to supply the needs of millions yet unborn. They promoted many similar projects simply to mulct a nation of speculators for the private benefit of the "Fittest."

With magnificent optimism these industrial leaders plunged forward for thirty years in Olympian combat among themselves for the spoils of the land and the people. Gradually, however, a new order began to emerge out of the chaos of brutal competition. Entrepreneurs were learning the profitable lessons of specialized and standardized production, of geographical concentration of plants, of centralized management. Corporations at war were learning that combination was a surer way to wealth and power. Above all, a small number of investment bankers were acquiring interests in great properties against which they had loaned large fortunes only to see them dissipated by wildcat managements, or to which they had extended liberal credit on condition that they participate in control. The nerve centers of the proliferating system, by the early 1890's, thus were becoming fewer and more complex, the instruments of control more centralized, the managers a select class of professional corporation directors. In the struggle for survival, competition had yielded to cooperation, individualism to combination. Corporations, in an age of gigantic personalities, had become super-persons, as incorporeal as angels and as little amenable to punishment, in mysterious ways directing the life of the new society, but seemingly outside its laws.

Railroad Imperialism. As industrial capitalism spread over Europe in the late nineteenth century and even across the world to Japan, Frenchmen, Germans, Belgians, Dutch, Italians, Russians, and Orientals joined the English who had preceded them in seeking raw materials, cheap labor, and free markets in Asia, Africa, and the uncharted islands of the seas. American industrialists, however, blessed with a fabulously rich continent of their own, a political system fashioned to their order, a legend irresistibly attractive to impoverished aliens eager to work for the meanest subsistence only to breathe the free air of the United States, did not have to venture so far afield. In America, obstacles were fewer, opportunities infinitely greater, than elsewhere in the world. Need we seek other explanations for the extraordinary vitality of our industrialism?

First to operate on a grand scale in the new atmosphere of business enterprise were American railroad men, and they made the greatest fortunes. Vigorous, violent, and corrupt, they showed by their accumulations of wealth that their business methods were best suited to the conditions of their time and place. Their contributions to the Gilded Age, however, were not limited to techniques of exploitation. Though they chased the Indian from western valleys and fertile plateaus, they peopled his territories with Europeans, orientals, and emigrants from eastern states, with farmers and cattlemen who improved the land and laborers who helped them in their tasks. To eastern imperialists they opened mines in Colorado, Nevada, Idaho, and Montana, and timberlands in Minnesota, Washington, Oregon, and California, where nature for countless millennia had stored prodigious wealth. On river shores and crossroads in the wilderness, they laid the cornerstones of future cities. From the Missouri, the Mississippi, and the Great Lakes, over the Rockies, Sierras, and Cascades, they joined in indissoluble union with older commonwealths the Pacific tier of states, ending the threat of other powers to our "continental destiny."

Between 1867 and 1873, more than 30,000 miles of new track were opened to traffic in the United States; and by 1893, though more than eight years of depression intervened, 150,000 miles had been laid since the war. Capital invested in American railroads jumped in this period from two to nearly ten billion dollars. Though most of this mileage and most of this capital went to complete old trunk lines and their links to new centers in the valleys of the Ohio, Mississippi, and Missouri, the most spectacular of all the roads and perhaps the most important were the transcontinentals. These really blazed the trail of American industry in the Gilded Age, gave great impetus to lesser western railroad building, and set the fashion in methods of construction and finance. These gave the nation its heroes, its Stanfords, Huntingtons, Hills, and Cookes, as well as its villains in the Crédit Mobilier and other construction companies. These were the governments within governments, the owners of executives, legislators, and judges, the leviers of taxes, the arbiters of the destiny of cities, counties, states, industries, and farms.

We need seek no further for the key to the power of American railroad men when we realize that in an age of corruption they knew best how to use their opportunities; that in a country of tremendous distances they were gaining a monopoly of long-haul transportation; that in regions where wealth was mainly land they were cornering the best of it. The promoters of the transcontinentals as well as lesser railroads spent millions in Washington, state capitals, county seats, and city halls to get land grants, loans and subsidies, and then spent millions more to maintain their grants inviolate. The Union Pacific, for instance, between 1866 and 1872 handed out $400,000 in graft; the Central Pacific, as late as the decade between 1875 and 1885, distributed $500,000 annually. Part of this went to fight water competition, to win rich mail contracts, to riddle with restrictions and objections bills for river and harbor improvements. Most of it, however, went to make private capital out of the public domain. When the fury of competitive building had run its course in the West and depression shrouded the countryside after 1893, it was found that railroads had been granted one-fourth of the whole area of Minnesota and Washington, one-fifth of Wisconsin, Iowa, Kansas, North Dakota, and Montana, one-seventh of Nebraska, one-eighth of California, and one-ninth of Louisiana. It was found that in 1872, to meet the demands of the Southern Pacific, Los Angeles County had donated the equivalent of a $100 tax on each of its six thousand inhabitants; that Superior, Minnesota, in 1880, had granted one-third of its "lands, premises and real estate" as well as a right of way to get the Northern Pacific to run through it; that between 1867 and 1892 forty-three sparsely settled Nebraska counties had voted almost $5,000,000 to railroad companies some of which never built a mile of track.

All told, Congress, in twenty-one grants between 1862 and 1872, chartered to the railroads 200,000,000 acres of land, of which, for one reason or another, slightly more than half actually came into their possession. In addition, federal loans to railroads totaled $64,623,512, the bulk of which went to the Union and Central Pacific. State land grants and state loans were even greater in the aggregate, and a few cities and counties which had not repudiated their liabilities remained in debt even in the twentieth century for railroad bonds issued in the seventies and eighties. All these subsidies supplied far from sufficient capital to build the roads to which they were granted and to yield as well an acceptable profit to the promoters. By using such grants to guarantee private loans, however, the promoters were able to supplement public gifts with private capital. Even so, they had their difficulties in raising money. Americans enriched by the war were finding other investments more attractive than transcontinentals that took seven to sixteen years to build, more attractive than shorter lines that traversed as yet untenanted western deserts. On the other hand, foreign rentiers who were eager to invest in booming America demanded higher interest rates than promoters generally cared to offer. Thus even with the support of public grants, the promoters were forced to sell their securities well below par, the Union Pacific, for instance, issuing $111,000,000 worth of bonds for $74,000,000 in cash.

Such practices burdened the roads with excessive capitalizations, forced them to charge high rates to service their debts, left them vulnerable to complaints of shippers at monopoly points and to cutthroat competition in shared territories from lines less speculative in conception and more economically constructed.

Though they encountered many difficulties in raising capital, *promoters* of the transcontinentals and other land-grant railroads, once having accumulated it, had little difficulty in making money. Many great American fortunes have been accumulated not by producing goods or supplying services but by manipulating securities and diverting to personal uses the *capital* these securities nominally represent. We have seen how Drew milked into his own bucket the construction funds of the Erie. Of that company's stock, Jay Gould testified before a court in 1869: "There is no intrinsic value to it, probably; it has speculative value; people buy and sell it, and sometimes they get a little too much." Another time, he said: "The Erie won't be a dividend-paying road for a long time on its common stock." Yet out of Erie, dilapidated and bankrupt as it frequently was, Gould and Fisk made their first millions. By similar methods, the promoters of the transcontinentals and other railroads compensated themselves for their public services. Instead of taking competitive bids, they formed themselves into construction companies and voted themselves the contracts for construction work and equipment. As directors of construction companies they billed their railroads at exorbitant rates; as directors of railroad companies, they gladly paid what was asked. Thus railroad capital was turned into construction profits, public money into private fortunes. Besides cash they paid themselves millions in stock for which there was no immediate market. As building steadily progressed, however, and buyers for such stock were found in Wall Street and on exchanges in other great cities in the East and Middle West, these tokens for speculation netted their holders hundreds of millions of dollars.

Since the government granted lands and loans only as mileage was completed, it put a premium upon speed in construction and length of track. The result was that almost all of the land-grant railroads were poorly built along the most tortuous paths. Within fifteen years after they were completed almost all of them had to be rebuilt to eliminate needless curves, shifting roadbeds, splintering "sleepers" and spreading rails too light to bear the weight of the engines. Thus besides supplying the land and the cash with which the roads were built, and paying rates based on notoriously high capitalizations and taxes to service railroad bonds issued by their governments, the people were soon burdened with new charges to make their roads usable even at minimum efficiency. Those roads that could not attract new capital after their promoters had diverted the original construction funds to their personal use were left to rot. . . .

If the promoters of the land-grant roads were corrupt or crooked according to the moralists of their age, it was mainly because, in an age of private enterprise and the competitive pursuit of profit, they could not otherwise have completed their tasks. If private corporations had to build the western railroads, they could hardly have been expected to do so without making a profit. Since there was little traffic while the roads were being built, profits had to be found from other sources. Through the construction companies, they were taken out of capital. Because that capital had been supplied by public agencies, or by private investors only with public grants as collateral, a hue and cry was raised when this practice was revealed. The crime of the railroad profiteers, however—if crime it may be called—was not that they, as great speculators, milked an army of little speculators either directly or through venal politicians. Their crime was that they built poor roads. It was not so much that their construction operations cost about 100 per cent more than was warranted by expenses for labor, materials, and reasonable dividends; it was that for all this expense the nation got a very extensive but very shaky railroad system.

The Industrial Scene. Though the new railroads were attracting swarms of cheap labor to the United States, opening up vast markets and incredible resources in mines and forests, they were also causing competitive havoc in other industries by their policies of rebates, "midnight tariffs," drawbacks, and special concessions. Such favoritism and secrecy, said the Cullom Senate committee in 1886, "introduce an element of uncertainty into legitimate business that greatly retards the development of our industries and commerce." And speaking of the period before 1887, Carnegie himself declared: "Railway officials, free from restrictions, could make or unmake mining and manufacturing concerns in those days."

Despite their subjection to such practices, however, American industrialists soon outstripped all rivals. By 1893, New England alone was producing manufactured goods more valuable per capita than those of any country in the world. In the manufacture of timber and steel, the refinement of crude oil, the packing of meat, and the extraction of gold, silver, coal, and iron, the United States surpassed all competitors. America had more telephones, more incandescent lighting and electric traction, more miles of telegraph wires than any other nation. In specialties like hardware, machine tools, arms, and ammunition, she retained the leadership assumed before the Civil War, while her pianos as well as her locomotives had become the best in the world.

In any age, this would have been a towering performance; in an age wedded to "bigness," it made an impression so profound that, even in the doldrums of the middle seventies, few cared to question the right of the industrial businessmen to leadership. Americans had much to complain of in this early age of industrial enterprise, and their most frequent complaint was of hard times. Yet there was no questioning of the "system," no lessening of faith in entrepreneurial leadership. This was an age of consistently falling prices, a period shaken by three financial panics and a severe depression of seven lean years. It closed on the precipice of another. Yet industrialists were certain that Civilization was safe in their hands, that their methods were those of God and Nature and were in the end as infallible. With their record of physical achievement to boast of and the unassailable authority of Spencer to support them, they had little difficulty convincing the nation they were right.

In the nineteenth century, depressions were viewed simply as the results of errors of judgment that would not be repeated. They were regarded merely as periods of penance for economic sins, and recovery was expected as soon as rituals of liquidation and reorganization could be performed. Thus, instead of destroying hope, depressions paid dividends for faith. They presented opportunities to expand and modernize plants at the lowest cost, to corner raw materials at bottom prices, to capture customers with attractive schedules of rates and deliveries. It was in the seventies that Carnegie built his first steel plant, that Rockefeller organized his oil monopoly, that Armour and Morris built their meat-packing empires, that the Comstock Lode was exploited and Boston capitalists began to finance Bell's telephone.

Of all the undeveloped regions in the world claiming the capital of English and European rentiers, the United States in the late nineteenth century remained the most attractive, not least because of this resiliency of her leaders after shocks of war, bankruptcies, repudiations, and bursting bubbles. In 1871 alone, $110,000,000 of American securities were marketed in London; and though American failures in the depression of the seventies cost Europeans about $600,000,000, by 1893, when a new debacle was impending, we owed abroad some $3,000,000,000. Most of this, to be sure, was in government, railroad, and mining securities, but it released proportionate amounts of American capital for use in industry and agriculture. It allowed Carnegie, for instance, to pour his savings back into steel with the assurance that he would have coal with which to make it and railroads to deliver it. It allowed Rockefeller to devote his energies to petroleum refining and Armour his capital to dressing and packing beef and pork, certain as they were that others would furnish transportation for them.

Perhaps even more important was the stimulus this great debt gave to American enterprise. As our borrowings increased, interest upon them grew proportionately. To meet annual payments, we had to export more and more goods. Just as our tremendously expanding economy was attracting European funds, so service charges for the use of these funds were further stimulating expansion. Since farm products composed most of our exports, it was agriculture that grew fastest under this pressure. To industry, however, it meant greater orders for iron and steel to manufacture farm machinery and to build and maintain railroads in expanding farm areas. It meant extravagant demands for coal and timber for fuel and construction. Starting in these basic industries, it stimulated expansion in every other kind of commodity production. It created in confident America an overwhelming faith in perpetual growth, leaving us at the same time ever more intricately involved in international finance.

Just as we were beckoning capital from abroad, so were we inviting foreign ideas in science and invention and cheap labor to put these ideas to work. International capitalism was creating a world-wide exchange of patents and processes stimulated by expositions, fairs, new trade and technical journals, and foreign travel by businessmen of all nations. The *Commercial and Financial Chronicle* published its first number in 1865. The American Iron and Steel Association *Bulletin* first appeared in 1867. Early in the seventies, Pillsbury and other northwestern millers went to Europe and brought back from Hungary the roller process for making grain. At the same time Carnegie went to England and was converted to Bessemer's method for making steel. In 1867 the United States sent commissioners and exhibitions to the Paris International Exposition and captured many prizes. Nine years later, in the midst of the depression, we held our Centennial in Philadelphia, where the industrial and commercial exhibits were the greatest ever seen.

For all its tremendous records of physical growth and technical innovations, however, for all its magnetic attractiveness to capital and eager receptivity to new ideas, this iron age of American culture was marked from the start by gross inefficiency and waste. Its catalogue of great inventions fails to disclose any social Bessemer system to blow out the impurities of competition or any blueprint for scientific management to harness the potentialities of monopoly. To contemporaries, these deficiencies seemed but the results of partial adaptation to the new industrial environment. It is clear now that the costliness of competitive *laissez faire* was a defect of its qualities, and not simply the result of temporary conditions that would ultimately disappear.

In the three decades after the Civil War, as confident entrepreneurs raced to take advantage of every ephemeral rise in prices, of every advance in tariff schedules, of every new market opened by the railroads and puffed up by immigration, they recklessly expanded and mechanized their plants, each seeking the greatest share of the new melon. The more successful they were in capturing such shares and the more efficient they were in promptly satisfying the market, however, the greater was the number of buildings and machines left idle when the new market approached the saturation point and the rate of expansion declined. The result was that all the competitors were left with the problem of amortizing their new buildings and machines precisely at the time when the operation of those new buildings and machines was unable any longer to produce a profit. They were left with great plants, the symbols of great ambitions and with great silences in those plants to mourn their most recent failures. That was true of the whisky industry in which stills overbuilt in moments of prosperity were operated generally at no more than 40 per cent capacity. It was true of the iron industry in which, as the *Bulletin* of the American Iron and Steel Association said in 1884, "Indeed it might almost be rated the exception for half the works in condition to make iron to be in operation simultaneously." It was true in the manufacture of stoves, as the president of the National Association of Stove Manufacturers complained in 1888. "It is a chronic case," he said, "of too many stoves, and not enough people to buy them." And it was true even of the manufacture of bread, as the vice president of the National Millers Association also in 1888 informed his members. "Large output, quick sales, keen competition, and small profits are characteristic of modern trade," he declared. . . .

Pools, Trusts, and Corporations. Far from being "the life of trade," competition by the last decades of the nineteenth century had reduced efficiency in business, had encouraged colossal waste of natural resources, plant capacity, capital. It had not only destroyed many companies but had decimated the incomes even of those powerful enough to weather from time to time the periodic unbalancing of freely competitive markets. As conditions for such firms in any industry went from bad to worse and even the most liquid among them came to be threatened with destruction, their managers naturally sought some escape from the perils of cutthroat competition. Somehow, order had to be maintained among the anarchists of industry or imposed upon them from outside. Since businessmen feared government regulation even more than they had come to fear competition, their lobbyists, in the popular name of *laissez faire,* neatly eliminated the state as a possible peacemaker. Left to themselves, however, industrialists managed only to devise new schemes to devour one another. It was not until the 1890's, when large corporations had become as prominent in manufacturing as they had been for half a century in railroading, and private bankers thus could impose order in exchange for essential credit, that umpires of adequate stature were found to regulate industrial strife. Until that time, trade agreements, associations, and pools were made and remade only in the end to be broken.

Pools, or pooling agreements administered by trade associations, attempted to limit competition in many ways—by controlling output, by dividing the market among member firms, by establishing consolidated selling agencies, and later by controlling patents. Their object was artificially to keep prices at a profitable level. Their ultimate effect, because of constant breakdowns and reorganizations, was to increase the severity of price movements, thus dislocating business more than stabilizing it.

Unlike the cartels in Germany, where the government itself participated in the agreements, the pools in America, as in England, had no standing in common or statute law. They were obviously in restraint of trade, as restraint was interpreted by classical economists and Spencerian philosophers, and thus had to depend upon the good will of the members to attain their objectives. In a competitive society, this proved to be a precarious foundation. As we saw in the case of the New England Railroad Association of 1851, gentlemen's agreements only put a strain upon the integrity of the gentlemen who made them, tempting them secretly to evade their commitments the better to make profits. "A starving man will usually get bread if it is to be had," said James J. Hill, "and a starving railway will not maintain rates." . . .

Pools were a natural refuge for individuals who fought to keep as much of their independence as possible in situations calling desperately for cooperation. They began to disintegrate as soon as emergencies seemed to have passed, but, as in the whisky industry, such recurrent lapses into free competition brought also the recurrence of its evils, ultimately forcing businessmen to seek a more stable form of cooperative enterprise. It was in such situations that industrial trusts were formed.

The trust was a device through which the stock of many competing corporations was assigned to a group of trustees in exchange for trustee certificates, ownership remaining in the same hands as before, management now being concentrated in a single board of directors. Trusts could appear only in a society in which the corporation had become the dominant type of business organization, in which property rights were represented not by land or other physical assets, but by negotiable paper easily convertible into other types of negotiable paper. As a business organization the trust was really identical with a large corporation though it was created by different legal contrivances and functioned under somewhat different laws. The Standard Oil Company set the trust pattern in 1879, and so effectively did it operate under this new type of business enterprise that in the next decade appeared the Cottonseed Oil Trust, the Linseed Oil Trust, the Salt Trust, the Lead Trust, the Leather Trust, the Cordage Trust, and the Sugar Trust, until by the 1890's the term "trust" was applied invidiously to every seeming monopoly. In 1894, Henry Demarest Lloyd could write:

> In an incredible number of the necessaries and luxuries of life, from meat to tombstones, some inner circle of the "fittest" has sought, and very often obtained, the sweet power which Judge Barrett found the sugar trust had: It "can close every refinery at will, close some and open others, limit the purchases of raw material (thus jeopardizing, and in a considerable degree controlling, its production) artificially limit the production of refined sugar, enhance the price to enrich themselves and their associates at the public expense, and depress the price when necessary to crush out and impoverish a foolhardy rival.

In whisky, salt, vegetable oil, leather, and other commodities, trusts were evaded as long as possible. In a few lines like petroleum refining, meat packing, and steel, however, where strong leaders had the perspicacity to see the trend of the times before it bludgeoned them into submission and where they had the vigor and unscrupulousness to apply their foresight, trusts and giant corporations were forcibly imposed upon lesser competitors despite their stubborn resistance. John D. Rockefeller was easily the most outstanding among these leaders. . . .

Rockefeller had little use for half measures. When he went into oil, he gave up his other interests. When he set out to organize Cleveland refiners, he tackled "the largest concerns first." When dependence upon railroads became too troublesome and expensive, he built his own pipe lines. When producers of crude oil combined against him, they found that he had cornered transportation facilities. When he embarked upon retail distribution, he undersold great wholesalers and little grocers until they either became his agents or collapsed. When he extended his empire beyond the borders of the United States, he employed in competition with alien companies the same rigorous price policies that had proved so profitable at home.

Rockefeller abhorred waste. Having first eliminated it from every nook and cranny of his own business, mainly by vertical integration and complete utilization of by-products, he was ready to attack it in the entire oil refining industry and thus give scope to his imperial ambitions. Aided by the panic of 1873 and the ensuing long depression, by 1879 he had accomplished his objective.

As early as 1867, Rockefeller had become the greatest refiner in Cleveland and had extracted his first rebate from the Lake Shore & Michigan Southern Railroad. With this club he pounded into submission his Ohio competitors, and by 1872 he was ready to battle refiners in New York, Pittsburgh, and Philadelphia. Before the panic of 1873 they resisted him; but once the debacle came they were less unwilling to join the Standard or abdicate in its favor. Rockefeller's managerial genius had prepared his firm to weather any financial storm, and the strength of his position enabled him to demand from the railroads the greatest rebates on his own freight payments, and drawbacks from the rates paid by other refiners. No company could long resist an opponent so well armed, and by 1879 Rockefeller controlled about 90 per cent of America's refining industry. By 1877, with the aid of the New York Central and Erie railroads, he had crushed the efforts of Tom Scott of the Pennsylvania to enter the refining business; and in 1884, by building his own pipe lines, he forced into submission the Tidewater Pipeline Company, the last of his competitors.

Expansion meant economy, said Rockefeller, and in pursuit of economy he was relentless. He was hated by his contemporaries for his methods, but it was chiefly because he was more adept than they at using means that lay to his hand. By 1879, he said,

we had taken steps of progress that our rivals could not take. They had not the means to build pipe lines, bulk ships, tank wagons; they couldn't have their agents all over the country; couldn't manufacture their own acid, bungs, wicks, lamps, do their own cooperage—so many other things; it ramified indefinitely. They couldn't have their own purchasing agents as we did, taking advantage of large buying.

In a society which strove to apply the laws of individualism to the activities of corporations, Rockefeller found plenty of company among the successful seekers after loopholes and evasions. As always, business conditions in the Gilded Age were changing faster than the legal system; and, being ever in the van among businessmen, Rockefeller was generally more than two jumps ahead of the law. . . .

Much more ebullient than Rockefeller was Andrew Carnegie, and it was quite in character that while the oil nabob's genius was management Carnegie's was salesmanship. Nevertheless, they often used similar methods to achieve like results. Both were wonderfully astute in selecting the right men for the right jobs and pushing them to the limit of their capacities. Both abhorred pools, being the best competitors in their lines and needing no protection. And both believed in the justice of monopoly. "Pullman monopolized everything," wrote Carnegie after he had successfully merged the Woodruff and Pullman sleeping-car companies in 1869. "It was well that it should be so. The man had arisen who could manage and the tools belonged to him." In pressing their pursuit of order and organization both scrupled little over methods, making the ends justify rebates, drawbacks, and, if occasion required, violence. And in achieving their ends, both were materially aided by the panic of 1873. In the depression that followed, Carnegie said afterward,

so many of my friends needed money, that they begged me to repay them. I did so and bought out five or six of them. That was what gave me my leading interest in this steel business.

When other iron moguls were waiting for the depression to run its course, Carnegie was erecting his model rail factory at Braddock's Field, and just as Rockefeller was capturing the refining business from his less efficient rivals, so Carnegie was capturing the market for steel from under the noses of his competitors. On terms of perfect intimacy with Gould, Vanderbilt, Huntington, and Sidney Dillon, he "went out," as he said, "and persuaded them to give us orders."

By 1890, Carnegie had "obtained almost absolute control of the steel-rail business in the Pittsburgh district." In 1892, all his holdings were consolidated into the Carnegie Steel Company, capitalized at $25,000,000 and composed of the former Edgar Thomson Steel Works, and Duquesne Steel Works, the Homestead Steel Works, the Union Mills, the Beaver Falls Mills, the Lucy Furnaces, and the Keystone Bridge Company. In addition the new corporation owned coal and iron mines and coke ovens. The British Iron Trade Commission said in 1892:

Modern iron making in America began . . . in 1881. . . . It became firmly established when Andrew Carnegie was the first to recognize and act on the necessity for the successful iron producer to control his own material, and it gained international importance when this wonderful man joined to plants and mines the possession of railroads and ships.

Besides the Carnegie Company, by 1892 three other great corporations had organized regional monopolies in the steel industry, preparing the stage for the gigantic consolidations of the twentieth century. In the South was the Tennessee Coal & Iron Company, which in 1892 absorbed its largest competitor and emerged with a capitalization of $18,000,000. In the mountain region was the Colorado Fuel & Iron Company, capitalized at $13,000,000. In the Middle West was the Illinois Steel Company, formed in 1889, a giant equal in capitalization to Carnegie's firm and "believed to have a larger output than any other steel company in the world."

Outside steel and oil, similar combinations were being pushed to completion by Armour and Swift in meat packing, Pillsbury in flour milling, Havemeyer in sugar, and Weyerhaeuser in lumber. By 1893 all had become leaders of great corporations composed in part of shoestring competitors that had fallen in every financial storm.

Other People's Money. The first general use of the "modern" corporation in America was for the construction of railroads which required more capital than any single person could subscribe. As manufacturing expanded and became more and more mechanized, however, it also began to require large funds, and its managers used the corporate device to raise them. Gradually, therefore, a market was created for industrial stocks as well as for railroad securities and government bonds. As the property represented by such certificates seemed to yield attractive dividends, a greater part of American savings was drawn to them, and competition among investors was creating speculative fluctuations in many issues. To Americans inured to risky enterprises these fluctuations only enhanced the appeal of common stocks, and the stock market in the decades after the Civil War came to play each year a more important role in the breathtaking development of the country. Since the greatest stock exchange was located in New York, that city strengthened its position as the real capital of the nation. From every section the savings of millions flowed there, and with these savings came the sharpest minds bidding for their use.

As new institutions appear or old ones develop new functions, old controls grow obsolete before new ones are perfected. In the interim, adventurers improve the opportunities for profit. In the case of the stock exchange, no one illustrated this better than Jay Gould. Cornelius Vanderbilt unified his railroads while making large speculative profits on the side and Morgan sold securities to fund his mergers and reorganizations, but Gould "played the market" for itself alone. He knew his instrument like a virtuoso, knew every permutation and combination of its possibilities, knew how to exploit them till he hovered again and again on the very brink of failure but never once fell over. "I did not care at that time about the mere making of money," he said with reference to his Missouri Pacific exploits. "It was more to show that I could make a combination and make it a success." Careless of social approval, he was unscrupulous in flouting the unwritten standards of business. The exclusive New York Yacht Club refused him admittance, and Mrs. Astor never invited his family to her quadrilles. With nothing to lose in that direction he was yet freer to fleece high society. By his raids and ripostes in the market he made enemies who did not hesitate to reply with violence; and though he was protected day and night by a detachment of plain-clothes men he suffered physical beatings. His retaliation was invariably to arrange a neat transaction that would cost his assailant dearly.

While his contemporaries among manufacturers, therefore, were competing in commodity markets and organizing industrial trusts, and his railroad contemporaries were unifying their systems and making and breaking transportation pools, Gould was also following the monopolistic trend, using the stock market as his lever to force combinations. He learned early that, as long as people could be persuaded to advance money, there was more profit to be made by wrecking concerns than by building them up, that there was more to gain from reorganization proceedings than from management that made such proceedings unnecessary. Having learned this, he became expert in attracting investors, clairvoyant in determining when they had reached the limit of tolerance. Through the New York *World,* of which he became owner in 1879, and Western Union, which he dominated after 1881, he blasted at the credit of companies in which he was interested. Thus getting bear raids under way, he purchased stock in such companies at the nadir of their decline. Gaining control of their resources, he then told his readers how strong his companies had suddenly become, proved his contentions by paying liberal dividends out of capital, and then sold out at the zenith of the speculative course of their securities. Between times, he milked the assets of his companies until they became in fact the carcasses he had claimed they were when he started his bearish machinations.

Gould improvised many variations on this favorite theme of profits through destruction. In one of his earliest ventures in Erie, he, Fisk and Drew merely converted construction bonds into $7,000,000 worth of unauthorized stock, sold these to Vanderbilt who was seeking control of Erie, and then bribed the New Jersey legislature to legalize the transaction. Getting out of Erie in a strong cash position on the eve of the panic of 1873, he was ready to attack the Union Pacific. Running down its stock with ingenious bearish tactics, he bought a controlling interest for very little and then forced the directors to purchase from him the Denver Pacific and Kansas Pacific, both of which he had acquired for a song. Clearing $10,000,000 in this transaction, he made about $10,000,000 more by successively damning and praising Union Pacific and trading its stock accordingly. By 1879 he abandoned it, still keeping control of various western roads which gave him a trunk line of his own to the Pacific. . . .

Gould's next venture was in Western Union, which he forced into submission by typical bear raids. When he got control he increased the capitalization of the company 25 per cent, using part of the funds for his private purposes. Turning next to the New York Elevated Railway, he slashed its stock by advertising that the state Attorney General (one of his men) was going to sue for revocation of the company's charter. In control, he again increased capital and imposed a ten-cent fare, thus making the general public as well as investors his dupes.

Though Gould was the master trader of his time he was not alone in exploiting the new capital that was drawn to the great stock market in New York. Every merger that was consummated, every trust whose stock was offered to the public in the decades after the Civil War, was capitalized at a higher figure than was warranted by the actual physical assets involved. Promoters hoped that the elimination of competition would insure profits sufficient to pay higher fixed charges on new bonds and regular dividends on common stocks, or else they counted on making *managerial* profits simply out of the new money they attracted. In most cases their calculations proved incorrect, and when the panic of 1893 once again rocked the business world the burden of these additional capital charges proved too great. The attractiveness of the stock market had made industrial financing in America much more speculative than ever before, and the collapse was proportionately severe.

As we shall see, this situation prepared the stage for the dramatic entrance of the investment banker as the director of the business life of the nation. Just as competition had made businessmen prey to their own contrivances, so the ceaseless pursuit of speculative profits brought their combinations to the edge of disaster. From competitive anarchy within single industries they had sought to escape through combination. Because they overcapitalized the resulting giants, they had to appeal for succor to the investment banker. That his price was high was due mainly to their own desperate condition, and though they argued and bargained and made a brave show of independence, they knew they must concede his demands in the end. Until 1893 Morgan was the leader in financing corporate reorganizations, and his work was limited mainly to railroads. After the panic his interests spread to other lines, and other private bankers entered the field. In most cases their price was the same: a large fee for services, and participation in the management of the reorganized company. Here was the nursery of the interlocking directorates and imperial holding companies that concentrated the management of American industrial enterprise in the few strong hands of the bankers. They dealt not in steel or meat or salt or coal, they supplied no essential industrial services. They controlled only the avenues to the savings of a maturing industrial society, and thus they controlled its life.

Industrial Society. Just as modern industrialism in the western world profoundly affected such distant places as China, India, and South Africa in the nineteenth century, so industrial leaders in the great cities of America affected life in every distant hamlet in the land. They controlled the railroads that brought the farmer's produce to market, the flour mills that ground his wheat, the slaughterhouses that purchased his pigs, the machine shops that supplied his tools, the shoe factories that made his shoes, the salt and sugar refineries that supplied his table with these necessities, and the oil refineries that gave him kerosene by which to read. There was in America no miner who did not depend upon machine-made tools, no lonely cultivator who did not strive in vain to keep his sons on the farm, his daughters from some wicked metropolis.

The growth of the railroads, the perfection of the telephone and Atlantic cable, the development of the telegraph, the improvement of postal and express services in the decades after the Civil War, all gave businessmen almost instantaneous communication with every department of their far-flung economic empires—with their lieutenants at the sources of raw materials, their managers at fabrication centers, their salesmen in the markets of the nation and the world. Often they had but to sit in their offices in great cities and press the proper buttons, call the proper clerks, dictate the pertinent letters, and their wishes would be transmitted to the proper subordinates and carried out a hundred, a thousand, three thousand miles away. No village was too distant to escape the influence of New York, Chicago, St. Louis, or San Francisco. No region was too secluded to escape the net cast by the imperialists of every great center to catch the labor, capital, and natural resources of the ever more accessible hinterlands.

While the new technology was annihilating distance, helping to speed and centralize the administration of proliferating business enterprises, businessmen were developing new techniques designed to accelerate these trends. They were coming more and more in their fiscal transactions to deal in stocks and bonds, in rights to property rather than in physical property itself. They were using checks canceled through central clearinghouses, rather than cumbersome commercial paper. Their commodity transactions were increasingly conducted through negotiable bills rather than in raw products themselves. In almost all our large cities in these decades commodity exchanges began bringing buyers and sellers into immediate contact, standardizing quality, codifying trade practices and developing systems of business ethics that speeded all transactions by making unnecessary the legal paraphernalia of competitive contract making—the jargon, the endless details, the interminable oaths and affidavits. There was little need, now, to go to the warehouses to test the quality of the wheat or to the docks to test the cotton. Varying qualities were classified by the exchanges and offered for what they were. As in stocks, frauds were perpetrated. Poor produce was passed off as the best, just as unauthorized stocks were sold as gilt-edged securities. But the markets responded each time with better regulations. Their very existence depended upon trust, upon the faith businessmen had in the reliability of their representations. It was axiomatic, therefore, that the exchanges must extend themselves to preserve this trust. They were generally successful in doing so, though raiders like Gould, who depended upon this general faith for the success of their own malpractices, frequently did their unwitting best to shatter business confidence.

While the centrifugal force of expanding industrialism was extending the power of American businessmen to the farthest reaches of the land, other industrial factors were drawing more and more people each year to the centers from which this force issued. Rural mills and forges closed down in the decades after the Civil War, and their owners went to work in Minneapolis or Pittsburgh; cobblers went to Lynn and Rochester; packers, to St. Louis and Chicago. Once thriving villages in every section of the land were left deserted while their residents thronged to the cities seeking the bright lights, the education, the glowing opportunities that were promised them. There they joined with aliens imported from every section of Europe to create an adequate labor supply for enterprising businessmen. At least as important in drawing business to the cities were the rate policies of the railroads. It was to the advantage of individual roads to keep business as decentralized as possible, so that they might charge monopoly rates from as many points as they could make dependent solely upon their lines. By overcharging businessmen at these points, however, the railroad forced them to move their plants to the larger cities, where alternative lines were available and competitive rates were in force. By becoming great distributing centers for the products of farms, mines and factories, metropolises also offered businessmen advantages in purchasing raw materials, fuel, and machinery. All these conditions brought businessmen swarming to the great cities of the East and Middle West, whose continual growth gave additional incentives by bringing always more and more buyers and sellers together, enhancing the value of urban real estate, and combining the funds of tens of thousands into great capital available at reasonable rates for industrial and speculative enterprises.

While business expansion and business competition were drawing millions to the cities of America, technological inventions and improvements were encouraging city life. Refrigerator cars on the railroads after 1875 helped to feed large landless populations. Structural steel, introduced in the late seventies, helped to house them in their work. Urban rapid transit, beginning in 1869 with the Ninth Avenue Elevated in New York, helped them to move quickly and cheaply to and from their offices and factories.

It is impossible to exaggerate the role of business in developing great cities in America, and it is impossible to exaggerate the role of the cities in creating our business culture. The cities subjected hundreds of thousands of people to identical pressures, at the same time exporting to every rural river valley, plain, and plateau uniform factory products. Creating a national market for standardized goods, they also created a national model of the successful man: the thrifty, shrewd, and practical clerk or mechanic who rose from the ranks to leadership. "The millionaires who are in active control," wrote Carnegie, "started as poor boys and were trained in the sternest but most efficient of all schools—poverty." And he held up as examples, besides himself, McCormick, Pullman, Westinghouse, and Rockefeller in manufacturing; Stanford, Huntington, Gould, Sage, and Dillon, in finance; Wanamaker, Stewart, Claflin, Marshall Field, Phelps, and Dodge in merchandising. Boys in the cities saw the stately mansions of these great men, saw their princely carriages, their gigantic offices and stores. Boys on the farms heard of them or studied their photographs in newspapers and magazines that were achieving national circulation. They read how these leaders of business society had acquired their rewards, and the ambitious set out to emulate them. Thus the ideals of our business leaders became the ideals of the great majority of the people, though only a few were themselves endowed with talent for leadership.

Frances W. Gregory

and Irene D. Neu

The Industrial Elite

in the 1870s

In the previous selection, Andrew Carnegie—himself an immigrant lad who became an industrial giant and, hence, a living symbol of the rags-to-riches dream—said that the millionaire business leaders of the Gilded Age had "started as poor boys and were trained in the sternest but most efficient of all schools—poverty." Tradition, historians, biographers of business leaders, and legend have all supported this view. In fact, this theme was embroidered into American folklore. Using comparative statistical data and historical analysis, the authors of the following essay challenge the "rags-to-riches" theme. Their findings, based on a study of the social origins of approximately three hundred leaders of American industry in the 1870s, suggest that even in these formative years, social stratification in the United States, as in much of Europe, had a great deal to do with the recruitment of business leaders. This evidence also suggests that even though the upward mobility in the social structure was broader in the United States than abroad, the business leaders could be considered, in effect, members of a baronial class.

In any case, this essay offers an example of how the historian's research can replace long-held assumptions with interpretive data based on solid evidence. [Reprinted by permission of the publishers from William Miller, editor, Men in Business: Essays in the History of Entrepeneurship. *Cambridge, Mass: Harvard University Press. Copyright 1950, 1952 by the President and Fellows of Harvard College.]*

Despite the importance of business in the United States, as elsewhere, the social origins of business leaders, the social sources of business leadership, have received but little attention from scholars. A few biographies and autobiographies have tended to point up the spectacular and the unusual, with the result that the origins of a handful have been attributed to the many, though the grounds of attribution have remained vague. What have been the actual origins of American business leaders? And what have been the consequences, for the business community and for society at large, of the actual process of recruitment? These are questions of great magnitude and are not to be resolved by the findings of a single study. It is felt, however, that the information presented in this paper is a contribution toward the eventual answers.

The characteristics of the industrial leader in the United States, as tradition had sketched him, reflect the idealism of the American heritage. Specifically, his was the Carnegie story. A poor immigrant boy arrived on the shores of a new nation which abounded in endless opportunity. As the boy was the son of a workingman, he had little or no formal education and was forced by circumstances to seek employment at a tender age. His first job was a lowly one, but in short order he rose to prominence, usually as a result of cleverness, diligence, or luck. In this manner, the top-level businessman was but a generation removed from poverty and anonymity.

This story was not unheard of before the golden age of American industrial expansion that followed the Civil War. It was already frequently told in the early decades of the nineteenth century when the merchant was at the apex of the business ladder. It is the theme of the short biography of Amos Lawrence, suggestively entitled *The Poor Boy and Merchant Prince.* Nathan Appleton, the Boston textile magnate and backer of Webster, also voiced this thesis of freedom of ascent to financial success and industrial prominence, and always projected himself, indeed with more or less accuracy, as an example of this fluidity of social and economic structure. It was only with the appearance on the American scene of such businessmen as Carnegie, Vanderbilt, and Rockefeller, however, that this thesis found its major exemplars, and in the history books and biographies of succeeding generations their lives continue to be used to buttress the tradition.

Only within the last twenty years has this tradition been seriously questioned. F. W. Taussig and C. S. Joslyn in *American Business Lead-*

ers: A Study in Social Origins and Social Stratification, published in
1932, cast doubt upon the widely held belief in the easy ascent of the
poor boy to business prestige and financial power. They showed that the
way was considerably more accessible to the sons of the middle and upper
classes, and advanced the hypothesis that the absence of representation of
the lower classes among business leaders was chiefly the result of a lack of
innate ability, not lack of opportunity. Studies of this subject by other
scholars have appeared from time to time in learned journals. For the
most part, these have been concerned with but small groups, and their
value has been limited for these reasons.

Recently William Miller published two essays in which he analyzed the
backgrounds of 190 American business leaders of the first decade of the
twentieth century and compared their social characteristics with those of
the population generally. In these essays he set forth the conclusion that
the men who held the top positions—essentially presidencies or board
chairmanships—in the largest industrial and financial institutions in the
United States during this period were recruited, in great part, from a
highly select segment of the population. Typical of these magnates in the
early twentieth century was the son of a professional or business man of
colonial American heritage, born in some American city or town of more
than 2500 persons. This executive very likely had attended high school
and had had a 40 per cent chance of reaching college. Moreover, he
certainly was over 16 and was likely to be over 19 before going to work.
In all probability, he was a member of the middle or upper class. Unlike
Taussig and Joslyn, who offer no acceptable evidence for their thesis of
innate ability among the business elite, Miller presents verifiable data to
support his contention that certain social characteristics marked a man as
good material for the leading business positions.

These findings prompted the Research Center in Entrepreneurial History at Harvard University to conduct an investigation into the origins of
a group of business leaders of an earlier period and to compare the
findings with Miller's for the period 1901–1910. This is the first report of
that investigation.

At the outset it was decided that the period for study should be the
decade 1870–1879, one recent enough to assure adequate biographical
information for a considerable number of men, yet not too close to that
of 1901–1910 for purposes of comparison and contrast. To keep the number of business leaders within manageable limits, men were chosen from
three major fields only: textiles, steel, and railroads. Textiles and steel
were selected because the first was the oldest large-scale industry in America and the second was then the newest. Railroads were an obvious choice
for they represented by far the largest agglomeration of capital in the
period.

Once these three industries had been decided upon, the next step was
to ascertain the key top jobs in the major companies. In textiles the

treasurer and agent of each establishment were used. The treasurer was the chief executive officer and had charge of the financial end of the business, including the purchase of cotton from the South. The agent was the local authority on the job and supervised the construction of the factory, the manufacture of cloth, and the employment of labor. In steel corporations the top men were taken to be the president, the vice-president, and the general manager or superintendent. This industry, however, was still organized largely on a partnership basis, and since there was no general way of determining the relative interests of the several partners in an establishment, all known partners were included. The top men in the railroads were taken to be presidents, vice-presidents, and general managers.

The men in textiles represented all cotton manufacturing concerns having an authorized capital of more than $1,000,000 and a spindlage of at least 70,000; all wool manufacturing companies with an authorized capital of $600,000 or more and at least 49 sets of cards; and the single American silk company which had a capital of $1,000,000. The men in steel covered all eleven Bessemer and all fifteen open-hearth plants in the United States in 1878, as well as the six crucible plants which produced 10,000 tons or more that year, or were attached to ironworks having a combined production of iron and steel in excess of 10,000 tons. The railroaders represented all companies in their field capitalized in excess of $24,000,000 and having construction and equipment accounts in excess of $38,000,000, according to the census 1880.

In all, seventy-seven companies supplied men for the list. These were the thirty largest textile companies, the thirty largest steel manufacturers, and the seventeen largest railroads in the country. The names of the leaders themselves were found, for the most part, in industrial directories. The final aggregate of 303 men includes 102 from textiles, 100 from steel, and 101 from railroads. No men known to have held the positions named above in any of these companies were omitted from the list, though, of course, for some not all the information sought could be found. . . .

Though the men with whom this study is concerned were all industrialists and represented but three industries in an economy which was already highly diversified, these three industries were among the four largest in the United States. Since the results of this study will be compared with Miller's for the period 1901–1910, other things should also be noted here. While about 20 per cent of Miller's men were bankers and life insurance executives, and an additional 15 per cent were in public utilities, these activities are represented in the present study only by executives who were also in textiles, steel, or railroads. Further, it must be remembered that Miller writes largely of the bureaucratic business hierarchies which had become common by 1910, while the present essay is concerned with an age when even some of the topmost companies were still organized as family concerns. This certainly was largely the case in steel but much less so in textiles in which most firms were largely incorporated and career lines of a professional, managerial type could be found. A bureaucracy, it is true, was emerging in railroads by the 1870's but even here its organization was far from complete.

Whether bureaucrats or family-made men or general entrepreneurs, however, it is clear that the men both in Miller's sample and our own were among the topmost business leaders of their time.

The businessmen in Miller's group, averaging approximately 50 years of age in 1900, were considerably younger than men in similar positions today. The men of the 1870's, in turn, were younger still; their average age, brought down, to be sure, by the sizable representation of men other than those at the very top, was 45. But even these men were already in the prime of life, nor had they, as the tradition would have it, spent much of their time in becoming accustomed to a strange culture in a strange land. Some, of course, like English-born John Fallon in textiles and Scotsman Thomas Carnegie in steel, were born abroad. These men, however, were exceptional, not typical, among the industrial elite of the 1870's, as among the business leaders of the later decade. . . .

Besides Fallon, five other textile men are known to have been born abroad. Two were the Cumnock brothers (a third brother was born in America) whose father, a freeholder of Glasgow, was "a man of fair estate." Andrew F. Swapp, another immigrant, like Fallon, was from a working-class family. Of all those born abroad, only Alexander G. Cumnock ever reached the treasurership and he, of a company too small to be included in this study. The others were agents only. In steel, ten men in addition to Carnegie were born outside the United States. At least six of these—the three Chisholms, Reginald H. Bulley, William Butcher, and Otto Wuth—appear to have come from substantial middle-class backgrounds. In the railroad group there is not a single instance of a "poor immigrant" working his way up the ladder. Of the eight men known to have been born in foreign countries, Jacob D. Cos, John Murray Forbes, and Azariah Boody were the children of American parents and therefore could hardly be called "immigrants." Of the five men who may properly be so labeled, James B. Hodgskin, James McHenry, and Gustavus A. Nicolls were the sons of well-established professional men, Alexander Mitchell was the son of a "well-to-do" farmer, and Peter H. Watson apparently had been trained in the law before the time at which he arrived in the United States, after having been forced to leave Canada for his part in the rebellion of 1837.

Not only were few of these business leaders immigrants; but few were the sons of immigrants. Of the native-born in the group about whom information is available, only 3 per cent were the sons of foreign-born fathers. . . .

It would seem, therefore, that the top-level leadership in American industry in the 1870's, as in the 1900's, was native-born and of native families. Indeed, the immigrant ancestors of these families, in all likelihood, had come over to America in the seventeenth century. Not John Fallon, therefore, who came to this country as an expert in calico-printing, but George Atkinson, Edmund Dwight, or Augustus Lowell, men born in New England whose fathers and grandfathers were also born there, would seem to be characteristic of the topmost men in textiles. In steel the typical leader was not Thomas Carnegie, but such a man as James I. Bennett or William Sellers, both born in Pennsylvania to fathers who were native Pennsylvanians. A typical railroader might be John H. Devereaux, who was born in Boston, and whose father was a native of Massachusetts; or Charles E. Perkins, who was born in Cincinnati of New England parents and whose relatives were still prominent Bostonians.

Perkins' history, moreover, illustrates the shift in the geographic origins of American business leaders away from storied New England, a shift that took place, perhaps, a good deal earlier than has commonly been supposed. By the 1900's, indeed . . . fewer than two in ten of the men studied were themselves born in New England; more striking, fewer than three in ten of their fathers had been born there. For the 1870's, of course, the proportions of New Englanders are considerably greater; but even so, including the almost 100 per cent representation of the textile sample, about half the whole group was born there; and of those not in the textile group, considerably less than half had New England-born fathers. . . .

The decline of New England as a source of business leadership is paralleled by the falling off between the 1870's and the 1900's in men of British but especially of English origins. Even so, such men continued to be represented at the top of American business far out of proportion to their representation in the population generally.

Most of the leaders of the 1870's had been reared in a period of religious ferment and fragmentation of some of the older established sects. Aside from the Unitarians, however, most of whom must either have embraced this faith themselves or been the sons of men who did, only fourteen of the group are known to have shifted from one denomination to another, and among these it was more often a shift to the older elite Episcopal church than to any of the more zealous or more intellectual ones. This . . . served to bring those who shifted into closer conformity with their associates in the business community.

There is in American literature considerable evidence of the view that the business leader, if not a refugee from abroad, was at any rate a refugee from the farm. Nor is this theme confined to fiction. Andrew Carnegie, himself the son of a city worker, was but stating a popular belief when he wrote in 1886, "Most great men, it is true, have been born and brought up in the country." In speaking of the 1870's, one of the outstanding historians of our own day has said, "The cities were full of wealthy newcomers of rural antecedents"; but he cites as his only reference William Dean Howells' Silas Lapham, a fictional Boston capitalist who was born and reared on a Vermont farm. Certainly there were such cases in real life, too, in the 1870's as in all periods of American history, but the statistics . . . show that these cases were hardly representative in our period, and this at a time, be it remembered, when by far the larger part of the nation's population was composed of farm dwellers. . . .

Half the industrial leaders of 1870–1879 were born in places with more than 2500 persons as compared with 59 per cent of the business leaders of 1901–1910. But even the remaining half in the 1870's was not necessarily of rural origin. A population below 2500 is roughly the measure used by the Bureau of the Census, both in designating modern rural areas and in going back into the past for purpose of comparison. Yet it is scarcely sound to suggest, on that account, that every community having a population of less than 2500 in 1825 (the year in which the "average" industrial leader of 1870–1879 was born), was essentially rural. Take, for instance, St. Albans, Vermont, which even as late as 1830 falls into our "rural" category population-wise, but which, when J. Gregory Smith, the railroad man, was born there in 1818, was already a flourishing community with many of the refinements of the urban life of the time. Smith's father was a lawyer and businessman, and of Smith himself it has been said, "established position and affluence were his birthright." Another example is Erie, Pennsylvania, in which railroad man John F. Tracy was born in 1827. With a population of 1465 in 1830, Erie was a bustling lake port, and a rapidly expanding business center. Tracy's father was a railroad contractor; the academy which the boy attended had been a feature of Erie life since 1806.

Nor are Erie and St. Albans the only examples. It is perhaps a fairer measure, therefore, to count as having been brought up in rural surroundings only those men actually born on farms. When this is done, the rural classification in the 1870's . . . drops from 50 to 25 per cent, and the farm boy who becomes a successful businessman appears a much less frequent phenomenon. . . .

The prevalence of businessmen among the fathers of the leaders in our group is noteworthy. While the term "businessman" is interpreted to include such widely separated occupations as bank president and peddler, only two fathers fit into the first category and but one in the second. One-third of the fathers designated as businessmen were merchants; another third were manufacturers. Among the remaining third were three contractors or builders, two sea captains, a supercargo, a river captain, a railroad superintendent, a gristmill operator, the owner of a country store, a newspaper publisher, and a bookseller. The fathers of seventeen textile leaders were themselves textile men, while the fathers of a like number in the steel industry had preceded their sons as iron and steel manufacturers. Only seven railroaders were the sons of men who had engaged in railroading.

Such crude occupational categories as we have used are not necessarily precise criteria of social status in any of its various meanings. "Farmer" may include men who were able to afford education for their children, while some petty businessmen could not do so. And if, at one end of the scale among business and professional men we find those who could not give their children higher education, at the other end are fathers who were already at the top in their respective fields and men of more than local power and prestige. Precise calculations of class or status do not seem feasible, but every effort to take all known factors into account re-emphasizes the general impression that most—perhaps 90 per cent—of the industrial leaders in our group were reared in a middle- or upper-class milieu.

The education of most of these men was not limited to what the little red schoolhouse had to offer; . . . the majority at least attained the equivalent of high school training, while a sizable number also had a taste of college. This is particularly apparent in the textile group, almost half the men whose education is known having attended college. Among the railroad men, moreover, while not as many had gone to college, almost half had had professional training, usually in law or engineering. . . .

A natural consequence of a longer educational period is delay in starting to earn a living. . . . Almost half the men for whom data were to be had did not go to work before they had reached their nineteenth birthday. Less than one-quarter were set to work when they were younger than sixteen. These figures and Miller's for the later decade point up the fact that in the earlier period, as in the later, we are dealing with a favored segment of the population. . . .

Was the typical industrial leader of the 1870's, then, a "new man," an escapee from the slums of Europe or from the paternal farm? Did he rise by his own efforts from a boyhood of poverty? Was he as innocent of education and of formal training as has often been alleged? He seems to have been none of these things. American by birth, of a New England father, English in national origin, Congregational, Presbyterian, or Episcopal in religion, urban in early environment, he was rather born and bred in an atmosphere in which business and a relatively high social standing were intimately associated with his family life. Only at about eighteen did he take his first regular job, prepared to rise from it, moreover, not by a rigorous apprenticeship begun when he was virtually a child, but by an academic education well above average for the times.

Sidney Fine

Laissez-Faire and

the Businessman

*In the Gilded Age, the businessman—
who had become the most admired of
Americans—set the tone for practically all of society. In the following
essay a judicious historian explains
why, and analyzes the dominant
philosophy of the industrial entrepreneurs. He shows how they lauded
the concepts of Social Darwinism and
of laissez-faire economics, but with a
practical purpose—mainly to maintain a* status quo *favorable to themselves. Their application of theory to practice was inconsistent, primitive,
and even naïve. Yet their distorted use of theory to justify their position
received wide support, particularly from the Protestant clergy. The clergy,
like the businessman, was captivated by the image and reality of success.
So were most Americans of the Gilded Age; they seemed to find the
ideas of the business leaders not only congenial but also acceptable as
social and economic philosophy. [Reprinted from* Laissez Faire and
the General-Welfare State: A Study of Conflict in American Thought,
1865–1901 *by Sidney Fine, by permission of The University of Michigan
Press. Copyright 1956 by The University of Michigan Press, Ann Arbor,
Michigan.]*

It is, of course, extremely difficult to speak in general terms of the views
of the business community as a whole with respect to the functions of
government. Manufacturers, merchants, bankers, railroad entrepreneurs,
and small businessmen in the period after the Civil War did not necessarily regard the problem all in the same light, nor were individuals
within these groups equally articulate in the expression of such opinions
as they did entertain. One finds among the businessmen protectionists
and free traders, friends of hard money and of soft money, opponents of
any real government control of corporate enterprise and advocates of
government regulation of corporations as creatures of the state. What
follows, therefore, is largely an attempt to focus upon what appear to
have been some of the dominant elements in the thought of the business
community regarding the role of state and, particularly, although by no
means exclusively, the thought of the industrial capitalists.

   With the triumph of the North in the Civil War the industrial capitalist became for the first time the regnant figure in American life. No
longer did he have to contend with the slaveholding aristocrat for control
of the state. The policies he favored—a national banking system, a high
protective tariff, generous land grants to railway corporations, and the
authorized importation of contract labor—were put into effect during the
war years by a government amenable to his will, and after Appomattox
the national administration remained responsive to his wishes. As the
Nation caustically pointed out, what the national government inter-

preted as the common good was, in actuality, "the good of those . . . rich and powerful enough to make their influence felt at Washington."

Since the businessman was the admired social type of the Gilded Age, large sections of the American public acquiesced in his views. Warren Miller, a former United States senator from New York, expressed a desire to see more businessmen in American legislatures because he regarded them as "more competent to deal with the live questions of the hour than any other class"; and Godkin noted that Americans had "an inordinate respect for the opinions on all subjects of 'successful business men.' " . . .

Not content merely to be the most influential figure on the American scene, the businessman felt the need for a philosophy to explain and to justify his preeminent position. To a great extent, he found what he sought in the precepts of social Darwinism and laissez-faire economics. The businessman, to be sure, did not accept the doctrines of Spencer and the economists *in toto:* he took from their thought only what suited his needs. His version of laissez faire, unlike theirs, was essentially a rationalization of the *status quo.* The theorists of laissez faire were, after all, reformers in their own manner and were opposed to the use of government for the benefit of any particular class. They denounced evidences of governmental favoritism, such as the protective tariff, that were dear to the heart of the businessman. The businessman, for his part, saw no wrong in government activities that were conducive to his welfare: he did not ordinarily object to the use of state power to promote business enterprise. He tended to become an opponent of the state only when it sought to regulate his economic endeavors or to cater to the needs of other economic groups. Laissez faire to him meant, "Leave things as they now are." "If asked what important law I should change," Andrew Carnegie declared, "I must perforce say none; the laws are perfect."

One element of the businessman's defense of the *status quo* was a formula for success. The success of the businessman, it was explained, was the result of his possessing certain simple virtues and abilities; the failure of the poor man resulted from his lack of these same virtues and abilities. In his book *The Successful Man of Business,* Benjamin Wood explained that success was "nothing more or less than doing thoroughly what others do indifferently." In a lecture delivered at Cornell University in 1896, Carnegie gave it as his opinion that success "is a simple matter of honest work, ability, and concentration." . . .

Not only did the businessman equate success with virtue and concentration, but he sought to impress upon one and all the view that there was ample room at the top for those who were willing to make the effort. "The storehouse of opportunity is open to all," proclaimed Benjamin Wood. Henry Wood thought that "examples on every hand" proved how simple it was to move into the "independent class." This was not a matter of theory, but of "universal experience." Wall Street's Henry Clews also emphasized the numerous opportunities for acquiring wealth in the United States. It required neither genius, education, breeding, nor even luck to gather "the nimble dollar"; it was necessary for one only to begin "aright."

The businessman's interpretation of success found popular literary expression in the biographies of William Roscoe Thayer and the novels of Horatio Alger. These two authors were among the chief representatives of a veritable "cult of success" that glorified the self-made man and trumpeted the idea that the road to the top lay open to those with the requisite qualities. The implications of such a version of success were obvious—it would be fatuous to interfere with an economic system that so readily rewarded ability and that provided an opportunity for all to gain riches. This, indeed, was the theme of Carnegie's paean of praise to the system that had made his rise to fame possible, *Triumphant Democracy*, published in the year of the Haymarket Affair. "The publication of it is very timely," George Pullman wrote to Carnegie, "as owing to the excesses of our turbulent population, so many are uttering doubts just now as to whether democracy has been a triumph in America." . . .

In further support of his position and of the *status quo*, the man of wealth pointed to the teachings of Spencer. That part of Spencer's thought that dealt with the struggle for existence, the survival of the fittest as the result of natural selection, and the inevitability of progress was readily adaptable to the pattern of American economic life and to the needs of the businessman. It took no great imagination to see that Spencer offered a rationale for the business triumphs of the industrial leaders and for opposition to all proposals of state intervention on behalf of the unsuccessful. "Upon reading Darwin and Spencer," Carnegie remarked, "I remember that light came as in a flood and all was clear."

Competition, the success of some and the failure of others, and the consolidation of industry into ever larger units were all readily explainable by the businessman in the terms that Spencer had made popular. "Competition in Economics," the publisher Richard R. Bowker proclaimed, "is the same as the law of the 'survival of the fittest,' or 'natural selection,' in nature." The great Southern textile manufacturer Daniel A. Tompkins informed an audience that "in a businessman's every-day life he sees this law of the survival of the fittest at work, thinning out the ranks of his competitors, introducing new material." "Competition, the very essence of business life," Tompkins continued, "puts down some and elevates others. The fittest survive. It must be so, else there is no life, no progress. Whatever the socialist and other sentimentalists may think, the survival of the fittest is, has been, and will always be the law of progress in national affairs, in business and in all other walks of life." It would be "the silliest kind of sentimentalism" to fret about those who were "defeated" in this struggle for existence. . . .

Not only did the businessman describe the success of individuals in Darwinian terms, but he was able to explain and justify the consolidation of industry in similar terms. The concentration of capital, Carnegie declared, "is an evolution from the heterogeneous to the homogeneous, and is clearly another step in the upward path of development." Carnegie was, moreover, quite certain that "this overpowering, irresistible tendency toward aggregation of capital and increase of size . . . cannot be arrested or even greatly impeded." Rockefeller, too, explained the growth of the "large business" as "merely a survival of the fittest . . . the working out of a law of nature and a law of God." It was obviously futile, in the view of business advocates of social Darwinism, for the state to attempt to interfere with the process that brought the fittest individuals and concerns to the fore. . . .

And it is clear that, just as the theories of the social Darwinists were readily adaptable to the needs of the captains of industry, so was there much in the doctrines of the laissez-faire economists that fitted the specifications of a businessman's philosophy. Like the economists, the businessman was prone to talk of the inexorable natural laws that governed the economic order, of competition as the great regulator, and of the virtues of self-interest.

The doctrine of self-interest was particularly attractive to the businessman, for it supplied him with a truly potent argument with which to defend the existing order. If each individual in his pursuit of wealth unconsciously promoted the general good, did not those who were most successful in the quest for economic gain promote the general welfare more effectively than all others? The millionaires, declared Carnegie, "are the bees that make the most honey, and contribute most to the hive even after they have gorged themselves full." The millionaire "cannot evade the law which . . . compels him to use his millions for the good of the people." What need was there then for the state to seek by positive action to promote the well-being of the mass of the people. The captains of industry, said John F. Scanlan, of the Western Industrial League, "are fathers to guide the masses to higher conditions."

Like the laissez-faire economists and the social Darwinists, whose views they found so palatable, businessmen generally cautioned the state to pursue a hands-off policy with respect to economic matters. The Chicago banker Lyman Gage, eventually to become McKinley's secretary of the treasury, informed a committee of Congress that insofar as the industrial affairs of the country were concerned, the legislature should "simply . . . define the obligations of the citizens to each other, and . . . secure the enforcement of individual rights." The state, businessmen thought, should protect property and enforce contracts, but they did not wish it to interfere with prices, wages, or profits. "The more the legislature and the people let these things alone, the better they will work out their own solution," asserted the president of the Wholesale Grocers' Association of New York City. If trade were untrammeled, the head of the sugar trust informed the United States Industrial Commission, no economic group would enjoy any special advantage, and the country would benefit. Of course, if one concern managed to get rid of its competitors in the process, that was trade, and nothing could be done about it.

The businessman was prone to contrast the beneficent natural laws which, in his view, governed the economic order with the clumsy, artificial laws devised by man. "Oh, these grand immutable, all-wise laws of natural forces," exulted Carnegie, "how perfectly they work if human legislators would only let them alone! But no, they must be tinkering" The president of the American Exchange Bank and the onetime president of the American Bankers Association, George S. Coe, thought the laws of economics "as sacred and as obligatory as . . . those of the decalogue." He spoke of the "impotence and limitations of human law" and insisted that "all material values are governed by influences far beyond the reach of human vision and legislation." In Charles Flint's view, industrial progress was assured so long as "natural conditions" were undisturbed. However, if legal restraints were imposed, then, Flint warned the "wheels which have been driving all this vast machinery will come to rest." The nation was already "overwhelmed . . . by useless legislation," according to J. G. Batterson, the president of the New England Granite Works, and more was to be gained from the repeal than from the enactment of any law. "The universal law of supply and demand," he averred, "is superior to any law which can be enacted by Congress or any other power on earth."

Not only did the businessman compare man-made law unfavorably with natural law, but he also found virtue on the side of private enterprise as contrasted to government enterprise. "It is better always," said the merchant Danford Knowlton, "to leave individual enterprise to do most that is to be done in the country." Even the Post Office, Jay Gould thought, should be in private hands, "because individual enterprise can do things more economically and more efficiently than the Government can."

In his approach to such problems of the day as labor relations, money, railroads, and trusts, the businessman generally adhered closely to the laissez-faire doctrine. He naturally looked with disfavor on attempts by workers to interfere with the *status quo*. Regarding himself as the benefactor of the community in general and of the laborer in particular, the industrialist exhorted the workingman to remain quiescent and to trust to his employer and to natural law to improve his position. The entrepreneur, he informed the worker, was entitled to a large share of the total product because he was "the most important factor in the modern economy" and made the major contribution to production. It was altogether proper for him to earn more than the laborer because he possessed "superior judgment, skill, and sagacity." Moreover, since the efforts of the few had served to raise wages and increase purchasing power, the laborer had no cause for complaint. If the worker succeeded somehow in reducing the margin of profits, the capitalist would be unable to put forth his best efforts, and the total product would be diminished, to the detriment of all.

Trade unions that sought to reduce the hours of labor or to improve wage rates were reminded that matters of this sort were determined by inexorable laws of supply and demand that unions, as well as employers, were powerless to set aside. Some businessmen, indeed, insisted that trade unions not only were an "intrusion" upon the domain of natural law, but that they were withal destructive of the rights of the individual laborer and, in effect, subversive of the existing order. One manufacturer referred to unions as "fierce, cruel, arbitrary, dictatorial—in a word, tyrannical!" The *Portage Lake Mining Gazette,* reflecting the views of employers in Michigan's copper country, declared that "nothing more thoroughly un-American, in practice and in principle, can well be conceived than trades unionism." . . .

The state as well as the trade union was cautioned by employers to entrust the labor contract to the bargaining of the individual worker and his employer. "I say the legislature has no right to encroach upon me as to whether I shall employ men eight hours, or ten, or fifteen," the clothing manufacturer Henry V. Rothschild informed a committee of the House of Representatives. "It is a matter of mutual agreement, and the legislature has no right, according to the principles of our government, according to the principles of the Declaration of Independence, to impose upon me what hours of labor I shall have between myself and my employees." Jane Addams has informed us that the Illinois labor legislation of the 1890's "ran counter to the instinct and tradition, almost to the very religion of the manufacturers of the state."

With respect to the great currency problems that troubled the nation in the three and one-half decades after the Civil War, the business community was in essential agreement with the laissez-faire economists. Although some businessmen were sympathetic to the cause of greenbacks, businessmen in general and the banking community in particular favored specie resumption. The battle of the standards found business leaders generally arrayed on the side of gold and using the conventional arguments as to the limited role government should play in this sphere.

The advent of the railroad and the practices which railway managers found it necessary to employ raised doubts in the minds of some businessmen regarding the virtues of a completely unregulated economic order. Merchants and shippers disadvantageously affected by personal or place discrimination or by railway-rate agreements decided that the railway business was not one that could be safely entrusted to the free play of economic forces and that in this field at least the power of the state would have to be invoked. The pro-rata movement in the East during the 1850's and the 1860's was led by members of the business community; merchants and shippers played the crucial role in the framing of the so-called Granger laws in Illinois, Iowa, Wisconsin, and Minnesota; and commercial elements in New York City were instrumental in securing the Hepburn investigation of the New York State Assembly and the railway legislation that the state subsequently adopted and were, according to one scholar, "the single most important group" behind the passage of the Interstate Commerce Act.

Railroad officials sought for a time to stave off state and federal railroad regulation and were not at all pleased with the regulatory legislation that was enacted. Charles Elliott Perkins, of the Chicago, Burlington and Quincy, expressed the wish that the "intelligent people" could "be made to see that the let alone policy as regards railroads is the safe one and that any other policy is full of danger." Confronted by the Hepburn investigation, Presidents William H. Vanderbilt of the New York Central and H. J. Jewett of the New York, Lake Erie and Western Railroad spoke of the attack on the railroads as evidence of the "growth of a disregard to the rights of property in this country." "This growing tendency to socialistic principles," they declared, "is one of the most dangerous signs of the times, and if not checked, will produce scenes of disaster that would now appal the country." This was not, Vanderbilt and Jewett thought, a matter with which individual states might cope, and unless Congress could somehow interpose its authority, all concerned would have to "wait for time either to furnish a remedy or permit the great laws of trade, now trammeled by destructive competition, to work out the result." When Congress finally did "interpose its authority" by enacting the Interstate Commerce Act, railroad officials were not, however, altogether satisfied with the result. The great railroad entrepreneur John Murray Forbes branded the measure "a cross between socialism and paternalism," and other railroad leaders were equally critical of the statute.

Persuaded, however, to recognize the folly of unlimited competition in an industry in which fixed costs are so prominent a factor, railroad presidents became eager for federal legislation that would legalize the pooling arrangements that the roads might themselves devise. Railroad officials nevertheless, made it clear to the United States Industrial Commission at the turn of the century that although they were prepared to accept legislation of this sort, they, like the laissez-faire economists, were firmly opposed to the grant of full rate-making authority of the Interstate Commerce Commission and to the "sublime folly" of government ownership. President E. B. Thomas of the Erie Railroad was doubtless giving expression to the thought of many of these officials at this time when he asked the Commission why public authorities did not permit the railways, which had done so much for the country, "to work out their own solution instead of hampering them so much with investigation, legislation, and all that line of procedure."

Like the advent of the railroad, the trend toward business consolidation and the growth of trusts and industrial combinations in the last decades of the nineteenth century caused many persons to question the validity of the businessman's argument that competition equitably regulates the economic life of the nation and that state intervention is therefore unnecessary. Since one of the chief reasons for the formation of trusts was the desire of the interested parties to avoid the rigors of competition, there was some difficulty in fitting these combinations into the businessman's picture of the self-regulating economic order. Many merchants and small businessmen, indeed, frightened by the implications of the consolidation movement, advocated anti-monopoly action that would be more favorable to them and more in consonance with the American ideal of equality of opportunity. Other businessmen, however, and particularly those associated with the larger concerns, insisted that the trusts were a natural and inevitable product of industrial progress and a source of benefit to the community. Most of the businessmen who argued in this fashion maintained that the trusts did not interfere with competition in any essential way. Some, however, averred that competition had served its purpose and that the era of competition was being replaced by a new era of cooperation.

Those who maintained that the trust in no way violated the principles of competition generally pointed to the factor of potential competition. It was alleged that if a trust should attempt to secure more than the average return from capital, new competitors would invade the field, and this would force prices down. Competition and the natural laws of supply and demand could therefore be relied on to secure to the consumer a fair price even in areas of the economy that were dominated by industrial combinations. S. C. T. Dodd, of Standard Oil, and Hermon B. Butler, of Ryerson and Son, insisted the formation of business consolidations had actually improved the quality of competition and that any antitrust action would constitute an unwarranted restraint of trade. In similar fashion, Charles Elliott Perkins argued that the experience of many industries had demonstrated that combination was "a necessary part . . . of the natural law of competition" and that its results were of benefit to the public at large.

A few businessmen, however, spoke of the "debauch of competition" and extolled the trust as the harbinger of a new era of cooperation and industrial peace. The virtues of competition, these businessmen contended, had been exaggerated, and all should rejoice that industry was moving on to a higher level. The vice president of the National Bank of the Republic informed the American Bankers Association in 1896 that competition was the life of trade "within well defined limits, but beyond those limits it [was] far from profitable and wise." . . .

Though businessmen who defended the trusts differed in their views as to the vitality of competition, the vast majority of them were agreed that industrial combinations were not properly the concern of the state. If a particular combination effectively served the needs of the people, they maintained, it would survive; if not, it would perish. Legislation, at all events, could in no way affect the survival of the fittest business concerns. Henry O. Havemeyer, president of the American Sugar Refining Company, summed up the views of many businessmen in this matter when he informed the United States Industrial Commission that "the Government should have nothing to do with them [trusts] in any way, shape, or manner." The public, he argued, needs no information about monopoly. "Let the buyer beware; that covers the whole business. You cannot wet-nurse people from the time they are born until the time they die. They have got to wade in and get stuck, and that is the way men are educated and cultivated."

Although the businessman was prone to argue the virtues of the nega-tive state, he was hardly consistent in his application of laissez-faire theories. To be sure, he criticized state action that might circumscribe his activities or that would aid other groups in the community, but he did not oppose such activities of the state as served to promote business enterprise or to enhance business profits. Andrew Carnegie regularly de-nounced legislative tinkering but nevertheless advocated government construction of a Lake Erie and Ohio River Ship Canal that would lower ton-mile rates from the Lakes to the Carnegie works in Pittsburgh. The National Association of Manufacturers, organized in 1895, criticized the manufacture and free distribution to farmers by the Department of Agri-culture of vaccine designed to combat blackleg but importuned the fed-eral government to promote foreign trade by chartering an international American bank, subsidizing the merchant marine, enacting a protective tariff, and reforming the consular service so as to make it more solicitous of the export needs of American manufacturers. Railway officials who attacked rate-making as an improper exercise of legislative authority saw nothing amiss in legislation to prevent strikes from interfering with in-terstate commerce, to define liabilities in case of bankruptcy, and to require tests for color blindness; and many of them had perhaps forgot-ten that they were speaking for railroads that had benefited from federal land grants and from the largesse of state and local governments.

One of the most patent violations of the laws of trade in the period after the Civil War was the protective tariff; and yet most businessmen, and particularly industrialists, approved of this form of government bounty. Henry Clews, who told the workingman not to organize but to rely on the laws of trade, was not so convinced of the benign effects of natural law when it came to the tariff: he bitterly criticized Grover Cleveland's famous tariff message of 1887. Henry Wood and Charles Flint, who thought the state should do little more than protect property and provide for the enforcement of contracts, approved the enactment of tariff legislation that afforded protection to American industries. After declaring that he did not "believe in attempting to control the business of the citizen by legislative enactment," the banker E. R. Chapman went on to say that he was a high protectionist. Andrew Carnegie, although an acknowledged disciple of Herbert Spencer, was not disposed to interpret natural law in the same manner as the English philosopher when it came to the subject of the tariff. To the American ironmaster, the protective tariff was a necessary means of implementing the "evident law of nature" that many nations should enjoy "the blessings of diversified industries."

At the National Tariff Convention of 1881 representatives from virtually all the major industries of the country announced their adherence to the principle of protection. Laissez-faire economists were denounced at this convention because of their support of free trade, but words of praise were directed at Francis Bowen, who, although an advocate of laissez faire, was, at the same time, a friend to protection. Most of the witnesses connected with manufacturing industries who testified before the United States Industrial Commission spoke in favor of the protective tariff and yet denounced projects for regulating the trusts as contrary to the laws of trade. The businessman thus refused to carry laissez faire to its logical conclusion. He was quite willing to sanction state interference with the laws of trade when that interference offered hope of higher profits. But when the state sought to embark on programs of social reform, the businessman became an opponent of state action, an advocate of laissez faire.

The laissez-faire philosophy of the businessman culminated, in a sense, in Andrew Carnegie's "Gospel of Wealth." The businessman had found support for his exalted position in the doctrines of social Darwinism and laissez faire and in the actual conditions of American life. He had expounded the virtues of the system of private enterprise and had pointed out that the capitalist in his pursuit of wealth necessarily serves the common good. But he was forced to recognize that social problems still existed and that the state was being called on to solve these problems. Perhaps the public, even if it would not sanction any significant state interference with the laws of trade, would demand that the state recapture some of the gains of the wealthy by way of an income tax and use the funds so obtained to advance the general welfare. As if to meet this problem, Carnegie, who considered an income tax "perhaps the most pernicious form of taxation which has ever been conceived since human society has settled into peaceful government," devised his Gospel of Wealth.

Carnegie, who had pledged himself as early as 1868 to spend "for benevolent purposes" that portion of his annual income which exceeded fifty thousand dollars, first set forth his philosophy of wealth in popular form in an article that appeared in the *North American Review* in June, 1889. In this statement of his position, Carnegie accepted individualism, private property, competition, and the accumulation of wealth as the highest results of human experience. He insisted that the accumulation of wealth in the hands of the few was not only the inevitable result of the basic laws of civilization but that it was "essential for the future progress of the race." Carnegie did not, however, believe that the millionaire had discharged his responsibilities to mankind simply because he had amassed a fortune. He maintained that the man who had been wise enough to accumulate wealth was under an obligation to administer that wealth wisely. To Carnegie, this meant that the millionaire should not simply bequeath his wealth to his children or to the state, for that was contrary to the best interests of all concerned, but should rather utilize his fortune during his lifetime for the benefit of the community. After having provided for the legitimate wants of his dependents, the rich man was to treat all "surplus revenues" as "trust funds" that he was obligated "to administer in the manner which, in his judgment, is best calculated to produce the most beneficial results for the community—the man of wealth thus becoming the mere agent and trustee for his poorer brethren, bringing to their service his superior wisdom, experience, and ability to administer, doing for them better than they would or could do for themselves." "Such, in my opinion," said Carnegie, "is the true Gospel concerning Wealth."

In a second article, Carnegie detailed the types of gifts he thought most advisable. He recommended the donation of funds for the establishment of universities, the founding or extension of hospitals, medical colleges, and laboratories, the creation of public parks, and the construction of music halls, swimming pools, and churches. He considered the wisest gift to a community to be a free library, provided the community would maintain it as a public institution.

Carnegie's Gospel of Wealth rested on the usual laissez-faire assumptions as to the sufficiency of an unregulated economic order. However, Carnegie's program represented, in a sense, an addition to the laissez-faire doctrine of self-interest. Whereas the advocate of laissez faire ordinarily contended that the individual in seeking and acquiring wealth thereby unconsciously serves the interests of the whole, Carnegie went one step further and maintained that the individual who accumulates wealth should consciously use this wealth during his lifetime for the general welfare.

Carnegie did not regard his Gospel of Wealth as a mere sop to the general public but rather as an actual solution for the social problems of the day. He referred to his plan as "the true antidote for the temporary unequal distribution of wealth," as a solution for the problem of rich and poor. As once it had been maintained that political rule should be vested in the well-to-do, so now Carnegie was saying that the promotion of the general welfare of the community should be entrusted to those who had managed to make the most money rather than to the representatives of the people. Identifying wealth with intelligence, he insisted that the millionaires would know better than the people's government how to expend funds for the common good and that resort to the paternalism of the state was therefore unnecessary. Carnegie's Gospel of Wealth was thus a challenge to the democratic service state and represented a recrudescence of the principles of aristocracy and stewardship. . . .

Of a piece with the Gospel of Wealth were the programs of "welfare capitalism" instituted by businessmen in the last two decades of the nineteenth century. This development stemmed, to a certain extent at least, from the desire of businessmen to persuade employees to identify their best interests with their employer rather than with a trade union or the general-welfare state. To that end employers established insurance funds for sick and injured employees, provided their workers with libraries and music halls, constructed model towns, and instituted schemes of profit sharing. A study of the subject of welfare capitalism by the Department of Labor in 1900 revealed fifteen different plans of industrial betterment in operation. Although the movement of welfare capitalism in the 1880's and 1890's in no way reached the proportions of the similar movement in the 1920's, it is none the less significant as a manifestation of the businessman's philosophy.

Since the businessman was the dominant figure on the American scene during the years from 1865 to 1901, his views received strong support from most elements in American life. Nowhere, however, did the business spirit find greater favor than in the Protestant church. In the Gilded Age, "urban Protestantism cultivated the middle and upper classes who possessed the ultimate power in American society." Never before had wealth mattered so much to the church. Wealthy business figures were appointed to church boards in increasing numbers, and men of business ability were in demand to serve as church officials. Even the Baptists, who had prided themselves on being a poor man's denomination, ceased to express contempt for wealth and decided that the man of wealth was also "a man of talent." The churches were fast becoming "social and religious clubs for the privileged classes."

Ministers who resented the "aristocratic drift of Protestantism" denounced the alliance between church and market. "No Christian minister," charged the Reverend Franklin M. Sprague, "can deny that the church is crippled, yea, bound and gagged, because of her alliance with wealth." "The simple fact," said the Reverend Arthur T. Pierson, "is . . . that the communion of saintliness is displaced by the communion of respectability. Our churches are becoming the quarters of a monopoly." . . .

The Protestant minister, like the businessman, gave his support to laissez-faire and the *status quo*. He provided religious sanction for the businessman's views with respect to property, inequality, stewardship, state aid, and labor. Property was defended by churchmen as an exclusive right. The general well-being and progress of society were declared to be in proportion to the freedom of the individual to acquire property and to be secure in its possession. Love requires the acquisition of property, declared Mark Hopkins, the eminent Congregational minister and president of Williams College, "because it is a powerful means of benefiting others." Those who have done the most for our institutions have been men with "a strong desire of property." "As men now are," Hopkins concluded, "it is far better that they should be employed in accumulating property honestly . . . than that there should be encouraged any sentimentalism about the worthlessness of property." . . .

Like the businessman, the churchman accepted inequalities among men as inevitable and desirable and maintained that those who had risen to the top were the men of ability whereas those who had failed had only themselves to blame. "God," said Henry Ward Beecher, "has intended the great to be great, and the little to be little." But, in Beecher's view, it was not only predestination that served to make a man poor. He thought it a "general truth" that "no man in this land suffers from poverty unless it be more than his fault—unless it be his *sin.*" In the long run, said the Bishop of Massachusetts, wealth comes to the man of morality. To desire wealth is a sign of strong character and is both "natural and necessary." Religious sanction should not be given to any attempt to suppress this desire. In his celebrated lecture, *Acres of Diamonds,* the Baptist clergyman Russell Conwell preached the "gospel of success." "I say that you ought to get rich, and it is your duty to get rich." The richest people are generally those of the best character. It is wrong to be poor.

The Reverend A. J. F. Behrends, who looked upon inequality as "an original, ultimate, and unalterable fact," deprecated talk of limiting individual wealth because it involved "the right of the state to regulate personal ability, to prescribe to the Almighty how much brains a man shall be permitted to have." Roswell D. Hitchcock, of Union Theological Seminary, agreed with Behrends. Capital, he stated, represents intelligence, self-denial, and control and is "finer than labor, just as brain is finer than muscle." "At bottom, it is an immorality to fight against the inequality of condition, which simply corresponds with inequality of endowment."

Carnegie's Gospel of Wealth accorded perfectly with Protestant ideas of stewardship and hence was warmly endorsed by Protestant clergymen. "If ever Christ's words have been obeyed to the letter," stated Bishop Lawrence, "they are obeyed to-day by those who are living out His precepts of the stewardship of wealth." Speaking to the American Association for the Advancement of Science, President Joseph Cummings of Wesleyan University declared that "the great remedy for social wrongs" was to "be found in the Christian use of money." . . .

The majority of Protestant churchmen, like the businessmen, took a completely negative view of social reform and state action. They considered reform a matter of individual regeneration rather than of improved social conditions. Character, they said, determines conditions more than conditions determine character. Like their business friends, they were opposed to any significant legislative interference with the laws of trade. They advised the state to protect property and enforce contracts and, in effect, to ignore the general welfare.

The idea that "government should be paternal and take care of the welfare of its subjects and provide them with labor" was denounced by the eminent divine Henry Ward Beecher as "un-American." "The American doctrine," Beecher declared, "is that it is the duty of the Government merely to protect the people while they are taking care of themselves—nothing more than that. 'Hands off,' we say to the Government." Roswell D. Hitchcock looked on most types of state action as communistic in character. Although recognizing that social evils existed,

Hitchcock thought that the remedies for these evils were not to be prescribed by the state. Government, he asserted, may not meddle with wages, limit the number of working hours (except for minors), set up labor exchanges, or run any industry. "The questions to be settled are questions of political economy, which ought, on every account, to be settled dispassionately. Men may vote as they please, but the laws of production and of trade are as inexorable as the laws of nature."

The Reverend A. J. F. Behrends differed but little in his social philosophy from that great opponent of social reform, William Graham Sumner. A policy that relieves individuals of "worry" or the "fear of want," he argued, "only degrades, pauperizes and brutalizes them." All that justice requires is that each individual be left free to work at his chosen task and to reap the fruits of his labor. If the responsibility is "individualized" and competition unchecked, the nation will enjoy the benefits of a cheap and abundant production. Like Sumner, Behrends feared the rule of the majority and contended that what characterizes the free state is the existence of restraints imposed on the majority by the minority.

Even giving aid to the poor was criticized by some clergymen as an unwarranted exercise of state authority and as a task that was more properly entrusted to private charity. Bishop Harris of Michigan attacked state poor relief as injurious to both the poor and the rich. Relief of this sort, he held, encourages improvidence in the needy and paralyzes the bounty of the wealthy, thus depriving the poor of the personal sympathy of the rich and the rich of the gratitude of the poor. The poor and the rich, he concluded, are indispensable to one another and should be brought together "by flinging all classes . . . back on the old law of mutual helpfulness and sympathy; by discontinuing charity by law, and relying on the charity of love."

The workingman received no more sympathy from most Protestant clergymen than he did from the businessman. Labor, in the view of conservative church leaders, was but a commodity and like all other commodities was to be "governed by the imperishable laws of demand and supply." "It is all right to talk and declaim about the dignity of labor," declared the *Watchman and Reflector*. "But when all has been said of it, what is labor but a matter of barter and sale."

The advice offered to the laborer by clergymen was to remain passive. The Reverend W. D. Wilson told the workingman that Jesus' advice was that he be content with his wages. If he were entitled to higher wages, in the Lord's good time he would receive them. What injustice he suffered in this world would be turned to his account in the hereafter. "Be quiet," declared Wilson. "Whatsoever your hands find to do, do it, and be content with your wages. God will take care of the rest."

Other clergymen also found laissez faire to be the proper nostrum for the ills of labor, and they therefore condemned all of labor's weapons: trade unions, strikes, and labor legislation. Trade unions, they alleged, served but to drag down the superior workman to the level of the inferior and to introduce class lines into American society. "The Trades' Unions," charged the *Christian Advocate,* "are despotic and revolutionary in tendency. . . . The worst doctrines of Communism are involved in these unions. . . . Legislate Trades' Unions out of existence. . . ."

The Reverend Joseph Cook, who won for himself a reputation as a reformer but who was denounced by the labor editor John Swinton as a "noisy and empty-headed preacher," recognized that female and child laborers required the protection of government but insisted that adult male laborers should seek to improve their competitive position through self-help rather than by invoking the aid of the state. Politicians who advised workers to enlist the support of the state were attacked by Cook as "enemies of social progress."

An especially bitter foe of labor was the influential Princeton clergyman-economist Lyman Atwater, a frequent contributor to Presbyterian journals and "a force in public opinion only slightly below Sumner." Atwater looked upon most trade unions as "conspiracies against the laws of God, the rights of man, and the welfare of society," and believed, consequently, that they must be repressed. He was similarly opposed to strikes and was virtually thrown into a panic by the great railroad strikes of 1877. . . .

Bishop Harris was as critical of labor's methods as was Atwater and viewed them as being essentially socialistic. Labor legislation, the Bishop declared, is useless because the industrial world is governed by natural laws that man cannot annul. "The best legislation in the industrial and commercial sphere of human activity has long since been enacted by the Supreme Lawgiver; and every interposition by human government is both impertinent and harmful."

From the point of view of economics, the clergymen thus advocated laissez-faire as the solution for existing labor difficulties. As Bishop Harris put it: "So far as economical agencies are concerned, there is no doubt that the great principle of *laissez faire,* advanced by Adam Smith, is the correct one." From the religious point of view, however, the ministers proposed Christianity as a supplement to laissez faire. The capitalist was exhorted to apply Protestant ideas with respect to the stewardship of wealth, to treat his employees properly, and to adopt such "Christian" devices as profit sharing. "The power of Christian love," said one clergyman, "should smooth and sweeten all the relations of capitalists and labor."

The close alliance between the Protestant church and wealth and the attitude of Protestant clergymen toward the labor struggle were among the factors that contributed to the decline in the church attendance of Protestant workingmen in the decades after the Civil War. The workers, Samuel Gompers declared in response to a query as to why laborers had become alienated from the church, "have come to look upon the church and ministry as the apologists and defenders of the wrongs committed against the interests of the people, simply because the perpetrators are the possessors of wealth." Clergymen, he charged, were using "their exalted positions to discountenance all practical efforts of the toilers to lift themselves out of the slough of despondency and despair." "We believe much in Jesus and in his teachings, but not much in the teachings of his pretended followers," one workingman declared. "A civilization that permits man to be the greatest enemy of man . . . is a cheat and a sham; the political economy that permits it is a falsehood and a fraud; and a religion that allows it without constant, earnest, and persistent protest is a humbug." It was from conditions such as these that the social-gospel movement sought to rescue the Protestant church.

Critics writing about the 1870s and '80s have characterized these as years of vulgarity, speculation, waste, economic disorder, and low political morality. Since all this was covered by a gaudy exterior, the crusading journalist Edward L. Godkin spoke of a "chromo civilization," and Mark Twain of "the Gilded Age." It is Twain's term that has passed into common usage, because it quickly conveys the idea that there was something unsavory beneath the surface glitter.

2
POLITICS AND MORALITY IN THE GILDED AGE

The social philosophy of this age, it has been said, could be summarized by the term "the acquisitive society." Its political philosophy may be described in similar terms, for politics appeared wholly opportunistic. Americans, it seemed, looked upon political parties primarily as instruments to be used in extorting wealth from the government for private use. The Gilded Age, in other words, witnessed the flowering of the spoils system on an unprecedented scale.

Since Andrew Jackson's day the spoils system had made organized politics directly dependent on the government treasury, but now parties also gained support from the new capitalists who expected their contributions to organized politics to be repaid through favors from politicians in government service. In short, the alliance between the new capitalism and politics gave impetus to official corruption to an extent never before seen in the United States.

The very nature of American political organization at this time made the corruption easy, for it blurred the line between proper and improper conduct in government service. The political parties lived on patronage, and the politicians needed public offices to survive. These professional politicians, who made up the core of party organization, operated in a no-man's-land where the pressure for survival often made the distinction between legal and illegal action appear merely theoretical. When these men were placed in control of government departments, they frequently aided the entrepreneurs who had helped them gain office, took a share of the proceeds for such assistance for themselves, and diverted another portion of this wealth to their party organization so that the party would prosper and they themselves could continue to enjoy the fruits of power.

Throughout most of the Gilded Age, the Republican politicians were the ones who enjoyed the fruits of power, for their party retained control of the federal government. Under Ulysses S. Grant the Republicans spread what has been called a huge barbecue. Through Congress they bestowed rich gifts in lands, preferential tariffs, cash subsidies, and favors of all sorts. Politics and government became the servants of a material progress that in fact favored the few, such as the industrial barons, at the expense of the nation.

Greed, or the lust for spoils, was not the only cause for this barbecue for the few. Another reason was the lack of a generally accepted philosophy concerning the proper role of government in economic life. The nation's leaders took for granted the pragmatic idea that the business of America was to create private wealth and that political action at all levels should contribute to this task.

As a result, politics declined in prestige. Men now began to use the word "politician" as though it were dirty. In 1870 the historian Henry Adams expressed some of this disgust. "The government," he said, "does not govern; Congress is inefficient, and shows itself more and more incompetent." Yet, of the three branches of government, Congress was predominant. It overshadowed the Presidency and the judiciary. Between 1868 and 1888, in fact, none of the Presidents could be called truly strong or dynamic leaders.

Never before had politics been so much in the hands of professionals as in the Gilded Age. Even the strife between parties appeared to be merely a noisy show put on by professionals whose main concern was with the distribution of the spoils. They fought not for principles, political analysts have concluded, but for the uninterrupted use and enjoyment of their offices.

To the businessmen—considered by many to be the real leaders of America—the outcome of the political battles was not vitally important. Regardless of the results of virtually any election, their own interests were not endangered. One party's defeat and the other's victory made no appreciable difference in national direction. The Republican and Democratic parties were amorphous entities whose primary commitment seemed to be to the *status quo*. A new administration in Washington usually meant only that a different set of professional officeholders had taken power.

This commitment to inaction did not mean that America lacked problems worthy of the government's attention; the political stagnation stemmed from the refusal of politicians to recognize and act upon issues. No priority was given to statesmanship. Diplomacy and finance, as well as military, naval, and internal administration, one of Grant's Cabinet officers explained, are "relegated to such odds and ends as may be snatched from the greater cares of office."

If few issues of importance divided Democrats and Republicans, it might be assumed that the frequent splitting of the dominant Republican party resulted from a concern for principle. Such was not the case; the factions within the party fought mainly for more of the fruits of the repeated victories. In the 1870s, for instance, the Half-Breed faction, led by James G. Blaine of Maine, and the Stalwart group, headed by Roscoe Conkling of New York, detested each other but did not disagree on policy. They differed mainly over the distribution of the mounting spoils. The Half-Breeds insisted that they should control the assignment of federal jobs, and the Stalwarts contended that *they* should.

So lucrative were the spoils that politics became a big business in its own right—hence its spreading professionalization. Party leaders would not willingly adopt policies that might jeopardize their chances of gaining and holding public office. In both parties these leaders refused to take clear-cut positions on major issues for fear of alienating substantial blocs of voters and losing elections. To them the very essence of politics was the winning and the taking of the spoils. The ever-swelling patronage at the disposal of the victors—in national, state, and city governments—added to the incentive to win rather than to serve.

Regardless of the incentive of spoils, somebody had to lose. Why didn't the losers seek change on the basis of principle? The party in power, obviously, did not wish to tamper with a profitable system. But neither did the leaders of the minority party, for they looked forward to the day when they would take office and profit from the same system. The professional politicians, therefore, practiced their trade apart from real needs of society, as though their deeds did not affect the mainstream of life.

Many Americans apparently were willing to go along with this state of affairs, for there was a general conformity of opinion in the country. Most voters, contemporary evidence suggests, did not think they were avoiding genuine issues or participating in sham battles. They seemed to believe that there were no economic issues or other problems of sufficient importance to merit decisive action by the government. As a consequence, until the 1890s the real problems of the period—such as those of currency, tariff schedules, farm distress, the rise of labor, and the emergence of business monopoly—developed beneath the gilded surface of the times.

The civil-service reform in 1883 seriously weakened the spoils system, upon which rested the political corruption of the Gilded Age. Competitive examinations rather than political favoritism became the means of obtaining government posts; competence on the job rather than the use of the job to advance party interests became the requirement for retaining government employment. Scandals and corruption still occasionally rocked the government and shocked most Americans, but they no longer gave tone to an entire age. America's political institutions, instead of being used by the professional politicians to advance their own interests, became useful in solving national problems and in helping the people realize their legitimate economic and social desires. A political observer like Lord Bryce could no longer truthfully argue that the best men refused to enter politics. Many of them, from big business and elsewhere, did seek public office and helped to restore and preserve the essentially democratic features of America's political institutions.

In theory the consolidation of the triumph of the industrial capitalists over the agrarians in the Gilded Age did not change the basic structure of America's political institutions. The parties continued to function under old concepts, and the governmental machinery operated within the established constitutional framework. Yet, in practice, a fundamental change had taken place. Big business had become so powerful and the drive to obtain wealth through government favors had become so strong that the traditional safeguards against tyranny and political abuses were not sufficient to protect the national interest in an industrialized and increasingly urbanized America. Only through political parties could Americans peacefully curb the abuses. Thus, just as political action had been an instrument of corruption in the Gilded Age, it also became a means of checking the power of the corrupters.

Even the weakness of government, which Woodrow Wilson saw as a growing trend, was reversed. Although there was a relapse into "congressional government" from 1921 to 1933, this did not become a permanent feature of the American system. Instead, in recent years, there have been alarmed cries over the expanding power of the Presidency. In summary, America's political system is a living institution. It became stagnant in the Gilded Age, but it has continued to grow and to be shaped by living people and by history.

The selections that follow all probe beneath the surface of the Gilded Age by focusing on some aspect of politics or corruption. Each explores one problem, and all attempt to explain why conditions were as they were.

Leonard D. White

PUBLIC SERVICE

ETHICS

Leonard D. White was a political scientist whose historical writings have won praise, admiration, and prizes from professional historians. His main concern was administrative history— the study of institutions and their development. He also tried to round out and give depth to his histories by analyzing and explaining the motives of the men who operated these institutions, most of which were political. In the following selection, White is concerned with political corruption in the Gilded Age and with its institutional ties. He agrees with critics such as Charles Francis Adams that the corruption stemmed, in part at least, from the system of party organization in the United States. He also points out that the basically high ethical standards of the American people were not seriously impaired by the low morality of those in government. Yet he admits that the built-in weaknesses and temptations for corruption in the political system were difficult to reform. One should note his analysis of why and how moral reform finally overcame the worst features of the American political system as exposed in the Gilded Age. [Reprinted with per-

mission of the publisher from The Republican Era: 1869–1901 *by Leonard D. White. Copyright 1958 by The Macmillan Company.*]

The Republican era opened in moral chaos. It remained sunk in moral degradation throughout Grant's two terms, during which members of Congress, high executive officials, and subordinate administrative agents were guilty of one dereliction after another. Improvement began with Hayes and was sustained by Garfield and Arthur. Cleveland did much, and the quality of presidential and Cabinet leadership during and after his administration helped restore the reputation of the government. In this long trend toward higher standards Washington preceded the states and cities, but all were bound together.

The deplorable levels of public and business morality from the 1860's into the 1880's were deprecated by reformers and journalists alike, but for years theirs were voices crying in the wilderness. Edwin L. Godkin wrote in 1868: "Another striking change which has occurred in the commercial world, and which is doing something to promote unscrupulousness, is what may be called the diminished value of character. . . . both here and in England the outer edge of the well-established and respectable circle of the commercial world swarms with adventurers whom no one knows, and to whom character is not necessary in order to do a considerable amount of business, and whom no number of failures seems to daunt or drive from the field." . . .

Charles Francis Adams [in 1876] traced political corruption to an indefensible party system. "The single great end to which all reformers, whatever their private theories may be, must look is distinct enough; it is to overcome the tendency of our political system to corruption. All political systems, no doubt, have some tendency, greater or less, towards corruption. The peculiarity of ours is that it moves, and for fifty years has moved, in that direction with accelerating pace, and it has now arrived at a point where even the blindest patriots see that, unless the evil is checked, our political system must break down and some new experiment must be substituted in its place." He put the blame on the system of party organization, "bred in the gutter of New York politics," and adopted by the entire nation.

The Moral Slump. The eight years of Grant's administration rocked with one scandal after another. Citizens defrauded the government in the acquisition of land and in claims for pensions; contractors supplying the army and navy were often venal; and unscrupulous lawyers levied toll on ignorant and defenseless Indians. Members of Congress were bribed and disgraced. Cabinet officers were investigated and impeached. Subordinate officials and employees were revealed in outright betrayal of the public trust. Never had the Republic sunk to so low an estate of official morality.

The condition in the rank and file of many government offices has already been revealed in previous chapters. During the 1870's there was both incompetence and dishonesty in the large customhouses; discipline and integrity among the navy-yard labor forces were at a low ebb; the Indian service had been roundly condemned by Garfield; land agents connived at irregularities, and surveyors made fraudulent claims for work not performed. The story of betrayal of trust at some points, however, must be kept in perspective—the smaller customhouses were substantially untouched by the evils that flourished in New York or Philadelphia; most postmasters in cities large and small were entirely reliable; rascals among the accountable officers were gratifyingly few; the majority of the departmental clerks in Washington held high ethical standards and performed their duties faithfully.

The tone of the eight years of Grant's administration was nevertheless set by a small number of weak and unreliable persons holding seats in Congress and in high executive office. It was during these years that the most resounding scandals occurred, not only in Washington but in many states and cities. When the mighty wandered far from the paths of rectitude, it was not surprising that some of the lesser ranks followed their example. To a few of the scandals of these years we turn for brief review.

The Crédit Mobilier. This corporation, originally organized to finance railroad construction, fell into the control of a group of adventurers, including a member of Congress, Oakes Ames. The corporation was awarded a lucrative but fraudulent contract for the construction of a long section of the Union Pacific Railroad, the effect of which was to double the face value of its stock. Ames offered to sell shares of this stock to leading members of both the House and Senate at par value, for the purpose of protecting the interests of the railroad. "We want more friends in this Congress." The transactions were eventually exposed and a House investigation followed, resulting in the expulsion of two members of the House, Oakes Ames and James Brooks, the disgrace of Vice Presidents Colfax and Wilson, a recommendation in the Senate to expel James W. Patterson of New Hampshire, and a cloud on the reputation of Henry L. Dawes, James A. Garfield, and others. The *Nation* of January 30, 1873, summarized the consequences as "total loss, one Senator; badly damaged, and not serviceable for future political use, two Vice-Presidents and eight Congressmen. The condition of Ames's reputation language is inadequate to describe."

The Case of the Secretary of War, William W. Belknap. Laxness or corruption in the award of Indian trading posts had been suspected for some time under General Belknap's administration of the War Department. A House committee took evidence in the winter of 1876 that revealed both.

Secretary Belknap's busybody wife, anxious for social display and needing income beyond her husband's salary, had secured from her husband a post tradership for a New York contractor, Caleb P. Marsh. The then incumbent of the post, John S. Evans, offered Marsh $12,000 a year to be let alone; Marsh accepted and agreed to give one half to Mrs. Belknap. Shortly after the first payment of $1,500 she died, but Belknap continued to receive the payments. Other favorites of the administration were also taking illegitimate profits, amounting to at least $100,000 a year.

The outcome was sudden, dramatic, and symptomatic. The House Committee on Expenditures in the War Department found "at the very threshold of their investigations" uncontradicted evidence of Secretary Belknap's malfeasance in office and recommended that he be impeached. One of Belknap's friends privately informed him of his impending fate, whereupon, before the committee could report, he dashed to the White House and presented his resignation. Grant accepted it "with great regret" without realizing, as he later confided to the Cabinet, that acceptance was not a matter of course.

Articles of impeachment were brought against Belknap despite his hasty resignation and his claim that as a private citizen impeachment proceedings would not lie against him. The Senate repudiated this construction of the impeachment clause. When, however, the proceedings came to an end, Belknap was acquitted for lack of a two-thirds majority. On the fifth article (the most serious) thirty-seven Senators voted guilty, twenty-three not guilty for want of jurisdiction, and two more not guilty on the evidence. As to Belknap's moral guilt, there could be no doubt.

The Case of Attorney General George H. Williams. Williams was Attorney General from 1872 to 1875. In 1873 Grant nominated him as Chief Justice of the Supreme Court. A passage from the diary of Hamilton Fish tells the story of Williams' subsequent embarrassments. Fish was called to the White House by the President, who revealed that the nomination would probably fail for highly discreditable reasons.

He [President Grant] did not think that he (Williams) had done anything corrupt or illegal, but that there had been indiscreet things done. That Mrs. Williams had given orders for the purchase of an expensive carriage and liveries for two servants and that the expenses for those had been paid out of the contingent fund of the Department of Justice; as were also the wages of the two men who were employed as private servants. He manifested much regret at having learned this. . . . It was also alleged that Judge Williams had mingled his accounts with those of the Department, and that during the panic, when the banks were not paying private checks, it was said that the money for meeting the expenses of his house had been paid from the funds of the government; that he understood it had all been made good, but that this appropriation of government funds was unjustifiable.

Conkling reported the nomination favorably from the Judiciary Committee, but the Senate recommitted the matter and Grant shortly thereafter withdrew the nomination. Nevertheless the President allowed Williams to continue as Attorney General of the United States for another year and a half.

The Case of the Secretary of the Navy, George M. Robeson. A House investigation of the Navy Department in 1876, colored no doubt by partisanship, nevertheless disclosed operations highly dishonorable to the Secretary, if not outright corrupt. When Robeson took office in 1869 he had a small amount of property and a modest law practice. Once in office he formed a business connection with A. G. Cattell and Company of Philadelphia, a grain, feed, and flour commission firm. By reason of its connection with Robeson, the firm was enabled to levy percentages upon other contractors' engagements with the navy, always a heavy purchaser of flour and other supplies. Both the Cattells and Robeson grew rich. The House Committee proved through Robeson's bank books that between July 1, 1869, and April 4, 1876, he had deposited over $300,000 beyond his apparent income.

The Democratic majority of the House Committee thought impeachment was in order, but the disputed presidential election of 1876 foreclosed further proceedings. Godkin declared in the *Nation:* "we believe no man in his senses can read the evidence taken and doubt that a secret partnership existed between the Secretary and the Cattells, by virtue of which they levied toll on contracts and he levied toll on them."

So far as the wasteful and extravagant operation of the navy yards was concerned, Robeson sought protection by alleging that he left all details to the bureau chiefs. The evidence contradicted him. The bureau chiefs sought excuse by trying to pass responsibility to the yard commandants. They declared that they had to obey orders, and could show repeated instances of gross mismanagement for political purposes due directly to the instructions of Robeson or the bureau heads. These offenses were less than high crimes and misdemeanors and could hardly lead to impeachment, but they revealed a sad state of official morality in eminent circles.

The Sanborn Contracts. Since Hamilton's day in the Treasury the revenue laws had authorized informers to collect a moiety of delinquent customs and other revenue due the government. The Forty-second Congress repealed all laws providing such moieties for delinquent internal revenue taxes, but a seemingly innocuous rider to an appropriation act empowered the Secretary of the Treasury to appoint not more than three persons "to assist the proper officers of the government in discovering and collecting" money due the United States. A bold scandal eventually developed from this rider, involving a protégé of Benjamin Butler, John D. Sanborn, Secretary of the Treasury William A. Richardson, and two of his high official associates.

Despite the fact that Sanborn was already a special agent of the Treasury, he applied for and received appointment as one of the three assistants and secured a series of contracts to ferret out delinquent taxpayers. Successful on a small scale, he persuaded Secretary Richardson on July 7, 1873, to add to his contract the names of 592 railroad companies—a list taken from a railroad guide and including practically all the railroads in the United States. The law required Sanborn to make affidavit of personal knowledge of delinquency. Sanborn admitted some knowledge concerning not more than 150 of them, but nevertheless swore that all were delinquent.

The law specified that Sanborn's duties were *to assist* the regular internal revenue officers; the contract authorized Sanborn *to proceed to collect,* and the regular employees were directed to assist him. The theory of the law, as the House Ways and Means Committee declared, was thus completely reversed—a fact which the committee asserted, correctly enough, would demoralize the entire internal revenue force.

The contract was a huge success for Sanborn. He collected $427,000 and received his moiety, $213,500. The House Committee declared that most, if not all, of this huge sum "would have been collected by the Internal Revenue Bureau in the ordinary discharge of their duty." Thus the contract in substance authorized a political favorite to require the assistance of the regular internal revenue staff in discovering delinquent taxpayers, then to substitute himself for the government officials in suit for recovery, all for the purpose of diverting one-half of the amount collected out of the Treasury into Sanborn's own pockets. The Commissioner of Internal Revenue made written protest to the Secretary of the Treasury against this arrant trickery, but his letter remained unanswered. The arrangements were concluded at the departmental level.

The House Committee on Ways and Means sought in vain to discover precisely who was to blame. Secretary Richardson testified, "I do not know the least thing about it any more than about ten thousand other things that are done in the different divisions of the Department. . . . I sign without reading." The Assistant Secretary disclaimed any knowledge or recollection of his signature and said the papers were prepared by the solicitor. This officer testified that he had consulted with the Secretary or Assistant Secretary, that he had acted in obedience to the directions of his superiors, and that the contracts were well known to the Secretary and Assistant Secretary. The committee looked "with serious apprehension upon the apparent effort of these gentlemen to transfer the responsibility each from himself to the other."

Although the report of the Committee on Ways and Means condemned the Sanborn transaction and severely criticized the principals, the committee found nothing to impeach their integrity or to demonstrate corrupt motives. The Assistant Secretary, Frederick A. Sawyer, and the solicitor, E. C. Banfield, resigned. The fate of Secretary Richardson was astonishing and symptomatic; he was appointed a member of the Court of claims. Godkin was struck dumb: "The transfer to the judicial bench of a person found guilty of the gross negligence and incapacity which Mr. Richardson has displayed in the Treasury needs no comment."

The Whiskey Ring. The most dramatic and perhaps the most damaging evidence of official corruption during the Grant administration involved the evasion of internal revenue taxes on distilleries. Fraud had long been suspected, and protests by honest distillers against the unfair competition of the dishonest were known during the administration of President Johnson and the first term of President Grant. Shortly after the appointment of Benjamin H. Bristow as Secretary of the Treasury on June 4, 1874, he received private information that offered him the opportunity to attack the Whiskey Ring. The events that followed were full of excitement, frustration, misunderstanding, and eventual triumph against evildoers but at the cost of Bristow's loss of the secretaryship.

The Whiskey Ring included General John A. McDonald, collector of internal revenue in St. Louis (one of the principal centers), other collectors, notably in Chicago, Milwaukee, and San Francisco, subordinate personnel in considerable numbers, the chief clerk of the internal revenue division of the Treasury Department in Washington, and an unknown number of informants to the ring in Washington and elsewhere. It also included General Orville E. Babcock, President Grant's private secretary, who was subsequently indicted but who escaped conviction. So widely was the net of the ring flung that Bristow dared trust no one in the Department except the solicitor, Bluford Wilson.

The campaign to secure evidence of tax evasion was planned by Bristow and Wilson, initially with the aid of three private citizens of St. Louis and later with the help of departmental agents who were sent on apparently innocent missions to check railroad shipments—among others of whiskey. The ring became uneasy, but never penetrated the disguise under which Bristow's agents operated. The trap was sprung simultaneously in St. Louis, Chicago, and Milwaukee. At the end of the first day of seizures sixteen of the largest distilleries and sixteen rectifying houses were in the possession of the government; others were seized thereafter; and illegal shipments were taken into custody from Boston to Galveston.

Indictments were served against 47 distillers, 60 rectifiers, 10 wholesale dealers, and 86 field agents of the internal revenue service ranging from collectors and deputy collectors to gaugers and storekeepers. All in all 230 persons were indicted, about 100 pleaded guilty, about 20 were convicted, and a dozen fled the country.

These events were damaging enough, but equally disconcerting were the apparent efforts to hamstring Bristow and to thwart the prosecutions. President Grant sustained Bristow until General Babcock's complicity was suspected, but then grew cool toward the proceedings, which were made to appear as a movement to strike at him through his secretary. Grant's mind was continuously poisoned against Bristow, who at one point saw no alternative but to resign in midstream. A forged telegram even made it appear that the President was being shadowed on a trip to St. Louis with Babcock, and set off an attempt to remove Solicitor Wilson. At one point Grant himself determined to go to St. Louis to testify on behalf of Babcock, and actually did make a deposition in his favor. The weight of this deposition was influential in his acquittal. Babcock returned momentarily to the White House and received Grant's appointment as inspector of lighthouses, but his influence in national affairs had been destroyed.

Meanwhile Grant had become convinced that Bristow was strengthening his claim on the Republican nomination of 1876 by attacking the President through an innocent secretary, and determined to remove Bristow as soon as Babcock's trial was at an end. Formally Bristow resigned; actually Grant made it clear that he was no longer welcome in the Cabinet. Thus left the public stage a man of high character, moral strength, and unyielding courge. Bluford Wilson also went out, and so did many of the lesser persons who had been active in the prosecution of the Whiskey Ring. Punishment fell heavily upon this devoted group of men.

The fate of Secretary of the Treasury Richardson and of Secretary of the Treasury Bristow presented a melancholy contrast. Richardson, caught in dubious official operations, was rescued by a quasi-judicial appointment to the Court of Claims. Bristow, successfully fighting corruption in the revenue service, was forced into private life. "His reward," declared Godkin, "has been a practical isolation at Washington, the enmity of the whole political class, dastardly accusations of corruption in office, and a forced retirement at the very time when his honesty and good faith were most needed to protect the Treasury from being turned over to a corrupt gang of officeholders to keep themselves in power."

Treasury Contingent Funds. The public service began a long period of moral renovation with the reform of the New York customhouse in Hayes' administration, but recovery was slow. A Senate investigation of the Treasury contingent fund in 1881–82 revealed a mass of petty graft and of apparent conversion of public funds to the advantage of a committee seeking the nomination of John Sherman (then Secretary of the Treasury) for the presidency in 1880. Senator William B. Allison reported that stationery and other items had been furnished by the Treasury to the Sherman campaign committee in the amount of $502, for which vouchers were made out calling for fileholders. No fileholders nor any other article on these vouchers were received by the Treasury. Upon discovery, the amount was reimbursed. In the early winter of 1880 gas fixtures were installed in the campaign committee rooms under cover of a requisition on the Treasury contingent fund for repairs. This amount was repaid after discovery. In the summer of 1880 a local druggist sold the Treasury Department three dozen bottles of Colgate's violet water paid for on a voucher calling for friction matches. Under the heading of an expenditure for ice, payment was made for 250 geranium plants. These were never delivered; in fact someone got 35 yards of evergreen, 6 wreaths, and a basket of cut flowers. Three payments were made ostensibly for billiard cloth, but actually delivered were ulster overcoats for employees driving wagons.

More damaging to Sherman's reputation were payments made by the Treasury for repairs and labor on his residence and for architectural drawings for his new house. Herman Blau relaid some of Sherman's carpets and was directed to bill the Treasury; James A. Rodbird put on weather strips, rehung sash, made horse troughs and hay mangers, and two bookshelves for the Secretary's basement, all on Treasury time. A Treasury draftsman worked ten days during office hours on plans for Sherman's new house. Later he worked at night and on Sundays but with no other compensation than his regular pay.

Sherman emphatically denied all knowledge of these encroachments on Treasury funds. The investigating committee admitted there was no testimony that he was aware of these payments "for his individual benefit." The committee nevertheless noted "gross abuses and frauds perpetrated through false and fictitious vouchers," and set forth the duties of department heads and bureau chiefs. "It is absolutely necessary that the heads of the several departments and chiefs of bureaus shall exercise a constant supervision over the actions of all their subordinates, and make each one feel his personal responsibility for the faithful and honest discharge of every duty, and that his absolute personal integrity alone can secure his retention in the service. . . ." These admonitions were richly deserved. Also needed was the kind of administrative assistance, then wanting, that would enable a department head to know what was taking place among his subordinates. Congress was laggard in providing the necessary, if only partial, administrative remedy to a moral problem.

The Star Route Frauds. The star route frauds in the post office, occurring during Hayes' administration and exposed during Arthur's, gave evidence that unremitting caution was still essential. They were reminiscent of the problems faced by the Post Office Department in the early years of Jackson's administration, involving collusion between postal officials and unscrupulous contractors.

In the settled portions of the country the mails were carried by rail, steamboat, and messenger. In the western states and territories mail contracts (by stage, horseback riders, or otherwise) were awarded to the lowest bidders who would engage to carry the mail with "certainty, celerity, and security." These words were indicated on the clerks' registers by three stars, and the routes thus came to be known as star routes. Since the contracts were let for a four-year period it was natural that changes might be required in the interest of greater speed or more frequent delivery. The Post Office Department was accordingly vested with discretion to make extra allowances under certain circumstances and subject to safeguards, an authority which proved vulnerable in the 1870's. Responsibility for contract changes was in the hands of Thomas J. Brady, Second Assistant Postmaster General, appointed by Grant in 1876 and continued through Hayes' administration and Garfield's brief term into Arthur's administration.

Hayes had not been decisive when in January 1880 the House Committee on Appropriations questioned the extravagant, if not fraudulent, acts of Brady. The President appeared to regard the situation as one involving merely a dispute over restricted or liberal western mail facilities. He noted after he left the presidency that he had repeatedly called the attention of Postmaster General Key and his First Assistant Tyner to the matter, but that both saw in it only a controversy over policy. Hayes finally directed that no more increases should be allowed except by the Postmaster General after consideration by the President and the Cabinet. This raised the adjustments of contracts on remote mail routes to the highest political level—a solution, as Hayes declared, that should prevent crookedness, but at a heavy administrative cost in time of the President and Cabinet.

Garfield quickly became aware of strange occurrences in the star route contracts and at once ordered an investigation. Brady and other subordinates were replaced and prosecutions were started. It appeared that in the western division of the post office alone, Brady had approved additional trips and greater "celerity," the effect of which was to increase original contract terms by about two million dollars a year. P. H. Woodward, special investigator for Postmaster General Thomas L. James, reported by way of illustration the case of route No. 40,116 from Phoenix to Prescott, Arizona, which was twice expedited at a change of compensation from $680 to $32,640.32 without readvertisement or competition; and route No. 32,024 from Las Vegas, New Mexico, to Vinita, where the annual compensation went from $6,330 up to $150,592.03. Favored contractors offered impossibly low bids to freeze out competitors and then, once secure, proceeded to "improve" their service. An honest bidder was at an impossible disadvantage.

Conviction on charges of conspiracy to defraud the government proved impossible despite the confession, later repudiated, of one of the participants. The defense argued that the disputed increases of compensation were due (1) to those required by increase of population; (2) to those made in response to requests of influential members of Congress; and (3) to those allowed because of misinformation or mistaken, though honest, judgment. General William T. Sherman testified for the defense, explaining that the needs of the army on the frontier had required improvements in the mail. Senator Henry M. Teller testified that he had frequently urged better mail facilities for his constituents in Colorado. Amidst allegations of bribery of the jury, the trial came to an end in disagreement on September 11, 1882. A second trial from December 7, 1882, to June 14, 1883, with more charges of jury tampering, resulted in a verdict of "not guilty." Civil suits for restitution likewise failed.

The United States Marshals. The abuse of the Treasury contingent fund and the star route frauds were not the only evidence that old evils tended to persist. A shocking mass of corruption and extortion was revealed by the House Committee on Expenditures in the Department of Justice in 1884. Marshals and their deputies, supervisors of elections, court commissioners, and others rendered false accounts on a huge scale, failed to report their fees, and in some cases conspired to arrest and harass innocent persons in order to increase their official income. . . .

The fiscal officers of the Department of Justice disallowed over $340,-000 in the accounts of these field agents from 1882 to 1884. The House committee surmised that this was a small sum compared to total stealings. The committee's indignation was extreme: "We cannot expect the people to have an affection for the Government when, instead of having their rights and liberties protected by it, the most egregious wrongs are perpetrated upon them; and when the officers not only bring the public service into contempt, but actually convert the machinery of the courts of justice into an engine of oppression."

Recovery. The misfeasance and corruption that flourished in the federal government during the Grant administration receded in later years. If comparison be made of ethical standards during McKinley's administration with those during Grant's, the change is marked and dramatic. Before McKinley's day, indeed, progress had been substantial. The transformation was gradual; no sharp transition occurred, and no outstanding events demonstrated the arrival of a new era. To close observers the direction of change was, however, readily perceptible, although progress was slow and victories were mixed with defeats.

What were the circumstances that favored moral reform in the federal administration? Those most fundamental were probably lost from sight and will remain undisclosed until a history of morality reveals the aspirations and standards of the people. It must be remembered that even in the years of the most rampant corruption, old Puritan ideals of conduct, although apparently submerged, prevailed among the masses of plain men and women. Honesty, reliability, and trustworthiness in dealings between man and man were the rule, crookedness was the exception. The churches did not waver in holding man's duty to his fellowman before him, and it may be asserted with justification that the loss of character, widespread though it was in business, politics, and government, never undermined the mores of the community. The basic ethical standards of the American people were untouched; most persons would have declared that it was wrong to steal from the public treasury, to give or to accept bribes, to deceive and to misrepresent. These basic standards were steadily opposed to skulduggery in public as well as private affairs.

The character of the Presidents following Grant was such as to encourage decency in government. Hayes was a deeply religious man of highest personal rectitude; in his Cabinet were men of integrity; their influence was steady if not spectacular, and in favor of honest performance of public duty. President Arthur may have lost renomination for a second term by his insistence on prosecuting some delinquent marshals. Cleveland was speaking for Hayes, Garfield, and Arthur as well as for himself and his successors when he declared that public office was a public trust. The advent of a reforming Democratic administration in

1885 after nearly a quarter century of one-party domination was itself a renovating influence.

Leadership in Congress slowly improved. Benjamin Butler disappeared with Grant. The intended expulsion of Patterson from the Senate served notice that even in the depths of degradation discovery of corruption would reap its due and proper punishment. The evil influence of Senator Conklin ended early in Garfield's administration; the dubious influence of Blaine was diminished by his loss of the 1884 election. The quality of Congressmen and Senators depended, however, on the quality of the party system, election procedures, the integrity of state legislatures, and local leadership; these were hard to change, and progress was slow.

The reformers were in the forefront of the moral regeneration that slowly took place from the late 1870's to the 1890's. They were at best a small minority, but they were deeply stirred by the need for moral reconstruction of American democracy. They were based in New England and New York, as the Jacksonian ideas of democracy had been based in the Middle West. They were characterized by integrity, earnestness, intelligence, and determination. They could write and they could speak. They were in the line of moral succession from the antislavery advocates of the pre-Civil War period. Strong in their convictions, they faced the entrenched party system with demands for its purification and a higher standard of public morals.

Among the various wings of the reformers the civil service reform group was the earliest on the stage, and the first to gain substantial initial success. The story has already been told, and it is sufficient here merely to relate civil service reform to the improvement of public service standards. The connection is an obvious one. Before 1883 a considerable proportion of the rank-and-file federal employees were political hacks, active in the small intrigues of the big city machines, well-informed concerning the corrupt practices that flourished in the winning of elections, disinterested in public office except as a livelihood, and expecting to hold their jobs only so long as their party, or faction, was predominant. There was little incentive to honest performance of official work; much inducement to do party work, pay party assessments, and carry out party obligations and orders.

The enactment of the civil service law built a wall around a steadily larger segment of the public service, access to which was on the basis of competence tested by open competitive examinations, continuance in which was contingent upon good work and good character. This wing of public office was protected in considerable measure from party obligation, and in its own interest gradually developed an ethical system that abjured neglect of the public interest, that bespoke a collective morale founded on a permanent work association, and that in some quarters, notably Agriculture, was permeated by ideals of professional conduct. From any point of view, civil service reform ranks high as a source of steady improvement in the standards of the government service.

Another wing of the reformers was attacking corruption and intimidation at the ballot box. Before the Civil War voting was generally viva voce; after the war it was by privately printed ballots publicly distributed, and so marked as to make secrecy difficult. Purchase of votes and intimidation of voters were common. . . . According to a Senate report in 1880, men were frequently marched or carried to the polls in their employers' carriages. They were then supplied with ballots, and sometimes compelled to hold their hands up with the ballots in them so that they could be watched until the ballots were safely deposited in the box.

The Australian ballot provided the formal remedy for lack of secrecy and for open intimidation.This ballot, introduced on a state-wide basis in Massachusetts in 1888, was printed officially, was distributed only in the polling place, and was marked in secrecy. Although it did not eliminate all corrupt practices in elections, it represented a major advance. The unprecedented use of money in the election of 1888 gave impetus to this reform. Between 1888 and 1892 thirty-two states and two territories adopted the Australian ballot, and by 1896 seven other states had followed this example. Thus was laid another cornerstone for the reduction of corruption in public life.

A third wing of the reformers meanwhile was battling corruption in cities, whose government was described by James Bryce as the most conspicuous failure of the American commonwealth. Americans had been accustomed to the management of their rural communities and small towns, but the rapid growth of big cities, with large expenditures and emerging utility corporations, presented problems beyond their experience. The general relaxation of moral standards after the close of the Civil War had some of its worst consequences in New York, Philadelphia, Chicago, and other large cities. In 1890 Andrew D. White, former president of Cornell University, declared: "Without the slightest exaggeration we may assert that, with very few exceptions, the city governments of the United States are the worst in Christendom—the most expensive, the most inefficient, and the most corrupt."

Even temporary success in the overthrow of a corrupt municipal gang was usually followed by a relapse from civic virtue. The Tweed Ring was dispersed in 1871, but Tammany was soon back again in the city hall. The Gas Ring was overthrown in Philadelphia in 1887, but corruption could be discovered in the City of Brotherly Love in subsequent years. Most cities alternated between subjection to local bosses, occasional reform victories, and early loss again to the professional political rings.

The municipal situation was exceedingly complex and from the point of view of the reformers uncompromisingly stubborn. Cities grew rapidly during the 1870's and 1880's. Numbers were swollen by newly arrived immigrants who proved ready recruits to the professional politicians. The "better elements" were too often indifferent to laxness in city affairs or were the complaisant beneficiaries. It was relatively easy, moreover, for a hardened machine to compel a reluctant businessman to "go along" by threat of annoyance through building or license inspectors, or by delaying municipal services. The prizes to be won in the era of streetcar franchises, gas and utility franchises, and other special privileges were enormous—so great that the machine could be bought by reckless businessmen for corrupt franchise bargains. The machine used its power over the little men as well by favors and threats. The New York Citizens' Association estimated in 1871 that Tweed could influence about half of New York City's 130,000 votes. A decade later it was estimated that the Philadelphia Gas Ring could control at least 20,000 votes. Obviously the task of the municipal reformers was stupendous.

Slowly and with discouraging setbacks the cause of reform advanced. It took institutional form in local organizations of civic-minded persons, of which there were in 1894 more than eighty. The two most active—the City Club of New York and the Municipal League of Philadelphia— joined hands in 1894 to call the first National Conference for Good City Government. The object was to determine the best means of forwarding the cause of honest and intelligent municipal government and to unite the scattered forces fighting for better cities. Within a few months this Conference organized the National Municipal League, the outstanding center for improvement in the politics, administration, and morals of American cities for the next half century and more.

We may repeat that the moral quality of the federal government was dependent upon the ethical standards of cities and states, and the people thereof. State legislators elected Senators, party conventions nominated Presidents, voters elected Congressmen. Corruption in city government was bound up with the character of the local party organization and often proceeded directly from it. The same party organization comprised the local machine and played an important role in the state organization. It could make its voice felt in the halls of Congress and in the executive departments. Presidents, Senators, and Congressmen were dependent on party organizations for re-election; and they in turn drew much of their sustenance from the patronage and perquisites of their Washington representatives.

Civil service reform, ballot reform, and municipal reform had accomplished much, but had left substantially untouched the dubious connection between amoral business and utility corporations on the one hand and city and state governments on the other. Lincoln Steffens was still to write *The Shame of the Cities* and *The Struggle for Self-Government*. While there had been marked and salutary progress from Grant to McKinley, vigilance was still necessary.

A perceptive Rip Van Winkle who fell into slumber on the banks of the Potomac at the close of the Civil War and awoke at the close of the Spanish-American War would have remarked both the tenacity of tradition and the inevitability of change. . . .

Before reviewing the two major institutional developments and some of their consequences—the presidency and civil service reform—it will be convenient to comment on a few of the underlying changes that were in motion. A new ideal of the standards of prosecuting the public business was slowly gathering force; the great body of federal employees, which the Civil War and its aftermath had perforce based on the North and West, was again becoming national, not sectional, in character; the universality of the "clerk" and of handwritten manuscripts was yielding to the typewriter, while the tempo of action was speeded by the telephone.

Trend toward Businesslike Administration. The country was slowly moving from one broad ideal of the nature of its administrative system to another. For decades this ideal had been a system political in character, serving the interests of party at an admitted cost in competence and integrity, as well as, or often in preference to, the interests of good administration. This ideal was challenged and gradually subdued to the ideal of a "businesslike" government.

The ferment was more strenuously at work in municipal government than in the capital city, but it could be sensed in Washington as well as in New York. It was symbolized by the occasional appearance of businessmen at the heads of departments, such as John Wanamaker in the Post Office, William C. Whitney in the Navy, Stephen B. Elkins in War, and Ethan A. Hitchcock in Interior. It was implicit in the gradual extension of the merit system and in the demands of the merchant importers of New York for less politics and more attention to duty in the customhouse.

Bearing on the same tendency was the appointment of university faculty men to important government posts. As long as college and university curricula were based on classical studies, philosophy, and theology, the faculty were hardly prepared to serve in executive positions. As the newer disciplines of economics and statistics, political science, and the agricultural sciences found a place in the institutions of higher learning, specialists in these fields became useful in practical affairs.

Many of the larger institutions contributed faculty members to the public service, notably the state universities. Among these the University of Michigan was one of the most conspicuous. The first chairman of the Interstate Commerce Commission, Thomas M. Cooley, was professor of history and dean of the School of Political Science at this institution and earlier had been a member of its law department. The chief statistician of the Commission, Henry C. Adams, had taught at Johns Hopkins and Cornell, and at the time of his appointment was professor of political economy at Michigan. James B. Angell, noted educator and president of the University of Michigan, was appointed by both Republican and Democratic administrations to a series of important posts: minister to China (1880), Canadian Fisheries Commission (1887), chairman, Deep Waterways Commission (1896), and minister to Turkey (1897). Edwin Willits, president of Michigan Agricultural College and graduate of the

University of Michigan, became Assistant Secretary of Agriculture in 1889.

The faculties of other universities were also called upon for government service, consulting or administrative. A rare early example of the scholar in politics who also rose to high administrative post was William Lyne Wilson, Postmaster General from 1895 to 1897. After service in the Confederate army, he was assistant professor of the ancient languages at Columbian College and eventually president of West Virginia University. He was a member of the House from 1883 to 1895, and in 1892 permanent chairman of the Democratic National Convention. He thus had impressive political as well as academic credentials. James Wilson, a member of the faculty of Iowa State College and Secretary of Agriculture under three Presidents, was another distinguished academician, equally successful in administration. John W. Foster, a member of the faculty of George Washington University, served as minister to Mexico, Russia, and Spain, and for a short period (1892–93) was Secretary of State. Many one-time faculty men were attracted to Washington for scientific research in such agencies as the Department of Agriculture and the Geological Survey; some of them took on administrative duties. Their appointment again was a symbol of the nonpolitical ideal.

The emerging concept of administration as properly businesslike rather than political in nature was still novel and was disputed in many quarters. Thus James S. Clarkson, Harrison's First Assistant Postmaster General, explained that the United States government was a political, not a business machine. It was indeed both, but its political character was receding, its business quality advancing.

Trend from a Sectional to a National Service. Prior to the Civil War the public service was drawn freely from all sections of the country, and southern influence was strong. Congressional interest in office had already introduced a form of apportionment in the 1850's, and in accordance with immemorial tradition local appointments of federal officials were confined to the locality. During the war many southern clerks and probably most southern officials withdrew from Washington. The service became northern and western. Prejudice against southerners remained strong after the war. The fourteenth amendment forbade the employment of former members of Congress or state officials who had given aid or comfort to enemies of the United States, until after civic rehabilitation. This was accomplished by a series of enactments applying to named persons and in 1872 by a general amnesty, with a few exceptions.

On the higher levels the *de facto* southern proscription was tempered by Hayes' appointment of Postmaster General David McKendree Key, an ex-Confederate officer from Tennessee. Thereafter most Cabinets contained at least one representative from the Deep South and others from the border states.

Veterans' preference was a powerful factor in maintaining northern and western predominance in the public service. The thirty years after the Civil War were par excellence the generation of army officers in the middle and higher ranks, and of the rank and file of the Grand Army of the Republic in the subordinate positions. The strength of the former lay in a sense of public gratitude and their active participation in politics; that of the latter in statutory preference as well. Promptly at the close of the war Congress for the first time required preference in civil office to persons honorably discharged from the military and naval service, if found to possess the necessary business capacity.

Both Congress and Presidents saw to it that appointing officers did their duty to veterans. In 1882 the Senate ordered an investigation to discover whether the law had been faithfully executed—obviously suspecting that it had not. The Civil Service Act of 1883 renewed the enactment of 1865. In 1885 Cleveland wrote the New York collector of customs, "It is exceedingly important that the force of this law should be scrupulously regarded. Indeed, this *must* be done." Departmental reports, however, justified the record of the appointing officers. In Treasury over 50 per cent of appointments from 1887 to 1882 were veterans, their widows, or orphans; in the War Department (1865–1882) more than 60 per cent; in Interior, about one-third. Other departments were less explicit, but all asserted their determination to favor the veterans. The authority of the Grand Army of the Republic was the potent political sanction weighing upon all concerned.

The effect of this preference, from the point of view of the present analysis, was to enforce the regional character of the federal service. Veterans' preference was not enjoyed by the men in gray.

Party continued to play a role also in geographical dislocation. Except for Cleveland's eight years in the White House, the country was governed by the Republicans. There were few Republicans in the South and southern officeholders were often northerners or Negroes—members of the Republican organization. In the classified competitive service a reasonable balance was gradually achieved; in the rest of the service the disproportion persisted as Republican party control pushed into the twentieth century. It was in the North, too, that the business ideal flourished, and the Republican party was its home.

Trend from the Age of the Copy Clerk to the Dawn of the Age of the Technician. For a full century the characteristic figure in the rank and file was the person who sat at a desk and used a pen: the auditing clerks and the department copy clerks. Immense masses of handwritten accounts, letterbooks, and manuscripts accumulated in every agency, the product of painstaking, laborious, and usually excellent penmanship. Now began the transition to employees trained and skillful in the use of office machines, one of the earliest of which was the typewriter. By the 1890's the telephone was coming into use in government offices and a new class of employment came into existence, the telephone operator. The automobile mechanic was almost entirely a mark of the twentieth century. In the scientific agencies men skilled in instrumentation were the characteristic type. The geologist's hammer, the chemist's reagents, the plant pathologist's microscope became the marks of a new kind of public service.

Involved in these tendencies was another intimately related to them, the transition from a public service calling primarily for persons with a common school, academy, or high school education to one requiring college and professional training. In numbers they were a small minority, but in significance they loomed large. It cannot be said that the Civil Service Commission sought college or university men and women, apart from the scientific and technical fields; indeed it had to protect itself against allegations that it was building up an intellectual aristocracy. The task of keeping the machine in order was that of the chief clerks, who were formed by experience, not by study.

It is deeply to be regretted that it is impossible with the material at hand to do justice to the chief clerks, whose collective history began in 1789. Of them it could be said, to borrow the words of Secretary Jacob D. Cox, "An experienced clerk is a repository of the law, the history and the traditions of the department, and may often, by a word or suggestion, expose a fraud, which might otherwise escape unnoticed, indicate an important fact of which there is no record, or in a thousand ways save his superior from imposition or from a long and laborious investigation."

The quality of the chief clerks was exemplified in the career of Robert S. Chew, chief clerk of the State Department, who was memorialized in 1874 by Congressman James B. Sener. "He . . . was forty years in the service of the State Department, serving with sixteen Secretaries of State, under twelve Presidents, and dying as he had lived, a most honest, faithful, and capable public servant, enjoying under all administrations the confidence of his superiors and the respect and esteem of all with whom he was brought into intercourse."

One suspects that as a class chief clerks were meticulous, masters of detail, proud of their unique knowledge of forms and precedents, devoted to *status quo* and not inclined to innovation, quick to bend to the wishes of their immediate superiors but apt in blunting such policies as seemed to them in error. We may guess also that many of them were martinets, and we may be sure that as a group they were far from being partisans. Without continuity in their offices, Secretaries would indeed have been at a loss in the management of their departments.

The Presidency. If now we turn to the institutional framework of the administrative system we note the gradual restoration of authority to the Chief Magistrate. The office had been nearly wrecked during Johnson's administration and from 1865 to 1877 the country in effect had been governed by a Senate oligarchy. Hayes challenged this small group and Garfield defeated it. Cleveland succeeded in securing the repeal of the Tenure of Office Act, the highwater mark of Senate pretensions. The Senate, however, remained powerful and no President argued during these years that he represented the people as truly as Congress.

As an executive the office of President was handicapped both by public expectations and by the absence of an administrative staff. It was not supposed that Presidents (or governors, and mayors for that matter) would take an active part in the management of the public business. So long as the departments ran smoothly and avoided serious congressional or public criticism they were generally left alone by the White House. Department heads were expected to keep Presidents informed and to warn them of impending trouble, but the responsibility of day-by-day affairs was theirs. Apart from the civil service system, indeed, there was almost no government-wide operation.

The executive staff to which a later age became accustomed was not even thought of. There were no administrative assistants, although Cleveland wished for one. There was no budget bureau. The Civil Service Commission was not understood to be a part of the executive office but (erroneously) an independent agency to police the departments. There was no agency directly serving the President to inquire, to report, and to advise. In the absence of such administrative aids he was necessarily barred from an active role in management. His mind was directed primarily to Congress, not to the executive departments.

Civil Service Reform. Without doubt the achievement of civil service reform in 1883 was a fundamental turning point in the history of the federal administrative system. Limited as was its initial application and bitter as was the hostility of the professional politicians, it was nevertheless the foundation on which the public service was to be built in succeeding decades. The government simply could not have supported the tasks that the country imposed upon it in the twentieth century without the stable, competent, and responsible public service which the Pendleton Act made possible.

Some of the consequences that were feared as a result of the merit system did not materialize. The friends of Jacksonian democracy discovered that an obnoxious officeholding class did not arise to vex them. The party managers learned that they could win elections with the patronage resources that remained at their command. The reformers learned that the merit system was not the wonder-working solution of all the problems of government. There was no transformation of the relations of the President to Congress, and of Congressmen to the White House and the executive departments.

One consequence, however, was quickly evident. The quality of the public service began a steady improvement. The quadrennial disruption was lessened in violence. The competence of the rank and file improved. Their loyalty to their work strengthened; to their party it diminished. The moral standards of the public offices improved, even if marred by some scandals.

Other corollaries of the merit system were not slow in emerging. Primary among these was the partial formation of a government-wide establishment in lieu of a loose collection of mutually independent departments and agencies. Before 1883 the only important element of a government-wide administrative system was found in the auditing offices. The settlement of accounts was presumably on the same principles, no matter what the department in which the expenditure occurred. The broad legal limits within which administration was confined were fixed by statute, such as the eight-hour day; and by the rulings of the Attorney General and the comptrollers. Most of the decisions of these offices, however, dealt with particulars, not with problems of a service-wide nature.

The civil service rules, to the contrary, were universal, so far as the classified competitive service was concerned. They were the same in every department, and in the field offices of every establishment. They were prescribed by the President, not by the Commission; they consequently had the highest authority and were a direct obligation upon every agency. They comprised the first major recognition both of a service-wide administrative system and of the President as the active head of that system.

The recognition of tenure for the classified competitive system raised in more acute form the problem of superannuation. Serious discussion of the plight of the aged clerk began in the decade following the Pendleton Act, but official opinion was hostile to pensions for civil employees. This element of a service-wide system was not to become effective until 1920.

The Civil Service Act also brought discussion of the proper line of demarcation between the subordinate nonpolitical employees and the directing personnel. McKinley's roll back of the classified competitive service doubtless had a strong political motivation, but it also was based upon a preliminary rational analysis of a basic distinction. Where "to draw the line," indeed, was a dimly understood problem for succeeding decades and first received an adequate analysis only in 1953.

A final consequence of the merit system was to lay the foundation for the organization of civil service employees. Without the guarantee of stable employment, organization even for beneficial objects was hardly worthwhile. The Pendleton Act also coincided with powerful labor movements in the industrial world and with a slowly changing climate of opinion, conducive to tolerating unions in some branches of the public service. Tenure was the essential element for the civil service union movement.

The Civil Service Act thus foreshadowed many emerging tendencies. Modest as were its early accomplishments, the merit system deserves to rank as one of the decisive administrative achievements of the period.

Improvement in Moral Standards. To obtain a proper perspective on the course of moral standards in the public service from Grant to McKinley it is necessary to assert at the outset that the vast majority of federal officials and employees were men and women of character, of whose integrity there could be no question. This had been the case during the rise and dominance of the patronage system before the Civil War and remained the case in the years of degradation after the war.

Riding on top of this solid mass of men of good will and honest devotion to duty, there was a layer of adventurers who had no hesitation in defrauding the public, stealing government funds, and shamefully abusing helpless government clients such as the Indians. Their number and audacity were greatest during Grant's administration, when even members of the Cabinet and of the President's official family were involved in dishonorable transactions. The official climate altered abruptly when Hayes became President, although unsuspected evil-doing continued in some quarters. The change in party control consequent upon Cleveland's election in 1884 was the occasion for a general housecleaning; Cleveland, indeed, had won success in large measure because the country believed him to be a stubbornly honest man.

The Civil Service Act was conducive to higher standards of official conduct. The rank and file, at least, had new motives for sobriety, attention to duty, and propriety in their departmental conduct. It became less important to seek political endorsement (at whatever price) as a condition of steady employment, and more important to earn a reputation for diligence and trustworthiness. Some breaks in the dykes did occur in civil service ranks, notably in the Post Office. The influence of the merit system was nevertheless pronounced in cultivating proper observance of official morality.

Thirty Years of Intellectual Stagnation. Considering the state of administrative doctrine from 1870 to 1900, we must conclude that these were years of stagnation. Congress repeatedly investigated the public service, but its committee reports made no contributions to an understanding of the nature of administration. None of them approached the excellence of the 1842 report of the Gilmer Select Committee on Retrenchment. Presidents had little to say beyond recommendations for particular reforms. None of them, so far as noted, offered a program suggestive of an interest in the art of management as such. A department head occasionally evidenced an awareness of the administrative inadequacies of his own position and of the necessities of active management on his part, but none of them developed a systematic analysis of management at the departmental level.

What contributions there were to administrative doctrine came from outside government, from the pens of reformers and students of government. Only three of these were remembered by succeeding generations: Charles Francis Adams, whose masterly articles on the relation of the state to railroads and on the character of the public service were fundamental in character; Woodrow Wilson, whose single contribution in the *Political Science Quarterly* (1887) was the first recognition of the field of public administration as an object of study and a potential area of generalization; and Frank J. Goodnow, who published his *Comparative Administrative Law* in 1893. Reform was the dominant concern of the country, not the formulation of doctrine.

These writings, and others concerned with special problems, foreshadowed the emergence of a field of study and a systematic formulation. The latter was still a good quarter-century in the future; the former was recognized in a few institutions at the close of the century. Foremost among them was Columbia University where, under the leadership of Frank J. Goodnow, the study of administrative law and public administration was vigorously pursued.

The course of administrative history, after Grant, was one of recovery from the abuses of the Civil War and of the first twelve years thereafter. Hard battles were fought between Congress and the executive branch, between an older generation wedded to politics and a new generation emerging in an age of business, between reformers and skeptics. Although improvement was painfully slow, there was substantially no regression. A Potomac Rip Van Winkle, stirring into consciousness at the end of McKinley's first term, would have found relative satisfaction in the state of the administrative system. It was not yet fully prepared to tackle the emerging problems of the near future—colonial government, the regulation of business and banking, war administration, and a host of lesser responsibilities—but some essential foundations had been laid. Far-reaching transformations were to follow.

Woodrow Wilson

Congressional

Government

Woodrow Wilson grew to manhood in the Gilded Age and was disgusted by the American political system as he saw it operate. "Eight words contain the sum of the present degradation of our political parties," he wrote; "no leaders, no principles; no principles, no parties." Presidential leadership, as he viewed it, was lacking or ineffectual. As a result, he assumed that Congress was the central and predominant power in the American system. In later years, after the turn of the century, he took a different view.

Nonetheless, in 1883, when he was 27 and a graduate student at Johns Hopkins University, he began to describe the American political system and the breakdown of government as he had seen and studied it. The resulting book, completed in the following year and published in 1885, was the first analysis of the American constitutional system as it operated while Congress predominated. Under congressional government, Wilson argued, power and responsibility disintegrate, for congressional government is in fact committee government. The result, he believed, was bad government. He concluded, erroneously, that the government by committee that prevailed in his youth had become a normal and permanent part of the American political system . . .

In the selection that follows, Wilson attempts to explain why Congress was becoming the one sovereign authority in government. He also points out what he considered to be the defects and weaknesses in government in the Gilded Age. [Woodrow Wilson, Congressional Government: A Study in American Politics *(Boston: Houghton Mifflin Co., 1885; republished by Meridian Books, The World Publishing Company, 1956).]*

Congress is fast becoming the governing body of the nation, and yet the only power which it possesses in perfection is the power which is but a part of government, the power of legislation. Legislation is but the oil of government. It is that which lubricates its channels and speeds its wheels; that which lessens the friction and so eases the movement. Or perhaps I shall be admitted to have hit upon a closer and apter analogy if I say that legislation is like a foreman set over the forces of government. It issues the orders which others obey. It directs, it admonishes, but it does not do the actual heavy work of governing. A good foreman does, it is true, himself take a hand in the work which he guides; and so I suppose our legislation must be likened to a poor foreman, because it stands altogether apart from that work which it is set to see well done. Members of Congress ought not to be censured too severely, however, when they fail to check evil courses on the part of the executive. They have been denied the means of doing so promptly and with effect. Whatever intention may have controlled the compromises of constitution-making in 1787, their result was to give us, not government by discussion, which is the only tolerable sort of government for a people which tries to do its own governing, but only *legislation* by discussion, which is no more than a small part of government by discussion. What is quite as indispensable as the debate of problems of legislation is the debate of all matters of administration. It is even more important to know how the house is being built than to know how the plans of the architect were conceived and how his specifications were calculated. It is better to have skillful work—stout walls, reliable arches, unbending rafters, and windows sure to "expel the winter's flaw"—than a drawing on paper which is the admiration of all the practical artists in the country. The discipline of an army depends quite as much upon the temper of the troops as upon the orders of the day.

It is the proper duty of a representative body to look diligently into every affair of government and to talk much about what it sees. It is meant to be the eyes and the voice, and to embody the wisdom and will of its constituents. Unless Congress have and use every means of acquainting itself with the acts and the disposition of the administrative agents of the government, the country must be helpless to learn how it is being served; and unless Congress both scrutinize these things and sift them by every form of discussion, the country must remain in embarrassing, crippling ignorance of the very affairs which it is most important that it should understand and direct. The informing function of Congress should be preferred even to its legislative function. The argument is not only that discussed and interrogated administration is the only pure and efficient administration, but, more than that, that the only really self-governing people is that people which discusses and interrogates its administration. The talk on the part of Congress which we sometimes justly condemn is the profitless squabble of words over frivolous bills or selfish party issues. It would be hard to conceive of there being too much talk about the practical concerns and processes of government. Such talk it is which, when earnestly and purposefully conducted, clears the public mind and shapes the demands of public opinion.

Congress could not be too diligent about such talking; whereas it may easily be too diligent in legislation. It often overdoes that business. It already sends to its Committees bills too many by the thousand to be given even a hasty thought; but its immense committee facilities and the absence of all other duties but that of legislation make it omnivorous in its appetite for new subjects for consideration. It is greedy to have a taste of every possible dish that may be put upon its table, as an "extra" to the constitutional bill of fare. This disposition on its part is the more notable because there is certainly less need for it to hurry and overwork itself at lawmaking than exists in the case of most other great national legislatures. It is not state and national legislature combined, as are the Commons of England and the Chambers of France. Like the Reichstag of our cousin Germans, it is restricted to subjects of imperial scope. Its thoughts are meant to be kept for national interests. Its time is spared the waste of attention to local affairs. It is even forbidden the vast domain of the laws of property, of commercial dealing, and of ordinary crime. And even in the matter of caring for national interests the way has from the first been made plain and easy for it. There are no clogging feudal institutions to embarrass it. There is no long-continued practice of legal or of royal tyranny for it to cure,—no clearing away of old debris of any sort to delay it in its exercise of a common-sense dominion over a thoroughly modern and progressive nation. It is easy to believe that its legislative purposes might be most fortunately clarified and simplified, were it to square them by a conscientious attention to the paramount and controlling duty of understanding, discussing, and directing administration.

If the people's authorized representatives do not take upon themselves this duty, and by identifying themselves with the actual work of government stand between it and irresponsible, half-informed criticism, to what harassments is the executive not exposed? Led and checked by Congress, the prurient and fearless, because anonymous, animadversions of the Press, now so often premature and inconsiderate, might be disciplined into serviceable capacity to interpret and judge. Its energy and sagacity might be tempered by discretion, and strengthened by knowledge. One of our chief constitutional difficulties is that, in opportunities for informing and guiding public opinion, the freedom of the Press is greater than the freedom of Congress. It is as if newspapers, instead of the board of directors, were the sources of information for the stockholders of a corporation. We look into correspondents' letters instead of into the Congressional Record to find out what is a-doing and a-planning in the departments. Congress is altogether excluded from the arrangement by which the Press declares what the executive is, and conventions of the national parties decide what the executive shall be. Editors are self-constituted our guides, and caucus delegates our government directors.

Since all this curious scattering of functions and contrivance of frail, extra-constitutional machinery of government is the result of that entire separation of the legislative and executive branches of the system which is with us so characteristically and essentially constitutional, it is exceedingly interesting to inquire and important to understand how that separation came to be insisted upon in the making of the Constitution. Alexander Hamilton has in our own times, as well as before, been [according to Henry Cabot Lodge] "severely reproached with having said that the British government was the 'best model in existence.' In 1787 this was a mere truism. However much the men of that day differed they were all agreed in despising and distrusting *a priori* constitutions and ideally perfect governments, fresh from the brains of visionary enthusiasts, such as sprang up rankly in the soil of the French revolution. The Convention of 1787 was composed of very able men of the English-speaking race. They took the system of government with which they had been familiar, improved it, adapted it to the circumstances with which they had to deal, and put it into successful operation. Hamilton's plan then, like the others, was on the British model, and it did not differ essentially in details from that finally adopted." It is needful, however, to remember in this connection what has already been alluded to, that when that convention was copying the English Constitution, that Constitution was in a stage of transition, and had by no means fully developed the features which are now recognized as most characteristic of it. Mr. Lodge is quite right in saying that the Convention, in adapting, improved upon the English Constitution with which its members were familiar,—the Constitution of George III and Lord North, the Constitution which had failed to crush Bute. It could hardly be said with equal confidence, however, that our system as then made was an improvement upon that scheme of responsible cabinet government which challenges the admiration of the world today, though it was quite plainly a marked advance upon a parliament of royal nominees and pensionaries and a secret cabinet of "king's friends." The English Constitution of that day had a great many features which did not invite republican imitation. It was suspected, if not known, that the ministers who sat in parliament were little more than tools of a ministry of royal favorites who were kept out of sight behind the strictest confidences of the court. It was notorious that the subservient parliaments of the day represented the estates and the money of the peers and the influence of the King rather than the intelligence

and the purpose of the nation. The whole "form and pressure" of the
time illustrated only too forcibly Lord Bute's sinister suggestion, that
"the forms of a free and the ends of an arbitrary government are things
not altogether incompatible." It was, therefore, perfectly natural that the
warnings to be so easily drawn from the sight of a despotic monarch
binding the usages and privileges of self-government to the service of his
own intemperate purposes should be given grave heed by Americans, who
were the very persons who had suffered most from the existing abuses. It
was something more than natural that the Convention of 1787 should
desire to erect a Congress which would not be subservient and an executive which could not be despotic. And it was equally to have been expected that they should regard an absolute separation of these two great
branches of the system as the only effectual means for the accomplishment of that much desired end. It was impossible that they could believe
that executive and legislature could be brought into close relations of co-
operation and mutual confidence without being tempted, nay, even
bidden, to collude. How could either maintain its independence of action unless each were to have the guaranty of the Constitution that its
own domain should be absolutely safe from invasion, its own prerogatives
absolutely free from challenge? "They shrank from placing sovereign
power anywhere. They feared that it would generate tyranny; George III
had been a tyrant to them, and come what might they would not make a
George III." They would conquer, by dividing, the power they so much
feared to see in any single hand.

"The English Constitution, in a word," says our most astute English
critic [Walter Bagehot], "is framed on the principle of choosing a single
sovereign authority, and making it good; the American, upon the principle of having many sovereign authorities, and hoping that their multitude may atone for their inferiority. The Americans now extol their
institutions, and so defraud themselves of their due praise. But if they
had not a genius for politics, if they had not a moderation in action
singularly curious where superficial speech is so violent, if they had not a
regard for law, such as no great people have ever evinced, and infinitely
surpassing ours, the multiplicity of authorities in the American Constitution would long ago have brought it to a bad end. Sensible shareholders,
I have heard a shrewd attorney say, can work *any* deed of settlement; and
so the men of Massachusetts could, I believe, work *any* constitution." It is
not necessary to assent to Mr. Bagehot's strictures; but it is not possible to
deny the clear-sighted justice of this criticism. In order to be fair to the
memory of our great constitution-makers, however, it is necessary to remember that when they sat in convention in Philadelphia the English
Constitution, which they copied, was not the simple system which was
before Mr. Bagehot's eyes when he wrote. Its single sovereign authority
was not then a twice-reformed House of Commons truly representative of
the nation and readily obeyed by a responsible Ministry. The sovereignty
was at see-saw between the throne and the parliament,—and the throne-

end of the beam was generally uppermost. Our device of separated, individualized powers was very much better than a nominal sovereignty of
the Commons which was suffered to be overridden by force, fraud, or
craft, by the real sovereignty of the King. The English Constitution was
at that time in reality much worse than our own; and, if it is now
superior, it is so because its growth has not been hindered or destroyed by
the too tight ligaments of a written fundamental law.

The natural, the inevitable tendency of every system of self-government like our own and the British is to exalt the representative body, the
people's parliament, to a position of absolute supremacy. That tendency
has, I think, been quite as marked in our own constitutional history as in
that of any other country, though its power has been to some extent
neutralized, and its progress in great part stayed, by those denials of that
supremacy which we respect because they are written in our law. The
political law written in our hearts is here at variance with that which the
Constitution sought to establish. A written constitution may and often
will be violated in both letter and spirit by a people of energetic political
talents and a keen instinct for progressive practical development; but so
long as they adhere to the forms of such a constitution, so long as the
machinery of government supplied by it is the only machinery which the
legal and moral sense of such a people permits it to use, its political
development must be in many directions narrowly restricted because of
an insuperable lack of open or adequate channels. Our Constitution, like
every other constitution which puts the authority to make laws and the
duty of controlling the public expenditure into the hands of a popular
assembly, practically sets that assembly to rule the affairs of the nation as
supreme overlord. But, by separating it entirely from its executive agencies, it deprives it of the opportunity and means for making its authority
complete and convenient. The constitutional machinery is left of such a
pattern that other forces less than that of Congress may cross and compete
with Congress, though they are too small to overcome or long offset it;
and the result is simply an unpleasant, wearing friction which, with other
adjustments, more felicitous and equally safe, might readily be avoided.

Congress consequently, is still lingering and chafing under just such
embarrassments as made the English Commons a nuisance both to themselves and to everybody else immediately after the Revolution Settlement
had given them the first sure promise of supremacy. The parallel is
startlingly exact.

In outer seeming the Revolution of 1688 had only transferred the sovereignty
over England from James to William and Mary. In actual fact it had given a
powerful and decisive impulse to the great constitutional progress which was
transferring the sovereignty from the King to the House of Commons. From
the moment when its sole right to tax the nation was established by the Bill
of Rights, and when its own resolve settled the practice of granting none but
annual supplies to the Crown, the House of Commons became the supreme
power in the State. . . . But though the constitutional change was complete,

the machinery of government was far from having adapted itself to the new conditions of political life which such a change brought about. However powerful the will of the Commons might be, it had no means of bringing its will directly to bear on the control of public affairs. The ministers who had charge of them were not its servants but the servants of the Crown; it was from the King that they looked for direction, and to the King that they held themselves responsible. By impeachment or more indirect means the Commons could force a king to remove a minister who contradicted their will; but they had no constitutional power to replace the fallen statesman by a minister who would carry out their will.

The result was the growth of a temper in the Lower House which drove William and his ministers to despair. It became as corrupt, as jealous of power, as fickle in its resolves and factious in its spirit as bodies always become whose consciousness of the possession of power is untempered by a corresponding consciousness of practical difficulties or the moral responsibilities of the power which they possess. It grumbled . . . and it blamed the Crown and its ministers for all at which it grumbled. But it was hard to find out what policy or measures it would have preferred. Its mood changed, as William bitterly complained, with every hour. . . . The Houses were in fact without the guidance of recognized leaders, without adequate information, and destitute of that organization out of which alone a definite policy can come [John Richard Green].

The cure for this state of things which Sunderland had the sagacity to suggest, and William the wisdom to apply, was the mediation between King and Commons of cabinet representative of the majority of the popular chamber,—a first but long and decisive step towards responsible cabinet government. Whether a similar remedy would be possible or desirable in our own case it is altogether aside from my present purpose to inquire. I am pointing out facts,—diagnosing, not prescribing remedies. My only point just now is, that no one can help being struck by the closeness of the likeness between the incipient distempers of the first parliaments of William and Mary and the developed disorders now so plainly discernible in the constitution of Congress. Though honest and diligent, it is meddlesome and inefficient; and it is meddlesome and inefficient for exactly the same reasons that made it natural that the post-Revolutionary parliaments should exhibit like clumsiness and like temper: namely, because it is "without the guidance of recognized leaders, without adequate information, and destitute of that organization out of which alone a definite policy can come."

The dangers of this serious imperfection in our governmental machinery have not been clearly demonstrated in our experience hitherto; but now their delayed fulfillment seems to be close at hand. The plain tendency is towards a centralization of all the greater powers of government in the hands of the federal authorities, and towards the practical confirmation of those prerogatives of supreme overlordship which Congress has been gradually arrogating to itself. The central government is constantly becoming stronger and more active, and Congress is establishing itself as the one sovereign authority in that government. In constitutional theory and in the broader features of past practice, ours has been what Mr. Bagehot has called a "composite" government. Besides state and federal authorities to dispute as to sovereignty, there have been within the federal system itself rival and irreconcilable powers. But gradually the strong are overcoming the weak. If the signs of the times are to be credited, we are fast approaching an adjustment of sovereignty quite as "simple" as need be. Congress is not only to retain the authority it already possesses, but is to be brought again and again face to face with still greater demands upon its energy, its wisdom, and its conscience, is to have ever-widening duties and responsibilities thrust upon it, without being granted a moment's opportunity to look back from the plough to which it has set its hands.

The sphere and influence of national administration and national legislation are widening rapidly. Our populations are growing at such a rate that one's reckoning staggers at counting the possible millions that may have a home and a work on this continent ere fifty more years shall have filled their short span. The East will not always be the centre of national life. The South is fast accumulating wealth, and will faster recover influence. The West has already achieved a greatness which no man can gainsay, and has in store a power of future growth which no man can estimate. Whether these sections are to be harmonious or dissentient depends almost entirely upon the methods and policy of the federal government. If that government be not careful to keep within its own proper sphere and prudent to square its policy by rules of national welfare, sectional lines must and will be known; citizens of one part of the country may look with jealousy and even with hatred upon their fellow-citizens of another part; and faction must tear and dissension distract a country which Providence would bless, but which man may curse. The government of a country so vast and various must be strong, prompt, wieldy, and efficient. Its strength must consist in the certainty and uniformity of its purposes, in its accord with national sentiment, in its unhesitating action, and in its honest aims. It must be steadied and approved by open administration diligently obedient to the more permanent judgments of public opinion; and its only active agency, its representative chambers, must be equipped with something besides abundant powers of legislation.

As at present constituted, the federal government lacks strength because its powers are divided, lacks promptness because its authorities are multiplied, lacks wieldiness because its processes are roundabout, lacks efficiency because its responsibility is indistinct and its action without competent direction. It is a government in which every officer may talk about every other officer's duty without having to render strict account for not doing his own, and in which the masters are held in check and offered contradiction by the servants. Mr. Lowell has called it "government by declamation." Talk is not sobered by any necessity imposed upon those who utter it to suit their actions to their words. There is no day of reckoning for words spoken. The speakers of a congressional majority may, without risk of incurring ridicule or discredit, condemn what their own Committees are doing; and the spokesmen of a minority may urge what contrary courses they please with a well-grounded assurance that what they say will be forgotten before they can be called upon to put it into practice. Nobody stands sponsor for the policy of the government. A dozen men originate it; a dozen compromises twist and alter it; a dozen offices whose names are scarcely known outside of Washington put it into execution.

This is the defect to which, it will be observed, I am constantly recurring; to which I recur again and again because every examination of the system, at whatsoever point begun, leads inevitably to it as to a central secret. It is the defect which interprets all the rest, because it is their common product. It is exemplified in the extraordinary fact the utterances of the Press have greater weight and are accorded greater credit, though the Press speaks entirely without authority, than the utterances of Congress, though Congress possesses all authority. The gossip of the street is listened to rather than the words of the law-makers. The editor directs public opinion, the congressman obeys it. When a presidential election is at hand, indeed, the words of the political orator gain temporary heed. He is recognized as an authority in the arena, as a professional critic competent to discuss the good and bad points, and to forecast the fortunes of the contestants. There is something definite in hand, and he is known to have studied all its bearings. He is one of the managers, or is thought to be well acquainted with the management. He speaks "from the card." But let him talk, not about candidates, but about measures or about the policy of the government, and his observations sink at once to the level of a mere individual expression of opinion, to which his political occupations seem to add very little weight. It is universally recognized that he speaks without authority, about things which his vote may help to settle, but about which several hundred other men have votes quite as influential as his own. Legislation is not a thing to be known beforehand. It depends upon the conclusions of sundry Standing Committees. It is an aggregate, not a simple, production. It is impossible to tell how many persons' opinions and influences have entered into its composition. It is even impracticable to determine from this year's law-making what next year's will be like.

Speaking, therefore, without authority, the political orator speaks to little purpose when he speaks about legislation. The papers do not report him carefully; and their editorials seldom take any color from his arguments. The Press, being anonymous and representing a large force of inquisitive news-hunters, is much more powerful than he chiefly because it *is* impersonal and seems to represent a wider and more thorough range of information. At the worst, it can easily compete with any ordinary individual. Its individual opinion is quite sure to be esteemed as worthy of attention as any other individual opinion. And, besides, it is almost everywhere strong enough to deny currency to the speeches of individuals whom it does not care to report. It goes to its audience; the orator must depend upon his audience coming to him. It can be heard at every fireside; the orator can be heard only on the platform or the hustings. There is no imperative demand on the part of the reading public in this country that the newspapers should report political speeches in full. On the contrary, most readers would be disgusted at finding their favorite columns so filled up. By giving even a notice of more than an item's length to such a speech, an editor runs the risk of being denounced as dull. And I believe that the position of the American Press is in this regard quite singular. The English newspapers are so far from being thus independent and self-sufficient powers,—a law unto themselves,—in the politics of the empire that they are constrained to do homage to the political orator whether they will or no. Conservative editors must spread before their readers verbatim reports not only of the speeches of the leaders of their own party, but also of the principal speeches of the leading Liberal orators; and Liberal journals have no choice but to print every syllable of the more important public utterances of the Conservative leaders. The nation insists upon knowing what its public men have to say, even when it is not so well said as the newspapers which report them could have said it. There are only two things which can give any man a right to expect that when he speaks the whole country will listen: namely, genius and authority. Probably no one will ever contend that Sir Stafford Northcote was an orator, or even a good speaker. But by proof of unblemished character, and by assiduous, conscientious, and able public service he rose to be the recognized leader of his party in the House of Commons; and it is simply because he speaks as one having authority,— and not as the scribes of the Press,—that he is as sure of a heedful hearing as is Mr. Gladstone, who adds genius and noble oratory to the authority of established leadership. The leaders of English public life have something besides weight of character, prestige of personal service and experience, and authority of individual opinion to exalt them above the anonymous Press. They have definite authority and power in the actual control of government. They are directly commissioned to control the policy of the administration. They stand before the country, in parliament and out of it, as the responsible chiefs of their parties. It is their business to lead those parties, and it is the matter-of-course custom of the constituencies to visit upon the parties the punishment due for the mistakes made by these chiefs. They are at once the servants and scapegoats of their parties.

It is these well-established privileges and responsibilities of theirs which make their utterances considered worth hearing,—nay, necessary to be heard and pondered. Their public speeches are their parties' platforms. What the leader promises his party stands ready to do, should it be intrusted with office. This certainty of audience and of credit gives spice to what such leaders have to say, and lends elevation to the tone of all their public utterances. They for the most part avoid buncombe, which would be difficult to translate into Acts of Parliament. It is easy to see how great an advantage their station and influence give them over our own public men. We have no such responsible party leadership on this side the sea; we are very shy about conferring much authority on anybody, and the consequence is that it requires something very like genius to secure for any one of our statesmen a universally recognized right to be heard and to create an ever-active desire to hear him whenever he talks, not about candidates, but about measures. An extraordinary gift of eloquence, such as not every generation may hope to see, will always hold, because it will always captivate, the attention of the people. But genius and eloquence are too rare to be depended upon for the instruction and guidance of the masses; and since our politicians lack the credit of authority and responsibility, they must give place, except at election-time, to the Press, which is everywhere, generally well-informed, and always talking. It is necessarily "government by declamation" and editorial-writing.

It is probably also this lack of leadership which gives to our national parties their curious, conglomerate character. It would seem to be scarcely an exaggeration to say that they are homogeneous only in name. Neither of the two principal parties is of one mind with itself. Each tolerates all sorts of difference of creed and variety of aim within its own ranks. Each pretends to the same purposes and permits among its partisans the same contradictions to those purposes. They are grouped around no legislative leaders whose capacity has been tested and to whose opinions they loyally adhere. They are like armies without officers, engaged upon a campaign which has no great cause at its back. Their names and traditions, not their hopes and policy, keep them together.

It is to this fact, as well as to short terms which allow little time for differences to come to a head, that the easy agreement of congressional majorities should be attributed. In other like assemblies the harmony of majorities is constantly liable to disturbance. Ministers lose their following and find their friends falling away in the midst of a session. But not so in Congress. There, although the majority is frequently simply conglomerate, made up of factions not a few, and bearing in its elements every seed of discord, the harmony of party voting seldom, if ever, suffers an interruption. So far as outsiders can see, legislation generally flows placidly on, and the majority easily has its own way, acting with a sort of matter-of-course unanimity, with no suspicion of individual freedom of action. Whatever revolts may be threatened or accomplished in the ranks of the party outside the House at the polls, its power is never broken inside the House. This is doubtless due in part to the fact that there is no freedom of debate in the House; but there can be no question that it is principally due to the fact that debate is without aim, just because legislation is without consistency. Legislation is conglomerate. The absence of any concert of action amongst the Committees leaves legislation with scarcely any trace of determinate party courses. No two schemes pull together. If there is a coincidence of principle between several bills of the same session, it is generally accidental; and the confusion of policy which prevents intelligent cooperation also, of course, prevents intelligent differences and divisions. There is never a transfer of power from one party to the other during a session, because such a transfer would mean almost nothing. The majority remains of one mind so long as a Congress lives, because its mind is very vaguely ascertained, and its power of planning a split consequently very limited. It has no common mind, and if it had, has not the machinery for changing it. It is led by a score or two of Committees whose composition must remain the same to the end; and who are too numerous, as well as too disconnected, to fight against. It stays on one side because it hardly knows where the boundaries of that side are or how to cross them.

Moreover, there is a certain well-known piece of congressional machinery long ago invented and applied for the special purpose of keeping both majority and minority compact. The legislative caucus has almost as important a part in our system as have the Standing Committees, and deserves as close study as they. Its functions are much more easily understood in all their bearings than those of the Committees, however, because they are much simpler. The caucus is meant as an antidote to the Committees. It is designed to supply the cohesive principle which the multiplicity and mutual independence of the Committees so powerfully tend to destroy. Having no Prime Minister to confer with about the policy of the government, as they see members of parliament doing, our congressmen confer with each other in caucus. Rather than imprudently expose to the world the differences of opinion threatened or developed among its members, each party hastens to remove disrupting debate from the floor of Congress, where the speakers might too hastily commit themselves to insubordination, to quiet conferences behind closed doors, where frightened scruples may be reassured and every disagreement healed with a salve of compromise or subdued with the whip of political expediency. The caucus is the drilling-ground of the party. There its discipline is renewed and strengthened, its uniformity of step and gesture regained. The voting and speaking in the House are generally merely the movements of a sort of dress parade, for which the exercises of the caucus are designed to prepare. It is easy to see how difficult it would be for the party to keep its head amidst the confused cross-movements of the Committees without thus now and again pulling itself together in caucus, where it can ask itself its own mind and pledge itself anew to eternal agreement.

The credit of inventing this device is probably due to the Democrats. They appear to have used it so early as the second session of the eighth Congress. Speaking of that session, a reliable authority [Statesman's Manual] says: "During this session of Congress there was far less of free and independent discussion on the measures proposed by the friends of

the administration than had been previously practiced in both branches
of the national legislature. It appeared that on the most important subjects, the course adopted by the majority was the effect of caucus arrangement, or, in other words, had been previously agreed upon at meetings of
the Democratic members held in private. Thus the legislation of Congress
was constantly swayed by a party following feelings and pledges rather
than according to sound reason or personal conviction." The censure
implied in this last sentence may have seemed righteous at the time when
such caucus pledges were in disfavor as new-fangled shackles, but it
would hardly be accepted as just by the intensely practical politicians of
to-day. They would probably prefer to put it thus: That the silvern
speech spent in caucus secures the golden silence maintained on the floor
of Congress, making each party rich in concord and happy in cooperation.

The fact that makes this defense of the caucus not altogether conclusive is that it is shielded from all responsibility by its sneaking privacy. It
has great power without any balancing weight of accountability. Probably its debates would constitute interesting and instructive reading for
the public, were they published; but they never get out except in rumors
often rehearsed and as often amended. They are, one may take it for
granted, much more candid and go much nearer the political heart of the
questions discussed than anything that is ever said openly in Congress to
the reporters' gallery. They approach matters without masks and handle
them without gloves. It might hurt, but it would enlighten us to hear
them. As it is, however, there is unhappily no ground for denying their
power to override sound reason and personal conviction. The caucus
cannot always silence or subdue a large and influential minority of dis-
sentients, but its whip seldom fails to reduce individual malcontents and
mutineers into submission. There is no place in congressional jousts for
the free lance. The man who disobeys his party caucus is understood to
disavow his party allegiance altogether, and to assume that dangerous
neutrality which is so apt to degenerate into mere caprice, and which is
almost sure to destroy his influence by bringing him under the suspicion
of being unreliable,—a suspicion always conclusively damning in practical life. Any individual, or any minority of weak numbers of small
influence, who has the temerity to neglect the decisions of the caucus is
sure, if the offense be often repeated, or even once committed upon an
important issue, to be read out of the party, almost without chance of
reinstatement. And every one knows that nothing can be accomplished in
politics by mere disagreement; they are forever shut out from the privilege of confidential cooperation. They have chosen the helplessness of a
faction.

It must be admitted, however, that, unfortunate as the necessity is for
the existence of such powers as those of the caucus, that necessity actually
exists and cannot be neglected. Against the fatal action of so many elements of disintegration it would seem to be imperatively needful that

some energetic element of cohesion should be provided. It is doubtful whether in any other nation, with a shorter inheritance of political instinct, parties could long successfully resist the centrifugal forces of the committee system with only the varying attraction of the caucus to detain them. The wonder is that, despite the forcible and unnatural divorcement of legislation and administration and the consequent distraction of legislation from all attention to anything like an intelligent planning and superintendence of policy, we are not cursed with as many factions as now almost hopelessly confuse French politics. That we have had, and continue to have, only two national parties of national importance or real power is fortunate rather than natural. Their names stand for a fact, but scarcely for a reason.

An intelligent observer of our politics has declared that there is in the United States "a class, including thousands and tens of thousands of the best men in the country, who think it possible to enjoy the fruits of good government without working for them." Every one who has seen beyond the outside of our American life must recognize the truth of this; to explain it is to state the sum of all the most valid criticisms of congressional government. Public opinion has no easy vehicle for its judgments, no quick channels for its action. Nothing about the system is direct and simple. Authority is perplexingly subdivided and distributed, and responsibility has to be hunted down in out-of-the-way corners. So that the sum of the whole matter is that the means of working for the fruits of good government are not readily to be found. The average citizen may be excused for esteeming government at best but a haphazard affair, upon which his vote and all of his influence can have but little effect. How is his choice of a representative in Congress to affect the policy of the country as regards the questions in which he is most interested, if the man for whom he votes has no chance of getting on the Standing Committee which has virtual charge of those questions? How is it to make any difference who is chosen President? Has the President any very great authority in matters of vital policy? It seems almost a thing of despair to get any assurance that any vote he may cast will even in an infinitesimal degree affect the essential courses of administration. There are so many cooks mixing their ingredients in the national broth that it seems hopeless, this thing of changing one cook at a time.

The charm of our constitutional ideal has now been long enough wound up to enable sober men who do not believe in political witchcraft to judge what it has accomplished, and is likely still to accomplish, without further winding. The Constitution is not honored by blind worship. The more open-eyed we become, as a nation, to its defects, and the prompter we grow in applying with the unhesitating courage of conviction all thoroughly-tested or well-considered expedients necessary to make self-government among us a straightforward thing of simple method, single, unstinted power, and clear responsibility, the nearer will we approach to the sound sense and practical genius of the great and honorable statesmen of 1787. And the first step towards emancipation from the timidity and false pride which have led us to seek to thrive despite the defects of our national system rather than seem to deny its perfection is a fearless criticism of that system. When we shall have examined all its parts without sentiment, and gauged all its functions by the standards of practical common sense, we shall have established anew our right to the claim of political sagacity; and it will remain only to act intelligently upon what our opened eyes have seen in order to prove again the justice of our claim to political genius.

James Bryce

Why the Best Men

Do Not Go

into Politics

Probably the most learned and penetrating student of American politics and government in the Gilded Age was an Englishman—Lord Bryce. A jurist, statesman, and historian of note, he began his study of American life and institutions in 1870 when he made the first of a series of visits to the United States. He began putting the results of his observations into a book in 1883 and published it in 1888. That book, called The American Commonwealth, *was the first important broad study of American politics, and it became a classic of its kind. It is still studied with profit by political scientists. In the following selection, Bryce explains why few men of social and intellectual eminence in the America of the Gilded Age entered public life. Although he considers this situation unfortunate, he sees hope for improvement in the future. Remember, Bryce is analyzing conditions contemporary with his own time. [Reprinted with permission of the publisher from* The American Commonwealth *by James Bryce. Copyright 1910 by The Macmillan Company. Renewed 1938 by Elizabeth M. Bryce.]*

"But," some one will say, who has read the reasons just assigned for the development of a class of professional politicians, "you allow nothing for public spirit. It is easy to show why the prize of numerous places should breed a swarm of office-seekers, not so easy to understand why the office-seekers should be allowed to have this arena of public life in a vast country, a free country, an intelligent country, all to themselves. There ought to be patriotic citizens ready to plunge into the stream and save the boat from drifting towards the rapids. They would surely have the support of the mass of the people who must desire honest and economical administration. If such citizens stand aloof, there are but two explanations possible. Either public life must be so foul that good men cannot enter it, or good men must be sadly wanting in patriotism."

This kind of observation is so common in European mouths as to need an explicit answer. The answer is two-fold.

In the first place, the arena is not wholly left to the professionals. Both the Federal and the State legislatures contain a fair proportion of upright and disinterested men, who enter chiefly, or largely, from a sense of public duty, and whose presence keeps the mere professionals in order. So does public opinion, deterring even the bad men from the tricks to which they are prone, and often driving them, when detected in a serious offence, from place and power.

However, this first answer is not a complete answer, for it must be admitted that the proportion of men of intellectual and social eminence who enter public life is smaller in America than it has been during the present century in each of the free countries of Europe. Does this fact indicate a want of public spirit?

It is much to be wished that in every country public spirit were the chief motive propelling men into public life. But is it so anywhere now? Has it been so at any time in a nation's history? Let any one in England, dropping for the moment that self-righteous attitude of which Englishmen are commonly accused by foreigners, ask himself how many of those whom he knows as mixing in the public life of his own country have entered it from motives primarily patriotic, how many have been actuated by the love of fame or power, the hope of advancing their social pretensions or their business relations. There is nothing necessarily wrong in such forms of ambition; but if we find that they count for much in the public life of one country, and for comparatively little in the public life of another, we must expect to find the latter able to reckon among its statesmen fewer persons of eminent intelligence and energy.

Now there are several conditions present in the United States, conditions both constitutional and social, conditions independent either of political morality or of patriotism, which make the ablest citizens less disposed to enter political life than they would otherwise be, or than persons of the same class are in Europe. I have already referred to some of these, but recapitulate them shortly here because they are specially important in this connection.

The want of a social and commercial capital is such a cause. To be a Federal politician you must live in Washington, that is, abandon your circle of home friends, your profession or business, your local public duties. But to live in Paris or London is of itself an attraction to many Englishmen and Frenchmen.

There is no class in America to which public political life comes naturally, scarcely any families with a sort of hereditary right to serve the State. Nobody can get an early and easy start on the strength of his name and connections. as still happens in several European countries.

In Britain or France a man seeking to enter the higher walks of public life has more than five hundred seats for which he may stand. If his own town or county is impossible he goes elsewhere. In the United States he cannot. If his own district is already filled by a member of his own party, there is nothing to be done, unless he will condescend to undermine and supplant at the next nominating convention the sitting member. If he has been elected and happens to lose his own re-nomination or re-election, he cannot re-enter Congress by any other door. The fact that a man has served gives him no claim to be allowed to go on serving. In the West, rotation is the rule. No wonder that, when a political career is so precarious, men of worth and capacity hesitate to embrace it. They cannot afford to be thrown out of their life's course by a mere accident.

Politics are less interesting than in Europe. The two kinds of questions which most attract eager or ambitious minds, questions of foreign policy and of domestic constitutional change, are generally absent, happily absent. Currency and tariff questions and financial affairs generally, internal improvements, the regulation of railways and so forth, are important, no doubt, but to some minds not fascinating. How few people in the English or French legislatures have mastered them, or would relish political life if it dealt with little else! There are no class privileges or religious inequalities to be abolished. Religion, so powerful a political force in Europe, is outside politics altogether.

In most European countries there has been for many years past an upward pressure of the poorer or the unprivileged masses, a pressure which has seemed to threaten the wealthier and more particularly the landowning class. Hence members of the latter class have had a strong motive for keeping tight hold of the helm of state. They have felt a direct personal interest in sitting in the legislature and controlling the administration of their country. This has not been so in America. Its great political issues have not hitherto been class issues. On the contrary there has been, till within the last few years, so great and general a sense of economic security, whether well or ill founded I do not now inquire, that the wealthy and educated have been content to leave the active work of politics alone.

The division of legislative authority between the Federal Congress and the legislatures of the States further lessens the interest and narrows the opportunities of a political career. Some of the most useful members of the English Parliament have been led to enter it by their zeal for philanthropic schemes and social reforms. Others enter because they are interested in foreign politics or in commercial questions. In the United States foreign politics and commercial questions belong to Congress, so no one will be led by them to enter the legislature of his State. Social reforms and philanthropic enterprises belong to the State legislatures, so no one will be led by them to enter Congress. The limited sphere of each body deprives it of the services of many active spirits who would have been attracted by it had it dealt with both these sets of matters, or with the particular set of matters in which their own particular interest happens to lie.

In America there are more easy and attractive openings into other careers than in most European countries. The settlement of the great West, the making and financing of railways, the starting of industrial or commercial enterprises in the newer States, all offer tempting fields to ambition, ingenuity, and self-confidence. A man without capital or friends has a better chance than in Europe, and as the scale of under-takings is vaster, the prizes are more seductive. Hence much of the prac-tical ability which in the Old World goes to Parliamentary politics or to the civil administration of the state, goes in America into business, espe-cially into railways and finance. No class strikes one more by its splendid practical capacity than the class of railroad men. It includes administra-tive rulers, generals, diplomatists, financiers, of the finest gifts. And in point of fact (as will be more fully shown later) the railroad kings have of late years swayed the fortunes of American citizens more than the poli-ticians.

The fascination which politics have for many people in England is largely a social fascination. Those who belong by birth to the upper classes like to support their position in county society by belonging to the House of Commons, or by procuring either a seat in the House of Lords, or the lord-lieutenancy of their county, or perhaps a post in the royal household. The easiest path to these latter dignities lies through the Commons. Those who spring from the middle class expect to find by means of politics an entrance into a more fashionable society than they have hitherto frequented. Their wives will at least be invited to the party receptions, or they may entertain a party chieftain when he comes to address a meeting in their town. Such inducements scarcely exist in America. A congressman, a city mayor, even a State governor, gains noth-ing socially by his position. There is indeed, except in a few Eastern cities with exclusive sets, really nothing in the nature of a social prize set before social ambition, while the career of political ambition is even in those cities wholly disjoined from social success. The only exception to this rule occurs in Washington, where a senator or cabinet minister enjoys *ex officio* a certain social rank.

None of these causes is discreditable to America, yet, taken together, they go far to account for the large development of the professional element among politicians. Putting the thing broadly, one may say that in America, while politics are relatively less interesting than in Europe and lead to less, other careers are relatively more interesting and lead to more.

It may however be alleged that I have omitted one significant ground for the distaste of "the best people" for public life, viz. the bad company they would have to keep, the general vulgarity of tone in politics, the exposure to invective or ribaldry by hostile speakers and a reckless press.

I omit this ground because it seems insignificant. In every country a

politician has to associate with men whom he despises and distrusts, and
those whom he most despises and distrusts are sometimes those whose so-
called social rank is highest—the sons or brothers of great nobles. In
every country he is exposed to misrepresentation and abuse, and the most
galling misrepresentations are not the coarse and incredible ones, but
those which have a semblance of probability, which delicately discolour
his motives and ingeniously pervert his words. A statesman must soon
learn, even in decorous England or punctilious France or polished Italy,
to disregard all this, and rely upon his conscience for his peace of mind,
and upon his conduct for the respect of his countrymen. If he can do so
in England or France or Italy, he may do so in America also. No more
there than in Europe has any upright man been written down, for
though the American press is unsparing, the American people are shrewd,
and sometimes believe too little rather than too much evil of a man
whom the press assails. Although therefore one hears the pseudo-Euro-
pean American complain of newspaper violence, and allege that it keeps
him and his friends from doing their duty by their country, and although
it sometimes happens that the fear of newspaper attacks deters a good
citizen from exposing some job or jobber, still I could not learn the name
of any able and high-minded man of whom it could be truly said that
through this cause his gifts and virtues had been reserved for private life.
The roughness of politics has, no doubt, some influence on the view
which wealthy Americans take of a public career, but these are just the
Americans who think that European politics are worked, to use the common phrase, "with kid gloves," and they are not the class most inclined
anyhow to come to the front for the service of the nation. Without
denying that there is recklessness in the American press, and a notable
want of refinement in politics generally, I doubt whether these phenomena have anything like the importance which European visitors are
taught, and willingly learn, to attribute to them. Far more weight is to be
laid upon the difficulties which the organization of the party system
throws in the way of men who seek to enter public life. There is much
that is disagreeable, much that is even humiliating, in the initial stages of
a political career, and doubtless many a pilgrim turns back after a short
experience of this Slough of Despond.

To explain the causes which keep so much of the finest intellect of the
country away from national business is one thing, to deny the unfortunate results would be quite another. Unfortunate they certainly are.
But the downward tendency observable since the end of the Civil War
seems to have been arrested. When the war was over, the Union saved,
and the curse of slavery gone for ever, there came a season of contentment
and of lassitude. A nation which had surmounted such dangers seemed to
have nothing more to fear. Those who had fought with tongue and pen
and rifle, might now rest on their laurels. After long-continued strain and
effort, the wearied nerve and muscle sought repose. It was repose from
political warfare only. For the end of the war coincided with the opening

of a time of swift material growth and abounding material prosperity, in which industry and the development of the West absorbed more and more of the energy of the people. Hence a neglect of the details of politics by the better class of voters such as had never been seen before. The last few years have brought a revival of interest in public affairs, and especially in the management of cities. There is more speaking and writing and thinking, practical and definite thinking, upon the principles of government than at any previous epoch. Good citizens are beginning to put their hands to the machinery of government; and it is noticed that those who do so are, more largely than formerly, young men, who have not contracted the bad habits which the practice of politics has engendered among many of their elders, and who will in a few years have become an even more potent force than they are now. If the path to Congress and the State legislatures and the higher municipal offices were cleared of the stumbling-blocks and dirt heaps which now encumber it, cunningly placed there by professional politicians, a great change would soon pass upon the composition of legislative bodies, and a new spirit be felt in the management of State and municipal as well as of national affairs.

Dramatic social and economic changes accompanied the mushrooming industrialism of the decades following the Civil War. None felt the impact of change more deeply than those who worked with their hands, and among the workers none were more helpless in the industrial society than the immigrants. In these years, the workers—whether native American or foreign born—were forced to adjust to the demands of machines without sharing in the increased wealth produced by the new industrialism. The immigrants came, or were brought, to the United States in response to the labor needs of this industrialism, and their escape from the demands of the machines seemed impossible. To the native American workers, the laborer status imposed by the machines was new and unpleasant. At first they resisted or sought to escape this status. They tried to find a way out of a system where they now became one cog in the machinery of mass production.

3

LABOR AND IMMIGRATION IN THE INDUSTRIAL SOCIETY

Now that the unskilled could do what had formerly been done by the skilled, labor became a commodity that could be bought and sold like other elements in production. The craftsman could no longer produce and sell his own goods. He lost not only the bargaining power he had once enjoyed, but also the status of being his own employer. All that the individual worker could do was to sell his own labor for a wage. In the factory, mill, or foundry, he became part of a wage system in which he had little contact with his employer and in which his interests and those of the employer were different. The employer sought to buy labor as cheaply as possible, and the worker tried to obtain a larger share of the profits he helped to create. This new status was at first confusing to the American workingman. Unable to adjust easily to the industrial order, the worker was uncertain of where his true long-term interests lay. Unlike the European laborer or the new immigrant, the native American worker lacked the feeling and tradition of belonging to a distinct class. As a result, he rejected the wage system and looked upon his job as temporary—as merely a steppingstone to something higher socially and economically. Even the unions that the workers organized refused at first to accept the wage system.

The National Labor Union and the Knights of Labor—the first two unions to dominate the labor movement from the end of the Civil War to the late 1880s—both sought escape from the wage system. Their leaders apparently believed that the capitalist system of production had been devised to enslave the worker and drive the craftsman out of existence.

The unions fought back with programs that would aid the workers in becoming their own employers, or even small-scale entrepreneurs, because union leaders looked upon self-employment as the ultimate salvation for labor.

The National Labor Union, for example, embraced the idea of a cooperative industrial society wherein the workers would take over and direct the economic system. In cooperative enterprises the workers would pool their resources, supply their own labor, and manage the factories themselves. Organized labor thus concentrated on political and economic measures designed to promote ownership of the means of production and on cooperative production as a way of supplanting the wage system.

In the 1880s, many craftsmen came to recognize that the wage system, as an integral part of mass production, was permanent—as was a more or less fixed working class, concerned primarily with the sale of its labor at favorable prices. During the depression of 1884–85, in fact, labor organizations assumed the characteristics of a class movement, and the idea of the solidarity of labor began to take form. The acceptance of the innovation of the wage system, along with the trend toward concentration of economic power in business and politics, transformed the American labor movement from an amorphous entity into a compact body fighting for limited but concrete economic gains.

This narrow attitude became basic in the labor philosophy of the third national organization, the American Federation of Labor, which was formed in 1886. Accepting the new industrial order, the Federation concentrated on the practical task of improving the position of its own trade-union followers within the wage system instead of seeking to escape from the system into ownership. The head of the Federation, Samuel Gompers, held a pragmatic view of labor's objectives. He shunned cooperative enterprises and confined labor activity to the immediate economic problems of the wage earners, such as wages, hours, accidents, and other working conditions. This was pure and simple trade unionism.

The new trade unionism tried to forge an organization strong enough to engage in economic struggle with employers, using the strike, the boycott, and the union label as its weapons. This new unionism frankly accepted the existence of a fundamental conflict between employer and employee, as well as the fact that relatively few wage earners could become employers; but it rejected socialist theory and the radical concepts of class struggle.

In theory, trade unionism avoided partisan politics, in the sense of allying itself with any one political movement or party. It did not, however, avoid politics altogether. The trade unions participated actively in elections and legislative affairs, but with conservative views on the means and end of political action. They believed that politics should serve the basic goals of the wage earners. Political activity for broad general reforms, they held, would only dissipate energies in causes remote from labor's immediate interests. Pure and simple trade unionism, in brief, required nonpartisan politics—that is, the support of any candidate who would espouse the union's legislative demands, such as the legal use of pickets. Such support became the business politics of trade unionism.

No one can study the growth of organized labor without realizing that it was joined to another social movement—the immigration of millions of young men, from southern and eastern Europe, who worked in America's mines, mills, and factories. Their unskilled labor provided the sinew for the phenomenal industrial expansion of the late nineteenth century. Before the century ended these foreign-born workers constituted the mass of wage earners in industry after industry. In proportion to their numbers they performed more of the nation's labor than did the native-born. This, however, is only part of the immigrant story, for the human flood from Europe in the last decades of the nineteenth century was one of the forces that truly transformed American society.

From the beginning, immigration from Europe has been a central force in the making of the American nation. Wave after wave of immigrants were washed up on America's shores, so that, ultimately, almost all Americans were either immigrants or descendants of immigrants. While it is true that Europe spread her sons and daughters over many lands, it is also true that no other country has been so strong in its attraction for immigrants as has the United States. It has been the host for the greatest folk migration yet recorded. Of the seventy million or more Europeans who have migrated since 1600, about two-thirds made their way to the United States. No other country, furthermore, has been settled by so many nationalities as has the United States.

Historians and others have long used a hierarchical classification for immigrants. Those who reached American shores before 1776, mostly from the British Islands, were called "colonists" or "settlers"; those who arrived mainly between 1815 and 1880, primarily from northwest Europe, were known as "old" immigrants; and those who came after 1880, mainly from southeast Europe, were referred to as "new" immigrants. Such distinctions may be pertinent in stressing the main source of each immigrant stream, but they were also used as the basis for social stratification and discrimination. Such stratification has little true meaning. Even though the various streams of immigrants may have shown marked cultural differences, the social origins and motives of all immigrants, from the earliest to the latest, were much alike. All immigrants went through a similar experience of being uprooted from old surroundings, coping with a strange environment, and adjusting to a new status. As a social process, immigration in American history has shown little variation and an essential continuity.

Nonetheless, many regarded the coming of the new immigrants in the 1880s as precipitating a fundamental change in the character of American immigration and of American life itself. As a result, the immigrant from southeast Europe encountered bitter hostility from Americans who had lived longer in the land. Although all immigrants, in the process of settling, had raised vexing problems of adjustment, the new immigrant seemed far different in behavior, language, and religion than foreigners Americans had previously known. Earlier, Americans had accepted immigration as a central formative element in American life, but now the native-born did not want to see the new strangers plant their customs in the land. This attitude, reflected in daily living, marked a change in the status of the immigrant in American society.

This changed status was also reflected in the experience of the newcomers themselves. As had many of those before them, the new immigrants came to the United States mainly to improve their economic lot; many were peasants who sought land. Few realized their dreams. Almost immediately they found themselves at the bottom of the economic and social scale. Unable to finance their journey beyond the Atlantic seaboard, many became stranded in the large eastern cities. New York, Boston, and Philadelphia swarmed with the newly arrived Europeans. At first they clung to those of their own kind and to the known ways of their homelands, because they were crushed by an intense loneliness and the frightening realization that they were truly strangers in the land. Few of the new immigrants, consequently, came to terms with American life. They found themselves trapped by a degrading status and by conditions that had been weighted against them from the start.

Some Americans, notably social reformers and humanitarians such as Jane Addams, tried to soften the adjustment of the immigrant to a harsh and alien society. These reformers encouraged immigrants to express their own culture and attempted to foster an appreciation for the unique contributions the new strangers could make to American society. Other Americans, especially members of patriotic organizations such as the Daughters of the American Revolution, stressed assimilation, or Americanization. They wanted the immigrants to abandon their old ways and quickly conform to the dominant American customs. A third category of Americans, primarily native-born and Protestant, wished to insulate the land from further alien influence by restricting immigration. They argued that the experience of migration itself could no longer guarantee that immigrants would be converted to an appreciation of American values and be assimilated.

To justify this view, intellectual opponents of immigration—mainly from New England—concocted a social theory that went something like this. American society had prospered because it had been founded on Anglo-Saxon institutions brought by the colonists, who were themselves descendants of Anglo-Saxons and hence innately superior to other peoples. The new immigrants, coming from different biological stock, were not so capable of adjusting to American life as their predecessors had been, earlier in the century. Obviously, therefore, the national origin of an immigrant, governed by his biological proximity to the Anglo-Saxon norm, determined his capacity for Americanization. There should be, in other words, degrees of Americanization based on the concept of race.

This attitude ran counter to two basic characteristics of American life: diversity and social mobility. Many immigrants had been attracted to the United States principally because of its relatively open society and fluid social structure. But with the growing industrialization, the new immigrant met hostility even in the labor force, of which he was a large and vital part. In rejecting the unskilled laborer, for example, the trade-union movement in effect rejected the immigrant. This hostility did not last, of course, for when the immigrant became self-conscious about his place in American society, he demanded a share of what that society in theory offered to all. And more often than not, he made his economic and sometimes his social demands known through the labor movement.

Two of the following selections explain how labor and immigration helped shape modern America. They offer insight into powerful social forces that have endowed the United States with some of its unique characteristics. The third essay analyzes immigration as a historical process and describes how it has been treated by historians.

Carl N. Degler

Machines, Men and Socialism

This selection by Carl N. Degler is taken from a broad social history of the United States in which the author explores what he calls the origins of the American character. He believes that ideas are basic forces in history and that they have a life of their own. In his analysis, therefore, he concentrates on the role of ideas in the shaping of modern America. By ideas he means the beliefs, assumptions, and values of the people themselves rather than the concepts of the great thinkers. He focuses on Americans as a people and on the qualities that have made them unique or different from other peoples.

In this segment, Degler concerns himself with the unique characteristics of the labor movement after the Civil War, when it assumed its modern form and became one of the forces that shaped the nation. He sees the labor unions in three roles: (1) as the workers' instrument for defense—not offense—against industrialization; (2) as the workers' basically conservative response to the radical challenge of capitalism; and (3) as the workers' refuge in reaction to their loneliness and loss of status in a capitalistic society. Since socialism has usually been concomitant to labor movements in other capitalistic societies, Degler also explains why organized socialism has been historically weak, if not a complete failure, in the United States. [From "Machines, Men and Socialism" in Out of Our

To say that the labor movement was affected by the industrialization of the postwar years is an understatement; the fact is, industrial capitalism created the labor movement. Not deliberately, to be sure, but in the same way that a blister is the consequence of a rubbing shoe. Unions were labor's protection against the forces of industrialization as the blister is the body's against the irritation of the shoe. The factory and all it implied confronted the workingman with a challenge to his existence as a man, and the worker's response was the labor union.

There were labor unions in America before 1865, but, as industry was only emerging in those years, so the organizations of workers were correspondingly weak. In the course of the years after Appomattox, however, when industry began to hit a new and giant stride, the tempo of unionization also stepped up. It was in these decades, after many years of false starts and utopian ambitions, that the American labor movement assumed its modern shape.

Perhaps the outstanding and enduring characteristic of organized labor in the United States has been its elemental conservatism, the fantasies of some employers to the contrary notwithstanding. Indeed, it might be said that all labor unions, at bottom, are conservative by virtue of their being essentially reactions against a developing capitalism. Though an established capitalist society views itself as anything but subversive, in the days of its becoming and seen against the perspective of the previous age, capitalism as an ideology is radically subversive, undermining and destroying many of the cherished institutions of the functioning society. This dissolving process of capitalism is seen more clearly in Europe than in America because there the time span is greater. But, as will appear later, organized labor in the United States was as much a conservative response to the challenge of capitalism as was the European trade union movement.

Viewed very broadly, the history of modern capitalism might be summarized as the freeing of the three factors of production—land, labor, and capital—from the web of tradition in which medieval society held them. If capitalism was to function, it was necessary that this liberating process take place. Only when these basic factors are free to be bought and sold according to the dictates of the profit motive can the immense production which capitalism promises be realized. An employer, for example, had to be free to dismiss labor when the balance sheet required it, without being compelled to retain workers because society or custom demanded it. Serfdom, with its requirement that the peasant could not be taken from the land, was an anachronistic institution if capitalism was to become the economic ideology of society. Conversely, an employer needed to be unrestricted in his freedom to hire labor or else production could not expand in accordance with the market. Guild restrictions which limited apprenticeships were therefore obstacles to the achievement of a free capitalism.

The alienability of the three factors of production was achieved slowly and unevenly after the close of the Middle Ages. By the nineteenth century in most nations in the West, land had become absolutely alienable—it could be bought and sold at will. With the growth of banking, the development of trustworthy monetary standards, and finally the gold standard in the nineteenth century, money or capital also became freely exchangeable. Gradually, over the span of some two centuries, the innovating demands of capitalism stripped from labor the social controls in which medieval and mercantilistic government had clothed it. Serfdom as an obstacle to the free movement of labor was gradually done away with; statutes of laborers and apprenticeships which fixed wages, hours, and terms of employment also fell into disuse or suffered outright repeal. To avoid government interference in the setting of wage rates, the English Poor Law of 1834 made it clear that the dole to the unemployed was always to be lower than the going rate for unskilled labor. Thus supply and demand would be the determinant of wage levels. Both the common law and the Combination Acts in the early nineteenth century in England sought to ensure the operation of a free market in labor by declaring trade unions to be restraints on trade.

Like land and capital, then, labor was being reduced to a commodity, freely accessible, freely alienable, free to flow where demand was high. The classical economists of the nineteenth century analyzed this long historical process, neatly put it together, and called it the natural laws of economics.

To a large extent, this historical development constituted an improvement in the worker's status, since medieval and mercantilist controls over labor had been more onerous than protective. Nevertheless, something was lost by the dissolution of the ancient social ties which fitted the worker into a larger social matrix. Under the old relationship, the worker belonged in society; he enjoyed a definite if not a high status; he had a place. Now he was an individual, alone; his status was up to him to establish; his urge for community with society at large had no definite avenue of expression. Society and labor alike had been atomized in pursuit of an individualistic economy. Herein lay the radical character of the capitalist ideology.

That the workingman sensed the radical change and objected to it is evident from what some American labor leaders said about their unions. Without rejecting the new freedom which labor enjoyed, John Mitchell, of the Mine Workers, pointed out that the union "stands for fraternity, complete and absolute." Samuel Gompers' eulogy of the social microcosm which was the trade union has the same ring. "A hundred times we have said it," he wrote, "and we say it again, that trade unionism contains within itself the potentialities of working class regeneration." The union is a training ground for democracy and provides "daily object lessons in ideal justice; it breathes into the working classes the spirit of unity"; but above all, it affords that needed sense of community. The labor union "provides a field for noble comradeship, for deeds of loyalty, for self-sacrifice beneficial to one's fellow-workers." In the trade union, in short, the workers could obtain another variety of that sense of community, of comradeship, as Gompers put it, which the acid of individualistic capitalism had dissolved.

And there was another objection to the transformation of labor into an exchangeable commodity. The theoretical justification for the conversion of the factors of production into commodities is that the maximum amount of goods can be produced under such a regime. The increased production is deemed desirable because it would insure greater amounts of goods for human consumption and therefore a better life for all. Unfortunately for the theory, however, labor cannot be separated from the men who provide it. To make labor a commodity is to make the men who provide labor commodities also. Thus one is left with the absurdity of turning men into commodities in order to give men a better life!

"Labor is a commodity of a peculiar sort," John Mitchell pointed out. "It is a part of the very being of the man who sells it. The commodity sold is a human creature, whose welfare in the eyes of the law should be of more importance than any mere accumulation of wealth on the part of the community." For the very same reason, Samuel Gompers bestowed the label "Labor's Magna Carta" upon Section 14 of the Clayton Act, which specifically denied that labor was a commodity.

Seen in this light, the trade union movement stands out as a truly conservative force. Almost instinctively, the workers joined labor unions in order to preserve their humanity and social character against the excessively individualistic doctrines of industrial capitalism. Eventually the workers' organizations succeeded in halting the drive to the atomized society which capitalism demanded, and in doing so, far from destroying the system, compelled it to be humane as well as productive.

The essential conservatism of the labor movement is to be seen in particular as well as in general. The organizations of American labor which developed in the course of industrialization were conspicuous for their acceptance of the private property, profit-oriented society. They evinced little of the radical, anticapitalist ideology and rhetoric so common among European trade unions. Part of the reason for this was the simple fact that all Americans—including workers—were incipient capitalists waiting for "the break." But at bottom it would seem that the conservatism of American labor in this sense is the result of the same forces which inhibited the growth of socialism and other radical anticapitalist ideologies. . . .

"The overshadowing problem of the American labor movement," an eminent labor historian has written, "has always been the problem of staying organized. No other labor movement has ever had to contend with the fragility so characteristic of American labor organizations." So true has this been that even today the United States ranks below Italy and Austria in percentage of workers organized (about 30 per cent as compared, for instance, with Sweden's 90 per cent). In such an atmosphere, the history of organized labor in America has been both painful and conservative. Of the two major national organizations of workers which developed in the latter half of the nineteenth century, only the cautious, restrictive, pragmatic American Federation of Labor lived into the twentieth century. The other, the Knights of Labor, once the more powerful and promising, as well as the more deviant in policies, succumbed to Selig Perlman's disease of fragility.

Founded in 1869, the Noble Order of the Knights of Labor recorded its greatest successes in the 1880's, when its membership rolls carried 700,000 names. As the A.F. of L. was later to define the term for Americans, the Knights did not seem to constitute a legitimate trade union at all. Anyone who worked, except liquor dealers, bankers, lawyers, and physicians, could join, and some thousands of women workers and Negroes were members in good standing of this brotherhood of toilers. But the crucial deviation of the Knights from the more orthodox approach to labor organization was its belief in worker-owned producers' co-operatives, which were intended to make each worker his own employer. In this way, the order felt, the degrading dependence of the worker upon the employer would be eliminated. "There is no good reason," Terence V. Powderly, Grand Master Workman of the order, told his followers, "why labor cannot, through co-operation, own and operate mines, factories and railroads."

In this respect the order repudiated the direction in which the America of its time was moving. It expressed the small-shopkeeper mentality which dominated the thinking of many American workers, despite the obvious trend in the economy toward the big and the impersonal. As the General Assembly of 1884 put it, "our Order contemplates a radical change, while Traders' Unions . . . accept the industrial system as it is, and endeavor to adapt themselves to it. The attitude of our Order to the existing industrial system is necessarily one of war." Though the order called this attitude "radical," a more accurate term, in view of the times, would have been "conservative" or "reactionary."

In practice, however, the Knights presented no more of a threat to capitalism than any other trade union. Indeed, their avowed opposition to the strike meant that labor's most potent weapon was only reluctantly drawn from the scabbard. The Constitution of 1884 said, "Strikes at best afford only temporary relief"; members should learn to depend on education, co-operation, and political action to attain "the abolition of the wage system."

Though the order officially joined in political activity and Grand Master Workman Powderly was at one time mayor of Scranton, its forays into politics accomplished little. The experience was not lost on shrewd Samuel Gompers, whose American Federation of Labor studiously eschewed any alignments with political parties, practicing instead the more neutral course of "rewarding friends and punishing enemies."

In a farewell letter in 1893, Powderly realistically diagnosed the ills of his moribund order, but offered no cure: "Teacher of important and much-needed reforms, she has been obliged to practice differently from her teachings. Advocating arbitration and conciliation as first steps in labor disputes she has been forced to take upon her shoulders the responsibilities of the aggressor first and, when hope of arbitrating and conciliation failed, to beg of the opposing side to do what we should have applied for in the first instance. Advising against strikes we have been in the midst of them. While not a political party we have been forced into the attitude of taking political action."

For all its fumblings, ineptitude, and excessive idealism, the Knights did organize more workers on a national scale than had ever been done before. At once premature and reactionary, it nonetheless planted the seeds of industrial unionism which, while temporarily overshadowed by the successful craft organization of the A.F. of L., ultimately bore fruit in the C.I.O. Moreover, its idealism, symbolized in its admission of Negroes and women, and more in tune with the mid-twentieth century than the late nineteenth, signified its commitment to the ideals of the democratic tradition. For these reasons the Knights were a transitional type of unionism, somewhere between the utopianism of the 1830's and the pragmatism of the A.F. of L. It seemed to take time for labor institutions to fit the American temper.

In the course of his long leadership of the American Federation of Labor, Samuel Gompers welcomed many opportunities to define the purposes of his beloved organization. But probably none tried his soul so much as that day in 1914 when Morris Hillquit of the Socialist party questioned him before the United States Commission on Industrial Relations. In the course of the colloquy, the sharp contrast between the highly philosophical and theoretical aims of the Socialists and the stubbornly unphilosophical, practical spirit of the Federation's eminent leader was spread upon the record for all to see.

After sparring for a while, Hillquit asked "whether the American Federation of Labor and its authorized spokesman have a general social philosophy or work blindly from day to day?" Obviously nettled, Gompers refused to answer on the ground that the question was an insult. Finally, when Hillquit withdrew the words "blindly from day to day," the trade union leader launched into a recital of the A.F. of L.'s aims, carefully avoiding any theoretical formulations. It sought, he said, to "accomplish the best results in improving the conditions of the working people, men and women and children, today and tomorrow and tomorrow—and tomorrow's tomorrow; and each day making it a better day than the one that had gone before."

Pressed by Hillquit for some measure of what "better" meant, Gompers irascibly replied that anyone knew, without benefit of philosophy, that a wage of $3 a day was better than one of $2.50 and an eight-hour day superior to one of twelve. To Hillquit's leading suggestion that $4 and seven hours were even better, the union chief readily agreed, saying, "the best possible conditions obtainable for the workers is the aim." But Hillquit's effort to expose the philosophical poverty of the union's aims and Gompers' stubborn defense of cautious, practical unionism can best be appreciated the way it happened:

Mr. Hillquit: Yes, and when these conditions are obtained—

Mr. Gompers: (interrupting) Why, then we want better.

Mr. Hillquit: (continuing) You will strive for better?

Mr. Gompers: Yes.

Mr. Hillquit: Now my question is, Will this effort on the part of organized labor ever stop until it has the full reward for its labor?

Mr. Gompers: It won't stop at all.

Hillquit, working hard to convince Gompers that labor and socialism had common aims, pushed his questioning still further. The old cigarmaker, however, knew what he was doing.

Mr. Hillquit: Then, the object of the labor union is to obtain complete social justice for themselves and for their wives and for their children?

Mr. Gompers: It is the effort to obtain a better life every day.

Mr. Hillquit: Every day and always—

Mr. Gompers: Every day. That does not limit it.

Mr. Hillquit: Until such time—

Mr. Gompers: Not until any time.

Mr. Hillquit: In other words—

Mr. Gompers: (interrupting) In other words we go further than you. (Laughter and applause in the audience.) You have an end; we have not.

In the final words of Gompers, "You have an end; we have not" are summed up the great gulf which separated successful trade unionism in America from socialism. Dedicated as Gompers obviously was to organized labor and more specifically to the A.F. of L., he did not permit utopian idealism to influence his clear-eyed view of the American scene. The almost mystical identification with all workers which both the Knights and the Socialists exhibited had no analogue in the American Federation of Labor, which confined itself to the welfare of craft workers and the preservation of that group's position as the elite of the working class. Any other course, the Federation felt, would bring disintegration to the labor movement. This was business unionism, neither idealistic brotherhood nor belief in the unity of the proletariat.

"The trade unions are the business organizations of the wage-earners," Gompers explained in 1906, "to attend to the business of the wage-earners." Later he expressed it more tersely: "The trade union is not a Sunday school. It is an organization of wage-earners, dealing with economic, social, political and moral questions." As Gompers' crossing of swords with Hillquit demonstrated, there was no need or place for theories. "I saw," the labor leader wrote years later, in looking back on his early life in the labor movement, "the danger of entangling alliances with intellectuals who did not understand that to experiment with the labor movement was to experiment with human life. . . . I saw that the betterment of workingmen must come primarily through workingmen."

In an age of big business, Samuel Gompers made trade unionism a business, and his reward was the survival of his Federation. In a country with a heterogeneous population of unskilled immigrants, reviled and feared Negroes, and native workers, he cautiously confined his fragile organization to the more skilled workers and the more acceptable elements in the population. The result was a narrow but lasting structure.

Though never ceasing to ask for "more," the A.F. of L. presented no threat to capitalism. "Labor Unions are *for* the workingman, but against no one," John Mitchell of the United Mine Workers pointed out. "They are not hostile to employers, not inimical to the interests of the general public. . . . There is no necessary hostility between labor and capital," he concluded. Remorselessly pressed by Morris Hillquit as Gompers was, he still refused to admit that the labor movement was, as Hillquit put it, "conducted against the interests of the employing people." Rather, Gompers insisted, "It is conducted for the interests of the employing people." And the rapid expansion of the American economy bore witness to the fact that the Federation was a friend and not an enemy of industrial capitalism. Its very adaptability to the American scene—its conservative ideology, if it was an ideology at all—as Selig Perlman has observed, contained the key to its success. "The unionism of the American Federation of Labor 'fitted' . . . because it recognized the virtually inalterable conservatism of the American community as regards private property and private initiative in economic life."

This narrow conception of the proper character of trade unionism—job consciousness, craft unionism, lack of interest in organizing the unskilled, the eschewing of political activity—which Gompers and his Federation worked out for the American worker continued to dominate organized labor until the earthquake of the depression cracked the mold and the Committee for Industrial Organization issued forth.

"By any simple interpretation of the Marxist formula," commented Socialist Norman Thomas in 1950, "the United States, by all odds the greatest industrial nation and that in which capitalism is most advanced, should have had long ere this a very strong socialist movement if not a socialist revolution. Actually," he correctly observed, "in no advanced western nation is organized socialism so weak." Nor was this the first time Socialists had wondered about this. Over fifty years ago, in the high noon of European socialism, Marxist theoretician Werner Sombart impatiently put a similar question: *"Warum gibt es in den Vereinigten Staaten keinen Sozialismus?"*

The failure of the American working class to become seriously interested in socialism in this period or later is one of the prominent signs of the political and economic conservatism of American labor and, by extension, of the American people as a whole. This failure is especially noteworthy when one recalls that in industrialized countries the world over—Japan, Italy, Germany, Belgium, to mention only a few—a Socialist movement has been a "normal" concomitant of industrialization. Even newly opened countries like Australia and New Zealand have Labour parties. Rather than ask, as Americans are wont to do, why these countries have nurtured such frank repudiators of traditional capitalism, it is the American deviation from the general pattern which demands explanation.

In large part, the explanation lies in the relative weakness of class consciousness among Americans. Historically, socialism is the gospel of the *class-conscious* working class, of the workingmen who feel themselves bound to their status for life and their children after them. It is not accidental, therefore, that the major successes of modern socialism are in Europe, where class lines have been clearly and tightly drawn since time immemorial, and where the possibility of upward social movement has been severely restricted in practice if not in law. Americans may from time to time have exhibited class consciousness and even class hatred, but such attitudes have not persisted, nor have they been typical. As Matthew Arnold observed in 1888, "it is indubitable that rich men are regarded" in America "with less envy and hatred than rich men in Europe." A labor leader like Terence Powderly was convinced that America was without classes. "No matter how much we may say about classes and class distinction, there are no classes in the United States. . . . I have always refused to admit that we have classes in our country just as I have refused to admit that the labor of a man's hand or brain is a commodity." And there was a long line of commentators on American society, running back at least to Crèvecoeur, to illustrate the prevalence of Powderly's belief.

The weakness of American class consciousness is doubtless to be attributed, at least in part, to the fluidity of the social structure. Matthew Arnold, for example, accounted for the relative absence of class hatred on such grounds, as did such very different foreign observers as Werner Sombart and Lord Bryce. The British union officials of the Mosely Commission, it will be recalled, were convinced of the superior opportunities for success enjoyed by American workers.

Men who are hoping to move upward on the social scale, and for whom there is some chance that they can do so, do not identify themselves with their present class. "In worn-out, king-ridden Europe, men stay where they are born," immigrant Charles O'Connor, who became an ornament of the New York bar, contended in 1869. "But in America a man is accounted a failure, and certainly ought to be, who has not risen above his father's station in life." So long as Horatio Alger means anything to Americans, Karl Marx will be just another German philosopher.

The political history of the United States also contributed to the failure of socialism. In Europe, because the franchise came slowly and late to the worker, he often found himself first an industrial worker and only later a voter. It was perfectly natural, in such a context, for him to vote according to his economic interests and to join a political party avowedly dedicated to those class interests. The situation was quite different in America, however, for political democracy came to America prior to the Industrial Revolution. By 1865, all adult males could vote and, for the most part, they had already chosen their political affiliations without reference to their economic class; they were Republicans or Democrats first and workers only second—a separation between politics and economics which has become traditional in America. "In the main," wrote Lord Bryce about the United States of the 1880's, "political questions proper have held the first place in the voter's mind and questions affecting his class second." Thus, when it came to voting, workers registered their convictions as citizens, not as workingmen. (In our own day, there have been several notable failures of labor leaders to swing the labor vote, such as John L. Lewis' attempt in 1940 and the C.I.O.'s in 1950 against Senator Taft.) To most workers, the Socialist party appeared as merely a third party in a country where such parties are last resorts.

Nor did socialism in America gain much support from the great influx of immigration. It is true that many Germans came to this country as convinced Socialists and thus swelled the party's numbers, but they also served to pin the stigma of "alien" upon the movement. Even more important was the fact that the very heterogeneity of the labor force, as a result of immigration, often made animosities between ethnic groups more important to the worker than class antagonism. It must have seemed to many workers that socialism, with its central concern for class and its denial of ethnic antagonism, was not dealing with the realities of economic life.

In the final reckoning, however, the failure of socialism in America is to be attributed to the success of capitalism. The expanding economy provided opportunities for all, no matter how meager they might appear or actually be at times. Though the rich certainly seemed to get richer at a prodigious rate, the poor, at least, did not get poorer—and often got richer. Studies of real wages between 1865 and 1900 bear this out. Though prices rose, wages generally rose faster, so that there was a net gain in average income for workers during the last decades of the century. The increase in real wages in the first fifteen years of the twentieth century was negligible—but, significantly, there was no decline. The high wages and relatively good standard of living of the American worker were patent as far as the twenty-three British labor leaders of the Mosely Commission were concerned. The American is a "better educated, better housed, better clothed and more energetic man than his British brother," concluded the sponsor, Alfred Mosely, a businessman himself.

But America challenged socialism on other grounds than mere material things. Some years ago an obscure socialist, Leon Samson, undertook to account for the failure of socialism to win the allegiance of the American working class; his psychological explanation merits attention because it illuminates the influence exercised by the American Dream. Americanism, Samson observes, is not so much a tradition as it is a doctrine; it is "what socialism is to a socialist." Americanism to the American is a body of ideas like "democracy, liberty, opportunity, to all of which the American adheres rationalistically much as a socialist adheres to his socialism—because it does him good, because it gives him work, because, so he thinks, it guarantees him happiness. America has thus served as a substitute for socialism."

Socialism has been unable to make headway with Americans, Samson goes on, because "every concept in socialism has its substitutive counter-concept in Americanism." As Marxism holds out the prospect of a class-less society, so does Americanism. The opportunities for talent and the better material life which socialism promised for the future were already available in America and constituted the image in which America was beheld throughout the world. The freedom and equality which the oppressed proletariat of Europe craved were a reality in America—or at least sufficiently so to blunt the cutting edge of the Socialist appeal. Even the sense of mission, of being in step with the processes of history, which unquestionably was one of the appeals of socialism, was also a part of the American Dream. Have not all Americans cherished their country as a model for the world? Was not this the "last, best hope of earth?" Was not God on the side of America, as history, according to Marx, was on the side of socialism and the proletariat?

Over a century ago, Alexis de Tocqueville predicted a mighty struggle for the minds of men between the two giants of Russia and the United States. In the ideologies of socialism and the American Dream, his forecast has been unexpectedly fulfilled.

Industrialization was a new and potent force in American life; even when only emergent, it was reshaping the face of America. The factory, in league with the city, would eventually transform the America of Jefferson and Jackson. But these were not the only forces at work in the years after 1865—the wave after wave of immigrants which washed over America also left their impress on the American.

Maldwyn Allen Jones

New Sources

of Immigration,

1860–1914

The selection that follows, written
by Maldwyn Allen Jones, a Briton
who knows Americans and the
documents of American history, is
part of a larger synthesis on American immigration whose theme is
the interaction of the immigrant
inheritance with the American environment. There are several distinctive features that should be
noted in this particular essay. Unlike many who have written on the
subject, Jones does not restrict himself to the American scene. He views
American immigration in its world perspective and gives the reader an
analysis of the newcomer as both emigrant and immigrant. In particular, he explains how and why conditions in Europe brought about a
change in the character of American immigration in the 1880s. He also
shows precisely why southeastern Europeans chose to emigrate at this
time and why they chose the United States. Jones's objective treatment
of the myths and misunderstandings that have distorted the nature,
motivation, and attitudes of the new immigrants merits special attention.
He not only challenges the traditional interpretations concerning this immigration, but also exposes the statistical and historical flaws on which
those interpretations have been based. Such corrective analysis can be seen,
for example, in his assessment of the role of the "transportation revolution" in making immigration easier. He also explains the basic forces behind the new immigration, and compares them with the essential forces
underlying the earlier immigration. [Reprinted from American Immigration by Maldwyn Allen Jones by permission of The University of Chicago
Press. Copyright 1960 by The University of Chicago Press, Chicago,
Illinois.]

A single assumption ran through the forty-one-volume report of the Dillingham Commission set up by Congress in 1907 to investigate the question of immigration. This was that the early 1880's had seen a fundamental change in the character of American immigration. Up to that
time immigration had come almost exclusively from the countries of
northern and western Europe and, according to the Commission, had
been very largely a movement of families seeking a permanent home in
the New World. Those who had constituted this "old" immigration had,
it was claimed, "entered practically every line of activity in nearly every
part of the country," a considerable number having taken up farming.
And despite the fact that a large proportion had been non-English-speak-
ing, they had "mingled freely with . . . native Americans" and had
therefore been quickly assimilated.

Far different, however, was the Commission's view of the movement which had begun about 1883 from the countries of southern and eastern Europe. This "new" immigration had consisted, it declared, largely of unskilled male laborers, a large proportion of whom had come to the United States not as permanent settlers but simply as transients. Almost entirely avoiding agriculture, they had flocked to the industrial centers of the East and Middle West, where they had "congregated together in sections apart from native Americans and the older immigrants to such an extent that assimilation [had] been slow."

For half a century these sharply drawn distinctions have been almost universally accepted. The concept of an "old" and a "new" immigration, differing from each other in many essentials, has exerted a decisive influence upon American immigration policy and has served as a framework for a great deal of historical writing about nineteenth-century immigration. Historians have in fact often been more emphatic than the Immigration Commission in distinguishing the "new" immigration from the "old." The two movements, it has been claimed, differed from each other just as much in their motivation as in their composition. Whereas the immigration from northern and western Europe is accepted to have been largely spontaneous and self-directed, that from southern and eastern Europe is alleged to have been involuntary and artificially induced. The rise of the "new" immigration, we have been led to believe, was due mainly to steamship and railroad advertising and to the efforts of American employers to import cheap labor.

That there was a significant shift in the geographical origins of American immigration toward the end of the nineteenth century is beyond dispute. Of the three great waves which made up the century-long mass migration, the first two—covering the years 1815–60 and 1860–90, respectively—came from the same general areas in Europe. Both the five million immigrants who composed the pre–Civil War wave and the ten million who arrived in the succeeding thirty years were predominantly from the British Isles, Germany, Scandinavia, Switzerland, and Holland. But the last and greatest of the three waves, which brought to the United States a total of fifteen million immigrants between 1890 and 1914 was drawn very largely from Austria-Hungary, Italy, Russia, Greece, Rumania, and Turkey.

The extent of the change can be measured by comparing the immigration of 1882 with that of 1907, the years in which the two post–Civil War waves reached their respective crests. Of the 788,000 immigrants who arrived in 1882, 87 per cent came from the countries of northern and western Europe and 13 per cent from the countries of southern and eastern Europe. But in 1907, when 1,285,000 immigrants reached the United States, the proportions were 19.3 and 80.7 per cent, respectively. The "old" immigration had thus declined absolutely as well as relatively. Yet the shift came both later and with less suddenness than we are sometimes told. Not until 1896 did the volume of the "new" immigration exceed that of the "old," and the disparity between the two groups became really marked only after the turn of the century.

Despite the fact that the period saw a marked change in the sources of the movement, the interpretation favored by the Dillingham Commission and by many historians is open to serious objection. The coming of the southern and eastern Europeans did not reflect a change in the pattern of immigrant recruitment; steamship lines, railroad companies, and American industry were no more responsible for the "new" immigration than they had been for the "old." Moreover, as we have already shown, urban concentration and clannishness were by no means unknown among pre–Civil War immigrants. The fundamental weakness of the traditional interpretation, however, is that it is based upon a completely artificial distinction. In no real sense could either the immigration from northern and western Europe or that from southern and eastern Europe be regarded as a collective entity possessing common attributes; on the contrary, each of the two groups of immigrants was composed of a great variety of contrasting types who deserve to be treated as such. Any other approach is not only unobjective but misleading.

This much is glaringly evident from an examination of the data upon which the Dillingham Commission based its distinctions. The Commission attempted to show statistically that the "new" immigration differed from the "old" in having a higher percentage of males and of unskilled laborers, in being more illiterate, and in having a greater tendency to impermanence. But the Commission's own data did not bear out these conclusions. Had specific groups of immigrants been considered individually, instead of being lumped together in two arbitrarily chosen categories, a very different picture would have emerged. It was undeniable that Italian and Slavic immigrants, for instance, were predominantly male, unskilled, illiterate, and transient. But there were larger percentages of males among German, Scandinavian, and English immigrants than there were among Jewish, Bohemian, and Portuguese; Bohemians, Moravians, and Finns had lower percentages of illiteracy than had the Irish and Germans; Englishmen, Germans, and Scandinavians showed a greater tendency to return to Europe than did Armenians, Dalmatians, Jews, and Portuguese; Jews had a higher percentage of skilled laborers than any group except the Scots, and the Irish had a smaller percentage than the Italians.

The Commission also neglected to take into account the duration of settlement of each of the immigrant groups. Had it done so, it could not have failed to notice a marked correlation between the percentage of males and the recency of immigration. There was a much higher proportion of males among the Greeks, whose immigration had begun on a large scale only about 1900, than among the Italians, who had been coming for a decade longer; the Italians in turn had a much higher proportion than the Bohemians, whose immigration had begun in the 1860's. In this respect, therefore, what the Commission's statistics tended to show was that post–Civil War immigration adhered closely to the pattern established by Irish immigrants at the very beginning of the nineteenth century. That is to say, the initial phase of immigration from any given area was generally composed largely of unaccompanied males; but as soon as the first comers had established themselves, they were usually joined by their wives and families.

Still another defect in the Commission's reasoning resulted from the narrow chronological limits of its inquiries. The Commission drew attention to the fact that in the period 1899–1909 the percentage of skilled laborers among immigrants from northern and western Europe was twice as great as among those from southern and eastern Europe. But this was a misleading comparison to make for the simple reason that, in the period named, the proportion of unskilled laborers from northern and western Europe was as low as it was only because of the extent of the competition from south and east Europeans. A more proper comparison would have been between the "new" immigration in the period 1899–1909 and the "old" immigration in the period 1871–82—that is, before the "new" immigration had begun. This would have shown that the "old" immigration had only a slightly higher proportion of skilled laborers than had the "new"—22.9 per cent as against 18.1 per cent.

The belief that the "new" immigration was artificially induced in some distinctive way rested in large part upon a mistaken view of the promotional activities of steamship companies in southern and eastern Europe. The Dillingham Commission reported that, although steamship company propaganda circulated in every European country, "the attempted promotion of emigration by steamship ticket agents" was carried on chiefly in Austria-Hungary, Greece, and Russia. In those countries a vast army of agents and sub-agents was said to be feverishly at work to induce the peasants to leave; in Galicia alone, it was reported, two of the leading steamship companies employed no fewer than five thousand agents in "a great hunt for emigrants." By means of "highly colored posters," circulars, and other advertising matter attempts were being made to impress the peasants with the belief that employment at high wages could promptly be secured on landing in the United States. Some lines, indeed, had even established their own labor bureaus in American cities to assist immigrants in finding work. Such activities, the Commission believed, proved that the steamship lines were largely responsible for "this unnatural immigration."

But it was not the case that the steamship lines adopted novel methods to drum up custom in southern and eastern Europe; they simply used the same advertising techniques there that had proved successful elsewhere. Steamship labor bureaus, for example, were first advertised not in Austria-Hungary or Italy during the eighties, but in Scandinavia during the sixties. In any case job inducements were nowhere a regular feature of steamship advertising, except perhaps in the earliest stages of immigration from any given area. Individual sub-agents may well have continued to hold out the bait of high American wages—just as they had done from the beginning of mass emigration; but the steamship companies themselves soon found it both impossible and unnecessary to encourage emigration. Impossible, because the practice was strictly forbidden by nearly every European government; unnecessary, because emigrants offered themselves in sufficient numbers without solicitation. The highly colored posters in nearly every case simply gave particulars of sailings. As for the thousands of agents whom the Dillingham Commission pictured as working surreptitiously to flood the United States with an "unnatural immigration," these were for the most part inoffensive storekeepers who sold steamship tickets on commission as a profitable and not very demanding sideline. Similar agencies existed also in northern and western Europe; they had done so ever since the immigrant trade had first become organized in the 1830's. Thus to ascribe the "new" immigration simply to steamship advertising was, as a shrewd contemporary remarked, a mere "rhetorical commonplace," which appealed to observers in inverse ratio to their knowledge of the subject.

Nevertheless, the transition from sail to steam in the transatlantic immigrant trade was an event of enormous significance for the history of immigration. It meant, first, that the Atlantic crossing lost virtually all of its hazards and that the perils of the journey were much less of a deterrent than before. More than this, the opening-up of new steamship routes made immigration possible for the peoples of the entire European continent. By the beginning of the twentieth century, passage to the United States was as easy to obtain from Odessa as from Queenstown, from Palermo as from Bergen. Finally, by introducing the possibility of seasonal migration across the Atlantic, the steamship altered the whole character of the movement to the United States. . . .

A drastic reduction in the length of passage was the outstanding benefit brought about by this transportation revolution. Whereas the crossing had taken between one and three months in sailing vessels, it now took a mere ten days. Unlike the sailing packets the new steamers were built primarily as passenger-carriers, and therefore had better steerage accommodations. To be sure, there was still room for improvement. The steerage remained dark and poorly ventilated, access to the deck was restricted, and overcrowding was still a problem, especially in rush seasons. Moreover, epidemics did not completely disappear. An outbreak of cholera caused hundreds of deaths among German immigrants traveling from Rotterdam on National Line steamers in 1866; and a similar outbreak in 1892 among Russian Jewish immigrants traveling on Hamburg-Amerika liners forced the United States to apply quarantine measures which brought all immigration to a halt for a time. But these were isolated occurrences which in any case were not attributable to conditions on board the ships. As early as 1873 a congressional investigation of the immigrant trade could find no serious abuses; the general opinion of the investigators was rather that "the cruelty, ill-usage, and general discomfort of the steerage belong to the history of the past." . . .

The steamship not only bridged the Atlantic from areas which until then had contributed little to the westward flow; it led to a tremendous expansion of the prepaid passage system. By 1890 hardly a town of any size in the United States was without its steamship agencies where passages for relatives and friends could be purchased; the Hamburg-Amerika Line alone had 3,200 American agencies, the Red Star Line 1,800, the Anchor Line more than 1,500. In that year, according to the testimony of passenger agents before a congressional Committee on Immigration and Naturalization, between one-quarter and one-third of all immigrants were arriving on prepaid tickets. In 1901 the United States Industrial Commission found that between 40 and 65 per cent of all immigrants now came either on prepaid tickets or on fares paid for with money sent to them by relatives in the United States. The proportion, incidentally, was the same among "new" immigrants like the Italians as among "older" groups like the Irish and Swedes.

It is also important to recognize that it was the steamship, and not the shift in the sources of immigration, that was responsible for the beginning of temporary European immigration to the United States. No sooner had the Atlantic crossing become regular, fast, and tolerably comfortable than a substantial transient movement set in. British and German skilled workers began in the seventies to shuttle back and forth across the Atlantic in response to wage movements in America and the homeland. Great numbers began to go out to the United States each spring with the fixed intention of returning in the fall. This was the practice of house decorators and quarrymen whose trades shut down in the American winter, and also of miners, potters, and textile workers whose purpose in migrating was simply to obtain temporary employment at high wages. Thus the transatlantic steerage traffic became for the first time a two-way movement. There were even times during the long American depression of the seventies when the eastbound movement exceeded that in the opposite direction.

Though the steamship companies did little directly to stimulate immigration, there were a number of agencies which did. The most active were those established by individual American states and by the land-grant railroads. The northwestern states had a double reason for trying to attract immigrants; they were anxious to dispose of their unsold lands, and they recognized that increased population was essential to material growth. Though some states—Michigan and Wisconsin, for instance—attempted even before the Civil War to turn the immigrant stream in their direction, it was not until later that their example was at all widely followed. After 1865, however, practically every northwestern state and territory from Wisconsin to Oregon embarked upon a policy of encouraging immigration. State immigration bureaus advertised extensively in the press of the eastern states and of Europe, published and distributed many thousands of pamphlets and maps, and dispatched immigration agents to numerous places in Europe and America. Just how effective these efforts were is impossible to judge, but Wisconsin, Minnesota, and Iowa particularly seem to have owed a significant part of their foreign-born population to the vigor of their advertising campaigns. . . .

Less sporadic and more systematic than those of the states were the colonizing activities of the land-grant railroads. For them, it was vital that the empty lands contiguous to their tracks should be settled as soon as possible. Accordingly, many of them spent large sums of money in efforts to attract immigrants, both from Europe and from longer-settled regions in the United States. First in the field was the Illinois Central, whose promotional campaign was initiated as early as 1855. But the heyday of railroad colonization did not come until the seventies and eighties, when the Northern Pacific, Burlington and Missouri, Santa Fe, Southern Pacific, and many other roads operated land and immigration departments. Apart from being conducted upon a more lavish scale, railroad advertising in Europe and the eastern states closely resembled that of the state immigration bureaus. But the railroads were able to offer immigrants greater inducements than could the states. Free "land-exploring" tickets, reduced steamship and railroad fares, liberal sales policies, and long-term financing plans were only some of the baits the railroads held out to prospective land-purchasers. Many of the roads built immigrant houses on the plains where buyers could stay free of charge while they selected suitable tracts; some, like the Great Northern, offered to educate settlers in plains agriculture, and a few roads even went so far as to build churches and schools for the communities they planted. Altogether the colonization activities of the railroads were marked by a benevolence which contrasted strangely with some of their other contemporary practices.

Railroad colonization, characterized as it was by a tendency to establish compact, homogeneous settlements, did more than a little to determine the ethnic pattern of the trans-Mississippi West. The Burlington planted numerous German, British, and Scandinavian colonies in Nebraska and Iowa; the Northern Pacific fathered an even greater number in Minnesota, Dakota, and the Pacific Northwest; and the Santa Fe was responsible for bringing to Kansas some thousands of Russo-German Mennonites. Each of these colonies, moreover, acted in succeeding decades as a lodestone for immigrants of similar background.

Yet it is all too easy both to exaggerate and to misinterpret the role of railroad and state immigration promotion. Both types of agency directed their European advertising almost exclusively toward the British Isles, Germany, and Scandinavia; the "new" immigration owed virtually nothing to their efforts. And even their attempts to attract immigrants from northern and western Europe were less a matter of stimulating the movement than of directing it. Neither state bureaus nor railroad land departments undertook grass-roots campaigns to induce Europeans to leave;

instead they stationed agents at strategic points along immigrant routes with the object simply of tapping a movement already under way.

Still less concerned with the process of immigration was American industry which, together with the steamship lines, occupied a prominent place in nativist demonology. Not only nativists but the mass of contemporary opinion assumed that between 1864, when Congress legalized contract labor, and 1885, when the Foran Act forbade it, American industry imported on contract vast numbers of unskilled laborers from southern and eastern Europe for the purpose of lowering wages and breaking strikes. This, too, has been the view of most historians. But recent research has disclosed an entirely different situation. It has been shown that, although mine operators and railroad contractors were glad enough to employ those immigrants who found their own way to America, they did not import masses of unskilled labor on contract. Contract labor was in fact extremely rare in America in the post–Civil War era, largely because manufacturers found it too unreliable. . . .

Somewhat akin to contract labor was the *padrone* system, a method of immigrant recruitment which first developed in connection with the movement from southern Italy. During the eighties some *padroni,* or labor bosses, collected children from the hillsides of Italy and carried them to America, practically in the condition of slaves, to be employed as wandering musicians and street acrobats. This practice was soon prohibited by law, however, and by 1880 had virtually ceased to exist. Yet the *padrone* system, even from the first, was concerned less with child labor than with that of adults. Either on his own initiative, or in association with an Italian immigrant "bank"—an institution which combined banking with the sale of passage tickets and also acted as an employment agency—a *padrone* would go to Italy to recruit unskilled labor on contract at a fixed wage, usually paying the fares of those he engaged. On arrival in the United States the recruits were supplied in gangs to American employers at rates which gave the *padrone* a substantial profit. In this form the *padrone* system flourished only during the early stages of Italian immigration. After about 1890 the movement from Italy reached such proportions that it was no longer necessary for contractors to go abroad to import labor. By this time, the *padrone* had become, for Italian immigrants at least, simply a special kind of employment agent. Newly arrived Italians, ignorant of American conditions, were glad enough to place themselves in the hands of a *padrone* who, though he often exploited them, could be relied upon not only to find them work but to supply them with food and lodging. As Italians became better acquainted with American conditions, however, and learned how they were being exploited by the *padrone,* they tended to dispense with his services.

The *padrone* system was also a feature of Greek and Syrian immigration. Among the Syrians it flourished chiefly in merchandising, the practice being for Syrian merchants to control a number of immigrant peddlers. These they lodged and boarded, and sent out daily to peddle notions and dry goods in the larger cities. There seems to be no evidence that Syrian *padroni* were responsible for the immigration of those they employed; and in any case the system soon declined because Syrian immigrants preferred factory or railroad work to peddling. Among the Greeks, on the other hand, *padroni* often financed the immigration of youths whom they employed as fruit and candy peddlers or, more often, as shoeblacks. That by 1910 practically every American city had its Greek-operated shoeshine parlors was due to the steady importation of youths during the previous fifteen years from the Greek province of Arcadia.

Though all these agencies, from steamship lines to *padroni*, did much to stimulate immigration in the post–Civil War era, the essential forces underlying the movement were to be found elsewhere. These forces were precisely those which had brought to the United States the first great wave of mass immigration in the decades immediately after 1815. Among them were political and religious discontent, as well as increasing knowledge of American opportunity. But the successive extension of the frontiers of European emigration in the period between 1860 and 1914 was due basically to the widening impact of economic change. In northern and western Europe, as we saw earlier, the collapse of the old agrarian order and the rise of the factory system had transformed social and economic life and, in conjunction with the pressure of mounting population, had provided the impetus for emigration. Now, in the later decades of the nineteenth century, the same thing happened in other parts of Europe.

Although between 1860 and 1890 the bulk of the immigrants to the United States came as before from the British Isles, Germany, and Scandinavia, from none of these regions was the geographical source of the movement quite the same as in pre–Civil War days. The Irish exodus, though still considerable, was very much smaller than during the famine and, in the movement from the British Isles, Englishmen, Welshmen, and Scots replaced Irishmen as the most numerous element. In Scandinavian emigration, Swedes came to the forefront at the expense of Norwegians, and in that from Germany, Bavarians and Württembergers gave way to Prussians and Saxons. In each of the three main areas of emigration, therefore, the center of gravity of the movement moved appreciably to the eastward.

Mainly responsible for the change was the competition of cheap foreign grain. England, Sweden, and Germany east of the Elbe were all grain-producing regions which were hard hit in the sixties and seventies by the sweep of technical progress. Thanks to the railroad and the cargo steamer the cost of transporting grain fell dramatically, with the result that the wheat farmers of the United States, Russia, India, and other distant countries could for the first time compete successfully in the European market. Upon European farming the effect was immediate and catastrophic. Germany, now linked by rail to the Russian black earth zone, the Polish and Hungarian plains, and the Rumanian wheatlands, changed within a single decade—1865-75—from a grain-exporting to a grain-importing country. In England a searing agricultural depression in the seventies, originating in the competition of American wheat, spelled the doom of the old agrarian economy; between the sixties and the eighties the price of wheat and the acreage of land under wheat both fell by almost 50 per cent. In Sweden, which turned to free trade in 1865, the agrarian crisis was heightened by disastrous crop failures between 1861 and 1869 which produced famine conditions in many areas.

In each of the areas affected tens of thousands of farmers and agricultural laborers were driven to emigrate. To be sure, the agricultural crisis does not wholly explain the exodus. In Sweden the decline of the timber industry caused by the transition from wooden to iron ships, and the depression of the iron and steel industry as a result of American tariff policy, both helped to swell the number of departures. Special factors were at work in Germany, too, such as the widespread hostility to military service after 1866 when the formation of the North German Confederation brought into being a centralized military system under Prussian control. Industrial depression, particularly in the early eighties, had a marked effect upon the character of German immigration, which at all times included a substantial proportion of artisans. From the Ruhr came thousands of coal-miners and iron and steel workers; from the textile districts of Saxony, Bavaria, and Silesia a steady stream of weavers and spinners; and from Westphalia and Rhenish Prussia great numbers of glassworkers, cutlers, and leatherworkers. From Britain, a sizable part of the outflow bore a similar character. In the late sixties began a large-scale movement of Lancashire textile workers, followed shortly afterward by one of Yorkshire woolen operatives and a smaller but no less significant exodus of Macclesfield silkworkers, who felt the pinch after Cobden's treaty of 1860 had admitted French silks to Britain free of duty. Yet the most numerous group of British industrial emigrants were probably coal-miners from Durham, Scotland, and Wales, and iron puddlers and rollers from the Black Country.

Even so it was the European agricultural crisis which was mainly responsible for the postwar wave of emigration from Germany, the British Isles, and Scandinavia. That the wave should reach its crest in the early eighties was a consequence less of industrial depression than of a steadily worsening agricultural situation. German farming had been under a blight for almost a decade, Swedish commodity prices were the lowest for half a century, the English farmer was reeling under a succession of disastrous harvests, and Ireland had just been revisited by famine. In 1882, therefore, with the American economy booming, the volume of immigration rose to an unprecedented 788,000. German arrivals amounted to 250,000, an all-time record, British and Irish immigrants to 179,000, and those from Sweden, Norway, and Denmark to 105,000.

After 1890 immigration from all these countries showed a sharp decline. During the succeeding quarter of a century the annual arrivals from the British Isles only rarely exceeded 100,000 and in many years came to less than half that figure. Scandinavian immigration showed an even greater drop, and that from Germany became almost negligible. After 1894 the annual movement from Germany never exceeded 40,000, and by 1912 had fallen below 20,000.

One reason for the decline was that the countries of northwestern Europe now had fewer men to spare. The fall in the birthrate, which began in the last decades of the nineteenth century and which became precipitate after 1900, brought to an end a period of more than a century of rapid population increase in that area. In Germany and Scandinavia, moreover, rapid industrialization created new employment for those displaced from the land. So tremendous was the absorptive capacity of German industry that after 1890 German agriculture experienced a labor shortage which was met only by the large-scale importation of foreign labor for harvesting and other seasonal work. Then, too, the international rivalries of the late nineteenth century brought a new awareness of the military and economic value of manpower, a change which was reflected in official attitudes to emigration. Germany now made strenuous efforts to keep her people at home; some of Bismarck's social legislation as well as the laws to broaden land-ownership were inspired partly by this aim. Sweden pursued a similar course, with the government giving its blessing to a society for the prevention of emigration which sought to achieve its object by promoting land reform. Britain, by contrast, did nothing to check departures but attempted to divert her emigrants away from the United States and toward her own dominions and colonies. How successful she was is shown by the fact that between 1901 and 1912 the proportion of British and Irish emigrants choosing the United States declined from 61 per cent to 25 per cent—Canada, Australasia, and South Africa now claimed the great majority. Finally, there were now fewer opportunities in the United States for north and west Europeans. After 1890 the empty lands of the American West were no longer there to beckon the would-be farmer. Equally important, the unskilled labor market was now being pre-empted by south and east Europeans.

Even if other circumstances had been favorable, emigration from southern and eastern Europe could hardly have begun before it did because of official hostility. For the first two-thirds of the nineteenth century most countries in this region strictly forbade their subjects to emigrate, the prohibitory laws being especially severe in the states of southern Italy and in those areas of the Balkans under Turkish rule. The growth of more liberal attitudes was closely related to major European political changes. In Italy it was the success of the unification movement in 1859–60 which brought about the removal of existing restraints. In Austria-Hungary freedom of emigration was officially conceded in 1867 in the course of the political reorganization marked by the *Ausgleich;* this concession, however, did not prevent the Austrian and Hungarian governments from attempting to impede emigration for more than a decade longer. For large parts of the Balkans the right to emigrate came after the Russo-Turkish War of 1877, when large Slavic areas—Serbia, Bulgaria, Montenegro, Bosnia, and Herzegovina—were emancipated from Turkish rule. Although by the beginning of the twentieth century there was a general tendency to deplore emigration as a drain upon national resources and military strength, all European countries, except perhaps Russia and Turkey, had come to recognize the right of their peoples to emigrate freely. Even the Russian and Turkish prohibitory laws were largely dead letters.

With the disappearance of official restraint and the simultaneous development of new transportation facilities, emigration to the New World was free to develop to the extent determined by local conditions. As economic change spread southward and eastward in the last decades of the nineteenth century, it was thus able to have the same expulsive effect that we have already noted in other regions. First to be affected was the sprawling, ramshackle empire of the Hapsburgs with its ethnic hodgepodge of Germans, Magyars, Rumanians, and half a dozen varieties of Slavs. Though conditions in Austria-Hungary varied from province to province the basic situation producing emigration was everywhere the same, namely, one of dislocation resulting from the breakup of the age-old peasant economy. The abolition of feudal dues in 1848 transformed the peasant into a free proprietor, thus ending the medieval conditions which had hitherto persisted. But it was not until the sixties that the emancipated peasant was given the right to divide his land. Once that happened subdivision took place at an extremely rapid rate so that the land became split up into tiny holdings quite incapable of supporting those who lived on them. Then, as had happened elsewhere, the peasant emigrated to avoid an inevitable fall to the status of a propertyless day laborer.

In its earliest stages, during the sixties and seventies, the bulk of Austro-Hungarian emigration consisted of Bohemians and Moravians, or Czechs as they later became known. But as the movement from Austria-Hungary increased, rising from 17,000 in 1880 to 114,000 in 1900 and reaching a peak of 338,000 in 1907, it became increasingly heterogeneous. By the eighties the stream included considerable numbers of Poles, Jews, and Ruthenians from Galicia, and Slovaks and Magyars from Hungary; a decade later these groups were being accompanied by Rumanians from Bukovina and Croats, Serbs, Slovenes, and Dalmatians from the southern provinces of Carniola, Carinthia, and Styria. In each of these areas local economic difficulties helped swell the outgoing throng. In Bohemia the McKinley Tariff of 1890 destroyed the local pearl-button industry, causing its transplantation to the United States; in parts of Carniola and Croatia, the destruction of the vineyards by phylloxera proved to be the last straw for the struggling peasants; in Dalmatia, emigration was stimulated by the Italian-Austrian treaty of 1890, which admitted Italian wines free of duty, thus crippling local vineyards. But these were minor influences. The outflow was in essence one of displaced peasants and agricultural laborers, whose departure could be attributed to more widespread and permanent economic influences.

Similar forces were at work in Italy, particularly in the South, which groaned under a vicious land system reminiscent in many respects of that prevailing in Ireland in pre-famine days. Southern Italy was predominantly a region of large estates owned by absentee landlords who made little effort to return profits to the soil or to make capital improvements; short leases and high rents encouraged tenants to exploit the land and precluded the introduction of modern agricultural methods. Nor were matters any better on small estates cultivated by their owners, for here excessive subdivision—*frazionamento* the Italians called it—produced its usual results. Throughout the region obsolete and unscientific methods of cultivation kept productivity low, and the wholesale deforestation which followed upon the abolition of feudalism and the secularization of church lands added still further to the difficulties of cultivation. Considering also that southern Italy had only recently emerged from centuries of Spanish and Bourbon neglect and misrule, and that in the latter half of the nineteenth century population was increasing by leaps and bounds, it was hardly surprising that the region as a whole presented a picture of chronic poverty unparalleled in Europe.

In the late eighties the precariously balanced rural economy of southern Italy sustained a double shock. Owing to a rapid increase in subtropical fruit production in Florida and California, American imports of Italian lemons and oranges fell precipitately, ruining thousands of growers in Calabria, Basilicata, and Sicily. Simultaneously, France built a prohibitive tariff wall against the Italian wines, thus depriving Apulian, Calabrian, and Sicilian winegrowers of their chief export market. These events ushered in a period of unprecedented hardship and set in motion the first large-scale Italian emigration to the United States. A substantial exodus from northern Italy to South America was already in progress, and the movement from southern Italy would probably have taken the same direction but for the fact that South American conditions in the late eighties were temporarily uninviting. A yellow fever outbreak in Brazil had carried off 9,000 Italian victims and had led the Italian government temporarily to ban emigration to that country; in Argentina, political disturbance, financial crisis, and a war with Paraguay brought economic life almost to a halt. Hence the south Italian current set toward the United States and, having once chosen its course, rapidly gathered momentum. Italian arrivals in the United States rose from 12,000 in 1880 to 52,000 a decade later; by 1900 the figure had passed 100,000 and after averaging over 200,000 in the succeeding decade reached a peak of almost 300,000 in 1914. From about the turn of the century, when emigration to Brazil declined as a result of a crisis in coffee-growing, the north Italians too tended to choose the United States. But their numbers were never more than a fraction of those from southern Italy.

Emigration from Russia differed from the Slavic and Italian movements in that its origin was not primarily economic but political and religious. The first sizable group to leave Russia for the United States consisted of Russo-German Mennonites from the Volga and Black Sea areas. These people had settled in Russia at the end of the eighteenth century in response to the invitation of Catherine the Great, who had granted them immunity from military service, freedom of worship, and a substantial degree of autonomy. But with the withdrawal of these privileges in 1870 as a result of rising Russian nationalism, the Mennonites determined to seek homes elsewhere. Thanks to the attraction of railroad lands, several thousand of them settled in Kansas, Nebraska, the Dakotas, and other western states during the seventies and eighties, and here they were subsequently joined by even larger numbers of non-Mennonite Russo-Germans.

This exodus was completely overshadowed, however, by that of Russian Jews for whom the rise of Pan-Slav nationalism betokened a renewal of persecution. The assassination of Tsar Alexander II in 1881 set off a wave of anti-Jewish riots and led to strict enforcement of the requirement that all Jews must reside within the Pale of Settlement, an area bordering on Germany, Austria, and Rumania. A year later came the notorious May Laws, which placed restrictions upon Jewish worship, virtually debarred Jews from agriculture, industry, and the professions, excluded them from public office, and denied them educational opportunities. Persecution now became systematic, persistent, and ruthless; worst of all there were the frightful pogroms of 1881–82, 1891, and 1905–6 in which countless Jews were massacred. Largely in consequence, Russian arrivals in the United States rose from 5,000 in 1880 to 81,000 in 1892 and then bounded upward to a peak of 258,000 in 1907.

After 1900, however, the Russian outflow was more varied. Between 1899 and 1910, Poles accounted for fully a quarter of the total immigration from Russia, and Lithuanians, Finns, and Russo-Germans together made up a similar proportion. But Jews were still easily the largest single group, comprising 43.8 per cent of the total. Immigration from Russia to the United States was thus composed almost entirely of what was known as the "alien element" in the Russian population. During the period named less than 5 per cent of the westward exodus could be classified as Russian. This was not because Russians proper were averse to movement; vast numbers of them moved eastward both before and after 1900 in order to colonize the empty wastelands of Siberia.

While Austria-Hungary, Italy, and Russia were by far the most important sources of the "new" immigration, substantial numbers came from other areas. The collapse of the French market for Greek currants in the early nineties, resulting from France's adoption of a protective policy, gave the initial impetus to emigration from Greece, more particularly from the currant-producing regions around Tripolis and Sparta. From Portugal, a backward, densely peopled, agricultural country, emigration took place chiefly to Brazil, on account of the linguistic, historical, and religious ties between the two countries. But a steady trickle of Portuguese emigrants found their way to the United States. They came not only from Portugal itself but from the Azores—whence emigration first developed out of the circumstance that American whalers had long called there to recruit sailors—and from the Cape Verde Islands. In Rumania and Bulgaria the transition from a peasant economy to large-scale modern agriculture gave emigration its usual stimulus, and in Finland the same result was brought about by a declining demand for agricultural labor, coupled with Russia's repressive policy from 1899 onward. It was oppression, too, in the form of the "Armenian massacres" of 1894–96, which set emigration in motion from Armenia, a Christian island in the Mohammedan world of the Ottoman Empire. Turkish misrule also brought about the wholesale expatriation of another Christian minority, the Syrians, about a million of whom emigrated between 1870 and 1900. Most of them went to Egypt, South America, and India, but in the 1890's, thanks mainly to the influence of American Protestant missionaries who told of the opportunities America offered, discontented Syrians began to go to the United States.

Not all of those who immigrated to the United States in this period came from across the Atlantic. A very large though indeterminate number came overland from Canada, both from the Maritime Provinces and Quebec, whence the movement had been in progress continuously since before the Civil War, and to an increasing extent from Ontario, where the limit of desirable agricultural settlement was reached in the seventies and where the competition of western wheat brought about a major shift in land use. For a generation after the Civil War, emigration to the United States took place on such a scale as to threaten the Dominion with depopulation; only at the very end of the century, when the frontier of settlement reached the prairie provinces of Manitoba and Saskatchewan did the human tide at last begin to flow in the opposite direction.

Finally, there was a relatively small but highly significant influx from across the Pacific. The first Oriental arrivals were the Chinese, of whom 300,000 came to the Pacific coast of the United States between 1850 and the passage of the Chinese Exclusion Act in 1882. Though contemporaries generally referred to Chinese immigrants as coolies, implying that they had been imported in a servile state, those who came to the United States were voluntary immigrants who had paid their own fares from Hong Kong to San Francisco. Large-scale Chinese immigration, like that of the Irish, originated in economic catastrophe; the great Taiping rebellion, beginning in 1848, paralyzed trade and industry in southeastern China and brought famine and ruin to millions. News of the high wages paid to laborers in gold-rush California was thus all that was needed to start an exodus from the hard-hit province of Kwangtung. Having once begun, Chinese emigration from this region to California went on un-interruptedly until the law of 1882 brought it virtually to an end.

Three years later a second Oriental movement got under way when the Japanese emperor removed a long-standing ban on the emigration of his subjects. For the first time Japan had men to spare, as a result of a population increase without parallel in the Western world. In the eighties and nineties most Japanese emigrants went to Hawaii as contract laborers to work on American sugar plantations. But after Hawaii had been annexed in 1898, the Japanese were free to move to the continental United States, which they did at the rate of about 10,000 a year. The Gentlemen's Agreement of 1907–8, whereby Japan undertook not to issue passports to unskilled laborers wishing to enter the United States, checked without halting the influx. Since the agreement permitted Japa-nese residents in the United States to send for their wives, thousands of Japanese women continued to come, many of them as "picture brides" who had been married by proxy in Japan to men they had never seen.

It is thus apparent that the widening of the frontiers of emigration, which was perhaps the outstanding feature of migration history in the latter half of the nineteenth century, implied no fundamental change in the pattern of the movement to the United States. With the exception only of the east European Jews, the Armenians, and the Syrians, who were driven from their homes by persecution, post–Civil War immigrants were everywhere uprooted by a common set of economic influences and had much the same objects in coming to America that men had had for centuries. The belief that the motives of the "new" immigrants were more sordid and mercenary than those of their predecessors runs quite contrary to the facts. And if immigrants tended in the late nineteenth century to revisit their homelands more frequently than before, this was largely because such a practice had hitherto been impossible.

Though immigrant motives were pretty much alike, the immigrants themselves were not. In refuting the traditional view that nineteenth-century immigrants to the United States can be divided into two mutu-ally exclusive categories, one should not lose sight of the fact that the bulk of the southern and eastern Europeans were culturally very different both from native Americans and from immigrants born in northern and western Europe. The fact and the extent of cultural difference shaped much of the new immigrant's experience in the United States. One must not forget, though, that while the type of immigrant was changing, so was America herself. And from the point of view of immigrant adjustment, perhaps the latter circumstance was the more important.

Oscar Handlin

Immigration in

American Life:

A Reappraisal

*Oscar Handlin is one of the most articulate and perceptive of contemporary historians of immigration. He has written widely on the subject, and one of his books—*The Uprooted *(1951), a moving account of immigrant adjustment in industrial America—won the Pulitzer Prize. In the following essay, Handlin looks at how historians have treated American immigration as a subject of investigation, and he offers a theme for reassessing and reformulating the study of immigration in broad terms that will add to our understanding of American social history and the world of the 1960s. Earlier studies, he points out, have focused on the immigrant as a foreign element thrust into American life. But it is also possible, he suggests, to view the process of immigration from within American society, as an event experienced by native-born Americans as well as by foreigners. For instance, he maintains that a study of the collapse of traditional communities as a result of internal migration, such as the movement of poor whites and Negroes from the agrarian South to the industrial North, can give us deeper understanding of American social history. Note also Handlin's explanations of why immigrants and other Americans faced problems in adjusting to the demands of industrial America, particularly to the impersonal factory system and the anonymity of urban life. Finally, note how he explains the immigrants' positive contributions to American life and how he relates the tragedy and triumph of the immigrant saga to the whole of American history. [From* Immigration and American History: Essays in Honor of Theodore C. Blegen, *edited by Henry Steele Commager. University of Minnesota Press, Minneapolis. Copyright 1961 by the University of Minnesota.]*

In July 1921, the *American Journal of Sociology* published a forceful article by Arthur Meier Schlesinger entitled "The Significance of Immigration in American History." The paper was widely read and, no doubt, contributed to the revival of interest in what had theretofore been a relatively neglected field.

The aim of the essay was to set the record straight. It devoted itself to two major themes. In the first place, it pointed to the mixed antecedents of the American population in rebuttal of the argument that the culture of the nation derived from a single overseas source. In the second place it outlined the contributions of immigrants since the colonial period to the material, political, artistic, and idealistic life of the United States.

To the modern reader these points are so familiar as to seem almost commonplace. But they were far from being so in 1921. Four years earlier, under the pressure of wartime emotions, the Congress over President Wilson's veto had enacted a literacy test, the first genuine restriction on immigration in American history. And in 1921, a new law went even farther. It not only set a maximum limit on the number of immigrants who could enter the United States but also established the principle of national quotas as a means of differentiating among the various types of people who sought entry.

These measures were the culmination of a lengthy, bitter struggle in which a sustained intellectual attack against immigrants was mounted. This attack questioned the utility of immigration to the United States and challenged the capacity of the natives of a large part of Europe to be assimilated into American life.

The Schlesinger essay should thus be seen in terms of the issues of its time. The record had to be set straight in order to eliminate the distortion the restrictionists had introduced into it, and the means of doing so was to prove that immigrants really belonged in the United States by showing the extent of their contributions.

Professor Schlesinger was himself the son of immigrants and was, no doubt, moved to take the position he did by emotional attachments as well as by the intellectual problem itself. In the four decades since then a substantial group of scholarly contributions has added immensely to our knowledge and has helped further to set the record straight. Many of these contributions too were made by immigrants or the sons of immigrants. The names of Marcus L. Hansen, Theodore C. Blegen, and Carl Wittke come immediately to mind. But, however aware these authors were of their own European roots, their products were far removed from the filiopietistic writings of the earlier part of the century. Adhering to rigid codes of scholarship and using scientific methods, these historians did much to create a healthier climate of opinion and to develop an understanding of the place of immigration in American history. Although a great deal still remains to be done, particularly when it comes to the history of such newer immigrant groups as the Poles, the Italians, the Armenians, and the Greeks, the research of the past forty years in this field has made a substantial contribution to American historiography in general.

Those who aspire to treat the subject of immigration in the 1960's, however, must take up the task of that earlier generation in a quite different environment. Both as historian and as citizen the student of today faces new kinds of questions. As a scholar he has been challenged by recent comparative studies and by the development of the social sciences. As a citizen he finds that immigration to the United States is no longer a factor of contemporary importance. But his world is still seriously troubled by the divisive forces of racial and ethnic prejudice and in the East it faces an unprecedented challenge to the American way of life. It is his obligation to apply what knowledge he can assemble to the issues of his own society.

A reappraisal of the role of immigration in American life, therefore, calls not for a restatement or elaboration of the earlier point of view. It demands rather a reassessment and reformulation of the problem in terms that will add meaning to the world of the 1960's and that will draw upon the accumulated knowledge in all the social sciences of the past forty years.

The focus of earlier studies was upon the immigrant as a foreign element injected into American life. They were designed to discover whether the addition of these outsiders to the existing population had beneficial or deleterious effects. Although almost all these works came to a positive conclusion, they approached the immigrant as a newcoming and extraneous addition to indigenous society. Hence in a good many of these works—although not in the best—a concern with the degree to which one group or another was unique, or different from the rest, in its adaptability to American conditions. Hence also that pathetic eagerness to take credit for contributions which produced such futile arguments as those over the nationality of Columbus or the ethnic identity of the Scotch-Irish. Such issues too have lost whatever relevance they ever had.

It is however, also possible to view the process of immigration from within American society. Such a reversal of perspective does not draw so sharp a line between the immigrants and other Americans. It starts rather with the assumption that the entire population of the United States almost from the start was a composite, made up of elements from a multitude of sources. Among these heterogeneous multitudes those who had actually been born in other countries represented only the extreme of a condition that was general to the whole society. The differences between them and the native-born of various sorts, while real, were differences of degree rather than of kind.

Such an approach makes the experience of immigration far more meaningful. By taking the immigrant as a type of American, it also contributes to an understanding of the development of civilization in the United States and sets overseas immigration in a more comprehensive context.

For a long time in American history the movement of peoples across the Atlantic was only one of several types of migration. It was not by coincidence that Frederick Jackson Turner who did so much to call attention to the westward movement also emphasized the importance of immigration. He surmised, although not clearly, that the arrival of millions of newcomers from across the national boundaries was only one aspect of a more general process which also comprehended radical internal shifts of population. Since the international movement was more readily visible than the internal one, the experience of the Irishmen or Italians of the nineteenth century may throw light on the lives of the New Englanders who moved to New York State or Iowa. It may also supply clues to the problems of the "Oakies" who went to California in the 1930's or the southern hillbillies who went to Detroit in the 1940's or the Puerto Ricans and Negroes who arrived in New York in the 1950's.

More generally, insights derived from the extreme experiences of the immigrants have significant implications also for men who themselves never made a move. For in America even those who stubbornly stayed in the place of their birth often found themselves made aliens by changes in the world about them. Many a Brahmin, grown old on Beacon Hill, looked across the Common in the 1890's and found himself almost as much a stranger to his city as the newcomers who had transformed it. His reactions and theirs were linked; only theirs were more visible.

Among the themes upon which the process of migration throws light is one that has been particularly important in the shaping of modern society. The immigrants experienced in an extreme form what other modern men have felt—the consequences of the breakdown of traditional communal life. This decisive development, about which little is yet known, has significantly influenced American character. One need not feel any sense of nostalgia for the old community to recognize its importance and also the importance of its passing. Whatever judgment one may make upon them, these phenomena are worthy of study. What follows will briefly illustrate the ways in which that breakdown, most clearly to be perceived among the immigrants, influenced significant sectors of American life.

The traditional community embraced a complex of comprehensive, integrated, cohesive, and self-contained institutions. In it people worked out habitual patterns of action and thought. The community was traditional both in the sense that its forms reached back to times out of the minds of living men and also in the sense that it resisted innovations.

The immigrants had destroyed that community in the coming to America. The shock of having done so and the adjustments necessary to compensate were their fundamental social experiences. Persistently but unsuccessfully the immigrants strove to restore their communities. But the disruption was irreparable, with profound effects for American culture in general.

Virtually all immigrants made valiant efforts to reconstruct the old communities on the soil of the New World. True, the setting was different; but group after group expressed the longing to perpetuate the forms and to preserve the values which seemed to extend from far back in the past. Even the handfuls of conscious and deliberate rebels who accompanied the larger streams of peasants and artisans were guided by visions formed in the Old World. Only a few men, like Carl Schurz, were sensitive enough to the unfamiliar environment to adjust their sights to the new horizons. The great mass of newcomers could not allow the coming to America to extinguish their heritage. Fear of the possible guilt of having let that happen created a persistent tension among those who strove to preserve the inherited virtues.

The impulse to re-establish the old community was as characteristic of the earliest as of the latest immigrants. In the very first generation of Puritan settlement in New England, the cry was already heard concerning the necessity of preserving the manners and habits of the past. The same appeal was to be pathetically reiterated by the offspring of the Puritans as they advanced into the west. On every frontier, beginning with that on the Connecticut River, and extending in the eighteenth and nineteenth centuries through upper New York State and across Ohio, Indiana, Illinois, on into Iowa, the migrants from New England wistfully urged themselves to preserve that which they were leaving behind. In the architecture and the social order of towns that dot the path of that migration there appear the repeated patterns of the section that was left behind.

George Bates, at the Forefathers' Celebration in San Francisco, thus explained the "New England triumphs on the Pacific." Mentioning the extent of Yankee enterprise in the city, he nevertheless directed his audience to "look upward to the many . . . houses whose pointed spires, rising heavenward, show that they are dedicated to God. The bell summons us to enter, and we do so; and there, with suppressed breath, we listen to New England sermons, we join in New England psalms; we look around upon New England wives, New England husbands, New England children." And, the orator added, when "we leave the house of God . . . we enter the school houses of the city. . . . These are New England school houses, New England scholars, New England teachers." Indeed even in the twentieth century the young man who left New England for the great city could find a church supper in New York's Washington Heights identical with that he had known at home.

Historians have rarely perceived the tenacious grip on the inherited culture of the old community. In the 1840's and 1850's, for instance, the clusters of New England settlements across the country formed links in a chain that held together the reform movements of the period. One of the significant aspects of reform in those decades was precisely the effort to preserve the values of the Puritan community under the changing conditions of American society. These agitations often reveal an anxiety about the future and an intention to guard, even if in new forms, the ideals of the past—concerns that also emerge later in the prohibition crusade and account for the intensity with which that issue was debated in the 1920's and 1930's.

So too the negativism and intolerance of the immigration restriction movement and of nativism in general become more comprehensible when viewed in the light of the motives of Americans anxious to prevent their world from changing. Narrow nationalism of this sort was the refuge of men frustrated in the effort to restore the old community. It had numerous counterparts among other American groups; Fenianism and Zionism and a host of similar quests for a homeland embodied the same need for a community to which to belong.

All that of course was futile. No group could restore the old community or preserve the traditional values against the corrosive forces that transformed these people. Indeed the very process of resistance furthered change.

Yet the struggle was not altogether without results, although not always those anticipated. The most constructive were those in which groups of men turned from the dream of a great all-encompassing community to fill some immediate need in their own lives.

The immigrants in the United States could not restore the community destroyed by migration. But they devised a multitude of organizations to replace it. Mutual assistance, fraternal, religious, and cultural associations supplied them in a fragmentary way with the services the community had performed at home. These organizations have been both more durable and of wider import than is commonly supposed. They have been durable in the sense that they continued to serve a function long after the disappearance of the original immigrating group. They have carried over from the second generation in most groups to play an important role in the lives of the third generation and beyond. Furthermore, such associations have not been confined to peoples conventionally recognized as immigrants through visible differences of language and customs. Analogous organizations developed among the British and also emerged from internal migrations. What was more, the prevalence of this pattern of social action imposed it even on groups not set off by national or sectional differences. It became linked to religious organization and contributed to the ethnic character of American sectarianism.

Such efforts at organization met particular needs but they did not reconstruct the coherent, comprehensive community of the past. The consequences are reflected to this day in the dominant features of American group life. A society compelled to tolerate a multitude of significant ethnic differences had to develop in a pluralistic fashion, recognizing the right of each group to operate in its own way and yet to suffer in consequence no discrimination or deprivation of the rights of citizenship. Then, too, such a society had to give a wide scope of activity to voluntary as distinguished from governmental organizations. The logical corollary of pluralism in a free society was the abstention by government from interference in spheres in which the points of view of the people it served were not uniform or homogeneous. From the eighteenth century to the present, a continuing adjustment has set the limits within which the state could act and outside of which action could come only through voluntary and fragmented means.

That process had a profound effect upon American institutions, although historians have not yet worked out the details. Bernard Bailyn's study of education in the colonial period reveals clearly and incisively the consequences in one sphere of the disruption of the community caused by migration. Other investigations would show results of comparable significance in philanthropy, in religion, and in the variety of media through which American culture found expression. Much of their history can be written in terms of the collapse of traditional communities, an experience most vividly illustrated in the experience of the immigrants.

A closer view of two primary areas of social activity will reveal some of the ways in which changes in communal life were influential and also the ways in which the development of immigration can illuminate those changes.

The disintegrating influences that grew steadily more important in the eighteenth and nineteenth centuries quickly altered the situation of the family in the community. Observers were quick to notice the disruptive impact of movement upon the families of immigrants, from the Puritans to the Puerto Ricans. What was not so readily evident was that the disorder in such groups was but an acute form of difficulties all Americans encountered.

All the characteristics of strain in the immigrant family had native counterparts. The new conditions that created a difference between the generations and that deprived parents of their educational function, the instability of authority in the absence of communal sanctions, and the constant readjustment in the roles of husband, wife, father, mother, and children have subtly reshaped the family as an institution in the United States. It is not surprising that the subject should have supplied themes for such writers as Mark Twain and Sherwood Anderson. What is surprising is its neglect at the hands of historians.

Some of the tensions that accompanied this transformation have been explored, but rarely with any awareness of the importance of the changing nature of the family. The historians of the women's rights movement, for instance, have generally been content to deal with the demand for equality as if it were simply a product of abstract intellectual propositions. Yet beneath the surface claim to specific legal privileges was a deep emotional unrest generated by the altered position of the woman in the family and by her consequent uncertain status in society.

Other related subjects have not been touched at all. No student of modern society can minimize the importance of changes in the rates of divorce or juvenile delinquency, in family size or attitudes toward birth control and sexuality. Yet general historians have neglected these matters not because the material for an understanding of them is lacking, but because of the difficulty of fitting them into any larger conception of their relationship to society as a whole.

The historians of immigration have been almost alone in dealing with such problems because they had a framework ready-made for doing so. The disorganization of the old extended family in the course of migration and the developing individualization of its members were readily described as aspects of the move from the Old World to the New. But these phenomena have also been embedded in the general American experience and can be advantageously explored as consequences of the transformation of the traditional community in the United States.

The breakdown of the community also had important effects upon the relationship of the American to his economy. In the case of the immigrant the shift from one country to another involved a change in occupation that was troublesome enough. But even more troublesome was the fact that the dislocation detached all the modes of earning and spending from their familiar communal settings. The native Americans who migrated across the continent encountered similar difficulties. The hardship of moving from one physiographic region to another or from rural areas to the cities was deepened by the weakness of communal institutions which in turn were further weakened by those very moves.

The consequences were important although they have not yet been historically evaluated. Sons in the United States in the nineteenth century did not often follow the occupations of their parents. The break between the callings of one generation and its successor has been readily related to expanding opportunities, to the ideal of success, and to the utilization of talent to its maximum. But there were also heavy costs in the loss of continuity. Altogether apart from the failures, the hardships, the mistakes, and the wrong decisions that may have been as numerous as the correct ones, the break between the occupational experience of each generation and its successor produced an all-pervasive running tension among Americans.

The economic effects of that tension appeared at every level of American society. It was a concomitant, for instance, of the process by which the market farm took the place of the traditional family farm. The cultivator of the soil in the United States produced not to satisfy his own wants but to sell his crops. As a result he was torn between the incompatible impulses to treat his farm as a home and as a business. On the one hand, he clung to his homestead at any cost. On the other, he concentrated upon staple crops, became involved in commercial speculation, and mechanized and rationalized his modes of production. The resultant difficulties echo through the farmers' grievances from the seventeenth century to the present.

That tension also must be recognized in the problems of labor. We are only at the beginning of our understanding of the phenomena involved in industrialization and urbanization. These processes were not merely economic in character, with the sole issues those of dollars and cents. The experience of the immigrants reveals other more important dimensions.

The immigrant who entered the industrial labor force was not simply oppressed by relatively low wages or by long and difficult conditions of work. Nor, in settling in an urban place, was he troubled only by the physical problems of adjustment. Slums, new habits dictated by life under congested circumstances, the change from living conditions of the countryside that sapped his health—these were all matters of grave concern to him. But they were only part of the story.

To the newcomers life in the cities and labor in the factories seemed to derogate from their qualities as human beings. However harsh their existence had been at home—and often it had been more demanding of their energies than in America—they had been sustained by a community within which they had lived a round of life that was comprehensible in its own terms. All the incidents of the year's labor back there had possessed a meaning and had accorded them a satisfaction, conditioned on no external criteria and validated by the harmony with the world that was their own way from birth to death.

The factory destroyed that. It introduced a new impersonal relationship between employer and employee, subjected the laborer to a routine that took no account of his individuality, and treated him as a piece of machinery less valuable than those of iron because more easily replaced.

More important, the activities of the factory were intrinsically meaningless. Often the laborer had only an approximate impression of the end-product he toiled to produce and rarely did he understand the relationship of his own toiling to it. In time he grasped the central fact of industrialism—that the value of work was not a factor of its productiveness but rather of an inexplicable process that led some men to success and others to failure. By the same token the city was frightening in its anonymity. In it men quickly were overwhelmed by the fear of being lost, for it seemed unrelated to any reality they had earlier known.

The fear, the bewilderment, and the loneliness of the industrial order certainly compounded the difficulties created by low incomes and poor living conditions. These emotional factors undoubtedly shaped the forms taken by efforts to organize labor in the half-century after 1880. The violence and irrational bitterness that then became endemic in American industrial life owed much to the awareness that more was at stake than wages or hours of work. From Homestead to Paterson to Lawrence, the men who resorted to strikes against their employers were aggrieved by the denial of their human dignity.

The difficult adjustment to urban industrial life was not limited to the immigrants or to the lowest sectors of the labor force. The process, most visible among Italian millworkers or Jewish tailors, also touched the experiences of natives of Maine or Ohio or Kentucky. After the depression of 1873, the roads of the nation suddenly seemed thronged with homeless men. For the next four decades the tramp became a characteristic American figure. Estimates of the number of these people at any given time, which range as high as two million, are of course unreliable. But that they were a sizable group seems certain. They merged at times with the armies of migratory workers who took seasonal jobs in agriculture, and in the forests and mines. But some of them also were skilled, like the familiar tramp printer, actor, or promoter who moved from town to town. And these latter figures were, in turn, not far removed from the revivalist, the folk doctor, and the traveling salesman who occupied the faded rooms of countless modest hotels or rooming houses.

We catch only reflected glimpses of these transients in the observations of more settled people. But these are enough to inform us that the wanderers were men of native birth and antecedents whose restlessness derived from an unwillingness to accept such fixed places as the economy made available to them. Having more opportunity for choice than the foreign-born, they rejected the degradation of factory work and city life and accepted rootlessness as a permanent status.

The cities of mid-nineteenth-century America also contained an enormous population of clerks, bookkeepers, salesmen, foremen, and petty shopkeepers, most of them native-born and almost all of them newcomers from the rural countryside. Their problems of income and housing were not as difficult as those of the unskilled immigrants. But the young men and women who lived in block after block of boarding houses or in monotonous rows of apartments faced social adjustments fully as strenuous as those of the foreigners. The short stories of O. Henry and many of the naturalistic novels of the turn of the century provide documentary evidence of the strains of this process. Such people did not join unions or go out on strike. But their ambitions, frustrations, and grievances received political and social expression, in forms that would be better understood were their sources more clearly recognized.

Among all such groups one can perceive, as among the immigrants, the disruptive effects of the breakdown of the community. In family life and in the economy, the isolation of the individual, the erosion of traditional functions, and the pressure of new conditions form a situation within which many of the characteristic traits of American society were molded.

The consequences for American culture of the breakdown of traditional communities are more subtle, but none the less significant. In the disorganization that followed upon migration, controls of every sort grew weaker and leaders found it ever more difficult to shape the desires, attitudes, or tastes of their followers. Furthermore pluralism and voluntarism deprived most groups of any external means of coercion over their members. Individuals who did not wish to conform could break away without fear of any sanctions but those of informal disapproval. Only so long as a tightly knit community life was maintained was effective oversight of the cultural life of the people possible; and that was but rarely achieved except by such millennialist sects as the seventeenth-century Puritans, the Pennsylvania Amish, and the Rappites.

The breakdown was particularly rapid among new immigrants and on the frontier where the lines of communication were most attenuated; and the process was already well advanced in the eighteenth century as the observations of William Byrd revealed.

For somewhat less than a century after the Revolution a good deal of energy went into the effort to develop new and distinctly American forms. Not much then came of the grandiloquent appeals for a national literature or national architecture. But the atmosphere nevertheless encouraged a thriving and genuine folk culture, of which the minstrel show and the circus, the penny press and the lyceum were representative. Inchoate and divided among numerous sectional and ethnic variants, that culture nevertheless responded to authentic popular needs. Within it the immigrants readily found a place.

Indeed it was the immigrant who proved most capable of resisting the later efforts to cram American culture into an artificially defined strait jacket. In the half-century after 1870, the development of American society produced forces that sought to impose an official orderly pattern upon the chaos of folk culture, to define what was good music, good art, good literature, and to exclude from the canons of good taste that which did not fit. The stultifying result, referred to at the time as the genteel tradition, was damaging both to the audience for, and the creators of, art.

The immigrants stood apart. Their separateness enabled them to preserve forms of expression, in the theater, in literature, and in the press, that remained close to their lives. Their culture seemed to outsiders vital and authentic at a moment when a heavy formalism descended elsewhere. After the turn of the century the most creative spirits in the United States were attracted by the immigrants whose "warm, pagan blood" flowed rich by contrast with the austerity about them. Stephen Crane, Theodore Dreiser, Sherwood Anderson, and Hutchins Hapgood, among others, discovered in the urban and rural ethnic enclaves a genuineness of emotions and a reality they could not find elsewhere.

That was why many of them made immigrants of themselves, either by expatriation or by settling in the Bohemias which were the lands of an inner migration. It was not by coincidence that Greenwich Village and Beacon Hill were in close proximity to the immigrant quarters, for here were settled those who deliberately chose the alienation that the immigrant, unwittingly and unwillingly, made part of his situation. And no doubt that association influenced some of the most vital developments of American culture in the twentieth century. In the movies of Charlie Chaplin, in the realistic drama, in the naturalistic novel, and in the music of jazz are refracted impulses of the shattered communities and traditions of which the immigrants were representative.

If it seems paradoxical that in the 1920's many of those who were most eager to rediscover America should have sought to do so by emigrating among the foreign-born, that is of a piece with the other paradoxes with which the history of the United States abounds. Perhaps a nation of immigrants was necessarily too much preoccupied with its own quest for identity and tradition to be aware of the fact that its only identity derived from the diversity of its origins and that its only tradition was that of ceaseless change.

Now that we have arrived at the end of the long process of immigration, some of the elements of a reassessment may have fallen into place.

Such a reassessment would reveal the immense achievements of both the immigrants and the nation as a whole. The story of immigration is a tale of wonderful success, the compounded biography of thousands of humble people who through their own efforts brought themselves across great distances to plant their roots and to thrive in alien soil. Its only parallel is the story of the United States which began in the huddled settlements at the edge of the wilderness and pulled itself upward to immense material and spiritual power.

But the magnitude of the achievement has sometimes blinded observers to the elemenets of tragedy that were intermixed with it. The history of the United States has been written almost entirely about the smiling aspects of life: rise, progress, growth were the figures of speech that flowed naturally from the pen of the historian. Yet he did less than justice to the drama of the American experience in neglecting its tragic depths.

Certainly tragedy was an intimate part of the life of all immigrants, from those who came to Jamestown to those who only yesterday fled from Hungary. Even those who earned all the exterior measures of success nonetheless carried forever the marks of the losses they suffered from migration.

But this was not the experience of immigrants alone. Nor indeed only of the depressed and underprivileged peoples like the Negroes or Indians. Millions of Americans, native-born and prosperous, lived lives of quiet desperation, the pain of which they compounded by their own inability to recognize its source. But then only a few of their more perceptive contemporaries, and fewer still of the historians, perceived the character of their plight.

It was always tempting, for example, to describe the advance of the frontier as the march of a triumphal army. The frontiersman was a conquering hero, even if he attacked with no banners flying. But this plausible figure of speech concealed a falsification of reality. It glided too readily over the hardships of new settlement, over the debasement of personality and the deterioration of culture that accompanied this process. It left out of account the deserted villages and the abandoned farmhouses. Most important of all it obscured the fact that every man who turned his back upon his home was, in one sense at least, defeated. These restless people were on the move because old homes and families could no longer contain them. Therein their experience paralleled that of the immigrants.

Indeed, in this perspective such American achievements as the absorption of the immigrants and the settlement of the frontier have the quality of greatness precisely because these were not simply success stories. To recall that these immense accomplishments were rooted in tragic origins, were accompanied by the disruption of traditional communities, and were paid for in heavy human costs is to add the dimension of grandeur to American history.

In the twentieth century, by a steadily increasing majority, Americans have become city dwellers. It was not always so. Even though there have always been cities in the United States, in the eighteenth and nineteenth centuries most Americans lived on farms or in small rural towns. In 1850, for example, less than 13 per cent of the people lived in cities, of which there were only nine whose population exceeded 50,000. Perhaps even more important is the social impact of this rural heritage. Most Americans grew to man-hood within an agrarian tradition that glorified those who tilled the soil and that engendered a distrust of those who worked and lived in the city. In fact, the theme of conflict between city and farm cuts through the history of nine-teenth-century America just as the Mis-sissippi River winds through the heart of the nation.

4

THE CITY AND THE AGRARIAN TRADITION

The clash between the city and the countryside became most pronounced after the Civil War, when the process of urbanization was stepped up. So rapidly did the city expand that American life experienced what was in effect an urban revolution. The decade of the 1880s wit-nessed the greatest urban growth. In these years the older cities of the Northwest and Middle West burst their original limits to become budding metropolitan centers. Census figures tell us that in that decade more than a hundred cities with populations of 8,000 or more doubled their size. Kansas City, Kansas, for instance, increased its population by 1,000 per cent. Minneapolis and other cities experienced similarly spec-tacular growth.

At the same time, America's farms and rural communities were losing people. In the years between 1880 and 1890, about 40 per cent of the nation's townships reported a decline in population. In addition, more than 50 per cent of the rural townships in states such as Illinois and Ohio, which were increasing in population, lost people. In the 1880s, in other words, the city became a controlling factor in American life, and for the first time reached a position where it could challenge the pre-dominance of rural America.

As urbanization spread across the nation, the city became the focal point of the new industrialism that was transforming America. Nowhere, in fact, was the impact of social and economic change more discernible than in the city. Into it flocked the sons and daughters of native-stock farmers in search of wider opportunities than were available in the coun-tryside. There too went the millions of new immigrants looking for the fulfillment of their quest for a better life than they had known. Thus into the city poured labor, capital, and raw materials, and from it spilled a variety of finished products. These manufactured goods from the city displaced the homemade products of the farm. In the 1880s and 1890s, the cities, to a degree unknown in the past, became centers of manufacture, hubs of transportation, holders of liquid wealth, dormitories for labor, and reservoirs of managerial skill.

The vibrating heart of the city was commerce. All other human activity branched out from business, creating ultimately a social and cultural as well as an economic community. This community was not, however, self-sufficient. As rural leaders never hesitated to point out, the city depended on the farm. Among the complex causes for urban growth, a main one, paradoxically, was the vast increase in agricultural output after the Civil War. As more and more food could be produced by fewer and fewer hands, increasing numbers of men were freed from toil on the land to enter the business life of the city.

Technological change also stimulated urban growth in other ways. The steam locomotive, for example, made possible the movement of vast quantities of food into the cities from the farms, and rapid transit made possible movement within the city's densely packed living areas. The metropolis of the late nineteenth century thus resulted from improvements in farming, manufacturing, and transportation, as well as from surplus rural population.

Urban growth, of course, spawned new problems. The very existence of the metropolis deepened social and economic cleavage within the nation. Rural folk resented their loss of influence and power to forces bred by the city. They looked upon the city as the corrupter of those who lived in it, and they also considered it the enslaver of the farmer. In the cities were gathered all the forces—such as banks, railroad financiers, and manufacturers of farm machinery—of the omnipotent capitalism that was revolutionizing agriculture and seemingly preying on it. Upon the cities, therefore, America's rural majority focused its hatred.

Country people feared the strange new interests and activities that urban leisure made possible, and they saw something sinister in the relationship between the immigrant and the city. Those wedded to the agrarian tradition often considered the new immigrant as the typical city dweller. Regardless of how ill-founded rural suspicion was, the growth of the city did profoundly alter small-town and rural patterns of culture. Urban attitudes spread into the life of the state and nation and could be seen transforming the traditions—most of which were rooted in the rural past—of the entire nation.

Rural distrust was also mixed with envy. Farm people envied the increasing population, cultural advantages, wealth, and power of the cities. While denouncing the city for its sinfulness and strangeness, ironically, they were also irresistibly attracted to its gaiety, bright lights, and mystery, as well as to the sheer variety of living that could be found there. Rural communities felt that their mode of life—what their people considered to be the traditional way of American life—was threatened by the forces of the city. Heirs of the agrarian tradition, therefore, prepared themselves to do battle with the hosts of the industrial city.

Although there was a widening gap caused by the farmers' deteriorating economic status and the increasing urban wealth, the city was merely a symbol of agrarian difficulties and not in itself the source. After the Civil War, agriculture, like industry and the city, expanded with revolutionary speed. Between 1865 and 1900, America's farms, stimulated by technological advances and ever widening markets, disgorged prodigious amounts of foodstuffs and raw materials. Within the nation, the railroad lines provided improved marketing facilities for whatever the land yielded. Yet the agricultural output outdistanced even the rapidly growing internal market. By the 1880s, American agriculture had become dependent on export markets. Wheat, for example, was poured into all parts of Europe, where it upset long-established markets.

This commercialization of agriculture, and its dependence on growing urban centers and foreign markets, stripped the American farmer of his old self-sufficiency—a loss he was willing to accept in return for increased profits. The commercialization also deprived him of any semblance of control over his market and the prices he could obtain for his goods. The price of wheat, for example, was now subject to the fluctuations of worldwide supply and demand. This meant that the farmer, even with the aid of state governments that he might control, could not tamper with the price and market system of which he had become a part.

In the last decades of the nineteenth century, commercialized agriculture brought a loss instead of the profits that farmers had anticipated. With the expansion of world agricultural production, of which America's was only one element, came a steady fall in farm prices. Agricultural prices, in fact, fell more rapidly than did prices in general. This prolonged drop, plus the fact that the farmers did not grasp the full significance of the impersonal price and market system, convinced many that they were the innocent victims of an urban conspiracy and economic squeeze. Whether real or imaginary, the farmers' basic complaint was that costs were too high and prices too low. They maintained that the banks and creditors charged arbitrarily high interest rates, the railroads unreasonable freight rates, and merchants steep prices for essential agricultural machinery.

Similarly, the farmers attributed low prices to a currency shortage forced on the people by the selfish policies of Wall Street bankers who controlled the flow of the nation's fluid wealth. Many farmers felt that their status could be improved only by breaking the grip of the financiers on the economy.

Seeking to arrest the deterioration in the farmers' economic position, and motivated in part at least by a hatred of urban capitalism, a number of agrarian protest movements sprang into existence in the 1870s and '80s. The first of these, a secret society called the Patrons of Husbandry, began as an organization devoted to improving the farmers' social life.

The farmers met in local units called Granges, as well as in other associations. Soon they became impatient with social activities and began thinking of ways to meet the challenge of falling prices.

Although the farmers in the Grange movement made some limited gains against the middlemen and the railroads—both of which were held responsible for agrarian ills—economic pressure seemed incapable of improving the farmers' worsening position, particularly when hard times set in about 1881 and farm prices dropped again. As a result, the organized farmers turned to political action as a means of attacking the agents of industrial capitalism on a broad front. They worked through new associations: the Grand State Alliance of Texas, the Agricultural Wheel (which originated in Arkansas), the Farmers' Clubs of South Carolina—all of which emerged as the Southern Alliance—and the National Farmers' Alliance of the Northwest, strongest in the states of the upper Mississippi Valley. These two main groups sought the same reforms, such as inflation and the nationalization of railroads and telegraph lines.

From 1890, the Alliances voiced the demands of the farmers in local and state politics throughout most of the West and South. In St. Louis in 1892, out of a convention of Alliances, was born the Populist Party. In the presidential election of that year, the Populist candidate, James B. Weaver of Iowa, attracted more than a million votes. Substantial gains, at the expense of the two major parties, were made in governorships and in Congress, mainly by the agrarian states south of the Ohio and west of the Mississippi. Out of agrarian unrest had arisen an effective protest party.

Although the real source of agrarian difficulty lay in surplus—the farmer was simply producing more than the world could absorb—the Populists became obsessed with the need for monetary reform. They apparently could not escape their history of hostility toward the absentee and perhaps usurious creditor, a hostility intensified by plummeting prices. They were convinced that the city—the stronghold of their alleged oppressors—was a parasite that sucked its wealth from a victimized countryside, primarily through currency manipulation.

The farmers' revolt reached its high point in the campaign of 1896. With William Jennings Bryan as their standard bearer, the Populists fused with the Democrats to lead the forces of rural America on a crusade for government aid to the distressed farmers; they particularly sought inflation through coinage of silver. The conservative, wealthy Republicans in the eastern and even middle-western cities, on the other hand, built a huge war chest and fought back in defense of property and sound values based on the gold standard.

Despite Bryan's remarkable success in winning 45 per cent of the vote, the defeat of rural America was decisive. The election revealed weaknesses too great to enable the Populists to continue as a third party in American politics. Decisive majorities in the big cities gave evidence of distrust of the Populist program by voting Republican. The workers in the cities, despite the Populist effort to woo them, would have nothing to do with the agrarian movement. Even though the farmers and workers had a common interest in redressing the balance of power against capitalism, they were too far apart in basic sympathy to combine effectively. They were incapable, furthermore, of overcoming the heritage of distrust between farm and city.

Populism, in one sense, represented the last effort to preserve the agrarian tradition in the face of economic reality. After 1896, the farmer adopted the methods of the businessman and tried to improve his position within the price-market system. As entrepreneur and manipulator of pressure groups, the farmer in the twentieth century became far more successful in gaining political and popular support than he had in openly fighting the forces of urban capitalism. But even though he had become a businessman, he still clung to an agrarian tradition whose precepts did not fit an industrialized and urbanized society.

In the selections that follow, interpretation and analysis rather than factual data are central. Each essay advances special points of view on the reasons for the rise of the city, on the relationship between free land and surplus urban labor, and on the realities of the agrarian tradition in an industrial society. Each probes beneath the surface of events to deal with ideas and concepts.

Arthur M. Schlesinger

The City

in American

Civilization

Despite the importance of urban environment and activity in American social history, the city was, until the 1930s a neglected field of study—one that suffered, from a lack of specialized scholarly works. Since that time, however, interest in its unique problems has steadily mounted, and the result has been the development of an increasingly sophisticated scholarly literature on the history of the city and its place in the growth of the nation. No man did more to arouse scholarly activity in urban studies than Arthur M. Schlesinger of Harvard University. In the following essay, Professor Schlesinger suggests, in broad terms rather than in monographic style, what the significance of the city has been in the shaping of America. He points out, for example, that urban life brought with it tensions that were not evident in rural America. Even the nation's basic political institutions were developed under relatively simple rural conditions. To cope with the complex conditions of crowded city life, those institu-

tions had to be modified or reshaped. His conclusion is, in effect, a call for recognition that the city has been a major factor in the development of the nation. [Reprinted with permission of the publisher from Paths to the Present *by Arthur M. Schlesinger. Copyright 1949 by The Macmillan Company.]*

"The true point of view in the history of this nation is not the Atlantic Coast," declared Frederick Jackson Turner in his famous essay of 1893, "it is the Great West." Professor Turner, writing in Wisconsin, had formed his ideas in an atmosphere of profound agrarian unrest, and the announcement of the Superintendent of the Census in 1890 that the frontier line could no longer be traced impelled him to the conclusion that "the first period of American history" had closed. His brilliant paper occasioned a fundamental reappraisal of the mainsprings of national development.

Today, however, it seems clear that in the zeal to correct older notions he overlooked another order of society which, rivaling the frontier even in the earliest days, eventually became the major force. The city marched westward with the outposts of settlement, always injecting exotic elements into pioneer existence, while in the older sections it steadily extended its dominion over politics, economics and all the other interests of life. The time came, in 1925, when Turner himself confessed the need of "an urban reinterpretation of our history." A true understanding of America's past demands this balanced view—an appreciation of the significance of both frontier and city. The broad outlines of the particular role of the city are here suggested.

The Atlantic shore constituted the original frontier. Though the great bulk of colonists took up farming, the immediate object of the first settlers was to found a village or town, partly for mutual protection and partly as a base for peopling the near-by country. Other advantages presently gave these places more lasting reasons for existence. There persons could enjoy friendly intercourse with their neighbors as in Europe and there, too, ply a variety of occupations. These communities, besides taking in farm produce for consumption and export, developed local manufactures, arts and crafts and carried on fisheries and an active overseas trade. Without the articles so provided—hardware, firearms, medicine, books and the like—the colonial standard of living would have greatly suffered.

In time the coastline became beaded with towns, many of them so well situated with respect to geographic and trading advantages as to grow into the great cities of today. The establishment of settlements like Albany, New York, and Lancaster, Pennsylvania, moreover, foreshadowed the rise of urban communities inland. If colonial towns seem small by modern standards, it is well to remember that this was also true of contemporary English provincial towns, for industrialization had not yet concentrated populations in the homeland. Philadelphia with thirty thousand people on the eve of Independence was one of the metropolises of the British Empire.

From the outset townsfolk were plagued with what would today be called urban problems. There were disadvantages as well as advantages in living closely together, and as these disadvantages became flagrant, the citizens were moved to action. Though they seldom assumed community responsibilities willingly, their record compares favorably with that of provincial cities in the mother country. To combat the increase of crime the public-spirited in some places maintained night watches out of their own purses, while in others the city fathers required persons to take turns guarding the streets by night on pain of fines. Sooner or later, however, the taxpayers accepted such policing as a normal municipal charge. The fire hazard early prodded the authorities to regulate the construction of chimneys, license chimney sweeps and oblige householders to keep water buckets; and when these measures fell short of the requirements in the eighteenth century, the people formed volunteer companies which, long after the colonial period, continued to be the chief agency of fire fighting. The removal of garbage generally devolved upon roving swine and goats, while drainage remained pretty much an unsolved problem, though occasional individuals laid private sewers. The pressure of urban needs also fertilized American inventiveness, producing Franklin's lightning rod and the fireplace stove.

Thanks to the special conditions of town life, the inhabitants developed a sense of collective responsibility in their daily concerns that increasingly distinguished them from the individualistic denizens of the farm and frontier. Other circumstances served to widen the distance. As cities grew in size and substance, they engaged in economic rivalry with one another which tended to ignore the interests of the intervening countryside. Boston, New England's metropolis, possessed special mercantile advantages which enabled her for nearly a century to maintain a position of primacy in British America, with New York, Philadelphia and lesser centers hardly more than commercial satellites. These other ports, however, contended as best they could for their share of ocean-borne traffic and briskly cultivated their local trading areas.

New Yorkers, for example, successfully fought the proposal of the East New Jersey authorities to erect a competing port at Perth Amboy, and for a time prevailed upon the provincial legislature to tax and otherwise hinder Boston's commerce with eastern Long Island. The fur trade with the Iroquois brought Manhattan and Albany businessmen immense profits, but watchful of every advantage, the New Yorkers contested with Philadelphia for the trade of the Susquehanna region. Farther to the south, Charleston and Virginia merchants staged a similar struggle for the deerskins of the back country, with the South Carolinians emerging victorious. An unpremeditated result of this fierce competition for pelts was a notable stimulus to westward exploration and settlement.

As the eighteenth century advanced, Boston's rivals came to stand securely on their own feet, aided by their rapidly developing hinterlands. New York now completed its sway over western Connecticut and eastern New Jersey, while Philadelphia merchants annexed western Jersey, Delaware and northern Maryland. So eager was the pursuit of business that the chambers of commerce of New York and Charleston, formed respectively in 1768 and 1774, antedated all others in English-speaking lands. Meanwhile, in the tributary areas, these early indications of urban imperialism bred jealousies and resentments which were to reach critical intensity in later times. The metropolis of a given region became a symbol of deception and greed. "A Connecticut Farmer," venting his spleen against New York in the *New-London Gazette*, August 17, 1770, expressed the fervent hope that "the plumes of that domineering city may yet feather the nests of those whom they have long plucked."

Happily for America's future independence, Britain's new revenue policy after 1763 struck deeply at the roots of urban prosperity. The business classes rallied promptly to the defense of their interests and, heedless of the dangers of playing with fire, secured the backing of the artisan and mechanic groups. Throughout the decade of controversy the seaports set the pace of resistance, supplying most of the militant leaders, conducting turbulent demonstrations at every crisis, and mobilizing farmer support when possible. Even in rural commonwealths like Virginia and Maryland the most effective steps of opposition were taken when the colonists consulted together at the provincial capitals while attending legislative sessions. Boston's foremost position in the proceedings may well have arisen from the fact that, having recently fallen behind Philadelphia and New York in the commercial race, she was resolved at any cost to stay the throttling hand of Parliament. With the assembling of the First Continental Congress the direction of the movement shifted to Philadelphia, the principal city, presently to become first capital of the new Republic.

The colonial town, however, was more than an embodiment of political and economic energies or a means of gratifying the gregarious instinct. Cities, then as now, were places where one found a whole gamut of satisfactions. Ports of entry for European settlers and goods, they were also ports of entry for European thought and standards of taste. At the same time their monopoly of printing presses, newspapers, bookstores and circulating libraries exposed the residents to a constant barrage of mental stimuli. Hence the spirit of innovation expressed itself quite as much in intellectual as in commercial undertakings. It was townsfolk who led in founding schools and colleges. The protracted battle to establish inoculation as a preventive against smallpox was fought out in the cities. The first great victory for freedom of the press was won by a Philadelphia lawyer defending a New York editor. Besides, mere numbers of people made it possible for the professions to become more clearly differentiated, so that a merchant need no longer plead cases before the courts nor a clergyman practice medicine. Before the colonial period ended, bar associations and medical societies were flourishing in New York, Boston and elsewhere, and medical schools were drawing students to Philadelphia and New York.

The man whom a biographer has called the "first civilized American" was the scion of not one but many cities. Boston, Philadelphia, London and Paris, all contributed to Benjamin Franklin's intellectual growth and social understanding. Few elements of American culture but are indebted to his fostering care: printing, publishing, journalism, belles-lettres, education, the postal service, theoretical and applied science. All these achievements rested in final analysis on that interest, encouragement and financial support which a populous community alone could provide. How diligently Franklin utilized these advantages appears in his autobiography, which reveals, for instance, how he set about arousing his fellow Philadelphians to the need of such projects as a lending library, a hospital and the American Philosophical Society.

Yet Franklin with all his many-sidedness was less "civilized" than urban society as a whole: his ambit of interests did not embrace the theater, architecture or an active concern with art. In all these lines the pre-Revolutionary town, with the steady increase of wealth and leisure, showed a growing maturity. Cities, for example, vied with one another for the services of outstanding portraitists. Robert Feke, a Newport artist, painted also in Boston, New York and Philadelphia. John Singleton Copley of Boston found on a visit to New York "so many that are impatient to sit that I am never at a loss to fill up all my time." Like the Philadelphian Benjamin West, however, Copley eventually removed to London.

The city, both in its internal life and external relations, deeply affected colonial society politically, economically and culturally. Though in 1776 only about one in twenty-five Americans dwelt in places of eight thousand or more, the urban influence, thanks to its concentrated character, carried far greater weight than its fractional representation in the population indicated. Moreover, city residents evolved a pattern of life which not only diverged from, but increasingly challenged, that of countryside and frontier. These restless, aspiring urban communities foreshadowed the larger role that cities would play in the years ahead.

That role townsfolk began to assume in the struggle for a strong central government following the Revolution. As a contemporary newspaper observed, "The citizens in the seaport towns . . . live compact; their interests are one; there is a constant connection and intercourse between them; they can, on any occasion, centre their votes where they please." Faced by interstate trade restrictions, stay laws and growing social turmoil, the urban business and creditor classes feared for their future welfare and the sanctity of property rights. The framing and ratification of the Constitution represented in considerable degree their triumph over the debtor groups and small farmers of the interior. In the circumstances the first Congress under the new instrument was greeted with petitions from Philadelphia, New York, Boston and Baltimore for a tariff to protect American manufactures.

The underlying strife between city and country led also to the formation of the first national parties under the Constitution. Hamilton's famous financial plan, intended to benefit urban capitalists and thus indirectly the nation, formed the rallying point of the Federalists, while Jefferson, imbued with physiocratic notions, organized the Republican opposition. The Virginia planter, unlike the New York lawyer, dreaded the growth of a powerful moneyed class, and in the spread of cities he foresaw a repetition of the social miseries typical of the Old World. "For the general operations of manufacture," he declared, "let our work-shops remain in Europe." He could even regard calmly the destructive yellow-fever epidemics in Philadelphia and other ports in the 1790's, since the pestilence might teach people to avoid populous centers.

The contrasting social ideals and economic motives reflected in this early alignment of parties evoked differing views of constitutional interpretation and of particular measures. From that day to this the chief business of American politics has been to reconcile these interests in furtherance of the national welfare. True, the relative purity of the original groupings gradually became diluted. With the multiplication of urban voters through the years, Jefferson's political progeny, confident of the agricultural South, sought also to appeal to city wage earners. By the same token, the opposition party tended to be a coalition of city businessmen and Northern farmers. Hence each party came in time to constitute a battleground of contending urban and rural elements within its own ranks, a situation which continues to characterize American politics.

The westward surge of population beginning shortly after the Revolution has obscured the fact that the leading Atlantic cities, though hard hit by the war, soon resumed their growth, and that with the coming of the nineteenth century the rate of urban development in the nation at large far surpassed that of rural development. Between 1800 and 1860 the number of townsfolk increased twenty-four times while the rural population merely quadrupled. By 1810 one out of every twenty Americans lived in communities of eight thousand or more, by 1840 one out of every twelve, and by 1860 nearly one in every six.

Paradoxically enough, westward migration itself helped to bring this about, for the transappalachian region bred its own urban localities. Serving at first chiefly as distributing centers for commodities from the seaboard, these raw settlements quickly developed into marts where local manufacturer and farm dweller exchanged products. Pittsburgh early began to make glass, shoes, iron castings, nails and textiles, and already in 1814 the *Pittsburgh Gazette* was complaining of the sooty atmosphere.

By that time Cincinnati, farther down the river, boasted of two woolen mills and a cotton factory, and its meat-packing business was winning it the sobriquet of Porkopolis. Emboldened by such achievements, apparently every cluster of log huts dreamed of equal or greater eminence. The Indiana pioneers, for example, hopefully named their forest hamlets Columbia City, Fountain City, Saline City, Oakland City and Union City or, setting their sights still higher, called them New Philadelphia, New Paris, Rome City and even New Pekin.

Meanwhile, in the East, scores of cities sprang into being, generally at the fall line of the rivers, where water power was available for manufacturing. As the budding industrialists looked about for new worlds to conquer, they, together with the Eastern merchants and bankers, perceived their El Dorado in the settling West. Soon New York, Philadelphia and Baltimore were racing for the trade of the transappalachian country. This clash of urban imperialisms appeared most strikingly perhaps in the rivalry for transportation routes to the interior. The Baltimoreans led off by building a turnpike to tap the eastern terminus of the Cumberland Road, which the federal government by 1818 had completed as far as Wheeling on the Ohio. In order to counter this move, Pennsylvania promoted Philadelphia's wagon trade with the West by subsidizing a chain of roads to Pittsburgh. New York City, utilizing her natural advantages, now secured state backing for an all-water artery through upstate New York from the Hudson to Lake Erie.

The instant success of the Erie Canal, opened in 1825, forced a change of strategy on Manhattan's competitors. Philadelphia with legislative help promptly instituted a part-water, part-land route through the mountains, while Baltimore pushed the project of a Chesapeake and Ohio canal. Other citizens in the Maryland metropolis, however, conceived a bolder plan. Just as the canal had bested the turnpike, why should not the newly invented railroad best the canal? The construction of the Baltimore and Ohio Railroad, begun in 1828, once more altered the major weapons in the contest. In the next quarter of a century Baltimore and Philadelphia completed their rail connections with the West, New York acquired two lines, and Boston, which had lagged behind during the turnpike and canal eras, recovered some of the lost ground with a railroad linking up with the eastern extremity of the Erie Canal.

Middle Western towns, following the Eastern example, meanwhile entered upon a somewhat similar struggle, each seeking to carve out its own economic dependencies and spheres of influence and to profit from the new ties with the seaboard. By 1840 a network of artificial waterways joined Cleveland and Toledo on Lake Erie with Portsmouth, Cincinnati and Evansville on the Ohio. As in the East, however, the arrival of the steam locomotive changed the situation. Now every up-and-coming municipality strove by hook or crook to become a railroad center, sometimes plunging heavily in debt for the purpose. And looking to the commercial

possibilities of the remoter West, Chicago, St. Louis, Memphis and New
Orleans concocted rival plans for a Pacific railroad—a maneuvering for
position that had political repercussions in Congress and contributed to
the passage of the Kansas-Nebraska Act in 1854, which it was thought
would facilitate the building of a transcontinental line from St. Louis.
This law, by authorizing slavery by "popular sovereignty" in a region
hitherto closed to it, helped to set the stage for the Civil War.

The progress in transportation facilities, confined largely to the North,
spurred urban development throughout that part of the country. The
Erie Canal, reinforced by the rail arteries to the West and the magnificent harbor at the mouth of the Hudson, established conclusively New
York's pre-eminence on the seaboard and in the nation. From only sixty
thousand inhabitants in 1800 its population (not counting Brooklyn)
climbed to eight hundred thousand by 1860, outdistancing Philadelphia
and placing it next to London and Paris in size, while Philadelphia with
more than half a million was in 1860 larger than Berlin. Brooklyn, Baltimore and Boston came next in size. Indicative of the westward movement
of the urban frontier was the fact that at the latter date all the other
places of over a hundred thousand—New Orleans, Cincinnati, St. Louis
and Chicago—were in the heart of the country. Chicago, though the
smallest of these cities in 1860, had already gathered the economic sinews
which would make it New York's chief rival before the century closed.
Anthony Trollope, observing the Midwest in 1861, remarked that except
for a few river and lake sites "settlers can hardly be said to have chosen
their own localities. These have been chosen for them by the originators
of the different lines of railway." Urban communities greatly augmented
the demand for farm products, accelerated the invention of labor-saving
implements like the steel plow and the reaper and thus furthered commercial agriculture, which in turn speeded city growth.

To master the new complexities of urban living demanded something
more than the easygoing ways of colonial towns. Enlarged populations
called for enlarged measures for the community safety and welfare,
whether by government or otherwise. As might be expected, the bigger
cities set the pace. After the lethal yellow-fever visitations of the 1790's
frightened Philadelphia into installing a public water works, other places
fell into line, so that more than a hundred systems came into existence
before the Civil War. Unfortunately, ignorance of the yet to be discovered germ theory of disease fastened attention on clear water instead of
pure water, thus leaving the public health still inadequately protected. To
cope with the growing lawlessness the leading cities now supplemented
night watches with day police. In 1822 Boston instituted gas lighting and
in 1823 set the example of a municipally owned sewerage system. About
the same time regular omnibus service was started on the streets of New
York, to be followed in the next decade by horsecars running on tracks.

Fire fighting, however, continued generally in the hands of volunteer
companies. Though Boston organized a paid municipal department in

1837 and Cincinnati and other Western towns greatly improved the apparatus by introducing steam fire engines in the 1850's, New York and Philadelphia, thanks to the political pull of volunteer brigades, resisted changes in equipment and waited respectively till 1865 and 1871 to municipalize their systems. The cities did nothing at all to combat the evil of slums, an unexpected development due to the great inrush of foreign immigrants into the Atlantic ports in the forties and fifties. Even more serious for the ordinary citizen was the growth of political machines, rooted in the tenement-house population, the fire companies and the criminal classes, and trafficking in franchises for the new public utilities. Appointments to government office for partisan services, first practiced in Eastern cities, preceded and led directly to the introduction of the spoils system into state and national politics.

The "diversities of extreme poverty and extreme wealth," which Edwin H. Chapin etched so sharply in *Humanity in the City* (1854), distressed the tenderhearted and gave rise to most of the reform crusades of the pre-Civil War generation. Compact living facilitated the banding together of such folk and also the collection of funds. Never before had America known so great an outpouring of effort to befriend the poor and the handicapped. Under urban stimulus arose the movement for free schools, for public libraries, for married women's property rights, for universal peace, for prison reform, for a better deal for the insane. The new conditions of city life begot a social conscience on the part of townsfolk which would be lasting of effect and which increasingly differentiated them from their brethren on the farm and frontier.

In these crowded centers, too, the labor movement took form, for the vaunted safety valve of the frontier failed to work for the mass of the wage earners. "The wilderness has receded," declared Orestes A. Brownson in 1840, "and already the new lands are beyond the reach of the mere laborer, and the employer has him at his mercy." Early in the preceding decade trade-unions began to appear, first along the seaboard, then at such inland points as Buffalo, Pittsburgh, Cincinnati and St. Louis; and for a short time a national federation flourished. But the long economic slump following the Panic of 1837 shattered most of the organizations and turned the thoughts of men like George Henry Evans, a New York labor editor, to plans for siphoning excess urban inhabitants into the federal domain by means of free farms. During the discussions over the homestead bill of 1852, even an Alabama member urged Congress "to help the cities to disgorge their cellars and their garrets of a starving, haggard, and useless population." But the House measure failed in the Senate, and until the Civil War further attempts went awry because of Southern fears that antislavery Northerners would fill up the Western territories. In any event the farm population would have been the chief beneficiaries, for it is unlikely that urban workingmen could have been enticed to exchange known ills for the hazards and uncertainties of pioneering.

Besides, along with the known ills went cultural opportunities and advantages absent from the countryside. The fast-growing cities afforded the largest public America had yet known for the appreciation and patronage of letters and the arts, and greatly increased the chances for the discovery and recruitment of talent in all fields. Townsfolk, moreover, were the first to feel the bracing impact of new currents of European thought. A varied and vital intellectual life resulted which directly or indirectly affected all members of the community, including the children, for whom municipal authorities now began to provide free high schools.

Newspapers and magazines proliferated. The first modern publishing houses sprang up. The theater became firmly established, native players like Charlotte Cushman and Edwin Booth winning additional laurels in England. Artists multiplied, being at last assured of adequate support at home, and the founding of the National Academy of Design in 1826 raised New York to the position of the country's chief art center. In literature also this richly creative period demonstrated urban superiority, with Boston, Cambridge and Concord largely responsible for the "flowering of New England," and New York and Philadelphia, even Cincinnati and St. Louis, making their own bids for fame. Only in architecture did the city botch the possibilities, for the mushroom growth of population forced new construction at a pace that ignored aesthetic considerations. The typical city, even in its wealthy residential sections, exhibited a fantastic patchwork of styles.

Whatever the attractions of town life, the elevenfold leap in urban population between 1820 and 1860 aroused increasing dismay and foreboding among rural folk who saw their own sons and daughters succumbing to the lure. "Adam and Eve were created and placed in a garden. Cities are the results of the fall," cried Joseph H. Ingraham, a popular religious novelist. Country preachers joined in denouncing these human agglomerations "cursed with immense accumulations of ignorance and error, vice and crime," while farm journals implored the young not to sacrifice their manly independence in order "to fetch and carry" and "cringe and flatter" for a miserable pittance. Political attitudes further mirrored the deepening distrust. Western opposition to the Second United States Bank sprang largely from alarm at the control of credit facilities by the "great cities of the Northeast, which," according to Missouri's senator Thomas Hart Benton, "have been for forty years, and that by force of federal legislation, the lion's den of Southern and Western money—that den into which all the tracks point inward; from which the returning track of a solitary dollar has never yet been seen."

Since, however, the West was growing its own towns and cities, it was becoming steadily more like the Northeast, whereas the South, chained by Negro slavery to agriculture, contained few sizable cities and those mostly at its edges. The widening breach between North and South was in no small part due to these divergent tendencies. Every year sharpened the contrast between the urban spirit of progress animating the one section and the static, rural life of the other. Few important industries existed below the Mason and Dixon line. Though illiteracy prevailed among the mass of whites as well as blacks, little or nothing was done to further free schools, and the North's humanitarian crusades were derided as Yankee fanaticism. Moreover, the Southerners, lacking the nerve centers for creative cultural achievement, fell behind in arts, letters and science. "It would have been surprising had they not desired secession," remarked Anthony Trollope, in America shortly after Fort Sumter. "Secession of one kind, a very practical secession, had already been forced upon them by circumstances. They had become a separate people, dissevered from the North by habits, morals, institutions, pursuits and every conceivable difference in their modes of thought and action." Beyond the tie of language, he went on, "they had no bond but that of a meagre political union in their Congress at Washington."

In addition, their economic life lay under thrall to the Northern business community. "It is a hopeless task," affirmed the South Carolinian William Gregg, "to undertake to even approximate to the vast sums of wealth which have been transferred from the South to the North by allowing the Northern cities to import and export for us." For twenty years before the war, Southern commercial conventions sought ways and means to escape this bondage, but the hope of creating their own trading and financial centers was vain so long as lands and Negroes held a superior attraction for capital. It was no mere coincidence that Charleston, dropping rapidly behind the Northern ports, initiated every disunionist movement in the entire South from Jackson's time onward; and the *Charleston Mercury's* bitter comment in 1858 that "Norfolk, Charleston, Savannah, Mobile, are suburbs of New York" suggests that other places shared the bitterness.

Withdrawal from the Union coupled with free trade with England seemed the answer, since then, it was believed, "Charleston in the course of ten years will become a New York"; and other localities nursed similar hopes. Under the circumstances the leading towns and cities strongly supported the movement for separation. Even New Orleans, despite its large infusion of Northerners and foreign-born, chose twenty secessionists and only four unionists to the state convention summoned to take action. Not surprisingly, the Confederate authorities on assuming power invalidated the private indebtedness—estimated variously at forty to four hundred millions—owing to Northern merchants, bankers and manufacturers. But the North's industrial might and greater man power overwhelmed the South in war as well as in peace.

In the generation following the Civil War the city took supreme command. Between 1860 and 1900 the urban population again quadrupled while the rural merely doubled. With one out of every six people inhabiting communities of eight thousand or over in the earlier year, the proportion rose to nearly one out of four in 1880 and to one out of three in 1900. Considerably more than half of the urban-moving throng gravitated to places of twenty-five thousand and upwards. Since every town dweller added to his effectiveness by association with his fellows, even these figures understate the city's new role in the nation. Nevertheless the sheer growth of particular localities is amazing. By 1890 New York (including Brooklyn) had about caught up with Paris, while Chicago and Philadelphia, with over a million each as compared with New York's two and a half million, then outranked all but five cities in Europe. In the Far West, Los Angeles jumped from fewer than 5000 in 1860 to more than 100,000 in 1900, and Denver from nothing at all to 134,000, while in the postwar South, Memphis with a bare 23,000 in the former year surpassed 100,000 in the latter. "The youngest of the nations," wrote Samuel L. Loomis in 1887, "has already more large cities than any except Great Britain and Germany." Thanks to the progress of settlement in the West and the burgeoning of industry in a South emancipated from slavery, the city had at last become a national instead of a sectional institution.

As urban centers grew in size and wealth, they cast an ever stronger spell over the American mind. Walt Whitman, returning to Greater New York in September, 1870, after a short absence, gloried in the "splendor, picturesqueness, and oceanic amplitude of these great cities." Conceding that Nature excelled in her mountains, forests and seas, he rated man's achievement equally great "in these ingenuities, streets, goods, houses, ships—these hurrying, feverish, electric crowds of men." (More tersely, Dr. Oliver Wendell Holmes, weary of hearing Cowper's line, "God made the country and man made the town," retorted, "God made the *cavern* and man made the *house!*") Little wonder that the young and the ambitious yielded to the temptation. "We cannot all live in cities, yet nearly all seem determined to do so," commented Horace Greeley, adding that with "millions of acres" awaiting cultivation "hundreds of thousands reject this and rush into the cities."

The exodus from the older countryside was especially striking. While the cities of Maine, Vermont, Massachusetts, Rhode Island, New York, Maryland and Illinois gained two and a half million people between 1880 and 1890, the rural districts of these states lost two hundred thousand. The drain of humanity from backwoods New England left mute witnesses in deserted hill villages and abandoned farms. In the nation as a whole, 10,063 townships out of 25,746 in thirty-nine states and territories shrank in population during the decade. Some of the rural decline was due to the shifting of agriculturalists from older regions to the free unworked lands of the trans-Mississippi West, but the phenomenon was so widespread—and, indeed, as characteristic of Europe during these years as of America—as to evidence the more potent and pervasive influence of the city. True, the 1880's merely climaxed a historic trend. In the century from 1790 to 1890 the total population had grown 16-fold while the urban segment grew 139-fold. Hence the celebrated announcement of the Superintendent of the Census in 1890 that a frontier line no longer existed can hardly be said to have marked the close of "the first period of American history." Rather it was a tardy admission that the second period was already under way.

The lusty urban growth created problems which taxed human resourcefulness to the utmost. Though European precedent helped solve some of the difficulties, American ingenuity in most respects outdistanced that of Old World cities. The record is extraordinary. Hardly had New York in 1870 opened the first elevated railway than San Francisco contrived the cable car, and hardly had the cable car begun to spread over the country than Richmond demonstrated the superiority of the electric trolley system, and Boston at the end of the century added the subway. The need for better lighting prompted the invention of Brush's outdoor arc lamp and Edison's incandescent bulb for indoors, and in another application of electric power the telephone brought townsfolk into instant communication. By means of the apartment house and the department store cities simplified problems of housing and shopping, while by means of the steel-framed skyscraper they saved further ground space by building their business districts upward. Density of population also led to more effective protection of the public health by turning to account the principles of the germ theory of disease just being discovered abroad. Before the century's close nearly every municipality of ten thousand or over had one or more officials charged with the duty of charting and checking communicable maladies. The bigger cities had become healthier places to live than many rural sections.

These civic advances, however, came at a price already beginning to be evident before the Civil War. Americans had developed their political institutions under simple rural conditions; they had yet to learn how to govern cramped populations. Preyed upon by unscrupulous men eager to exploit the expanding public utilities, municipal politics became a byword for venality. As Francis Parkman wrote, "Where the carcass is, the vultures gather together." New York's notorious Tweed Ring denoted a sickness that racked Philadelphia, Chicago, St. Louis, Minneapolis and San Francisco as well. "With very few exceptions," declared Andrew D. White, "the city governments of the United States are the worst in Christendom—the most expensive, the most inefficient, and the most corrupt."

Though an irate citizenry succeeded now and then in "turning the rascals out," the boss and the machine soon recovered control. Nevertheless, the good-government campaigns ventilated the abuses of municipal misrule and aroused the humane to the worsening plight of the urban poor. Under reform prodding, the New York legislature from 1865 onward adopted a series of laws to combat the slum evil in America's metropolis, though with disappointing results. More fruitful were the steps taken by private groups in Manhattan and elsewhere to establish social settlements and playgrounds and to replace the indiscriminate almsgiving of earlier times with a more rational administration of charity. Religion, awakening to the social gospel, helped out with slum missions and institutional churches. In the city, too, trade-unions made a new start, organizing the swelling army of urban workers on a nation-wide basis, joining with the reformers in securing factory legislation and gradually winning concessions from the employing class. Occasional voices with a foreign accent advocated socialism or anarchism as the remedy for the city's gross disparities of wealth and want, while Edward Bellamy in *Looking Backward* offered a home-grown version of communism in his fanciful account of Boston as it would be in the year 2000.

The increasing tension of living was evidenced in a variety of ways. Masses of people reared in a rustic environment had suddenly to adapt themselves to the frantic urban pace. One outcome was a startling growth of neurasthenia, a word coined by Dr. George M. Beard of New York in his work *American Nervousness* (1881), which traced the malady to the hurry and scurry, the din of the streets, the frenzied struggle for existence, the mental excitements and endless distractions. From the ranks of the high-strung, Mary Baker Eddy gathered most of her converts to the new religion of Christian Science, and for much the same reason towns-folk now gave enthusiastic support to organized sports. Flabby muscles unfitted most persons for direct participation, but they compromised by paying professional contestants to take their exercise for them. If, as a magazine writer said, nervousness had become the "national disease of America," baseball, partly as an antidote, became America's national game.

The stress of existence seemed only to enhance creative powers, however. The cities, re-enacting their role of the "fireplaces of civilization"—Theodore Parker's phrase—provided compelling incentives to cultural achievement, multiplying colleges, public libraries and publishing houses and founding art museums, art schools and conservatories of music. A Henry James might still find Europe an intellectually more congenial milieu, but William Dean Howells, Mark Twain and Joel Chandler Harris discovered the needed stimulus at home; and the same held true of all or nearly all the leading painters, sculptors, architects, composers, playwrights and scholars. A statistical study showed that localities of eight thousand and more gave birth to almost twice as many men of note as their proportionate share, and that in fields like science, engineering, art and literature the ratio was far greater. But even such computations do less than justice to the city, for there, too, gifted newcomers from the countryside and foreign shores entered their Promised Land. Civic pride prompted the holding of two great expositions, one at Philadelphia in 1876 and the other at Chicago in 1893. That the second and grander took place in an inland metropolis revealed how decisively urbanization had altered the face of traditional America.

The new age of the city rested upon an application of business enterprise to the exploitation of natural resources such as mankind had never known. The city, as insatiable as an octopus, tended to draw all nutriment to itself. Railroads, industrial combinations, investment capital, legislative favors, comprised the means. There arose a complex of urban imperialisms, each striving for dominion, each battling with rivals and each perforce yielding tribute to the lord of them all. "Every produce market, every share market," observed James Bryce, "vibrates to the Produce Exchange and Stock Exchange of New York."

As the city forged ahead, imposing its fiat on less developed regions, the rift between country and town widened portentously. Historians speak of a new sectionalism aligning West and South against East in these years, but Charles B. Spahr in *The Distribution of Wealth in the United States* (1896) pointed out more acutely that the antagonism "only exists in so far as the East is the section of the cities, while the South and West are the sections containing the great body of the farmers." Everywhere rural life was in chains: "The people on the farms and in the villages in the East have shared no more in the advancing wealth of the past quarter of a century than the people on the farms and in the villages of the South and West." He estimated that city families possessed on the average almost three times as much as country families.

The passage of years heightened the husbandman's conviction of being a second-class citizen, of losing out in the technological and cultural progress that dowered townsfolk. He lacked the telephone, electric lights, central heating, plumbing, sewerage, street cars, recreational facilities. Herbert Quick in after years remembered the women as "pining for neighbors, for domestic help, for pretty clothes, for schools, music, art, and the many things tasted when the magazines came in." The drift of youth to the cities emphasized the shortcomings, embittering those who stayed behind, even though they loved the land and would not have left it if they could. The farmer, moreover, accepted too readily the urban estimate of his calling. Once acclaimed by orators as the "embodiment of economic independence," now, remarked a magazine writer, he was the butt of humorists: "The 'sturdy yeoman' has become the 'hayseed.' "

This feeling of rural inferiority, this growing sense of frustration, underlay the political eruptions in the farming regions: the Granger movement in the 1870's, the Farmers' Alliances of the eighties and the Populist conflagration in the nineties. Each time specific economic grievances like steep freight rates, high interest charges and low crop prices stirred the smoldering embers into blaze. These were tangible hardships which the farmers demanded the government remove by such measures as railroad regulation and silver inflation. It fell to the greatest of the agrarian champions, addressing the Democratic national convention in 1896, to hurl the ultimate challenge at urban imperialism. "Burn down your cities and leave our farms, and your cities will spring up again as if by magic," cried William Jennings Bryan of Nebraska in a speech that won him the nomination, "but destroy our farms and the grass will grow in the streets of every city in the country." In the election that followed, the big cities of the East and Midwest, including New York which for the first time went Republican, responded by casting decisive majorities against the Democrats and free silver.

No one in 1900 could have foreseen the transformation which the twentieth century was to effect in both town and country. In the cities the reformers made steady progress in bridling the predatory forces which, in James Bryce's familiar phrase, had made municipal government "the one conspicuous failure of the United States." Early in the century a crusading type of mayor rode into power—men like "Golden Rule" Jones and Brand Whitlock in Toledo, Tom Johnson in Cleveland and Emil Seidel in Milwaukee—who aroused the citizens from their apathy and showed that elected officials could zealously promote the public good. Even more important was the introduction of the commission-manager plan of government, which by 1948 came to prevail in nearly eight hundred places. A radical departure from the clumsy older form, which imitated the checks and balances of state governments, the new system copied the streamlined structure of business corporations, with the commission corresponding to the board of directors and the city manager resembling the president or general manager named by the board to conduct detailed affairs. In nearly every case the reform quickly justified itself, though eternal vigilance by the voters continued to be the price of ensuring the best results.

Alongside these improvements occurred the first sustained attempts at city planning. Instead of letting urban communities evolve in hit-and-miss fashion, the endeavor now was to guide their growth in the interests of sightliness and the people's convenience, safety and health. By an extensive use of zoning ordinances, appropriate locations were mapped for business and factory districts, residential neighborhoods, recreational facilities; and the New York legislature's adoption of an effective tenement-house code in 1901 inspired other states and municipalities to a vigorous attack on the slum evil, though it was not till the 1930's that the federal authorities took a hand in the matter. Already by 1922 a hundred and eighty-five towns and cities had set up official bodies to chart over-all programs of development, and by 1940 the number had risen to well over a thousand. City planning, moreover, stimulated interest in county planning and state planning and helped create the atmosphere for the New Deal's ventures in regional and national planning.

These advances went hand in hand with a further piling up of townsfolk. By 1930 approximately half the nation dwelt in localities of eight thousand or more and nearly a third in centers of one hundred thousand or more. Urban dominance was further enhanced by the emergence of great metropolitan districts or regions. These "city states" had begun to form in the nineteenth century as swifter means of transportation and communication flung the inhabitants outward into the suburbs, but it was the coming of the automobile and motor truck and the extension of electricity and other conveniences into the surrounding territory that gave these supercommunities their unprecedented size and importance.

Each consisted of one or more core cities with satellite towns and dependent rural areas, the whole knit together by economic, social and cultural ties. The hundred and thirty-three metropolitan regions in 1930 grew to a hundred and forty by 1940, when they contained almost half the total population. New York's region overlapped four states, an irregular tract twice the area of Rhode Island with 272 incorporated communities and intervening farm lands. Chicago's embraced 115 incorporated places, and San Francisco's 38. Subdivided into independent municipalities, the people faced enormous difficulties in looking after such common governmental concerns as policing, sewage disposal, public health and schooling. Some students, despairing of any other solution, proposed separate statehood for the larger metropolitan regions. New and unanticipated strains have been placed on a federal system framed in the eighteenth century for a simple agrarian economy.

Of all the new trends in urban development, however, none had such profound effects as the altered relationship of country and city. Historians generally attribute the decline of the free-silver movement in the late nineties to the discovery of fresh sources of gold supply and an uptrend of crop prices, but probably the more fundamental cause was the amelioration of many of the social and psychological drawbacks of farm existence. The introduction of rural free delivery of mail after 1896, the extension of good roads due to the bicycle craze, the expanding network of interurban trolleys, the spread of party-line neighborhood telephones after the basic Bell patents expired in 1893, the increase of country schools—all these, coming shortly before 1900, helped dispel the aching isolation and loneliness, thereby making rustic life pleasanter.

Yet these mitigations seem trifling compared with the marvels which the twentieth century wrought. The automobile brought farm families within easy reach of each other and of the city; the motorbus facilitated the establishment of consolidated schools with vastly improved instruction and equipment; while the radio introduced new interests and pleasures into the homes themselves, shedding its benefits impartially on country and town. At the same time the mechanical energy used in agriculture grew eightfold between 1900 and 1935, thus lightening the husbandman's toil and adding to his opportunities for leisure. Moreover, the state and national governments increasingly employed their powers to improve the farmer's economic and social status. The Smith-Lever Act, passed by Congress in 1914, provided for agricultural-extension work in rural communities through county agents; the Federal Farm Loan Board, created in 1916, offered long-term loans at relatively low rates of interest; and the Smith-Hughes Act of 1917 appropriated public funds for teaching vocational agriculture and home economics in country high schools. Such enactments reached a climax in the 1930's when the New Deal embarked upon far-reaching programs of rural betterment like the Tennessee Valley and Columbia River developments, the Triple-A, government-aided electrification and measures to boost farm tenants up the ladder to ownership. Though inequalities remained, the tiller of the soil had come to share many of the comforts and refinements once belonging only to townsfolk. He had attained a position in American society of which his Populist forebears could hardly have dreamed.

Just as rural life became more urbanized, so urban life became more ruralized. Wooded parks, tree-shaded boulevards, beautified waterfronts, municipal golf courses, athletic fields and children's playgrounds multiplied, while an increasing army of white-collar workers and wage earners piled into motorcars and buses each night to go farther and farther into the suburbs. Within the metropolitan regions population actually grew faster in the rustic outskirts between 1930 and 1940 than in the central cities. Retail trade too felt the centrifugal tug, and even factories showed a tendency to move into outlying villages where taxes, rent and food cost less. The extension of giant power will doubtless speed the trend, affording more and more townsfolk a chance to live and work and bring up their children in country surroundings. The dread specter of atomic-bomb attacks may operate to the same end in the interests of national military security.

Thus the twentieth century has been spinning a web in which city and country, no longer separate entities, have been brought ever closer together. When the city encroaches sufficiently on the country and the country on the city, America may hope to arrive at a way of life which will blend the best features of both the traditional ways. The people will have within grasp the realization of Plato's vision of a society in which "youth shall dwell in a land of health amid fair sights and sounds and imbibe good from every quarter; and beauty, the emanation of noble works, will flow into the eye and ear like an invigorating breeze from a purer region and imperceptibly woo the soul from infancy into harmony and sympathy with the beauty of reason."

From humble beginnings in the early seventeenth century the city thus traced a varied course. In Europe the modern urban community emerged by gradual stages out of the simple town economy of the Middle Ages; by comparison, the American city leaped into being with breath-taking speed. At first servant to an agricultural order, then a jealous contestant, then an oppressor, it now gives evidence of becoming a comrade and co-operator in a new national synthesis. Its economic function has been hardly more important than its cultural mission or its transforming influence upon rural conceptions of democracy. The city, no less than the frontier, has been a major factor in American civilization. Without an appreciation of the role of both the story is only half told.

Henry Nash Smith

The Garden

of the World

as Safety Valve

In this selection, Henry Nash Smith of the University of California analyzes a theoretical aspect of the agrarian tradition that was prominent in the popular thought of the late nineteenth century. It is the idea that the vacant lands of the West would absorb the surplus laborers of the eastern cities, who would become independent and self-subsisting farmers. Free Western land as a safety valve, according to an extreme expression of the idea, would overcome the blight of urban social problems, such as slums, and would eliminate serious unemployment in the United States.

Professor Smith's analysis is based on a broad study of the agrarian tradition in which he portrays the United States as a society dedicated to the principle that government should reflect the influence and interests of the independent farmer. Basic to this tradition is the idea of the "garden of the world"—an agricultural empire embodying the virtues of the Good Society. This poetic idea—thought by many to express the assumptions of a whole society and to define the promise of American life—is something of a myth, Smith maintains. Nonetheless, the idea long survived as a force in American thought and politics.

Smith points out that the Homestead Act of 1862 did not fulfill the expectations of the agrarian tradition, that the Western safety valve did not function according to theory, and that the agrarian tradition itself failed to comport with the realities of the industrial society of the late nineteenth century. The chasm between the realities of industrial life and the prevalent agrarian theory undoubtedly contributed to the disillusionment evident in the farmers' crusades of the last decades of the century. [Reprinted by permission of the publishers from Henry Nash Smith, Virgin Land: The American West as Symbol and Myth. *Cambridge, Mass.: Harvard University Press. Copyright 1950, 1952 by the President and Fellows of Harvard College.]*

The Homestead Act failed to help the Eastern urban laborer as woefully as it failed to help the farmer in the West. This failure was less important than the frustration of the frontier farmer's effort to acquire land, but it shows equally well how poor a tool the agrarian tradition was for dealing with nineteenth-century industrial society. American agrarians had long maintained that the West, the free lands beyond the frontier, would operate as a safety valve to keep down social and economic conflict in the East. The best known exponent of this notion was Horace Greeley. His constant emphasis on it, in the New York *Tribune* and on the lecture platform, is the basis for his great but not wholly deserved reputation as a spokesman for the westward movement. Greeley's famous slogan, "Go West, young man, go forth into the Country" dates from 1837, when he turned to the plan of encouraging emigration westward as means of relief from the poverty and unemployment caused by the Panic. In 1846, when he adopted Evans's National Reform program, he showed his loyalty to agrarian tradition by prophesying that the operation of the safety valve would establish an independent, substantial yeomanry on the public domain. A typical explanation of Greeley's theory appeared in the *Tribune* in 1854:

Make the Public Lands free in quarter-sections to Actual Settlers and deny them to all others, and earth's landless millions will no longer be orphans and mendicants; they can work for the wealthy, relieved from the degrading terror of being turned adrift to starve. When employment fails or wages are in-adequate, they may pack up and strike westward to enter upon the possession and culture of their own lands on the banks of the Wisconsin, the Des Moines or the Platte, which have been patiently awaiting their advent since creation. Strikes to stand still will be glaringly absurd when every citizen is offered the alternative to work for others or for himself, as to him shall seem most advantageous. The mechanic or laborer who works for another will do so only because he can thus secure a more liberal and satisfactory recompense than he could by working for himself.

The general notion embodied in this paragraph is very old and at various times has been invoked by writers of every possible political orientation. Frederick Jackson Turner found a version of it in a state-ment made by Governor John Winthrop of Massachusetts Bay in 1634. It appeared in the eighteenth century in discussions of British colonial policy, to persuade the authorities that there was no danger of a signifi-cant development of manufacturing in the American colonies. The Lon-don merchant Joshua Gee, for example, wrote to the Council of Trade and Plantations in 1721 that colonists would not be attracted into manu-facturing even though abundance of good workmen had emigrated to America.

The reason is plain [he argued], there is so much an easier subsistence to be made, where land is of so smal a value, by a little farme and a smal stock of cattle, that most of them slight manufacturies, and even in New England (the poorest of all the Colonies and the fullest of people) those few that do work will have near five times as much for manufacturing nails and other things, as is given for manufacturing in England . . .

Sir William Keith, royal customs official and Governor of Pennsylvania and Delaware, urged the British government in 1731 to make a grant of land for a colony beyond the Alleghenies on the ground that without such a new outlet for their energies, the colonists would be forced into manufacturing by a glut of tobacco, rice and corn. The anonymous author of the preface to the London edition of John Bartram's *Observa-tions* (1751) used a similar argument to urge the central government to encourage frontier settlement in America. In the same year Franklin stressed the idea in his *Observations Concerning the Increase of Mankind,* again with the intention of influencing British policy. "Labour will never be cheap here," he wrote, "where no Man continues long a Labourer for others, but gets a Plantation of his own."

With the establishment of American independence the bearing of this kind of economic analysis was altered. The criterion of policy was no longer the interests of British merchants. Instead, a developing American nationalism embraced the humanitarian conception of the West as a refuge for the oppressed of all the world. George Washington wrote with unaccustomed playfulness to Lafayette at the end of the Revolution:

I wish to see the sons and daughters of the world in Peace and busily employed in the . . . agreeable amusement of fulfilling the first and great commandment—*Increase and Multiply:* as an encouragement to which we have opened the fertile plains of the Ohio to the poor, the needy and the oppressed of the Earth; anyone therefore who is heavy laden or who wants land to cultivate, may repair thither & abound, as in the Land of promise, with milk and honey . . .

A similar conception of the function of the West furnished Jefferson with a perfectly logical basis for revising his theoretical hostility to the growth of industry in the United States. In 1805, when he was contemplating a new edition of the *Notes on Virginia,* he wrote that he planned to qualify several expressions in the nineteenth chapter which attacked manufacturing. These expressions, he said, applied only to "the manufacturers of the great cities in the old countries, at the time present." In Europe the poverty of urban laborers had begotten a depravity, a dependence and corruption which would make them undesirable citizens in a republic. But America had not yet reached the condition of Europe, because of the fortunate influence of free land:

As yet our manufacturers [that is, industrial workers] are as much at their ease, as independent and moral as our agricultural inhabitants, and they will continue so as long as there are vacant lands for them to resort to; because whenever it shall be attempted by the other classes to reduce them to the minimum of subsistence, they will quit their trades and go to laboring the earth.

Such a hopeful conception of the role of the West is one of the principal foundations of the myth of the garden. It occurs on every hand, and in a wide variety of forms through most of the nineteenth century. New England industrialists, for example, were accused of trying to restrict westward emigration in order to maintain a surplus of laborers and keep down wages. It was such a charge by Senator Robert Y. Hayne in 1829 that led to the famous Webster-Hayne debate. Hayne's colleague in this forensic encounter, Thomas H. Benton, developed the charge against New England at length, inveighing against the horrid policy of making paupers by law—against the cruel legislation which would confine poor people in the Northeast to work as journeymen in the manufactories, instead of letting them go off to new countries, acquire land, become independent freeholders, and lay the foundation of comfort and independence for their children.

Eastern mill owners, he declared,

are now realizing what was said by Dr. Franklin forty-five years ago, that they need great numbers of poor people to do the work for small wages; that these poor people are easily got in Europe, where there was no land for them, but that they could not be got in America until the lands were taken up. . . . This resolution, which we are now considering, is the true measure for supplying the poor people which the manufactories need.

Twenty years later Congressman Josiah Sutherland of New York opposed the Homestead Bill for reasons exactly like those Benton had attributed to factory owners. The bill, he said, would take labor from the manufacturing states to the land states, increasing the cost of labor and thus the cost of manufactures.

Karl Marx accepted the same theory about the relation between the status of American laborers and free land. It formed an important part of the radical tradition in this country, especially through the influence of George Henry Evans and his National Reform movement. Evans's safety-valve theory became official Republican doctrine in the 1850's when the party adopted the homestead principle. One of the earliest groups that used the name "Republican" was formed at Ripon, Wisconsin, in 1854 by Alvan E. Bovay, who had been a close associate of Evans before he moved West. Horace Greeley made strenuous efforts to publicize the safety-valve doctrine as an argument in favor of the party. In 1859 he published a stirring appeal in the *Tribune:*

Laboring men! remember that the Republican is the only national party committed to the policy of making the public lands free in quarter-sections to actual settlers, whereby every worker will be enabled to hew out for his family a home from the virgin soil of the Great West.

To cite only one other Republican spokesman, Senator James R. Doolittle of Wisconsin declared in 1860:

I sustain this [homestead] measure . . . because its benign operation will postpone for centuries, if it will not forever, all serious conflict between capital and labor in the older free States, withdrawing their surplus population to create in greater abundance the means of subsistence.

But the Homestead Act did not make an end of unemployment and social problems. On the contrary, the three decades following its passage were marked by the most bitter and widespread labor trouble that had yet been seen in the United States. Recent scholars have accordingly raised the question whether the public domain ever operated as a safety valve for eastern laborers, and the trend of the discussion has been strongly toward the conclusion that the theory, at least in the form endorsed by Greeley and his associates, had very little foundation. Unemployed workmen in eastern cities were not ordinarily able to go West and succeed as farmers. They seldom had the money needed to transport their families to the free public lands and to feed and shelter them until a crop could be made; and even if such a worker managed to establish himself on a western farm, he was not likely to succeed without skills that could be obtained only through long apprenticeship. Franklin had seen the West as a refuge for the laborer "that understands Husbandry"—a simple matter perhaps in the fertile Ohio Valley during the eighteenth century but a very difficult one after the Civil War on the sub-humid plains. Frontier settlers usually were farmers of some experience from nearby states. Except for European immigrants who were taken to the West by railway companies and other agencies with lands to sell, few settlers on the agricultural frontier came directly from eastern industrial centers.

But if the theory of the safety valve was largely false, how can we account for its almost universal acceptance during the nineteenth century? The question is a difficult one if we take into account only the facts of frontier settlement. The prevalence of the belief is easier to account for, however, if we realize that it was an important part of the myth of the garden of the world. The doctrine of the safety valve was an imaginative construction which masked poverty and industrial strife with the pleasing suggestion that a beneficent nature stronger than any human agency, the ancient resource of Americans, the power that had made the country rich and great, would solve the new problems of industrialism. Just as the theory that rain follows the plow was the myth of the garden expanded to include meteorology, the safety-valve theory was the form taken by the myth on the plane of economic analysis.

True or not, the theory was a two-edged weapon. Useful in the hands of humanitarian reformers who wished to open up opportunities for the poor and the exploited, or for Westerners who wished to foster the rapid development of their region, the theory had the disadvantage of implying that the future prosperity of the nation depended on the availability of land open to settlement. So long as the supply of land could be considered practically limitless, the theory of the safety valve could be invoked without risk to prove the uniquely fortunate destiny of America. But if opportunity, happiness, social harmony, and even liberty itself depended on the presence of free land beyond the frontier, what became of these values in the event that the available land should after all prove to be limited in extent? The doctrine of the safety valve implied that in these circumstances American society would become like crowded Europe. The ills of the Old World, which had been depicted with an invidious energy by men who insisted on the unprecedented good fortune of the United States, would become the ills of the New. The growth of population that had once seemed the surest omen of a glorious future for the American empire would become a curse on this side of the Atlantic as Malthus had declared it was in Europe.

Jefferson had hinted at such an outcome. The people of the United States will remain virtuous, he wrote to James Madison from Paris in 1787, as long as they are primarily agricultural, and this will be the case while vacant lands are available in any part of America. But when the lands are exhausted, Americans will "get piled upon one another in large cities as in Europe, and go to eating one another as they do there." Jefferson of course thought that day was comfortably remote. The first Americans who considered the closing of the safety valve imminent were Southern apologists for slavery searching for flaws in the Northern cult of free labor. As early as 1836 Thomas R. Dew of William and Mary College raised the question of what would happen when the supply of free land ran out:

the time must come [he said] when the powerfully elastic spring of our rapidly increasing numbers shall fill up our wide spread territory with a dense population—when the great safety valve of the west will be closed against us—when millions shall be crowded into our manufactories and commercial cities—then will come the great and fearful pressure upon the engine. . . .

This pressure would lead to class war:

then will the line of demarkation stand most palpably drawn between the rich and the poor, the capitalist and the laborer—then will thousands, yea millions arise, whose hard lot it may be to labor from morn till eve through a long life, without the cheering hope of passing from that toilsome condition in which the first years of their manhood found them, or even of accumulating in advance that small fund which may release the old and infirm from labor and toil, and mitigate the sorrows of declining years. . . .

When these things shall come [Dew inquired of the propertied men of the North]—when the millions, who are always under the pressure of poverty, and sometimes on the verge of starvation, shall form your numerical majority, (as is the case now in the old countries of the world) and universal suffrage shall throw the political power into their hands, can you expect that they will regard as sacred the tenure by which you hold your property? I almost fear the frailties and weakness of human nature too much, to anticipate confidently such justice.

The probable result was indeed lurid:

First comes disorganization and legislative plunder, then the struggle of factions and civil war, and lastly a military despotism, into whose arms all will be driven by the intolerable evils of anarchy and rapine.

With its allusion to the example of Rome and its gloomy realism, this is hardly in the key of the optimism that was the official American attitude in the period of manifest destiny. The Southerners were a minority of dissent from the doctrine of progress which underlay so much Northern and Western thought. In 1857 the Virginian George Fitzhugh asserted in his *Cannibals All!* that the social tensions resulting from population increase as the West was settled would force the North to resort to slavery as a means of controlling an insubordinate and menacing laboring class. A writer for the *Southern Literary Messenger* in the following year predicted that increase of population, by causing pressure on the available means of subsistence, would bring to the North a chain of grisly evils—mobs and violence in the cities, pulpits defiled by fanaticism and political passions, legislation tainted by demagoguery.

A celebrated letter from Lord Macaulay written in 1857 to an American biographer of Jefferson developed the same theme. Macaulay asserted that Jeffersonian democracy was feasible only in a society possessing a boundless extent of fertile and unoccupied land. When the United States should be as thickly populated as England, "You will have your Manchesters and Birminghams and hundreds of thousands of artisans will assuredly sometimes be out of work. Then your institutions will be fairly brought to the test." Having made the grievous error of giving the ballot to everyone, the upper classes would then be powerless to prevent legislation confiscating their property. Like the Southern apologists for slavery, Macaulay foresaw a Roman decadence for the American democracy:

Either some Caesar or Napoleon will seize the reins of government with a strong hand, or your republic will be as fearfully plundered and laid waste by barbarians in the twentieth century as the Roman Empire was in the fifth; with this difference, that the Huns and Vandals who ravaged the Roman Empire came from without and that your Huns and Vandals will have been engendered within your own country by your own institutions.

In passages like these the overtones of the phrase "safety valve" become apparent. The valve affords safety for the property of the rich against the potential violence of the poor, who are withheld from their vandal attack on the possessions of others by being enticed away to the West. It is worth recalling that Greeley urged his homestead program as an alternative to strikes, which he considered foolish and unnecessary when the worker had the opportunity to settle on his own farm from the public domain.

The antidemocratic tendency of the notion of the safety valve comes out very explicitly in Melville's *Clarel* (1876). Rolfe, the "straight" American, is discussing the destiny of the United States with Ungar, the "clouded man" and "malcontent," an expatriate Confederate veteran who expresses many of the ideas of Dew and Fitzhugh.

> Those waste-weirs [says Rolfe] which the New World yields
> To inland freshets—the free vents
> Supplied to turbid elements;
> The vast reserves—the untried fields;

> These long shall keep off and delay
> The class-war, rich-and-poor-man fray
> Of history. From that alone
> Can serious trouble spring.

But Ungar, in the manner of the *Southern Literary Messenger*, refuses to accept this flattering unction. History moves faster in modern times; the slumberous combustibles are sure to explode, and before very long.

> 'Twill come, 'twill come!
> One demagogue can trouble much:
> How of a hundred thousand such?
> And universal suffrage lent
> To back them with brute element
> Overwhelming?

A Thirty Years' War between the classes is fated; its probable sequel will be a dead level of rank commonplace, an Anglo-Saxon China which for Ungar (if indeed not for Melville himself) is significantly located in the West, on the vast plains where the garden of the world had been expected to materialize. There, in an almost explicit contrast with the confident earlier prophecies of a Western flowering of the arts and of civic virtue, the American society of the future will "shame the race / In the Dark Ages of Democracy." Even Clarel's companions are jolted into half-agreement with him:

> Nor dull they were in honest tone
> To some misgivings of their own:
> They felt how far beyond the scope
> Of elder Europe's saddest thought
> Might be the New World sudden brought
> In youth to share old age's pains—
> To feel the arrest of hope's advance,
> And squandered last inheritance;
> And cry—"To Terminus build fanes!
> Columbus ended earth's romance:
> No New World to mankind remains!"

Richard Hofstadter

The Agrarian Myth

and Commercial

Realities

Like Henry Nash Smith, Richard Hofstadter—a prominent social and intellectual historian—is concerned with the mythical elements of the agrarian tradition as they developed against the realities of an industrial society. In this selection, Hofstadter analyzes the agrarian myth, which he says was based on a sentimental attachment to rural living and utopian notions about rural people and rural life. This myth, he maintains, became embedded in the country's folklore and nationalist ideology. In the following essay, part of a larger intellectual history, the author's interpretations are of interest—particularly the interpretations on the nature of Populism; on the closing of the frontier as a cause for agrarian discontent; on the farmer as businessman; and on the status of the farmer, socially and economically, in comparison to that of the urban middle and upper classes. It should be kept in mind that this essay is a venture in ideas and that Professor Hofstadter's interpretations of the agrarian tradition, though provocative, may not be the most widely accepted among scholars. [Copyright 1955 by Richard Hofstadter. Condensed from The Age of Reform *by Richard Hofstadter, by permission of Alfred A. Knopf, Inc.]*

The Yeoman and the Myth. The United States was born in the country and has moved to the city. From the beginning its political values and ideas were of necessity shaped by country life. The early American politician, the country editor, who wished to address himself to the common man, had to draw upon a rhetoric that would touch the tillers of the soil; and even the spokesman of city people knew that his audience had been in very large part reared upon the farm. But what the articulate people who talked and wrote about farmers and farming—the preachers, poets, philosophers, writers, and statesmen—liked about American farming was not, in every respect, what the typical working farmer liked. For the articulate people were drawn irresistibly to the noncommercial, nonpecuniary, self-sufficient aspect of American farm life. To them it was an ideal. Writers like Thomas Jefferson and Hector St. Jean de Crevecoeur admired the yeoman farmer not for his capacity to exploit opportunities and make money but for his honest industry, his independence, his frank spirit of equality, his ability to produce and enjoy a simple abundance. The farmer himself, in most cases, was in fact inspired to make money, and such self-sufficiency as he actually had was usually forced upon him by a lack of transportation for markets, or by the necessity to save cash to expand his operations. For while early American society was an agrarian society, it was fast becoming more commercial, and commercial goals made their way among its agricultural classes almost as rapidly as elsewhere. The more commercial this society became, however, the more reason it found to cling in imagination to the noncommercial agrarian values. The more farming as a self-sufficient way of life was abandoned for farming as a business, the more merit men found in what was being left behind. And the more rapidly the farmers' sons moved into the towns, the more nostalgic the whole culture became about its rural past. The American mind was raised upon a sentimental attachment to rural living and upon a series of notions about rural people and rural life that I have chosen to designate as the agrarian myth. The agrarian myth represents a kind of homage that Americans have paid to the fancied innocence of their origins.

Like any complex of ideas, the agrarian myth cannot be defined in a phrase, but its component themes form a clear pattern. Its hero was the yeoman farmer, its central conception the notion that he is the ideal man and the ideal citizen. Unstinted praise of the special virtues of the farmer and the special values of rural life was coupled with the assertion that agriculture, as a calling uniquely productive and uniquely important to society, had a special right to the concern and protection of government. The yeoman, who owned a small farm and worked it with the aid of his family, was the incarnation of the simple, honest, independent, healthy, happy human being. Because he lived in close communion with beneficent nature, his life was believed to have a wholesomeness and integrity impossible for the depraved populations of cities. His well-being was not merely physical, it was moral; it was not merely personal, it was the central source of civic virtue; it was not merely secular but religious, for God had made the land and called man to cultivate it. Since the yeoman was believed to be both happy and honest, and since he had a secure propertied stake in society in the form of his own land, he was held to be the best and most reliable sort of citizen. To this conviction Jefferson appealed when he wrote: "The small land holders are the most precious part of a state"

In origin the agrarian myth was not a popular but a literary idea, a preoccupation of the upper classes, of those who enjoyed a classical education, read pastoral poetry, experimented with breeding stock, and owned plantations or country estates. It was clearly formulated and almost universally accepted in America during the last half of the eighteenth century. As it took shape both in Europe and America, its promulgators drew heavily upon the authority and the rhetoric of classical writers—Hesiod, Xenophon, Cato, Cicero, Virgil, Horace, and others—whose works were the staples of a good education. A learned agricultural gentry, coming into conflict with the industrial classes, welcomed the moral strength that a rich classical ancestry brought to the praise of husbandry. In France the Physiocrats preached that agriculture is the only true source of wealth. In England the rural entrepreneurs, already interested in breeding and agricultural improvement, found the praise of husbandry congenial. . . .

Wherever the peasantry was being displaced by industry or commercial farming, and particularly in England, where rustic life was devasted by the enclosures, such literature took on special poignancy. Oliver Goldsmith's classic statement, "The Deserted Village," became well over a hundred years later the unchallenged favorite of American Populist writers and orators. Chiefly through English experience, and from English and classical writers, the agrarian myth came to America, where, like so many other cultural importations, it eventually took on altogether new dimensions in its new setting. In America such men as Jefferson and Crevecoeur, Thomas Paine, Philip Freneau, Hugh Henry Brackenridge, and George Logan propagated the myth, and after them a multitude of writers whose lives reach well into the nineteenth century. So appealing were its symbols that even an arch-opponent of the agrarian interest like Alexander Hamilton found it politic to concede in his *Report on Manufactures* that "the cultivation of the earth, as the primary and most certain source of national supply, . . . has intrinsically a strong claim to pre-eminence over every other kind of industry." And Benjamin Franklin, urban cosmopolite though he was, once said that agriculture was "the only *honest way*" for a nation to acquire wealth, "wherein man receives a real increase of the seed thrown into the ground, a kind of continuous miracle, wrought by the hand of God in his favour, as a reward for his innocent life and virtuous industry."

Among the intellectual classes in the eighteenth century the agrarian myth had virtually universal appeal. It was everywhere: in tracts on agricultural improvement and books on economics, in pastoral poetry and political philosophy. At once primitivist and rationalist, it could be made congenial to almost every temperament. Some writers used it to give simple, direct, and emotional expression to their feelings about life and nature; others linked agrarianism with a formal philosophy of natural rights. The application of the natural-rights philosophy to land tenure became especially popular in America. Since the time of Locke it had been a standard argument that the land is the common stock of society to which every man has a right—what Jefferson called "the fundamental right to labour the earth"; that since the occupancy and use of land are the true criteria of valid ownership, labor expended in cultivating the earth confers title to it; that since government was created to protect property, the property of working landholders has a special claim to be fostered and protected by the state.

At first, as I have said, the agrarian myth was a notion of the educated classes, but by the early nineteenth century it had become a mass creed, a part of the country's political folklore and its nationalist ideology. The roots of this change may be found as far back as the American Revolution, which, appearing to many Americans as the victory of a band of embattled farmers over an empire, seemed to confirm the moral and civic superiority of the yeoman, made the farmer a symbol of the new nation, and wove the agrarian myth into its patriotic sentiments and republican idealism. Still more important, the myth played a role in the first party battles under the Constitution. The Jeffersonians appealed again and again to the moral primacy of the yeoman farmer in their attacks on the Federalists. The family farm and American democracy became indissolubly connected in Jeffersonian thought, and was inherited from the Jeffersonians by exponents of popular causes in the Jackson era. By 1840 even the more conservative party, the Whigs, took over the rhetorical appeal to the common man, and elected a President in good part on the strength of the fiction that he lived in a log cabin.

The Jeffersonians, moreover, made the agrarian myth the basis of a strategy of continental development. Many of them expected that the great empty inland regions would guarantee the preponderance of the yeoman—and therefore the dominance of Jeffersonianism and the health of the state—for an unlimited future. In his first inaugural address Jefferson spoke of the United States as "a chosen country, with room enough for our descendants to the thousandth and thousandth generation." The opening of the trans-Allegheny region, its protection from slavery, and the purchase of the Louisiana Territory were the first great steps in a continental strategy designed to establish an internal empire of small farms. Much later the Homestead Act, though temporarily blocked by the South (the only section of the country where the freehold concept was seriously contested as an ideal), was meant to carry to its completion the process of continental settlement by small homeowners. The failure of the Homestead Act "to enact by statute the fee-simple empire" was, as we shall see, one of the original sources of Populist grievances, and one of the central points at which the agrarian myth was overrun by the commercial realities.

Above all, however, the myth was powerful because the United States in the first half of the nineteenth century consisted predominantly of literate and politically enfranchised farmers. Offering what seemed harmless flattery to this numerically dominant class, the myth suggested a standard vocabulary to rural editors and politicians. Although farmers may not have been much impressed by what was said about the merits of a noncommercial way of life, they could only enjoy learning about their special virtues and their unique services to the nation, could hardly mind hearing that their life was intrinsically more virtuous and closer to God than the lives of many people who seemed to be better off. Moreover, the editors and politicians who so flattered them need not in most cases have been insincere. More often than not they too were likely to have begun life in little villages or on farms, and what they had to say stirred in their own breasts, as it did in the breasts of a great many townspeople, nostalgia for their early years, and perhaps relieved some residual feelings of guilt at having deserted parental homes and childhood attachments. They also had the satisfaction in the early days of knowing that in so far as it was based upon the life of the largely self-sufficient yeoman the agrarian myth was a depiction of reality as well as the assertion of an ideal.

Oddly enough, the agrarian myth came to be believed more widely and tenaciously as it became more fictional. At first it was propagated with a kind of genial candor, and only later did it acquire overtones of insincerity. There survives from the Jackson era a lithograph that shows Joseph Ritner, Governor of Pennsylvania, standing by a primitive plow at the end of a furrow. There is no pretense that the Governor has actually been plowing—he wears broadcloth pants and a silk vest, and his tall black beaver hat has been carefully laid in the grass beside him—but the picture is meant as a reminder of both his rustic origin and his present high station in life. By contrast, Calvin Coolidge posed almost a century later for a series of photographs that represented him as haying in Vermont. In one of them the President sits on the edge of a hay rig in a white shirt, collar detached, wearing highly polished black shoes under a fresh pair of overalls; in the background stands his Pierce Arrow, a secret-service man on the running board, plainly waiting to hurry the President away from his bogus rural labors. That the second picture is so much more pretentious and disingenuous than the first is a measure of the increasing hollowness of the myth as it became more and more remote from the realities of agriculture. Well on into the twentieth century eminent Americans continued to pay this ritualistic obeisance to what one writer has called "agricultural fundamentalism." . . .

Throughout the nineteenth century hundreds upon hundreds of thousands of farm-born youths had set the example that Coolidge . . . only followed: they sang the praises of agriculture but eschewed farming as a vocation and sought their careers in the towns and cities. For all the rhetoric of the pastoral tradition, nothing could keep the boys on the farm, and nothing could conceal from the farm population itself the continuous restless movement not merely to farms farther west but to urban areas, East and West. Particularly after 1840, which marked the beginning of a long cycle of heavy country-to-city migration, farm children repudiated their parents' way of life and took off for the cities, where in agrarian theory, if not in fact, they were sure to succumb to vice and poverty. Farm journals were full of editorials, stories, and poems voicing the plaintive theme: "Boys, Stick to the Farm!" and of advice to farmers on how to rear their sons so that farming as a way of life would be attractive to them. . . .

In the imagery of these appeals the earth was characteristically a mother, trade a harlot, and desertion of ancestral ways a betrayal that invited Providential punishment. When a correspondent of the *Prairie Farmer* in 1849 made the mistake of praising the luxuries, the "polished society," and the economic opportunities of the city, he was rebuked for overlooking the fact that city life *"crushes, enslaves, and ruins so many thousands of our young men* who are insensibly made the victims of *dissipation,* of *reckless speculation,* and of *ultimate crime."* Such warnings, of course, were futile. "Thousands of young men" wrote the New York agriculturist Jesse Buel, "do annually forsake the plough, and the honest profession of their fathers, if not to win the fair, at least from an opinion, too often confirmed by mistaken parents, that agriculture is not the road to wealth, to honor, nor to happiness. And such will continue to be the case, until our agriculturists become qualified to assume that rank in society to which the importance of their calling, and their numbers, entitle them, and which intelligence and self-respect can alone give them."

Rank in society! That was close to the heart of the matter, for the farmer was beginning to realize acutely not merely that the best of the world's goods were to be had in the cities and that the urban middle and upper classes had much more of them than he did but also that he was losing in status and respect as compared with them. He became aware that the official respect paid to the farmer masked a certain disdain felt by many city people. In time the eulogies of country life that appeared in farm journals lost their pleasantly complacent tone and took on some of the sharpness of a "defensive gesture against real or imagined slurs." "There has . . . a certain class of individuals grown up in our land," complained a farm writer in 1835, "who treat the cultivators of the soil as an inferior caste . . . whose utmost abilities are confined to the merit of being able to discuss a boiled potato and a rasher of bacon." The city was symbolized as the home of loan sharks, dandies, fops, and aristocrats with European ideas who despised farmers as hayseeds. One writer spoke in a magnificent stream of mixed metaphor of "the butterflies who flutter over them in British broadcloth, consuming the fruits of the sweat of their brows."

The growth of the urban market intensified this antagonism. In areas like colonial New England, where an intimate connection had existed between the small town and the adjacent countryside, where a community of interests and even of occupations cut across the town line, the rural-urban hostility had not developed so sharply as in the newer areas where the township plan was never instituted and where isolated farmsteads were more common. As settlement moved west, as urban markets grew, as self-sufficient farmers became rarer, as farmers pushed into commercial production for the cities they feared and distrusted, they quite correctly thought of themselves as a vocational and economic group rather than as members of a neighborhood. In the Populist era the city was totally alien territory to many farmers, and the primacy of agriculture as a source of wealth was reasserted with much bitterness. "The great cities rest upon our broad and fertile prairies," declared Bryan in his Cross of Gold speech. "Burn down your cities and leave our farms, and your cities will spring up again as if by magic; but destroy our farms, and the grass will grow in the streets of every city in the country." Out of the beliefs nourished by the agrarian myth there had arisen the notion that the city was a parasitical growth on the country. Bryan spoke for a people raised for generations on the idea that the farmer was a very special creature, blessed by God, and that in a country consisting largely of farmers the voice of the farmer was the voice of democracy and of virtue itself. The agrarian myth encouraged farmers to believe that they were not themselves an organic part of the whole order of business enterprise and speculation that flourished in the city, partaking of its character and sharing in its risks, but rather the innocent pastoral victims of a conspiracy hatched in the distance. The notion of an innocent and victimized populace colors the whole history of agrarian controversy, and indeed the whole history of the populistic mind.

For the farmer it was bewildering, and irritating too, to think of the great contrast between the verbal deference paid him by almost everyone and the real status, the real economic position, in which he found himself. Improving his economic position was always possible, though this was often done too little and too late; but it was not within anyone's power to stem the decline in the rural values and pieties, the gradual rejection of the moral commitments that had been expressed in the early exaltations of agrarianism. It was the fate of the farmer himself, as we shall see, to contribute to this decline. Like almost all good Americans he had innocently sought progress from the very beginning, and thus hastened the decline of many of his own values. Elsewhere the rural classes had usually looked to the past, had been bearers of tradition and upholders of stability. The American farmer looked to the future alone, and the story of the American land became a study in futures. In the very hours of its birth as a nation Crevecoeur had congratulated America for having, in effect, no feudal past and no industrial present, for having no royal, aristocratic, ecclesiastical, or monarchical power, and no manufacturing class, and had rapturously concluded: "We are the most perfect society now existing in the world." Here was the irony from which the farmer suffered above all others: the United States was the only country in the world that began with perfection and aspired to progress.

The Farmer and the Realities. To what extent was the agrarian myth actually false? When it took form in America during the eighteenth century, its stereotypes did indeed correspond to many of the realities of American agricultural life. There were commercial elements in colonial agriculture almost from the earliest days, but there were also large numbers of the kind of independent yeomen idealized in the myth, men who had remarkable self-sufficiency and bequeathed to their children a strong penchant for craftsmanlike improvisation and a tradition of household industry. For a long time the commercial potentialities of agriculture were held in check by severe obstacles. Only the farmers very near to the rivers and the towns had adequate transportation. The small industrial population provided a very limited domestic market, and the villagers raised a large part of their own food. Outside the South operations above the size of the family farm were cramped by the absence of a force of wage laborers. At the beginning of the nineteenth century, when the American population was still living largely in the forests, poised at the edge of the Appalachians, and standing on the verge of the great drive across the prairies that occupied settlers for half a century, the yeoman was by no means a fiction.

The early panegyrists of the agrarian myth were, of course, aware of the commercial farmers, but it was this independent yeoman who caught their fancy. Admiring the natural abundance produced and consumed by the family on its own farm, they assumed that the family farm would always be, as it so frequently was in the early days, a diversified and largely self-sufficient unit. Even Jefferson, who was far from a humble yeoman, and whose wants were anything but simple, succeeded to a remarkable degree in living up to the ideal of self-sufficiency. Like many planters, he numbered among his slaves a balanced group of craftsmen; and even if the luxuries of Jefferson the planter had to be imported, the necessities at least of Jefferson the farmer, and of all his "people," were yielded by his own land. This was also the goal set by the theorists for the yeoman. Making at home almost everything he needed, buying little, using each year but a pocketful of cash, he would be as independent of the marketplace as he was of the favors of others. The yeoman, too, valued this self-sufficiency and the savings it made possible, but he seems to have valued it more often than not as a means through which he could eventually enter the marketplace rather than as a means of avoiding it. "My farm," said a farmer of Jefferson's time, "gave me and my family a good living on the produce of it; and left me, one year with another, one hundred and fifty silver dollars, for I have never spent more than ten dollars a year, which was for salt, nails, and the like. Nothing to wear, eat, or drink was purchased, as my farm provided all. With this saving, I put money to interest, bought cattle, fatted and sold them, and made great profit." Here, then, was the significance of self-sufficiency for the characteristic family farmer: "great profit." Commercialism had already begun to enter the American Arcadia.

From colonial days there had always been before the eyes of the yeoman farmer in the settled areas alluring models of commercial success in agriculture: the tobacco, rice, and indigo planters of the South, the grain, meat, and cattle exporters of the middle colonies. In America the spirit of emulation was exceptionally strong, the opportunities were considerable. The farmer knew that without cash he could never rise above the hardships and squalor of pioneering and log-cabin life. Self-sufficiency produced savings, and savings went into the purchase of more land, of herds and flocks, of better tools; they erected barns and silos and better dwellings, and made other improvements. When there was spare time, the farmer often worked off the farm to add to his cash resources, at first in trapping, hunting, fishing, or lumbering, later in the maintenance and repair of railroads. Domestic politics were persistently affected by his desire for the means of getting a cash crop to market, for turnpikes and canals. The foreign policy of the early Republic was determined again and again by the clamor of farmers to keep open the river outlets for American produce.

Between 1815 and 1860 the character of American agriculture was transformed. The independent yeoman, outside of exceptional or isolated areas, almost disappeared before the relentless advance of commercial agriculture. The rise of native idustry created a home market for agriculture, while at the same time demands arose abroad, at first for American cotton and then for American foodstuffs. A network of turnpikes, canals, and railroads linked the planter and the advancing Western farmer to these new markets, while the Eastern farmer, spurred by Western competition, began to cultivate more thoroughly the nearby urban outlets for his products. As the farmer moved out onto the flat, rich prairies, he found possibilities for the use of machinery that did not exist in the forest. Before long he was cultivating the prairies with horse-drawn mechanical reapers, steel plows, wheat and corn drills, and threshers. The cash crop converted the yeoman into a small entrepreneur, and the development of horse-drawn machinery made obsolete the simple old agrarian symbol of the plow. Farmers ceased to be free of what the early agrarian writers had called the "corruptions" of trade. They were, to be sure, still "independent," in the sense that they owned their own land. They were a hardworking lot in the old tradition. But no longer did they grow or manufacture what they needed: they concentrated on the cash crop and began to buy more and more of their supplies from the country store. To take full advantage of mechanization, they engrossed as much land as they could. To mechanize fully, they borrowed cash. Where they could not buy or borrow they might rent: by the 1850's Illinois farmers who could not afford machines and large barns were hiring itinerant jobbers with machines to do their threshing. The shift from self-sufficient to commercial farming varied in time throughout the West and cannot be dated with precision, but it was complete in Ohio by about 1830 and twenty years later in Indiana, Illinois, and Michigan. All through the great Northwest, farmers whose ancestors might have lived in isolation and self-sufficiency were surrounded by jobbers, banks, stores, middlemen, horses, and machinery; and in so far as this process was unfinished in 1860, the demands of the Civil War brought it to completion. . . .

The triumph of commercial agriculture not only rendered obsolete the objective conditions that had given to the agrarian myth so much of its original force, but also showed that the ideal implicit in the myth was contesting the ground with another, even stronger ideal—the notion of opportunity, of career, of the self-made man. The same forces in American life that had made Jacksonian equalitarianism possible and had given to the equalitarian theme in the agrarian romance its most compelling appeal had also unleashed in the nation and entrepreneurial zeal probably without precedent in history, a rage for business, for profits, for opportunity, for advancement. If the yeoman family was to maintain itself in the simple terms eulogized in the myth, it had to produce consistently a type of character that was satisfied with a traditional way of life. But the Yankee farmer, continually exposed to the cult of success that was everywhere around him, became inspired by a kind of personal dynamism which called upon the individual to surpass traditions. He was in terms that David Riesman has made familiar, not a tradition-directed but an inner-directed man. Agrarian sentiment sanctified labor in the soil and the simple life, but the prevailing Calvinist atmosphere of rural life implied that virtue was rewarded, after all, with success and material goods.

From the standpoint of the familiar agrarian panegyrics, the supreme irony was that the immense interior that had been supposed to underwrite the dominion of the yeoman for centuries did as much as anything else to destroy the yeomanlike spirit and replace it with the spirit of the businessman, even of the gambler. Cheap land invited extensive and careless cultivation. Rising land values in areas of new settlement tempted early liquidation and frequent moves, and made of the small entrepreneur a land speculator. Already in the late eighteenth century writers on American agriculture noticed that American farmers were tempted to buy more land than they could properly cultivate. . . .

Frequent and sensational rises in land values bred a boom psychology in the American farmer and caused him to rely for his margin of profit more on the process of appreciation than on the sale of crops. It took a strong man to resist the temptation to ride skyward on lands that might easily triple or quadruple their value in one decade and then double again in the next. It seemed ultraconservative to improve existing possessions if one could put savings or borrowings into new land. What developed in America was an agricultural society whose real attachment was not to the land but to land values. . . .

The penchant for speculation and the lure of new and different lands bred in the American farmer a tremendous passion for moving—and not merely, as one common view would have it, on the part of those who had failed, but also on the part of those who had succeeded. For farmers who had made out badly, the fresh lands may have served on occasion as a safety valve, but for others who were beginning a farming "career," it was equally a risk valve—an opportunity to exploit the full possibilities of the great American land bubble. Mobility among farmers had serious effects upon an agricultural tradition never noted for careful cultivation: in a nation whose soil is notoriously heterogeneous, farmers too often had little chance to get to know the quality of their land; they failed to plan and manure and replenish; they neglected diversification for the one-crop system and ready cash. There was among them little attachment to land or locality; instead there developed the false euphoria of local "boosting," encouraged by railroads, land companies, and farmers themselves; in place of village contacts and communal spirit based upon ancestral attachments, there was professional optimism based upon hopes for a quick rise in values.

In a very real and profound sense, then, the United States failed to develop (except in some localities, chiefly in the East) a distinctively *rural* culture. If a rural culture means an emotional and craftsmanlike dedication to the soil, a traditional and pre-capitalist outlook, a tradition-directed rather than career-directed type of character, and a village community devoted to ancestral ways and habitually given to communal action, then the prairies and plains never had one. What differentiated the agricultural life of these regions from the practices widespread in European agriculture—or, for that matter, from the stereotype of the agrarian myth—was not simply that it produced for a market but that it was so speculative, so mobile, so mechanized, so "progressive," so thoroughly imbued with the commercial spirit.

Immigrant farmers, who really were yeomen with a background of genuine agrarian values, were frequently bewildered at the ethos of American agriculture. Marcus Hansen points out: "The ambition of the German-American father, for instance, was to see his sons on reaching manhood established with their families on farms clustered about his own. To take complete possession of a township with sons, sons-in-law and nephews was not an unrealizable ideal. To this end the would-be patriarch dedicated all his plodding industry. One by one, he bought adjacent farms, the erstwhile owners joining the current to the farther West. Heavily timbered acres and swamp lands which had been lying unused were prepared for cultivation by patient and unceasing toil. 'When the German comes in, the Yankee goes out,' was a local proverb that varied as Swedes, Bohemians or other immigrant groups formed the invading element. But the American father made no such efforts on behalf of his offspring. To be a self-made man was his ideal. He had come in as a 'first settler' and had created a farm with his ax; let the boys do the same. One of them perhaps was kept at home as a helper to his aging parents; the rest set out to achieve beyond the mountains or beyond the river what the father had accomplished in the West of his day. Thus mobility was fostered by family policy." The continuing influx of immigrants, ready to settle on cleared and slightly improved land, greatly facilitated the Yankee race across the continent.

American agriculture was also distinguishable from European agriculture in the kind of rural life and political culture it sustained. In Europe the managers of agriculture and the owners of land were characteristically either small peasant proprietors, or substantial landholders of traditional and conservative outlook with powerful political and military connections. The American farmer, whose holdings were not so extensive as those of the grandee nor so tiny as those of the peasant, whose psychology was Protestant and bourgeois, and whose politics were petty-capitalist rather than traditionalist, had no reason to share the social outlook of the rural classes of Europe. In Europe land was limited and dear, while labor was abundant and relatively cheap; in America this ratio between land and labor was inverted. In Europe small farmers lived in villages, where generations of the same family were reared upon the same soil, and where careful cultivation and the minute elimination of waste were necessary to support a growing population on a limited amount of land. Endless and patient labor, including the labor of peasant women and children exploited to a degree to which the Yankee would not go except under the stress of pioneering conditions, was available to conserve and tailor the land and keep it fertile. On limited plots cultivated by an ample labor force, the need for machinery was not urgent, and hence the demand for liquid capital in large amounts was rare. Diversification, self-sufficiency, and the acceptance of a low standard of living also contributed to hold down this demand. Much managerial skill was required for such an agricultural regime, but it was the skill of the craftsman and the traditional tiller of the soil. Village life provided a community and a co-operative milieu, a pooling of knowledge and lore, a basis of common action to minimize risks.

In America the greater availability of land and the scarcity of labor made for extensive agriculture, which was wasteful of the soil, and placed a premium on machines to bring large tracts under cultivation. His demand for expensive machinery, his expectation of higher standards of living, and his tendency to go into debt to acquire extensive acreage created an urgent need for cash and tempted the farmer into capitalizing more and more on his greatest single asset: the unearned appreciation in the value of his land. The managerial skill required for success under these conditions was as much businesslike as craftsmanlike. The predominance in American agriculture of the isolated farmstead standing in the midst of great acreage, the frequent movements, the absence of village life, deprived the farmer and his family of the advantages of community, lowered the chances of association and co-operation, and encouraged that rampant, suspicious, and almost suicidal individualism for which the American farmer was long noted and which organizations like the Grange tried to combat. The characteristic product of American rural society was not a yeoman or a villager, but a harassed little country businessman who worked very hard, moved all too often, gambled with his land, and made his way alone.

The Frontier or the Market? The American farmer was unusual in the agricultural world in the sense that he was running a mechanized and commercialized agricultural unit of a size far greater than the small proprietary holdings common elsewhere, and yet he was running it as a family enterprise on the assumption that the family could supply not only the necessary capital and managerial talent but also most of the labor. This system, however applicable to the subsistence farm or the small yeoman's farm, was hardly adequate to the conditions of commercial agriculture. As a businessman, the farmer was appropriately hardheaded; he tried to act upon a cold and realistic strategy of self-interest. As the head of a family, however, the farmer felt that he was investing not only his capital but his hard work and that of his wife and children, that when he risked his farm he risked his home—that he was, in short, a single man running a personal enterprise in a world of impersonal forces. It was from this aspect of his situation—seen in the hazy glow of the agrarian myth—that his political leaders in the 1890's developed their rhetoric and some of their concepts of political action. The farmer's commercial position pointed to the usual strategies of the business world: combination, co-operation, pressure politics, lobbying, piecemeal activity directed toward specific goals. But the bathos of the agrarian rhetoric pointed in a different direction: broad political goals, ideological mass politics, third parties, the conquest of the "money power," the united action of all labor, rural and urban. When times were persistently bad, the farmer tended to reject his business role and its failures to withdraw into the role of the injured little yeoman. This made the differences between his situation and that of any other victim of exploitation seem unimportant to him. As a Southern journalist wrote of the situation in the cotton country: "The landowner was so poor and distressed that he forgot that he was a capitalist . . . so weary of hand and sick of spirit that he imagined himself in precisely the same plight as the hired man . . ."

The American farmer thus had a dual character, and one way of understanding our agrarian movements is to observe which aspect of the farmer's double personality is uppermost at a given time. It is my contention that both the Populist rhetoric and the modern liberal's indulgent view of the farmers' revolt have been derived from the "soft" side of the farmer's existence—that is, from agrarian "radicalism" and agrarian ideology—while most farm organizations since the decline of the Populists have been based primarily upon the "hard" side, upon agricultural improvement, business methods, and pressure politics. Populism itself had a hard side, especially in the the early days of the Farmers' Alliance and the Populist Party, but this became less and less important as the depression of the nineties deepened and other issues were dropped in favor of the silver panacea.

Most of our views of the historical significance of Populism have been formed by the study of the frontier process and the settlement of the internal empire. This approach turned attention to some significant aspects of American agrarian development, but also diverted attention from others. To a writer like Frederick Jackson Turner the farmer on the plains was significant above all as the carrier of the traditions of the frontier. To Turner the frontier, or the West, was the primary source of most of "what has been distinctive and valuable in America's contributions to the history of the human spirit. . . ." Hence the primary interest of the Populist lay in the fact that he was "a survival of the pioneer, striving to adjust present conditions to his old ideals." While Turner did on occasion comment on the capitalistic and speculative character of the

farmer, he saw this as something of no special importance, when compared with the farmer's role as the bearer of the yeoman tradition and
"the old pioneer ideals of the native American. . . ." The chief difference
between Populist thinking and the pioneer tradition, Turner felt, was
that the Populists showed an increasing sense of the need for governmental help in realizing the old ideals. His explanation of this change in
philosophy—indeed, of the entire agrarian revolt of the 1890's—was formulated in the light of the frontier theory and the alleged exhaustion of
"free" land. "Failures in one area can no longer be made good by taking
up land on a new frontier," he wrote in 1896. "The conditions of settled
society are being reached with suddenness and with confusion. . . . The
frontier opportunities are gone. Discontent is demanding an extension of
governmental activity in its behalf. . . . A people composed of heterogeneous materials, with diverse and conflicting ideals and social interests,
having passed from the task of filling up the vacant spaces of the continent, is now thrown back upon itself and is seeking an equilibrium."
The idea that the agrarian uprising was precipitated by the disappearance of the frontier and the exhaustion of the public domain has also
been given the scholarly support of John D. Hicks's standard history of
The Populist Revolt. Earlier discontents, Hicks concluded, had been
lightened by the departure of the restless and disgruntled for the West, a
process that created new opportunities for them and eased the pressure
on those they left behind. But by the nineties, "with the lands all taken
and the frontier gone, this safety valve was closed. The frontier was
turned back on itself. The restless and discontented voiced their sentiments more and fled from them less."

The conclusion that it was the West, the frontier spirit, that produced
American democracy, and that Populism was the logical product of this
spirit, is a deceptive inheritance from the Turnerian school. The decisive
role played by the South in Populism suggests instantly the limitations of
this view. Terms that are superficially appealing when applied to Kansas
become meaningless when applied to Georgia. Southern Populism, which
could hardly have been close to the frontier spirit, was at least as strong
as the Western brand and contained the more radical wing of the agrarian revolt of the nineties. Moreover, the extent to which "the West" as a
whole supported the agrarian revolt has commonly been exaggerated, as
the distribution of Populist votes in 1892 and of Bryan votes in 1896
clearly shows. Populism had only three compact centers. Each was over-
whelmingly rural. Each was dominated by a product whose price had
catastrophically declined: the South, based chiefly upon cotton; a narrow
tier of four Northwestern states, Kansas, Nebraska, and the two Dakotas,
based upon wheat; and the mountain states, based chiefly upon silver.
Silver is a special case, though strategically an important one, and we can
for the moment postpone consideration of it, except to remark that the
free-silver Populism of the mountain-states variety was not agrarian
Populism at all, but simply silverism. Elsewhere agrarian discontent,

where it reached a peak of local intensity sufficient to yield an independent Populist Party of notable strength or to win a state for Bryan in 1896, was roughly coterminous with the cash-staple export crops and the burden of heavy mortgage indebtedness.

The common tendency to focus upon the internal frontier as the matrix of Populism has obscured the great importance of the agrarian situation in the external world, which is profoundly relevant to both Southern and Western Populism. The frontier obsession has been identified in America with a kind of intellectual isolationism. The larger and more important answer to the causes of the agrarian crises of the 1890's must be found not in the American West, but in the international market. While American Populism has been seen almost solely in terms of domestic events and the internal frontier, the entire European and American world was shaken by an agrarian crisis that knew no national boundaries and that struck at several nations without internal frontiers on the verge of real or imagined exhaustion. "Almost everywhere," declared an English observer in 1893, "certainly in England, France, Germany, Italy, Scandinavia, and the United States, the agriculturists, formerly so instinctively conservative, are becoming fiercely discontented, declare they gain less by civilization than the rest of the community, and are looking about for remedies of a drastic nature."

During the last three decades of the nineteenth century a revolution took place in international communications. For the first time the full effects of steam locomotion and steam navigation were felt in international trade. In 1869 the Suez Canal was opened and the first transcontinental railroad in the United States was completed. Europe was connected by submarine cable with the United States in 1866, and with South America in 1874. A great network of telegraph and telephone communication was spun throughout the world. Huge tracts of new land being settled in Argentina, Australia, Canada, and the American West were now pulled together in one international market, while improvements in agricultural technology made possible the full exploitation of areas susceptible to extensive and mechanized cultivation. Agrarian depressions, formerly of a local or national character, now became international, and with them came international agrarian discontent, heightened by the almost uninterrupted international price decline that occurred from the early 1870's to the 1890's. It is hardly accidental that the products of the American staple-growing regions showing the highest discontent were the products most dependent upon exports.

The notion that the unavailability of free land for further expansion of the American farming system was chiefly responsible for the remarkable surge of agrarian discontent no longer seems credible. It is true that many Americans, including some Populist spokesmen, were concerned during the 1890's about what they thought to be the imminent disappearance of the public domain. There was also a school of thought among those interested in the agrarian problem that took pleasure in the prospect that the approaching exhaustion of new lands would lower the expansion of the agricultural economy to the point at which the values of already settled land would begin to rise sharply, and thus put an end to the problem of settled farmers. However, the entire conception of exhausted resources has been re-examined and found to be delusive; actually an abundance of new land was available long after the so-called disappearance of the frontier in 1890. During the decade 1890–1900, in which the discontent was most acute, 1,100,000 new farms were settled, 500,000 more than the number in the previous decade. In the twenty years after the farmers' organizations met in 1890 at Ocala, Florida, to formulate their demands, 1,760,000 new farms and 225,600,000 new acres were added to the nation's agricultural domain. More land, indeed, was taken up after 1890 under the terms of the Homestead Act and its successors than had been taken up before. True, a high proportion of this was suitable only for grazing and dry farming, but the profitability of land is a result not merely of soil chemistry or soil humidity but also of the economic circumstances under which the land is cultivated; the condition of the market in the early years of the twentieth century admitted of more profitable cultivation of these relatively barren lands than of much richer lands in the depressed period. Finally, there were after 1890 still more supplies of rich land in Canada, which farmers from the United States did not hestitate to occupy. In 1914, Canadian officials estimated that 925,000 Americans had moved, chiefly during the sixteen years past, across the border to the lands of Alberta and Saskatchewan. Lavish opportunities to settle on new lands or open new acres were still available after 1890, and in fact much use was made of these opportunities during the nineties. In so far as farmers were deterred from further settlement, it was not by the absence of land but because the international agrarian depression made the nineties a hazardous time to begin a farm.

The conception that the end of free or cheap land was primarily responsible for precipitating discontent implies that the existence of such land had been effective in alleviating it, and suggests that the effects of the Homestead Act up to about 1890 were what had been hoped for at the time of its passage. But the Homestead Act had never been successful in creating the inland freehold empire that agrarian reformers had dreamed of. Its maladministration and its circumvention by speculators and railroads is by now well known. From 1860 to 1900, for every free farm entered and kept by a bona fide farmer under the act there were about nine bought from railroads or speculators or from the government itself. Speculators, engrossing immense tracts of land under the privilege of unrestricted "entry," which was not abolished until 1888, did far more damage to rural society in the West than merely transmitting "free" land to farmers at substantial prices. They drove immigrants to remote parts of the frontier; they created "speculators' deserts"—large tracts of uncultivated absentee-owned land—and thus added to the dispersal of the population, making the operation of roads and railroads far more costly than necessary; they refused to pay taxes, thus damaging local government finances and limiting local improvements; they added to all the characteristic evils of our rural culture while they built up land prices and kept a large portion of the farm population in a state of tenancy.

The promise of free Homestead land or cheap land was self-defeating. The Homestead Act itself, which required five years of residence before title to a free farm was granted, was based upon the assumption that settlement would take place in a gradual and stable way, after the manner of the mythical yeoman. It made no allowance for the mobile habits of the American farmer. The number of forfeited entries under the Homestead Act was extraordinary. What effect the Homestead Act *might* have had if the West had been gradually settled by yeoman farmers protected from speculators and living after the fashion of the myth seems no more than a utopian conjecture. As it worked out, the Homestead Act was a triumph for speculative and capitalistic forces, and it translated cheap or free land into a stimulus for more discontent than it could quiet. The promise of the Homestead Act was a lure for over-rapid settlement in regions where most settlers found, instead of the agrarian utopia, a wilderness of high costs, low returns, and mortgages. . . .

It is evident that Western Populism was, among other things, the outgrowth of a period of incredible expansion, one of the greatest in the world history of agriculture. From 1870 to 1900 more new farm land was taken up than in all previous American history. By the mid-eighties a feverish land boom was under way, and it is the collapse of this boom that provides the immediate background of Western Populism. We may take the experience of Kansas as illustrative. The boom, originally based on the high prices of farm produce, had reached the point of artificial inflation by 1885. It had swept not only the country, where the rapid advance in prices had caused latecomers to buy and mortgage at hopelessly inflated values, but also the rising towns, which were all "bonded to the limit for public improvements [and] public utilities." . . . In the winter of 1887–8 this boom, which had been encouraged by railroads, newspapers, and public officials, abruptly collapsed—in part because of drought in the western third of the state, in part because farm prices had stopped going up, and in part because the self-created confidence upon which the fever fed had broken.

The fathers of the Homestead Act and the fee-simple empire had acted upon a number of assumptions stemming from the agrarian myth which were out of date even before the act was passed. They trusted to the beneficence of nature, to permanent and yeomanlike nonspeculative settlement; they expected that the land really would pass without cost into the hands of the great majority of settlers; and they took it for granted that the native strength of the farmer would continue to rest upon the abundance produced on and for the farm. These assumptions were incongruous with the Industrial Revolution that was already well under way by 1862 and with the Communications Revolution that was soon to come; they were incongruous even with the natural character of the plains, with their winds, sandstorms, droughts, and grasshoppers. And the farmer, caught in the toils of cash-crop commercial farming, did not, and could not, reckon his prosperity by the abundance produced on the farm but rather by the exchange value of his products as measured by the supplies and services they could buy. His standard of living, as well as the security of his home, became dependent upon his commercial position, which in turn was dependent upon the vicissitudes of the world market.

In pointing to the farmer's commercial role I am not trying to deny the difficulties of his position or the reality and seriousness of his grievances: the appreciation of debts through deflation, the high cost of credit, inequitable tax burdens, discriminatory railroad rates, unreasonable elevator and storage charges. Populism can best be understood, however, not as a product of the frontier inheritance, but as another episode in the well-established tradition of American entrepreneurial radicalism, which goes back at least to the Jacksonian era. It was an effort on the part of a few important segments of a highly heterogeneous capitalistic agriculture to restore profits in the face of much exploitation and under unfavorable market and price conditions. It arose as a part of a transitional stage in the history of American agriculture, in which the commercial farmer was beginning to cast off habits of thought and action created almost as much by the persistence of the agrarian myth as by the realities of his position. He had long since taken from business society its acquisitive goals and its speculative temper, but he was still practicing the competitive individualism that the most advanced sectors of industry and finance had outgrown. He had not yet learned much from business about its marketing devices, strategies of combination, or skills of self-defense and self-advancement through pressure politics. His dual identity itself was not yet resolved. He entered the twentieth century still affected by his yeoman inheritance but with a growing awareness of the businesslike character of his future.

The war with Spain marks a watershed in the history of the United States. As a result of the war, the United States, hitherto without overseas possessions, acquired territory and interests in the Caribbean and in the Pacific, and as a result became a colonial power. Why the United States went to war and accepted an empire is still a major question in American historiography.

At one time it was fashionable to place sole responsibility for wars and imperial adventures on ambitious industrial and financial interests that sought outlets abroad for capital and products. The eminent British economist J. A. Hobson, in his study of imperialism, gave this view classic form. Subsequently, Marxists and other economic determinists made it the basis for their own interpretations. The economic explanation is, of course, plausible.

As a cause for America's going to war against Spain in 1898, and as a reason for annexing territory, the economic motivation is not the principal one. There were probably some Americans who wished war and supported imperialism for economic advantage, but in general the business community opposed the war, and for quite understandable reasons. Wars disrupt prosperity, endanger currency, and interrupt normal channels of trade. The *Magazine of Wall Street* put it neatly in 1931 on the occasion of another crisis: "War is a profligate paymaster and a reckless buyer. . . . War spends lavishly and collects brutally. War 'bulls' commodities and generates 'a howling war boom' but is followed by a terrific collapse and a period of painful adjustment." As a prominent Boston cotton broker wrote to Senator Henry Cabot Lodge in 1898, "The business interests of the state require peace and quiet, not war." Business was just recovering from the depression of 1893 and feared the effect of a war.

The researches of Julius W. Pratt indicate conclusively that the leading business, financial, and commercial newspapers and periodicals, the chambers of commerce and boards of trade, and the individuals most concerned with the economic life of the nation opposed involvement. Indeed, those who wanted war—Henry Cabot Lodge, Theodore Roosevelt, Albert Beveridge, Henry Adams, Alfred Thayer Mahan—thoroughly castigated businessmen as sordid money-grubbers, as men who were traitorous and unpatriotic, who lacked heroism and virility. This was not the first time that the business community had reacted against those who would involve the country in war. It is worth recalling that some three years earlier, when Secretary of State Richard Olney assumed a war-like posture during a crisis with Great Britain over the Venezuela boundary, stocks dropped a half-billion dollars on the New York Stock Exchange, and Wall Street panicked. At that time, Henry Adams wrote

5

THE NEW MANIFEST DESTINY

179

to his brother, "State Street [the Boston counterpart of Wall Street] is furious, pathetic, and desperate about Olney's manners." And Theodore Roosevelt was revolted by the "patriots of the ticker."

As for acquiring colonies, manufacturing interests did not generally consider colonies necessary or even desirable as markets or as sources of raw materials. Colonies were expensive to maintain and to defend, and their people did not always serve as willing purchasers or suppliers. Having long since abandoned the mercantilist doctrines of the seventeenth and eighteenth centuries, and operating within the framework of the British liberal Manchester school of economics, the American manufacturers believed that the best guarantee of a foreign market was to produce goods of highest quality at the cheapest price. It is true, however, that at the end of the century certain developments—such as the race for "spheres of influence" in China, as well as a move by some European countries to keep American imports out—tended to limit the area of free competition in Europe and Asia and inclined the manufacturers to seek colonial spheres for themselves.

To understand why America fought in 1898, one must look beyond economic motivation. One possibility is the disgust felt by Americans over Spain's treatment of Cuban revolutionaries. Americans knew, however, before war was declared, that a new liberal government in Spain had overhauled its Cuban policy, had dismissed General Valeriano Weyler—the man responsible for much of the savagery—and had, to some degree, humanized its method of suppressing the revolt. It is also true that the American people were furious with Spain over the sinking of the battleship *Maine* in Havana harbor. But an international incident such as the destruction of the *Maine,* exciting though it may be, is never in itself a cause for war unless there is a will to war. The sinking of the *Lusitania* in 1915 was just as troublesome an incident, but war did not come for two years.

It is, therefore, the will to war that must be investigated. Why, in April 1898, did the American people want to fight Spain? Why were they, in the words of Samuel Flagg Bemis, "ready for new adventures, new excitements, a new position in the world?" These questions are especially important in view of the fact that in the '70s and '80s Americans had turned their backs on war and expansion. The Cuban revolt had been going on since 1868, but few people in the United States had clamored to fight for the rebels.

The explanation for the change lies in a new intellectual climate created by Charles Darwin's theory of evolution through natural selection, which he proposed in *Origin of Species* (1859). Darwin's idea that in the struggle for existence in the natural world only the fittest survive was carried by himself and others into the realm of human affairs, resulting in the glorification of the Anglo-Saxons and Teutons as those most capable of surviving in the international arena of conflict. Various agencies of dissemination (lecturers, essayists, politicians, the press, and churches) spread these views across America in the last fifteen years of the century, popularized them, and translated them into a program for positive action and into a mission for Americans. By the end of the century, the American people—under continual exhortation to assert their greatness by subjugating lesser folk—found Spain the perfect target for their crusade. It was in the Spanish possessions that they would fulfill their destiny to carry their civilization to benighted peoples; and so they fought.

Historian John Fiske, clergyman Josiah Strong, political scientist John Burgess and naval historian Alfred Thayer Mahan were the principal literary figures who contributed to the new climate. Fiske, in numerous books, essays, and lectures, told of the superiority of the Anglo-Saxons and their institutions. Strong, in *Our Country* (1885), stated with confidence that "the Anglo-Saxon is the representative of two great ideas . . . civil liberty . . . [and] pure *spiritual* Christianity. . . . As the depository of these two great blessings . . . [he] is divinely commanded to be . . . his brother's keeper." Burgess, in *Political Science and Comparative Constitutional Law* (1890), extolled the virtues of the race. And Mahan, in books and articles, urged his fellow countrymen to build a great navy, increase their merchant fleet, extend their commerce, gain coaling stations, and, in general, be aggressive and vigorous.

Admittedly, such speeches and writings reached only those who attended lectures and read scholarly books and magazines such as *Harper's* and *Forum*. But the message reached a wider circle of ordinary Americans through other means. Politicians like Theodore Roosevelt, Henry Cabot Lodge, Albert Beveridge, and Henry M. Teller adopted the new views from conviction or for political capital and supported them in speeches to constituents. Churchmen—Protestant and Catholic—saw opportunities for missionary endeavor in the new ideas and made them subjects of sermons. Newspapermen like Joseph Pulitzer and William Randolph Hearst found the new spirit useful for selling newspapers and featured it in their respective New York dailies, the *World* and the *Journal,* which were then in the midst of a struggle for primacy in circulation.

As Richard Hofstadter has pointed out, this avalanche of propaganda fell on ears most receptive. The American people at the end of the century were taut, frustrated, discontented, and despondent; they were in the throes of a "psychic crisis." Corruption existed on every level, public and private; farmers were impoverished, labor oppressed, free competition curtailed by the giant trusts, and opportunities diminished by the disappearance of the frontier (solemnly stated in the census report of 1890); all these problems caused Americans to wish to seek release in a bold adventure.

It must not be supposed that America spoke with one voice in support of war and expansion. Throughout the '90s, important and articulate people such as Carl Schurz, David Starr Jordan, William James, and

Mark Twain opposed war and expansion. They warned that fighting a war and acquiring colonies violated every precept upon which the Republic was based and ignored every warning of the Founding Fathers and their successors. They quoted the Declaration of Independence to prove that no people should be ruled without their own consent. They cited George Washington's Farewell Address to urge Americans not to involve themselves in foreign entanglements. They predicted the destruction of American democracy if alien peoples unsuited to democratic practices were joined to the United States.

But the anti-imperialists could not halt the tide. They could not prevent the war or the acquisition of colonies. Their defeat, as Fred H. Harrington has noted, can be attributed in part to their differences on other questions—differences that prevented them from presenting a really united front. Gold Democrats of the Grover Cleveland type felt uneasy alongside William Jennings Bryan silverites; conservative Republicans like George F. Hoar loathed Mugwumps like Carl Schurz. Chiefly, however, it was the imperialists' call to positive action at a time in our history when the soil was peculiarly suitable that defeated the anti-imperialists.

After the war with Spain, the spirit of manifest destiny and the excitement of 1898 receded. Nonetheless, the expansionist movement had made the United States an imperial power with possessions in distant places. The past could not easily be undone. We had an empire that we were not vitally interested in maintaining, and one that involved us in the politics and diplomacy of distant continents.

The selections in this chapter describe and illustrate business's opposition to war, the connection between Darwinism and imperialism, and the anti-imperialist movement.

Julius W. Pratt

Expansionists

of 1898

Julius W. Pratt, for many years a professor of history at the University of Buffalo, is the author of important studies on two of America's wars, 1812 and 1898. For both wars, he challenged existing interpretations and presented new theses on the origins of the conflicts. In relation to the war with Spain, his principal contribution was to demolish the view that the business interests of the country propelled the nation to war and led the movements to acquire colonies. After examining the writings of prominent businessmen, editorials in financial and trade journals, resolutions of boards of trade and chambers of commerce, and letters from interested citizens to the Department of State, he concluded that the business community opposed both the war and the acquisition of colonies. He sampled opinion from a wide variety of industries and businesses located in different parts of the country, and thus provided a broad base for his conclusions. [Julius W. Pratt, Expansionists of 1898 (Baltimore: The Johns Hopkins Press, 1936). Reprinted by permission.]

So reliable a scholar as Professor H. U. Faulkner has asserted that "the great cause for the war" with Spain is to be found in the fact that by 1898 the United States was "sufficiently advanced for financial imperialism," implying that the war was fought for markets and fields for investment. This interpretation was directly contradicted by the late James Ford Rhodes, who declared quite as categorically that "the financial and business interests of the country were opposed to the war." We may well enquire, therefore, what was, in reality, the attitude of American business both to the war (or to the intervention in Cuba, which brought on the war) and to the question of territorial expansion.

We may begin with a generalization, the evidence for which will be presented as the chapter proceeds. American business, in general, had strongly opposed action that would lead to war with Spain. American business had been either opposed or indifferent to the expansionist philosophy which had arisen since 1890. But almost at the moment when the war began, a large section of American business had, for reasons that will become apparent, been converted to the belief that a program of territorial expansion would serve its purposes. Hence business, in the end, welcomed the "large policy" and exerted its share of pressure for the retention of the Spanish islands and such related policies as the annexation of Hawaii and the construction of an isthmian canal.

One public man to whom the welfare of American business was of so much concern that he may almost be considered its spokesman in the Senate, was McKinley's friend, Mark Hanna. No one was more unwilling than he to see the United States drift into war with Spain. To Hanna, in the words of his biographer, "the outbreak of war seemed to imperil the whole policy of domestic economic amelioration which he placed before every other object of political action." Hanna's attitude appears to have been identical with that of leading business men. This conclusion is based not only upon the few published biographies of such men, but also upon the study of a large number of financial and trade periodicals, of the proceedings of chambers of commerce and boards of trade, and of material in the *Miscellaneous Files* of the Department of State, containing numerous letters and petitions from business men and organizations.

That business sentiment, especially in the East, was strongly anti-war at the close of 1897 and in the opening months of 1898, is hardly open to doubt. Wall Street stocks turned downward whenever the day's news seemed to presage war and climbed again with information favorable to peace. Bulls and bears on the market were those who anticipated, respectively, a peaceable and a warlike solution of the Cuban question. The "jingo," in Congress or the press, was an object of intense dislike to the editors of business and financial journals, who sought to counteract his influence by anti-war editorials in their columns. Boards of trade and chambers of commerce added their pleas for the maintenance of peace to those of the business newspapers and magazines. So marked, indeed, was the anti-war solidarity of the financial interests and their spokesmen that the jingoes fell to charging Wall Street with want of patriotism. Wall Street, declared the Sacramento *Evening Bee* (March 11, 1898), was "the colossal and aggregate Benedict Arnold of the Union, and the syndicated Judas Iscariot of humanity." Senator Thurston, of Nebraska, charged that opposition to war was found only among the "money-changers," bringing from the editor of *The American Banker* the reply that "there is not an intelligent, self-respecting and civilized American citizen anywhere who would not prefer to have the existing crisis culminate in peaceful negotiations."

This anti-war attitude on the part of several leading financial journals continued up to the very beginning of hostilities. The New York *Journal of Commerce and Commercial Bulletin* declared on February 28 that the only possible excuses for war would be (1) a finding by the naval board investigating the "Maine" disaster that the ship had been destroyed by an official act of the Spanish Government; or (2) a refusal by Spain to make reparation if the board should hold that she had failed to exercise due diligence in safeguarding the vessel. Either of these events it held to be almost inconceivable. The *Commercial and Financial Chronicle* expressed the belief on March 12 that the opposition of the financial interests would yet prevent war; and on April 2 the same journal branded as "monstrous" the proposition to settle the Cuban and "Maine" questions by war while the slightest chance remained for a peaceful solution. On April 16, after the House of Representatives had passed the Cuban resolutions, the Boston *Journal of Commerce* declared: "Sober second thought had but little to do with the deliberations. . . . The members were carried off their feet by the war fever that had been so persistently worked up since the Maine explosion."

The reasons for this attitude on the part of business are not far to seek. Since the panic of 1893 American business had been in the doldrums. Tendencies toward industrial revival had been checked, first by the Venezuela war scare in December, 1895, and again by the free silver menace in 1896. But in 1897 began a real revival, and before the end of the year signs of prosperity appeared on all sides. The New York *Commercial* conducted a survey of business conditions in a wide variety of trades and industries, from which it concluded that, "after three years of waiting and of false starts, the groundswell of demand has at last begun to rise with a steadiness which leaves little doubt that an era of prosperity has appeared." January, 1898, said the same article, is "a supreme moment in the period of transition from depression to comparative prosperity." This note of optimism one meets at every turn, even in such a careful and conservative sheet as the *Commercial and Financial Chronicle*. As early as July, 1897, this paper remarked: "We appear to be on the eve of a revival in business"; and in December after remarking upon the healthy condition of the railroads and the iron industry, it concluded: "In brief, no one can study the industrial conditions of today in America without a feeling of elation." The *Wall Street Journal* found only two "blue spots" in the entire country: Boston, which suffered from the depressed demand for cotton goods, and New York, where senseless rate cutting by certain railroads caused uneasiness. "Throughout the west, southwest and on the Pacific coast business has never been better, nor the people more hopeful."

A potent cause for optimism was found in the striking expansion of the American export trade. A volume of exports far in excess of those of any recent year, a favorable balance of trade of $286,000,000, and an especially notable increase in exports of manufactures of iron, steel, and copper, convinced practically every business expert that the United States was on the point of capturing the markets of the world. "There is no question," said one journal, "that the world, generally, is looking more and more to the United States as the source of its supply for very many of the staple commodities of life." Especially elated were spokesmen of the iron and steel industry. Cheaper materials and improved methods were enabling the American producer to undersell his British competitor in Europe and in the British possessions, and Andrew Carnegie was talking of a great shipbuilding yard near New York to take advantage of these low costs. The *Iron Age,* in an editorial on "The Future of Business," foretold the abolition of the business cycle by means of a better planned economy, consolidation of railroads and industries, reduction of margins of profit, higher wages, and lower prices to consumers.

To this fair prospect of a great business revival the threat of war was like a spectre at the feast. A foreign complication, thought the *Commercial and Financial Chronicle* in October, 1897, would quickly mar "the trade prosperity which all are enjoying." Six months later (April 2, 1898), after a discussion of the effect of war rumors on the stock exchange, it declared: "Every influence has been, and even now is, tending strongly towards a term of decided prosperity, and that the Cuban disturbance, and it alone, has arrested the movement and checked enterprise." The *Banker and Tradesman* saw in the Cuban complication the threat of a "material setback to the prosperous conditions which had just set in after five years of panic and depression." The same journal summarized a calculation made by the Boston *Transcript* showing that in February, 1898, the wave of prosperity had carried the average price of twenty-five leading stocks within 5½ points of the high for the preceding ten years and 30 points above the low of 1896, and that the Cuban trouble had, in a little over two months, caused a loss of over ten points, or more than one-third of the recent gain. "War would impede the march of prosperity and put the country back many years," said the *New Jersey Trade Review*. The *Railway Age* was of the opinion that the country was coming out of a depression and needed peace to complete its recovery. "From a commercial and mercenary standpoint," it remarked, "it seems peculiarly bitter that this war should have come when the country had already suffered so much and so needed rest and peace."

The idea that war could bring any substantial benefits to business was generally scouted. It would endanger our currency stability, interrupt our trade, and threaten our coasts and our commerce, thought the *Commercial and Financial Chronicle*. It would "incalculably increase the loss to business interests," said the *Banker's Magazine;* while the *United States Investor* held that war was "never beneficial from a material standpoint, that is, in the long run." The *Railroad Gazette* predicted that war would result in "interruption of business enterprise of every kind, stopping new projects and diminution of the output of existing businesses and contraction of trade everywhere." Railroads would lose more than they would gain. Even arms manufacturers were not all agreed that war would be desirable. Journals speaking for the iron and steel industry also argued that war would injure business. It "would injure the iron and steel makers ten times as much as they would be benefited by the prevailing spurt in the manufacture of small arms, projectiles and steel plates for war ships," in the opinion of one of these. The *American Wool and Cotton Reporter* of New York and the *Northwestern Miller* of Minneapolis agreed that war was never materially beneficial in the long run, while trade journals in Atlanta, Chattanooga, and Portland, Oregon, saw as fruits of the approaching conflict only destruction, debt, and depressed industry.

Many conservative interests feared war for the specific reason that it might derange the currency and even revive the free-silver agitation, which had seemed happily dead. The subsidence of that agitation and the prospect of currency reform were among the hopeful factors at the close of 1897. It was not uncommonly charged that the jingoes were animated in part by the expectation that war would lead to inflation in paper or silver. The New York *Journal of Commerce,* in an editorial on "The Breeding Grounds of Jingoism," had called attention to the fact that the jingoes were generally silverites, including in their number "the financiers who desire to force bankruptcy on the country as a means of breaking down the gold standard," and had quoted with approval an editorial from another paper charging that Senator Morgan's championship of the Cuban insurgents was part of "his wild scheming in the interest of the silver standard." The *Commercial and Financial Chronicle* endorsed this view, declaring that many of the Cuban agitators "are only interested in the establishment of a free-silver standard, a plan which they think war would advance." Similar views were expressed by the *American Banker* of New York, the *United States Investor* of Boston, and the *Rand-McNally Bankers' Monthly* of Chicago. The last-named quoted from a speech of Secretary of the Treasury Gage, delivered in Chicago in February, 1898, in which he had declared that "it would be scarcely possible for this nation to engage in war in its present condition . . . without a suspension of specie payments and a resort to further issues of Government notes." A war of any duration, in the opinion of the *United States Investor,* would certainly derange the currency and reduce business to a gambling basis. . . .

It remains to examine the attitude of certain American business men and corporations having an immediate stake in Cuba, or otherwise liable to be directly affected by American intervention. Much American capital, as is well known, was invested in the Cuban sugar industry. Upon this industry the civil war fell with peculiarly devasting effect, not only cutting off profits on capital so invested, but also crippling a valuable carrying trade between Cuba and the United States. Naturally enough, some firms suffering under these conditions desired to see the United States intervene to end the war, though such intervention might lead to war between the United States and Spain. In May, 1897, a memorial on the subject bearing over three hundred signatures was presented to John Sherman, Secretary of State. The signers described themselves as "citizens of the United States, doing business as bankers, merchants, manufacturers; steamship owners and agents in the cities of Boston, New York, Philadelphia, Baltimore, Savannah, Charleston, Jacksonville, New Orleans, and other places, and also other citizens of the United States, who have been for many years engaged in the export and import trade with the Island of Cuba." They called attention to the serious losses to which their businesses had been subjected by the hostilities in Cuba and expressed the hope that, in order to prevent further loss, to reestablish American commerce, and also to secure "the blessings of peace for one and a half millions of residents of the Island of Cuba now enduring unspeakable distress and suffering," the United States Government might take steps to bring about an honorable reconciliation between the parties to the conflict.

Another memorial, signed by many of the same subscribers, was presented to President McKinley on February 9, 1898, by a committee of New York business men. It asserted that the Cuban war, which had now continued for three entire years, had caused an average loss of $100,-000,000 a year, or a total loss of $300,000,000 in the import and export trade between Cuba and the United States, to which were to be added "heavy sums irretrievably lost by the destruction of American properties, or properties supported by American capital in the Island itself, such as sugar factories, railways, tobacco plantations, mines and other industrial enterprises; the loss of the United States in trade and capital by means of this war being probably far greater and more serious than that of all the other parties concerned, not excepting Spain herself."

The sugar crop of 1897–1898, continued the memorial, appeared for the most part lost like its two predecessors, and unless peace could be established before May or June of the current year, the crop of 1898–1899, with all the business dependent upon it, would likewise be lost, since the rainy season of summer and fall would be required "to prepare for next winter's crop, by repairing damaged fields, machinery, lines of railways, &c." In view of the importance to the United States of the Cuban trade and of American participation "in the ownership or management of Cuban sugar factories, railways and other enterprises," the petitioners hoped that the President would deem the situation "of sufficient importance as to warrant prompt and efficient measures by our Government, with the sole object of restoring peace . . . and with it restoring to us a most valuable commercial field."

How much weight such pressure from special interest had with the administration there is no way of knowing. But it is to be noted that the pressure from parties directly interested was not all on one side. Mr. E. F. Atkins, an American citizen who divided his time between Boston and his sugar plantation of Soledad near Cienfuegos, Cuba, which he had developed at a cost of $1,400,000, had been able, through protection received from the Spanish Government and through a corps of guards organized and paid by himself, to continue operations throughout the period of the insurrection. He was frequently in Washington, where he had influential friends, during both the Cleveland and McKinley administrations and worked consistently against the adoption of any measures likely to provoke war.

Unlike some of the sugar plantations, American-owned iron mines in Cuba continued to do active business despite the insurrection. Three American iron and manganese enterprises in the single province of Santiago claimed to have an investment of some $6,000,000 of purely American capital, a large proportion of which was in property which could easily be destroyed. "We are fully advised as to our status in case of war," wrote the representative of one company to the Assistant Secretary of State, "and that this property might be subject to confiscation or destruction by the Spanish Government." War between Spain and the United States, wrote the president of another company, "will very likely mean the destruction of our valuable plant and in any event untold loss to our Company and its American stockholders." An American cork company with large interests in Spain; a New York merchant with trade in the Mediterranean and Black Sea; a Mobile firm which had chartered a Spanish ship to carry a cargo of timber—these are samples of American business interests which saw in war the threat of direct damage to themselves. They are hardly offset by the high hopes of an enterprising gentleman of Norfolk, "representing a party of capitalists who are enthusiastic supporters of the Government," who applied to the State Department for a letter of marque "to enable us to lawfully capture Spanish merchant vessels and torpedo boats," adding: "We have secured option on a fine steam vessel, and on receipt of proper documents will put to sea forthwith."

It seems safe to conclude, from the evidence available, that the only important business interests (other than the business of sensational journalism) which clamored for intervention in Cuba were those directly or indirectly concerned in the Cuban sugar industry; that opposed to intervention were the influence of other parties (including at least one prominent sugar planter) whose business would suffer direct injury from war and also the overwhelming preponderance of general business opinion. After the middle of March, 1898, some conservative editors came to think intervention inevitable on humanitarian grounds, but many of the most influential business journals opposed it to the end.

We can now turn to the question whether American business was imperialistic; whether, in other words, business opinion favored schemes for acquiring foreign territory to supply it with markets, fields for capital investment, or commercial and naval stations in distant parts of the world. American business men were not unaware of the struggle for colonies then raging among European nations. Did they feel that the United States ought to participate in that struggle?

We have seen above that the rising tide of prosperity was intimately connected with the increase in American exports, particularly of manufactured articles. That the future welfare of American industry was dependent upon the command of foreign markets was an opinion so common as to appear almost universal. The New York *Journal of Commerce* pointed out, early in 1897, that the nation's industrial plant had been developed far beyond the needs of domestic consumption. In the wire nail industry there was said to be machinery to make four times as many nails as the American markets could consume. Rail mills, locomotive shops, and glass factories were in a similar situation. "Nature has thus destined this country for the industrial supremacy of the world," said the same paper later in the year. When the National Association of Manufacturers met in New York for its annual convention in January, 1898, "the discussion of ways and means for extending this country's trade, and more particularly its export business, was, in fact, almost the single theme of the speakers," according to *Bradstreet's* which added the comment: "Nothing is more significant of the changed attitude toward this country's foreign trade, manifested by the American manufacturer today as compared with a few years ago, than the almost single devotion which he pays to the subject of possible export-trade extension."

But if business men believed, prior to the opening of the war with Spain, that foreign markets were to be secured through the acquisition of colonies, they were strangely silent about it. To the program of colonial expansion which for almost a decade had been urged by such men as Mahan, Albert Shaw, Lodge, Roosevelt, and Morgan, business had remained, to all appearances, either indifferent or antagonistic. To the business man, such a program was merely one form of dangerous jingoism. A large section of business opinion had, indeed, favored plans for the building of a Nicaraguan canal with governmental assistance, and some spokesmen for business had favored annexation of the Hawaiian Islands. But beyond these relatively modest projects few business men, apparently, wished to go. Two of the most important commercial journals, the New York *Journal of Commerce* and the *Commercial and Financial Chronicle,* had stoutly opposed both the canal scheme and Hawaiian annexation. The former satirized the arguments of the proponents of both schemes. "We must certainly build the canal to defend the islands, and it is quite clear that we must acquire the islands . . . in order to defend the canal." The canal was not only unnecessary, but unless fortified at each end and patrolled by two fleets, it would be a positive misfortune. Such protection—"the price of jingoism"—might "easily cost us $25,000,000 a year, besides the lump sum that will be required for the original investment, and there is absolutely no excuse whatever in our commercial or our political interests for a single step in this long procession of expenses and of complications with foreign powers." As for Hawaii and Cuba, neither was fit for self-government as a state,—and the American constitution provided no machinery for governing dependencies. The Hawaiian Islands would have no military value unless the United States were to build a great navy and take an aggressive attitude in the Pacific. The *Commercial and Financial Chronicle* saw in colonies only useless outposts which must be protected at great expense, and the St. Louis *Age of Steel* warned lest the expansion of the export trade might "lead to territorial greed, as in the case of older nations, the price of which in armaments and militarism offsets the gain made by the spindle and the forge."

Colonies were not only certain to bear a fruit of danger and expense; they were valueless from the commercial point of view. Did not the colonies of Great Britain afford us one of the most valuable of our export markets? Did we not trade as advantageously with Guiana, a British colony, as with independent Venezuela? "Most of our ideas of the commercial value of conquests, the commercial uses of navies and the commercial advantages of political control," said the New York *Journal of Commerce,* dated back to times when colonial policies were designed to monopolize colonial trade for the mother country. The *Commercial and Financial Chronicle* believed that the current European enthusiasm for colonies was based on false premises; for although trade often followed the flag, "the trade is not always with the home markets of the colonizer. England and the United States are quite as apt to slip in with their wares under the very Custom-House pennant of the French or German dependency." Outright opposition, such as this, to the idea of colonial expansion is not common in the business periodicals examined; much more common is complete silence on the subject. Positive and negative evidence together seem to warrant the conclusion that American business in general, at the opening of 1898, was either indifferent to imperialism, or definitely opposed.

Confidence in the continued expansion of the export trade was based

upon faith in the working of natural forces in a world given over largely
to a system of free trade. American industry had reached a point where it
could meet the world on more than even terms in both the price and the
quality of its products. Given a fair chance, these products would make
their own way. Government could aid them, not by acquiring colonial
markets but by removing or lowering the barriers that restricted imports
of raw materials and exchange commodities.

Richard Hofstadter

Racism and Imperialism

*It was Charles Darwin who
provided the American im-
perialists at the end of the
nineteenth century with a
scientific basis for their
expansionist ideas. Using
the British biologist as a
starting point, they justified war with Spain and the acquisition of
colonies in terms of the racial superiority of the Anglo-Saxon strain.
Richard Hofstadter, a professor of history at Columbia University,
analyzes the connection between racism and imperialism in the selection
that follows. He points to the group of historians, clergymen, political
scientists, and philosophers who preached the doctrine of racial superiority in books, articles, and lectures. The effect of their efforts was to
awaken Americans to a sense of mission and destiny and to create
popular support for expansionism. [Richard Hofstadter, Social Darwinism in American Thought (Boston: Beacon Press, Inc., 1955). Reprinted by permission of the American Historical Association and the
author.]*

In 1898 the United States waged a three-month war with Spain. It took
the Philippine Islands from Spain by treaty and formally annexed the
Hawaiian Islands. In 1899 the United States partitioned the Samoan
Islands by agreement with Germany, and expressed its policy toward
western interests in China in the "Open Door" note. In 1900 Americans
took part in suppressing the Chinese Boxer Rebellion. By 1902 the Army
had finally suppressed insurrection in the Philippines; and in that year
the islands were made an unorganized territory.

As the United States stepped upon the stage of empire, American
thought turned once again to the subjects of war and empire; opponents
and defenders of expansion and conquest marshaled arguments for their
causes. After the fashion of late nineteenth-century thought, they sought
in the world of nature a larger justification for their ideals.

The use of natural selection as a vindication of militarism or imperialism was not new in European or American thought. Imperialists,

calling upon Darwinism in defense of the subjugation of weaker races, could point to *The Origin of Species,* which had referred in its subtitle to *The Preservation of Favored Races in the Struggle for Life.* Darwin had been talking about pigeons, but the imperialists saw no reason why his theories should not apply to men, and the whole spirit of the naturalistic world-view seemed to call for a vigorous and unrelenting thoroughness in the application of biological concepts. Had not Darwin himself written complacently in *The Descent of Man* of the likelihood that backward races would disappear before the advance of higher civilizations? Militarists could also point to the harsh fact of the elimination of the unfit as an urgent reason for cultivating the martial virtues and keeping the national powder dry. After the Franco-Prussian War both sides had for the first time invoked Darwinism as an explanation of the facts of battle. "The greatest authority of all the advocates of war is Darwin," explained Max Nordau in the *North American Review in* 1889. "Since the theory of evolution has been promulgated, they can cover their natural barbarism with the name of Darwin and proclaim the sanguinary instincts of their inmost hearts as the last word of science."

It would nevertheless be easy to exaggerate the significance of Darwin for race theory or militarism either in the United States or in western Europe. Neither the philosophy of force nor doctrines of *Machtpolitik* had to wait upon Darwin to make their appearance. Nor was racism strictly a post-Darwinian phenomenon. Gobineau's *Essai sur l'Inégalité des Races Humaines,* a landmark in the history of Aryanism, was published in 1853–55 without benefit of the idea of natural selection. As for the United States, a people long familiar with Indian warfare on the frontier and the pro-slavery arguments of Southern politicians and publicists had been thoroughly grounded in notions of racial superiority. At the time when Darwin was still hesitantly outlining his theory in private, racial destiny had already been called upon by American expansionists to support the conquest of Mexico. "The Mexican race now see in the fate of the aborigines of the north, their own inevitable destiny," an expansionist had written. "They must amalgamate or be lost in the superior vigor of the Anglo-Saxon race, or they must utterly perish."

This Anglo-Saxon dogma became the chief element in American racism in the imperial era; but the *mystique* of Anglo-Saxonism, which for a time had a particularly powerful grip on American historians, did not depend upon Darwinism either for its inception or for its development. It is doubtful that such monuments of English Anglo-Saxon historical writing as Edward Augustus Freeman's *History of the Norman Conquest of England* (1867–79) or Charles Kingsley's *The Roman and the Teuton* (1864) owed much to biology; and certainly John Mitchell Kemble's *The Saxons in England* (1849) was not inspired by the survival of the fittest. Like other varieties of racism, Anglo-Saxonism was a product of modern nationalism and the romantic movement rather than an outgrowth of biological science. Even the idea that a nation is an organism that must either grow or fall into decay, which doubtless received an additional impetus from Darwinism, had been invoked before 1859 by the proponents of "Manifest Destiny."

Still, Darwinism was put in the service of the imperial urge. Although Darwinism was not the primary source of the belligerent ideology and dogmatic racism of the late nineteenth century, it did become a new instrument in the hands of the theorists of race and struggle. The likeness of the Darwinian portrait of nature as a field of battle to the prevailing conceptions of a militant age in which von Moltke could write that "war is an element of the order of the world established by God . . . [without which] the world would stagnate and lose itself in materialism," was too great to escape attention. In the United States, however, such frank and brutal militarism was far less common than a benevolent conception of Anglo-Saxon world domination in the interests of peace and freedom. In the decades after 1885, Anglo-Saxonism, belligerent or pacific, was the dominant abstract rationale of American imperialism.

The Darwinian mood sustained the belief in Anglo-Saxon racial superiority which obsessed many American thinkers in the latter half of the nineteenth century. The measure of world dominion already achieved by the "race" seemed to prove it the fittest. Also, in the 1870's and 1880's many of the historical conceptions of the Anglo-Saxon school began to reflect advances in biology and allied developments in other fields of thought. For a time American historians fell under the spell of the scientific ideal and dreamed of evolving a science of history comparable to the biological sciences. The keynote of their faith could be found in E. A. Freeman's *Comparative Politics* (1874), in which he allied the comparative method with the idea of Anglo-Saxon superiority. "For the purposes of the study of Comparative Politics," he had written, "a political constitution is a specimen to be studied, classified, and labeled, as a building or an animal is studied, classified, and labeled by those to whom buildings or animals are objects of study."

If political constitutions were to be classified and compared by Victorian scholars as if they were animal forms, it was highly probable that the political methods of certain peoples would be favored over others. Inspired by the results of the comparative method in philology and mythology, particularly by the work of Edward Tylor and Max Müller, Freeman tried, using this method, to trace the signs of original unity in the primitive institutions of the Aryans, particularly in the "three most illustrious branches of the common stock—the Greek, the Roman, and the Teuton."

When Herbert Baxter Adams set up his great historical seminar at Johns Hopkins, it was with the official blessing of Freeman; and Freeman's dictum, "History is past politics and politics is present history," was emblazoned on the historical studies that came pouring forth from Adams' seminar. A whole generation of historians receiving their inspiration from the Johns Hopkins school could have said with Henry Adams,

"I flung myself obediently into the arms of the Anglo-Saxons in history."
The leading notion of the Anglo-Saxon school was that the democratic
institutions of England and the United States, particularly the New England town meeting could be traced back to the primitive institutions of
the early German tribes. In spite of differences in detail, the Hopkins
historians were in general agreement on their picture of the big, blond,
democratic Teuton and on the Teutonic genealogy of self-government.
The viewpoint of the school was given a fitting popular expression in
1890 with the publication of James K. Hosmer's *Short History of Anglo-
Saxon Freedom,* which drew upon the whole literature of Anglo-Saxondom to establish the thesis that government of the people and by the
people is of ancient Anglo-Saxon origin. Wrote Hosmer:

> Though Anglo-Saxon freedom in a more or less partial form has been
> adopted (it would be better perhaps to say imitated) by every nation in Europe,
> but Russia, and in Asia by Japan, the hopes for that freedom, in the future,
> rest with the English-speaking race. By that race alone it has been preserved
> amidst a thousand perils; to that race alone is it thoroughly congenial; if we
> can conceive the possibility of the disappearance among peoples of that race,
> the chance would be small for that freedom's survival . . .

Hosmer shared the optimism of his English contemporary John Richard Green, who believed that the English-speaking race would grow in
enormous numbers and spread over the New World, Africa, and Australia. "The inevitable issue," concluded Hosmer, "is to be that the primacy of the world will lie with us. English institutions, English speech,
English thought, are to become the main features of the political, social,
and intellectual life of mankind." Thus would the survival of the fittest
be written large in the world's political future.

What Hosmer did for Anglo-Saxon history, John W. Burgess did for
political theory. His *Political Science and Comparative Constitutional
Law,* published in the same year as Hosmer's book, serves as a reminder
of German as well as English influences in the American Anglo-Saxon
cult; for Burgess, like Herbert Baxter Adams, had received a large part of
his graduate training in Germany. The peculiarity of his work, Burgess
declared, was its method. "It is a comparative study. It is an attempt to
apply the method, which has been found so productive in the domain of
Natural Science, to Political Science and Jurisprudence." It was Burgess'
contention that political capacity is not a gift common to all nations, but
limited to a few. The highest capacity for political organization, he believed, has been shown, in unequal degrees, by the Aryan nations. Of all
these, only "the Teuton really dominates the world by his superior political genius."

> It is therefore not to be assumed that every nation must become a state. The
> political subjection or attachment of unpolitical nations to those possessing
> political endowment appears, if we may judge from history, to be as truly a
> part of the world's civilization as is the national organization of states. I do

not think that Asia and Africa can ever receive political organization in any other way. . . . The national state is . . . the most modern and complete solution of the whole problem of political organization which the world has yet produced; and the fact that it is the creation of Teutonic political genius stamps the Teutonic nations as the political nations *par excellence,* and authorizes them, in the economy of the world, to assume the leadership in the establishment and administration of states. . . . The Teutonic nations can never regard the exercise of political power as a right of man. With them this power must be based upon capacity to discharge political duty, and they themselves are the best organs which have as yet appeared to determine when and where this capacity exists.

Theodore Roosevelt, who had been Burgess' student at Columbia Law School was also inspired by the drama of racial expansion. In his historical work, *The Winning of the West,* Roosevelt drew from the story of the frontiersman's struggle with the Indians the conclusion that the coming of the whites was not to be stayed and a racial war to the finish was inevitable. "During the past three centuries," wrote the young scholar-in-politics, "the spread of the English-speaking peoples over the world's waste spaces has been not only the most striking feature in the world's history, but also the event of all others most far-reaching in its effects and its importance." This great expansion he traced back many centuries to the days when German tribes went forth to conquest from their marshy forests. American development represents the culminating achievement of this mighty history of racial growth.

The writings of John Fiske, one of the earliest American synthesizers of evolutionism, expansionism, and the Anglo-Saxon myth, show how tenuous could be the boundary between Spencer's ideal evolutionary pacifism and the militant imperialism which succeeded it. A kindly man, whose thought was grounded in Spencer's theory of the transition from militancy to industrialism, Fiske was not the sort to advocate violence as an instrument of national policy. Yet even in his hands evolutionary dogma issued forth in a bumptious doctrine of racial destiny. In his *Outlines of Cosmic Philosophy,* Fiske had followed Spencer in accepting the universality of conflict (outside of family relationships) as a fact in savage society; he believed it an effective agent in selection. But the superior, more differentiated and integrated societies had come to prevail over the more backward by natural selection, and the power of making war on a grand scale had become concentrated in the hands of "those communities in which predatory activity is at the minimum and industrial activity at the maximum." So warfare or destructive competition gives place to the productive competition of industrial society. As militancy declines, the method of conquest is replaced by the method of federation.

Fiske, who had long believed in Aryan race superiority, also accepted the "Teutonic" theory of democracy. This doctrine sanctified any conquest incidental to Anglo-Saxon expansion. English victories over France in the eighteenth-century colonial struggles represented a victory for industrialism over militancy. The American victory over Spain and the acquisition of the Philippines Fiske interpreted as the high point in a conflict between Spanish colonization and superior English methods.

In 1880, when he was invited to speak before the Royal Institute of Great Britain, Fiske gave a series of three lectures on "American Political Ideas" which became widely known as a statement of the Anglo-Saxon thesis. Fiske praised the ancient Roman Empire as an agency of peace, but argued that it had been inadequate as a system of political organization because it failed to combine concerted action with local self-government. The solution to this ancient need could be provided by representative democracy and the local self-government embodied in the New England town. By retaining the rustic democracy of America's Aryan forefathers, American federal organization would make possible an effective union of many diverse states. Democracy, diversity, and peace would be brought into harmony. The dispersion of this magnificent Aryan political system over the world, and the complete elimination of warfare, was the next step in world history.

With characteristic Darwinian emphasis upon race fertility, Fiske dwelt upon the great population potential of the English and American races. America could support at least 700,000,000; and the English people would within a few centuries cover Africa with teeming cities, flourishing farms, railroads, telegraphs, and all the devices of civilization. This was the Manifest Destiny of the race. Every land on the globe that was not already the seat of an old civilization should become English in language, traditions, and blood. Four-fifths of the human race would trace its pedigree to English forefathers. Spread from the rising to the setting sun, the race would hold the sovereignty of the sea and the commercial supremacy which it had begun to acquire when England first began to settle the New World. If the United States would only drop its shameful tariff and enter into free competition with the rest of the world, it would exert such pressure, peacefully of course, that the states of Europe would no longer be able to afford armaments and would finally see the advantages of peace and federation. Thus, according to Fiske, would man finally pass out of barbarism and become truly Christian.

Even Fiske, who was accustomed to platform success, was astonished at the enthusiasm evoked by these addresses in England and at home. The lecture on "Manifest Destiny," published in *Harper's* in 1885, was repeated more than twenty times in cities throughout the United States. By request of President Hayes, Chief Justice Waite, Senators Hoar and Dawes of Massachusetts, General Sherman, George Bancroft, and others, Fiske gave his lectures again at Washington, where he was feted by the politicos and presented to the Cabinet.

As a spokesman of expansion, however, Fiske was but a small voice compared with the Rev. Josiah Strong, whose book *Our Country: Its Possible Future and Its Present Crisis,* appeared in 1885 and soon sold 175,000 copies in English alone. Strong, then secretary of the Evangelical

Society of the United States, wrote the book primarily to solicit money for missions. His uncanny capacity for assimilating the writings of Darwin and Spencer to the prejudices of rural Protestant America makes the book one of the most revealing documents of its time. Strong exulted in the material resources of the United States, but he was dissatisfied with its spiritual life. He was against immigrants, Catholics, Mormons, saloons, tobacco, large cities, socialists, and concentrated wealth—all grave menaces to the Republic. Still he was undaunted in his faith in universal progress, material and moral, and the future of the Anglo-Saxon race. He employed the economic argument for imperialism; and a decade before Frederick Jackson Turner he saw in the imminent exhaustion of the public lands a turning point in national development. It was Anglo-Saxonism, however, that brought him to the highest pitch of enthusiasm. The Anglo-Saxon people, the bearers of civil liberty and pure spiritual Christianity, said Strong,

. . . is multiplying more rapidly than any other European race. It already owns one-third of the earth, and will get more as it grows. By 1980 the world Anglo-Saxon race should number at least 713,000,000. Since North America is much bigger than the little English isle, it will be the seat of Anglo-Saxondom.

If human progress follows a law of development, if "Time's noblest offspring is the last," our civilization should be the noblest; for we are "The heirs of all the ages in the foremost files of time," and not only do we occupy the latitude of power, but *our land is the last to be occupied in that latitude.* There is no other virgin soil in the North Temperate Zone. If the consummation of human progress is not to be looked for here, if there is yet to flower a higher civilization, where is the soil that is to produce it?

Strong went on to show how a new and finer physical type was emerging in the United States, bigger, stronger, taller than Scots or Englishmen. Darwin himself, Strong noted triumphantly, had seen in the superior vigor of Americans an illustration of natural selection at work, when he wrote in *The Descent of Man:*

There is apparently much truth in the belief that the wonderful progress of the United States, as well as the character of the people, are the results of natural selection; for the more energetic, restless, and courageous men from all parts of Europe have emigrated during the last ten or twelve generations to that great country, and have there succeeded best. Looking to the distant future, I do not think that the Reverend Mr. Zincke takes an exaggerated view when he says: "All other series of events—as that which resulted in the culture of mind in Greece, and that which resulted in the empire of Rome—only appear to have purpose and value when viewed in connection with, or rather as subsidiary to . . . the great stream of Anglo-Saxon emigration to the west."

Returning to his theme that the unoccupied lands of the world were filling up, and that population would soon be pressing upon subsistence in the United States as in Europe and Asia, Strong declared:

Then will the world enter upon a new stage of its history—*the final competition of races for which the Anglo-Saxon is being schooled.* If I do not read amiss, this powerful race will move down upon Mexico, down upon Central and South America, out upon the islands of the sea, over upon Africa and beyond. And can anyone doubt that the result of this competition of races will be the "survival of the fittest"?

Although concrete economic and strategic interests, such as Chinese trade and the vital necessity of sea power, were the prominent issues in the imperial debate, the movement took its rationale from more general ideological conceptions. The appeal of Anglo-Saxonism was reflected in the adherence to it of political leaders of the expansion movement. The idea of inevitable Anglo-Saxon destiny figured in the outlook of Senators Albert T. Beveridge and Henry Cabot Lodge and of John Hay, Theodore Roosevelt's Secretary of State, as well as the President himself. During the fight for the annexation of the Philippines, when the larger question of imperial policy was thrown open for debate, expansionists were quick to invoke the law of progress, the inevitable tendency to expand, the Manifest Destiny of Anglo-Saxons, and the survival of the fittest. Before the Senate in 1899, Beveridge cried:

> God has not been preparing the English-speaking and Teutonic peoples for a thousand years for nothing but vain and idle self-admiration. No! He has made us the master organizers of the world to establish system where chaos reigns. . . . He has made us adepts in government that we may administer government among savages and senile peoples.

In the most memorable of his imperialist exhortations, "The Strenuous Life" (1899), Theodore Roosevelt warned of the possibility of national elimination in the international struggle for existence:

> We cannot avoid the responsibilities that confront us in Hawaii, Cuba, Porto Rico, and the Philippines. All we can decide is whether we shall meet them in a way that will redound to the national credit, or whether we shall make of our dealings with these new problems a dark and shameful page in our history. . . . The timid man, the lazy man, the man who distrusts his country, the over-civilized man, who has lost the great fighting, masterful virtues, the ignorant man, and the man of dull mind, whose soul is incapable of feeling the mighty lift that thrills "stern men with empires in their brains"— all these, of course, shrink from seeing the nation undertake its new duties. . . .
>
> I preach to you, then, my countrymen, that our country calls not for the life of ease but for the life of strenuous endeavor. The twentieth century looms before us big with the fate of many nations. If we stand idly by, if we seek merely swollen, slothful ease and ignoble peace, if we shrink from the hard contests where men must win at hazard of their lives and at the risk of all they hold dear, then the bolder and stronger peoples will pass us by, and will win for themselves the domination of the world.

John Hay found in the impulse to expand a sign of an irresistible "cosmic tendency." "No man, no party, can fight with any chance of final success against a cosmic tendency; no cleverness, no popularity avails against the spirit of the age." "If history teaches any lesson," echoed another writer a few years later, "it is that nations, like individuals, follow the law of their being; that in their growth and in their decline they are creatures of conditions in which their own volition plays but a part, and that often the smallest part." The question of the Philippines was sometimes pictured as the watershed of American destiny; our decision would determine whether we should undergo a new expansion greater than any in the past, or fall back into decline as a senile people. Said John Barrett, former minister to Siam:

> Now is the critical time when the United States should strain every nerve and bend all her energies to keep well in front in the mighty struggle that has begun for the supremacy of the Pacific Seas. If we seize the opportunity we may become leaders forever, but if we are laggards now we will remain laggards until the crack of doom. The rule of the survival of the fittest applies to nations as well as to the animal kingdom. It is a cruel, relentless principle being exercised in a cruel, relentless competition of mighty forces; and these will trample over us without sympathy or remorse unless we are trained to endure and strong enough to stand the pace.

Charles A. Conant, a prominent journalist and economist troubled about the necessity of finding an outlet for surplus capital, "if the entire fabric of the present economic order is not to be shaken by a social revolution," argued that

> . . . the law of self-preservation, as well as that of the survival of the fittest, is urging our people on in a path which is undoubtedly a departure from the policy of the past, but which is inevitably marked out by the new conditions and requirements of the present.

Conant warned against the possibility of decadence if the country did not seize upon its opportunities at once. Another writer denied that a policy of colonial expansion was anything novel in American history. We had colonized the West. The question was not whether we should now enter upon a colonial career but whether we should shift our colonizing heritage into new channels. "We must not forget that the Anglo-Saxon race is expansive."

Although the Anglo-Saxon *mystique* was called upon in the interests of expansion by might, it also had its more pacific side. Its devotees had usually recognized a powerful bond with England; the historians of the Anglo-Saxon school, stressing the common political heritage, wrote about the American Revolution as if it were a temporary misunderstanding in a long history of common political evolution, or a welcome stimulant to flagging Anglo-Saxon liberties.

One outgrowth of the Anglo-Saxon legend was a movement toward an Anglo-American alliance which came to rapid fruition in the closing years of the nineteenth century. In spite of its unflagging conviction of racial superiority, this movement was peaceful rather than militaristic in its motivation; for its followers generally believed that an Anglo-American understanding, alliance, or federation would usher in a "golden age" of universal peace and freedom. No possible power or combination of powers would be strong enough to challenge such a union. This "English-speaking people's league of God for the permanent peace of this war-worn world," as Senator Beveridge called it, would be the next stage in the world's evolution. Advocates of Anglo-American unity believed that Spencer's transition from militant to pacific culture, and Tennyson's "Parliament of Man, the Federation of the World," were about to become a reality.

James K. Hosmer had appealed in 1890 for an "English-Speaking Fraternity" powerful enough to withstand any challenge by the Slavs, Hindus, or Chinese. This coalescence of like-minded states would be but the first step toward a brotherhood of humanity. Yet it was not until 1897 that American interest in an English alliance resulted in a movement of consequence, which received the support of publicists and statesmen as well as littérateurs and historians. During the war with Spain, when continental nations took a predominantly hostile attitude toward American interests, Britain's friendliness stood out in welcome relief. Common fears of Russia and a feeling of identity of interests in the Far East were added to the notion of a common racial destiny. The Anglophobia which had been so persistent among American politicians—Roosevelt and Lodge had been among the bitterest—was considerably relieved. The anti-imperialist Carl Schurz felt that what he rather prematurely took to be the complete dissipation of anti-English feeling was one of the best results of the Spanish-American War. Richard Olney—who as Cleveland's Secretary of State during the Venezuela dispute had defiantly told Britain that the fiat of the United States is law in the Western Hemisphere—now wrote an article on "The International Isolation of the United States" to point out the benefits of British trade and to warn against pursuing an anti-British policy at a time when our country stood alone in the world. Arguing that "family quarrels" were a thing of the past, Olney expressed his hope for Anglo-American diplomatic coöperation, and reminded his readers: "There is a patriotism of race as well as of country." Even the navalist Mahan approved of the British, and although he had felt for some time that a movement for union was premature, he was sufficiently friendly to be content to let the British retain naval supremacy. For a short time at the close of the century the Anglo-Saxon movement became the rage among the upper classes, and statesmen spoke seriously of a possible political alliance.

The Anglo-Saxon cult, however, had to pull against the great mass of the population, whose ethnic composition and cultural background rendered them immune to its propaganda; and even among those of Anglo-Saxon lineage the dynamic appeal of the cult was confined to the years of excitement at the turn of the century. The term "Anglo-Saxon" offended many people, and meetings of protest against Anglo-Saxonism were called in some of the western states. Suspicion of England, traditional in American politics, could not be overcome. John Hay complained in 1900 of "a mad-dog hatred of England prevalent among newspapers and politicians." When the movement for Anglo-American Union was revived again during the First World War, the term "English-speaking" was used in preference to "Anglo-Saxon," and racial exclusiveness was no longer featured. The powerful undertow of American isolation that followed the war, however, swept away this movement once again.

Anglo-Saxonism in politics was limited both in scope and in duration. It had its day of influence as a doctrine of national self-assertion, but as a doctrine of Anglo-Saxon world order its effects were ephemeral. Even the benevolent ideal of the dreamers of a Pax Anglo-Americana found practical meaning only as a timely justification of a temporary rapprochement inspired by the needs of *Realpolitik*. The day had not come when world peace could be imposed by a "superior" race confident in its biological blessings and its divine mission.

Lacking an influential military caste, the United States never developed a strong military cult audacious enough to glorify war for its own sake. Such outbursts as Roosevelt's "Strenuous Life" speech were rare; and it was also rare for an American writer to extol war for its effects upon the race, although Rear Admiral Stephen B. Luce, one of Mahan's patrons, once declared that war is one of the great agencies of human conflict and that "strife in one form or another in the organic world seems to be the law of existence. . . . Suspend the struggle, well called the battle of life, for a brief space, and death claims the victory." Most writers on war seemed to agree with Spencer that military conflict had been highly useful in developing primitive civilization but had now long outlived its value as an instrument of progress.

The advocates of preparedness did not usually take the stand that there is anything inherently desirable in war, but rather quoted the old maxim, "If you wish for peace, prepare for war." "Let us worship peace, indeed," conceded Mahan, "as the goal at which humanity must hope to arrive; but let us not fancy that peace is to be had as a boy wrenches an unripe fruit from a tree."

Others took the position that strife is inherent in the nature of things and must be anticipated as an unhappy necessity. Once the martial fever of the short and easy war with Spain had subsided, the psychology of the American people between 1898 and 1917 was surprisingly nervous and defensive for a nation that was rapidly rising in stature as a world power. Encouraged by the eugenics movement, men talked of racial degeneracy, of race suicide, of the decline of western civilization, of the effeteness of the western peoples, of the Yellow Peril. Warnings of decay were most commonly coupled with exhortations to revivify the national spirit.

One of the most popular among the pessimistic writers was an Englishman, Charles Pearson, who had formerly served the Empire as minister of education in Victoria. His melancholy book, *National Life and Character*, published in England and the United States in 1893, offered a discouraging prognosis for western culture. The higher races, Pearson believed, can live only in the temperate zone, and will be forever barred from effective colonization in the tropics. Overpopulation and economic exigencies will give rise to state socialism, which will extend its tentacles into every corner of western national life. Because of the increasing dependence of the citizen upon the state, nationalism will grow, and religion, family life, and old-fashioned morality will decline. There will also be a consolidation of peoples into great centralized empires, for only these will have the capacity to survive. Large armies, great cities, huge national debts will hasten cultural eclipse. The decline of competition, coupled with state education, will render the intellect more mechanical in its operations and deprive it of the initiative that alone is capable of outstanding achievement in the arts. The result will be a world of old people, scientific rather than esthetic, unprogressive, stable, without adventure, energy, brightness, hope, or ambition. Meanwhile other races will not fail in vitality, for biology shows that the lower are more prolific than the higher. Chinese, Hindus, Negroes cannot be exterminated, but will on the contrary be likely to challenge the supremacy of western civilization by industrial rather than military means. Perhaps the best that the governing races can do is to face the future with courage and dignity.

It is idle to say that if all this should come to pass our pride of place will not be humiliated. We were struggling among ourselves for supremacy in a world which we thought of as destined to belong to the Aryan races and to the Christian faith; to the letters and arts and charm of social manners which we have inherited from the best times of the past. We shall wake to find ourselves elbowed and hustled, and perhaps even thrust aside by peoples whom we looked down upon as servile, and thought of as bound always to minister to our needs. The solitary consolation will be that the changes have been inevitable. It has been our work to organize and create, to carry peace and law and order over the world, that others may enter in and enjoy. Yet in some of us the feeling of caste is so strong that we are not sorry to think we shall have passed away before that day arrives.

Pearson's fears were the beginning of a reaction from the optimism expressed by Fiske and Strong in the 1880's. For middle-class intellectuals, reeling under the shock of the panic of 1893 and the deep social discontents of the prolonged depression that followed, his prophecies of doom had a ring of truth. They were particularly suited to the dark mood that overcame Henry Adams in the 1890's. He wrote to C. M. Gaskell:

I am satisfied that Pearson is right, and that the dark races are gaining on us, as they have already done in Haiti, and are doing throughout the West Indies and our Southern States. In another fifty years, at the same rate of movement, the white races will have to reconquer the tropics by war and nomadic invasion, or be shut up, north of the fortieth parallel.

To his brother, Brooks Adams, pessimism was more than a matter of private despair. In his study of *The Law of Civilization and Decay* (1896), he set forth his own version of the deeper historical principles behind the façade of social change. The law of force and energy is universal, said Adams in a passage somewhat reminiscent of Spencer, and animal life is only one of the outlets through which solar energy is dissipated. Human societies are forms of animal life, differing in energy according to their natural endowments; but all societies obey the general law that the social movement of a community is proportionate to its energy and mass, and that its degree of centralization is proportionate to its mass. The surplus energetic material not expended by a society in the daily struggle for life can be stored as wealth, and the stored energy is transmitted from one community to another either by conquest or by superiority in economic competition. Every race sooner or later reaches the limit of its warlike energy and enters upon a phase of economic competition. Surplus energy, when accumulated in such bulk as to preponderate over productive energy, becomes the controlling social force. Capital becomes autocratic. The economic and scientific intellect grows at the expense of imaginative, emotional, and martial arts. A stationary period may supervene, lasting until it is terminated by war or exhaustion or both.

The evidence, however, seems to point to the conclusion that, when a highly centralized society disintegrates, under the pressure of economic competition, it is because the energy of the race has been exhausted. Consequently, the survivors of such a community lack the power necessary for renewed concentration, and must probably remain inert until supplied with fresh energetic material by the infusion of barbarian blood.

In subsequent volumes, *America's Economic Supremacy* (1900) and *The New Empire* (1902), Adams worked out a materialistic interpretation of society based upon physics, biology, geography, and economics. Surveying the rise and decline of historic states, he attributed changes in supremacy to changes in basic trade routes. The center of economic civilization, now once again in transit, he saw coming to rest in the United States; but he warned that "supremacy has always entailed its sacrifices as well as its triumphs, and fortune has seldom smiled on those who, beside being energetic and industrious, have not been armed, organized, and bold."

Nature tends to favor organisms that operate most cheaply—that is, with the most economic expenditure of energy. Wasteful organisms are rejected by nature; they can be eliminated by commerce if not by conquest. Adams was particularly anxious about a possible conflict with Russia in the east, for which he thought the United States should be well armed. Concerning the tendency toward centralized empires, he wrote:

Moreover, Americans must recognize that this is war to the death,—a struggle no longer against single nations but against a continent. There is not room in the economy of the world for two centres of wealth and empire. One organism, in the end, will destroy the other. The weaker must succumb. Under commercial competition, that society will survive which works cheapest; but to be undersold is often more fatal to a population than to be conquered.

More influential than Brooks Adams was Captain Alfred Thayer Mahan, whose book *The Influence of Sea Power upon History* (1890) had made him the world's most prominent exponent of navalism. In *The Interest of America in Sea Power* (1897), in which he urged that the country pursue a stronger policy than the present one of "passive self-defense," Mahan pointed out:

All around us now is strife; "the struggle of life," "the race of life," are phrases so familiar that we do not feel their significance till we stop to think about them. Everywhere nation is arrayed against nation; our own no less than others.

Theodore Roosevelt was among those who tried to stir the nation against the eventualities predicted by Pearson and foreseen by Brooks Adams. For Pearson's pessimism he saw little excuse; although he conceded that civilized nations were not destined to rule the tropics, he could not believe that the white races would lose heart or become intimidated by the tropic races. When western institutions, and democratic government itself, spread to the tropics, the danger of an overpowering industrial competition would be considerably less; and it seemed unlikely that high industrial efficiency would be achieved without a marked degree of westernization. He was somewhat more favorably impressed with the work of his friend Brooks Adams, but again the most pessimistic prophecies aroused Roosevelt to reply. He did not believe that the martial type of man necessarily decays as civilization progresses; pointing to the examples of Russia and Spain, he argued that the phenomenon of national decline should not be too closely identified with advancing industrialism. Only when Adams mentioned the failure to produce enough healthy children did he touch upon the real danger to our society. This was a theme dear to Roosevelt's heart. Vociferously fearful of the menace of race decadence through decline in the birth rate, he never tired of the theme of reproduction and motherhood. If marriages did not produce an average of four children, the numbers of the race could not be maintained. He warned that if the process of racial decay continued in the United States and the British Empire, the future of the white race would rest in the hands of the German and the Slav.

Associated with fears of racial decline and of the loss of fighting fiber was the menace of the Yellow Peril, which was much talked about between 1905 and 1916. The prevailing western attitude toward Japan had been friendly until the Japanese victory over Russia in 1905. However, with the convincing demonstration of the Japanese martial prowess, attitudes changed, just as they had toward Germany after her victory in 1871. In the United States, fear of the Japanese was especially strong in

California, where oriental immigration had been resented for over thirty
years. The sensational press took up the Japanese menace and exploited
it to the point of stimulating occasional war scares.

In 1904 Jack London, always a strenuous advocate of racial assertive-
ness, warned in an article in the *San Francisco Examiner* of the potential
threat to the Anglo-Saxon world if the organizing and ruling capacities of
the Japanese should ever gain control of the enormous working capacity
of the great Chinese population. The impending racial conflict, he
thought, might come to a head in his own time.

The possibility of race adventure has not passed away. We are in the midst
of our own. The Slav is just girding himself up to begin. Why may not the
yellow and brown start out on an adventure as tremendous as our own and
more strikingly unique?

Hugh H. Lusk believed that the Japanese menace was only a small part
of a general reawakening of the Mongolian race, whose urge to expansion, motivated by the age-old population problem, might soon send it
out over the Pacific and ultimately to southwestern America and to the
gates of the United States via Mexico. Talk of the Yellow Peril reached
its height just before the First World War, when congressmen spoke
openly of inevitable conflict in the Pacific.

Perhaps the closest American approximation to the German militarist
writer General von Bernhardi was General Homer Lea, a colorful military adventurer who fought against the Boxer Rebellion, and later became an adviser to Sun Yat-sen. Lea's militarism was based directly upon
biology. He believed that nations are like organisms in their dependence
upon growth and expansion to resist disease and decay.

As physical vigor represents the strength of man in his struggle for existence,
in the same sense military vigor constitutes the strength of nations; ideals, laws
and constitutions are but temporary effulgences, and are existent only so long
as this strength remains vital. As manhood marks the height of physical vigor
among mankind, so the militant successes of a nation mark the zenith of its
physical greatness.

Militancy may be divided into three phases: the militancy of the struggle
to survive, the militancy of conquest, and the militancy of supremacy or
preservation of ownership. It is in the first stage, the struggle to survive,
that the genius of a people reaches its height; the harder this struggle, the
more highly developed is the military spirit, with the result that con-
querors often arise from desolate wastes or rocky islands. The laws of
struggle and survival are universal and unalterable, and the duration of
national existence is dependent upon the knowledge of them.

Plans to thwart them, to short-cut them, circumvent, to cozen, to scorn and
violate [them] is folly such as man's conceit alone makes possible. Never has this
been tried—and man is ever at it—but what the end has been gangrenous and
fatal.

Lea warned of the possibility of Japanese invasion of the United States, and argued that a war with Japan would be settled by land campaigns, for which the country needed a much larger army. Without such a military establishment, the West Coast would stand in deadly danger of invasion. The strategy of such an invasion Lea had planned in full detail.

Lea further warned that the Saxon races were flouting the laws of nature by permitting the militancy of their people to decline. A decadent tendency to let individual wants take precedence over the necessities of national existence threatened Anglo-Saxon power throughout the world, he believed. The United States, submerged by a flood of non-Anglo-Saxon immigrants, was ceasing to be the stronghold of a Saxon race. The British Empire was in serious danger from the colored races. The day of the Saxon was ending. For the impending struggle between the Germans and the Saxon race, the latter was ill equipped. There was only one antidote for Anglo-Saxon decline: greater militancy. A confederation would be weak in war, but universal compulsory military service might check the already alarming decline.

The advocates of preparedness made a biological appeal similar to Lea's. Hudson Maxim, an inventor of smokeless powder, and brother of Hiram Maxim, the inventor of the Maxim gun, published a volume called *Defenseless America* (1914), which was widely distributed by Hearst's International Library. "Self-preservation," Maxim warned, "is the first law of Nature, and this law applies to nations exactly as it applies to individuals. Our American Republic cannot survive unless it obeys the law of survival." He argued that man is by nature a struggling animal, that human nature has always been more or less the same. To be unprepared for the struggle would be to risk extinction, but preparedness might avert war.

A similar philosophy could be found among the wartime leaders of the organized preparedness movement. S. Stanwood Menken, chairman of the National Security League's Congress of Constructive Patriotism, warned the delegates that the law of the survival of the fittest applied to nations, and that the United States could assert its fitness only through a national reawakening. General Leonard Wood was skeptical of the possibility of suppressing war, which, he said, "is about as difficult as to effectively neutralize the general law which governs all things, namely the survival of the fittest." Although the biological argument for militarism was hardly the dominant note among American leaders, it did give them a cosmic foundation that appealed to a Darwinized national mentality.

Fred H. Harrington

The Anti-Imperialist

Movement

Not all Americans shared the passion for the imperialist adventure at the end of the century. A sizable number of them fought expansionism and urged their countrymen to surrender the spoils of war. Fred H. Harrington, president of the University of Wisconsin and a historian of American foreign policy, has investigated the anti-imperialist movement and has found its achievements meager. In the selection that follows, he analyzes the basis of the opposition to expansionism, describes the principal leaders of the movement, narrates the creation of an organization to spearhead the fight, and examines the reasons for the failure of the movement. [Fred H. Harrington, "The Anti-Imperialist Movement in the United States," Mississippi Valley Historical Review, XXII (1935). Reprinted by permission.]

On May 1, 1898, the Asiatic Squadron of the United States Navy, under the command of Commodore George Dewey, engaged and virtually annihilated a Spanish fleet at anchor under the batteries of Cavite in Manila Bay. This victory, which gave the United States the first foothold in the Philippines, marks a turning point in the history of American territorial expansion. It marks as well the beginning of a protest movement of proportions, a movement led by a strangely assorted group of citizens who fought expansion tooth and nail, and, in the face of overwhelming odds, urged renunciation of the spoils of war. Although it failed to achieve its purposes, the movement is of importance, for it held the political stage in the United States for two full years, and attracted to its ranks such public men as Bryan and Cleveland, Reed and Carnegie, Schurz and Hoar.

In approaching the anti-imperialist movement, it is well to bear in mind that it was based almost exclusively on grounds of abstract political principle. The anti-imperialists did not oppose colonial expansion for commercial, religious, constitutional, or humanitarian reasons. They opposed it because they thought that an imperialist policy ran counter to the political doctrines of the Declaration of Independence, Washington's Farewell Address, and Lincoln's Gettysburg Address—the doctrines which asserted that a government could not rule peoples without their consent, and that the United States, having been conceived as an instrument of and for its own people, should not imitate the methods or interfere in the affairs of the Old World nations in any way.

However these doctrines may be regarded today, there can be no doubt that they had a very real meaning for the citizens who organized the anti-imperialist movement. Almost to a man the anti-expansionists sincerely

believed that abandonment of these "guiding principles" would mean
the doom of the republic. This feeling was reflected time after time in the
articles, speeches, and private correspondence of the leaders. It was proclaimed in the utterances of Carl Schurz, David Starr Jordan, William
Jennings Bryan, Grover Cleveland, and Thomas B. Reed—men who represented five distinct groups in the movement. Schurz, for example, defined his position in the fall of 1898, when he wrote:

> I believe that this Republic, in that sense, can endure so long as it remains
> true to the principles upon which it was founded, but that it will morally
> decay if it abandons them. I believe that this democracy, the government of,
> by, and for the people, is not fitted for a colonial policy, which means con-
> quest by force, or, as President McKinley called it, "criminal aggression" and
> arbitrary rule over subject populations. I believe that, if it attempts such a
> policy on a large scale, its inevitable degeneracy will hurt the progress of
> civilization more than it can possibly further that progress by planting its flag
> upon foreign soil on which its fundamental principles of government cannot
> live.

David Starr Jordan, one of the first of many educators to declare
against expansion, voiced the same sentiment when he told a San Francisco audience that to hold Cuba or the Philippines as colonies, "our
democracy must necessarily depart from its best principles and traditions." "There was great danger . . ." he thought, "that in easy victory
we might lose sight of the basal principles of the Republic, a coöperative
association in which 'all just government is derived from the consent of
the governed.' "

Nor were the words of the two great Democratic leaders different in
language or tone. "Our guns destroyed a Spanish fleet," Bryan told an
Omaha audience on June 14, "but can they destroy that self-evident
truth, that governments derive their just powers, not from superior force,
but from the consent of the governed?" Just a week later, in an address at
Lawrenceville, New Jersey, Cleveland asserted that "our government was
formed for the express purpose of creating in a new world a new nation,
the foundation of which should be man's self-government," and that to
embark on a career of colonial aggrandizement would be to "abandon . . . old landmarks and to follow the lights of monarchical hazards."

Speaker Reed, the most prominent Republican to oppose expansion,
made no public pronouncement on the subject. In private, however, he
let it be known that he would not support his party in opposing the
"foundation principles of our government."

It can readily be seen that, in each instance, the whole weight of
the argument is made to rest on the point of political principle. This
is the case with the other anti-imperialist speeches as well. It is true
that, in the later phases on the movement, economic, constitutional,
military, and humanitarian arguments were advanced against expansion,
but they were used to supplement the fundamental conception. Even

after the Philippine atrocities had caused many anti-expansionists to stress the humanitarian aspects of their case, the leaders continued to regard the question of political ideals as the real basis for their opposition to a colonial policy.

The anti-imperialist movement began to take shape almost immediately after the Battle of Manila Bay, as a protest against the wave of expansion sentiment set in motion by Dewey's victory. Expansionists were clamoring for the annexation of Hawaii and the "retention" of the Philippines. Whitelaw Reid's New York *Tribune* was declaring editorially that "this country will be bound, in honor and in morals, either itself to assume the administration of the islands or to empower some other competent authority to do so," even before the news of the naval victory had been confirmed. Other papers—the bulk of the administration press and some Democratic organs—followed the *Tribune's* lead, declaring for expansion on military, religious, commercial, humanitarian, and other grounds.

Those opposed to imperialism immediately took the field in reply. They came forward as individuals, with statements similar to those quoted above, and made themselves heard through the press. From the start they enlisted the services of the independent Democratic and the Mugwump press—papers like the New York *Evening Post,* the Springfield *Republican,* the Boston *Herald,* and the Baltimore *Sun.* These papers became the mainstays of the anti-imperialist support, but they were by no means alone in their denunciation of expansion. Many regular Democratic journals—the Chicago *Chronicle,* the Kansas City *Times,* the Charleston *News and Courier,* and the Richmond *Times,* to name but a few—followed the lead of Bryan or Cleveland in opposing imperialism. They were joined by a few Republican organs of independent leanings, among them the Boston *Transcript,* the Philadelphia *Ledger,* and the Pittsburgh *Dispatch.*

Despite this support, the anti-imperialist movement achieved no satisfactory organization in the early months of its existence. War feeling was still running high. It was as yet uncertain what the policy of the administration would be. And, most important of all, there was no feeling of common purpose among those opposed to a colonial policy. Cleveland and Bryan, though both anti-imperialists and both Democrats, had no love for each other, and their forces were not disposed to coöperate on short notice even in the face of common danger. Reed and Hoar and the other regular Republicans who feared expansion, recoiled at the thought of associating with Schurz and the other Mugwumps.

Thus handicapped, the anti-imperialists made slow progress at first. They were able to put up little opposition to the annexation of Hawaii, which the most prominent anti-imperialist organ termed a "letting out of the waters," the first step in a definitely imperialistic policy. Henry Cabot Lodge, leader of the imperialists in Congress, could dismiss the first large anti-imperialist meeting as one of the "comic incidents" of the war, and the Saratoga Conference, which was organized by Carl Schurz to impress on President McKinley the dangers of expansion, actually delivered itself into the hands of the enemy.

Organization, however, came in time. By the time of the cessation of hostilities, it had become reasonably certain that the administration would adopt an imperialist policy. Those opposed to expansion began to realize the absolute necessity of common action. The independents, convinced that anti-imperialism took precedence over all other reforms, led the way. In Boston, under Gamaliel Bradford and Moorfield Storey, two Mugwumps, they organized a non-partisan Committee of Correspondence, designed to unite workers for the cause irrespective of political faith. Elsewhere they showed a willingness to coöperate with anti-imperialists of every political faith. As time went on, the Bryan and Cleveland Democrats found that the issue might serve as a basis for a mutual understanding, and even the Republicans in the movement—strong party men most of them—displayed a tendency to draw closer to the other opponents of expansion. By January, 1899, George F. Hoar, who had called the Mugwumps the "vilest set of political assassins that ever disgraced this or any other country," was carrying on a close personal correspondence with two Mugwump leaders, Schurz and Storey. Andrew Carnegie, an anti-imperialist to whom the name of Bryan had been anathema two years before, was wishing the Nebraskan "god-speed" and warmly offering him "the hand of fellowship in the new issue before us."

It was this growing sense of common purpose that made possible the formation of the Anti-Imperialist Leagues in the months after November, 1898—leagues that included in their membership most of the prominent opponents of expansion, yet managed to carry on their work without much internal friction.

The first Anti-Imperialist League, like the earlier Committee of Correspondence, was brought into being by the Boston anti-imperialists. The Bostonians retained control of the executive committee, but membership was open to "any citizen of the United States, irrespective of party . . . if in sympathy with the objects of the League." The forty-one vice-presidents were drawn from all sections of the country.

An examination of the list of officers of this league and similar organizations (such as the New York Anti-Imperialist League) gives insight into the elements that were behind the anti-imperialist movement. In reviewing these lists, which contain the names of many of the nation's outstanding men, one is struck at first by the heterogeneous character of the league membership. A closer inspection serves to group most of the men into a few quite definite categories, the reformers, the political and economic groups, and the intellectuals.

Unquestionably the most active and enthusiastic of the anti-imperialists were those who had long fought for various political or social reforms. Included in the anti-imperialist movement were representatives of nearly every reform movement prominent in the United States in the second half of the nineteenth century. There were Liberal Republicans of 1872, Mugwumps, civil service enthusiasts—men like Carl Schurz, Charles Francis Adams, E. L. Godkin, Moorfield Storey, Edward Atkinson, and Samuel Bowles. There were municipal reformers—James Coolidge Carter, the Cuttings, and Edward M. Shepard of New York, Edwin Burritt Smith of Chicago, Hazen Pingree of Detroit, George G. Mercer and Herbert Welsh of Philadelphia, and many more. There were social welfare workers, among them Ernest Crosby, Jane Addams, Josephine Lowell, and William Potts. There were single taxers (Crosby, Charles B. Spahr, and Edward Osgood Brown), pacifists (Crosby, Atkinson, and Mercer), Prohibitionists (Senator Edward W. Carmack and John D. White), defenders of Indian rights (Mercer and Welsh), and free traders (Gamaliel Bradford and Albert S. Parsons). The remnant of the old abolition groups, represented by the son of Garrison, the son of Emerson, the son of James Birney, rallied to the cause, as did a number of clergymen, mustering in their ranks Bishop Henry Codman Potter, Henry Van Dyke, Charles H. Parkhurst, Leonard Woolsey Bacon, John White Chadwick, and Theodore Cuyler.

The political elements represented in the movement fall into four distinct groups—the independents, the Gold Democrats, the Bryan Democrats, and the regular Republicans. The independent group, most important of all, need only be mentioned here. It included Schurz, Adams, Storey, Godkin, Bradford, Bowles, Atkinson, and many others, men who have already been mentioned in consideration of their reform activities.

The Gold Democrats also made a notable contribution to the movement. Headed by ex-President Cleveland himself, the anti-imperialists in this classification numbered most of the prominent Democrats who had bolted Bryan and Free Silver two years before. No less than eight members of Cleveland's Cabinets,—Olney, Carlisle, Endicott, Morton, Vilas, Dickinson, Fairchild, and Harmon—came out against expansion, and among the leading anti-imperialists were such Gold Democrats as Bourke Cockran, A. Augustus Healy, Thomas Mott Osborne, Louis Ehrich, and Senator Donelson Caffery.

The Bryan Democrats were significant in the movement for their numbers rather than their leadership. Following Bryan, the majority of the Silverites embraced the anti-imperialist doctrine by 1900, but their advocacy of the cause noticeably lacked the enthusiasm displayed by the independents and the Cleveland men. Only one Bryan Democrat, Senator Ben Tillman, was on the roll of the forty-one vice-presidents of the Anti-Imperialist League, and a mere handful of others, among them Joe Bailey, Champ Clark, and Senator A. O. Bacon, opposed colonial expansion with more than a show of fervor.

The Republicans who joined the anti-imperialist movement were, almost without exception, Republicans of the older generation, former supporters of Fremont and Lincoln who believed they were carrying on the tradition of the party's antislavery days in opposing colonial expansion. They were ably represented in the movement by the president and secretary of the Anti-Imperialist League, George S. Boutwell and Erving Winslow; by Senators Hoar, Hale, and Justin Morrill (who died in December, 1898); by ex-Senators John Sherman, George F. Edmunds, and John B. Henderson, and former President Harrison. Notwithstanding their prominence in party politics, they brought few of the rank and file of the party with them.

A number of Silver Republicans, such as Charles S. Towne and Senator R. F. Pettigrew, a very few Republicans of the younger political generation, among them Henry U. Johnson and Governor William Larrabee, and a scattering of individuals from minor parties also were attracted to the ranks of the anti-imperialists. Few in number, they exercised no important influence on the character of the movement.

Turning from the reform and political classifications, one finds a number of intellectuals in the movement—men who cannot be classified either as reformers or as politicians. They fall into two general categories, the educators and the literary figures. A few college presidents were active anti-imperialists, David Starr Jordan of Stanford and Henry Wade Rogers of Northwestern being the leading examples. Many college professors took the same position, prominent among them being William Graham Sumner, William James, Charles Eliot Norton, Felix Adler, Adolph Cohn, Franklin Henry Giddings, Hermann E. von Holst, William Vaughn Moody, and I. J. McGinity. The literary group contained an equally noteworthy group of men, including Mark Twain, William Dean Howells, Henry B. Fuller, Thomas Wentworth Higginson, Thomas Bailey Aldrich, and Finlay Peter Dunne.

To complete the picture of the anti-imperialist movement, it is necessary to call attention to three economic classifications, the business men and industrialists, the labor leaders, and the "interested groups" in the movement. Though numerically insignificant, each of these groups deserves at least passing mention.

The business and industrial group, very small in size, should be noted because its members, as individuals, did much toward financing the movement. Andrew Carnegie was particularly generous in this respect, and others, including John J. Valentine, Dana Estes, Richard T. Crane, and George Foster Peabody, did their share.

Even smaller was the labor element. The anti-imperialists made great efforts to attract labor support, but, on the whole, were unsuccessful. Samuel Gompers, president of the American Federation of Labor, did show a lively interest in the question, but he was almost the only important labor leader to do so.

Nor did the "interested groups"—the growers of sugar beets, cane sugar, tobacco, and other agricultural products that presumably would suffer from Philippine competition—figure very greatly in the anti-imperialist movement of 1898–1900. Although this may appear surprising in view of the activities of those same groups in the Philippine independence movement thirty years later, it follows from a careful examination of the facts. Two directors of the American Sugar Beet Company were connected with the New York Anti-Imperialist League. At least one farm paper, the *American Agriculturist,* opposed expansion because of the menace of Philippine products. The secretary of the Anti-Imperialist League reported in 1899 that "the tobacco, the beet-sugar and the agricultural interests in general circulated our petitions and made canvasses among their own constituents to bring out remonstrances to the Senate." This, however, is virtually all that can be said of their activities. It does not appear that the "interested groups" contributed much money to the leagues, and certainly they gave the movement few leaders of note. The great majority of the anti-imperialists had no connection, direct or otherwise, with these activities.

It can be seen from this analysis that the anti-imperialists drew their support from a number of sources. This served to increase the prestige of the leagues, but it also served to limit their effectiveness. As each crisis came, in the years from 1898 to 1900, there were differences of opinion and desertions, which periodically threatened to wreck the movement, and finally did bring about its collapse. These dissensions are clearly revealed in the first great fight waged by the anti-imperialists, their struggle against ratification of the treaty of peace with Spain. . . .

The tangible results achieved by the anti-imperialists were few indeed. They may have had some slight influence on the American administration in the islands, by drawing attention to conditions in the Philippines, and, in the course of their long-continued battle for Philippine independence, they may have helped secure the enactment of the Jones Act of 1916. The movement also acted as the agency for restoring many Gold Democrats of party ranks, and for depriving certain Republicans of their influence in the party. But that is all. Beyond these incidental results, the movement seems to have left no perceptible trace in American history. The leaders never gained control of governmental machinery. They did not impress their message on more than a small fraction of the people, and when the Philippine independence bills were finally passed, more than three decades after the second defeat of Bryan, the passage was brought about by a combination of forces very different from those represented in the anti-imperialist movement of 1898–1900.

The reasons for the failure of the anti-imperialist movement are not hard to find. First was the strong position of the imperialists. In the early months of their agitation, the anti-imperialists had to contend with a widespread feeling of nationalism, a feeling engendered by the patriotism and enthusiasm incident to the war with Spain. The people were stirred by the thought of distant possessions, of an empire second to none, a "world power" on whose territories the sun would never set. In time, this feeling gave way to one of indifference, but by then expansion was an accomplished fact.

Second, the anti-imperialists were handicapped by the nature of their case. They were forced to preach abnegation rather than indulgence, to urge the pride of renunciation as against the pride of glory and possession. Their whole case rested on an abstract principle, the application of which was not altogether clear to the public at large. Although they could present a strong emotional argument based on traditions of liberty, the imperialists could more than match this with descriptions of future greatness.

Most tragic of all, however, was the failure to unite in support of a political leader. The majority of the great anti-imperialists—Cleveland and Reed and Hoar are examples—showed no disposition to head a great protest movement. The one available champion of the cause, William Jennings Bryan, was absolutely unacceptable to many anti-imperialists, and was followed by others with extreme reluctance. Men found themselves apologizing rather than fighting for the standard bearer of their cause. And in consequence, what had started as a glorious struggle for freedom ended in bickerings, dissension, and dissatisfaction, a great crusade without crusaders. The anti-imperialists, weakened by desertions and lack of morale, wavered every time they met the enemy, and, in 1900, suffered a rout from which they were never able to recover.

Toward the close of the nineteenth century, a new philosophy took root in the United States—a philosophy that became the prevailing mode of thought from the end of the war with Spain to America's entrance into World War I in 1917. Called by different names—empiricism, instrumentalism, pragmatism—it was a reaction against both idealism and "common-sense" realism, two systems that had been popular in the nineteenth century. Believers in pragmatism, as the philosophy was most usually labeled, rejected the view of the universe as a fixed, final, and static Newtonian machine; rather, they saw a dynamic world, always changing, always growing. They refused to accept a theory of knowledge rooted in God-implanted and innate ideas, substituting instead the conviction that knowledge came from experience and observation. They insisted that there were no eternal and absolute

6

PRAGMATISM

ethical principles but that good and bad were relative to time, place, and circumstance. Theirs was a philosophy that stressed the particular and not the universal. Their reasoning was *a posteriori,* not *a priori.* They favored the inductive over the deductive method; the Aristotelian over the Platonic; the concrete over the abstract. They tested an institution or an act not by any external yardstick but rather by asking a question: "Does it work?" or, "What are its consequences?" If the answers were "yes" or "good," then the institution or act was deemed worthy. As William James, the high priest of the new philosophy, stated, "Pragmatism is the attitude of looking away from first things, principles, 'categories,' supposed necessities; and of looking towards last things, fruits, consequences, facts."

That pragmatism appealed powerfully to Americans is not difficult to understand; it was superbly suited to the American temper. It was a philosophy of action that fitted well a practical, hard-headed, restless, utilitarian nation of innovators always on the move from one frontier to another and always eschewing the old, the traditional, the dogmatic. John Dewey, a James disciple and one of the great spokesmen of the movement, perceived the true marriage of the philosophy and the nation when he wrote, "The progressive and unstable character of American life and civilization has facilitated the birth of a philosophy which regards the world as being in a constant formation, where there is still a place for indeterminism, for the new, for a real future." Indeed, pragmatic ideas and values to some degree had always been present in the American character from the very beginnings of the Republic.

Pragmatism became popular at the end of the century for two reasons. One was the Darwinian theory of evolution, which was incompatible with the ideas of a static universe. For most thinking people, the great Englishman's *Origin of Species* had destroyed the world of absolutes, and they eagerly embraced a new philosophy that conformed to his dynamic concept. Second, the reformers of the Progressive Era found in pragmatism a perfect credo for their cause. They had an excellent instrument for testing the evil political, social, and economic institutions that resulted from industrialization, immigration, and urbanization. They found the justification for their hope that these institutions could be reformed and recast and that man's place in society could be improved, for the institutions were neither sacred nor permanent. As one observer put it, "The concept of a changing world meant the possibility of a better world."

The effect of pragmatism in American life in the first 15 years of the new century was great. It left few institutions untouched. Education, economics, religion, historical studies, the science of society, jurisprudence—all were influenced and in many ways remade by the new philosophy. Education stands as the discipline perhaps most radically altered. It became functional, progressive, and practical. Educators eliminated "dead and useless" subjects from the curriculum. Instead, industrial subject matter was stressed, everyday skills taught, and "meaningful tasks" cultivated. Teachers sought to develop instinctive and impulsive attitudes in their students and to rid them of formalism.

Similarly, economics underwent drastic change. A new school of economists arose, led by Thorstein Veblen, Wesley C. Mitchell, Richard T. Ely, and John R. Commons—all of whom saw economic institutions as constantly changing, always adapting to new conditions, and growing out of human experience. Veblen, in his *Theory of the Leisure Class* (1899), proposed a psychological and historical analysis of class relationships and of property, and he attacked the view that any economic or social institution was divinely ordained or fixed for eternity. Mitchell studied business cycles historically and statistically and concluded that depressions and recurrent economic crises could be averted by proper planning.

Historians abandoned the belief that history could be written objectively. Under the influence of pragmatism, they rejected the view that it could be studied irrespective of the attitudes, passions, and prejudices of the writer or of the pressures of the time. Each generation would have to rewrite its own history; every man would have to be his own historian. No historical event could be recorded finally and for all time, because truth was relative to time and to place. Reflecting the pragmatic view, Carl L. Becker, Charles A. Beard, Frederick Jackson Turner, and James Harvey Robinson blazed new trails in historical scholarship.

Jurisprudence could hardly escape the influence of the pragmatic view. The law came to be seen as constantly changing to meet the needs of a similarly changing society. The term "sociological jurisprudence" was invented to denote the idea that the law must fulfill "social ends." The new spirit may well be summed up in the neat phrase, "The law was made for man; man was not made for the law." Jurists and lawyers such as Roscoe Pound, Oliver Wendell Holmes, Benjamin N. Cardozo, Louis D. Brandeis, and John Wigmore rejected logic as the basis for interpreting the law, and for logic they substituted experience. As Pound pointed out, "The movement is for the adjustment of principles and doctrines to the human conditions they are to govern; for putting the human factor in the central place and relegating logic to its true place as an instrument." And from Holmes' pen: "The life of the law has not been logic; it has been experience. The felt necessities of the time, the prevalent moral and political theories, the institutions of public policy have had a good deal more than syllogisms in determining the rules by which men should be governed."

Religion, too, felt the impact. Churches focused their attention more on the "here" and the "now" and less on the "eternal" and the "everlasting." Many ministers seemed not so much interested in saving souls as in rescuing bodies and hearts and minds from poverty, misery, and despair. Club rooms, reading rooms, and gymnasiums became as important as church buildings. Ritual and dogma were de-emphasized in favor of the application of Christian principles to solving the mundane problems of everyday life. Alongside traditional subjects such as homiletics and Biblical exegesis, seminaries introduced courses on economics, sociology, and pastoral care. The "social gospel," indeed, became the central feature of Christianity, with men like Walter Rauschenbusch, Washington Gladden, and Josiah Strong serving as the chief spokesmen.

Obviously, not all Americans accepted pragmatism as a panacea. As the twentieth century moved toward war in 1914, many thoughtful people were becoming convinced that pragmatism, rather than solving the world's ills, was exacerbating them. They ascribed the national and international anarchy to the destruction of absolutes, of objective norms of good and evil, and of permanent yardsticks for measuring ethical conduct. If truth, justice, and all the other accepted virtues were transitory, ever-changing, and determined by each individual, then surely men and nations could pursue any course of action that experience might dictate. There was much questioning of a philosophy that abolished a common denominator and that eliminated a standard to which all men could rally.

The influence of pragmatism inevitably waned after the First World War. It was a philosophy unwelcome in the unfriendly climate of the nineteen twenties. There is no denying that in its heyday it did not solve all the problems that pressed down upon the nation and the world. This fact does not, however, prevent a fair appraisal of its place in the mainstream of American life. There is little doubt that almost every institution in the United States was improved by a philosophy that focused its attention on the individual and tried to improve his lot. That some institutions suffered from the excessive zeal of the pragmatists is also true. Certainly, progressive education seems to have carried the ideas of pragmatists to almost absurd lengths. But it is a truism of history that any fresh movement or idea tends to swing the pendulum too far to the other end of the arc, and that in time the pendulum eventually comes to rest near the middle, as the recent history of educational philosophy demonstrates. Above all, pragmatism's importance stems from the fact that it expressed and was perfectly suited to the prevailing optimistic and hopeful temper of the times and to the view that man was master of his own destiny and could shape society to better ends.

The selections in this chapter illustrate some of the important features of pragmatism. The first describes its nature, the next two analyze its effect on religion and education, and the last offers a somewhat disillusioned criticism.

William James

What Pragmatism

Means

The classic statement of the pragmatic philosophy appeared in 1907 in a volume of lectures entitled Pragmatism: A New Name for Some Old Ways of Thinking, *by William James. Born in 1842, he was the older brother of Henry James, the novelist. According to one prominent historian, William James was "the greatest of the American relativists, and perhaps the central figure of American intellectual history in the early twentieth century." Trained in chemistry, physiology, and medicine at Harvard, he was for many years an instructor there in physiology. His interests, however, soon shifted to the relation between physiology and psychology, which resulted in* Principles of Psychology (1890). *This work gained him an international reputation. His next intellectual excursion, in religion, came to fruition in another important work,* The Varieties of Religious Experience (1902). *Next he moved to philosophy. Dissatisfied with philosophic idealism, which he had studied in Germany and whose chief exponent in America was his friend Josiah Royce, and attracted to the views of John Stuart Mill and the British empiricists, he came to pragmatism quite easily.*

James did not coin the term pragmatism. As he points out in the following essay, it was first used by Charles S. Peirce, another Harvard philosopher, in January 1878. And James himself had exposed his pragmatic ideas well before his lectures were published in 1907. They may be seen quite clearly in the Principles *some 17 years earlier. It is in the lectures, however—the second of which is reprinted here—that one finds the most succinct and clearest statement. [William James,* Essays in Pragmatism, *edited by A. Castell (New York: Hafner Publishing Company, Inc., 1948). Reprinted by permission.]*

Some years ago, being with a camping party in the mountains, I returned from a solitary ramble to find every one engaged in a ferocious metaphysical dispute. The *corpus* of the dispute was a squirrel--a live squirrel supposed to be clinging to one side of a tree-trunk; while over against the tree's opposite side a human being was imagined to stand. This human witness tries to get sight of the squirrel by moving rapidly round the tree, but no matter how fast he goes, the squirrel moves as fast in the opposite direction, and always keeps the tree between himself and the man, so that never a glimpse of him is caught. The resultant metaphysical problem now is this: *Does the man go round the squirrel or not?* He goes round the tree, sure enough, and the squirrel is on the tree; but does he go round the squirrel? In the unlimited leisure of the wilderness, discussion had been worn threadbare. Every one had taken sides, and was obstinate; and the numbers on both sides were even. Each side, when I appeared, therefore appealed to me to make it a majority. Mindful of the scholastic adage that whenever you meet a contradiction you must make a distinction, I immediately sought and found one, as follows: "Which party is right," I said, "depends on what you *practically mean* by 'going round' the squirrel. If you mean passing from the north of him to the east, then to the south, then to the west, and then to the north of him again, obviously the man does go round him, for he occupies these successive positions. But if on the contrary you mean being first in front of him, then on the right of him, then behind him, then on his left, and finally in front again, it is quite as obvious that the man fails to go round him, for by the compensating movements the squirrel makes, he keeps his belly turned towards the man all the time, and his back turned away. Make the distinction, and there is no occasion for any further dispute. You are both right and both wrong according as you conceive the verb 'to go round' in one practical fashion or the other."

Although one or two of the hotter disputants called my speech a shuffling evasion, saying they wanted no quibbling or scholastic hair-splitting, but meant just plain honest English "round," the majority seemed to think that the distinction had assuaged the dispute.

I tell this trivial anecdote because it is a peculiarly simple example of what I wish now to speak of as *the pragmatic method.* The pragmatic method is primarily a method of settling metaphysical disputes that otherwise might be interminable. Is the world one or many?—fated or free?—material or spiritual?—here are notions either of which may or may not hold good of the world; and disputes over such notions are unending. The pragmatic method in such cases is to try to interpret each notion by tracing its respective practical consequences. What difference would it practically make to any one if this notion rather than that notion were true? If no practical difference whatever can be traced, then the alternatives mean practically the same thing, and all dispute is idle. Whenever a dispute is serious, we ought to be able to show some practical difference that must follow from one side or the other's being right.

A glance at the history of the idea will show you still better what pragmatism means. The term is derived from the same Greek word πρᾶγμα, meaning action, from which our words "practice" and "practical" come. It was first introduced into philosophy by Mr. Charles Peirce in 1878. In an article entitled "How to Make Our Ideas Clear," in the *Popular Science Monthly* for January of that year Mr. Peirce, after pointing out that our beliefs are really rules for action, said that, to develop a thought's meaning, we need only determine what conduct it is fitted to produce: that conduct is for us its sole significance. And the tangible fact at the root of all our thought-distinctions, however subtle, is that there is no one of them so fine as to consist in anything but a possible difference of practice. To attain perfect clearness in our thoughts of an object, then, we need only consider what conceivable effects of a practical kind the object may involve—what sensations we are to expect from it, and what reactions we must prepare. Our conception of these effects, whether immediate or remote, is then for us the whole of our conception of the object, so far as that conception has positive significance at all.

This is the principle of Peirce, the principle of pragmatism. It lay entirely unnoticed by any one for twenty years, until I, in an address before Professor Howison's Philosophical Union at the University of California, brought it forward again and made a special application of it to religion. By that date (1898) the times seemed ripe for its reception. The word "pragmatism" spread, and at present it fairly spots the pages of the philosophic journals. On all hands we find the "pragmatic movement" spoken of, sometimes with respect, sometimes with contumely, seldom with clear understanding. It is evident that the term applies itself conveniently to a number of tendencies that hitherto have lacked a collective name, and that it has "come to stay."

To take in the importance of Peirce's principle, one must get accustomed to applying it to concrete cases. I found a few years ago that Ostwald, the illustrious Leipzig chemist, had been making perfectly distinct use of the principle of pragmatism in his lectures on the philosophy of science, though he had not called it by that name.

"All realities influence our practice," he wrote me, "and that influence is their meaning for us. I am accustomed to put questions to my classes in this way: In what respects would the world be different if this alternative or that were true? If I can find nothing that would become different, then the alternative has no sense."

That is, the rival views mean practically the same thing, and meaning, other than practical, there is for us none. Ostwald in a published lecture gives this example of what he means. Chemists have long wrangled over the inner constitution of certain bodies called "tautomerous." Their properties seemed equally consistent with the notion that an instable hydrogen atom oscillates inside of them, or that they are instable mixtures of two bodies. Controversy raged, but never was decided. "It would never have begun," says Ostwald, "if the combatants had asked themselves what particular experimental fact could have been made different by one or the other view being correct. For it would then have appeared that no difference of fact could possibly ensue; and the quarrel was as unreal as if, theorizing in primitive times about the raising of dough by yeast, one party should have invoked a 'brownie,' while another insisted on an 'elf' as the true cause of the phenomenon."

It is astonishing to see how many philosophical disputes collapse into insignificance the moment you subject them to this simple test of tracing a concrete consequence. There can *be* no difference anywhere that doesn't *make* a difference elsewhere—no difference in abstract truth that doesn't express itself in a difference in concrete fact and in conduct consequent upon that fact, imposed on somebody, somehow, somewhere, and some-when. The whole function of philosophy ought to be to find out what definite difference it will make to you and me, at definite instants of our life, if this world-formula or that world-formula be the true one.

There is absolutely nothing new in the pragmatic method. Socrates was an adept at it. Aristotle used it methodically. Locke, Berkeley, and Hume made momentous contributions to truth by its means. Shadworth Hodgson keeps insisting that realities are only what they are "known as." But these forerunners of pragmatism used it in fragments: they were preluders only. Not until in our time has it generalized itself, become conscious of a universal mission, pretended to a conquering destiny. I believe in that destiny, and I hope I may end by inspiring you with my belief.

Pragmatism represents a perfectly familiar attitude in philosophy, the empiricist attitude, but it represents it, as it seems to me, both in a more radical and in a less objectionable form than it has ever yet assumed. A pragmatist turns his back resolutely and once for all upon a lot of inveterate habits dear to professional philosophers. He turns away from abstraction and insufficiency, from verbal solutions, from bad *a priori* reasons, from fixed principles, closed systems, and pretended absolutes and origins. He turns towards concreteness and adequacy, towards facts, towards action and towards power. That means the empiricist temper regnant and the rationalist temper sincerely given up. It means the open air and possibilities of nature, as against dogma, artificiality, and the pretence of finality in truth.

At the same time it does not stand for any special results. It is a method only. But the general triumph of that method would mean an enormous change in what I called in my last lecture the "temperament" of philosophy. Teachers of the ultra-rationalistic type would be frozen out, much as the courtier type is frozen out in republics, as the ultramontane type of priest is frozen out in protestant lands. Science and metaphysics would come much nearer together, would in fact work absolutely hand in hand.

Metaphysics has usually followed a very primitive kind of quest. You know how men have always hankered after unlawful magic, and you know what a great part in magic *words* have always played. If you have his name, or the formula of incantation that binds him, you can control the spirit, genie, afrite, or whatever the power may be. Solomon knew the names of all the spirits, and having their names, he held them subject to his will. So the universe has always appeared to the natural mind as a kind of enigma, of which the key must be sought in the shape of some illuminating or power-bringing word or name. That word names the universe's *principle,* and to possess it is after a fashion to possess the universe itself. "God," "Matter," "Reason," "the Absolute," "Energy," are so many solving names. You can rest when you have them. You are at the end of your metaphysical quest.

But if you follow the pragmatic method, you cannot look on any such word as closing your quest. You must bring out of each word its practical cash-value, set it at work within the stream of your experience. It appears less as a solution, then, than as a program for more work, and more particularly as an indication of the ways in which existing realities may be *changed.*

Theories thus become instruments, not answers to enigmas, in which we can rest. We don't lie back upon them, we move forward, and, on occasion, make nature over again by their aid. Pragmatism unstiffens all our theories, limbers them up and sets each one at work. Being nothing essentially new, it harmonizes with many ancient philosophic tendencies. It agrees with nominalism, for instance, in always appealing to particulars; with utilitarianism in emphasizing practical aspects; with positivism in its disdain for verbal solutions, useless questions and metaphysical abstractions.

All these, you see, are *anti-intellectualist* tendencies. Against rationalism as a pretension and a method pragmatism is fully armed and militant. But, at the outset, at least, it stands for no particular results. It has no dogmas, and no doctrines save its method. As the young Italian pragmatist Papini has well said, it lies in the midst of our theories, like a corridor in a hotel. Innumerable chambers open out of it. In one you may find a man writing an atheistic volume; in the next some one on his knees praying for faith and strength; in a third a chemist investigating a body's properties. In a fourth a system of idealistic metaphysics is being excogitated; in a fifth the impossibility of metaphysics is being shown. But they all own the corridor, and all must pass through it if they want a practicable way of getting into or out of their respective rooms.

No particular results then, so far, but only an attitude of orientation, is what the pragmatic method means. *The attitude of looking away from first things, principles, "categories," supposed necessities; and of looking towards last things, fruits, consequences, facts.*

So much for the pragmatic method! You may say that I have been praising it rather than explaining it to you, but I shall presently explain it abundantly enough by showing how it works on some familiar problems. Meanwhile the word pragmatism has come to be used in a still wider sense, as meaning also a certain *theory of truth.* I mean to give a whole lecture to the statement of that theory, after first paving the way, so I can be very brief now. But brevity is hard to follow, so I ask for your redoubled attention for a quarter of an hour. If much remains obscure, I hope to make it clearer in the later lectures.

One of the most successfully cultivated branches of philosophy in our time is what is called inductive logic, the study of the conditions under which our sciences have evolved. Writers on this subject have begun to show a singular unanimity as to what the laws of nature and elements of fact mean, when formulated by mathematicians, physicists and chemists. When the first mathematical, logical, and natural uniformities, the first *laws,* were discovered, men were so carried away by the clearness, beauty and simplification that resulted, that they believed themselves to have deciphered authentically the eternal thoughts of the Almighty. His mind also thundered and reverberated in syllogisms. He also thought in conic sections, squares and roots and ratios, and geometrized like Euclid. He made Kepler's laws for the planets to follow; he made velocity increase proportionally to the time in falling bodies; he made the law of the sines for light to obey when refracted; he established the classes, orders, families and genera of plants and animals, and fixed the distances between them. He thought the archetypes of all things, and devised their variations; and when we rediscover any one of these his wondrous institutions, we seize his mind in its very literal intention.

But as the sciences have developed further, notion has gained ground that most, perhaps all, of our laws are only approximations. The laws themselves, moreover, have grown so numerous that there is no counting them; and so many rival formulations are proposed in all the branches of science that investigators have become accustomed to the notion that no theory is absolutely a transcript of reality, but that any one of them may from some point of view be useful. Their great use is to summarize old facts and to lead to new ones. They are only a man-made language, a conceptual shorthand, as some one calls them, in which we write our reports of nature; and languages, as is well known, tolerate much choice of expression and many dialects.

Thus human arbitrariness has driven divine necessity from scientific logic. If I mention the names of Sigwart, Mach, Ostwald, Pearson, Milhaud, Poincaré, Duhem, Ruyssen, those of you who are students will easily identify the tendency I speak of, and will think of additional names.

Riding now on the front of this wave of scientific logic Messrs. Schiller and Dewey appear with their pragmatistic account of what truth everywhere signifies. Everywhere, these teachers say, "truth" in our ideas and beliefs means the same thing that it means in science. It means, they say, nothing but this, *that ideas (which themselves are but parts of our experience) become true just in so far as they help us to get into satisfactory relation with other parts of our experience,* to summarize them and get about among them by conceptual short-cuts instead of following the interminable succession of particular phenomena. Any idea upon which we can ride, so to speak; any idea that will carry us prosperously from any one part of our experience to any other part, linking things satisfactorily, working securely, simplifying, saving labor; is true for just so much, true in so far forth, true *instrumentally*. This is the "instrumental" view of truth taught so successfully at Chicago, the view that truth in our ideas means their power to "work," promulgated so brilliantly at Oxford.

Messrs. Dewey, Schiller, and their allies, in reaching this general conception of all truth, have only followed the example of geologists, biologists and philologists. In the establishment of these other sciences, the successful stroke was always to take some simple process actually observable in operation—as denudation by weather, say, or variation from parental type, or change of dialect by incorporation of new words and pronunciations—and then to generalize it, making it apply to all times, and produce great results by summating its effects through the ages.

The observable process which Schiller and Dewey particularly singled out for generalization is the familiar one by which any individual settles into *new opinions*. The process here is always the same. The individual has a stock of old opinions already, but he meets a new experience that puts them to a strain. Somebody contradicts them; or in a reflective moment he discovers that they contradict each other; or he hears of facts with which they are incompatible; or desires arise in him which they cease to satisfy. The result is an inward trouble to which his mind till then had been a stranger, and from which he seeks to escape by modifying his previous mass of opinions. He saves as much of it as he can, for in this matter of belief we are all extreme conservatives. So he tries to change first this opinion, and then that (for they resist change very variously), until at last some new idea comes up which he can graft upon the ancient stock with a minimum of disturbance of the latter, some idea that mediates between the stock and the new experience and runs them into one another most felicitously and expediently.

This new idea is then adopted as the true one. It preserves the older stock of truths with a minimum of modification, stretching them just enough to make them admit the novelty, but conceiving that in ways as familiar as the case leaves possible. An *outrée* explanation, violating all our preconceptions, would never pass for a true account of a novelty. We should scratch round industriously till we found something less excentric. The most violent revolutions in an individual's beliefs leave most of his old order standing. Time and space, cause and effect, nature and history, and one's own biography remain untouched. New truth is always a go-between, a smoother-over of transitions. It marries old opinion to new fact so as ever to show a minimum of jolt, a maximum of continuity. We hold a theory true just in proportion to its success in solving this "problem of maxima and minima." But success in solving this problem is eminently a matter of approximation. We say this theory solves it on the whole more satisfactorily than that theory; but that means more satisfactorily to ourselves, and individuals will emphasize their points of satisfaction differently. To a certain degree, therefore, everything here is plastic.

The point I now urge you to observe particularly is the part played by the older truths. Failure to take account of it is the source of much of the unjust criticism levelled against pragmatism. Their influence is absolutely controlling. Loyalty to them is the first principle—in most cases it is the only principle; for by far the most usual way of handling phenomena so novel that they would make for a serious rearrangement of our preconception is to ignore them altogether, or to abuse those who bear witness for them.

You doubtless wish examples of this process of truth's growth, and the only trouble is their superabundance. The simplest case of new truth is of course the mere numerical addition of new kinds of facts, or of new single facts of old kinds, to our experience—an addition that involves no alteration in the old beliefs. Day follows day, and its contents are simply added. The new contents themselves are not true, they simply *come* and *are*. Truth is *what we say about* them, and when we say that they have come, truth is satisfied by the plain additive formula.

But often the day's contents oblige a rearrangement. If I should now utter piercing shrieks and act like a maniac on this platform, it would make many of you revise your ideas as to the probable worth of my philosophy. "Radium" came the other day as part of the day's content, and seemed for a moment to contradict our ideas of the whole order of nature, that order having come to be identified with what is called the conservation of energy. The mere sight of radium paying heat away indefinitely out of its own pocket seemed to violate that conservation. What to think? If the radiations from it were nothing but an escape of unsuspected "potential" energy, pre-existent inside of the atoms, the principle of conservation would be saved. The discovery of "helium" as the radiation's outcome, opened a way to this belief. So Ramsay's view is generally held to be true, because, although it extends our old ideas of energy, it causes a minimum of alteration in their nature.

I need not multiply instances. A new opinion counts as "true" just in proportion as it gratifies the individual's desire to assimilate the novel in his experience to his beliefs in stock. It must both lean on old truth and grasp new fact; and its success (as I said a moment ago) in doing this, is a matter for the individual's appreciation. When old truth grows, then, by new truth's addition, it is for subjective reasons. We are in the process and obey the reasons. That new idea is truest which performs most felicitously its function of satisfying our double urgency. It makes itself true, gets itself classed as true, by the way it works; grafting itself then upon the ancient body of truth, which thus grows much as a tree grows by the activity of a new layer of cambium.

Now Dewey and Schiller proceed to generalize this observation and to apply it to the most ancient parts of truth. They also once were plastic. They also were called true for human reasons. They also mediated between still earlier truths and what in those days were novel observations. Purely objective truth, truth in whose establishment the function of giving human satisfaction in marrying previous parts of experience with newer parts played no rôle whatever, is nowhere to be found. The reasons why we call things true is the reason why they *are* true, for "to be true" *means* only to perform this marriage-function.

The trail of the human serpent is thus over everything. Truth independent; truth that we *find* merely; truth no longer malleable to human need; truth incorrigible, in a word; such truth exists indeed superabundantly—or is supposed to exist by rationalistically minded thinkers; but then it means only the dead heart of the living tree, and its being there means only that truth also has its paleontology, and its "prescription," and may grow stiff with years of veteran service and petrified in men's regard by sheer antiquity. But how plastic even the oldest truths nevertheless really are has been vividly shown in our day by the transformation of logical and mathematical ideas, a transformation which seems even to be invading physics. The ancient formulas are reinterpreted as special expressions of much wider principles, principles that our ancestors never got a glimpse of in their present shape and formulation.

Mr. Schiller still gives to all this view of truth the name of "Humanism," but, for this doctrine too, the name of pragmatism seems fairly to be in the ascendant, so I will treat it under the name of pragmatism in these lectures.

Such then would be the scope of pragmatism—first, a method; and second, a genetic theory of what is meant by truth. And these two things must be our future topics.

What I have said of the theory of truth will, I am sure, have appeared obscure and unsatisfactory to most of you by reason of its brevity. I shall make amends for that hereafter. In a lecture on "common sense" I shall try to show what I mean by truths grown petrified by antiquity. In another lecture I shall expatiate on the idea that our thoughts become true in proportion as they successfully exert their go-between function. In a third I shall show how hard it is to discriminate subjective from objective factors in Truth's development. You may not follow me wholly in these lectures; and if you do, you may not wholly agree with me. But you will, I know, regard me at least as serious, and treat my effort with respectful consideration.

You will probably be surprised to learn, then, that Messrs. Schiller's and Dewey's theories have suffered a hailstorm of contempt and ridicule. All rationalism has risen against them. In influential quarters Mr. Schiller, in particular, has been treated like an impudent schoolboy who deserves a spanking. I should not mention this but for the fact that it throws so much sidelight upon that rationalistic temper to which I have opposed the temper of pragmatism. Pragmatism is uncomfortable away from facts. Rationalism is comfortable only in the presence of abstractions. This pragmatist talk about truths in the plural, about their utility and satisfactoriness, about the success with which they "work," etc., suggests to the typical intellectualist mind a sort of coarse lame second-rate makeshift article of truth. Such truths are not real truth. Such tests are merely subjective. As against this, objective truth must be something non-utilitarian, haughty, refined, remote, august, exalted. It must be an absolute correspondence of our thoughts with an equally absolute reality. It must be what we *ought* to think unconditionally. The conditioned ways in which we *do* think are so much irrelevance and matter for psychology. Down with psychology, up with logic, in all this question!

See the exquisite contrast of the types of mind! The pragmatist clings to facts and concreteness, observes truth at its work in particular cases, and generalizes. Truth, for him, becomes a class-name for all sorts of definite working-values in experience. For the rationalist it remains a pure abstraction, to the bare name of which we must defer. When the pragmatist undertakes to show in detail just *why* we must defer, the rationalist is unable to recognize the concretes from which his own abstraction is taken. He accuses us of *denying* truth; whereas we have only sought to trace exactly why people follow it and always ought to follow it. Your typical ultra-abstractionist fairly shudders at concreteness: other things equal, he positively prefers the pale and spectral. If the two universes were offered, he would always choose the skinny outline rather than the rich thicket of reality. It is so much purer, clearer, nobler.

I hope that as these lectures go on, the concreteness and closeness to facts of the pragmatism which they advocate may be what approves itself to you as its most satisfactory peculiarity. It only follows here the example of the sister-sciences, interpreting the unobserved by the observed. It brings old and new harmoniously together. It converts the absolutely empty notion of a static relation of "correspondence" (what that may mean we must ask later) between our minds and reality, into that of a rich and active commerce (that any one may follow in detail and understand) between particular thoughts of ours, and the great universe of other experiences in which they play their parts and have their uses.

John Dewey

Pragmatism and

Education

No account of progressive education is complete without reference to John Dewey, its creator and guiding spirit. Born in 1859, he studied at Johns Hopkins University and taught philosophy at the Universities of Minnesota, Michigan, Chicago, and Columbia. A prolific writer on philosophy, pyschology, and education, it was in the latter field that he made his greatest imprint. Applying the concrete, practical, pragmatic approach to education, he envisaged it "as a process of living and not as a preparation for future living." The emphasis was, therefore, on learning for the purpose of social utility, "to reproduce on the child's level the typical doings and occupations of the larger, ma-

turer society into which he is finally to go forth." He saw the school not as a training ground for democracy but as democracy itself, and hence he objected to the traditional authoritarian position of the teacher with the birch rod poised over the unhappy student who missed the rote recitation of "dead" subject matter. The purpose of education was to "develop in each individual the knowledge, interests, ideals, habits, and powers whereby he will find his place and use that place to shape both himself and his society toward ever nobler aims." Dewey's ideas on education may be found in two key books, School and Society *(1899) and* Democracy and Education *(1916). But it is in his essay "My Pedagogic Creed," published in 1897 and reprinted here, that he stated most precisely his important and trail-blazing views. [From* Education Today *by John Dewey. Copyright 1940 by John Dewey. Reprinted by permission of G. P. Putnam's Sons.]*

Article I—What Education Is

I Believe that

—all education proceeds by the participation of the individual in the social consciousness of the race. This process begins unconsciously almost at birth, and is continually shaping the individual's powers, saturating his consciousness, forming his habits, training his ideas, and arousing his feelings and emotions. Through this unconscious education the individual gradually comes to share in the intellectual and moral resources which humanity has succeeded in getting together. He becomes an inheritor of the funded capital of civilization. The most formal and technical education in the world cannot safely depart from this general process. It can only organize it or differentiate it in some particular direction.

—the only true education comes through the stimulation of the child's powers by the demands of the social situations in which he finds himself. Through these demands he is stimulated to act as a member of a unity, to emerge from his original narrowness of action and feeling, and to conceive of himself from the standpoint of the welfare of the group to which he belongs. Through the responses which others make to his own activities he comes to know what these mean in social terms. The value which they have is reflected back into them. For instance, through the response which is made to the child's instinctive babblings the child comes to know what those babblings mean; they are transformed into articulate language, and thus the child is introduced into the consolidated wealth of ideas and emotions which are now summed up in language.

—this educational process has two sides—one psychological and one sociological—and that neither can be subordinated to the other, or neglected, without evil results following. Of these two sides, the psychological is the basis. The child's own instincts and powers furnish the material and give the starting-point for all education. Save as the efforts of the educator connect with some activity which the child is carrying on of his own initiative independent of the educator, education becomes reduced to a pressure from without. It may, indeed, give certain external results, but cannot truly be called educative. Without insight into the psychological structure and activities of the individual, the educative process will, therefore, be haphazard and arbitrary. If it chances to coincide with the child's activity it will get a leverage; if it does not, it will result in friction, or disintegration, or arrest of the child nature.

—knowledge of social conditions, of the present state of civilization, is necessary in order properly to interpret the child's powers. The child has his own instincts and tendencies, but we do not know what these mean until we can translate them into their social equivalents. We must be able to carry them back into a social past and see them as the inheritance of previous race activities. We must also be able to project them into the future to see what their outcome and end will be. In the illustration just used, it is the ability to see in the child's babblings the promise and potency of a future social intercourse and conversation which enables one to deal in the proper way with that instinct.

—the psychological and social sides are organically related, and that education cannot be regarded as a compromise between the two, or a superimposition of one upon the other. We are told that the psychological definition of education is barren and formal—that it gives us only the idea of a development of all the mental powers without giving us any idea of the use to which these powers are put. On the other hand, it is urged that the social definition of education, as getting adjusted to civilization, makes of it a forced and external process, and results in subordinating the freedom of the individual to a preconceived social and political status.

—each of these objections is true when urged against one side isolated from the other. In order to know what a power really is we must know what its end, use, or function is, and this we cannot know save as we conceive of the individual as active in social relationships. But, on the other hand, the only possible adjustment which we can give to the child under existing conditions is that which arises through putting him in complete possession of all his powers. With the advent of democracy and modern industrial conditions, it is impossible to foretell definitely just what civilization will be twenty years from now. Hence it is impossible to prepare the child for any precise set of conditions. To prepare him for the future life means to give him command of himself; it means so to train him that he will have the full and ready use of all his capacities; that his eye and ear and hand may be tools ready to command, that his judgment may be capable of grasping the conditions under which it has to work, and the executive forces be trained to act economically and efficiently. It is impossible to reach this sort of adjustment save as con-

stant regard is had to the individual's own powers, tastes, and interests—
that is, as education is continually converted into psychological terms.

In sum, I believe that the individual who is to be educated is a social
individual, and that society is an organic union of individuals. If we
eliminate the social factor from the child we are left only with an abstraction; if we eliminate the individual factor from society, we are left only
with an inert and lifeless mass. Education, therefore, must begin with a
psychological insight into the child's capacities, interests, and habits. It
must be controlled at every point by reference to these same considerations. These powers, interests, and habits must be continually interpreted—we must know what they mean. They must be translated into
terms of their social equivalents—into terms of what they are capable of
in the way of social service.

ARTICLE II—WHAT THE SCHOOL IS

I Believe that

—the school is primarily a social institution. Education being a social
process, the school is simply that form of community life in which all
those agencies are concentrated that will be most effective in bringing the
child to share in the inherited resources of the race, and to use his own
powers for social ends.

—education, therefore, is a process of living and not a preparation for
future living.

—the school must represent present life—life as real and vital to the
child as that which he carries on in the home, in the neighborhood, or on
the playground.

—that education which does not occur through forms of life, forms that
are worth living for their own sake, is always a poor substitute for the
genuine reality, and tends to cramp and to deaden.

—the school, as an institution, should simplify existing social life; should
reduce it, as it were, to an embryonic form. Existing life is so complex
that the child cannot be brought into contact with it without either
confusion or distraction; he is either overwhelmed by the multiplicity of
activities which are going on, so that he loses his own power of orderly
reaction, or he is so stimulated by these various activities that his powers
are prematurely called into play and he becomes either unduly specialized or else disintegrated.

—as such simplified social life, the school life should grow gradually out
of the home life; that it should take up and continue the activities with
which the child is already familiar in the home.

—it should exhibit these activities to the child, and reproduce them in
such ways that the child will gradually learn the meaning of them, and
be capable of playing his own part in relation to them.

—this is a psychological necessity, because it is the only way of securing continuity in the child's growth, the only way of giving a background of past experience to the new ideas given in school.

—it is also a social necessity because the home is the form of social life in which the child has been nurtured and in connection with which he has had his moral training. It is the business of the school to deepen and extend his sense of the values bound up in his home life.

—much of present education fails because it neglects this fundamental principle of the school as a form of community life. It conceives the school as a place where certain information is to be given, where certain lessons are to be learned, or where certain habits are to be formed. The value of these is conceived as lying largely in the remote future; the child must do these things for the sake of something else he is to do; they are mere preparations. As a result they do not become a part of the life experience of the child and so are not truly educative.

—the moral education centers upon this conception of the school as a mode of social life, that the best and deepest moral training is precisely that which one gets through having to enter into proper relations with others in a unity of work and thought. The present educational systems, so far as they destroy or neglect this unity, render it difficult or impossible to get any genuine, regular moral training.

—the child should be stimulated and controlled in his work through the life of the community.

—under existing conditions far too much of the stimulus and control proceeds from the teacher, because of neglect of the idea of the school as a form of social life.

—the teacher's place and work in the school is to be interpreted from this same basis. The teacher is not in the school to impose certain ideas or to form certain habits in the child, but is there as a member of the community to select the influences which shall affect the child and to assist him in properly responding to these influences.

—the discipline of the school should proceed from the life of the school as a whole and not directly from the teacher.

—the teacher's business is simply to determine, on the basis of larger experience and riper wisdom, how the discipline of life shall come to the child.

—all questions of the grading of the child and his promotion should be determined by reference to the same standard. Examinations are of use only so far as they test the child's fitness for social life and reveal the place in which he can be of the most service and where he can receive the most help.

ARTICLE III—THE SUBJECT-MATTER OF EDUCATION

I Believe that

—the social life of the child is the basis of concentration, or correlation, in all his training or growth. The social life gives the unconscious unity and the background of all his efforts and of all his attainments.

—the subject-matter of the school curriculum should mark a gradual differentiation out of the primitive unconscious unity of social life.

—we violate the child's nature and render difficult the best ethical results by introducing the child too abruptly to a number of special studies, of reading, writing, geography, etc., out of relation to this social life.

—the true center of correlation on the school subjects is not science, nor literature, nor history, nor geography, but the child's own social activities.

—education cannot be unified in the study of science, or so-called nature study, because apart from human activity, nature itself is not a unity; nature in itself is a number of diverse objects in space and time, and to attempt to make it the center of work by itself is to introduce a principle of radiation rather than one of concentration.

—literature is the reflex expression and interpretation of social experience; that hence it must follow upon and not precede such experience. It, therefore, cannot be made the basis, although it may be made the summary of unification.

—once more that history is of educative value in so far as it presents phases of social life and growth. It must be controlled by reference to social life. When taken simply as history it is thrown into the distant past and becomes dead and inert. Taken as the record of man's social life and progress it becomes full of meaning. I believe, however, that it cannot be so taken excepting as the child is also introduced directly into social life.

—the primary basis of education is in the child's powers at work along the same general constructive lines as those which have brought civilization into being.

—the only way to make the child conscious of his social heritage is to enable him to perform those fundamental types of activity which make civilization what it is.

—the so-called expressive or constructive activities are the center of correlation.

—this gives the standard for the place of cooking, sewing, manual training, etc., in the school.

—they are not special studies which are to be introduced over and above a lot of others in the way of relaxation or relief, or as additional accomplishments. I believe rather that they represent, as types, fundamental forms of social activity; and that it is possible and desirable that the child's introduction into the more formal subjects of the curriculum be through the medium of these activities.

—the study of science is educational in so far as it brings out the materials and processes which make social life what it is.

—one of the greatest difficulties in the present teaching of science is that the material is presented in purely objective form, or is treated as a new peculiar kind of experience which the child can add to that which he has already had. In reality, science is of value because it gives the ability to interpret and control the experience already had. It should be introduced, not as so much new subject-matter, but as showing the factors already involved in previous experience and as furnishing tools by which that experience can be more easily and effectively regulated.

—at present we lose much of the value of literature and language studies because of our elimination of the social element. Language is almost always treated in the books of pedagogy simply as the expression of thought. It is true that language is a logical instrument, but it is fundamentally and primarily a social instrument. Language is the device for communication; it is the tool through which one individual comes to share the ideas and feelings of others. When treated simply as a way of getting individual information, or as a means of showing off what one has learned, it loses its social motive and end.

—there is, therefore, no succession of studies in the ideal school curriculum. If education is life, all life has, from the outset, a scientific aspect, an aspect of art and culture, and an aspect of communication. It cannot, therefore, be true that the proper studies for one grade are mere reading and writing, and that at a later grade, reading, or literature, or science, may be introduced. The progress is not in the succession of studies, but in the development of new attitudes towards, and new interests in, experience.

—education must be conceived as a continuing reconstruction of experience; that the process and the goal of education are one and the same thing.

—to set up any end outside of education, as furnishing its goal and standard, is to deprive the educational process of much of its meaning, and tends to make us rely upon false and external stimuli in dealing with the child.

ARTICLE IV—THE NATURE OF METHOD

I believe that

—the question of method is ultimately reducible to the question of the order of development of the child's powers and interests. The law for presenting and treating material is the law implicit within the child's own nature. Because this is so I believe the following statements are of supreme importance as determining the spirit in which education is carried on:

—the active side precedes the passive in the development of the child-nature; that expression comes before conscious impression; that the muscular development precedes the sensory; that movements come before conscious sensations; I believe that consciousness is essentially motor or impulsive; that conscious states tend to project themselves in action.

—the neglect of this principle is the cause of a large part of the waste of time and strength in school work. The child is thrown into a passive, receptive, or absorbing attitude. The conditions are such that he is not permitted to follow the law of his nature; the result is friction and waste.

—ideas (intellectual and rational processes) also result from action and devolve for the sake of the better control of action. What we term reason is primarily the law of orderly or effective action. To attempt to develop the reasoning powers, the powers of judgment, without reference to the selection and arrangement of means in action, is the fundamental fallacy in our present methods of dealing with this matter. As a result we present the child with arbitrary symbols. Symbols are a necessity in mental development, but they have their place as tools for economizing effort; presented by themselves they are a mass of meaningless and arbitrary ideas imposed from without.

—the image is the great instrument of instruction. What a child gets out of any subject presented to him is simply the images which he himself forms with regard to it.

—if nine-tenths of the energy at present directed towards making the child learn certain things were spent in seeing to it that the child was forming proper images, the work of instruction would be indefinitely facilitated.

—much of the time and attention now given to the preparation and presentation of lessons might be more wisely and profitably expended in training the child's power of imagery and in seeing to it that he was continually forming definite, vivid, and growing images of the various subjects with which he comes in contact in his experience.

—interests are the signs and symptoms of growing power. I believe that they represent dawning capacities. Accordingly the constant and careful observation of interests is of the utmost importance for the educator.

—these interests are to be observed as showing the state of development which the child has reached.

—they prophesy the stage upon which he is about to enter.

—only through the continual and sympathetic observation of childhood's interests can the adult enter into the child's life and see what it is ready for, and upon what material it could work most readily and fruitfully.

—these interests are neither to be humored nor repressed. To repress interest is to substitute the adult for the child, and so to weaken intellectual curiosity and alertness, to suppress initiative, and to deaden interest. To humor the interests is to substitute the transient for the permanent. The interest is always the sign of some power below; the important thing is to discover this power. To humor the interest is to fail to penetrate below the surface, and its sure result is to substitute caprice and whim for genuine interest.

—the emotions are the reflex of actions.

—to endeavor to stimulate or arouse the emotions apart from their corresponding activities is to introduce an unhealthy and morbid state of mind.

—if we can only secure right habits of action and thought, with reference to the good, the true, and the beautiful, the emotions will for the most part take care of themselves.

—next to deadness and dullness, formalism and routine, our education is threatened with no greater evil than sentimentalism.

—this sentimentalism is the necessary result of the attempt to divorce feeling from action.

ARTICLE V—THE SCHOOL AND SOCIAL PROGRESS

I Believe that

—education is the fundamental method of social progress and reform.

—all reforms which rest simply upon the enactment of law, or the threatening of certain penalties, or upon changes in mechanical or outward arrangements, are transitory and futile.

—education is a regulation of the process of coming to share in the social consciousness; and that the adjustment of individual activity on the basis of this social consciousness is the only sure method of social reconstruction.

—this conception has due regard for both the individualistic and socialistic ideals. It is duly individual because it recognizes the formation of a certain character as the only genuine basis of right living. It is socialistic because it recognizes that this right character is not to be formed by merely individual precept, example, or exhortation, but rather by the influence of a certain form of institutional or community life upon the individual, and that the social organism through the school, as its organ, may determine ethical results.

—in the ideal school we have the reconciliation of the individualistic and the institutional ideals.

—the community's duty to education is, therefore, its paramount moral duty. By law and punishment, by social agitation and discussion, society can regulate and form itself in a more or less haphazard and chance way. But through education society can formulate its own purposes, can organize its own means and resources, and thus shape itself with definiteness and economy in the direction in which it wishes to move.

—when society once recognizes the possibilities in this direction, and the obligations which these possibilities impose, it is impossble to conceive of the resources of time, attention, and money which will be put at the disposal of the educator.

—it is the business of every one interested in education to insist upon the school as the primary and most effective instrument of social progress and reform in order that society may be awakened to realize what the school stands for, and aroused to the necessity of endowing the educator with sufficient equipment properly to perform his task.

—education thus conceived marks the most perfect and intimate union of science and art conceivable in human experience.

—the art of thus giving shape to human powers and adapting them to social service is the supreme art; one calling into its service the best of artists; that no insight, sympathy, tact, executive power, is too great for such service.

—with the growth of psychological service, giving added insight into individual structure and laws of growth; and with growth of social science, adding to our knowledge of the right organization of individuals, all scientific resources can be utilized for the purposes of education.

—when science and art thus join hands the most commanding motive for human action will be reached, the most genuine springs of human conduct aroused, and the best service that human nature is capable of guaranteed.

—the teacher is engaged, not simply in the training of individuals, but in the formation of the proper social life.

—every teacher should realize the dignity of his calling; that he is a social servant set apart for the maintenance of proper social order and the securing of the right social growth.

—in this way the teacher always is the prophet of the true God and the usherer in of the true kingdom of God.

Randolph S. Bourne

Twilight

of Idols

The roster of critics of pragmatism is long and contains many distinguished names. The selection that follows, originally published in 1917, is by one of the bitterest, Randolph S. Bourne. Bourne's death in 1918 at the age of 32 ended a brilliant literary career. An incisive essayist, he was one of the young radicals of the early years of the new century—a group that included Van Wyck Brooks, Walter Lippmann, Walter Weyl, Herbert Croly, and Waldo Frank— and he was a prominent contributor to New Republic, Dial, *and* Seven Arts. *Bourne was once an enthusiastic pragmatist and an eager disciple of John Dewey, under whom he had studied at Columbia, and whose ideas on education he had defended in two books. His disillusionment came as a consequence of America's entry into war in 1917. He believed the war would destroy the reform movement and the progressive spirit. He saw in the struggle in Europe a conflict between two opponents, both alien to the American democratic spirit and both fighting for much the same sordid ends. [From* War and the Intellectuals *by Randolph S. Bourne (edited by Carl Resek). Copyright © 1964 by Carl Resek. Used by permission of Harper & Row, Publishers, Incorporated.]*

Where are the seeds of American promise? Man cannot live by politics alone, and it is small cheer that our best intellects are caught in the political current and see only the hope that America will find her soul in the remaking of the world. If William James were alive would he be accepting the war-situation so easily and complacently? Would he be chiding the over-stimulated intelligence of peace-loving idealists, and ex-communicating from the ranks of liberal progress the pitiful remnant of those who struggle "above the battle"? I like to think that his gallant spirit would have called for a war to be gallantly played, with insistent care for democratic values at home, and unequivocal alliance with democratic elements abroad for a peace that should promise more than a mere union of benevolent imperialisms. I think of James now because the recent articles of John Dewey's on the war suggest a slackening in this thought for our guidance and stir, and the inadequacy of his pragmatism as a philosophy of life in this emergency. Whether James would have given us just that note of spiritual adventure which would make the national enterprise seem creative for an American future,—this we can never know. But surely that philosophy of Dewey's which we had been following so uncritically for so long, breaks down almost noisily when it is used to grind out interpretation for the present crisis. These articles on "Conscience and Compulsion," "The Future of Pacifism," "What America Will Fight For," "Conscription of Thought," which *The New Repub-*

lic has been printing, seem to me to be a little off-color. A philosopher
who senses so little the sinister forces of war, who is so much more concerned over the excesses of the pacifists than over the excesses of military
policy, who can feel only amusement at the idea that any one should try
to conscript thought, who assumes that the war-technique can be used
without trailing along with it the mob-fanaticisms, the injustices and
hatreds, that are organically bound up with it, is speaking to another
element of the younger intelligentsia than that to which I belong. Evidently the attitudes which war calls out are fiercer and more incalculable
than Professor Dewey is accustomed to take into his hopeful and intelligent imagination, and the pragmatist mind, in trying to adjust itself to
them, gives the air of grappling, like the pioneer who challenges the arid
plains, with a power too big for it. It is not an arena of creative intelligence our country's mind is now, but of mob-psychology. The soldiers
who tried to lynch Max Eastman showed that current patriotism is not a
product of the will to remake the world. The luxuriant releases of explosive hatred for which peace apparently gives far too little scope cannot be
wooed by sweet reasonableness, nor can they be the raw material for the
creation of rare liberal political structures. All that can be done is to try
to keep your country out of situations where such expressive releases
occur. If you have willed the situation, however, or accepted it as inevitable, it is fatuous to protest against the gay debauch of hatred and
fear and swagger that must mount and mount, until the heady and
virulent poison of war shall have created its own anti-toxin of ruin and
disillusionment. To talk as if war were anything else than such a poison
is to show that your philosophy has never been confronted with the
pathless and the inexorable, and that, only dimly feeling the change, it
goes ahead acting as if it had not got out of its depth. Only a lack of
practice with a world of human nature so raw-nerved, irrational, uncrea-
tive, as an America at war was bound to show itself to be, can account for
the singular unsatisfactoriness of these later utterances of Dewey. He did
have one moment of hesitation just before the war began, when the war
and its external purposes and unifying power seemed the small thing
beside that internal adventure which should find our American promise.
But that perspective has now disappeared, and one finds Dewey now
untainted by skepticism as to our being about a business to which all our
idealism should rally. That failure to get guaranties that this country's
efforts would obligate the Allies to a democratic world-order Dewey
blames on the defection of the pacifists, and then somehow manages to
get himself into a "we" who "romantically," as he says, forewent this
crucial link of our strategy. Does this easy identification of himself with
undemocratically-controlled foreign policy mean that a country is democratic when it accepts what its government does, or that war has a nar-
cotic effect on the pragmatic mind? For Dewey somehow retains his sense

of being in the controlling class, and ignores those anxious questions of democrats who have been his disciples but are now resenters of the war.

What I come to is a sense of suddenly being left in the lurch, of suddenly finding that a philosophy upon which I had relied to carry us through no longer works. I find the contrast between the idea that creative intelligence has free functioning in wartime, and the facts of the inexorable situation, too glaring. The contrast between what liberals ought to be doing and saying if democratic values are to be conserved, and what the real forces are imposing upon them, strikes too sternly on my intellectual senses. I should prefer some philosophy of War as the grim and terrible cleanser to this optimism-haunted mood that continues unweariedly to suggest that all can yet be made to work for good in a mad and half-destroyed world. I wonder if James, in the face of such disaster, would not have abandoned his "moral equivalent of war" for an "immoral equivalent" which, in swift and periodic saturnalia, would have acted as vaccination against the sure pestilence of war.

Dewey's philosophy is inspiring enough for a society at peace, prosperous and with a fund of progressive good-will. It is a philosophy of hope, of clear-sighted comprehension of materials and means. Where institutions are at all malleable, it is the only clue for improvement. It is scientific method applied to "uplift." But this careful adaptation of means to desired ends, this experimental working out of control over brute forces and dead matter in the interests of communal life, depends on a store of rationality, and is effective only where there is strong desire for progress. It is precisely the school, the institution to which Dewey's philosophy was first applied, that is of all our institutions the most malleable. And it is the will to educate that has seemed, in these days, among all our social attitudes the most rationally motivated. It was education, and almost education alone, that seemed susceptible to the steady pressure of an "instrumental" philosophy. Intelligence really seemed about to come into conscious control of an institution, and that one the most potent in moulding the attitudes needed for a civilized society and the aptitudes needed for the happiness of the individual.

For both our revolutionary conceptions of what education means, and for the intellectual strategy of its approach, this country is immeasurably indebted to the influence of Professor Dewey's philosophy. With these ideas sincerely felt, a rational nation would have chosen education as its national enterprise. Into this it would have thrown its energy though the heavens fell and the earth rocked around it. But the nation did not use its isolation from the conflict to educate itself. It fretted for three years and then let war, not education, be chosen, at the almost unanimous behest of our intellectual class, from motives alien to our cultural needs, and for political ends alien to the happiness of the individual. But nations, of course, are not rational entities, and they act within their most irrational rights when they accept war as the most important thing the nation can do in the face of metaphysical menaces of imperial prestige. What concerns us here is the relative ease with which the pragmatist intellectuals, with Professor Dewey at the head, have moved out their philosophy, bag and baggage, from education to war. So abrupt a change in the direction of the national enterprise, one would have expected to cause more emotion, to demand more apologetics. His optimism may have told Professor Dewey that war would not materially demoralize our growth—would, perhaps, after all, be but an incident in the nation's life—but it is not easy to see how, as we skate toward the bankruptcy of war-billions, there will be resources available for educational enterprise that does not contribute directly to the war-technique. Neither is any passion for growth, for creative mastery, going to flourish among the host of militaristic values and new tastes for power that are springing up like poisonous mushrooms on every hand.

How could the pragmatist mind accept war without more violent protest, without a greater wrench? Either Professor Dewey and his friends felt that the forces were too strong for them, that the war had to be, and it was better to take it up intelligently than to drift blindly in; or else they really expected a gallant war, conducted with jealous regard for democratic values at home and a captivating vision of international democracy as the end of all the toil and pain. If their motive was the first, they would seem to have reduced the scope of possible control of events to the vanishing point. If the war is too strong for you to prevent, how is it going to be weak enough for you to control and mould to your liberal purposes? And if their motive was to shape the war firmly for good, they seem to have seriously miscalculated the fierce urgencies of it. Are they to be content, as the materialization of their hopes, with a doubtful League of Nations and the suppression of the I.W.W.? Yet the numbing power of the war-situation seems to have kept them from realizing what has happened to their philosophy. The betrayal of their first hopes has certainly not discouraged them. But neither has it roused them to a more energetic expression of the forces through which they intend to realize them. I search Professor Dewey's articles in vain for clues as to the specific working-out of our democratic desires, either nationally or internationally, either in the present or in the reconstruction after the war. No programme is suggested, nor is there feeling for present vague popular movements and revolts. Rather are the latter chided, for their own vagueness and impracticalities. Similarly, with the other prophets of instrumentalism who accompany Dewey into the war, democracy remains an unanalyzed term, useful as a call to battle, but not an intellectual tool, turning up fresh sod for the changing future. Is it the political democracy of a plutocratic America that we are fighting for, or is it the social democracy of the new Russia? Which do our rulers really fear more, the menace of Imperial Germany, or the liberating influence of a socialist Russia? In the application of their philosophy to politics, our pragmatists are sliding over this crucial question of ends. Dewey says our ends must be intelligently international rather than chauvinistic. But this gets us little distance along our way.

In this difficult time the light that has been in liberals and radicals has become darkness. If radicals spend their time holding conventions to attest their loyalty and stamp out the "enemies within," they do not spend it in breaking intellectual paths, or giving us shining ideas to which we can attach our faith and conscience. The spiritual apathy from which the more naive of us suffer, and which the others are so busy fighting, arises largely from sheer default of a clear vision that would melt it away. Let the motley crew of ex-socialists, and labor radicals, and liberals, and pragmatist philosophers, who have united for the prosecution of the war, present a coherent and convincing democratic programme, and they will no longer be confronted with the skepticism of the conscientious and the impossibilist. But when the emphasis is on technical organization, rather than organization of ideas, on strategy rather than desires, one begins to suspect that no programme is presented because they have none to present. This burrowing into war-technique hides the void where a democratic philosophy should be. Our intellectuals consort with war-boards in order to keep their minds off the question of what the slow masses of the people are really desiring, or toward what the best hope of the country really drives. Similarly the blaze of patriotism on the part of the radicals serves the purpose of concealing the feebleness of their intellectual light.

Is the answer that clear formulation of democratic ends must be postponed until victory in the war is attained? But to make this answer is to surrender the entire case. For the support of the war by radicals, realists, pragmatists, is due—or so they say—to the fact that the war is not only saving the cause of democracy, but is immensely accelerating its progress. Well, what are those gains? How are they to be conserved? What do they lead to? How can we further them? Into what large idea of society do they group? To ignore these questions, and think only of the war-technique and its accompanying devotions, is to undermine the foundations of these people's own faith.

A policy of "win the war first" must be, for the radical, a policy of intellectual suicide. Their support of the war throws upon them the responsibility of showing inch by inch the democratic gains, and of laying out a charter of specific hopes. Otherwise they confess that they are impotent and that the war is submerging their expectations, or that they are not genuinely imaginative and offer little promise for future leadership.

It may seem unfair to group Professor Dewey with Mr. Spargo and Mr. Gompers, Mr. A. M. Simons, and the Vigilantes. I do so only because in their acceptance of the war, they are all living out that popular American "instrumental" philosophy which Professor Dewey has formulated in such convincing and fascinating terms. On an infinitely more intelligent plane, he is yet one with them in his confidence that the war is motivated

by democratic ends and is being made to serve them. A high mood of
confidence and self-righteousness moves them all, a keen sense of control
over events that makes them eligible to discipleship under Professor
Dewey's philosophy. They are all hostile to impossibilism, to apathy, to
any attitude that is not a cheerful and brisk setting to work to use the
emergency to consolidate the gains of democracy. Not, Is it being used?
but, Let us make a flutter about using it! This unanimity of mood puts
the resenter of war out of the arena. But he can still seek to explain why
this philosophy which has no place for the inexorable should have adjusted itself so easily to the inexorable of war, and why, although a
philosophy of the creative intelligence in using means toward ends, it
should show itself so singularly impoverished in its present supply of
democratic values.

What is the matter with the philosophy? One has a sense of having
come to a sudden, short stop at the end of an intellectual era. In the crisis,
this philosophy of intelligent control just does not measure up to our
needs. What is the root of this inadequacy that is felt so keenly by our
restless minds? Van Wyck Brooks has pointed out searchingly the lack of
poetic vision in our pragmatist "awakeners." Is there something in these
realistic attitudes that works actually against poetic vision, against concern for the quality of life as above machinery of life? Apparently there
is. The war has revealed a younger intelligentsia, trained up in the
pragmatic dispensation, immensely ready for the executive ordering of
events, pitifully unprepared for the intellectual interpretation or the
idealistic focussing of ends. The young men in Belgium, the officers'
training corps, the young men being sucked into the councils at Washington and into war-organization everywhere, have among them a definite element, upon whom Dewey, as veteran philosopher, might well
bestow a papal blessing. They have absorbed the secret of scientific
method as applied to political administration. They are liberal, enlightened, aware. They are touched with creative intelligence toward the
solution of political and industrial problems. They are a wholly new
force in American life, the product of the swing in the colleges from a
training that emphasized classical studies to one that emphasized political and economic values. Practically all this element, one would say, is
lined up in service of the war-technique. There seems to have been a
peculiar congeniality between the war and these men. It is as if the war
and they had been waiting for each other. One wonders what scope they
would have had for their intelligence without it. Probably most of them
would have gone into industry and devoted themselves to sane reorganization schemes. What is significant is that it is the technical side of the
war that appeals to them, not the interpretative or political side. The
formulation of values and ideals, the production of articulate and suggestive thinking, had not, in their education, kept pace, to any extent
whatever, with their technical aptitude. The result is that the field of
intellectual formulation is very poorly manned by this younger intelli-

gentsia. While they organize the war, formulation of opinion is left largely in the hands of professional patriots, sensational editors, archaic radicals. The intellectual work of this younger intelligentsia is done by the sedition-hunting Vigilantes, and by the saving remnant of older liberals. It is true, Dewey calls for a more attentive formulation of war-purposes and ideas, but he calls largely to deaf ears. His disciples have learned all too literally the instrumental attitude toward life, and, being immensely intelligent and energetic, they are making themselves efficient instruments of the war-technique, accepting with little question the ends as announced from above. That those ends are largely negative does not concern them, because they have never learned not to subordinate idea to technique. Their education has not given them a coherent system of large ideas, or a feeling for democratic goals. They have, in short, no clear philosophy of life except that of intelligent service, the admirable adaptation of means to ends. They are vague as to what kind of a society they want, or what kind of society America needs, but they are equipped with all the administrative attitudes and talents necessary to attain it.

To those of us who have taken Dewey's philosophy almost as our American religion, it never occurred that values could be subordinated to technique. We were instrumentalist, but we had our private utopias so clearly before our minds that the means fell always into its place as contributory. And Dewey, of course, always meant his philosophy, when taken as a philosophy of life, to start with values. But there was always that unhappy ambiguity in his doctrine as to just how values were created, and it became easier and easier to assume that just any growth was justified and almost any activity valuable so long as it achieved ends. The American, in living out this philosophy, has habitually confused results with product, and been content with getting somewhere without asking too closely whether it was the desirable place to get. It is now becoming plain that unless you start with the vividest kind of poetic vision, your instrumentalism is likely to land you just where it has landed this younger intelligentsia which is so happily and busily engaged in the national enterprise of war. You must have your vision and you must have your technique. The practical effect of Dewey's philosophy has evidently been to develop the sense of the latter at the expense of the former. Though he himself would develop them together, even in him there seems to be a flagging of values, under the influence of war. *The New Republic* honorably clamors for the Allies to subordinate military strategy to political ends, technique to democratic values. But war always undermines values. It is the outstanding lesson of the whole war that statesmen cannot be trusted to get this perspective right, that their only motto is, first to win and then grab what they can. The struggle against this statesman-like animus must be a losing one as long as we have not very clear and very determined and very revolutionary democratic ideas and programmes to challenge them with. The trouble with our situation is not only that values have been generally ignored in favor of technique, but that those who have struggled to keep values foremost, have been too bloodless and too near-sighted in their vision. The defect of any philosophy of "adaptation" or "adjustment," even when it means adjustment to changing, living experience, is that there is no provision for thought or experience getting beyond itself. If your ideal is to be adjusted to your situation, in radiant co-operation with reality, then your success is likely to be just that and no more. You never transcend anything. You grow, but your spirit never jumps out of your skin to go on wild adventures. If your policy as a publicist reformer is to take what you can get, you are likely to find that you get something less than you should be willing to take. Italy in the settlement is said to be demanding one hundred in order to get twenty, and this machiavellian principle might well be adopted by the radical. Vision must constantly outshoot technique, opportunist efforts usually achieve less even than what seemed obviously possible. An impossibilist élan that appeals to desire will often carry further. A philosophy of adustment will not even make for adjustment. If you try merely to "meet" situations as they come, you will not even meet them. Instead you will only pile up behind you deficits and arrears that will some day bankrupt you.

We are in the war because an American Government practised a philosophy of adjustment, and an instrumentalism for minor ends, instead of creating new values and setting at once a large standard to which the nations might repair. An intellectual attitude of mere adjustment, of mere use of the creative intelligence to make your progress, must end in caution, regression, and a virtual failure to effect even that change which you so clear-sightedly and desirously see. This is the root of our dissatisfaction with much of the current political and social realism that is preached to us. It has everything good and wise except the obstreperous vision that would drive and draw all men into it.

The working-out of this American philosophy in our intellectual life then has meant an exaggerated emphasis on the mechanics of life at the expense of the quality of living. We suffer from a real shortage of spiritual values. A philosophy that worked when we were trying to get that material foundation for American life in which more impassioned living could flourish no longer works when we are faced with inexorable disaster and the hysterias of the mob. The note of complacency which we detect in the current expressions of this philosophy has a bad taste. The congruous note for the situation would seem to be, on the contrary, that of robust desperation,—a desperation that shall rage and struggle until new values come out of the travail, and we see some glimmering of our democratic way. In the creation of these new values, we may expect the old philosophy, the old radicalism, to be helpless. It has found a perfectly definite level, and there is no reason to think that it will not remain there. Its flowering appears in the technical organization of the war by an earnest group of young liberals, who direct their course by an opportunist programme of State-socialism at home and a league of benevo-lently-imperialistic nations abroad. At their best they can give us a gov-ernment by prudent, enlightened college men instead of by politicians. At their best, they can abolish war by making everybody a partner in the booty of exploitation. That is all, and it is technically admirable. Only there is nothing in the outlook that touches in any way the happiness of the individual, the vivifying of the personality, the comprehension of social forces, the flair of art,—in other words, the quality of life. Our intellectuals have failed us as value-creators, even as value-emphasizers. The allure of the martial in war has passed only to be succeeded by the allure of the technical. The allure of fresh and true ideas, of free specu-lation, of artistic vigor, of cultural styles, of intelligence suffused by feel-ing, and feeling given fibre and outline by intelligence, has not come, and can hardly come, we see now, while our reigning philosophy is an instrumental one.

Whence can come this allure? Only from those who are thorough mal-contents. Irritation at things as they are, disgust at the continual frustra-tions and aridities of American life, deep dissatisfaction with self and with the groups that give themselves forth as hopeful—out of such moods there might be hammered new values. The malcontents would be men and women who could not stomach the war, or the reactionary idealism that has followed in its train. They are quite through with the profes-sional critics and classicists who have let cultural values die through their own personal ineptitude. Yet these malcontents have no intention of being cultural vandals, only to slay. They are not barbarians, but seek the vital and the sincere everywhere. All they want is a new orientation of the spirit that shall be modern, an orientation to accompany that technical orientation which is fast coming, and which the war accelerates. They will be harsh and often bad-tempered, and they will feel that the break-up of things is no time for mellowness. They will have a taste for spiritual adventure, and for sinister imaginative excursions. It will not be Puritanism so much as complacency that they will fight. A tang, a bitterness, an intellectual fibre, a verve, they will look for in literature, and their most virulent enemies will be those unaccountable radicals who are still morally servile, and are now trying to suppress all free specula-tion in the interests of nationalism. Something more mocking, more ir-reverent, they will constantly want. They will take institutions very lightly, indeed will never fail to be surprised at the seriousness with which good radicals take the stated offices and systems. Their own con-tempt will be scarcely veiled, and they will be glad if they can tease, provoke, irritate thought on any subject. These malcontents will be more or less of the American tribe of talent who used either to go immediately to Europe, or starved submissively at home. But these people will neither go to Europe, nor starve submissively. They are too much entangled emotionally in the possibilities of American life to leave it, and they have no desire whatever to starve. So they are likely to go ahead beating their heads at the wall until they are either bloody or light appears. They will give offense to their elders who cannot see what all the concern is about, and they will hurt the more middle-aged sense of adventure upon which the better integrated minds of the younger generation will have compromised. Optimism is often compensatory, and the optimistic mood in American thought may mean merely that American life is too terrible to face. A more skeptical, malicious, desperate, ironical mood may actually be the sign of more vivid and more stirring life fermenting in America today. It may be a sign of hope. That thirst for more of the intellectual "war and laughter" that we find Nietzsche calling us to may bring us satisfactions that optimism-haunted philosophies could never bring. Malcontentedness may be the beginning of promise. That is why I evoked the spirit of William James, with its gay passion for ideas, and its freedom of speculation, when I felt the slightly pedestrian gait into which the war had brought pragmatism. It is the creative desire more than the creative intelligence that we shall need if we are ever to fly.

The problems confronting the United States at the beginning of the twentieth century were numerous and grave. Since the close of the Civil War, there had been a tremendous increase in national wealth, in industrial and agricultural productivity, in population, and in the standard of living. But, as Woodrow Wilson noted some years later, "The evil has come with the good, and much fine gold has been corroded. With riches has come inexcusable waste. . . . We have been proud of our

industrial achievement but we have not hitherto stopped thoughtfully enough to count the cost, the cost of lives snuffed out, of energies overtaxed and broken, the fearful physical and spiritual cost to the men and women and children upon whom the dead weight and burden of it all has fallen pitilessly the years through. . . . With the great government went many deep secret things which we too long delay to look into and scrutinize with fearless eyes. The great government we love has too often been made use of for private and selfish purposes, and those who use it have forgotten the people."

7

THE
PROGRESSIVE
ERA

There was, indeed, great wealth, but it was unevenly distributed, with 12 per cent of the population owning 90 per cent of the national wealth. Great cities there were, but disease, vice, crime, and slums flourished in each of them. Industry thrived, yet the laboring classes lived in squalor. Graft, corruption, and bribery existed on every political level—city, state, and federal—and the word democracy had a hollow ring. Trusts and monopolies had destroyed many an independent businessman. They controlled every phase of many of the important industries, and politicians frequently did their bidding.

These conditions brought forth a protest and a demand for reform in the period from 1900 to 1917, known as the Progressive Era. The Progressives attacked every evil—political, social, and economic—as they sought to restore government to the people, to make democracy effective, and to enable the common man to share in the benefits of America's great progress.

The Progressives were not revolutionaries. They blazed no new trails, but rather followed in the footsteps of earlier reformers: Greenbackers, Grangers, and Populists. To the Populists they were most akin, and William Allen White labeled them "Populists without silver." There were, of course, essential differences between Populism and Progressivism. The former was a rural movement begun in depression by impoverished farmers, while the latter flourished during prosperous times and attracted supporters of the comfortable middle class. Both movements, however, aimed at improving conditions and reforming the evils of their time.

The Progressives were liberal, not radical; optimistic, not pessimistic; pragmatic, not visionary. They did not wish to remake American society or to found a new order. John Chamberlain, a noted Progressive, characterized them most aptly in his *Farewell to Reform* as "On the side of individualism as against socialism, and democracy as against plutocracy; on the side of collectivism where necessary to curb monopoly or unfair competition . . . but not for the type of collectivism where all stood on the same level of production and compensation regardless of individual differences in capacity; for a progressive income tax but not for a single tax on land; for an inheritance tax to prevent swollen fortunes but not for common ownership of capital."

Progressives wanted only to cleanse and purify existing institutions and to restore them to what they considered their pristine nature. In addition, they wanted a strong national government capable of being the instrument to right the wrongs and to maintain the balance between the various competing groups in society. As Herbert Croly put it in his influential *Promise of American Life,* which became almost the philosophic basis for Progressivism, they wished to use "Hamiltonian means to achieve Jeffersonian, or democratic, ends."

Progressives came from every class, group, section, and political party. Democrats joined Republicans; merchants and lawyers were alongside farmers and laborers; middle-class entrepreneurs were with plutocrats; there were the native born and immigrants. The leaders, however, were to be found, according to one historian of the movement, in the "middle class, to a remarkable extent college-educated, self-employed, professional men or small businessmen, of native-born, Protestant background. . . . financially secure civic leaders who had earlier been McKinley Republicans." The rank and file consisted chiefly of white-collar workers.

Most useful to the Progressive movement were the Muckrakers—the journalists and authors who wrote books and articles exposing conditions that required correction. Their objective was to excite the public to demand and the legislators to enact legislation to remedy the evils. Jacob Riis's *How the Other Half Lives,* Ida M. Tarbell's *History of Standard Oil,* Lincoln Steffens' *The Shame of the Cities,* and Upton Sinclair's *The Jungle* were only a few of a long list of incisive revelations and hard-hitting exposures.

Many Progressives were not satisfied merely to expose and to castigate. They sought to ameliorate conditions by helping the poor, the underprivileged, and the oppressed. Their chief vehicle was the settlement house in the slums of every large city; it served as the beacon for all who needed help. Hull House, founded by Jane Addams in Chicago, and Henry Street Settlement in New York, begun by Lillian Wald, were among hundreds of oases in the desert of injustice. To these social agencies came the widow, the injured laborer, the deserted wife, for assistance in claiming insurance, damages, and support. The sick were directed to hospitals, the insane to asylums, the penniless to welfare homes. Baby clinics, free milk, day nurseries, and similar services were provided.

It was perfectly clear to the reformers that, valuable as these humanitarian efforts might be, they were dealing only with the consequences and the symptoms of a disease. The disease was lack of political democracy, control of politics by big business, corruption and dishonesty in politics, lack of public control over the corporations, and absence of social legislation. This disease would have to be rooted out. The reformers, therefore, agitated for civil-service reform; direct primary elections; secret ballots; popular election of senator; initiative, referendum, and recall; prosecution of the trusts in violation of the Sherman Act; regulation of child labor; the eight-hour day; fair wages; unemployment and sickness insurance; safety devices in mine and factory; and a host of other measures.

Theodore Roosevelt played an important part in the movement. His contribution lay not so much in the legislation enacted during his administration, which was rather meager, as in his capacity for popularizing and dramatizing the movement's purpose. His vigorous support of reform and equally vehement denunciation of "the malefactors of great wealth" were crucial in making Americans aware of the problems of the day. He spoke frequently in all parts of the country, and his bristling mustache and clenched fist became symbols of the aggressive and dynamic crusade against fraud, corruption, and wrong doing.

Dissatisfied with William H. Taft's record in the White House, and unwilling to accept him as the Republican standard bearer in that year, Roosevelt left the "Grand Old Party" when he realized he could not gain the nomination. He welded the Progressives into a new political party in 1912, with himself as the presidential candidate. The Progressive Party convention, which met in Chicago in August, was in many ways the culmination of Progressivism. All the fire and enthusiasm of the reform spirit were unleashed there. The delegates wildly acclaimed Roosevelt and agreed with him that they "stood at Armageddon and battled for the Lord."

Roosevelt's defeat at the polls did not mark the end of Progressivism. The victor, Woodrow Wilson, brought to the White House his own brand of Progressivism, and in the years of his Presidency before 1917, he enacted a large body of Progressive legislation. America's entry into the war, however, put an end to the Progressive movement. Immersed in a worldwide struggle, the nation had little time for social legislation. Indeed, much of the wartime legislation and executive action that restricted individual rights and freedom seemed a negation of the spirit of Progressivism. Yet in the previous 17 years, a great body of Progressive legislation had been achieved. Although skeptics such as John Chamberlain did not believe any real gains had been made, an examination of the laws enacted in that period on national, state, and municipal levels leads to the conclusion that, in terms of the greatest good for the greatest

number, much progress had taken place. On the federal level there were
such notable statutes as the Hepburn, Mann-Elkins, Smith-Lever, and
Pure Food and Drug Acts; amendments that included the Sixteenth (income tax) and Seventeenth (popular election of senators); numerous additions to the civil-service lists of many jobs hitherto political; and successful prosecutions of numerous trusts. A series of powerful and dedicated
governors—Hiram Johnson, Albert Cummins, Robert M. LaFollette,
Woodrow Wilson, and Charles E. Hughes—virtually revolutionized state
governments and placed numerous pieces of social legislation on the
statute books. In the cities, there were spectacular successes against
bossism by men such as Tom L. Johnson, Sam Jones, Emil Seidel, Mark
Fagan, and Fremont Older. In fact, two of the most lasting reforms
designed to separate municipal administration from politics—the city
manager form and the city commission plan—were introduced into many
cities as a consequence of Progressivism.

Certainly, not all the evils in American life had been eradicated, but
Progressivism had clearly made a successful assault on the citadel of
privilege and had charted a new role for government.

Lincoln Steffens

The Shame of Minneapolis

*The roster of Muck-
rakers was long and
their targets were ex-
haustive. Although
they wrote books,
magazines served as
their chief vehicle,*
with McClure's Magazine, Everybody's, Collier's, Cosmopolitan, *and*
American Magazine *the most prominent. No cause was too holy, no area
too sacrosanct for their sharp pen. Life in the slums, exploitation of the
Negro, the white slave traffic, corporate malpractice, political corruption,
the plight of labor, the administration of justice—all were fair game.
John Spargo, David Graham Phillips, Ben Lindsey, Gustavus Myers,
Thomas Lawson, Ray Stannard Baker, Ida M. Tarbell and Lincoln
Steffens were the most effective practitioners of the art, with the last
two, perhaps, the most famous.*

*Lincoln Steffens specialized in the politics of the cities. Born in 1866,
he worked on various newspapers and magazines as editor and reporter.
It was while a reporter that he began an investigation of a number of
leading municipalities to lay bare the corrupt alliance of business and
politics. He found all the cities remarkably similar in that they were all
ruled by bosses indulging in the most fraudulent practices. Minneapolis,
St. Louis, Pittsburgh, Philadelphia—all were the same. Without fear, and
with accuracy, he named names and exact sums and revealed the various
links and connections. It was a superb piece of reporting. The selection*

below is representative of his work. [*Lincoln Steffens, "The Shame of Minneapolis,"* McClure's Magazine, XX *(January 1903).* From THE AUTOBIOGRAPHY OF LINCOLN STEFFENS, copyright, 1931, by Harcourt, Brace & World, Inc.; renewed, 1959, by Peter Steffens. Reprinted by permission of the publishers.]

Whenever anything extraordinary is done in American municipal politics, whether for good or for evil, you can trace it almost invariably to one man. The people do not do it. Neither do the "gangs," "combines," or political parties. These are but instruments by which bosses (not leaders; we Americans are not led, but driven) rule the people, and commonly sell them out. But there are at least two forms of the autocracy which has supplanted the democracy here as it has everywhere it has been tried. One is that of the organized majority by which, as in Tammany Hall in New York and the Republican machine in Philadelphia, the boss has normal control of more than half the voters. The other is that of the adroitly managed minority. The "good people" are herded into parties and stupefied with convictions and a name, Republican or Democrat; while the "bad people" are so organized or interested by the boss that he can wield their votes to enforce terms with party managers and decide elections. St. Louis is a conspicuous example of this form. Minneapolis is another. Colonel Ed. Butler is the unscrupulous opportunist who handled the non-partisan minority which turned St. Louis into a "boodle town." In Minneapolis "Doc" Ames was the man.

Minneapolis is a New England town on the upper Mississippi. The metropolis of the Northwest, it is the metropolis also of Norway and Sweden in America. Indeed, it is the second largest Scandinavian city in the world. But Yankees, straight from Down East, settled the town, and their New England spirit predominates. They had Bayard Taylor lecture there in the early days of the settlement; they made it the seat of the University of Minnesota. Yet even now, when the town has grown to a population of more than 200,000, you feel that there is something Western about it too—a Yankee with a small Puritan head, an open prairie heart, and a great, big Scandinavian body. The Roundhead takes the Swede and Norwegian bone out into the woods, and they cut lumber by forests, or they go out on the prairies and raise wheat and mill it into fleet-cargoes of flour. They work hard, they make money, they are sober, satisfied, busy with their own affairs. There isn't much time for public business. Taken together, Miles, Hans, and Ole are very American. Miles insists upon strict laws, Ole and Hans want one or two Scandinavians on their ticket. These things granted, they go off on raft or reaper, leaving whoso will to enforce the laws and run the city.

The people who were left to govern the city hated above all things strict laws. They were the loafers, saloon keepers, gamblers, criminals, and the thriftless poor of all nationalities. Resenting the sobriety of a staid, industrious community, and having no Irish to boss them, they delighted to follow the jovial pioneer doctor, Albert Alonzo Ames. He was the "good fellow"—a genial, generous reprobate. Devery, Tweed, and many more have exposed in vain this amiable type. "Doc" Ames, tall, straight, and cheerful, attracted men, and they gave him votes for his smiles. He stood for license. There was nothing of the Puritan about him. His father, the sturdy old pioneer, Dr. Alfred Elisha Ames, had a strong strain of it in him, but he moved on with his family of six sons from Garden Prairie, Ill., to Fort Snelling reservation, in 1851, before Minneapolis was founded, and young Albert Alonzo, who then was ten years old, grew up free, easy, and tolerant. He was sent to school, then to college in Chicago, and he returned home a doctor of medicine before he was twenty-one. As the town waxed soberer and richer, "Doc" grew gayer and more and more generous. Skilful as a surgeon, devoted as a physician, and as a man kindly, he increased his practice till he was the best-loved man in the community. He was especially good to the poor. Anybody could summon "Doc" Ames at any hour to any distance. He went, and he gave not only his professional service, but sympathy, and often charity. "Richer men than you will pay your bill," he told the destitute. So there was a basis for his "good-fellowship." There always is; these good fellows are not frauds—not in the beginning.

But there is another side to them sometimes. Ames was sunshine not to the sick and destitute only. To the vicious and the depraved also he was a comfort. If a man was a hard drinker, the good Doctor cheered him with another drink; if he had stolen something, the Doctor helped to get him off. He was naturally vain; popularity developed his love of approbation. His loose life brought disapproval only from the good people, so gradually the Doctor came to enjoy best the society of the barroom and the streets. This society, flattered in turn, worshipped the good Doctor, and, active in politics always, put its physician into the arena.

Had he been wise, or even shrewd, he might have made himself a real power. But he wasn't calculating, only light and frivolous, so he did not organize his forces and run men for office. He sought office himself from the start, and he got most of the small places he wanted by changing his party to seize the opportunity. His floating minority, added to the regular partisan vote, was sufficient ordinarily for his useless victories. As time went on he rose from smaller offices to be a Republican mayor, then twice at intervals to be a Democratic mayor. He was a candidate once for Congress; he stood for governor once on a sort of Populist-Democrat ticket. Ames could not get anything outside of his own town, and after his third term as mayor it was thought he was out of politics altogether. He was getting old, and he was getting worse.

Like many a "good fellow" with hosts of miscellaneous friends down town to whom he was devoted, the good Doctor neglected his own family. From neglect he went on openly to separation from his wife and a second establishment. The climax came not long before the election of 1900. His wife was dying, and his daughter wrote to her father a note saying that her mother wished to see and forgive him. The messenger found him in a saloon. The Doctor read the note, laid it on the bar, and scribbled across it a sentence incredibly obscene. His wife died. The outraged family would not have the father at the funeral, but he appeared, not at the house, but in a carriage on the street. He sat across the way, with his feet up and a cigar in his mouth, till the funeral moved; then he circled around, crossing it and meeting it, and making altogether a scene which might well close any man's career.

It didn't end his. The people had just secured the passage of a new primary law to establish direct popular government. There were to be no more nominations by convention. The voters were to ballot for their party candidates. By a slip of some sort, the laws did not specify that Republicans only should vote for Republican candidates, and only Democrats for Democratic candidates. Any voter could vote at either primary. Ames, in disrepute with his own party, the Democratic, bade his followers vote for his nomination for mayor on the Republican ticket. They all voted; not all the Republicans did. He was nominated. Nomination is far from election, and you would say that the trick would not help him. But that was a Presidential year, so the people of Minneapolis had to vote for Ames, the Republican candidate for Mayor. Besides, Ames said he was going to reform; that he was getting old, and wanted to close his career with a good administration. The effective argument, however, was that, since McKinley had to be elected to save the country, Ames must be supported for Mayor of Minneapolis. Why? The great American people cannot be trusted to scratch a ticket.

Well, Minneapolis got its old mayor back, and he was reformed. Up to this time Ames had not been very venal personally. He was a "spender," not a "grafter," and he was guilty of corruption chiefly by proxy; he took the honors and left the spoils to his followers. His administrations were no worse than the worst. Now, however, he set out upon a career of corruption which for deliberateness, invention, and avarice has never been equalled. It was as if he had made up his mind that he had been careless long enough, and meant to enrich his last years. He began early.

Immediately upon his election, before he took office (on January 7th), he organized a cabinet and laid plans to turn the city over to outlaws who were to work under police direction for the profit of his administration. He chose for chief his brother, Colonel Fred W. Ames, who had recently returned under a cloud from service in the Philippines. The Colonel had commanded a Minnesota regiment out there till he proved a coward under fire; he escaped courtmartial only on the understanding that he should resign on reaching San Francisco, whither he was immediately shipped. This he did not do, and his brother's influence at Washington saved him to be mustered out with the regiment. But he was a weak vessel for chief of police, and the mayor picked for chief of detectives an abler man, who was to direct the more difficult operations. This was Norman W. King, a former gambler, who knew the criminals needed in the business ahead. King was to invite to Minneapolis thieves, confidence men, pickpockets, and gamblers, and release some that were in the local jail. They were to be organized into groups, according to their profession, and detectives were assigned to assist and direct them. The head of the gambling syndicate was to have charge of the gambling, making the terms and collecting the "graft," just as King and a Captain Hill were to collect from the thieves. The collector for women of the town was to be Irwin A. Gardner, a medical student in the Doctor's office, who was made a special policeman for the purpose. These men looked over the force, selected those men who could be trusted, charged them a price for their retention, and marked for dismissal 107 men out of 225, the 107 being the best policemen in the department from the point of view of the citizens who afterward reorganized the force. John Fitchette, better known as "Coffee John," a Virginian (who served on the Jeff Davis jury), the keeper of a notorious coffee-house, was to be a captain of police, with no duties except to sell places on the police force.

And they did these things that they planned—all and more. The administration opened with the revolution on the police force. They liberated the thieves in the local jail, and made known to the Under World generally that "things were doing" in Minneapolis. The incoming swindlers reported to King or his staff for instructions, and went to work, turning the "swag" over to the detectives in charge. Gambling went on openly, and disorderly houses multiplied under the fostering care of Gardner, the medical student. But all this was not enough. Ames dared to break openly into the municipal system of vice protection.

There was such a thing. Minneapolis, strict in its laws, forbade vices which are inevitable, then regularly permitted them under certain conditions. Legal limits, called "patrol lines," were prescribed, within which saloons might be opened. These ran along the river front, out through part of the business section, with long arms reaching into the Scandinavian quarters, north and south. Gambling also was confined, but more narrowly. And there were limits, also arbitrary, but not always identical with those for gambling, within which the social evil was allowed. But the novel feature of this scheme was that disorderly houses were practically licensed by the city, the women appearing before the clerk of the Municipal Court each month to pay a "fine" of $100. Unable at first to get this "graft," Ames's man Gardner persuaded women to start houses, apartments, and, of all things, candy stores, which sold sweets to children and tobacco to the "lumber Jacks" in front, while a nefarious traffic was carried on in the rear. But they paid Ames, not the city, and that was all the reform administration cared about.

The revenue from all these sources must have been enormous. It only whetted the avarice of the mayor and his Cabinet. They let gambling privileges without restriction to location or "squareness"; the syndicate could cheat and rob as it would. Peddlers and pawnbrokers, formerly licensed by the city, bought permits now instead from "Gardner's father," A. L. Gardner, who was the mayor's agent in this field. Some two hundred slot machines were installed in various parts of the town, with owner's agent and mayor's agent watching and collecting from them enough to pay the mayor $15,000 a year as his share. Auction frauds were instituted. Opium joints and unlicensed saloons, called "blind pigs," were protected. Gardner even had a police baseball team, for whose games tickets were sold to people who had to buy them. But the women were the easiest "graft." They were compelled to buy illustrated biographies of the city officials; they had to give presents of money, jewelry, and gold stars to police officers. But the money they still paid direct to the city in fines, some $35,000 a year, fretted the mayor, and at last he reached for it. He came out with a declaration, in his old character as friend of the oppressed, that $100 a month was too much for these women to pay. They should be required to pay the city fine only once in two months. This puzzled the town till it became generally known that Gardner collected the other month for the mayor. The final outrage in this department, however, was an order of the mayor for the periodic visits to disorderly houses, by the city's physicians, at from $5 to $20 per visit. The two physicians he appointed called when they willed, and more and more frequently, till toward the end the calls became a pure formality, with the collections as the one and only object.

In a general way all this business was known. It did not arouse the citizens, but it did attract criminals, and more and more thieves and swindlers came hurrying to Minneapolis. Some of them saw the police, and made terms. Some were seen by the police and invited to go to work. There was room for all. This astonishing fact that the government of a city asked criminals to rob the people is fully established. The police and the criminals have confessed it separately. Their statements agree in detail. Detective Norbeck made the arrangement, and introduced the swindlers to Gardner, who, over King's head, took the money from them. Here is the story "Billy" Edwards, a "big mitt" man, told under oath of his reception in Minneapolis:

"I had been out to the coast, and hadn't seen Norbeck for some time. After I returned I boarded a Minneapolis car one evening to go down to South Minneapolis to visit a friend. Norbeck and Detective DeLaittre were on the car. When Norbeck saw me he came up and shook hands, and said, 'Hullo, Billy, how goes it?' I said, 'Not very well.' Then he says, 'Things have changed since you went away. Me and Gardner are the whole thing now. Before you left they thought I didn't know anything, but I turned a few tricks and now I'm It.' 'I'm glad of that, Chris,' I said. He says, 'I've got great things for you. I'm going to fix up a joint for you.' 'That's good,' I said, 'but I don't believe you can do it.' 'Oh, yes, I can,' he replied. 'I'm It now—Gardner and me.' 'Well, if you can do it,' says I, 'there's money in it.' 'How much can you pay?' he asked. 'Oh, $150 or $200 a week,' says I. 'That settles it,' he said; 'I'll take you down to see Gardner, and we'll fix it up.' Then he made an appointment to meet me the next night, and we went down to Gardner's house together."

There Gardner talked business in general, showed his drawer full of bills, and jokingly asked how Edwards would like to have them. Edwards says:

"I said, 'That looks pretty good to me,' and Gardner told us that he had 'collected' the money from the women he had on his staff, and that he was going to pay it over to the 'old man' when he got back from his hunting trip next morning. Afterward he told me that the mayor had been much pleased with our $500, and that he said everything was all right, and for us to go ahead."

"Link" Crossman, another confidence man who was with Edwards, said that Gardner demanded $1,000 at first, but compromised on $500 for the mayor, $50 for Gardner, and $50 for Norbeck. To the chief, Fred Ames, they gave tips now and then of $25 or $50. "The first week we ran," said Crossman, "I gave Fred $15. Norbeck took me down there. We shook hands, and I handed him an envelope with $15. He pulled out a list of steerers we had sent him, and said he wanted to go over them with me. He asked where the joint was located. At another time I slipped $25 into his hand as he was standing in the hallway of City Hall." But these smaller payments, after the first "opening, $500," are all down on the pages of the "big mitt" ledger, photographs of which illuminate this article. This notorious book, which was kept by Charlie Howard, one of the "big mitt" men, was much talked of at the subsequent trials, but was kept hidden to await the trial of the mayor himself.

The "big mitt" game was swindling by means of a stacked hand at stud poker. "Steerers" and "boosters" met "suckers" on the street, at hotels, and railway stations, won their confidence, and led them to the "joint." Usually the "sucker" was called, by the amount of his loss, "the $102 man" or "the $35 man." Roman Meix alone had the distinction among all the Minneapolis victims of going by his own name. Having lost $775, he became known for his persistent complainings. But they all "kicked" some. To Norbeck at the street door was assigned the duty of hearing their complaints, and "throwing a scare into them." "Oh, so you've been gambling," he would say. "Have you got a license? Well, then, you better get right out of this town." Sometimes he accompanied them to the station and saw them off. If they were not to be put off thus, he directed them to the chief of police. Fred Ames tried to wear them out by keeping them waiting in the anteroom. If they outlasted him, he saw them and frightened them with threats of all sorts of trouble for gambling without a license. Meix wanted to have payment on his check stopped. Ames, who had been a bank clerk, told him so, and then had the effrontery to say that payment on such a check could not be stopped.

Burglaries were common. How many the police planned may never be known. Charles F. Brackett and Fred Malone, police captains and detectives, were active, and one well-established crime of theirs is the robbery of the Pabst Brewing Company office. They persuaded two men, one an employee, to learn the combination of the safe, open and clean it out one night, while the two officers stood guard outside.

The excesses of the municipal administration became so notorious that some of the members of it remonstrated with the others, and certain county officers were genuinely alarmed. No restraint followed their warnings. Sheriff Megaarden, no Puritan himself, felt constrained to interfere, and he made some arrests of gamblers. The Ames people turned upon him in a fury; they accused him of making overcharges in his accounts with the county for fees, and laying the evidence before Governor Van Sant, they had Megaarden removed from office. Ames offered bribes to two county commissioners to appoint Gardner sheriff, so as to be sure of no more trouble in that quarter. This move failed, but the lesson taught Megaarden served to clear the atmosphere, and the spoliation went on as recklessly as ever. It became impossible.

Even lawlessness must be regulated. Dr. Ames, never an organizer, attempted no control, and his followers began to quarrel among themselves. They deceived one another; they robbed the thieves; they robbed Ames himself. His brother became dissatisfied with his share of the spoils, and formed cabals with captains who plotted against the administration and set up disorderly houses, "panel games," and all sorts of "grafts" of their own. The one man loyal to the mayor was Gardner, and Fred Ames, Captain King, and their pals, plotted the fall of the favorite. Now anybody could get anything from the Doctor, if he could have him alone. The Fred Ames clique chose a time when the mayor was at West Baden; they filled him with suspicion of Gardner and the fear of exposure, and induced him to let a creature named "Reddy" Cohen, instead of Gardner, do the collecting, and pay over all the moneys, not directly, but through Fred. Gardner made a touching appeal. "I have been honest. I have paid you all," he said to the mayor. "Fred and the rest will rob you." This was true, but it was of no avail.

Fred Ames was in charge at last, and he himself went about giving notice of the change. Three detectives were with him when he visited the women, and here is the women's story, in the words of one, as it was told again and again in court: "Colonel Ames came in with the detectives. He stepped into a side room and asked me if I had been paying Gardner. I told him I had, and he told me not to pay no more, but to come to his office later, and he would let me know what to do. I went to the City Hall in about three weeks, after Cohen had called and said he was 'the party.' I asked the chief if it was all right to pay Cohen, and he said it was."

The new arrangement did not work so smoothly as the old. Cohen was an oppressive collector, and Fred Ames, appealed to, was weak and lenient. He had no sure hold on the force. His captains, free of Gardner, were undermining the chief. They increased their private operations. Some of the detectives began to drink hard and neglect their work. Norbeck so worried the "big mitt" men by staying away from the joint, that they complained to Fred about him. The chief rebuked Norbeck, and he promised to "do better," but thereafter he was paid, not by the week, but by piece work—so much for each "trimmed sucker" that he ran out of town. Protected swindlers were arrested for operating in the street by "Coffee John's" new policemen who took the places of the negligent detectives. Fred let the indignant prisoners go when they were brought before him, but the arrests were annoying, inconvenient, and disturbed business. The whole system became so demoralized that every man was for himself. There was not left even the traditional honor among thieves.

It was at this juncture, in April, 1902, that the grand jury for the summer term was drawn. An ordinary body of unselected citizens, it received no special instructions from the bench; the county prosecutor offered it only routine work to do. But there was a man among them who was a fighter—the foreman, Hovey C. Clarke. He was of an old New England family. Coming to Minneapolis when a young man, seventeen years before, he had fought for employment, fought with his employers for position, fought with his employees, the lumberjacks, for command, fought for his company against competitors; and he had won always, till now he had the habit of command, the impatient, imperious manner of the master, and the assurance of success which begets it. He did not want to be a grand juryman, he did not want to be a foreman; but since he was both, he wanted to accomplish something.

Why not rip up the Ames gang? Heads shook, hands went up; it was useless to try. The discouragement fired Clarke. That was just what he would do, he said, and he took stock of his jury. Two or three were men with backbone; that he knew, and he quickly had them with him. The rest were all sorts of men. Mr. Clarke won over each man to himself, and interested them all. Then he called for the county prosecutor. The prosecutor was a politician; he knew the Ames crowd; they were too powerful to attack.

"You are excused," said the foreman.

There was a scene; the prosecutor knew his rights.

"Do you think, Mr. Clarke," he cried, "that you can run the grand jury and my office, too?"

"Yes," said Clarke, "I will run your office if I want to; and I want to. You're excused."

Mr. Clarke does not talk much about his doings last summer; he isn't the talking sort. But he does say that all he did was to apply simple business methods to his problem. In action, however, these turned out to be the most approved police methods. He hired a lot of local detectives who, he knew, would talk about what they were doing, and thus would be watched by the police. Having thus thrown a false scent, he hired some other detectives whom nobody knew about. This was expensive; so were many of the other things he did; but he was bound to win, so he paid the price, drawing freely on his own and his colleagues' pockets. (The total cost to the county for a long summer's work by this grand jury was $259.) With his detectives out, he himself went to the jail to get tips from the inside, from criminals who, being there, must have grievances. He made the acquaintance of the jailor, Captain Alexander, and Alexander was a friend of Sheriff Megaarden. Yes, he had some men there who were "sore" and might want to get even.

Now two of these were "big mitt" men who had worked for Gardner. One was "Billy" Edwards, the other "Cheerful Charlie" Howard. I heard too many explanations of their plight to choose any one; this general account will cover the ground: In the Ames mêlée, either by mistake, neglect, or for spite growing out of the network of conflicting interests and gangs, they were arrested, arraigned, not before Fred Ames, but a judge, and held in bail too high for them to furnish. They had paid for an unexpired period of protection, yet could get neither protection nor bail. They were forgotten. "We got the double cross all right," they said, and they bled with their grievance; but squeal, no, sir!—that was "another deal."

But Mr. Clarke had their story, and he was bound to force them to tell it under oath on the stand. If they did, Gardner and Norbeck would be indicted, tried, and probably convicted. In themselves, these men were of no great importance; but they were the key to the situation, and a way up to the mayor. It was worth trying. Mr. Clarke went into the jail with Messrs. Lester Elwood and Willard J. Hield, grand jurors on whom he relied most for delicate work. They stood by while the foreman talked. And the foreman's way of talking was to smile, swear, threaten, and cajole. "Billy" Edwards told me afterwards that he and Howard were finally persuaded to turn state's evidence, because they believed that Mr. Clarke was the kind of a man to keep his promises and fulfil his threats, "We," he said, meaning criminals generally, "are always stacking up against juries and lawyers who want us to holler. We don't, because we see they ain't wise, and won't get there. They're quitters; they can be pulled off. Clarke has a hard eye. I know men. It's my business to size 'em up, and I took him for a winner, and I played in with him against that whole big bunch of easy things that was running things on the bum." The grand jury was ready at the end of three weeks of hard work to find bills. A prosecutor was needed. The public prosecutor was being ignored, but his first assistant and friend, Al. J. Smith, was taken in hand by Mr. Clarke. Smith hesitated; he knew better even than the foreman the power and resources of the Ames gang. But he came to believe in Mr. Clarke, just as Edwards had; he was sure the foreman would win; so he went over to his side, and, having once decided, he led the open fighting, and, alone in court, won cases against men who had the best lawyers in the State to defend them. His court record is extraordinary. Moreover, he took over the negotiations with criminals for evidence, Messrs. Clarke, Hield, Elwood, and the other jurors providing means and moral support. These were needed. Bribes were offered to Smith; he was threatened; he was called a fool. But so was Clarke, to whom $28,000 was offered to quit, and for whose slaughter a slugger was hired to come from Chicago. What startled the jury most, however, was the character of the citizens who were sent to them to dissuade them from their course. No reform I ever studied has failed to bring out this phenomenon of virtuous cowardice, the baseness of the decent citizen.

Nothing stopped this jury, however. They had courage. They indicted Gardner, Norbeck, Fred Ames, and many lesser persons. But the gang had courage, too, and raised a defence fund to fight Clarke. Mayor Ames was defiant. Once, when Mr. Clarke called at the City Hall, the mayor met and challenged him. The mayor's heelers were all about him, but Clarke faced him.

"Yes, Doc. Ames, I'm after you," he said. "I've been in this town for seventeen years, and all that time you've been a moral leper. I hear you were rotten during the ten years before that. Now I'm going to put you where all contagious things are put—where you cannot contaminate anybody else."

The trial of Gardner came on. Efforts had been made to persuade him to surrender the mayor, but the young man was paid $15,000 "to stand pat," and he went to trial and conviction silent. Other trials followed fast—Norbeck's, Fred Ames's, Chief of Detectives King's. Witnesses who were out of the State were needed, and true testimony from women. There was no county money for extradition, so the grand jurors paid these costs also. They had Meix followed from Michigan down to Mexico and back to Idaho, where they got him, and he was presented in court one day at the trial of Norbeck, who had "steered" him out of town. Norbeck thought Meix was a thousand miles away, and had been bold before. At the sight of him in court he started to his feet, and that night ran away. The jury spent more money in his pursuit, and they caught him. He confessed, but his evidence was not accepted. He was sentenced to three years in state's prison. Men caved all around, but the women were firm, and the first trial of Fred Ames failed. To break the women's faith in the ring, Mayor Ames was indicted for offering the bribe to have Gardner made sheriff—a genuine, but not the best case against him. It brought the women down to the truth, and Fred Ames, retried, was convicted and sentenced to six and a half years in state's prison. King was tried for accessory to felony (helping in the theft of a diamond, which he afterward stole from the thieves), and sentenced to three and a half years in prison. And still the indictments came, with trials following fast. Al. Smith resigned with the consent and thanks of the grand jury; his chief, who was to run for the same office again, wanted to try the rest of the cases, and he did very well.

All men were now on the side of law and order. The panic among the "grafters" was laughable, in spite of its hideous significance. Two heads of departments against whom nothing had been shown suddenly ran away, and thus suggested to the grand jury an inquiry which revealed another source of "graft," in the sale of supplies to public institutions and the diversion of great quantities of provisions to the private residences of the mayor and other officials. Mayor Ames, under indictment and heavy bonds for extortion, conspiracy, and bribe-offering, left the State on a night train; a gentleman who knew him by sight saw him sitting up at eleven o'clock in the smoking-room of the sleeping-car, an unlighted cigar in his mouth, his face ashen and drawn, and at six o'clock the next morning he still was sitting there, his cigar still unlighted. He went to West Baden, a health resort in Indiana, a sick and broken man, aging years in a month. The city was without a mayor, the ring was without a leader; cliques ruled, and they pictured one another hanging about the grand-jury room begging leave to turn state's evidence. Tom Brown, the mayor's secretary, was in the mayor's chair; across the hall sat Fred Ames, the chief of police, balancing Brown's light weight. Both were busy forming cliques within the ring. Brown had on his side Coffee John and Police Captain Hill. Ames had Captain "Norm" King (though he had been convicted and had resigned), Captain Krumweide, and Ernest Wheelock, the chief's secretary. Alderman D. Percy Jones, the president of the council, an honorable man, should have taken the chair, but he was in the East; so this unstable equilibrium was all the city had by way of a government.

Then Fred Ames disappeared. The Tom Brown clique had full sway, and took over the police department. This was a shock to everybody, to none more than to the King clique, which joined in the search for Ames. An alderman, Fred M. Powers, who was to run for mayor on the Republican ticket, took charge of the mayor's office, but he was not sure of his authority or clear as to his policy. The grand jury was the real power behind him, and the foreman was telegraphing for Alderman Jones. Meanwhile the cliques were making appeals to Mayor Ames, in West Baden, and each side that saw him received authority to do its will. The Coffee John clique, denied admission to the grand-jury room, turned to Alderman Powers, and were beginning to feel secure, when they heard that Fred Ames was coming back. They rushed around, and obtained an assurance from the exiled mayor that Fred was returning only to resign. Fred—now under conviction—returned, but he did not resign; supported by his friends, he took charge again of the police force. Coffee John besought Alderman Powers to remove the chief, and when the acting mayor proved himself too timid, Coffee John, Tom Brown, and Captain Hill laid a deep plot. They would ask Mayor Ames to remove his brother. This they felt sure they could persuade the "old man" to do. The difficulty was to keep him from changing his mind when the other side should reach his ear. They hit upon a bold expedient. They would urge the "old man" to remove Fred, and then resign himself, so that he could not undo the deed that they wanted done. Coffee John and Captain Hill slipped out of town one night; they reached West Baden on one train and they left for home on the next, with a demand for Fred's resignation in one hand and the mayor's own in the other. Fred Ames did resign, and though the mayor's resignation was laid aside for a while, to avoid the expense of a special election, all looked well for Coffee John and his clique. They had Fred out, and Alderman Powers was to make them great. But Mr. Powers wobbled. No doubt the grand jury spoke to him. At any rate he turned most unexpectedly on both cliques together. He turned out Tom Brown, but he turned out also Coffee John, and he did not make their man chief of police, but another of some one else's selection. A number of resignations was the result, and these the acting mayor accepted, making a clearing of astonished rascals which was very gratifying to the grand jury and to the nervous citizens of Minneapolis.

But the town was not yet easy. The grand jury, which was the actual head of the government, was about to be discharged, and, besides, their work was destructive. A constructive force was now needed, and Alderman Jones was pelted with telegrams from home bidding him hurry back. He did hurry, and when he arrived, the situation was instantly in control. The grand jury prepared to report, for the city had a mind and a will of its own once more. The criminals found it out last.

G. E. Mowry

The Progressive Profile

One of the most interesting questions concerning the Progressives is that of their origin and motivation. In many ways they were much like the earlier reformers, but in more ways they were dissimilar. How and why they differed is described by George E. Mowry of the University of California, Los Angeles, and a specialist on early twentieth-century America. In the following selection, from Mowry's volume in the New American Nation series, he paints a picture of the typical Progressive—young, self-made, solid middle class, either in a profession or a merchant or manufacturer, of old American stock, and a conservative in the 1890s. Mowry describes his intellectual and ethical climate and his social and economic milieu. With perception he analyzes the Progressive's view of America; his dreams and aspirations; his loathing of extremes, rich or poor; his hatred of the cities as the arch polluter of society; his loss of prestige and power to the newly enriched industrialist; and his hope to return to an earlier America where education and intellect counted. [From The Era of Theodore Roosevelt, 1900–1912, *by George E. Mowry. Copyright © 1958 by George E. Mowry. Reprinted by permission of Harper & Row, Publishers, Incorporated.]*

As a group, the reform mayors and governors, their prominent supporters, and the muckrakers were an interesting lot. Considering the positions they held, they were very young. Joseph W. Folk was only thirty-five when elected governor, Theodore Roosevelt forty, Charles Evans Hughes and Hiram Johnson forty-four, and Robert La Follette forty-five. The average age of the important progressive leaders who upset the Southern Pacific Railroad machine in California was a little over thirty-eight. The tale of a rather typical young reformer was that of Joseph Medill Patterson of the Chicago *Tribune* family. Patterson's grandfather founded the *Tribune,* his father was general manager of the paper, and his cousin was Robert McCormick, who controlled the paper for over thirty years. Patterson sharply reacted against the reigning conservatism by winning a seat in the Illinois legislature at the age of twenty-four on a platform advocating the municipal ownership of all city utilities in the state. Two years later he resigned from the Chicago Commission of Public Works to become a Socialist because, he announced, it was impossible to reform the city and the country under capitalism. In 1906 he published a diatribe against wealth in the *Independent* entitled "The Confessions of a Drone," and followed it two years later with a book of similar tone. Obviously, this was a period, like the ones after the War of 1812 and in the 1850's, when energetic and incautious youth took command. And in each instance the departure of the elder statesmen portended great changes.

Some of these reformers, like Golden Rule Jones, Charles Evans Hughes, and Tom Johnson, were self-made men, although Hughes's father was a minister, and Johnson's, a Confederate colonel, had come from the upper stratum of Kentucky society. A surprising number of them came from very wealthy families, with names like du Pont, Crane, Spreckels, Dodge, Morgenthau, Pinchot, Perkins, McCormick, and Patterson. The quip was made that this was a "millionaire's reform movement." But the great majority of the reformers came from the "solid middle class," as it then was called with some pride. That their families had been of the economically secure is indicated by the fact that most of them had had a college education in a day when a degree stamped a person as coming from a special economic group. It is interesting to note that most of the women reformers and social workers had gone to college. Occupationally also the reformers came from a very narrow base in society. Of a sample of over four hundred a majority was lawyers, as might be expected of politicians, and nearly 20 per cent of them newspaper editors or publishers. The next largest group was from the independent manufacturers or merchants, with the rest scattered among varied occupations, including medicine, banking, and real estate. A statistical study of sixty of the wealthier reformers reveals that the largest single group of twenty-one was manufacturers or merchants, ten lawyers, six newspaper publishers, while nineteen more had inherited their wealth. Quite a few among the latter group had no definite occupation save that of preserving their family fortune and indulging in reform. Of the sixty only about half attended college, a figure much lower than that for the entire group of reformers. Of this number just 50 per cent came from three institutions, Harvard, Princeton, and Yale.

If names mean anything, an overwhelming proportion of this reform group came from old American stock with British origins consistently indicated. Except for the women, who were predominantly Midwestern, the reformers' places of origin were scattered over the country roughly in proportion to population densities. Practically all of them by 1900, however, lived in northern cities, most of the Southerners having left their section during early manhood. Religious affiliations were surprisingly difficult to get, and no really trustworthy national sample was obtained. The figures collected were not at all consonant with national church membership statistics. Representatives of the Quaker faith bulked large among the women reformers, as did members of the Jewish religion among the very wealthy. But for the group as a whole the religious descendants of Calvin and Knox predominated, with the Congregationalists, Unitarians, and Presbyterians in the vast majority. Thus it seems likely that the intellectual and religious influence of New England was again dominating the land.

Whether Democrats or Republicans, the overwhelming number of this group of twentieth-century reformers had been conservatives in the nineties. If Republican, they had almost to a man followed the way of Theodore Roosevelt, Robert La Follette, Lincoln Steffens, and William Allen White to support William McKinley. Most of the progressive Democrats had not been supporters of Bryan, but, like Woodrow Wilson, John Johnson, and Hoke Smith of Georgia, had either followed the Gold Democratic ticket or had remained silent during the election of 1896. Yet from four to six years later most of these men were ardent advocates of municipal gas and water socialism, and were opposed to their regular party machines to the extent of leading either nonpartisan movements in the municipalities or rebellious splinter groups in the states. Moreover, the new century found most of them, except on the currency issue, supporting many of the 1896 Populist and Bryanite demands. Before the Progressive years were finished they and their kind had not only secured the inception of a host of the Populists' reforms, but had contributed a few of their own.

Obviously, a good many questions arise about the motivation of this economically secure, well-educated, middle-class group. On the surface it looked as if the progressive movement was simply a continuation under different leadership of the Populist cause. According to William Allen White, Populism had "shaved its whiskers, washed its shirt, put on a derby, and moved up into the middle class." But White's remark scarcely probed beneath the surface. Populism arose from farmer distress in a period of acute depression. Its reforms were belly reforms. The movement was led by angry men and women not too far removed from the Grange hall. Except for the western silver men, they were incensed at the mounting figures of farm foreclosures and a withering countryside. To the contrary, progressivism arose in a period of relative prosperity. Its reforms were more the results of the heart and the head than of the stomach. Its leaders were largely recruited from the professional and business classes of the city. A good many were wealthy men; more were college graduates. As a group they were indignant at times, but scarcely ever angry. What caused them to act in the peculiar way they did? A part of the answer lies in the peculiar economic and social position in which this middle-class group found itself at about the turn of the century, a part in the intellectual and ethical climate of the age, a part in the significant cluster of prejudices and biases that marked the progressive mind.

"The world wants men, great, strong, harsh, brutal men—men with purpose who let nothing, nothing, nothing stand in their way," Frank Norris wrote in one of his novels. This worship of the strong man, so characteristic of the age, produced a cult of political leadership with ominous overtones for later years. Tempered at this time with the ethics of the social gospel, the cult produced an image far less frightening: an image of men dedicated to the social good, an image approximating the hope of Plato for his guardians. These strong good men, "the change-makers," Harold Frederic wrote, were the protectors of morality, the originators of progress. They were ambitious men and ruthless, but only ruthless in their zeal for human advancement. They were supremely alone, the causative individuals. Far from being disturbed when isolated, David Graham Phillips's hero Scarborough was only concerned when he was "propped up" by something other than his own will and intelligence. "I propose," he commented, "never to 'belong' to anything or anybody."

In 1872 a future progressive, Henry Demarest Lloyd, confessed that he wanted power above all things, but "power unpoisoned by the presence of obligation." That worship of the unfettered individual, the strong pride of self, the strain of ambition, and the almost compulsive desire for power ran through progressive rhetoric like a theme in a symphony. From Frank Norris's strong-minded heroes to Richard Harding Davis's men of almost pure muscle these feelings were a badge of a restless, sensitive, and troubled class. They were never far below the surface in the character of Theodore Roosevelt. Robert La Follette knew them, and Woodrow Wilson had more than his share of them. While still a scholar and teacher, Wilson poured out his frustration with the contemplative life: "I have no patience with the tedious world of what is known as 'research,' " he wrote to a friend. "I should be complete if I could inspire a great movement of opinion."

A few progressive leaders like William Jennings Bryan and Golden Rule Jones really thought of themselves as servants of the people, and almost completely identified themselves with their constituents. But most progressives set themselves apart from the crowd. Mankind was basically good and capable of progress, but benign change scarcely issued from the masses. Rather it was only accomplished through the instrumentality of a few great and good men. Woodrow Wilson believed that efficient government could come only from "an educated elite," William Kent thought that progress never came from the bottom, and Roosevelt often spoke of government as the process of "giving justice from above." Occasionally, when the electorate disagreed with them, the progressives contented themselves with the thought that truth "was always in the minority" and a possession alone of the "few who see." In 1912 Walter Lippmann wrote that since men could do anything but govern themselves, they were constantly looking for some "benevolent guardian." To the progressive politician that guardian, of course, was patterned after his image of himself.

"I am so sick of fraud and filth and lies," David Graham Phillips plaintively wrote to Senator Beveridge in 1902, "so tired of stern realities. I grasp at myths like a child." The myths Phillips reached for were the supposed realities of an older day, a day when the individual presumably had been able to make his way to the top by the strength of his abilities, and yet a day when there was enough opportunity left at the bottom so that mass poverty, slums, and crime were never evident enough to assault either the eye or the conscience of the successful. Things were different now even in the Valley of Democracy.

The Indiana town where Booth Tarkington's Magnificent Ambersons had benevolently ruled from their big house on Amberson Boulevard had now become a city. In the process of growth spanning the lives of just one generation, the fortunes of the Ambersons had declined until the grandson George was working as a clerk in a factory. As all the young George Ambersons set about to reassert their rightful power and prestige, they were confronted both by enormous and monopolizing wealth and by the rising labor unions. The United States, it seemed, had become almost what Bellamy's historian in *Equality* called it, a world of organized degraded serfs run by a plundering and tightly knit plutocracy. The continual clash between the serfs and the plutocrats engulfed almost everyone. It was enough to disenchant the bystander whose loyalties were neither to the plunderers nor the plundered, but rather to an older America where such social extremes, it was felt, had not existed. Morosely, Professor Barett Wendell observed that America had sold her democratic, equalitarian birthright and was becoming "just another part of the world." Europe no longer learned at America's feet, Walter Weyl, the economist and publicist, wrote with an air of nostalgia, but rather in some respects had become "our teacher." Obviously something needed to be done. Should it be the "return or reversion . . . to certain elementary doctrines of common sense" and the simple rural institutions of the past, as some progressives hoped, or a going forward to something approaching Howells' utopia, which combined the new urban industrialism and a concern for human values in a new type of ethical socialism?

A small reform-minded minority in 1900 was outspoken in defense of the large industrial and commercial city as the creator of the good life. Some of them saw the city as a place of refuge from an ugly countryside and from a hostile natural environment. Remembering his own bleak and lonely boyhood on an upstate New York farm, the novelist Harold Frederic condemned a daily communion with nature that starved the mind and dwarfed the soul. Theodore Dreiser bluntly described the natural processes as inimical to man as a species. Others felt the fascination of the city, a place of excitement and of opportunity. Lincoln Steffens recalled that he felt about the concrete canyons of New York as other youths felt about the wild West. For people like Jane Addams, Jacob Reis, and Hutchins Hapgood the city offered a place to work and an avenue to opportunity.

For the great majority of the new century's reformers, however, the city contained almost the sum of their dislikes. It was a "devilsburg of crime" sucking into its corrupt vortex the "young, genuine, strong and simple men from the farm." There, if successful, they became "financial wreckers" who made their money strangling legitimate enterprises and other human beings. If they were failures—that is, if they remained factory workers—they gradually became like the machine they tended, "huge, hard, brutal, strung with a crude blind strength, stupid, unreasoning." At the worst such unfortunates became the flotsam of the slums, making the saloon their church and the dive their home. The native American lost not only his morals in the city but also his talent for creative work and his sense of beauty. "Sometimes, I think, they'se poison in th' life in a big city," Mr. Dooley remarked, "the flowers won't grow there." If a man stayed in the city long enough, one of David Graham Phillips' characters remarked, he would almost inevitably lose those qualities that made him an American: one had to go West to see a "real American, a man or a woman who looks as if he or she would do something honest or valuable."

With such intense antiurban feelings, it is small wonder that the United States began to romanticize its pioneer past and its agrarian background. Following the Spanish War historical novels fairly poured from the publishers. The public appetite for western stories had one of its periodic increases, and the virtues of the countryside were extolled in even the best literature. In one of Ellen Glasgow's first novels the country, "with its ecstatic insight into the sacred plan of things," is contrasted with the city's "tainted atmosphere." Almost repeating William Jennings Bryan in 1896, Miss Glasgow wrote that the country was the world as God had planned it, the city as man had made it. The cult of the frontier, first introduced into historical scholarship by Frederic Jackson Turner in 1890, and the new emphasis upon agrarian virtues were zealously reflected by the more sensitive politicians. William Jennings Bryan, Theodore Roosevelt, Robert La Follette, and Woodrow Wilson all showed to varying degrees this national nostalgia, this reactionary impulse. Roosevelt in particular saw the great city as the creator of national weakness and possible disintegration, and the countryside as the nation's savior. It was the man on the farm, he wrote, who had consistently done the nation the "best service in governing himself in time of peace and also in fighting in time of war." Dangerous elements to the commonwealth lurked in every large city, but among the western farmers of the West "there was not room for an anarchist or a communist in the whole lot." What Professor Richard Hofstadter has called the agrarian myth, but which might better be called the agrarian bias, was one of the more important elements that went into the making of the progressive mind.

A part of the progressive's romantic attraction to the countryside at this particular time can be explained by the alien character of the urban population. In 1903 the Commissioner of Immigration reported that the past year had witnessed the greatest influx of immigrants in the nation's history. But far from being pleased, the Commissioner was plainly worried. An increasing percentage of these newcomers, he pointed out, belonged to an "undesirable foreign element," the "indigestible" aliens from south Europe. The public was neither surprised at the figures of the report nor shocked by its adjectives. It had been made increasingly sensitive to the changing patterns of immigration by numerous periodical articles and newspaper items calling attention to the alien nature of the eastern seaboard cities. As the immigrant tide welled stronger each year, the nativist spirit that had been so obviously a part of the mental complex leading to the Spanish War increased in intensity. Throughout the decade editors, novelists, and politicians competed with each other in singing the praises of the "big-boned, blond, long-haired" Anglo-Saxon with the blood of the berserkers in his veins, and in denigrating Jack London's "dark pigmented things, the half castes, the mongrel bloods, and the dregs of long conquered races." In Frank Norris's novels the really despicable characters run all to a type. Braun, the diamond expert in *Vandover;* Zerkow, the junk dealer in *McTeague;* the flannel-shirted Grossman in *The Pit;* and Behrman in *The Octopus* were all of the same religion and approximately from the same regions in Europe. One of the themes in Homer Lea's *The Vermillion Pencil* was the extranational loyalty of the Catholic bishop who intrigued endlessly for the Church and against the State. Although Chester Rowell frankly admitted that California needed "a class of servile labor," he was adamantly opposed to the admission of Orientals, who were dangerous to the state and to "the blood of the next generation."

The progressives, of course, had no monopoly of this racism. Such conservatives as Elihu Root, Henry Cabot Lodge, and Chauncey Depew, and even radicals like Debs, shared their views to a degree. But for one reason or another neither conservative nor radical was as vocal or specific in his racism as was the reformer. No more eloquent testimony to the power of racism over the progressive mind is evident than in the writings of the kindly, tolerant Middle Westerner William Allen White. In a book published in 1910 White explained nearly all of America's past greatness, including its will to reform, in terms of the nation's "race life" and its racial institutions, "the home and the folk moot." Nor would this genius, this "clean Aryan blood," White promised, be subjected to a debilitating admixture in the future despite the incoming hordes. "We are separated by two oceans from the inferior races and by an instinctive race revulsion to cross breeding that marks the American wherever he is found." Such diverse reformers as Theodore Roosevelt, Albert J. Beveridge, Chester Rowell, Frank Parsons, Hoke Smith, Richard W. Gilder, and Ray Stannard Baker, with more or less emphasis, echoed White's sentiments.

The attitude of the progressive toward race, religion, and color, and his attending views of the great city, was to have profound effects on both internal and external policy. Its consequences were already obvious by 1905 in the South; it was to provoke an international storm in California, and it was to keep alive and possibly nourish a strain of bigotry that was to bear bitter fruit for the United States after the First World War and for the entire world in post-depression Germany. But this is far from saying that the progressive was a spiritual father of either the Ku-Klux Klan of the twenties or the Nazi of the thirties. He might well have been anti-immigrant, anti-Catholic, and anti-Jewish, and he might have thought of himself as one of the racial lords of creation, but he was also extremely responsive to the Christian ethic and to the democratic tradition. It was just not in his character to be ruthless toward a helpless minority, especially when the minority was one of his own. The progressive's response to the big-city slum was the settlement-house movement and housing, fire, and sanitary regulations, not the concentration camp. It was probably not entirely politics that prompted Theodore Roosevelt to invite the first Negro to lunch in the White House or to appoint people of Jewish or of Catholic faith to the Cabinet. Roosevelt thoroughly sympathized with California's Oriental problem. But he insisted that the state live up to the nation's international agreements and to the Constitution in its treatment of American Orientals. True, he was worried about Japan's reaction, but elsewhere in international politics he was not so careful of the sensibilities of other nations.

The progressive had reasons beyond racial ones for disliking the big city. For him the metropolis was the home of great wealth, and excessive wealth was as much an enemy to civilization as excessive poverty. A surprising number of very wealthy men supported the progressive cause, and their feelings toward their wealth produced a most interesting psychic state. Taken together, their statements sounded something like those in a confessional session of an early Puritan congregation. Explaining that he had acquired his wealth by "special privilege," Joseph Fels sought expiation by proposing "to spend the damnable money to wipe out the system by which I made it." Medill Patterson and William Kent produced similar variations on the same theme, and Tom Johnson repeatedly used coups from his own career of money-making to illustrate the social viciousness of the system he was contending against in Cleveland. Professor Hofstadter has ascribed this sense of guilt to the Protestant mind as it made the transit from rural and village life to the urban world where great extremes of economic circumstance were the common condition. It is also probable that as the Protestant upper middle class lost its mystical religion, it compensated by more fiercely adhering to Protestant ethic. It may be of note that the very wealthy who maintained their belief in a mystical religion were never as earnest in social well-doing as their erring brothers. If no one is as zealous as a convert, then perhaps no one conserves what is left of his ideological inheritance more than the man who has lost part of it.

The less well-circumstanced progressive was just as critical of great wealth as his more fortunate colleague. Theodore Roosevelt, who had been left a comfortable but not a great fortune, disliked the American multimillionaire and felt that a society that created an ideal of him was in a very "rotten condition." Bryan once declared that great wealth and personal goodness was something of a paradox. And a reforming journalist from the midlands raised the question whether a man could honestly earn more than a few million dollars in one lifetime. By 1913 Walter Lippmann noted that great wealth, along with "the economic man of the theorists," was in public disrepute.

The reasons for this antimaterialist crusade of the progressive are an interesting study in complex human motivation. Some of the sentiment undoubtedly came from personal frustration and personal envy. Perhaps to the point is Lincoln Steffens' experience with the stock market. In 1900 he wrote his father that the boom in stocks had made him considerable profits and that he was joining the Republican organization in his district. A year later, after some reverses, he insisted that character was the important desideratum for a young man and not wealth, which often meant the loss of character. The rising intensity of competition for the small merchants and industrialists also played a part in the attack on great wealth. Occasionally one found a reformer who had lost his business. But more often than not in the new century such men were moderately prosperous. Their resentment, if it arose from economic causes, came not from despair but from other feelings, from their sense of lessened power, perhaps, from their regard for their good name, from their sensitivity to the opinion of their fellows. Their relative status and power in society had been going down consistently since the rise of the economic moguls following the Civil War. The gap between them and the Morgans and the Rockefellers had been steadily increasing, and their hopes for attaining the top of the economic heap were progressively dimming. As one commentator noted, the ambitious middle classes in society had "suffered a reduction less in income than in outlook."

This reduction in outlook that Walter Weyl perceived was even more acute for another class, the old American elite whose wealth, family, name, and social power had been secure long before the rise of the relatively new multimillionaires. The Adamses, the Lodges, the Roosevelts, the Bonapartes, and their local counterparts in the hinterlands were a self-consciously proud group. Although Theodore Roosevelt was well down academically in his 1880 Harvard class, he observed that "only one gentleman stands ahead of me." The turbulent and revolutionary waves of the new industrialism and finance had washed up on such polished shores some exceedingly rough gravel. The Rockefellers, the Hannas, and the Harrimans, to say nothing of the Jay Goulds, had not importuned for power in either industry or politics; they had seized it. As their names dominated the newspaper headlines and their ladies laid violent siege to formal society, old families and old ways seemed to have been forgotten. To the recent plutocrats, Henry Cabot Lodge acidly observed from the historic shores of Nahant, "the old American family" and society's long-tested "laws and customs" meant nothing. And far to the west in Cincinnati, it was reported, a social war had broken out between "the stick-ems" and "the stuck-ems." The first group was a "barbarous new class" of millionaires, just risen from the packing industry, who had assaulted an older class of "thousandaires," who had inherited their wealth made two generations before in the same industry. . . .

As the progressive looked at the sharply differentiated America of 1900, he saw "pyramids of money in a desert of want." For William Allen White the world was full of "big crooks" and the "underprivileged." The polar conditions of society assaulted the progressive conscience and threatened progressive security. Supremely individualistic, the progressive could not impute class consciousness, or, as he would have phrased it, class selfishness, to himself. His talk was therefore full of moral self-judgments, of phrases like "the good men," "the better element," "the moral crowd." From the Old Source, he paraphrased, "Thou shalt not respect the person of the poor, nor honor the person of the great; in righteousness shalt thou judge thy neighbor." His self-image was that of a "kind-hearted man" dealing in justice. William Kent publicly stated that he could not believe in the class struggle because every great reform of the past had been wrought by men who were not "selfishly interested." "I believe," he concluded, "altruism is a bigger force in the world than selfishness."

Since the progressive was not organized economically as was the capitalist and the laborer, he chose to fight his battles where he had the most power—in the political arena. And in large terms his political program was first that of the most basic urge of all nature, to preserve himself, and secondly to refashion the world after his own image. What the nation needed most, wrote a Midwestern clergyman, was an increase in the number of "large-hearted men" to counteract the class organization of both capital and labor. "Solidarity," Herbert Croly stated, "must be restored." The point of reconcentration around which the hoped-for solidarity was to take place, of course, was the middle class. It was to "absorb" all other classes, thought Henry Demarest Lloyd. It was to be both the sum and substance of the classless state of the future.

The progressive mentality was a compound of many curious elements.

It contained a reactionary as well as a reform impulse. It was imbued with a burning ethical strain which at times approached a missionary desire to create a heaven on earth. It had in it intense feelings of moral superiority over both elements of society above and below it economically. It emphasized individual dynamism and leadership. One part of it looked backward to an intensely democratic small America; another looked forward to a highly centralized nationalistic state. And both elements contained a rather ugly strain of racism.

The progressive mentality was generated in part from both a fear of the loss of group status and a confidence in man's ability to order the future. Had progressive militancy come in a more despondent intellectual and ethical climate and in a bleaker economic day, group fear might have won over group hope. Its more benign social ends might then have been transmuted into something more malignant. But in the warm and sunny atmosphere of 1900 the optimistic mood prevailed. For the year marking the beginning of the new century was a year of progressive success in the cities and the states. And within another year, by the ugly agent of an assassin's gun, Theodore Roosevelt had become President. With the shot in Buffalo, progressivism achieved a spokesman in the White House.

William E. Leuchtenburg

The New Nationalism

and the New Freedom

As Arthur S. Link has pointed out, there were two quite distinct types of Progressivists— the Rooseveltian and the Wilsonian. The former, exemplified by the New Nationalism, envisaged the goal of the Progressives as the creation of an equilibrium in American society among the various components—laborers, farmers, industrialists— for the purpose of achieving the greatest good for the greatest number. The monitor of the system, overseeing a "square deal" for all, would be the federal government. Its principal function would be to prevent any one component from riding roughshod over the others. It would not hesitate to intervene to prevent an imbalance. In such a system, bigness was not necessarily bad. Indeed, Roosevelt believed that large corporations had considerable virtue in promoting efficiency in production and distribution and that they were a national asset. They must not, however, become predatory.

Woodrow Wilson's view of the goals of Progressivism was also the greatest good for the greatest number, but it was to be achieved not by "regulating competition" but by "regulating monopoly." The role of the government was not to step in when one component of society tended to upset the balance; instead, government should create such conditions as *would prevent any one interest group from becoming powerful enough to tip the scales in its favor. This condition could best be achieved by destroying the monopolies that the great industrial combines were enjoying—a move that would restore competition to the system. The credo of the New Freedom became, therefore, to use "federal powers to eliminate economic maladjustments so that the economy might run freely."*

An excellent statement of the ideas of these two leaders appears in the introductions by William E. Leuchtenburg to collections of their speeches. A professor of history at Columbia and the author of two important books on twentieth-century America, Leuchtenburg analyzes the differences between Roosevelt's and Wilson's views of Progressivism. [William E. Leuchtenburg, ed., The New Nationalism *by Theodore Roosevelt and* The New Freedom *by Woodrow Wilson (Englewood Cliffs, N.J.: Prentice-Hall, Inc., 1961). Reprinted by permission.]*

Much of the confusion about Roosevelt's position came from a misguided attempt to classify him either as a progressive or a business-oriented conservative when Roosevelt, in fact, was neither. He approached the political problems of the day with quite different assumptions from the humanitarian reformer, committed to advancing the interests of the underprivileged, or from the business-minded conservative, opposed to any change that might jeopardize the interests of the propertied classes.

Roosevelt believed that the country faced the most serious crisis since the eve of the Civil War. Over and over again in his letters in 1910, he returned to the analogy between the division in the Republican party and the troubles which had destroyed the pre-war Whigs. As the occasion to introduce the New Nationalism, he chose the dedication ceremonies of John Brown's battlefield at Osawatomie. He held up to both factions the ideal of Abraham Lincoln, the Lincoln who was the saint of American nationalism, the man who had risked bloody civil strife to preserve the nation, and who, on the eve of triumph in a war to unite the nation, had been martyred on Good Friday. Americans of Roosevelt's generation came close to transforming the Lincoln legend into a secular cult; the California progressive leader William Kent's only religious affiliation was with the Abraham Lincoln Center of Chicago.

Roosevelt traced the source of the new crisis facing the country to the fact that men lacked a sense of national unity. The nation was still much too parochial in its outlook, too sectionally-minded in its attitude toward American politics, too provincial in its view of the world. More serious even than this parochialism were the actions of two warring classes, capital and labor, both of which pursued their private advantages heedless of the national interest. Roosevelt had the deep contempt of the patrician for the greedy businessman who lacked even a primitive sense of justice. He felt at the same time a horror of mob violence; he saw in each new labor leader, in each new tribune of the people, a potential Robespierre. Throughout his western trip, he warned that the Scylla of demagogism was as much to be dreaded as the Charybdis of conservatism; the reckless agitator and the unscrupulous reactionary both stood "on the same plane of obnoxiousness."

The factions which threatened to divide the nation were the very factions whose extreme members threatened to disrupt the Republican party, Roosevelt believed. The conservatives who fawned on business, he wrote Lodge in mid-September, were "really the heirs of the cotton Whigs, and not of the Republicanism of Lincoln." On the other hand, the radical wing of the insurgents posed the same threat to sane politics that John Brown once had. A few weeks before he went to Osawatomie, he explained: "At the moment, I am endeavoring to prevent the John Browns among the insurgents getting themselves in a position from which the Abraham Lincolns cannot extricate them." In December after the state campaigns had been fought and lost to the Democrats, a weary and melancholy Roosevelt made one more attempt to explain his position: "I wish to be radical, as Lincoln was radical compared to Buchanan and Fillmore, and conservative as he was conservative compared to Wendell Phillips and John Brown."

As the Lincoln who would reunite a fragmented nation, Roosevelt insisted that the national interest was prior to any individual right. At Osawatomie, he had made the bold assertion: "The man who wrongly holds that every human right is secondary to his profit must now give way to the advocate of human welfare, who rightly maintains that every man holds his property subject to the general right of the community to regulate its use to whatever degree the public welfare may require it." The rights of the community, greater than any individual rights, would best be advanced, Roosevelt argued, by a powerful central government. Since business had been nationalized, states and localities were no longer able to cope with "lawbreakers of great wealth"; only the federal government could do so. It should have power to complete its tasks, unfettered by the casuistries of judges who would shackle it. The hope of the people lay not in the courts but in a vigorous Chief Executive who would be "the steward of the public welfare."

Roosevelt had a peculiarly European concern with the health of the state. The great menace to the health of the nation, Roosevelt believed, lay in the utilitarianism of a business civilization, insensible to national honor, and that popular pursuit of ease which placed rights above duties, pleasures above the national interest. A people unwilling to sacrifice for the good of the state was a decadent people; the New Nationalism would seek, by teaching and by action, to reinvigorate American society. "Social efficiency," Roosevelt thought, derived from "love of order, ability to fight well and breed well, capacity to subordinate the interests of the individual to the interests of the community."

Many of Roosevelt's contemporaries believed that Roosevelt had drawn the doctrines of the New Nationalism directly from the American political philosopher, Herbert Croly. In the 1912 campaign, for example, the *American Magazine* described Croly as "the man from whom Colonel Roosevelt got his 'New Nationalism.' " Roosevelt had had his attention called to Croly's *The Promise of American Life,* published in 1909, by both Learned Hand and Henry Cabot Lodge, not in Africa, as is sometimes said, but on his tour of Europe as he headed home for America. Sometime in the late spring or early summer of 1910, Roosevelt read Croly's study. In late July, at a time when the Colonel was preparing his speeches for his western tour, he wrote Croly: "I do not know when I have read a book which I felt profited me as much as your book on American life." Roosevelt added: "I shall use your ideas freely in speeches I intend to make."

Such direct evidence of the influence of a writer on a public man is more than most historians ever hope to find, and it is little wonder that they have made so much of the impact of Croly on Roosevelt. They have not only suggested that he influenced the New Nationalism but have gone still further to argue that Croly converted Roosevelt from the conservatism of his White House years to the advanced progressivism of the Bull Moose campaign of 1912. Such a view of Croly's influence arises from the mistaken conviction that Roosevelt as President was a fraud, a conservative masquerading as a reformer. Since no one could deny that the Colonel made a radical appeal in 1912, historians who conceive of Roosevelt as a pseudo-progressive as president have felt compelled to explain the "change" in Roosevelt and to attribute it to some external agent.

The notion that the Colonel changed the views of a lifetime as the result of reading one book betrays a wistful faith in the power of the pen, but little else. There is scarcely a theme or a recommendation of the New Nationalism which Roosevelt had not already enunciated before Croly wrote his book. In three messages to Congress in 1907 and 1908, Roosevelt had spelled out almost the entire program of the New Nationalism: federal regulation of business, legislation to benefit labor, the inheritance and income taxes, and instrumentalities like postal savings banks. He had accused individual business leaders of "rottenness," of "flagrant dishonesty," and of "bitter and unscrupulous craft." He had urged that workers be guaranteed "a larger share of the wealth." He had assaulted the judiciary, and especially the federal courts, and had suggested that some judges were "incompetent." Well before 1907, in private letters and in some public acts, he had foreshadowed the main outlines of New Nationalist thought: nationalism, love of order, alarm at both corporation and union power, fear of revolution, distrust of the Jeffersonian tradition of reform, faith in a strong state and a powerful Chief Executive—the list could be extended to embrace every important tenet of the New Nationalism.

This is not to say Croly had no importance at all. The book could hardly have helped but have a great appeal to Roosevelt not only because it mirrored his own thinking but also because the Colonel was the hero of the book. It probably prodded Roosevelt to clarify his thoughts in the summer of 1910, and he may even, as many writers have suggested, have taken the very phrase "New Nationalism" from Croly, although this seems unlikely. Some of the words Roosevelt spoke at Osawatomie seemed to be a direct response to Croly's urging that he carry his thinking to its logical conclusion. But *The Promise of American Life* is less important for the impact Croly had on Roosevelt than as evidence of the impact Roosevelt had on Croly. In Croly's work, we can find a more systematic statement of Roosevelt's New Nationalism than Roosevelt himself ever found time to set down, and for this reason it commands our attention.

The central agrument of *The Promise of American Life* rests on the premise that the ills of American society can be traced to the persistence of Jeffersonian thinking. Croly believed that Jefferson, a man of "intellectual superficiality and insincerity," had started the country off on the wrong foot. Jefferson's "cant" about equal rights for all and special privileges for none had licensed greed and the pursuit of self-interest without regard to the national interest. Instead of seeking to create and sustain fluid elites, Jefferson had prattled about the equality of all men. By his suspicion of concentrated power, he had obscured the need for a strong central government which would direct the fortunes of the nation with a coherent sense of national purpose.

The familiar cliché about Croly is that he favored the achievement of Jeffersonian ends by Hamiltonian means. To say this is to misunderstand Croly altogether. Jefferson is the villain of *The Promise of American Life,* and Croly condemns Jeffersonian ends as well as Jeffersonian means. A truckler to the masses, Jefferson, Croly declared, wanted "a government of and by the people," when he should have sought "a government for the people by popular but responsible leaders." The gross error of Jeffersonianism was that it supposed that "the people were to guide their leaders, not their leaders the people."

Jefferson's "fatal policy of drift," Croly argued, fixed the course of American history for the next century. Jackson perpetuated the Jeffersonian errors, especially the equal rights fetishism and the suspicion of the expert. In the Jacksonian era, "Americans of intelligence" were subjected to "social equalitarianism." For a time, under Lincoln, when all of the resources of the nation were mobilized to wipe out slavery, the country did achieve a sense of national purpose. Lincoln rallied the nation to a sense of its responsibilities by refusing to allow local and individual rights to stand in his way; the war itself "began to emancipate the American national idea from an obscurantist individualism and provincialism." Unhappily, as soon as the war ended, the country slipped back into an aimless policy of drift.

In the years since the Civil War, Croly continued, the industrialization of the country had destroyed the homogeneous society of the early republic. Jefferson's ideas had been mischievous even then, but in the world of the early twentieth century, they were downright dangerous. The doctrine of equal rights had resulted, paradoxically, in the concentration of wealth and power in the hands of a few. The founding fathers had imagined neither such concentration of financial power nor the growth of special interests like labor unions; to cope with them, America needed to develop both a body of opinion and instrumentalities strong enough to discipline both in the national interest. To replace the instinctive homogeneity of 1800, the nation had to reconstruct a new "democratic social ideal." But every attempt to achieve "a national purpose" broke against the fatalistic faith in progress, the irresponsible optimism of a people who thought that, despite the revolutionary changes in American society, they could afford to drift along without taking conscious action in pursuit of a national ideal.

To be sure, there had been countless efforts at reform, Croly conceded, but the reform movement had been cursed by the old Jeffersonian emphases. The reformer's faith in individualism and equal rights had led him to reject the need for a stratified society and to embrace the folly of trust busting. A reformer like Bryan who was a Democrat started out with a fatal handicap, for his party distrusted the concentration of power in the state. Moreover, Bryan's idealization of the common man and his suspicion of the exceptional man meant that he stood for "the sacrifice of the individual to the popular average; and the perpetuation of such a sacrifice would mean ultimate democratic degeneration." An even greater danger came from Jacobins like William Randolph Hearst who abused businessmen by holding them up to public scorn instead of recognizing that politics must be grounded in "mutual confidence and fair dealing."

Fortunately, Croly wrote, there was one reformer "whose work has tended to give reform the dignity of a constructive mission": Theodore Roosevelt. Roosevelt's strength arose from the fact that he was even more a nationalist than a reformer. He had nationalized the reform movement by reviving "the Hamiltonian ideal of constructive national legislation," while at the same time being, as Hamilton was not, a democrat. Roosevelt, with his sense of the national interest, his faith in a strong state, and his willingness to give power to exceptional men, had served "to emancipate American democracy from its Jeffersonian bondage." He had given the Republican party, which had slipped back into the ineffectiveness of the old Whig party, some sense of "its historic mission."

But Roosevelt was not yet the perfect reformer, Croly observed, for he was not yet the perfect nationalist. He continued, at times, to talk the language of Jeffersonianism. What was "the square deal" but an unhappy revival of the assumptions of equal rights, including the demagogic assumption that businessmen had been acting like dishonest sharpers? Fortunately, Roosevelt was building better than he knew or would admit. He was, in fact, a thoroughgoing nationalist whose actions pointed him toward a complete break with the Jeffersonian tradition.

Nevertheless, Croly concluded, the danger remained that, so long as Roosevelt refused to acknowledge this fact, the reform movement with which he was associated might go astray.

In his western tour in 1910, Roosevelt did not altogether come to terms with Croly's strictures. Yet he did take another step along the path he had been moving away from the old reform tradition which emphasized natural rights, egalitarianism, and the limited state. His 1910 speeches anticipated the Progressive Party program of 1912. That year, in contrast to Woodrow Wilson's "New Freedom," with its emphasis on a return to the maxims of a nineteenth-century society, Roosevelt would advocate a great augmentation of power of the federal government. In 1912, he would say more than he had in 1910 about permitting the trusts to develop, rather than breaking them up; readers of *The New Nationalism* are often astonished to find that there is only a single passage about the trusts, that it is not at all a book about trusts. In 1912, too, he would come out for welfare measures that he had not yet come to advocate in 1910. But all the main features of the Bull Moose program had been sketched in 1910.

The New Nationalism would be the most fruitful doctrine of the Progressive era, for it stated the underlying assumptions of much of what was later to be known as the Welfare State. Liberated from the fear of centralized authority, political leaders could, for the first time, use the powers of the federal government to make an industrial society more humane. Freed from the unrealistic assumption that every worker was a potential entrepreneur, the government began to take steps to recognize rights of workingmen which previously had been denied. No longer bound by the view that the state should be, at most, an umpire, government officials could embark on bold new programs of regional planning, slum clearance, and public power development.

Yet the New Nationalism too raised disturbing questions about the relation of progressive values to the omnicompetent state. Roosevelt minimized the danger in unrestrained exercise of power by the Executive, yet he himself had demonstrated on many occasions the perils of the lawless use of power by a president who confused his own obsessions with the "national interest." He saw little danger in the cartelization of American society, yet the concentration of decision-making in the hands of a few government and corporation leaders raised a decided threat to individual liberties, quite apart from the question of whether corporations so powerful would not soon control the state.

Even more doubtful was the conception of Roosevelt and Croly that man should find fulfillment in service to the state, the nation-state which Croly insisted had an individuality of its own. Although Croly saw an important role for voluntaristic organization, he based most of his hopes on the state. The Promise of American Life was to be fulfilled not by a maximum grant of freedom, or by the abundant satisfaction of wants, "but by a large measure of individual subordination and self-denial . . .

to the fulfillment of a national purpose." Instead of speaking simply for a collectivity of individuals, the New Nationalists' state, Croly explained, would act for "the nation of yesterday and tomorrow, organized for its national historical mission." Both leaders and people would subordinate their desires to "a morally authoritative Sovereign will."

Much as in Bismarck's Germany, Roosevelt and many of the progressives who followed him used as their touchstone the health of the state and its mystical sense of national mission. The same state which promised new social benefits could also embark on nationalistic wars and crush out dissent, also in the name of patriotic ideals. The New Nationalism, Croly explained, was to be "unscrupulously" nationalistic. In 1916, the Progressive Party, which helped give birth to the idea of a positive state dedicated to social welfare, would be destroyed in the name of a positive state dedicated to chauvinism and military preparedness. In the end, as many had always feared, Roosevelt's nationalism ran deeper than his progressivism.

In the summer of 1912, Woodrow Wilson was a candidate in search of a program. The direction of Wilson's thought was clear; the content was not. In the early months of the 1912 campaign, Wilson had placed his chief stress on the need for tariff reform, but he could not arouse much excitement over that tired old issue. He sensed that he might find the program he wanted in the popular uneasiness about monopoly, but he did not know quite how to go about it. He had, in years past, fired some salvos at the trusts, but he had been distressingly unclear about what he proposed to do about them. He had recommended disciplining not the corporations but individual businessmen, who would have to be ferreted out of the corridors of corporate anonymity, but no one thought very much of this proposal. In short, he had found little constructive to say, and he had not been able to identify himself in any dramatic way with the trust issue. This was the situation when on August 18, 1912, at Sea Girt, New Jersey, Wilson and the brilliant Boston attorney, Louis Brandeis, met for the first time. In a single afternoon, Brandeis persuaded Wilson to base his campaign on the trust question. Wilson, Brandeis urged, should mark out a course sharply different from Roosevelt's by proposing that the government regulate not monopoly but competition. Like a teacher working with a promising pupil, Brandeis schooled Wilson in the precise tools the government could use to restore competition.

Brandeis, who had won a national reputation as a foe of monopoly in his war with the New Haven Railroad, contended that the trusts were too large to be efficient. They had been put together by financial manipulation with the aid or acquiescence of benign governments. To win special privileges, they had corrupted government. Once they had massed their power, they had used it to control credit and markets, to ward off competition from smaller, more efficient businesses, and to enrich themselves with excessive profits based on overcapitalization. Brandeis wanted to use government to prosecute existing concentrations of power, to enforce the rules of competition in the future, and to extend credit facilities to new entrepreneurs.

If Brandeis supplied him with the special knowledge he needed, Wilson's success in turning the trust issue into a crusade to preserve fundamental liberties was wholly his own achievement. Woodrow Wilson, as August Heckscher has remarked, was an unusual kind of political leader who led "through the power of style and more particularly through style in oratory." From the very beginning, Wilson felt that every significant political achievement resulted from the leadership of an inspired statesman who had found the precise words to move men. He was often less interested in finding the solution to a problem than the right language. Throughout his life, Wilson relied on the power of words as a political weapon to advance his career and the causes with which he was identified.

As a young man, Wilson aimed not for the presidency but for the Senate, for he went to college at a time when Congress held the reins of power. He fancied himself a member of Parliament, and he fastened his attention not on the work of government, but on the great debates in the House of Commons. Part of his vexation with the clandestine committee system came from a conviction that it was orators who moved men to act, and an awareness that his own strength lay in oratorical prowess. As a Princeton senior, he entered into "a solemn covenant" with a classmate in which, as he later explained, it was agreed "that we would drill ourselves in all the arts of persuasion, but especially in oratory . . . that we might have facility in leading others into our ways of thinking and enlisting them in our purposes." His long years as a teacher and scholar were years of fretful waiting and preparation for his true vocation as a political leader. In 1909, a year before he was to win election to the governorship, Wilson cried: "I wish there were some great orator who could go about and make men drunk with this spirit of self-sacrifice . . . whose tongue might every day carry abroad the golden accents of that creative age in which we were born a nation."

In the 1912 campaign, Wilson transmuted the trust question into "a second struggle for emancipation." At stake were no longer pecuniary matters like markets and profits but the eternal truths by which men live. Wilson identified the plight of the man seeking enough capital to start a small business with the ageless struggle of men for liberty. "Are you not eager for the time when the genius and initiative of all the people shall be called into the service of business? when newcomers with new ideas, new entries with new enthusiasm, independent men, shall be welcomed? when your sons shall be able to look forward to becoming, not employees, but heads of some small, it may be, but hopeful, business, where their best energies shall be inspired by the knowledge that they are their own masters, with the paths of the world open before them?" Wilson asked. "Surely you must feel the inspiration of such a new dawn of liberty."

To express the meaning of opening up opportunities to the new entrepreneur, Wilson used the symbolism of Eastertide, of renewal and resurrection. Society was to be renewed by the "constant rise of the sap from the bottom, from the rank and file of the great body of the people." "A people shall be saved," Wilson wrote, "by waters welling up from its own sweet, perennial springs. Not from above; not by patronage of its aristocrats. The flower does not bear the root, but the root the flower. Everything that blooms in beauty in the air of heaven draws its fairness, its vigor, from its roots. . . . Up from the soil, up from the silent bosoms of the earth, rise the currents of life and energy. Up from the common soil, up from the quiet heart of the people, rise joyously today streams of hope and determination bound to renew the face of the earth in glory."

Wilson had an unusual capacity for making mundane issues seem like moral questions of transcendent importance. Some men regarded this gift as a blessing, others as an annoyance. He could make men see the spiritual possibilities of matters to which they had been blind before, but he could also make of political issues more than was actually there. Even the short ballot could be made to seem an evidence of Divine Providence. "His mind," a contemporary critic remarked, "is like a light which destroys the outlines of what it plays upon; there is much illumination, but you see very little." He gave to the trust question in 1912 a spirit of elevated thought and action men had rarely heard before, but he left both many of his contemporaries and two generations of historians bewildered about precisely what he did propose to do about the trusts.

It is sometimes said that the distinction between the New Nationalism and the New Freedom is that Roosevelt wanted to permit the trusts to grow and regulate them, while Wilson wanted to break them up. This would be a logical distinction, but it does not seem to be an accurate one. Much of Wilson's rhetoric makes little sense unless one supposes he was advocating the dissolution of the trusts, yet on more than one occasion he made clear that he did not favor dismemberment. In 1912, Wilson declared: "I am not one of those who think that competition can be established by law against the drift of a world-wide economic tendency." If his faith in competition drove him in the direction of dissecting the trusts, his organic conception of society restrained him. Deeply influenced by Burke and Bagehot, he viewed society as the product of slow growth. He would not "tear up ancient rootages" and he understood that "you cannot make a *tabula rasa* upon which to write a political program." Society, he observed in *The State,* was formed "of the common habit, an evolution of experience, an interlaced growth of tenacious relationships, a compact, living, organic whole, structural, not mechanical." In his first inaugural address, Wilson stated: "We shall deal with our economic system as it is and as it may be modified, not as it might be if we had a clean sheet of paper to write upon."

While, on occasion, Wilson adopted Brandeis' view that bigness was, in itself, a curse, more often he insisted that he did not oppose bigness as such, so long as this great size had been acquired fairly. "I am not afraid of anything that is normal," Wilson asserted, and if trusts were the product of natural growth, he had no quarrel with them. There was no little casuistry in Wilson's distinction between big business and the trusts, and, in fact, he did almost nothing, either as governor or as president, to disturb existing agglomerations. He aimed rather at halting the process of concentration before it went any further. While he was worried about the tendency toward monopoly in particular industries, he was most alarmed by the "community of interest" created by "the combination of the combinations," and he wanted to use the power of government to insure intercorporate competition. "It has been said that you cannot 'unscramble eggs,' and I am perfectly willing to admit it," Wilson declared in 1912, "but I can see in all cases before they are scrambled that they are not put in the same basket and entrusted to the same groups of persons."

Wilson believed that only in a society of free enterprise could men be free. In 1910, he observed that in the modern business world, men were no longer individuals but "fractions." Having lost their independence of choice in business, they had "lost also their individual choice within the field of morals." In a truly competitive society, on the other hand, each man's rewards would be determined by his character. A believer in progress who was at the same time deeply aware of the sinfulness of man, he distrusted concentrating power in the hands of corporations or of governments which would determine a man's lot in life for him. If each man were free to follow his own self-interest, aware of his need to answer to his Maker, the interests of society would be best advanced. Only in such a society could each man be a "distinct moral agent," responsible for his own destiny and living his life with an almost overpowering sense of the presence of God. Man, observed Wilson, was "not the creature of the drawing room or the stock exchange, but a lonely, awful soul confronted by the Source of all souls."

Nothing distressed Wilson more than the fear that the middle class, the class which originated new enterprises, was "being crushed between the upper and nether millstones." He hoped he would never see an America which consisted only "of masters and employees," where the opportunities for the man who would take risks had been snuffed out. His New Freedom envisioned the kind of society the bourgeois French revolutionaries of 1789 had sought to create by ending privilege and declaring careers open to talents. They would destroy feudal privilege, he the privilege of the monopolists. By using the power of government to restore competition, Wilson hoped he could arrest the change from the old middle class of the independent professional and businessman to the new middle class of the white collar worker and the salaried professional.

He wanted to help not the established businessman, but the new entrepreneur. The real division in the country, he said in 1908, was not between capital and labor, but rather between large, concentrated capital and more dispersed economic forces. "Every new policy proposed has as its immediate or ultimate object the restraint of the power of accumulated capital for the protection and benefit of those who cannot command its use," Wilson observed. By 1910 he had become the paladin of the small businessman. "The trouble today is that you bankers are too narrow-minded," he scolded a meeting of New York financiers, including J. P. Morgan, that year. "You take no interest in the small borrower and the small enterprise which affect the future of the country, but you give every attention to the big borrower and the rich enterprise which has already arrived."

It is a little puzzling that a man like Wilson, who retreated from his brief contact with the harsh world of business and whose ideal in life was more that of the scholar or the English gentleman than the hustler, should have placed at the center of his political thought the "man on the make." His sympathy seems to have derived less from actual experience with the American salesman or shopkeeper or manufacturer than from his admiration of leaders of the British mercantile class like Richard Cobden and John Bright. He believed that while the farmer and the worker were confined by the limits of a rural village or the factory walls, the merchant had a wide-ranging view that swept the seven seas. Trade, he thought, was "the great nurse of liberal ideas." "Zeal for rational principles of trade," he declared, "changed simple unambitious men of business into diligent politicians, transformed them into orators, exalted them into statesmen."

Modern liberals have distinguished between the "moral" and the "business" viewpoints of Wilson—insofar as he was for business, he was less "moral." Such a viewpoint would have made little sense to a seventeenth-century Puritan or a nineteenth-century British liberal, and it made little sense to Wilson, who felt himself a part of both traditions. He told the Chicago Commercial Club in 1902: "Every great man of business has got somewhere . . . a touch of the idealist in him . . . this feeling of the subtle linking of all men together." "Business underlies every part of our lives," Wilson declared in 1912, "the foundation of our lives, of our spiritual lives included, is economic."

The growth of the trusts, Wilson believed, was the ultimate perversion of Whiggery. Government, he felt, should represent all the people, but should grant special privileges to none. His distinction between big business, which was acceptable, and the trusts, which were not, rested on the distinction that business had grown "naturally" while the trusts had not. The trusts had been fostered by the grant of special privileges like tariff protection. As Franklin K. Lane, who was later to serve in Wilson's cabinet, explained in 1911: "If men have made these tremendous fortunes out of privileges granted by the whole people, we can correct this by a change in our laws. They do not object to men making any amount of money so long as the individual makes it, but if the Government makes it for him, that is another matter." If the government denied special privileges, Wilson thought, these "artificial" creations of the trusts, stripped of their unfair advantage, would not be able to stand up in competition with businesses that had grown naturally.

Wilson charged that government had been rigged against the small entrepreneur not only because it had granted special privileges to trusts but because both governments and political parties were controlled by machines. The objection to the machine was the same as the objection to the trust: it used government for private purposes. Wilson sought to free government from its tie with any one class, and to divorce government from its association either with trusts or with machine bosses. His main disagreement with the Bull Moose Party of 1912 arose from his conviction that Theodore Roosevelt, instead of destroying these evil cabals, aimed to institutionalize the alliance of politics and business under the aegis of the super-trusts.

He believed that politics must be purified. The government had been defiled by its association with privileged monopolists and he would wash it clean. Repeatedly Wilson returned to the imagery of light, air, and sun; government had been besmirched and had to be cleansed. By removing tariff privileges, he would "let the sun shine through the clouds again as once it shone." "We are going into this garden and give the little plants air and light in which to grow," Wilson explained. "We are going to pull up every root that has so spread itself as to draw the nutriment of the soil from other roots." The energies of free men would then be able to find expression. To purify politics, he would break the nexus of government and special interests and arouse the citizenry to a moral awakening.

Wilson contended that the most important decisions in the country were being made in secret behind locked doors. Trustees in the board room made economic policy; bosses in caucuses shaped political policies. The people had no say at all. "It is a question of access to our own government," Wilson observed. "There are very few of us who have had any real access to the government." "Woodrow Wilson's new freedom," as Henry Wallace later commented, "was the right to discuss in public those governmental decisions which had so long been made by government on behalf of business, by devious methods, with big corporations working through our political bosses." Wilson believed that if actions were carried out in full view of the people, evil doings would quickly be scotched, for a moral people would not countenance them. He wanted, in short, open covenants openly arrived at.

Governor Wilson insisted that the government could claim that areas of life which were thought to be private lay in fact in the public domain. He was fascinated by the example of the city of Glasgow which treated the hallways and entries of the tenements as public streets and required that they be well lighted. Once again, he turned to the imagery of air, sun, and light. "You have got to cure diseased politics as we nowadays cure tuberculosis, by making all the people who suffer from it live out of doors," he explained. They would "always remain in the open, where they will be accessible to fresh, nourishing, and revivifying influences." "And so the people of the United States have made up their minds to do a healthy thing for both politics and big business," Wilson asserted. "Permit me to mix a few metaphors: They are going to open doors; they are going to let up blinds; they are going to drag sick things into the open air and into the light of the sun. They are going to organize a great hunt, and smoke certain animals out of their burrows."

The core of Wilson's thought was a protest against paternalism, and he disliked the paternalism of the welfare state almost as much as he objected to the egregiousness of the trusts. To be sure, he had come by 1912 to favor a number of welfare measures, although he did not go nearly so far as Roosevelt in this direction; yet his emphasis differed quite sharply from that of the statist progressives. He no more wished to grant special privileges to workers or farmers than to business corporations. He saw the state not as an agency to help direct society, but rather as an instrument to remove the shackles preventing men from having the same opportunity to compete. As Walter Lippmann put it: Wilson's political beliefs were "a fusion of Jeffersonian democracy with a kind of British Cobdenism. This meant in practical life a conviction that the world needs not so much to be administered as to be released from control."

Curiously, for a man who is taken as the exemplar of the intellectual in government, Wilson distrusted the new class of experts, and viewed with alarm the growth of commissions, which would provide the intellectuals with their home in government. He appeared to have for experts the tolerant disdain with which a university president views the claims to omniscience of his faculty. "I have lived with experts all my life," he observed, "and I know that experts . . . don't even perceive what is under their nose." His chief adviser, Brandeis, had the same suspicion of the planners, but he came to see more quickly than Wilson the need for expertise, and it was, of course, Brandeis who, by his brief in *Muller v. Oregon,* had given the intellectual new stature and a new role in securing progressive legislation. Under Brandeis's tutelage, Wilson modified some of his views. Yet even at the end of the campaign, he still remained suspicious of government commissions and arrogant intellectuals.

Nevertheless, no one who understood Wilson could have supposed that he wished to preside over an impotent government. Unlike a man such as Grover Cleveland, whose views he seemed to share, Wilson had the governing urge. However conservative his doctrines may have been at any given time, Wilson had the zeal of a change-maker who wanted to remake the world. Only one question faced a competent leader, Wilson declared in 1890: "There are men to be moved: how shall he move them? . . . It is the power which dictates, dominates; the materials yield. Men are as clay in the hands of the consummate leader." At times, Wilson sounded like a conservative politician who, once he achieved office, would be a *roi faineant*. In fact, he thought of himself—good Presbyterian that he was—as nothing less than an instrument of the Lord charged with altering the conditions of life for his fellow men.

When Wilson entered the White House, he quickly demonstrated that he had the power to command, and it was not long before he recognized that the ideology of Cobdenism had little relevance to America in the second decade of the twentieth century. Before he had ended his first term of office, he had jettisoned almost every one of the New Freedom doctrines. Even in his first months as president, when he adhered with reasonable faith to the philosophy of the New Freedom, he felt compelled to concede a good deal to the advocates of a positive state. By the end of 1916, he had gone virtually all the way. He had approved welfare legislation like the Child Labor Law and the La Follette Seamen's Act; he had fought for special interest measures like the Adamson Act and the Rural Credits Act; and he had surrendered to business demands for a tariff commission, protection against "dumping," and government sanction of export cartels. With scarcely a backward glance at the crusade for a New Freedom, he claimed in 1916 to have enacted the program of the Bull Moose Party as well as his own.

By 1916, Wilson's campaign of four years before already seemed curiously antiquated. When he had run for president for the first time, he had spoken to a nation that stood at a great divide, looking longingly at the nineteenth-century world it was leaving, peering, half-hopefully, half-anxiously, at the twentieth-century world it was about to enter. Wilson's campaign of 1912 caught perfectly the mood of America that year, a nation captivated by the new and yearning for the old. In the same sentence, he could say that he wanted "to express the *new* spirit of our politics and *restore* our politics to their full spiritual vigor again." He identified himself with progress, spoke of "the presence of a new organization of society," and in a year when America was excited by the New Theater and the New Poetry, called his political program the New Freedom. Yet at the same time he exploited the resentment at the impersonal nature of the modern world and the disappearance of the village. He talked of "restoration" and "return"; celebrated the "America of the fathers"; and resorted repeatedly to images of a pristine rural life: "voting populations of the countryside, men tramping over the mountains, men going to the general store up in the village, men moving in little talking groups to the corner grocery to cast their ballots." Never did he try to evoke a similar urban idyll. "You know what the vitality of America consists of," Wilson declared. "Its vitality does not lie in New York, nor in Chicago; it will not be sapped by anything that happens in St. Louis." Precisely at the point in time when the city was beginning to overtake the rural town, Wilson warned that "if America discourages the locality, the community, the self-contained town, she will kill the nation."

By 1916, America had already taken several long strides from the village world Wilson had held up as an ideal. Today, we have travelled so far from that world that much of *The New Freedom* no longer seems usable. "If America is not to have free enterprise," Wilson told a crowd in Denver in October 1912, "then she can have freedom of no sort whatever." A statement of this sort—one which pays such homage to "free enterprise"—has a curious ring for the modern liberal, and it is here that much of the difficulty of the usability of Wilson's words for the liberal of the 1960's lies. Wilson's New Freedom was a progressive response, but it was a special brand of progressivism. It was deeply rooted in nineteenth-century British liberalism. Wilson's Southern free trade heritage, his studies at Princeton, his reading of Godkin's *Nation,* the influence of Cobden and Bright and above all of his idol, Gladstone, had all made of him a disciple of the classical British economists. Wilson had that distrust of centralized power of a states rights Democrat whose family had lived in Augusta when Sherman was marching through Georgia.

Wilson conceived of every man as a potential businessman. It almost seemed as though he could not imagine a man's being free if he were an employee. If unborn children "open their eyes in a country where they must be employees or nothing," Wilson cried, "then they will see an America such as the founders of this Republic would have wept to think of." Apparently he never grasped the fact that America had become a land where most people were destined to be employees, or what the consequences of this development were. He had almost nothing to say to this employee class except to promise them a way out of their bondage, a way which, in the very nature of things, was open to very few of them.

In later years, many of the champions of the New Freedom opposed vigorously the advocates of an omnicompetent welfare state. In the 1920's, good New Freedom Democrats adjusted easily to the business ethos; after all, Wilson's "man on the make" was the prototype of the booster at the Rotary luncheon, and in the 1930's, many of the Wilsonian Democrats—men like McReynolds, Glass, and Baker—became bitter foes of the New Deal. For a time, Brandeis and his followers did leave their imprint on the New Deal, and in the summer of 1935, the ideological warfare revived memories of 1912. Brandeis wrote a friend: "F.D. is making a gallant fight and seems to appreciate fully the evils of bigness. He should have more support than his party is giving him; and the social worker-progressive crowd seems as blind as in 1912." Yet the animus of this faction of New Dealers was really quite different from that of Wilson in 1912. They were less concerned with advancing the interests of the "man on the make" than in arguing that business was the enemy of reform, and hence that Roosevelt, rather than seeking a coalition with business as he had in the NRA, should be trying to dynamite the great concentrations of power.

In only one important respect does *The New Freedom* speak directly to the liberal of today. In warning of the perils of "corporate philanthropy," Wilson anticipated the modern-day concern with the Organization Man. Wilson feared that the corporation might not only do economic mischief, but, more important, that it would swallow up the individual. The vast impersonality of modern business, Wilson warned, was destroying the independence of men. The country doctor was devoured by the city hospital, the village attorney by the mammoth law firm, the small businessman by the corporation. The menace came not simply from the malevolent corporation, but, perhaps even more, from the well-intentioned corporation which, through its profit-sharing and bonus plans, subtly destroyed men's wills by offering them security and contentment. In his alarm at the permeation of the values of the large organization through all of American culture, he expressed fears which a half-century later would be even more keenly felt.

The First World War wrought profound changes in the world. It caused a rearrangement of the map of Europe—new states were created, some old ones made smaller, others enlarged. It altered the balance—old states were weakened and relegated to second-rate status, and only one, the United States, emerged from the war with strength enhanced. Indeed, an irony of modern history is the undisputed primacy of America's power in the post-war world and her refusal to accept the responsibilities inherent in that position.

8

THE FIRST WORLD WAR

The outbreak of war in 1914 surprised most Americans. They had not expected a world war to follow the assassination of an Austrian archduke in an obscure corner of Europe. As a matter of fact, they had not expected war at all, and for two reasons. One was ignorance of the affairs in Europe. The majority of Americans had not paid much attention to foreign affairs in the period from 1900 to 1914. Their interest focused on domestic matters, such as the regulation of railroads and trusts, the tariff, social and political reform, immigration, and the exposures of the Muckrakers. They knew and understood little of the balance of power, the struggle for colonies and markets and raw materials, the race for supremacy on the seas, and other such elements of power politics. Hence, the developments following the assassination, which culminated in war, caught people unprepared.

The second reason for not expecting war was an idealistic one. Many Americans felt that war in the future was inconceivable. Man, they thought, was too rational and civilized to fight. He had learned from experience that wars never solve problems, but rather create new ones; that they are too expensive and destructive. Furthermore, the ensuing dislocation and disarrangement of international economy and channels of trade made war unthinkable. Nations were now capable of settling their differences by arbitration and by other peaceful means, Americans thought, just as individuals settled theirs by recourse to legal machinery rather than by vendettas. Charles W. Eliot observed a new moral climate, which he saw as putting an end to periods of strife, and Woodrow Wilson in 1913 spoke of a greater cordiality among nations, presaging an era of settled peace. A peace movement flourished in the United States as never before. It was more respectable, more affluent, supported by more distinguished people, engaging in more numerous activities, and teaching wider audiences than at any other time in the nation's history. The few voices raised in warning against such optimism by Henry and Brooks Adams, Lewis Einstein, and others went largely unheeded.

When finally the realization dawned upon the American people that a war of grand proportions was in progress, the vast majority wished to steer clear of the whole affair. Americans hailed as wise President Wilson's official proclamation of neutrality. To be sure, they could not help sympathizing with one or the other of the two sets of belligerents. The polyglot American nation had too many ties with Europe. But even those who felt most fervently attached to the country of their ancestry did not want to fight, nor did many of those who believed that America's destiny was interwoven with the European war. Why, then, did America enter the war two years and eight months after its beginning, and on the Allied side?

One thing appears certain: the United States would not have fought against the Allies alongside Germany. Americans resented the British treatment of American neutral commerce and the trampling of American rights on the high seas, but war against England and France was unthinkable. Too many Americans believed in the justice of the Allied cause; too many were certain that the Allies were defending civilization against German barbarism and Prussian militarism; too many had been reared on Shakespeare, Browning, Keats, Dickens, and the other great British writers; too many had been taught that American liberties sprang from the Magna Carta and the Glorious Revolution. Enforcing these ties of sentiment were economic attachments. From 1914 to 1917, most of America's exports and most of the money loaned had gone to Britain and France. Further, the experiences of the decade and a half before the war had led Americans to believe, rightly or wrongly, that Germany coveted possessions and influence in the Western Hemisphere, thereby endangering American hegemony in the area, while Britain, on the other hand, had seemed willing to see the United States assume mastery in its own backyard. If there was to be an enemy, it would have to be Germany.

The submarine was primarily responsible, however, for Germany's becoming the enemy. For two and a half years before America entered the war, German sinkings of Allied and neutral vessels without warning had outraged the American President and the public. Compared with this conduct, British violations seemed mild to Wilson. In his view, the British may have been thieves, but the Germans were murderers of innocent women and children and other noncombatants. After the British passenger liner *Lusitania* went down in May 1915, Wilson warned Berlin that the Kaiser's government would be held strictly accountable for the action of submarine commanders and the loss of ships and lives. When the French cross-channel steamer *Sussex* was torpedoed in March 1916, the President insisted that Germany discontinue her practices. The Germans did then pledge that no ships would be sunk without warning and without providing for the safety of the passengers. But the announcement by the German Imperial government on January 31, 1917, of unrestricted submarine warfare, and the subsequent destruction of American ships with loss of lives, led President Wilson to ask Congress for a declaration of war on April 2.

The President did not seek war with Germany, nor did the American people, in the main, wish to fight. During the period of neutrality, Wilson gave the Germans ample opportunity to alter their policy. Even in February, after the rupture in relations, he hoped still to remain at peace in a state of armed neutrality. But, finally, he could not tolerate any longer "the challenge . . . to all mankind." Germany's acts had to be halted even at the expense of war. The President alone made the decision to go to war, but he had behind him the support of the people, who had become, during neutrality, more and more aroused by the submarine.

Some people at the time, and some historians since, have accused the President of being the dupe and tool of bankers and financiers who wanted to go to war to aid the Allies when their military effort seemed to be sinking. They further have accused the President of showing partiality to the Allies from the outset. This partiality, they claimed, drove the Germans to use the submarine as the only weapon calculated to cut the supply line between the United States and the enemy. Had he really been neutral, he would have embargoed exports to both sets of belligerents so that neither would have received an advantage. He would also have prevented American merchant ships from sailing into the war zones and American passengers from traveling on belligerent merchant vessels, thus making impossible an incident with Germany and thereby providing no opportunity for war.

The President's request for a declaration of war was given overwhelming but not unanimous support in Congress. Fifty congressmen and six senators voted against war. The congressional attitude reflected the public sentiment. The vast majority of the American people supported the war effort, but there were many who throughout the eighteen months of the conflict questioned the wisdom of intervention and made every effort to hinder the successful prosecution of the war. Those in opposition represented diverse groups. Primarily, they were Americans of German extraction, but they were also Socialists, pacifists, and members of radical labor unions and other minority and fringe organizations. To suppress them, the government had a series of statutes enacted (Espionage Act, Trading with the Enemy Act, Sedition Act), which by their interpretations seriously curtailed the freedom of speech and violated many constitutional guarantees. As Frederic L. Paxson has said, "Moderation and reason had a hard time with democracy at war." It was a paradox, indeed, that "to make the world safe for democracy," democracy had to be in some measure sacrificed.

The climax of the period of the First World War was the negotiation of the treaty of peace and the refusal by the Senate of the United States on March 19, 1920, to approve it. The most significant consequence of the Senate's act was not the failure to bring the war with Germany officially and legally to an end, but rather the failure of the United States to join the League of Nations. Indeed, the League of Nations Covenant, which was imbedded in the treaty, was the basis for the treaty's rejection. So, in a sense, the United States reversed its position of 1917. Having entered the war to help determine the political balance in the Old World, it now served notice that it would not take part in maintaining that balance in the postwar period.

The readings in this chapter illustrate three major aspects of the war—the causes for intervention and Wilson's actions in that regard, the treatment of opponents of the war, and the defeat of the treaty in the Senate.

Arthur S. Link

Wilson the

Diplomatist

The controversy surrounding American intervention in the First World War and Wilson's role in that intervention has evoked a considerable literature, which is surveyed in "The Problem of American Intervention, 1917: An Historical Retrospect" by Richard W. Leopold (World Politics, II [April 1950], 405–425). Of all the historians who have written on the subject, Arthur S. Link and Edwin M. Borchard have presented the two opposing points of view most clearly and convincingly. Link seeks to demonstrate that the President tried honestly and honorably to steer a neutral course and sought to keep America out of the war. He shows that German submarine warfare, however, caused Wilson finally to enter the war. Continued sinkings of American vessels by German submarines hardened the President's position. Link has written widely on Wilson. He has published three volumes of a multi-volumed biography of the President and is the editor of his letters and papers. [Arthur S. Link, Wilson the Diplomatist (Baltimore: The Johns Hopkins Press, 1957). Reprinted by permission.]

All authorities, whether friendly or hostile to Wilson, would agree that the acid tests of his neutrality were the policies that he worked out and applied vis-à-vis the British from 1914 to 1917. He has been most condemned by that group of historians highly censorious of his policies, generally known as revisionists, on this score—for becoming the captive of pro-Allied influences within his administration, for condoning such sweeping British control of neutral commerce that the Germans were forced to resort to drastic countermeasures, for permitting American prosperity to become dependent upon loans and exports to the Allies, in short, for permitting a situation to develop that made it inevitable that the United States would go to war if the success of Allied arms was ever seriously threatened.

Like most fallacious arguments, this one contains a certain element of plausibility. Wilson did condone a far-reaching British maritime system. American neutrality did work greatly to the benefit of the Allies. The error arises in saying that these things occurred because Wilson and his advisers necessarily wanted them to occur.

Perhaps the best way to gain a clear understanding of why Anglo-American relations developed as they did from 1914 to 1917 is to see how the policies that decisively shaped those relations emerged in several stages in response to certain pressures, events, and forces. The first stage, lasting from August, 1914, to about August, 1915, was in many ways the most critical, because the basic American response to the war and to the British maritime system was formulated then. That response was governed in the first instance by two domestic realities: the overwhelming, virtually unanimous, American desire to be neutral, and the pressures in the United States for a large measure of free trade with Britain's enemies.

In view of the prevailing American sentiment at the outbreak of the war, a policy of strict official neutrality was the only possible course for the United States government. This fact prompted the President's official proclamations of neutrality, supplemented by his appeal to the American people for impartiality in thought; the subsequent working out by the State Department of the elaborate technical rules to preserve American neutrality; and the establishment of a Joint State and Navy Neutrality Board to advise the various departments upon the correct interpretation of international law.

One cannot read the records revealing how these policies were formulated without being convinced that their authors were high-minded in their determination to be fair to both sides. Indeed, Wilson and the man who chiefly influenced him in the formulation of the rules of neutrality, Secretary of State Bryan, were so intent upon being fair to the Germans that they adopted policies during the first months of the war that were highly disadvantageous to the British, if not unneutral. One was to prevent the sale of submarine parts, and hence parts for any naval craft, by a private American firm to the British government, on the ground that such a sale would be "contrary to . . . strict neutrality." Wilson persisted in supporting Bryan in this matter, in spite of advice from Counselor Lansing and the Joint Neutrality Board to the effect that their position was contrary to international law.

Infinitely more damaging to the Allies was the administration's second effort to lean over backward in being "strictly" neutral—the ban of loans by American bankers to the belligerent governments that the President permitted Bryan to impose in August, 1914. From a technical viewpoint, the ban was not unneutral, but it was highly prejudicial to the Allies because its effect was potentially to deny them their otherwise legal right to purchase supplies in the American market. These two incidents are not to be understood as revealing any anti-British bias on the part of Wilson and Bryan, although British officials at the time were convinced that they did. I mention them only to show what an important role the administration's desire to be impartial played in the formation of policies vis-à-vis the British during the early period of American neutrality.

The other pressure shaping American policies at this time was the force of combined demands at home for the virtually free transit of American ships and goods to the European neutrals and the belligerent Central Powers. So powerful were these demands, especially from cotton growers and exporters and their spokesmen in Congress, that Wilson personally sponsored two measures highly disadvantageous to the British and un-neutral in fact as well as in spirit. One was a change in the ship registry law, put into effect by an act approved August 18, 1914, which made it easy for German or other foreign shipping firms to take out American registry for their vessels. The other was a plan to establish a federal corporation to purchase German ships in American ports and to use them to carry supplies to the belligerents, particularly to Germany. Wilson applied heavy pressure to obtain congressional approval of this, the so-called ship-purchase bill, during the short term from December, 1914, to March, 1915; he failed only because of a stout senatorial filibuster.

In negotiations with the British government during the early months of the war, Wilson fought hard in response to domestic pressures to keep the channels of international commerce open to American ships and goods. He did not go as far in defense of neutral rights as some of his predecessors, but he did suggest a code so sweeping that an enforcement of it would have meant almost total destruction of the British system of maritime controls. Specifically, the President first proposed on August 6, 1914, that the belligerents adopt the rules of naval warfare laid down in the Declaration of London of 1909, a convention never ratified by Great Britain or the United States, which permitted the free transit of all goods except those obviously contraband. When the British rejected this sug-gestion, the President came back on October 16, proposing a compromise that would have still seriously impaired the effectiveness of British sea power. When this effort also failed, Wilson then announced that his government would assert and defend all its rights under international law and treaties.

I have described these policies and proposals because they so clearly reveal Wilson's neutral intentions and what he would have done in matters of trade had he been able to make the rules himself. But he obviously could not follow his personal preferences alone or respond only to domestic pressures. In seeking to assert and defend American neutral rights he ran head-on into a reality as important as the reality of the pressures at home. It was the British determination to use sea power to prevent American ships and goods from going to the sustenance of the German economy and military forces.

British assumption of a nearly absolute control of the seas washing western Europe began with relatively mild measures in August, 1914, and culminated in the suppression of virtually all commerce to the Central Powers in March, 1915. For the British, this was not a question of adher-ing to the laws of blockade or of violating them, or of doing things merely to be nice to American friends. It was a question of achieving their supreme objective, to deprive their enemies of vital raw materials and goods, without risking the alienation of the United States. The controlling fact for the British was the necessity of preserving American friendship, in order to assure the uninterrupted rhythm of the North Atlantic trade. As the British Foreign Secretary at the time frankly put it:

Blockade of Germany was essential to the victory of the Allies, but the ill-will of the United States meant their certain defeat. . . . It was better therefore to carry on the war without blockade, if need be, than to incur a break with the United States about contraband and thereby deprive the Allies of the resources necessary to carry on the war at all or with any chance of success. The object of diplomacy, therefore, was to secure the maximum of blockade that could be enforced without a rupture with the United States.

The crucial question all along, therefore, was whether the United States, the only neutral power strong enough successfully to challenge the British measures, would acquiesce or resist to the point of threatening or using force. The American response during the formative period of neutrality was, in brief, to accept the British system and to limit action against it to a vigorous assertion of American legal rights for future adjudication. All this is too well known to require any further exposition. What is not so well understood are the reasons why Wilson and his advisers acquiesced in a solution that denied the objectives that they and a large segment of the American public demanded. These reasons may be briefly summarized, as follows:

First, the British maritime system, in spite of American allegations to the contrary, enjoyed the advantage of being legitimate and usually legal, or nearly so, by traditional criteria. It was legitimate rather than fraudulent, and legal rather than capricious or terroristic, in its major aspects because the British did in fact hold undisputed sea supremacy and were therefore able to execute their controls in an orderly fashion. In asserting their own rights, the Americans could not well deny the advantages that accrued to the British by virtue of their sea power. The British, for example, had an undoubted right to establish a blockade of the Central Powers, and the American attempt to persuade the London government to use techniques effective only in the days of the sailing ship did not have much cogency in the twentieth century.

Second, much of the success of the British in establishing their control depended upon the way in which they went about it. Had they instituted their total blockade at the outset of the war, the American reaction would undoubtedly have been violent. Instead, the British applied their controls gradually, with a careful eye upon American opinion, using the opportunities provided by recurrent crises in German-American relations to institute their severest measures.

Third, the British were careful never to offend so many American interests at one time that retaliation would have been inevitable, or any single interest powerful enough by itself to compel retaliation. There was the case of cotton, which the officials in London were determined to prevent from going to Germany because it was an ingredient of gunpowder. Not until a year after the war began did they put cotton on the list of absolute contraband; even then they went to the extraordinary length of underwriting the entire American cotton market in order to avert an irresistible southern pressure in Congress for retaliation. In addition, although they were ruthless in enforcing their blockade, the British took careful pains to avoid any serious injury to American property interests. They confiscated only the most obvious contraband; in all doubtful cases they paid full value for cargoes or ships seized. Their objective was to control, not to destroy, American commerce.

Fourth, there was great significance in the language and symbolism that the British Foreign Office used in defending the measures of the Admiralty and Ministry of Blockade. By justifying their maritime system in terms of international law and the right of retaliation, and (at least before the summer of 1916) by making an honest effort to meet American objections half way when possible, the British made it almost inevitable that the Washington authorities would have to reply in the same language, thus giving a purely *legal* character to the issues involved and for the most part avoiding raising the issues of sovereignty and inherent national rights. The significance of this achievement can be seen in the conviction of Wilson and the majority of Americans that the Anglo-American disputes did involve only property rights, which should be vindicated only by an appeal to much-controverted international law. Moreover, by appealing to the American government and people in the name of friendship and by always professing their devotion to the cause of humanity, the British succeeded in evoking strong feelings of sympathy and understanding on the other side of the water.

Finally, the British were able partially to justify their own blockade measures as legitimate adaptations to a changing technology by pointing to precedents established by the Washington government itself during the American Civil War. To be sure, the British drew some incorrect analogies (as Lansing pointed out) between American and British practice; even so, their main contention—that the American government had also stretched the rules of blockade to allow for technological changes—was essentially correct.

Wilson's refusal to challenge the British maritime system, in short, to break the British blockade, was almost inevitable in view of the facts we have just reviewed, *if the President's objective was simply to maintain as best he could the neutral position of the United States.* An absolute neutrality was in any event impossible because of the total character of the war and America's importance in the world economy. It often happened that any action by the United States inevitably conferred a benefit on one side and thereby injured the other, at least indirectly. In these circumstances, neutrality often consisted of doing the things that would give the least unwarranted or undeserved advantages.

By this standard, it would have been more unneutral than neutral for Wilson to have broken the British maritime system by enforcing highly doubtful technical rights under international law. Judged by practical standards rather than by the often conflicting criteria of neutrality, Wilson's acceptance of the British system seems realistic and wise—indeed, the only choice that he could have made in the circumstances. This is true because the results of destroying the British blockade would have been the wrecking of American friendship with the two great European democracies and the probable victory of the Central Powers, without a single compensating gain for the interests and security of the United States. Only the sure achievement of some great political objective like a secure peace settlement, certainly not the winning of a commercial advantage or the defense of doubtful neutral rights, would have justified Wilson in undertaking a determined challenge to British sea power.

The second stage in Anglo-American relations, lasting from the summer of 1915 to the late spring of 1916, saw the development of the natural economic consequence of the American adjustment to tightening British control of the seas. That consequence was the burgeoning of an enormous war trade between the United States and the Allies. The United States became the storehouse and armory of the Allies neither because there was any conspiracy on the part of certain pro-Allied leaders in Washington to make American prosperity dependent upon an Allied victory, nor because American businessmen and bankers were willing to incur the risks of war in order to increase their profits. The United States became the storehouse of the Allies for the simple reason that Great Britain and not Germany controlled the seas.

The war trade itself was entirely neutral. Indeed, any action by the United States government to impede it, unless undertaken for overriding political motives, would have been grossly prejudicial and unneutral. If it had been permitted to develop in a normal way, this commerce would have raised no important problems in the relations of the United States with the Allies. A problem of the first magnitude did arise, however, because the President, in the summer of 1914, had permitted Secretary Bryan to enforce his own private moral views by imposing a ban on loans by American bankers to the belligerents.

There was no difficulty so long as the British and French governments could find gold and dollars to settle their adverse trade balances. By the summer of 1915, however, Allied gold and dollar resources were near the point of exhaustion; and American insistence upon a continuation of cash payments could result only in gravely damaging the Allied economies and ending the North Atlantic trade altogether. Credit could be found only in the United States, but credit meant floating loans, and loans to the belligerents were as much a political as an economic question because of the existence of Bryan's ban.

It is well known that the State Department under Bryan's direction substantially relaxed its credit embargo during the spring of 1915 and that Wilson and Bryan's successor, Lansing, lifted the ban altogether a

few months later, at a time when the credit needs of the Allied governments were demonstrably acute. Even though the full facts bearing upon
this matter have been available to scholars for more than twenty years,
the reasons for the administration's reversal are still not properly understood.

Bryan's ban could not survive the development of the war trade on a
large scale because, in the first place, it (like the Embargo of 1808) was
potentially nearly as disastrous to the United States as to the Allies.
American material well-being was in large measure dependent upon foreign trade, and particularly upon trade with the Allied world. Such trade
was possible during wartime only if American businessmen were willing
to do for the Allies what they always did for solvent customers in temporary straits, namely, sell them goods on credit.

The most important reason that Bryan's embargo could not survive,
however, was that it was an essentially unneutral policy that impeded the
growth of the chief economic consequence of American neutrality, the
legitimate war trade. The credit embargo and the war trade could not
both survive. The former gave way because Wilson finally realized that it
would be as unneutral to interfere with the extension of credit as it
would be to stop the flow of goods. Bryan's ban was in a sense, therefore,
a casualty chiefly of American neutrality.

The historian can talk himself blue in the face without really convincing his listeners that these simple facts are true. He can point out that
Britain's existence depended upon her ability to use sea power to keep
the channels of trade and credit open, just as Germany's existence depended upon the use of superior land power. He can demonstrate that
the sale of goods and the extension of credit to belligerents by private
parties were neutral in theory, tradition, and practice. He can show that
the effect of unwarranted interference with such intercourse would have
been seriously to penalize sea power to the advantage of land power. But
a historian arguing this way makes little impression upon an American
audience, because the issue is still too supercharged with emotionalism
and is still resolved within a framework of economic determinism, of
hostility to the business and financial classes, and of moralistic pacifism. . . .

So long as the British controlled the seas and the Germans commanded
the strategic territories and resources of Europe, the American task of
neutrality was the relatively easy one of accepting a *de facto* situation
and of pursuing the most impartial policies possible within this framework of power. Thus Wilson permitted the German invasion of Belgium
to pass without protest, even though some Americans contended that he
was morally obliged to denounce such a gross violation of international
law; thus he accepted the British maritime system. In this situation of
actual stalemate, there was little likelihood of an Anglo-American rupture and no possibility of a German-American conflict, because there

were no points of friction between the two governments. But the German decision to attempt to break the stalemate by using an untried weapon, the submarine, created a situation of great peril for the United States because it raised the issue of fundamental national rights and made it exceedingly difficult for the President to continue to steer a neutral course. Before we see how he struggled to find some adjustment to this new situation, let us consider for a moment some of the underlying factors that helped to govern German submarine policy and Wilson's response.

First, German decisions regarding the use of the submarine were determined almost exclusively by internal and objective considerations—the number of submarines on hand and their calculated effectiveness, the military situation in Europe and how it might be affected by American intervention, and the like—and in no essential way by American policies vis-à-vis the British, or by the rules of international law for cruiser warfare. Many historians have assumed that stern American resistance to the British maritime system, resulting in opening the channels of trade in noncontraband materials to the Central Powers, would have rendered the so-called submarine blockade unnecessary. This conclusion assumes that the Germans used the submarine only to force the British to abandon their own blockade. Actually, the chief and in the final showdown the only reason the Germans used the submarine was to cut Britain off from her indispensable sources of supply and thereby to win the war. To put the proposition in its strongest form, the Germans would have used the submarine to knock England out of the war when they had enough U-boats to accomplish this goal, even if the British had long since given up their maritime system altogether. That is to say, calculations of sheer military advantage or disadvantage and not American or even British maritime policies dictated the way in which the Germans would prosecute their underseas campaign.

Second, the submarine was in 1915 a new weapon of naval warfare. This was an important fact, for it meant that there was no special international law to govern its use when the rights of neutrals were involved. The only laws that could be applied were the rules of cruiser warfare, which required attacking warships to warn merchant ships before sinking them and to make provision for the safety of passengers and crew. The trouble was that the submarine was not a cruiser, but a frail craft that had to rely upon deception and quick striking power for safety and effectiveness. If its use had been an issue only between the belligerents, then international law would not have been much involved. But international law was directly involved, because its provisions defined not only the rights of neutrals, but their obligations to the belligerent powers as well. Having chosen a course of neutrality under international law, Wilson had to work within accepted rules in formulating his response to the submarine challenge insofar as American rights were concerned. The Allies, understandably, would not consent to modifications to permit enemy submarines to operate at their peak deadly efficiency; their refusal made it difficult for Wilson to insist upon changing the rules without seeming to be unneutral in spirit and without in fact conferring enormous advantages upon the Germans.

Third, all questions of international law aside, a great power like the United States could not view the submarine blockade as a legitimate weapon, one that should be considered and perhaps accepted on grounds of expediency or necessity. This was true because at the time of its inauguration in February, 1915, the submarine blockade was actually a sham, since the Germans were then able to keep at most only seven U-boats at one time in all the waters surrounding the British Isles. The Germans, in fact, inaugurated the "blockade" with four submarines in service in the area. A year later, at the time of the *Sussex* crisis, the German Admiralty could send only eleven or twelve submarines into western waters at one time. Knowledge of these facts decisively influenced the way in which Wilson and his advisers viewed the so-called blockade and formulated policies regarding it, for it was one of the oldest and most generally recognized rules of international law that a blockade must be effective in order to be legal.

Fourth, unlike the Anglo-American disputes over trading rights, which involved only property interests, the German submarine campaign as it was often prosecuted raised an issue which no great power should ever evade or arbitrate—the safety and welfare of its people in pursuits and areas where they have a right to be. It is almost inconceivable that Wilson and the American people could have thought of going to war with the British over issues of search and seizure or of blockade. It is also inconceivable that they would not have been willing to think in terms of war with a government that permitted, indeed, instructed, its naval commanders to slaughter Americans indiscriminately upon the high seas.

It would, however, be a mistake of almost fatal magnitude to conclude, as so many writers have done, that Wilson's response to the submarine challenge was a simple and automatic reaction governed entirely by these factors. Although they played an important role, Wilson actually formed and executed, not a single consistent submarine policy, but a series of policies in response to changing issues and circumstances and in response to his own larger diplomatic objectives.

His first policy was formed in answer to the original German proclamation of submarine warfare. Avoiding the more difficult issue raised, the one involving the right of Americans to travel in safety on belligerent ships, Wilson replied by simply but strongly affirming the right of American vessels to use the seas subject to limitations permitted by international law, and by warning that the United States would hold Germany to a "strict accountability" (Counselor Lansing's words) for lives and property lost as a consequence of illegal submarine attacks against *American neutral* shipping. It was the only position that the President could have taken without abandoning the pretense of neutrality and national dignity, and the Germans soon retreated and gave such sweeping guarantees regarding American ships that this issue was never again a point of conflict between the two governments before 1917.

There still remained the necessity of devising a policy to deal with the more controversial issue of the right of American citizens to travel and work on *belligerent* merchant ships under conditions of safety specified by international law. When a German submarine sank the British liner *Falaba* without warning in March, 1915, killing an American citizen, Wilson's advisers in the State Department squared off in a momentous debate over the formulation of a proper response. One group, headed by Secretary Bryan, argued that American interests were not sufficiently involved to warrant a stern protest against submarine attacks on Allied ships, even when Americans were traveling on them, and that the spirit of neutrality demanded that the United States condone German violations of international law as it had done with British violations. The other group, headed by Counselor Lansing, replied that the attack on the *Falaba* had been such a flagrant infraction of international law that the United States must protest uncompromisingly in order to defend its neutrality and honor.

The records reveal that Wilson would have preferred to avoid any involvement while the two giant belligerents fought it out on the seas. In legal theory he agreed with Lansing, but he was so strongly moved by Bryan's pleading that he had apparently decided by the end of the debate over a *Falaba* note to make no protest at all. This is the course that he would probably have followed in the future if the Germans, by confining their underseas campaign to attacks against Allied cargo ships and by showing a desire to avoid the loss of American life, had made it possible for him to find a means of adjusting to the new situation.

A policy of noninvolvement, however, became impossible when a German U-boat sank the British passenger liner *Lusitania* without warning on May 7, 1915, with the loss of almost 1,200 civilians, including 128 Americans, men, women, and children. Wilson had to make some positive response now, so atrocious was the deed in the eyes of the American people, so flagrant was the violation of elemental national rights, so unneutral and degrading would be an acceptance of the terror campaign against the North Atlantic passenger liners.

The strategic facts of the situation—the German inability to maintain any effective blockade of the British Isles and the consequent serious dangers to Germany from a break with the United States—would have justified the President in peremptorily demanding prompt disavowal and guarantees. Wilson's response, however, reflected his own desire and that of the majority of Americans to preserve neutrality and to avoid taking any position short of yielding essential rights that might lead to hostilities with Germany. Thus all during the summer of 1915 Wilson pounded out notes on his typewriter, for the sole purpose of persuading the German government to disavow the sinking of the *Lusitania* and to abandon its campaign against unarmed passenger vessels. Threatening to break relations after a U-boat sank the liner *Arabic* on August 19, 1915, Wilson finally won the promise that he demanded.

By the end of the summer of 1915 the President had thus worked through two stages of policy and had won immunity from ruthless submarine attacks on American neutral ships and unarmed belligerent passenger liners. Up to this time, at any rate, Wilson had been patient, conciliatory, and firm only in his demand that the Germans give up measures that had already taken American lives and threatened untold others.

The third stage in the formulation of Wilson's policies toward the submarine, lasting from the early autumn of 1915 through the *Sussex* crisis in the spring of 1916, saw the President attempting to reach a definitive understanding with the Berlin authorities over all phases of submarine warfare against merchant shipping. The issue was daily becoming more difficult to solve by the application of traditional law, because the Allies since March, 1915, had been arming some passenger and cargo ships and ordering them to attack submarines that showed "hostile intent." But Wilson and Lansing persisted in trying to find a solution in spite of the obstacles because they (or Wilson, at any rate) and the majority of Americans still earnestly desired to avoid conflict over merely technical issues.

By patient negotiation Lansing finally won something resembling a German apology for the loss of American lives on the *Lusitania* and an implicit reaffirmation of the *Arabic* pledge. In order to hasten this German concession and to avert even the possibility of future contention, Lansing proposed his *modus vivendi* of January 18, 1916 (already mentioned), designed to provide a new code to govern the German underseas campaign against maritime commerce. This was the proposal that the Allies disarm their merchant ships and that the German submarines observe the rules of cruiser warfare in attacking them.

Adoption of the proposal by the opposing belligerents, or by the United States and Germany alone, would have achieved Wilson's objective of a comprehensive settlement of the submarine issue. And yet, for reasons that we have already seen, Wilson jettisoned the *modus vivendi* in order to save the House-Grey Agreement. Soon afterward, during the *Sussex* controversy (as we have also seen), he launched a new campaign to force the German government to conduct submarine operations against all merchant ships, armed and unarmed, within the rules of cruiser warfare.

Wilson's rejection of the opportunity to come to a seemingly definitive understanding with Germany seems altogether logical and wise when we remember his objectives and the circumstances in which he made these decisions during the third stage in German-American relations. Wilson's supreme objective now was peace through his own mediation. Mediation seemed possible at this time only through the co-operation of the British government. But the British would co-operate only if they believed that the President was genuinely neutral, and certainly not if he insisted upon a code of submarine warfare that minimized the risks to Americans at the expense of British sea power to the advantage of an essentially illegitimate weapon.

Mediation was a noble objective with such great benefits to the United States that it justified taking a few risks to achieve. But Wilson could have followed no other course than the one he followed during the crises over armed merchantmen and the *Sussex*, even if his objective had been merely to maintain American neutrality. In the circumstances prevailing in the late winter of 1916, Wilson had to choose between continuing to accept the British maritime system, mooted by American Civil War precedents, or acquiescing in the challenge to that system, the German submarine blockade. The first was legitimate because it was based upon *de facto* power as well as legal precedent; the second was not legitimate because it was still a paper blockade without any power of effective enforcement. By insisting upon adherence to traditional rules insofar as the rights of Americans were concerned, Wilson was not at this time depriving the Germans of a weapon essential for their survival or one the free use of which would bring them victory at this time. This, essentially, was the reason that they yielded (for the time being) to Wilson's demands in the *Sussex* crisis. By insisting upon the adoption of Lansing's *modus vivendi*, on the other hand, Wilson in effect would have changed the traditional rules and aimed a heavy blow at the British maritime system, and only for the illusory purpose of averting the possibility of a conflict with Germany.

The final test of any foreign policy is whether it serves the national interest. If it was to the interest of the United States to avoid participation in the war at any cost, regardless of its outcome, and if implementing the *modus vivendi* would have averted all possibility of American involvement, then Wilson's policies at this time were unwise. This generalization, however, is faulty in all its assumptions. To begin with, American interests would be best served by a stalemate and by a peace of reconciliation through Wilson's mediation, not by driving the Allies into sullen opposition, thereby making mediation impossible, and not by promoting a German victory. More important was the fact that implementing the *modus vivendi* would not have prevented the conflict with Germany that Wilson wished to avoid. As we now know, and as Wilson did not know, conflict would come inevitably when the Germans had enough submarines to institute an effective blockade. In that event neither right nor law nor concessions by the United States would dissuade the Germans from making an all-out bid for victory through a devastating attack upon all maritime commerce to the Allied nations.

E. M. Borchard
and W. P. Lage
Neutrality for the
United States

Edwin M. Borchard and W. P. Lage take the position that Wilson was never really neutral in 1914–1917. All his policies were designed to aid the Allies, and he was so economically and sentimentally committed to the Allied cause that by 1917 intervention was inevitable. Indeed, the authors believe that from the very beginning of the war, Wilson inclined to intervention. [Reprinted by permission from Neutrality for the United States *by E. M. Borchard and W. P. Lage. Copyright 1940 by Yale University Press.]*

It is not a grateful task to record the diplomacy of the United States during the period 1914–17. Although President Wilson had enjoined on the nation the necessity for remaining neutral "in thought as well as in action," unfortunately he soon found himself entangled in an emotional drift toward intervention in the war. It is possible that he did not realize the extent to which he was committing himself. With little if any useful aid from Secretary Lansing, who seems to have fumbled nearly every legal issue, with an Ambassador in London who was less interested in his own country than in the success of what he supposed to be a crusade for civilization, and with a most adroit and effective propaganda operating to persuade the United States into seeing only one side of the issue, it required a strong, sophisticated, and detached mind, with a philosophical view of history, to resist the pressure and allurements to which President Wilson was subjected. Volumes have already been written, and more are likely to be written, analyzing the various factors which served to propel the United States into the European war. In this book no detailed examination of the diplomatic history of the time can be attempted; but it is possible to say that the conduct of the American Government during that period was a negation of nearly all the requirements of neutrality both in thought and in action. The difficulty was not decreased by the profession that we were acting as neutrals, for neutrality and unneutrality became inextricably confused. There is no doubt that the administration desired to see the Allies win and declined to take any action even in defense of American neutral rights which would seriously interfere with that objective. Perhaps the objective is understandable—this is not the place to discuss that question—but to suggest that the objective was consistent with the maintenance of American neutrality is a travesty of the truth. We were unneutral and we paid the price.

Our unneutrality began as early as August, 1914. If neutrality was to be the national policy, the struggle to attain it, if such it was, did not last long. As we shall observe, the effort to obtain British adherence to the

Declaration of London disclosed an obsequiousness on the part of Ambassador Page, Colonel House and Mr. Lansing which must have forfeited British respect for the American case and for the capacity of America's representatives to defend it. As Ray Stannard Baker says, "By October [1914], perhaps earlier, our case was lost."

Again, in the protest against the British "measures of blockade" which gradually exposed all American trade with the neutrals of Europe to British and Allied control, the United States as early as December, 1914, practically gave away the American case against Allied impositions with the pathetic admission that such trade could not be interfered with "unless such interference is manifestly an imperative necessity to protect their [Allied] national safety, and then only to the extent that it is a necessity." The note appealed to "the deep sense of justice of the British nation" in requesting it to "refrain from all unnecessary interference with the freedom of trade" and to "conform more closely" to the rules of international law. But as long as the belligerents were to be the judges of "imperative necessity," this friendly admonition had the effect of acquiescing in their illegal measures. The British seem so to have construed it. Baker remarks:

. . . One cannot avoid the impression, after a careful study of this document, that the Administration's defense of American policy was in reality a defense of the British blockade, and furnished the British government with a whole arsenal of arguments against our own criticism of that blockade.

Although on August 18, 1914, President Wilson had solemnly urged "every man who really loves America" to "act and speak in the true spirit of neutrality, which is the spirit of impartiality . . . and friendliness to all concerned," and had warned against "partisanship" and "taking sides," on August 30, 1914, only twelve days later, he is recorded as telling Colonel House "that if Germany won, it would change the course of our civilization and make the United States a military nation."

The submarine campaign initiated by Germany in February, 1915, seems to have deeply offended President Wilson and to have fixed his attachment to the Allied cause. This influenced both the tone and contents of his notes to Germany and he began to talk about "strict accountability." Even before the *Lusitania* sinking in May, 1915, Attorney General Gregory attended a Cabinet meeting which he described as follows:

While these conditions existed [i.e., the sinking of ships before the *Lusitania*] a cabinet meeting was held, at which several of Mr. Wilson's advisers expressed great indignation at what they considered violation [by Britain] of our international rights, and urged a more vigorous policy on our part.

After patiently listening, Mr. Wilson said, in that quiet way of his, that the ordinary rules of conduct had no application to the situation; that the Allies were standing with their backs to the wall, fighting wild beasts; that he would permit nothing to be done by our country to hinder or embarrass them in the prosecution of the war unless admitted rights were grossly violated, and that this policy must be understood as settled.

Like all true-hearted Americans, he hoped that the United States would not be drawn into the war; but he was of Scotch and English blood, and by inheritance, tradition and rearing at all times the friend of the Allies.

On September 22, 1915, Colonel House records Wilson's views as follows: "Much to my surprise, he [Wilson] said he had never been sure that we ought not to take part in the conflict, and, if it seemed evident that Germany and her militaristic ideas were to win, the obligation upon us was greater than ever."

Mr. Tumulty, the President's Secretary, reports the President as believing that the public demand that he keep England within legal bounds was actuated by a "sinister political purpose." The President is reported to have approved Sir Edward Grey's statement that "of course many of the restrictions that we have laid down and which seriously interfere with your trade are unreasonable, but America must remember that we are fighting her fight as well as our own to save the civilization of the world." The President thereupon adopted this idea as his own, stating, according to Mr. Tumulty: "England is fighting our fight and you may well understand that I shall not, in the present state of affairs, place obstacles in her way." He declined to take any action to embarrass England when she "is fighting for her life and the life of the world."

Secretary Lansing admits in his *Memoirs* that as early as July, 1915, he had concluded that "the German Government is utterly hostile to all nations with democratic institutions" and that "Germany must not be permitted to win this war or to break even, though to prevent it this country is forced to take an active part. This ultimate necessity must be constantly in our minds in all our controversies with the belligerents. American public opinion must be prepared for the time, which may come, when we will have to cast aside our neutrality and become one of the champions of democracy."

We shall have occasion to see that the legal positions of the United States in its controversies with the belligerents were highly colored by this view, to which Mr. Lansing gave repeated expression. Describing his notes to England, Mr. Lansing says:

The notes that were sent were long and exhaustive treatises which opened up new subjects of discussion rather than closing those in controversy. Short and emphatic notes were dangerous. Everything was submerged in verbosity. It was done with deliberate purpose. It insured continuance of the controversies and left the questions unsettled, which was necessary in order to leave this country free to act and even to act illegally when it entered the war.

On October 6, 1915, Colonel House wrote to Mr. Page: "We have given the Allies our sympathy and we have given them, too, the more substantial help that we could not offer Germany even were we so disposed—and that is an unrestricted amount of munitions of war and money. In addition to that, we have forced Germany to discontinue her submarine warfare . . ." In 1915, Mr. Lansing wrote to Colonel House: "In no event should we take a course that would seriously endanger our friendly relations with Great Britain, France, or Russia, for, as you say, our friendship with Germany is a thing of the past."

On January 11, 1916, Colonel House records a conference he held with British leaders in which they had asked "what the United States wished Great Britain to do." To this the neutral Colonel replied: "The United States would like Great Britain to do those things which would enable the United States to help Great Britain win the war." Page admired this "cleverness."

And Mr. Lansing discloses at least one reason for his insincere defense of American neutrality, by stating: "in dealing with the British Government there was always in my mind the conviction that we would ultimately become an ally of Great Britain." His point of view being that of a prospective ally, his conduct was in reasonable accord.

No wonder that Sir Cecil Spring-Rice's biographer could say of him: "As to his value in negotiation, it cannot be overlooked that during the period while America was neutral, all the issues in dispute between England and America were decided as England wished." And Lord Reading adds: "I believe it to be the case that the Allied governments were never forced to recede from their position in any important question owing to American opposition."

The American surrender was, unfortunately, not merely a betrayal of neutrality, of which Lansing declared we were to be the "champions"; it was a surrender of the independence of the United States and of American self-respect. Furthermore, it must have forfeited the respect of Great Britain and her Allies. The surrender was not made through malevolence but through shortsighted emotionalism, a confusion of ideas as to where America's interest lay. It set the mood for that partiality and that incapacity to take and stand upon correct legal positions which ultimately made of the United States an instrument of the foreign policy of certain European belligerents.

We need only refer to the agreement between Colonel House and Sir Edward Grey on February 22, 1916 (of all days!), for the contingent intervention of the United States on behalf of the Allies if the Central Powers failed to accept terms of peace suitable to the Allies. Such an agreement is unique in the history of "neutrality."

Nor need more than passing reference be made to the "Sunrise Breakfast Conference" in April, 1916, in which President Wilson sought to find out from Speaker Clark, Floor Leader Kitchin, and Chairman Flood of the Foreign Affairs Committee of the House whether Congress could be persuaded to approve war against Germany.

It is now established that the British Ambassador was often notified in advance that important notes of protest against British violations of American rights were merely formal and not to be taken too seriously. In connection with the American note of October 21, 1915, Ambassador Spring-Rice was requested to send Sir Edward Grey a cable preparing him for a protest. Spring-Rice assured his government that the note was due to the fact that "the United States must defend their rights and they must make a good showing before Congress meets, but that the correspondence should not take a hostile character but should be in the nature of a juridical discussion."

An entirely different attitude distinguishes the correspondence of the United States with Great Britain from that with Germany. Had there been no fundamental prejudice in favor of one group of belligerents, the legal questions might have been approached with greater felicity and understanding.

On the armed merchantmen question, the unsustainable position was taken that, notwithstanding the ability of a single shot to sink a submarine and notwithstanding the British Admiralty orders to ram or fire on submarines at sight, nevertheless the submarine had no right to fire on and sink an armed belligerent merchantman which had American citizens on board. Thus, the neutral United States undertook to defend British merchantmen from attack by their enemy, a practice new in history. The real legal issues involved in the *Lusitania* case—her naval status, her cargo, her course in the war zone, the risks the passengers assumed—were not carefully examined, but ultimata were sent to Germany which were not and have not since been justified. The administration declined to inform American citizens, notwithstanding Secretary Bryan's importunities, that they took passage on belligerent vessels at their own risk. It fought the Gore-McLemore Resolutions of 1916 which merely sought to declare this elementary rule of law.

No more than casual reference needs to be made to one of the more egregious lurches into unneutrality, whereby the United States and its people were led into financing the munitions supply of one set of the belligerents, the Allies. In August, 1914, the administration had announced that the flotation of loans for the belligerents was "inconsistent with the spirit of neutrality." In October, 1914, as the munitions traffic developed, a plausible argument was advanced by Mr. Lansing that bank credits for the purchase of supplies were not public loans and hence should not be banned. The President agreed, but was not willing to let the public know that he had approved this qualification of his original position. By August, 1915, this trade had developed to such proportions that the credits needed to be funded and, it was argued, the Allied governments had to have new money to buy their enormous supplies. The 1914 prohibition and its reasons stood in the way. The Secretary of the Treasury made an eloquent plea to the President for authority to permit the Federal Reserve banks to discount bills and acceptances, a flagrantly unneutral act of the United States Government, and to permit the Allied governments to float loans in the United States. Again the President yielded, but again not publicly. He thus committed himself to a policy which could have but one end, for as the need for Allied credit continued—the argument was that American prosperity could not be permitted to decline—and private lenders became reluctant, only public lending could meet the need, and that meant war. Like the impressment issue to the "War Hawks" of 1812, the German submarine note of January 31, 1917, must have been a godsend to the interventionists. The way to the public Treasury was now open. The subsequent record is current history.

The strange thing is that President Wilson apparently failed to perceive that he was inveigled from one misstep to the next and that the end of the trail was intervention. Perhaps his mental attitude in August, 1915, was already such that he conceived it legitimate to reverse Secretary Bryan's and his own sensible position of August, 1914. Those members of the Federal Reserve Board who in August, 1915, were reluctant to permit the Federal Reserve banks' participation in this violation of neutrality were denounced by Secretary McAdoo as "pro-German," then as later a form of psychological terrorism to discourage the well-balanced, the thoughtful, the really neutral devotees of America, its traditions and its independence. The remarkable fact is that under the impact of the mighty forces making for American involvement, including the consistently unneutral attitude of mind and action of the leaders of the administration, American intervention was nevertheless delayed for more than two years. That fact alone attests the fundamental detachment of the American people and their aversion to participation in European wars.

No wonder that the belated effort of President Wilson in December, 1916, to end the war fell in England on unresponsive ears. The British Government had no reason to believe that the United States would exert pressure on England or that it would even act impartially. The mediatory or constructive influence of the United States had been frittered away; only its physical power as a belligerent was now sought. That ultimate seduction was not difficult.

Great Britain, well aware of the situation in Washington, timed its replies so as to conceal the downright refusal of practically every American protest; they were almost invariably delivered when the administration was engrossed in the clouds of controversy incidental to American protests against the German submarine. Thus, the American note of October 21, 1915, was answered on April 19, 1916, when the *Sussex* controversy was at its height. This was excellent strategy, like the release of the Bryce reports on German atrocities in Belgium at the time of the *Lusitania* controversy. In like manner, Great Britain made cotton absolute contraband on August 20, 1915, the day following the sinking of the British steamer *Arabic*.

It is not necessary to extend the demonstration of American unneutrality by a discussion of the feeble protest at the seizure of American mails and the diversion of all northern transatlantic shipping into British ports for examination. Nor is it necessary to discuss the forcible removal of passengers from American ships on the high seas if they were thought to be German reservists.

President Wilson thought the "national honor" required him to fight for the right of American citizens to take passage unmolested on British merchant ships. As John Bassett Moore stated to the Senate Foreign Relations Committee in 1936: "We became involved in war directly as the result of our undertaking to guarantee the safety of belligerent merchantmen and our taking the position that armed belligerent merchantmen were to be considered as peaceful vessels." It is not necessary to emphasize the fact that scarcely a ton of cargo left an American port from 1915 to 1917 without the control of a British agent. And we need merely call attention to the submission of the United States to the impositions of the British black list which prevented an American citizen from trading with Germans or even Chileans in Chile if their names had been placed on the British black lists—this at a time when Canada refused to submit to such a black list and freely sent shipments to those very firms! . . .

The momentary effort to restore American neutrality by retracting an error, the consternation this aroused in interventionist circles, and the successful campaign to induce the return to error, had produced a confusion of counsels not altogether without its amusing features. In spite of the arguments employed by Lansing to prove the inconsistency between the American position of 1914, on armed merchantmen, and the further insistence on their immunity from submarine attack, President Wilson nevertheless declined to draw the natural inference that if armed merchantmen were subject to submarine attack, American citizens on such vessels were obviously exposed to the same danger. At Topeka on February 2, 1916, in the Preparedness Campaign, the President had urged the need to protect and safeguard "the rights of Americans no matter where they might be in the world." In a letter of February 24, 1916, to Senator Stone, Wilson pictured the right of American citizens to travel unmolested on armed belligerent merchantmen as a matter of national "honor," fundamental "principle," and "of the very essence of the things that have made America a sovereign nation." To yield on that point he regarded as a confession of "impotency as a Nation" and a "surrender" of American independence.

The introduction of the Gore-McLemore Resolutions in February, 1916, warning American citizens against taking passage on armed belligerent merchantmen, although approved, according to Speaker Clark's statement to the President, by a majority in Congress, was firmly opposed by the administration. The President summoned the Congressional leaders on February 21 and made the defeat of the resolutions a matter of personal prestige. Many members became convinced that the President would insist on the right of American citizens to travel unmolested on armed belligerent merchantmen, even at the risk of war. To clarify the issue Senator Stone wrote the President on February 24, giving his version of the conference of the twenty-first:

I have stated my understanding of your attitude to be substantially as follows:

That while you would deeply regret the rejection by Great Britain of Mr. Lansing's proposal . . . you were of the opinion that if Great Britain and her allies rejected the proposal and insisted upon arming her merchant ships she would be within her right under international law.

Also that you would feel disposed to allow armed vessels to be cleared from our ports; also that you are not favorably disposed to the idea of this Government taking any definite steps toward preventing American citizens from embarking upon armed merchant vessels.

Furthermore that you would consider it your duty, if a German warship should fire upon an armed merchant vessel of the enemy upon which American citizens were passengers, to hold Germany to strict account.

I find it difficult for my sense of duty and responsibility to consent to plunge this Nation into the vortex of this world war because of the unreasonable obstinacy of any one of the powers upon the one hand, or, on the other hand, of foolhardiness, amounting to a sort of moral treason against the Republic, of our people recklessly risking their lives on armed belligerent ships. I can not escape the conviction that such would be so monstrous as to be indefensible.

To this letter, the President immediately replied, in part, as follows:

. . . But in any event our duty is clear. No nation, no group of nations, has the right, while war is in progress, to alter or disregard the principles which all nations have agreed upon in mitigation of the horrors and sufferings of war; and if the clear rights of American citizens should very unhappily be abridged or denied by any such action, we should, it seems to me, have in honor no choice as to what our own course should be.

For my own part, I cannot consent to any abridgment of the rights of American citizens in any respect. The honor and self-respect of the Nation is involved. We covet peace, and shall preserve it at any cost but the loss of honor. To forbid our people to exercise their rights for fear we might be called upon to vindicate them would be a deep humiliation indeed. It would be an implicit, all but an explicit, acquiescence in the violation of the rights of mankind everywhere and of whatever nation or allegiance. It would be a deliberate abdication of our hitherto proud position as spokesman, even amid the turmoil of war, for the law and the right. It would make everything this Government has attempted and everything that it has accomplished during this terrible struggle of nations meaningless and futile.

It is important to reflect that if in this instance we allowed expediency to take the place of principle the door would inevitably be opened to still further concessions. Once accept a single abatement of right, and many other humiliations would certainly follow, and the whole fine fabric of international law might crumble under our hands piece by piece. What we are contending for in this matter is of the very essence of the things that have made America a sovereign nation. She cannot yield them without conceding her own impotency as a Nation and making virtual surrender of her independent position among the nations of the world.

The Gore-McLemore Resolutions were duly defeated, a result which was hailed in Washington and London as a vindication of the President's position. But it meant war. There is something tragic in making a moral issue out of a fundamental mistake. Wilson, of course, thought he was legally right and standing on solid ground. It exemplifies the tricks that emotionalism can play on intelligence. The solemnity of the avowal was inappropriate. Solemnity may well be evoked, however, by the painful consciousness that the President of the United States had by very poor advice been led into a blunder as preposterous as it was fatal.

Had the President been really interested in the law and sought competent advice, he would have been told that Congress needed no legislation to accomplish its object; it was elementary law, as we shall see, that a person sailing under a foreign flag takes his legal position and protection from that flag and cannot look to his own country to protect him from the risks of his location on belligerent "territory." Contrary to Mr. Lansing's view that there was no legal authority in the President to issue such a warning, the President merely had to announce the elementary rule of law, which requires no legislation to confirm it. Indeed, the only objection there is to legislation prohibiting or warning American citizens against taking passage on belligerent merchantmen or treating armed merchantmen as warships in our ports is that such legislation implies that this is not already established law.

The public as represented in Congress was for the most part really desirous of avoiding opportunities to enlist in a foreign war, and the Gore-McLemore Resolutions were a response to this demand. The objections, however, to the Lansing proposal of January 18, 1916, and President Wilson's determination to repudiate that proposal, caused the administration to concentrate all its pressure to bring about the defeat of the Gore-McLemore Resolutions which its own policy of January, 1918, had invited. The Congress tried to be neutral. The administration would not permit it.

Horace C. Peterson

Opponents

of War

Horace C. Peterson, for many years until his death in 1952 a professor of history at the University of Oklahoma, concentrated his writing on the period of the First World War. After writing a book on propaganda in the United States during the war, he turned his attention to a study of the treatment of the Opponents to War, 1917–1918. (Professor G. C. Fite completed the book after Peterson's death.) As he shows, the United States government persecuted and prosecuted the dissenters relentlessly. A flood of hate was loosened, which made a *mockery of constitutional liberties and guarantees. It is worth noting that in World War II the policy of the government towards dissenters and opponents was so exemplary as to merit an award from the American Civil Liberties Union.*

The selection that appears below is drawn from two chapters of the book—entitled, significantly, "The Implements of Repression" and "The American Reign of Terror." [Reprinted with permission of the Copyright owners, the Regents of the University of Wisconsin, from H. C. Peterson and G. C. Fite, Opponents of War, 1917–1918 *(Madison: The University of Wisconsin Press, 1957).]*

The declaration of war by the United States on April 6, 1917, left many Americans angry and bitter. Some, such as the Socialists, said openly that participation in the war was a crime. Many diverse elements in the country hated conscription and were not reluctant to express that hatred. Still others condemned governmental policies which tended to repress and restrict those who opposed the prosecution of the war. And there were, of course, those who expressed suspicion of the ultimate aims of the majority committed to the conflict.

This continuing opposition was now met by a progressive demand that critics be silenced. Some suggested that physical violence should be used to quiet pacifists. Others were to suggest that opponents of governmental policies be jailed.

One group—a small but effective minority—was typified by Theodore Roosevelt and his militant followers. This faction strongly favored smothering criticism of national war policies. These leaders were united, as some had been during the Spanish-American War, by an interest in international politics. They now longed to use American wealth and power in competition with other nations. Some of their interest developed from their belief in this particular war; some of it from a peculiar psychosis which would have made war palatable almost any time; part of it from a simple enjoyment of violence. In this particular conflict, there were special claims upon their enthusiasm. Here was an opportunity to fight alongside and against the leading nations of the world. For the first time, their country would be participating in what European statesmen identified as *la grande politique.* This idea alone was attractive to some, and for them it carried the obligation to silence opposition.

Joined with the proponents of international adventuring, and including some of the same people, were "moral fundamentalists," people whose tendency was to interpret all life as a struggle between God and the devil. For them, the American nationalist cause evoked by war assumed an almost religious character; and per contra, German militarism represented the forces of deepest evil. As in the history of religion, where ecclesiastical and doctrinal differences left no room for charity, there was no place for differences of opinion. The opponents of war were at once subjected to an unrelenting attack by believers in the moral righteousness of a conflict which they considered a holy war.

A strong third element, much larger than either of the others, which supported a policy of repression was made up of super-patriots who, either knowingly or unwittingly, tended to place their nation above the laws of morality or reason. To them the state could do no wrong. The attitude of "my country, right or wrong" controlled those minds which could not justify American prosecution of the war, even though they could not condone the cause of Germany and her allies.

There were also those whose demand for repression stemmed from economic motives. In the name of patriotism and loyalty conservatives were able to attack economic and political radicals, labor union members, and others who were demanding some kind of change or reform. This theme will be amply illustrated later.

In addition to these groups there were many people who simply had no concern about opposing repression. Some had sons or husbands in the armed forces and felt that hostility to the war was hostility to members of their family. Others, now that the die was cast, felt that nothing should be allowed to interfere. These moderates felt that clear and sudden danger overrode all questions of civil liberty. Moreover, the high idealism of war propaganda, particularly of Wilson's speeches, made them feel that participating in this war gave meaning and even a sense of nobility to their individual lives. Here was something worth while. The extremism of people who rejected freedom of thought and expression usually was disguised or hidden behind high-sounding phrases. To themselves as well as to others, their intolerances appeared as righteousness, their bigotry as idealism, and their hatreds as loyalty.

War advocates may have been moved by patriotism, by nationalism, by moralism, or perhaps by economic factors. But whatever the motivation, extreme supporters of the war very soon lashed out at all who stood in their way. And moderates, by their silence, gave them encouragement. Vituperation, epithet, ridicule, and abuse were heaped upon "pacifists." The swear word "isolationist" was applied to those who opposed war— and many sincere pacifists puzzled over its logic. Jane Addams wrote, "We were constantly accused of wishing to isolate the United States. . . . We were, of course, urging a policy exactly the reverse."

Very soon the verbal attacks were to be accompanied by implication or suggestion that pacifists should be silenced, jailed, or even killed. As early as April 10, 1917, the *New York Times* quoted Elihu Root as saying that "we must have no criticism now." Root told a cheering crowd at the Union League Club on August 15 that "there are men walking about the streets of this city tonight who ought to be taken out at sunrise tomorrow and shot for treason." Speaking before the Harvard Club the same evening, Theodore Roosevelt referred to those who wanted peace as pacifists, Socialists, I.W.W.'s, and "a whole raft of sexless creatures." Two days later, as reported by the *New York Times* of August 18, he was urging "vigorous police action against orators preaching veiled treason on street corners and elsewhere." Earlier, on July 4, according to the *New York Herald* of July 5, 1917, he had berated "half-hidden traitors" and had demanded "one allegiance, one flag, one language." Even high government officials fell into this pattern. In November Attorney General Gregory added to the attacks on war opponents with his remark, "May God have mercy on them, for they need expect none from an outraged people and an avenging Government." The President himself remarked in his Flag Day address, June 14, 1917, "Woe to the man or group of men that seeks to stand in our way in this day of high resolution. . . ."

Throughout April and May some individuals who attacked American entrance into the war were arrested. In such cases pacifists were usually charged with "disorderly conduct" or "unlawful assembly," and the result might be jail sentences of up to three months and occasionally a small fine. But there began to develop a desire on the part of war supporters to give stiffer sentences to anyone and everyone who spoke out against the war.

Even before the declaration of war on April 6 the Department of Justice had sought legal power to punish espionage. As early as February 8 the Attorney General had recommended legislation concerning "publication of information which might be useful to an enemy of the United States." After the declaration of war, Senator George E. Chamberlain of Oregon introduced a bill making the entire United States "a part of the zone of operations conducted by the enemy." This bill would have classified as a spy every person who published anything "endangering the success of the military forces" and would have made him subject to the death sentence by court-martial. However, the bill was defeated as a result of opposition by President Wilson.

During this period Congress evolved what was to become the Espionage Act. The bill, introduced on April 2, was an amalgamation of seventeen bills prepared in the Attorney General's office. Some of the original drafts were much more drastic than the one that came out of committee. There is reason to believe that supporters of the measure did not realize the power it had or how it could be used to strike down opponents of the war. The name indicates that it was intended to outlaw spies, and debate in Congress turned time and again to blueprints and photographs of military installations which spies might acquire. Congressman Edwin Y. Webb, who guided it through the lower house, stressed the fact that it was an attempt to "safeguard and protect our national defense secrets."

Senator Borah was suspicious. On April 19, 1917, when the bill to punish espionage was being discussed, he described it as "omnipotently comprehensive . . . though nebulous in its terms." "No man can foresee," he said, "what it might be in its consequences. . . ." Thomas E. Watson, editor of the Thomson, Georgia, *Jeffersonian*, attacked it in his newspaper with intense earnestness. It would establish, he said, "the same kind of autocracy in this country that the *lese majestie* [*sic*] laws create in

Germany. . . . Must we begin our war upon European autocracy *by
creating one,* here at home? . . . *Don't abuse me*—ANSWER ME!

The principal opposition turned upon a section which gave the President the right to censor the press. Newspapers throughout the country
objected. The American Newspaper Publishers petitioned Congress to
delete this section. The Los Angeles *Times* of May 3, 1917, called it un-
American. In reply the bill's sponsors in Congress emphasized time and
time again that the bill "gives you the right to criticize all you please."
They quoted the provision which said that "nothing in this section shall
be construed to limit or restrict . . . any discussion, comment, or criticism
of the acts or policies of the Government or its representatives, or the
publication of the same." But Senator Hiram Johnson of California was
dubious. He asked Senator Overman, "Would you have me think, sir,
that you have written one provision and then nullified it by the next?"
The purpose of this proposed statute, he said, was "to render impossible
legitimate criticism . . . of those who may lead during this war, and lead
in incompetence and in inefficiency." President Wilson also entered the
fight. He wrote a letter to Congressman Webb which appeared in the
New York Times on May 23, saying that the Administration must have
authority to censor the press. This was "absolutely necessary to the public
safety," he wrote.

The censorship provision was defeated, and after its elimination a
majority of the national lawmakers apparently believed that the bill
could not be used to suppress critical opinion. Actually, however, the aim
of curbing recalcitrant newspapers could be achieved under Title XII of
the Espionage Bill. Part of this section prohibited sending through the
mails any materials "advocating or urging treason, insurrection, or forcible resistance to any law of the United States." In effect, this was to give
the Postmaster General the right to determine mailable matter. And it
might be added that the elimination of the much quoted sentence which
gave citizens the right to criticize "the acts or policies of the Government or its representatives" was about as much of a victory for repression
as the original censorship provision would have been.

The real teeth of the Espionage Bill were to be found in the paragraph
which stated that whenever anyone

shall wilfully make or convey false reports or false statements with intent to
interfere with the operation or success of the military or naval forces . . . [or]
shall wilfully cause or attempt to cause insubordination, disloyalty, mutiny,
or refusal of duty in the military or naval forces of the United States, or shall
wilfully obstruct the recruiting or enlistment service of the United States . . .
[he] shall be punished by a fine of not more than $10,000 or imprisonment for
not more than twenty years or both.

On the surface this appeared to be innocuous. There apparently was
no threat to freedom of speech. In the debate in Congress this provision
received relatively little consideration. Congressman Harold Knutson

asked what would happen if someone revealed bad conditions in some army camp similar to those which had existed during the Spanish-American War. "Would that lay the writer open to a criminal prosecution?" Congessman Webb hastened to reply, "Certainly not. . . . Conditions, policies of the Government, and acts of its officers would always be open to criticism." He then stressed the fact that there could be prosecutions only when statements were "willfully false." Other questions were answered in about the same way.

On June 15, 1917, the Espionage Bill became law. Eventually, in *Schenck* v. *United States,* Mr. Justice Holmes wrote the majority decision which upheld the law. In this decision was propounded the theory of "clear and present danger." But this rather liberal interpretation quite apparently was not the guiding principle of American courts. Instead, courts often relied on the "bad tendency" doctrine. Zechariah Chafee stated that the Espionage Act, as interpreted by the courts, "renders civilians severely punishable during a war for questioning its justifiability or the methods of conducting it." Many court cases bearing out this judgment will be discussed later. Undoubtedly, one of the main purposes of the law was to minimize domestic opposition to the war. But regardless of the exact intent of Congress, when the law began to be interpreted by the judges and juries it became clear that opponents of war could and would be suppressed. For example, on August 16 a press notice announced that the Espionage Act might be used to provide punishment for anyone opposing the draft.

States and municipalities also joined in the move to quiet opposition against the war. The laws of some western states where the I.W.W. and the Nonpartisan League were strong were especially severe. For example, in Minnesota it was illegal to say "that men should not enlist in the military or naval forces of the United States or the state of Minnesota. . . ." Nine states passed laws making it a crime to use language opposing various aspects of the war effort. Several states passed some kind of sedition laws, and fifteen states enacted criminal syndicalism statutes. On the local level, an Indianapolis ordinance made it illegal "to incite, urge or advise strikes." The Maryland compulsory work law seems even more antilabor.

Many organizations co-operated to make local, state, and national laws successful. There already existed city, county, state, and national police and detective forces. These were expanded and new units were formed. In addition, numerous semiofficial and private organizations for the purpose of suppressing opposition to the war were set up throughout the country. Among these were the American Defense Society, the National Security League, the American Protective League, the Home Defense League, the Liberty League, the Knights of Liberty, the American Rights League, the All-Allied Anti-German League, the Anti-Yellow Dog League, the American Anti-Anarchy Association, the Boy Spies of America, the Sedition Slammers, and the Terrible Threateners.

The American Defense Society was extremely active. The *New York Herald* of August 18, 1917, reported, "More than one hundred men enrolled yesterday in the American Vigilante Patrol at the offices of the American Defense Society. . . . The Patrol was formed to put an end to seditious street oratory." On the twenty-second the organization's first capture was announced. An individual by the name of Bedford was accused of saying in front of a crowd at 37th and Broadway that he did not approve of sending U.S. troops to France to fight England's battles. The *New York Tribune* of August 22 reported that the Vigilantes had Bedford arrested and charged with disorderly conduct. In a letter to George Creel, H. D. Craig, secretary of this Society, recommended that stringent action be taken against all alien enemies and "enemy sympathizers whose conduct imperils or impedes the conduct of the war." In March, 1918, the Society attempted to get official sanction of the Council of National Defense "for the specific purpose of suppressing sedition." The honorary president of the group was Theodore Roosevelt, and honorary vice-presidents included Robert Bacon, Perry Belmont, Charles J. Bonaparte, and John G. Hibben.

The National Security League displayed much the same point of view. George Creel has stated that the League and the American Defense Society "were easily the most active and obnoxious [of chauvinist organizations]. At all times their patriotism was a thing of screams, violence, and extremes, and their savage intolerances had the burn of acid."

The state and municipal Councils of Defense were also active in hitting at opponents of the war. In each state, however, the situation varied. In some places these organizations led the war on pacifists. In others they participated feebly if at all. The parent body in Washington gave out the following instructions: "If you will continue to have your local councils, under your supervision, investigate and report upon cases of disloyalty and seditious utterances, communicating with the Department of Justice whenever it would appear to be advisable, we think you will be carrying out the policy of the Council of National Defense and fulfilling your obligation to your own legislature."

The most omnipresent of the repressive organizations was the American Protective League, sponsored by the Department of Justice. By June, 1917, it had units in some 600 cities and towns with a membership of nearly 100,000. In 1918 the membership had increased to around 250,000. The members of this League, one observer declared, were "the leading men in their communities. They were bankers, they were railroad men, they were hotel men, they were the choice of the citizens in their particular locality." A biographer of the League, Emerson Hough, wrote in 1919, "The mails are supposed to be sacred. . . . But let us call the A.P.L. sometimes almost clairvoyant as to letters done by suspects. . . . It is supposed that breaking and entering a man's home or office place without warrant is burglary. Granted. But the League has done that thousands of times and has never been detected!" Hough estimated that the League "brought to judgment three million cases of disloyalty."

Secretary of the Treasury McAdoo was disturbed. He objected to the fact that a person, for seventy-five cents or a dollar, could obtain membership in the American Protective League and have the authority "with the approval of the Department of Justice, to make investigations under the title of 'Secret Service.' " President Wilson wrote to Gregory, "It seems to me that it would be very dangerous to have such an organization operating in the United States, and I wonder if there is any way in which we could stop it." The Attorney General refused to withdraw his support, and Wilson did not press the matter.

An example of the more active state organized groups was the Minnesota Commission of Public Safety. This Commission, created by state law, was formed on April 23, 1917. It was headed by the Governor and was backed by a body of Home Guards. It closed saloons and moving picture theaters, directed a census of alien land ownership, established a policy of "work or fight," boosted the sale of Liberty bonds, examined and tested people for loyalty and pro-Germanism, and took other actions to bring conformity and all-out support of the war. On August 8, 1917, the *Minneapolis Journal* carried an appeal issued by this Commission "for all patriots to join in the suppression of anti-draft and seditious acts and sentiment." The official report of the Commission published in 1919 stated: "Misinterpreting the Constitutional guarantee of freedom of speech and of the press, these leaders of radical groups thought or pretended to think, that even in war times they could properly oppose the Government's policies in speech and writing." The Commission was referring to groups like the Nonpartisan League. The *St. Paul Daily News* on June 29, 1918, reported, "The Commission thinks that as a matter of law it cannot be restrained in the performance of its public functions by any Minnesota court."

As soon as these nationalistic societies were formed and the desired laws were passed, official and unofficial spokesmen of the groups urged people to become informers. The *New York Times,* June 6, 1917, editorialized, "It is the duty of every good citizen to communicate to the proper authorities any evidence of sedition that comes to his notice." The *Literary Digest* requested its readers to watch for sedition and "to clip and send to us any editorial utterances they encounter which seem to them seditious or treasonable." Attorney General Gregory announced that "complaints of even the most informal or confidential nature are always welcome." The Committee on Public Information issued advertisements urging readers to "report the man who spreads pessimistic stories. Report him to the Department of Justice." Even George Creel himself was known to have written, "I think this man might be watched with profit." Apparently Creel had in mind magazine and newspaper articles which he wanted to make the basis for legal prosecution.

President Wilson was also concerned with this problem. He wrote on one occasion, "Any item, great or small [dealing with pro-German activity], with which you would be kind enough to furnish us would be taken up and acted on with promptness. . . ." In August, 1917, Wilson asked the Attorney General what could be done about an individual opposing an expeditionary force. About a month later he asked if certain writings could not be made the basis for a treason trial. Gregory replied that this would not be possible, but that the writer might be silenced under the Espionage Act.

By 1918 the Attorney General was able to declare, "It is safe to say that never in its history has this country been so thoroughly policed." Many opponents of war had found this to be true through personal experience. . . .

Spring, 1918, in the United States was a time when strident voices filled the air, when mobs swarmed through the streets, when violence of all kinds was practiced upon the opponents of the war. The words and actions were not unlike those of earlier months, but the tones were heightened, the tempo accelerated.

A preacher was quoted by the *Detroit Free Press* on March 4, 1918, as saying, "The person who claims to be neutral ought to be exported, jailed, interned, labeled, or . . . rendered powerless." An editor exclaimed, "For goodness sake, when is the firing squad to get busy." Other editors spoke of firing squads, stone walls at sunrise, and telegraph poles. There were even those who almost regretted the "passing of the boiling-in-oil period of administering reprisal to traitors to their country." On August 3, 1918, the *New Republic* declared, "This [hysterical] state of mind is being assiduously cultivated by many of our newspapers, many of our respected fellow citizens, and certain public officials. Those who do not encourage it certainly fail to protest against it."

To guarantee orthodoxy, the prying into people's opinions continued unabated. An army official in South Carolina invited civilians to report to him any suspicious and disloyal activity, as well as any signs of sympathy for the enemy. The state Councils of Defense were flooded with complaints against individuals of doubted loyalty. In Nebraska, for example, it was at first the practice of the Council to have a representative call on the accused, question him, and warn or threaten him if that seemed necessary. But the complaints grew so numerous that this procedure had to be changed and offenders were forced to come before the Council. An official of this body reported, "When we summon offenders before our committee . . . we do not permit them to be represented by attorneys, and we do not reveal to them the names of the men who make the complaints." The writer added, "We are partial to the tender touch, to the educational process, and as I have said we find that in most cases it works successfully. But we have had cases—many of them—where the 'iron hand' was necessary, and we have not hesitated to use it."

The Councils of Defense in some other states carried on in much the same way. At one time in South Dakota, some thirty-five people were subpoenaed in order to find out if they were loyally supporting the war. A farmer and his wife, suspected of "anti-American" activities, fainted when the sheriff read the subpoena to them. Suspects in a Florida town were made to repeat a catechism of loyalty.

From the very beginning of the war there had been attacks upon things German. Now the cries of hate rose to a crescendo. Names of towns and individuals were changed. The lowly hamburger became the liberty sandwich, and sauerkraut was called liberty cabbage. Hymns, symphonies, and operas of German origin were looked upon with suspicion. And then, of course, there was hatred of the German language.

During the winter of 1917–18, there was a strong drive to abolish the teaching of German in the country's schools. Theodore Roosevelt backed it. So did the state Councils of Defense. The American Defense Society urged the mayor of New York to discontinue teaching the "Kaiser's tongue" in the city schools. At a national meeting on illiteracy, much of the session was given over to attacks upon the teaching of German. The argument was advanced that the German language had no cultural or practical value and that to teach it gave aid and comfort to the enemy. *The Manufacturers Record* said that German had been emphasized not because of its "intrinsic value" but because it was part of the "political propaganda intended to wean the people of this country away from Anglo-Saxon and Anglo-Celtic origins and ideals and divide the national interest and national sympathy." Professor Knight Dunlap of Johns Hopkins declared that the German language was a "barbarous tongue," lacking in cultural worth and without commercial importance.

With these sentiments predominating, the desired results were soon obtained. The use of the German language was forbidden in the pulpits and schools of Montana. In Iowa, the Governor ruled that German could not be used on streetcars, over the telephone, or anywhere else in public. News stories from all sections of the nation told of individual cities outlawing the use of German in public places and forbidding its teaching in the schools. On March 26, 1918, the Seattle *Post-Intelligencer* announced, "German Barred from Spokane's Public Schools." Again on April 9, the *Post-Intelligencer* headed a story, "Speech of Hated Hun Forbidden." As the Oklahoma schools dropped German from their curricula, the Tulsa *Daily World* declared, "German Deader than Latin Now." On the basis of a poll taken by the *Literary Digest,* 149 schools had discontinued German language study by March, 1918. Others were to follow.

On the same intellectual level was the move to burn German books. In Lewiston, Montana, a committee marched on the local high school and burned all the German textbooks it could find. A book-burning was announced as a part of a Fourth of July celebration in Shawnee, Oklahoma. Another was promised in Spartanburg, South Carolina. In a small Indiana town, German books were thrown into a muddy ditch.

A common punishment devised for people suspected of disloyalty or sedition was that of kissing the flag. The riot in Boston on July 4, 1917, was accompanied by flag-kissing. In December, a young man in Arkansas was compelled to wrap a flag about him, kiss it, and then salute army recruiting officers. By 1918 flag-kissing had become so frequent that it was hardly first-rate news. In Trenton, New Jersey, two sisters working in a pottery plant were reported to have made disparaging remarks about American soldiers. Other workers gave them the choice of being ducked in a canal or kissing the flag and pledging allegiance to the United States. The two chose the flag-kissing punishment. In California, the police forced a Russian to kiss the flag. A foreigner in New York was arrested for failing to register. He swore that he would be a "slacker as long as he lived." He was forced to kiss the flag several times and then wave it above his head as he paraded up and down the corridor. In New Jersey a man who refused to subscribe for a Liberty bond was compelled to go to his knees and kiss the flag.

A young man in Montana, E. V. Starr, fell into the hands of a mob bent upon vindicating its peculiar standard of patriotism by compelling him to kiss the flag. In the heat of the argument, Starr remarked, "What is this thing anyway? Nothing but a piece of cotton with a little paint on it and some other marks in the corner there. I will not kiss that thing. It might be covered with microbes." Starr was arrested under the state sedition act for using language "calculated to bring the flag into contempt and disrepute." He was fined five hundred dollars and costs, and given a long penitentiary sentence. In denying Starr a writ of habeas corpus, the district court said that he had been "more sinned against than sinning." The members of the mob, not Starr, "should have been punished," said the court. The judge then sharply criticized that brand of patriotism which descended to fanaticism. But the court held that Starr had no legal recourse, except to apply for a pardon.

Along with flag-kissing came a great sensitiveness about respect for the national anthem. A Croatian by the name of Frank Horrath failed to stand in a Pittsburgh theater when the anthem was played. A policeman took him away from an angry mob and put him in jail. He was charged with disorderly conduct and fined ten dollars. In Chicago an individual was fined fifty dollars for failing to stand when the "Star-Spangled Banner" was played. Similar incidents occurred elsewhere.

As mentioned before, yellow paint was customarily used to single out those who were considered disloyal. Sometimes homes, offices, and churches were marked with it. Frequently, even individuals were painted. For example, when some Nebraskans refused to participate in a Liberty Loan rally they were painted yellow, as were three men who made adverse comments about the loans in Kansas City. A grain elevator in Little Rock, Iowa, was painted yellow because the proprietor was accused of pro-

Germanism. When he tried to locate those who had done the painting job by using bloodhounds to follow them, "loyal citizens" beat him and drove him out of town.

Unique forms of violence were often devised by mobs to punish those charged with disloyalty or pro-Germanism. For instance, in San Rafael, California, a man had his hair clipped in the form of a cross, after which he was tied to a tree on the courthouse lawn. A person of German birth in Salt Lake City was thrown into a bin of dough where he almost suffocated. In Pennsylvania a man was taken from a hotel room, "severely beaten, made to walk up and down the street with a dog chain around his neck, forced to kiss the flag and doused into a large watering trough." At LaSalle, Illinois, Dr. J. C. Biemann, a pioneer physician, was ducked in a canal by several hundred men and boys. Then he was forced to kiss the flag and warned to leave the city. His "crime" was that he was supposed to have called Secretary of War Baker a "fat head."

In Berkeley, California, a large canvas tabernacle used by the Church of the Living God was burned down by a mob of men and boys. The pastor, the Reverend Joshua Sykes, and two elders were ducked in the baptismal tank. Along with other leaders, they were shortly arrested for their pacifist activities. They were accused of having told members of their church that they were citizens of God's kingdom and not of the United States, and that they should not assist with the war. Sykes and others were also accused of urging members not to contribute to the Red Cross, to buy Liberty bonds, to display the American flag, or to participate in war work. They were sentenced to various terms in McNeil Island Penitentiary.

Ernest Votaw, a Quaker and an outstanding opponent of militarism, was appointed real estate assessor in a small Pennsylvania town. However, when he appeared to take his job, a "committee" informed him he would have to resign or else be tarred and feathered and ridden out of town on a rail. Votaw resigned. Dr. James P. Warbasse was expelled from a county medical society in the same state because of his pacifist leanings. Later, however, he was restored to the roster.

Opponents of war often felt the pain of mob beatings. A man distributed handbills which advocated conscripting all incomes over five thousand dollars in order to finance the war. He had to be rescued from a mob. A Lithuanian woman packing-house worker, who supposedly made disloyal remarks, was badly beaten by other women when she refused to wear an American flag which they had pushed upon her. In Pocahontas, Arkansas, the sheriff gave a young man permission to "beat up" a worker in a button factory who had "hoped Germany would whip the entire world." The beaten employee was then made to kiss a Wilson button and salute the flag. Of course, he lost his job. A chap with a German name was severely beaten in a San Francisco saloon for saying that the United States "is not democratic. This Government is nothing but a hypocrite.

There is no difference between it and any other government." He was also sentenced to sixty days in jail.

During the spring of 1918 news stories from all sections of the country told of people being beaten by mobs of super-patriots. Sometimes it was for not displaying a flag, for objecting to the draft law, for criticizing American soldiers, or even soldiers of the associated powers; perhaps it was for not buying bonds, or for other reasons. But whatever the cause, the safest policy for one's physical well-being in many communities was to remain silent. Criticism of war aims and policies would not be tolerated.

Besides beating their victims, American mobs frequently resorted to the use of tar and feathers. There were a number of such cases in the fall of 1917. Perhaps the most notable incident was that of the seventeen I.W.W.'s at Tulsa. But throughout the late winter and spring of 1918, there was a veritable rash of tar and feather incidents. A few examples from various sections of the nation will illustrate the situation.

Joe Polaras, a Mexican living in Seattle, was tarred and feathered because he was supposedly unpatriotic. In Reno, Nevada, Elmer White was tied to a stake, lashed with a cat-o-nine-tails, tarred and feathered, and ordered out of town. A superintendent of schools in a Colorado town was given a coat of grease and feathers—a slight variation. At Emerson, Nebraska, Rudolph Schopke was tarred and feathered because he refused to contribute to the Red Cross. In Oklahoma O. F. Westbrook, a farmer living near Altus, was dragged from his bed by a masked and heavily armed mob and taken to a wooded area. There he was forced to kiss the flag and take the oath of "eternal allegiance to the Knights of Liberty." He was then lashed with a blacksnake whip and given a coat of tar and feathers. Similar incidents were reported in or near Muskogee, Wynne-wood, Elk City, and Henryetta—all in Oklahoma. At Electra, Texas, a confectioner by the name of George Geanapolus was tarred and feathered and driven out of town by some two hundred businessmen.

Students at Rutgers University approached one of their fellow students, Samuel H. Chovenson, an antiwar Socialist, and demanded that he speak at their Liberty Loan rally. When Chovenson refused, he was "stripped, covered with molasses and feathers, then blindfolded, and paraded through the streets of the town." Signs carried at the head of the procession bore the inscriptions, "This is what we do with pro-Germans!" "He's a Bolsheviki!" "He is against the Liberty Loan and the U.S.A."

The Milwaukee *Free Press* reported that in its section of the country mobs were "riding roughshod over law and order to punish instances of alleged disloyalty." And this was happening all over the nation. Furthermore, almost everywhere there was vicious, slanderous gossiping about people who did not accept the conventional view of the war.

Mobs had not been on the march long before they threatened the very lives of their victims. A Pennsylvania mob, composed of women munition workers, attempted to lynch a man who was supposed to have made seditious remarks. An Oregon supporter of the Russellites distributed a circular criticizing persons said to have suppressed the circulation of *The Finished Mystery*. For this a mob threatened to lynch him. When an Austrian employee of the Erie Railroad was accused of a lack of patriotism, he was "hauled thirty feet above ground at the end of a rope . . . and a fire hose was played upon him. He was cut down an hour later by friends who found him alive."

Those who committed such acts quite naturally prepared the way for other mobs to kill their victims. The precedent for mob killings was, of course, present in the United States. In the first six months of 1918 alone, there were thirty-five such events. The states of Alabama and Louisiana led in number of killings with eight each. But these were mostly racial killings. The new mob killings were to be "patriotic" affairs; they were murder in the name of liberty and democracy.

On March 24, 1918, in the small town of Hickory, Oklahoma, a Bulgarian was shot and killed by a policeman. It was alleged that he had said something "seditious," and, according to the policeman, the victim had fired first. On the same date an "operative" of the County Council of Defense in Tulsa shot and killed Joe Spring, a waiter in a restaurant. He accused Spring of making pro-German remarks. Two days later the County Council of Defense issued a statement declaring that "any person or persons who utter disloyal or unpatriotic statements do so at their own peril and cannot expect the protection of the loyal citizenship of this nation." On March 27, the Tulsa *Daily World* reported, "It wasn't S. L. Miller that was on trial for murdering Joe Spring yesterday. . . . It was the patriotism of Tulsa and the principle of a new unwritten law that makes it justifiable for a man to slay one who speaks out against the country that shelters and nurtures him." Miller was found not guilty. "The decision was received with cheers, and men, women, and children rushed to Miller to congratulate him, both for his patriotism and the outcome of the trial." On April 14, the *Daily World* reported that the policeman who had killed the Bulgarian was also acquitted. The presiding judge released the officer "after making a patriotic talk and warning pro-Germans not to speak their sentiments against the United States."

Southern Illinois was one of the most mob-ridden parts of the country. There was widespread discontent and unrest in the coal fields. Conflicts between employers and workmen were common. It was in this region that a labor lawyer and a union leader were tarred and feathered and driven out of town because they were causing "dissension among several thousand coal miners near Staunton." At the same time, according to an account in the files of the American Civil Liberties Union, "more than one hundred persons were made to sign pledges of loyalty." This news stimulated stern measures in Worden, Mount Olive, Gillespie, Williamson, Hillsboro, and several other small towns. There were numerous instances of people being taken from their homes and forced to make public professions of loyalty. Some were forced to kiss the flag; others had to sing the national anthem or play patriotic tunes on musical instruments. To protest such actions was in itself considered disloyal. It was said that the American Defense Society was trying to make the district "100 per cent American."

In the town of Christopher, a Polish Catholic priest, the Reverend John Kovalsky, was accused of having remarked that "God is with the Kaiser and the Kaiser will win the war." In spite of his fervent denials he was taken by a mob, and, with three other men, was tarred and feathered. What the others were accused of was not specified. In Benton Mrs. Frances Bergen got into an argument and apparently said some uncomplimentary things about President Wilson. Both Mrs. Bergen and Henry Baker, with whom she had argued, were arrested. While Baker's fine was paid by public subscription, the Loyalty League took Mrs. Bergen through town on a rail, forcing her to wave the American flag. One account stated, "At frequent intervals the procession paused, while Mrs. Bergen was compelled to shout praise for President Wilson."

Labor organizers were especially unpopular. At Hillsboro three union organizers, L. B. (Dad) Irvin, and Frank and Joseph Zib, had done effective work with the laborers. Among other things they had helped to bring about a large increase in the accident compensation received by injured miners. After the draft was passed, the Zib brothers registered as conscientious objectors. Although the questionnaires were supposed to have been private, the local editor immediately wrote a scathing article against them, and the private information was made public. Within a short time a group of citizens decided to take action against Irvin and the Zibs. On March 8, 1918, the vigilantes assembled, prepared tar and straw, and went in search of their intended victims. A report to the Civil Liberties Union stated: "Not finding the Zibs or Irvin at home after all their preparations, they became more enraged and with that frantically seized every possession—clothing, trunks, furniture, typewriter—their library, everything, and pulled them down the steps into the street where they offered them, in the name of freedom, to the flames prepared by the others of the group." Continuing their search, members of the mob descended in force upon a house where Irvin was believed to be hiding. When they knocked on the door—the occupants of the house apparently did not understand the purpose of a visit from the mob—a shot was fired, and a wild melee followed. Four men were wounded, including policeman Seaton Emory and a young man named Clifford Donaldson. Donaldson died later. He was twenty-four years old and had just enlisted in the navy.

The hysteria of the area spread into the small town of Collinsville just east of St. Louis. The local Council of Defense advocated "loyalty pledges," and there was severe criticism of a Baptist minister who felt that the church should not be used for Thrift Stamp meetings. Miners expressed uneasiness because some of their fellow workers were of foreign birth. Conservative elements were disturbed by union agitation. Members of a Loyalty committee began to agitate for the suppression of "disloyalty." Loud accusations were made against Robert Paul Prager, a

young man of German birth. A registered enemy alien, Prager was employed in a local bakery. He had applied for membership in a local
miners' union at which time he was supposed to have talked to the men
on the virtues of Socialism. However, so far as is known, he was not guilty
of directly opposing the war. He had made no seditious statements and
no incidents had occurred. In fact, he had tried to enlist in the navy but
was rejected because he had one glass eye.

Because of wild and irresponsible talk about disloyalty, the mayor
ordered the saloons closed on April 4, thus throwing a group of idle, half-
drunken men onto the streets. They began a search for Prager. When
they found him, "his shoes were stripped off and members of the mob
began pulling off his clothes, when someone produced an American flag.
It was wrapped around him and tied." In this condition, with only a flag
to cover him, he was dragged barefooted, stumbling through the streets.

At this point, the police rescued Prager and placed him in the city jail.
But the mob soon broke into the jail and took its victim out of town in
search of a convenient tree. This may have happened after the police
"insisted no violence be done inside the city limits." Prager was asked if
he were a German spy, and "if he had tried to blow up the Maryville
mine." One member of the mob was reported to have struck Prager on
the head and knocked him down. A participant in the mob action, Joseph Riegel, was quoted as saying, "All the time the crowd kept getting
more excited and angry. Someone shouted, 'Well if he won't come in
with anything, string him up.' A boy produced a handkerchief and his
hands were tied. I might have been the man who did the tying. I was
drunk, and because I had been in the army the crowd made me the big
man in the affair, and I guess I was sort of puffed over that." Before they
hanged Prager, he was allowed to write a note to his mother and father.
"Dear Parents:" he said, "I must this day, the fourth of April, 1918, die.
Please, my dear parents, pray for me. This is my last letter or testament.
Robert Paul." He was then given a few minutes to fall on his knees and
pray before members of the mob pulled him high in the air where he
gasped his last breath. As a report in the *New York Call* of April 16, 1918,
expressed it, "He was one, his pursuers were five hundred, who, after
baiting him to their heart's content, deliberately murdered him." The
New York Times of April 11 reported that his last request was to be
buried with an American flag over him.

At last the excesses of the super-patriots had reached such heights that
some people were jolted into realizing, for the first time, how serious mob
actions in the name of loyalty had become. That Prager had been guilty
of no crime, or of any overt acts of disloyalty, made the deed even more
dastardly. In referring to the case, Attorney General Gregory declared,
"From all the facts I have been able to gather concerning the lynching of
the man in Illinois, I doubt his having been guilty of any offense."

There was widespread condemnation of the lynching, even by those
who had previously spoken out most strongly against all aspects of dis-

loyalty. Theodore Roosevelt and William Howard Taft both immediately condemned the action. The most outspoken critic was Senator Sherman of Illinois. He referred to the mob and to city officials as follows: "The police followed this drunken mob to the edge of the city. . . . There are four policemen in that town to preserve the peace. That magnificent constabulary followed to the city limits; they said they had no jurisdiction beyond it; and the mob was allowed to wreak its bloody purpose upon the helpless victim." He also called the mayor a "poltroon" and a "renegade in public office."

The *New York Call* editorialized on April 16, 1918, "It is our national purpose to stand before the world as a clean and honorable nation. We do not want our Allies to be burdened with the necessity of apologizing for our Kultur." The Oklahoma City *Daily Oklahoman* printed a fine denunciation of mob law on April 22. It was a good article, but it was tardy—very tardy. On April 11, the *Chicago Herald* recommended "punishment of the guilty crew." The *Detroit Free Press* of April 6 carried a strong and forthright condemnation of mob lynchings. The *New York Times* said editorially that "a fouler wrong could hardly be done America." The editor declared that, in light of United States war aims, "we shall be denounced as a nation of odious hypocrites." The *Times* also called for punishment of those responsible.

Some papers, however, were quite reserved in their criticisms. This was probably because they did not want to take a position which might be interpreted as in any way lacking in patriotism. Their attitude, however, indicates a fundamental problem posed by modern nationalism. How can one safely attack an evil action when it is clothed in "patriotism"? It is quite apparent that many papers felt it could, and perhaps should, not be done. After the Prager lynching nationalists tried to lay the blame for mob actions on the victims themselves. Some elements of the press even seemed to approve the action. On April 12 the *Washington Post* commented, "In the East the public mind toward the war was much earlier divested of errors." Then it added, "In spite of excesses such as lynching, it is a healthful and wholesome awakening in the interior of the country."

Eventually a number of the leaders of the mob were indicted and tried. There was great difficulty in obtaining a jury, and the trial was a most unjudicial affair. Defendants wore red, white, and blue ribbons, and occasionally a band would play patriotic airs in the courthouse. The defense attorney's statement to the jury "was almost entirely a loyalty plea, mingled with an attack on the State for conducting the prosecution." The defense argued that Prager's lynching was a "patriotic murder" which served as a means of home protection. The jury returned the usual mob verdict of not guilty in twenty-five minutes. Those in the courtroom congratulated the defendants. There was cheering and hand-clapping, and one juryman shouted, "Well, I guess nobody can say we aren't loyal now." But he was wrong. The New York *Evening Post* of

June 3, 1918, said that the verdict was a "gross miscarriage of justice." Indeed, it was.

The sentiment of local patriots, however, was expressed in a story from Edwardsville, Illinois. It reported a feeling of "grim satisfaction" by the public in southern Illinois. Continuing, the account stated, "Having lynched an undesirable resident and escaped without unpleasant consequences, Madison County is ready for the next comer. Hanging is not an agreeable business and it may not be necessary to hang anybody else. That is entirely up to the other fellow. If a deserving victim should happen along there are other trees and plenty of unused rope." The "unhung traitors" idea had gained wide popularity and acceptance. On April 13, the *Seattle Union-Record* ran an editorial which stated ironically, "If you don't like your neighbor, shoot him! . . . Then declare he made seditious or pro-German statements and rely on the patriotism of the people to see that you are not punished. That is, in effect, the advice of the yellow press." After referring to certain local newspapers, the editorial in the *Union-Record* continued, "As a result of similar utterances we have had during the past few weeks a regular terror of tar and featherings, hangings, and even burnings of alleged traitors." Such was the spirit and action of early 1918.

Prager's hanging capped the climax of violence performed under the guise of patriotism. But even this ghastly incident did not bring people to their senses. It did not create a popular demand which might say in effect, mob law will no longer be tolerated. It did not end further patriotic excesses. Instances of violence in late April and early May of 1918 continued to be reported in all sections of the United States. When a Kentucky citizen later protested to President Wilson about "the persecution of a naturalized German-American in his town," a man who had bought war bonds liberally, Wilson commented to Tumulty, "I have no doubt that there are hundreds of cases like it."

The Prager affair, as well as the less violent actions by nationalists, seemed to call for vigorous action by the federal Government to protect innocent people against lawless and irresponsible mobs. Many moderate Americans, and even some of the super-patriots, objected and were publicly critical of current happenings. Also, stinging criticism of what was called American barbarism began coming from abroad. The German Government lodged an official protest through the Swiss legation, and even offered to pay Prager's funeral expenses. Needless to say, this offer was not accepted.

But President Wilson was distressingly slow in taking any forthright action. The Prager murder was discussed at the regular Cabinet meeting on the afternoon of April 5. Apparently, the President and his advisers decided to sidestep this touchy issue. The *New York Times* reported on April 6 that "from what was said after the meeting it was apparent that the President and his advisers decided that the federal Government had no warrant for interference." Speaking after the meeting, Attorney General Gregory said that it was a problem for Illinois to handle. To refuse to accept responsibility may have been an easy way out, but it did not satisfy a great many people.

On April 18 John Lord O'Brian of the Department of Justice prepared a memorandum which was sent to Wilson suggesting that some sort of statement should be issued by the Government "for the purpose of reassuring the people, quieting their apprehensions, and preventing so far as possible the spread of mob violence, evidence of which is now appearing in all parts of the country." Still Wilson held off. He did write on April 22 that he was "very deeply concerned" about the treatment of people "whose offense is merely one of opinion." Wilson added that he had "a very great passion for the principle that we must respect opinion even when it is hostile. . . ." But his silent concern did little good.

On June 11, a bulletin was issued by the Council of National Defense warning its local representatives against undertaking any repression unless they were "expressly requested or authorized by the . . . Department of Justice." It was not until July 26, after the "patriotic" jury in Illinois had proclaimed members of the mob innocent, and after other incidents had occurred, that Wilson finally spoke out. A few days earlier, he had asked Creel to prepare the way for his statement. "My only object," he told Creel, "is to fix the attention of the people on this protest of mine in the way that will give it the greatest possible emphasis." One observer stated that Wilson acted because of the "use made of the Prager case in the German Reichstag."

The President's statement said:

There have been many lynchings, and every one of them has been a blow at the heart of ordered law and humane justice. No man who loves America, no man who really cares for her fame and honor and character, or who is truly loyal to her institutions, can justify mob action while the courts of justice are open. . . .

We proudly claim to be the champions of democracy. If we really are, in deed and truth, let us see to it that we do not discredit our own. I say plainly that every American who takes part in the action of a mob or gives any sort of countenance is no true son of this great democracy, but its betrayer, and does more to discredit her by that single disloyalty to her standards of law and right, than the words of her statesmen or the sacrifices of her heroic boys in the trenches can do to make suffering peoples believe her to be their savior. How shall we commend democracy to the acceptance of other peoples if we disgrace our own by proving that it is, after all, no protection to the weak? Every mob contributes to German lies about the United States, what her most gifted liars cannot improve upon by the way of calumny. They can at least say that such things cannot happen in Germany except in times of revolution, when law is swept away!

I therefore very earnestly and solemnly beg that the Governors of all the States, the law officers of every community, and, above all, the men and women of every community . . . will co-operate . . . to make an end of this disgraceful evil.

The President spoke noble sentiments and, as usual, spoke them well. But his statement came too late to be very effective. Had he spoken out boldly a day or two after the Prager lynching, the weight of his words might have been felt. As it was, little was accomplished. It was only page seven news in the *New York Times*.

Referring to the Wilson proclamation, the *New Republic* commented:

The facts upon which the President's protest is based are notorious. Yet they meet with comparatively little reprobation or even notice either from the newspapers or from public speakers. There is no indication that the great majority of those people who do most to mould public opinion in this country are particularly shocked at the presence of mob violence and other evidences of collective moral disintegration.

A writer for the *New York Call* said on July 29, "The reaction of the press of our native von Bissings to the personal statement of the President in condemnation of lynching and terrorism is a sorry spectacle. Some papers have nothing to say in their editorial columns, while others come forward with a 'me too,' generally hedged with some 'ifs, buts, perhapses,' and other qualifications."

This condition, however, was by no means universal. The *New York Times* severely condemned the "mob mind" and expressed hope that the President's statement would help to curb the excesses of super-patriots. Yet even the *Times* praised the people's great patience and the "almost saintlike patience of the Government" in dealing with "disloyal agitators." Probably the *New Republic* was right in its judgment that leaders of public opinion were not especially "shocked at the presence of mob violence."

Thomas A. Bailey

Defeat in

the Senate

The quest to fix responsibility for the defeat of the Treaty of Versailles in the Senate has led to a large body of controversial literature. Historians have generally placed the blame on either Henry Cabot Lodge, a leading Republican senator and Chairman of the Senate Foreign Relations Committee, or on President Wilson. Thomas A. Bailey—a professor of history at Stanford University who has written on many aspects of the diplomatic history of the United States—has analyzed the course of the treaty in the Senate in a balanced, perceptive, and lively way. For him, the President is chiefly to blame, but he does not exonerate Lodge. In his view, both share the responsibility for the treaty's defeat, and both acted from motives less than lofty. [Reprinted

Blind partisanship, as much as any other single factor, ruined the League
of Nations in the United States. This is not to condemn any one individual or group of individuals; it is merely to state a fact which, in the
circumstances, was as inescapable as the law of gravitation.

The treaty was too much bound up with Wilson, and especially with
Wilson's League of Nations, to leave any room for hope that the issue
could escape the reefs of partisanship. One competent writer has estimated that four-fifths of the opposition to the League was nothing more
than unreasoning hatred of Wilson. This is probably an exaggeration,
but there can be no doubt that the Republican leaders, and many of the
Republican rank and file, hated the President with a consuming bitterness, and were prepared to stop at nothing to bring about his downfall
and at the same time (so they claimed) save the Republic.

The Republicans could not forgive Wilson for having beaten them in
1912, especially since his victory was their own fault. They could not
accustom themselves to the role of a minority party: this was contrary to
the natural order of things since 1861. They could not forgive Wilson for
having won again in 1916, by the narrowest of margins and with the
slogan, "He kept us out of war." It was in fact the first time an incumbent Democrat had been elected since the redoubtable Andrew Jackson,
in 1832.

The Republicans distrusted Wilson because he was a Southerner, with
Southerners in his Cabinet, and with long-lived Southern Democrats in
control of the Congressional committees. He was believed to be conspiring
to impoverish the North to the advantage of the South through the
income tax and other devices. The New York *Tribune* charged that
Wilson's internationalism was developed as a screen to cover his South-
ernism. William E. Dodd alleges that certain "eminent" Republicans
announced in his presence that it would have been better if the South
had won the Civil War, for "then we should have escaped Wilson."

Wilson believed that a President should lead, and he had stood over
Congress with a dictatorial rod. Worse than that, he had liberal ideas
about the tariff and trusts and income taxes, all of which notions were
anathema to Republican big business. Republican journals referred
angrily to the "crimes of Wilson"; and the oil magnate, Edward L.
Doheny, later to be besmeared with the Teapot Dome scandal, growled
that the President was a "college professor gone Bolshevik."

Bitterly though the Republicans reacted against Wilson's peacetime
leadership, their resentment increased when war came and Wilson ("Kaiser" Wilson) assumed the dictatorial powers that were lawfully his under
the Constitution. The Republicans could not reconcile themselves to the

fact, nor forgive themselves for it, that a Democrat was running the biggest of our wars up to that time. They cried out against huge expenditures of money, as if penny-pinching were in order when the fate of America was at stake; and their bitterness mounted to fury when, search though they did, they could find no real taint of scandal.

Wilson not only had run the war, but had kept prominent Republicans from winning glory and making political capital out of it. General Leonard Wood, a potential Republican President and a close friend of ex-President Theodore Roosevelt, was suddenly ordered away from the embarkation port and condemned to stay at home while the troops which he had trained went overseas. Colonel Theodore Roosevelt, who was regarded as the logical Republican nominee in 1920, almost got down on his knees before the hated Wilson, pleading for a chance to take a division of volunteers to France and inspirit the flagging Allied cause. Wilson austerely rebuffed him, thus visiting upon the graying Rough Rider the greatest disappointment of his life.

Wilson of course had good or at least plausible reasons for snubbing both Wood and Roosevelt; but the important point is that the Republicans neither forgot nor forgave. Roosevelt had once shown some friendliness to the idea of a league of nations, notably in his address accepting the Nobel Peace Prize. But when Wilson espoused the League, Roosevelt attacked it with all his unbridled vehemence. He literally plotted on his deathbed to defeat the yet unborn League of Nations.

The venom engendered by the Roosevelt-Wilson feud persisted, and gave strength to the foes of the League during those dark hours when it seemed as though theirs was a losing cause. Looking back through the mists of thirteen years, Mrs. Alice Roosevelt Longworth, the doughty Rough Rider's doughty daughter, could write, "How we did cherish and nourish our hatreds in those days!"

During the war, politics had been nominally "adjourned." Both partisanship and pro-Germanism took cover, but they were still very much alive. Now that the shooting had stopped, partisanship could flare forth with all the greater explosiveness for having been repressed.

Wilson, it must be conceded, played directly into the hands of the Republican partisans. Before going to Paris, he bluntly called upon the country for a Democratic Congress to uphold his policies; then, when the voters returned Republicans, he snubbed the Senate by refusing to consult with its leaders and by taking abroad a peace commission of five which contained no senators and only one Republican, a minor figure at that. Wilson was going to make a Wilsonian peace, a Democratic peace, with the glory unipartisan but with the responsibility partisan. All right, said the Republicans, that was a game that two could play.

Partisanship in some degree could not have been kept out of the death struggle over the treaty. Yet if Wilson had been more deferential to the Republicans, if he had honored them with prominent places in his councils, if he had accepted more of their ideas, he would no doubt have removed some of the sting. Certainly he would have given the Republicans less excuse for going before the country in a blaze of indignation crying that the President was playing politics with the treaty.

In short, the Republicans were forced to oppose the League, at least in unamended form, if for no other reason than that it was a Wilson League. As the Greenville (S.C.) *Piedmont* baldly put it, "The Senate's chief objection to the League idea is that Wilson is a Democrat." A few prominent Republicans, notably ex-President William Howard Taft, could rise above their dislike of Wilson and support the League with unflagging devotion. But such men were the exception. The Columbus *Ohio State Journal* whimsically remarked, "The attitude of most of us thoughtful Republicans seems to be that we're unalterably opposed to Article X, whether we know what's in it or not."

The high officials of both parties naturally considered their position on the League issue in the light of their political fortunes. The chairman of the Republican National Committee, Will H. Hays, was in constant touch with the party leaders, senatorial and otherwise, as to what attitude the Republicans should take. Should they accept the Wilson League? Should they strive to amend it slightly, or fundamentally? Or should they scrap the whole thing, as Senators Borah and Brandegee and Johnson were demanding? Would not the ringing cry of "Americanism versus internationalism" win the most votes in the end? The Republicans, in brief, were striving to find the winning issue; the Democrats, to maintain one.

Neither party ever lost sight of the relation of the League to the Presidential election of 1920. The Republicans were confident that on domestic issues alone they could defeat any possible Democratic candidate: they had merely to capitalize on war-weariness and a desire to get back to "normalcy." But if Wilson should shove his grandiose scheme through the Senate, his increased prestige would be dangerous. So overshadowing a world figure might he become that he would perhaps dictate a Democratic successor—possibly his son-in-law, William G. McAdoo.

Even more disquieting was another possibility. Once the League was approved, would it not be logical that Wilson should stay in office at least another term to see that it got off to a proper start? The two-term tradition was still strong, but world reorganization was a grave responsibility. Wilson might consent to run by persuading himself that he was the "indispensable man." Worse than that, he might be able to persuade the voters that he was the "indispensable man." The night-mare of four more years of Wilsonism caused cold chills to run down Republican spines.

The hated professor might even aspire to head the League of Nations and become president of the world. Possibly this was his desire. Irwin H. ("Ike") Hoover, the White House usher, referring to the period shortly after Wilson's return from Europe, recalls that the President once turned to him and asked if he would like to go back to Geneva. . . .

Closely associated with the "irreconcilables," at least in the public mind, was the leader of the "strong reservationists," Henry Cabot Lodge. He was so important in the treaty fight that one might almost say he was a group in himself.

Lodge was slender, narrow-shouldered, and aristocratically bewhiskered. Sprung from the stony soil of Massachusetts, and nurtured by the New England aristocracy, he fell heir to all the advantages of wealth, education, culture, travel, and social position. Educated at Harvard University, where he took the degree of Ph.D. in history, Dr. Lodge early undertook a literary career. From his pen poured a succession of books, chiefly on historical subjects, some of which had their brief day, but none of which has lived or has deserved to live. He also revealed a flair for politics, and by faithful party service he secured a strangle hold on his seat in the Senate, and became chairman of the Senate Committee on Foreign Relations. Cold, cautious, aloof, aristocratic as he was, one wonders at the secret of his appeal to the masses.

For many years Dr. Lodge enjoyed the distinction of being "the scholar in politics." Then came Professor Wilson, whose political and scholarly attainments eclipsed those of Lodge, and the senator's flattering sobriquet dropped into disuse. This was no doubt displeasing to the learned solon.

All of Lodge's forbears had reached America before the Revolutionary War; all of Wilson's had come well after the establishment of the Republic. Lodge took naturally to nationalism; Wilson more naturally to internationalism—possibly as a result, in part, of his heredity.

Yet Lodge, before the arrival of Wilson on the scene, had shown signs of broadening horizons, as had other leaders of the traditionally expansionist and imperialistic Republican party. He had warmly supported his bosom friend, "dear Theodore" Roosevelt, in the various international adventures upon which the brandisher of the Big Stick embarked. He had made speeches in favor of some kind of international organization for peace, and in 1915 had even come out for *a* league of nations. But shortly thereafter Wilson began to advocate *the* League, and Lodge found himself in the other camp. The senator in his apologia strongly denies that this was anything but mental growth. Chronology and circumstance suggest that it was not disassociated from the feud with Wilson.

Contrary to a general misconception, Lodge was not an isolationist of the Borah or Johnson stripe. On the eve of the Peace Conference he was willing to go even further than Wilson in making the United States a part-guarantor of the European settlement. He said repeatedly that, League or no League, the world could count on us again to spring to the defense of Western civilization against ruthless aggression.

The whole bent of Lodge's thinking had naturally predisposed him to entertain kindly thoughts toward the Covenant that Wilson brought back from Paris. But it was a Democratic League, from which the Democrats could make political capital, and all the partisan instincts of the senator rose to the surface.

Above all things Lodge was a partisan, a narrow and bitter partisan, who believed that the Republican party was the embodiment of all the virtues. In 1914 he had made an eloquent speech about politics stopping "at the water's edge"; but this was pure rhetoric. He probably would have denied that he would basely subordinate the interests of his country to those of his party, but so ingrained was his Republicanism that he did not find it difficult to convince himself that the interests of both were identical. With him party regularity was a religion.

Lodge realized as clearly as anyone that it would be politically unwise for the Republicans to permit Wilson and his Democratic following to garner all the glory from the League. The Republicans must be allowed to add something to it, just enough to pose as co-authors of the pact.

With disarming candor, Lodge outlines in his posthumous book the strategy which he employed. He would load the treaty down with Republican reservations, and in this way "Americanize" or "Republicanize" the document, thus safeguarding both the country and the party. If Wilson accepted the Lodge reservations, then the Republicans would be sharers of the glory; if he did not, then the onus for rejecting the entire pact would be on the President's shoulders, not on those of the Republicans. Either way the Republican party could make political capital.

When the corpse of the treaty was finally dragged from the senatorial arena, the friends of international cooperation pointed the finger of accusation at Lodge, and since then have kept it unwaveringly there.

This is a gross oversimplification. The struggle was exceedingly complex; there were all shades of opinion; there were varying and conflicting motives; there were currents and crosscurrents. To say that one senator alone killed Cock Robin is to betray obtuseness or mental inertia.

So poisonous were the hatreds stirred up by Lodge that his position has seldom been viewed in proper perspective. He was chairman of the Foreign Relations Committee. He was majority leader, not because of personal charm, but because men respected his skill as a party manager and parliamentarian. His speeches were able, dignified, and usually on a high plane. His two-hour condemnation of the League, on August 12, 1919, was delivered at a time when the galleries were crowded with marines who had returned from Château-Thierry. The unprecedented roar that greeted his peroration lasted for three minutes, and sounded like the ovation accorded the hometown hero who knocks the ball into the right-field bleachers.

Lodge's responsibilities were heavy and conflicting. He was a foremost defender of senatorial prerogative. He was leader of the party in the Senate and the official spokesman for the various factions within the party. His immediate task was twofold: first, to propose and carry through a specific program of reservations; second, to keep the party ranks intact, and prevent any such schism as had developed in 1912. His primary duty, as he conceived it, was not to unite the world but to unite the party.

The Massachusetts senator was in the plight of one attempting to ride three horses trying to go in three different directions. The body of the Republican senators—the "strong reservationists"—were not too difficult to manage; they were going down the middle of the track. But on one side the dozen "mild reservationists" were momentarily threatening to coalesce with the Democrats. On the other side the "bitter-enders" were threatening to bolt the party completely, or go over to the Democrats and vote through reservations objectionable to Lodge. At one time the Massachusetts senator complained that the "irreconcilables" were addressing him in language which "no man of my age should be obliged to hear."

While Lodge was trying to curb the three horses, he had to keep closely in touch with the party managers outside the Senate so that the strategy of the campaign of 1920 could be carefully mapped. Above all, he had to restrain his personal dislike of Wilson for fear that he would appear to be a "sorehead." It has been well said that Lodge had "a hard enough time keeping his temper without stopping to consult his conscience."

The bitterness of feeling between Lodge and Wilson was intense and was perhaps the most formidable single barrier in the way of compromise.

The two men simply rubbed each other the wrong way. Lodge insists that his distrust of Wilson was wholly on public grounds, and began with the administration's alleged misconduct of relations with Mexico. The feud broke out into the open in 1916, when Lodge accused Wilson of suppressing certain vital information regarding the *Lusitania* negotiations. Wilson, in a not altogether candid reply, delicately branded the senator a liar, and from then on the breach widened.

Colonel Bonsal talked with Lodge about the League Covenant in November, 1919. "As an English production it does not rank high," said Lodge, perhaps half jokingly. "It might get by at Princeton but certainly not at Harvard." Colonel House observed at Paris that President Wilson "bristled" whenever Lodge's name was mentioned. On the few occasions when the President and the senator had to meet, the interchanges were severely formal, and the atmosphere could seemingly be cut with a knife.

Both the senator and the President were bitter partisans, lasting haters. In life, Lodge outwardly restrained his innermost feelings, at least in public. But he forgot about the Old Testament patriarch who expressed the desire that his "adversary had written a book." The senator prepared an elaborate, posthumously published apology, in which his embittered spirit rose from the grave to reveal what he had previously been at pains to conceal.

"I never had the slightest personal hostility to Mr. Wilson," writes

Lodge. He goes on to say that Wilson was not a true scholar at all, and as proof stresses the fact that, unlike Lodge, the Princeton professor did not stud his speeches with classical allusions—which any sterile wit may crib from compilations of quotations.

The Senator finally convicts Wilson of not having been a scholar, and perhaps not even an educated man, when he gleefully reveals that on the one occasion when he found the Princetonian using a classical reference, it was used incorrectly. Wilson committed the terrible error of having Hercules, rather than Antaeus, renew his strength as he touched Mother Earth.

This does not prove that Wilson was unscholarly. All it proves is that Lodge had a jealous and petty spirit. . .

Is it true that the invalid in the White House really strangled the treaty to death with his own enfeebled hands?

It is seldom that statesmen have a second chance—a second guess. They decide on a course of action, and the swift current of events bears them downstream from the starting point. Only rarely does the stream reverse itself and carry them back.

In November, Wilson had decided that he wanted deadlock, because he reasoned that deadlock would arouse public opinion and force the Senate to do his bidding. The tidal wave of public opinion did surge in, and Wilson got his second chance. But he threw it away, first by spurning compromise (except on his terms), and then by spurning the Lodge reservations.

There had been much more justification for Wilson's course in November than in March. In November he was sick, secluded, was fed censored news, and was convinced by Hitchcock that the strategy of deadlock was sound. In March, he was much improved in health, far less secluded, more in touch with the press and with the currents of opinion, though probably still not enough. He consulted even less with the Senate, presumably because he had made up his mind in advance to oppose the Lodge reservations. In November, there was a fair possibility of reconsiderations; in March, it was clear that the only possibility lay in making the League an issue in the coming campaign. Wilson, with his broad knowledge of government and politics, should have seen that this hope was largely if not completely illusory. Perhaps he would have seen it had he not been blinded by his feeling for Lodge.

The evidence is convincing that Wilson wanted the issue cast into the hurly-burly of politics. He could not accept Lodge's terms; Lodge would not accept his terms. The only possible chance of beating the senator— and this was slim indeed—was to win a resounding mandate in 1920.

Yet this strategy, as already noted, meant further delay. At Paris, the feeling at times had been, "Better a bad treaty today than a good treaty four months hence." Europe was still in chaos, and increasingly in need of America's helping hand. Well might the Europeans cry, "Better a treaty with the Lodge reservations today than a probable treaty without reservations after the election." Or as Dr. Frank Crane wrote in *Current Opinion,* "It is vastly more needful that some sort of League be formed, *any sort,* than that it be formed *perfectly.*" (Italics Crane's.)

Yet Wilson, for the reasons indicated, could not see all this clearly. Four days after the fatal vote he wrote Hitchcock, praising him for having done all in his power to protect the honor of the nation and the peace of the world against the Republican majority.

Mrs. Wilson, no doubt reflecting her husband's views, later wrote, "My conviction is that Mr. Lodge put the world back fifty years, and that at his door lies the wreckage of human hopes and the peril to human lives that afflict mankind today."

To the very end Wilson was a fighter. When the Scotch-Irish in him became aroused, he would nail his colors to the mast. He said in 1916 that he was "playing for the verdict of mankind." His conception of duty as he saw it was overpowering. He once remarked that if he were a judge, and it became his duty to sentence his own brother to the gallows, he would do so—and afterwards die of a broken heart.

It is well to have principles; it is well to have a noble conception of duty. But Wilson, as he became warmed up in a fight, tended to get things out of focus and to lose a proper sense of values.

The basic issue in 1920 was the Hitchcock reservations or the Lodge reservations. Wilson accepted those of Hitchcock while rejecting those of Lodge, which, he said, completely nullified the treaty and betrayed his promises to the Allies and to the American dead.

This, as we have seen, was a gross exaggeration. Minds no less acute than Wilson's, and less clouded with sickness and pride, denied that the Lodge reservations completely nullified the treaty. To the man in the street—in so far as he gave the dispute thought—there was little discernible difference between the two sets of reservations. How could one decry statements which merely reaffirmed the basic principles of the Constitution and of our foreign policy? To a vast number of Americans the Lodge reservations, far from nullifying the treaty, actually improved it. This was so apparent to even the most loyal Democrats in the Senate that Wilson could barely keep them in line.

In the final analysis the treaty was slain in the house of its friends rather than in the house of its enemies. In the final analysis it was not the two-thirds rule, or the "irreconcilables," or Lodge, or the "strong" and "mild reservationists," but Wilson and his docile following who delivered the fatal stab. If the President had been permitted to vote he would have sided with Borah, Brandegee, Johnson, and the other "bitter-enders"— though for entirely different reasons.

Wilson had said that the reservation to Article X was a knife thrust at the heart of the Covenant. Ironically, he parried this knife thrust, and stuck his own dagger, not into the heart of the Covenant, but into the entire treaty.

This was the supreme act of infanticide. With his own sickly hands Wilson slew his own brain child—or the one to which he had contributed so much.

This was the supreme paradox. He who had forced the Allies to write the League into the treaty, unwrote it; he who had done more than any other man to make the Covenant, unmade it—at least so far as America was concerned. And by his action, he contributed powerfully to the ultimate undoing of the League, and with it the high hopes of himself and mankind for an organization to prevent World War II.

The preceding dogmatic observations are of course qualified by the phrase, "in the last analysis."

Many elements enter into a log jam. Among them are the width of the stream, the depth of the stream, the swiftness of the current, the presence of boulders, the size of the logs, and the absence of enough lumberjacks. No one of these factors can be solely responsible for the pile-up.

Many elements entered into the legislative log jam of March, 1920. Among them were isolationism, partisanship, senatorial prerogative, confusion, apathy, personal pride, and private feuds. No one of them was solely responsible for the pile-up. *But as the pile-up finally developed, there was only one lumberjack who could break it, and that was Woodrow Wilson.* If at any time before the final vote he had told the Senate Democrats to support the treaty with the Lodge reservations, or even if he had merely told them that they were on their own, the pact would almost certainly have been approved. So "in the last analysis" the primary responsibility for the failure in March rested with Wilson.

What about Lodge? If the treaty would have passed by Wilson's surrendering, is it not equally true that it would have passed by Lodge's surrendering?

The answer is probably "Yes," but the important point is that Lodge had far less responsibility for getting the treaty through than Wilson. If Lodge had yielded, he probably would have created a schism within his ranks. His ultimate responsibility was to keep the party from breaking to pieces, and in this he succeeded. Wilson's ultimate responsibility was to get the treaty ratified, and in this he failed. With Lodge, as with any truly partisan leader, the party comes before country; with the President the country should come before party, though unhappily it often does not.

It is possible that Wilson saw all this—but not clearly enough. He might have been willing to compromise if his adversary had been any other than Lodge. But so bitter was the feeling between the two men that Wilson, rather than give way, grasped at the straw of the election of 1920.

Lodge did not like Wilson either, but he made more of a show of compromising than the President. He actually supported and drove through amendments to his original reservations which were in line with Wilson's wishes, and he probably would have gone further had the "irreconcilables" not been on his back. He fought the crippling Irish reservation, as well as others supported by the "bitter-enders." Finally, he gave the Democrats a fair chance to reconsider their vote and get on the bandwagon, but they spurned it.

If Lodge's words mean anything, and if his actions were not those of a monstrous hypocrite, he actually tried to get the treaty through with his reservations. When he found that he could not, he washed his hands of the whole business in disgust.

The charge is frequently made that, if Wilson had yielded to his adversary, Lodge would have gleefully piled on more reservations until Wilson, further humiliated, would have had to throw out the whole thing.

The strongest evidence for this view is a circumstantial story which Secretary Houston relates. During a Cabinet meeting Wilson was called to the telephone, and agreed to make certain concessions agreeable to Lodge. Before adjournment the telephone rang again, and word came that Lodge would not adhere to his original proposal.

This story is highly improbable, because Wilson attended no Cabinet meetings between September 2, 1919, and April 13, 1920. By the latter date, all serious attempts at compromise had been dropped; by the earlier date the treaty was still before the Senate committee, and the Lodge reservations, though in an embryonic stage, were yet unborn. But, even if the story is true, it merely proves that Lodge veered about, as he frequently did under "irreconcilable" pressure.

In March, as in November, all Wilson had to do was to send over Postmaster General Burleson to the Senate a few minutes before the final vote with the quiet word that the Democrats were to vote "Yea." The treaty would then have passed with the Lodge reservations, and Lodge could hardly have dared incur for himself or his party the odium of moving to reconsider for the purpose of screwing on more reservations. Had he tried to do so, the "mild reservationists" almost certainly would have blocked him.

A few days after the disastrous final vote, Wilson's only comment to Tumulty was, "They have shamed us in the eyes of the world." If his previous words said what he really meant, he was hardly more shamed by the defeat of the treaty than by the addition of the Lodge reservations. In his eyes it all amounted to the same thing.

If the treaty had passed, would the President have been willing to go through with the exchange of ratifications? Would he not have pocketed it, as he threatened to do prior to the November vote?

Again, if Wilson's words may be taken at their face value, this is what he would have done. He had not backed down from his pre-November position. His Jackson Day message and his letter to Hitchcock made it unmistakably clear that he preferred the uncertainties of a political campaign to the certainties of ratification with the Lodge reservations. The addition of the indefensible Irish reservation provided even stronger justification for pocketing the entire pact.

It is probable that some of the loyal Democrats voted as they did partly because they were convinced that Wilson was going to pigeonhole the treaty anyhow. From their point of view it was better that the odium for defeat should seemingly rest on Lodge rather than on their President. It also seems clear that Wilson preferred, as in November, to have the blood of the treaty on the Senate doorstep rather than on his. As he wrote to Secretary Colby, on April 2, 1920, the slain pact lay heavily on the consciences of those who had stabbed it, and he was quite willing to have it lie there until those consciences were either awakened or crushed.

Yet it is one thing to say, just before Senate action, "I will pocket the treaty." It is another, after the pact is approved and sent to the White House, to assume this tremendous responsibility. The eyes of the world are upon the President; he is the only man keeping the nation out of the peace which it so urgently needs; he is the one man standing in the way of the rehabilitation which the world so desperately demands. Public pressure to ratify in such a case would be enormous—probably irresistible.

Some years later Senator Hitchcock said that in the event of senatorial approval Wilson would possibly have waited for the November election. If he had won, he would have worked for the removal of the Lodge reservations; if he had lost, then the compulsion to go through with ratification would have become overpowering. By November more than six months would have passed, and by that time Wilson might have developed a saner perspective.

But this is all speculation. Wilson gave orders that the treaty was to be killed in the Senate chamber. And there it died.

Rarely in American history has contemporary literature so sharply portrayed the mood of a period as in the 1920s. F. Scott Fitzgerald, Ernest Hemingway, John Dos Passos, E. E. Cummings, Sinclair Lewis, and H. L. Mencken, to name only the most prominent, caught the accents and nuances of the era, reflected its hopes and frustrations, and satirized its foibles and weaknesses in superb fashion.

The mood was disillusionment, disenchantment, and futility. The war had left an ineradicable mark on the "lost generation." Young people felt betrayed and duped. Their elders had led them into a war to save the world for democracy, but the war had turned out to be just another old-fashioned imperialist one—simply a contest between two alliances, as Reinhold Niebuhr said. Out of the Great Crusade had come not a rebirth of liberalism and a reinvigoration of democracy and Progressivism but repression and conservatism. Thus a generation of cynics came into being.

9

THE 1920s IN

LITERATURE

The feeling was strong in the '20s that elders could never again be depended upon for guidance; it was but a short and logical step to a revolt against and a rejection of all authority and tradition. By the same reasoning, the old and hallowed middle-class virtues were assailed and the Victorian amenities of the pre-war age were scorned. Skepticism and bitterness became the hallmark of the generation; idealism was spurned. Pious mouthings of ministers as well as noble utterances of patriots were ridiculed. "The spiritual affirmation had fallen so low," said Ludwig Lewisohn, "that every noble word was soiled and every idealistic notion discredited. Who will dare to use, for instance, the word 'service'?" Ernest Hemingway had his hero in *A Farewell to Arms* remark, "I am always embarrassed by the words 'sacred,' 'glorious,' 'sacrifice.' . . ." Long-standing heroes of the American saga such as Emerson and Thoreau were discredited while philosophers like Nietzsche were idolized. The beliefs and teachings of the New England liberals did not conform to the realities of the new age. Instead, the dour prophecies of the critics of middle-class democracy seemed fulfilled.

The "lost generation" had had enough of saving worlds and of building new societies. It was, as Fitzgerald noted, tired of great causes. It wanted no more of the tenseness and intellectualism of a Woodrow Wilson; instead, it welcomed the simple, warm, congenial Warren G. Harding with his unencumbered mind and his soothing injunction, "America's present need is not heroics but healing, not nostrums but normalcy, not revolution but restoration . . . not surgery but serenity." It gladly accepted his calm, unruffled, and taciturn successor, Calvin Coolidge.

America in the '20s was interested in the pursuit of pleasure. The decade called variously the Roaring Twenties, the Jazz Age, the Era of

Wonderful Nonsense, the Ten-Year-Long Weekend Party, and the Gaud-
iest Spree in History was heavily hedonistic. It was the era of the flapper,
bath-tub gin, speakeasies, the hip-flask, the short skirt, the rolled-down
hose, and bobbed hair. It was the age of the gay, the frivolous, the
carefree. Repressions and inhibitions were cast off and sexual freedom
was enshrined. Petting parties and companionate and trial marriages
became accepted practices. Sigmund Freud was the rage. Said one university president, "Rolled-down hose and low-cut gowns and short skirts
are born of the devil and his angels and are carrying the present and
future generations to chaos and destruction." Edna St. Vincent Millay's
famous quatrain "My Candle Burns at Both Ends" put it more poet-
ically.

Another major quest of the '20s was material well-being, and the successful businessman took his place alongside Freud as a symbol of the
decade. In the lush post-war economy, men were making money by specu-
lating in the ever spiraling stock market and by selling the ever increasing output of the American industrial machine. With the boosting of
American products by novel and imaginative techniques, the salesman
and business organizer came in for a new kind of glorification. In 1925
Bruce Barton published *The Man Nobody Knows,* an account of Jesus as
a business executive who molded twelve men into an efficient organization to sell Christianity. It became at once a best seller. Prosperity, indeed, seemed to be a permanent and eternal quality of American life.
People easily accepted Herbert Hoover's observation, "We in America
are nearer to the final triumph over poverty than ever before in the
history of any land."

All these attitudes and views of the decade of the '20s were reflected in
the novels, essays, and biographies written at the time. The literary output possessed certain well-defined, general characteristics. It was satiric,
iconoclastic, and irreverent. It reveled in the unorthodox and the bizarre.
It delighted in shocking Aunt Jane, as J. B. Priestley noted. It was realistic, frank, and bold, never mawkish. It refused to follow the genteel
authors who "purred sexless nothings in books read exclusively by respectable spinsters." It preferred, as Pierre Coalfleet, the Canadian critic,
noted, words that kicked and rhythm that jerked, much as Americans of
the time preferred jazz to chamber music and cocktails to wine. Although
many of these tendencies were not new in the '20s and had been apparent
before the war, they were more fully developed and reached their apogee
in the period.

John Dos Passos

The Backwash of

Our First Crusade

A number of sensitive young men who had been deeply affected by the First World War wrote novels and stories about it and about the decade that followed it. One of the most successful and eloquent of those writers was John Dos Passos. Born in Chicago in 1896 and educated at Harvard, where he graduated cum laude *in 1916, Dos Passos became a major literary figure in the 1920s. After returning from service in France as a private in the U.S. Medical Corps, he wrote* Three Soldiers *(1921), one of the first novels to protest against the war and to debunk the glory that many had associated with the fighting of that "first crusade." His other major works of the 1920s and '30s—*Manhattan Transfer *(1925) and the trilogy* U.S.A. *(1930–1936) —presented panoramas of American life at various levels of society; in fact, society has been called the hero of these novels. They were written as a kind of contemporary history, with literary skill and originality, and with a concern for detail and accuracy.*

Although in later years Dos Passos' political views shifted far to the right, his intense interest in social injustice and the underdog led him, in the '20s, into left-wing movements. In 1926 he helped to found the magazine The New Masses; *he served on its executive board and was a frequent contributor to it until the early 1930s. He also participated actively in the protests against the treatment of two Italian immigrants, Nicola Sacco and Bartolomeo Vanzetti, who were jailed for murder in Massachusetts in 1920. In June 1927—two months before Sacco and Vanzetti were executed—Dos Passos published in* The New Masses *a critical article on the case. This article appears below, along with a prologue and epilogue written in 1956 when the article was reprinted in a collection of Dos Passos' writings. The selection illustrates some of the main qualities of his work of the '20s: it rings out in protest; it deals with historical detail; and it shows a firm grasp of the social problems of his time. [*"The Backwash of Our First Crusade," *in* The Theme Is Freedom *by John Dos Passos (New York: Dodd, Mead & Company, 1956). Copyright by John Dos Passos. Reprinted by permission of the author.]*

[1956] It's hard to overestimate the revulsion wrought by the first world war in the minds of a generation that had grown up in the years of comparative freedom and comparative peace that opened the century. It's hard to remember in the middle fifties today that in those years what little military service there was in America was voluntary, that taxes were infinitesimal, that if you could scrape up the price of a ticket you could travel anywhere in the world except through Russia and Turkey, without saying boo to a bureaucrat. If you wanted to take a job it was nobody's business but yours and the boss's. Of course, as the labor people were busily pointing out, if you worked in a sweat shop for a pittance and happened to starve to death in the process it was nobody's business either. When Woodrow Wilson led the country into the European war, however little we approved this reversal of American tradition, most of us just out of college were crazy to see what war was like. We experienced to the full the intoxication of the great conflagration, though those of us who served as enlisted men could hardly be expected to take kindly to soldiering, to the caste system which made officers a superior breed or to the stagnation and opportunism of military bureaucracy. Waste of time, waste of money, waste of lives, waste of youth. We came home with the horrors. We had to blame somebody.

The reformers we admired, the Bull Moose people, the Progressives from Wisconsin, Eugene V. Debs and the old time Populists had tended to blame everything that went wrong on malefactors of great wealth. Capitalism was the bogey that was destroying civilization. Cut the businessman's profits we said. Production for use. We thrilled to the word cooperative. Industrial democracy was the refrain of our song. In Europe we had picked up some of the slogans of Marxists and syndicalists. We agreed with them that democratic self-government had sold out to capital. Capitalism was the sin that had caused the war; only the working class was free from crime.

Most of us had been brought up in easy circumstances. If we were enlisted men in the army we found ourselves suddenly instead of top dog, bottom dog. An enlightening experience, but we couldn't help some cries of pain. We came home with the feeling that bottom dog must be boss. We must restore selfgovernment at home. If the people had had their way none of these disasters would have happened.

Greenwich Village met us at the dock. American Bohemia was in revolt against Main Street, against the power of money, against Victorian morals. Freedom was the theme. Freedom from hard collars, from the decalogue, from parental admonitions. For Greenwich Village art and letters formed an exclusive cult. The businessman could never understand. It was part of the worldwide revolt of artists and would be artists and thinkers and would be thinkers against a society where most of the rewards went to people skillful in the manipulation of money. The would be artists and writers felt out of it. The revolt of Bohemia was the last eddy in the ebb of the romantic flood that had flowed in various great waves through the literature of nineteenth century Europe. When artists and writers found it hard to make themselves a niche in industrial society they repudiated the whole business. Greenwich Village was their refuge, the free commune of Montmartre on American soil. *Les bourgeois à la lanterne.*

Greenwich Village wanted freedom and so did the working class. Only the people who worked in factories wanted freedom from certain very definite things, especially from low pay and bad conditions of work. They wanted to be treated as first class citizens the way businessmen were. Greenwich Villagers, mostly the sons and daughters of professional people, clergymen and lawyers and doctors, felt a sudden kinship with the working class. Of all strata of society only the artists and writers and the people who worked with their hands were pure. Together they would overturn the businessman and become top dog themselves. From the alliance between the trade unions and Greenwich Village the American radical was born.

The war had left an aftermath of ruin. Dislocated populations were starving and sick. The apocalyptic vision of capitalism's collapse that had haunted the working people of Europe was coming true. Revolution was the cure. Only a complete new order could bring health and cleanness back into the world. It was ordained by the march of progress. Only the bankers and industrialists and the old feudal hierarchies stood in the way of the millennium. In Russia the soviets had seized power. To the artists and writers of Greenwich Village the soviets were New England town meeting on a larger scale. Selfgovernment come to life again. Through the soviets the people who did the work of the world would conduct their own affairs. War was ruining civilization. Everywhere the plain people wanted peace. Only the bankers and businessmen had profited by the war. Merchants of death. Down with the bankers and businessmen. With the working class in power, peace would be assured.

The American businessman met the failure of Woodrow Wilson's war to end war in two ways. He subscribed liberally to funds raised for the relief of the starving and the dispossessed abroad. For the first time relief became a career. At home he tried to root up discontent by force. Slackers and pacifists were hounded by vigilantes. The IWW was stamped out by the courts. Foreign agitators were deported by the boatload. Where Greenwich Village saw white the businessman saw black. After the radicals were suppressed new era financing would heal all wounds. Everybody would make a million on the stock exchange. Henry Ford had discovered that the wage earner was a consumer. Publicity began to be the national industry of the twenties. Instead of the full dinner pail, two chickens in every pot became the slogan; two cars in every garage.

Still even for Greenwich Villagers jobs were plentiful. In spite of the great literature of consent presided over by Lorimer's *Saturday Evening Post* the country was showing a certain taste for the literature of dissent. The twenties proved a golden age for the young people of the typewriter and the pen.

Dutifully we tried to throw our weight behind the working man's struggle to organize trade unions. In the meetings of strikers we saw new organs of selfgovernment. The class war must be reported. The old *Masses* had gone under in the massive wartime suppression of dissenting opinions. To report the class war we launched the *New Masses*. I forget who put up the money. Money was easy in those days. . . .

Class conformity was not in my mind when I helped revive the old

Masses. We wanted to raise a standard to which, in Washington's words, "the wise and good might repair." Most of us could hardly have been called Marxists. I hated classification the way the devil hates holy water. We radicals didn't all think alike. Damned if we would. Already an argument was on between the heretics like myself and the convinced militants of the gospel of Marx. It's amusing to remember that in those carefree days a Communist party-member and an anarcho-syndicalist and even some sad dog of a capitalist who believed in laissez faire could sit at the same table and drink beer together and lay their thoughts on the line. It wasn't that you respected the other fellow's opinions exactly, but you admitted his right to remain alive. Needless to say, this happy state didn't last very long. The right of a dissenter to remain alive has tended to go down the drain along with the other civil rights of the old order. . . .

The Marxists who are so skillful in the detection and the isolation of heresies used to inveigh against one particular heresy that pleased me particularly. They called it American exceptionalism. During these years of mounting protest against the way things were going in America that label was my refuge. It enabled me to join in the protests of the various breeds of Marxists who were being more and more effectively regimented by the Communist Party without giving up my own particular point of view. I could join my voice to theirs in the outcry against the wave of repression which culminated in the Sacco-Vanzetti case, whereby the great industrial manufacturers were able to use the machinery of the courts and the police power to harass every effort to organize working people into trade unions, without giving up the automatic responses of the plain American patriotism I'd been raised in. If we were going to bring about a revolution in America it must be an American revolution.

The year 1927 turned out to be one of protest meetings. It was a year of battle for the lives of Sacco and Vanzetti. Here I saw white where other good men saw black. I still think we were right, though it was a strange experience a couple of years ago to read a set of interviews by a reporter for the New Bedford paper with the surviving jurors that sat on the case. They were still convinced of Sacco's and Vanzetti's guilt.

Any man, I suppose, is capable of any crime, but having talked to Sacco and Vanzetti themselves it's impossible for me to believe they could have committed that particular crime. Oh Pilate, Pilate how sharp was your question.

". . . To this end was I born, and for this cause came I into the world, that I should bear witness unto the truth." . . . Pilate saith unto him, "What is the truth?"

It was in trying to help the Sacco-Vanzetti Defense Committee that I first came into personal touch with men of the anarchist faith. I found them to be simple and truthful. They were fanatics of course but there was humanity in their fanaticism. I never found among them that Marxist stirring up of envy, hatred and malice that corrodes the character of men and women. The anarchists had extravagant ideas but most of them seemed to me generous, selfsacrificing, warmhearted, really good people.

[1926–27] The evening of May 5, 1920, Nicola Sacco, an Italian, working as edger in a shoe factory, and Bartolomeo Vanzetti, also an Italian, a fishpeddler, were arrested in a streetcar in Brockton, Massachusetts. The two men were known as radicals and were active in Italian working class organizations.

A couple of weeks before, the afternoon of April 15, a peculiarly impudent and brutal crime had been committed in South Braintree, a nearby town, the climax of a long series of holdups and burglaries. Bandits after shooting down a paymaster and his guard in the center of the town had escaped in a Buick touring car with over $15,000 in cash. It was generally rumored that the bandits were Italians. The police had made a great fuss but found no clue to the identity of the murderers. Public feeling was bitter and critical. A victim had to be found. To prove the murderers to have been reds would please everybody. After a stormy trial they were convicted of murder in the first degree. Sentence was stayed by a series of defense motions for a new trial.

The most important new evidence brought forward by these motions consisted of a series of affidavits to the effect that operatives of the Department of Justice were active in the trial, and that lacking evidence on which to deport Sacco and Vanzetti as radicals, they helped in the frameup by which they were convicted as murderers.

"They were bad actors anyway and got what was coming to them," one detective was quoted as saying.

Another hearing of a motion for a new trial. Six have been denied so far. Sacco and Vanzetti have been six years in jail. This time there are no guards with riotguns, no state troopers riding round the courthouse. No excitement of any sort. Everyone has forgotten the great days of the Red Conspiracy, the passion to sustain law and order against the wave of radicalism, against foreigners, and the "moral rats gnawing at the foundations of the commonwealth" that Attorney General Palmer spoke of so eloquently. In this court there are no prisoners in a cage, no hysterical witnesses, no credulous jury under the sign of the screaming eagle. Quiet, dignity; almost like a class in lawschool. The case has been abstracted into a sort of mathematics. Only the lawyers for the defense and for the prosecution, Ranney from the Commonwealth's Attorney's office, Thompson and Ehrmann for the defense, two small tables of newspapermen, on the benches a few Italians, some professional liberals and radicals, plainclothesmen with rumpsteak faces occupying the end seats.

The court attendants make everybody get up. The judge comes in on the heels of a man in a blue uniform. Judge Thayer is a very small man with a little gray lined shingle face, nose glasses tilting out at the top across a sudden little hawknose. He walks with a firm bustling tread. The black gown that gives him the power of life and death (the gown of majesty of the blind goddess the law) sticks out a little behind. Another attendant walks after him. The judge climbs up to his high square desk. The judge speaks. His voice crackles dryly as old papers.

Affidavits, affidavits read alternately by counsel in the stillness of the yellowvarnished courtroom. Gradually as the reading goes on the courtroom shrinks. Tragic figures of men and women grow huge like shadows cast by a lantern on a wall; the courtroom becomes a tiny pinhole through which to see a world of huge trampling forces in conflict.

First it's the story of the life of Celestino Madeiros, a poor Portuguese boy brought up in New Bedford. He learned Americanism all right, he suffered from no encumbering ideas of social progress; the law of dawg eat dawg was morbidly vivid in his mind from the first. Hardly out of school he was up in court for "breaking and entering." No protests from him about the war. He and his sister and another man dressed up in uniform and collected money for some vaguely phony patriotic society: The American Rescue League. By the spring of 1920 he was deep in the criminal world that is such an apt cartoon of the world of legitimate business. He was making good. He was in with the Morelli brothers of Providence, a gang of freight-car robbers, bootleggers, pimps, hijackers and miscellaneous thugs. The great wave of highway robbery that followed the war was at its height. For three years the leaders of society had been proclaiming the worthlessness of human life. Is it surprising that criminals should begin to take them at their word?

Scared to death, blind drunk, Madeiros, an overgrown boy of eighteen, was in the back seat of the Buick touring car that carried off the tragic holdup outside the Rice and Hutchins shoefactory at South Braintree. Probably on his share of the payroll he went south, once he got out of the Rhode Island jail where another episode of breaking and entering had landed him. He came back north with his money spent and worked as a bouncer at the Bluebird Inn, a "disorderly" roadhouse at Seekonk, Massachusetts and fell at last into the clutches of the Massachusetts law through a miserable failure to duplicate the daring South Braintree holdup at Wrentham, where he shot an aged bank cashier and ran without trying to get any loot. At his trial he sat so hunched and motionless that he seemed an imbecile. Not even when his mother threw an epileptic fit in the courtroom and was carried out rigid and foaming did he look up.

At the Dedham jail he was put in the cell next to Sacco. He could see Sacco going out to meet his wife and kids when they came to see him. The idea of an innocent man going to the chair worried him. For him everything had crashed. It had been on his own confession that he had been convicted of the Wrentham murder. He seems to have puzzled for a long time to find some way of clearing Sacco and Vanzetti without inculpating his old associates, even though he had fallen out with them long ago. He tried to tell Sacco about it in the jail bathroom, but Sacco, seeing Department of Justice spies everywhere—and with good reason— wouldn't listen to him. So at last he sent the warden a written confession, asking him to forward it to the *Boston American*.

Nothing happened. The warden kept his mouth shut. Eventually Madeiros sent a new confession to Sacco enclosed in a magazine, begging him to let his lawyer see it. *"I hereby confess to being in the South Braintree Shoe Company crime and Sacco and Vanzetti were not in said crime.—Celestino F. Madeiros."*

Circumstances sometimes force men into situations so dramatic, thrust their puny frames so far into the burning bright searchlights of history that their shadows on men's minds become enormous symbols. Sacco and Vanzetti are all the immigrants who have built this nation's industries with their sweat and their blood and have gotten for it nothing but the smallest wage it is possible to give them and a helot's position under the bootheels of the Arrow Collar social order. They are all the wops, hunkies, bohunks, factory fodder that hunger drives into the American mills through the painful sieve of Ellis Island. They are the dreams of a saner social order of those who can't stand the law of dawg eat dawg. This tiny courtroom is a focus of the turmoil of an age of transition, the center of eyes all over the world. Sacco and Vanzetti throw enormous shadows on the courthouse walls.

William G. Thompson feels all this dimly when, the last affidavit read, he pauses to begin his argument. But mostly he feels that as a citizen it is his duty to protect the laws and liberties of his state and as a man to try to save two innocent men from being murdered by a machine set going in a moment of hatred and panic. He is a broadshouldered man with steely white hair and a broad forehead and broad cheekbones. He doesn't mince words. There is intense feeling in his words. The case is no legal game of chess for him.

"I rest my case on these affidavits, on the other five propositions that I have argued, but if they all fail, and I cannot see how they can, I rest my case on that rock alone, on the sixth proposition in my brief—innocent or guilty, right or wrong, foolish or wise men—these men ought not now be sentenced to death for this crime so long as they have the right to say, 'The government of this great country put spies in my cell, planned to put spies in my wife's house, they put spies on my friends, took money that they were collecting to defend me, put it in their own pocket and joked about it and said they don't believe I am guilty but will help convict me, because they could not get enough evidence to deport me under the laws of Congress, and were willing as one of them continually said to adopt the method of killing me for murder as one way to get rid of me.' "

The Commonwealth's Attorney's handling of his side of the argument has been pretty perfunctory throughout, he has contented himself with trying to destroy the Court's opinion of Madeiros' veracity. A criminal is only to be believed when he speaks to his own detriment. He presents affidavits of the Morellis and their friends denying that they had ever heard of Madeiros, tries to imply that Letherman and Weyand (who gave other affidavits favorable to the defendants) were fired from the government employ and had no right to betray the secrets of their department. He knows that he does not need to make much effort. He is strong in the inertia of the courts. The defense will have to exert six times the energy of the prosecution to overturn the dead weight of six other motions denied.

Thompson comes back at him with a phrase worthy of Patrick Henry.
. . . "And I will say to your honor that a government that has come to honor its own secrets more than the lives of its citizens has become a tyranny whether you call it a republic or a monarchy or anything else."

Then the dry, crackling, careful voice of Judge Thayer and the hearing is adjourned.

"Hear ye, hear ye, hear ye, all who have had business before the honorable the justice of the superior court of the southeastern district of Massachusetts will now disperse. The court is adjourned without delay.

"God Save the Commonwealth of Massachusetts."

The court has refused to grant a new trial. The court has decided that Sacco and Vanzetti must die.

God Save the Commonwealth of Massachusetts.

How is all this possible? Why were these men ever convicted in the first place? From the calm of the year of our Lord 1926 it's pretty hard to remember the delirious year of 1920.

On June 3, 1919 a bomb exploded outside the Washington house of Attorney General A. Mitchell Palmer. In the previous months various people had received bombs through the mail, one of them blowing off the two hands of the unfortunate housemaid who undid the package. No one, and least of all the federal detectives, ever seems to have discovered who committed these outrages or why they were committed. But their result was to put a scare into every public official in the country, and particularly into Attorney General Palmer. No one knew where the lightning would strike next. The signing of peace had left the carefully stirred up hatred of the war years unsatisfied. It was easy for people who knew what they were doing to turn the terrors of government officials and the distrust of foreigners of the average man into a great crusade of hate against reds, radicals, dissenters of all sorts. The Department of Justice, backed by the press, frenziedly acclaimed by the man on the street, invented an imminent revolution. All the horrors of Russian Bolshevism were about to be enacted on our peaceful shores. That fall the roundup began. Every man had his ear to his neighbor's keyhole. This first crusade culminated in the sailing of the *Buford*, the "Soviet Ark" loaded with alien "anarchists" and in the preparation of the famous list of eighty thousand radicals who were to be gotten out of the way.

The raids were particularly violent in the industrial towns round Boston and culminated in the captives being driven through the streets of Boston chained together in fours. There were raids in Boston, Chelsea, Brockton, Bridgewater, Norwood, Worcester, Springfield, Chicopee Falls, Lowell, Fitchburg, Holyoke, Lawrence and Haverhill. Unfortunate people after being beaten up and put through the third degree were concentrated at Deer Island under the conditions that have become public through U.S. Circuit Judge Anderson's decision on the cases that came up before him.

Now it is this ring of industrial towns round Boston that furnish the background of the Sacco-Vanzetti case. There is no doubt that the Americanborn public in these towns on the whole sympathizes with the activities of the detectives. The region has been for many years one of the most intense industrial battlegrounds in the country. People slept safer in their beds at the thought of all these agitators, bombsters, garlic-smelling wops, and unwashed Russians being under lock and key at Deer Island.

Eastern Massachusetts has a threefold population living largely from manufacturing of textiles and shoes and other leather goods. With the decline of shipping and farming the old simonpure New England stock, Congregationalist in faith, Republican in politics, has been pretty well snowed under by the immigration first of Irish Catholics, congenital Democrats and readers of Hearst papers, now assimilated and respectable, and then of Italians, Poles, Slovaks, transplanted European peasants tenderly known to newspaper readers as the scum of the Mediterranean or the scum of Central Europe. There's no love lost between the first two classes, but they unite on the question of wops, guineas, dagoes. The January raids, the attitude of press and pulpit, howling about atrocities, civilization endangered, women nationalized in Communist Russia, put the average right-thinking citizen into such a state of mind that whenever he smelt garlic on a man's breath he walked past quickly for fear of being knifed. A roomful of people talking a foreign language was most certainly a conspiracy to overturn the government. Read over the articles in the *Boston Transcript* on the Soviet conspiracy at that time and you will see what kind of stuff was being ladled out even to the intelligent highbrow section of the entrenched classes.

It was into this atmosphere of rancor and suspicion, fear of holdups and social overturn, that burst the scare headlines of the South Braintree murders. Pent-up hatred found an outlet when the police in Brockton arrested Sacco and Vanzetti, wops who spoke broken English, anarchists who believed neither in the Pope nor in the Puritan God, slackers and agitators, charged with a peculiarly brutal and impudent crime. Since

that moment these people have had a focus for their bitter hatred of the
new, young, vigorous, unfamiliar forces that are relentlessly sweeping
them on to the shelf. The people of Norfolk county and of all Massachusetts decided they wanted these men to die.

Meanwhile the red delirium over the rest of the country had slackened.
Something had happened that had made many people pause and think.

About dawn on May 3 the body of Andrea Salsedo, an anarchist
printer, was found smashed on the pavement of Park Row in New York.
He had jumped or been thrown from the offices of the Department of
Justice on the fourteenth floor of the Park Row building, where he and
his friend Elia had been secretly imprisoned for eight weeks. Evidently
they had tortured him during that time; Mr. Palmer's detectives were
"investigating" anarchist activity. A note had been smuggled out somehow, and a few days before Vanzetti had been in New York as the
delegate of an Italian group to try to get the two men out on bail. After
Salsedo's death Elia was hurried over to Ellis Island and deported. He
died in Italy. But from that time on the holy enthusiasm for red-baiting
subsided. The tortured body found dead and bleeding in one of the most
central and public spots in New York shocked men back into their senses.

When Sacco and Vanzetti were arrested in the trolley car in Brockton
the night of May 5, Sacco had in his pocket the draft of a poster announcing a meeting of protest against what they considered the murder of their
comrade. They were going about warning the other members of their
group to hide all incriminating evidence in the way of "radical" books
and papers so that, in the new raid that they had been tipped off to
expect, they should not be arrested and meet the fate of Salsedo.

Don't forget that people had been arrested and beaten up for distributing the Declaration of Independence.

But why were these men held as murderers and highwaymen and not
as anarchists and advocates of the working people?

It was a frameup.

That does not *necessarily* mean that any set of government and employing class detectives deliberately planned to fasten the crime of murder on Sacco and Vanzetti.

The frameup is often an unconscious mechanism. An unconscious
mechanism is a kink in the mind that makes people do something without knowing that they are doing it. A frameup is the subrational act of a
group.

Among a people that does not recognize or rather does not admit that
it recognizes the force and danger of ideas it is impossible to prosecute
the holder of unpopular ideas directly. Also there is a smoldering tradition of freedom that makes those who do it feel guilty. After all everyone
learned the Declaration of Independence and *"Give me liberty or give
me death"* in school, and however perfunctory the words have become
they have left a faint infantile impression on the minds of most of us.

Hence the characteristic American weapon of the frameup. If a cop wants to arrest a man he suspects of selling dope he plants a gun on him and arrests him under the Sullivan Law. If a man is organizing a strike in a dangerously lively way you try to frame him under the Mann Act or else you get hold of a woman to sue him for breach of promise. If a representative votes against war you have him arrested for breach of decency in an automobile on a Virginia roadside. If two Italians are spreading anarchist propaganda, you hold them for murder.

The frameup is a process that you can't help feeling, but like most unconscious processes it's very hard to trace step by step. Half the agents in such a process don't really know what they are doing. Hence the moderately fairminded newspaper reader who never has had personal experience of a frameup in action is flabbergasted when you tell him that such and such a man who is being prosecuted for wifebeating is really being prosecuted because he knows the origin of certain bonds in a District Attorney's safe.

In this neatly swept courtroom in Dedham with everything so varnished and genteel it is hardly possible to think of such a thing as a frameup and yet, under these elms, in these white oldtime houses of Dedham, in front of these pious Georgian doorways, the court has for the seventh time affirmed its will to send two innocent men to the electric chair.

What is this criminal garlic-smelling creed that the people of Massachusetts will not face openly?

For half a century anarchy has been the bogy of American schoolmasters, policemen, old maids and small town mayors. About the time of the assassination of McKinley a picture was formed in the public mind of the anarchist; redhanded, unwashed foreigner whom nobody could understand, sticks of dynamite in his pocket and a bomb in the paper parcel under his arm, redeyed housewrecker waiting only for the opportunity to bite the hand that fed him. Since the Russian Revolution the picture has merged a little with that of the sneaking, slinking, Communist Jew, enviously undermining Prosperity and Decency through secret organizations ruled from Moscow.

Gradually among liberals and intelligent people generally certain phases of anarchism have meanwhile been reluctantly admitted into respectable conversation under the phrase "philosophical anarchist," which means an anarchist who shaves daily, has good manners and is guaranteed not to act on his beliefs. Certain people of the best society, such as Kropotkin and Tolstoy, princes both, having through their diverse types of anarchy made themselves important figures in European thought and literature, it was impossible to exclude them longer from the pale of decency.

What is this outlaw creed?

When Christianity flourished in the Mediterranean basin, slave and emperor had the hope of the immediate coming of Christ's kingdom, the golden Jerusalem that would appear on earth to put an end to the tears and aches of the faithful. After the first millennium, the City of God, despaired of on earth, took its permanent place in the cloudy firmament with the Virgin Mary at the apex of the feudal pyramid. With the decay of feudalism and the coming of the kingdoms of this world the church became more and more the instrument of the governing orders. Undermined by the eighteenth century, overthrown by the French revolution, the church was restored by the great reaction as the strongest bulwark of privilege. But in the tough memories of peasants and fishermen—their sons worked in factories—there remained a faint trace of the vanished brightness of the City of God. All our city dwelling instinct and culture has been handed down to us from these countless urban generations, Cretans, Greeks, Phoenicians, Latins of the Mediterranean basin, Italians of the hilltowns. It is natural that the dwellers on those scraggy hills in sight of that always blue sea should have kept alight in their hearts the perfect city, where the strong did not oppress the weak, where every man lived by his own work at peace with his neighbors, the white commune where man could reach his full height free from the snarling obsessions of priest and master.

It is this inner picture that is the core of feeling behind all anarchist theory and doctrine. Many Italians planted the perfect city of their imagination in America. When they came to this country, many of the more ardent spirits, when they found the reality did not match their imagining, reverted to the anarchist creed. There have been terrorists among them, as in every other oppressed and despised sect since the world began. Respectable people generally have contended that anarchism and terrorism were the same thing, a silly and usually malicious error much fostered by private detectives and police bomb-squads.

An anarchist workman who works for the organization of his fellow workmen is a man who costs the factory owners money; thereby he is a bombthrower and possible murderer in the minds of the majority of American employers.

In his charge to the jury in the Plymouth trial Judge Thayer definitely instructed them that the crime of highway robbery was consistent with Vanzetti's ideals as a radical.

Yet, under the conflict between employer and workman and the racial misunderstanding, in themselves material enough for the creation of a frameup, might there not be a deeper bitterness? The people of Massachusetts centuries ago suffered and hoped terribly for the City of God.

This little white courthouse town of Dedham, neat and exquisite under its elms, is the symbol of a withered hope, mortgaged at six per cent to the kingdoms of the world. It is natural that New Englanders, who feel in themselves a lingering of the passionate barbed desire of perfection of their ancestors, should hate with particular bitterness, anarchists, votaries of the Perfect Commune on earth. The irrational features of this case of attempted communal murder can only be explained by a bitterness so deep that it has been forgotten by the very people it moves most fervidly.

During the spring of 1920 Bartolomeo Vanzetti was peddling fish in the pleasant little Italian and Portuguese town of North Plymouth. He was planning to go into fishing himself in partnership with a man who owned some dories. Early mornings, pushing his cart up and down the long main street, ringing his bell, chatting with housewives in Piedmontese, Tuscan, pidgin English, he worried about the raids, the imprisonment, the lethargy of the working people. He was an anarchist, after the school of Galeani. Between the houses he could see the gleaming stretch of Plymouth Bay, the sandy islands beyond, the white dories at anchor. About three hundred years before, men from the west of England had first sailed into the gray shimmering bay that smelled of woods and wild grape, looking for something; liberty . . . freedom to worship God in their own manner . . . space to breathe. Thinking of these things, worrying as he pushed the little cart loaded with eels, haddock, cod, halibut, swordfish, Vanzetti spent his mornings making change, weighing out fish, joking with housewives. It was better than working at the great cordage works that own North Plymouth. Some years before he had tried to organize a strike there and been blacklisted. The officials and detectives at the Plymouth Cordage, the largest cordage in the world, thought of him as a red, a slacker and troublemaker.

At the same time Nicola Sacco was living in Stoughton, working an edging machine at the Three K's Shoe Factory, where star workmen sometimes made as high as eighty or ninety dollars a week. He had a pretty wife and a little son named Dante. There was another baby coming. He lived in a bungalow belonging to his employer, Michael Kelly. The house adjoined Kelly's own house and the men were friends. Often Kelly advised him to lay off this anarchist stuff. There was no money in it. It was dangerous the way people felt nowadays. Sacco was a clever young fellow and could soon get to be a prosperous citizen, maybe own a factory of his own someday, live by other men's work.

But Sacco, working in his garden in the early morning before the whistles blew, hilling beans, picking off potatobugs, letting grains of corn slip by twos and threes through his fingers into the finely worked earth, worried about things. He loved the earth and people, he wanted them to walk straight over the free hills, not to stagger bowed under the ordained machinery of industry; he worried mornings working in his garden at the lethargy of the working people. It was not enough that he was happy and had fifteen hundred or more dollars in the bank for a trip home to Italy.

Three years before Sacco and Vanzetti had both of them had their convictions put to the test. In 1917, against the expressed vote of the majority, Woodrow Wilson had allowed the United States to become involved in a war with Germany. When the law was passed for compulsory military service a registration day for citizens and aliens was announced. Most young men submitted whatever their convictions were. A few of those who were opposed to any war or to capitalist war had the nerve to protest. Sacco and Vanzetti and some friends ran away to Mexico. There, some thirty of them lived in a set of adobe houses. Those who could get jobs worked. It was share and share alike. Everything was held in common. There were in the community men of all trades and conditions: bakers, butchers, tailors, shoemakers, cooks, carpenters, waiters. It was a momentary realization of the hope of anarchism. But living was difficult in Mexico and they began to get letters from the States telling that it was possible to avoid the draft, telling of high wages. Little by little they filtered back across the border. Sacco and Vanzetti went back to Massachusetts.

There was an Italian club that met Sunday evenings in a hall in Maverick Square, East Boston, under the name of the Italian Naturalization Society. Workmen from the surrounding industrial towns met to play bowls and to discuss social problems. There were anarchists, syndicalists, socialists of various colors. The Russian revolution had fired them with new hopes. The persecution of their comrades in various parts of America had made them feel the need of mutual help. While far away across the world the hope of a new era flared into the sky, at home the great machine they slaved for seemed more adamant, more unshakeable than ever. To the war heroes who had remained at home any foreigner seemed a potential Bolshevik, a menace to the security of Old Glory and liberty bonds and the bonus. When Elia and Salsedo were arrested there was great alarm among the Italian radicals around Boston. Vanzetti went down to New York to try to hire a lawyer for the two men. There he heard many uneasy rumors. The possession of any literature that might be interpreted as subversive by ignorant and brutal agents of the Departments of Justice and Labor was dangerous. It was not that deportation was so much to be feared, but the beating up and third degree that preceded it.

It was on May 3, 1920 that Salsedo was found dead on Park Row. A rumor went around that a new raid was going to be made in the suburbs of Boston. There was a scurry to hide pamphlets and newspapers. At the same time the Italians of Boston couldn't let this horrible affair go by without a meeting of protest. Handbills announcing a meeting in Brockton were printed. Vanzetti was to be one of the speakers.

On the evening of May 5, Sacco and Vanzetti with the handbills on them went by trolley from Stoughton to West Bridgewater. They thought they were being trailed and had put revolvers in their pockets out of some confused feeling of bravado. If the police pounced on them at least they would not let themselves be tortured to death like Salsedo. The idea was to hide the handbills somewhere until after the expected raid. When they found they couldn't use Boda's car they started back to Stoughton. They were arrested as the trolley entered Brockton. They thought they were being arrested as reds in connection with the projected meeting. When they were questioned at the police station their main care was not to implicate any of their friends. They kept remembering the dead body of Salsedo, smashed on the pavement of Park Row.

When Sacco and Vanzetti were first grilled by the chief of police of Brockton they were questioned as reds and lied all they could to save their friends. Particularly they would not tell where they had got their pistols. Out of this Judge Thayer and the prosecution evolved the theory of "the consciousness of guilt" that weighed so heavily with the jury. After they had been held two days they were identified, Sacco as the driver of the car in the South Braintree holdup and Vanzetti as the "foreign looking man" who had taken a potshot at a paytruck of the L. Q. White company at Bridgewater early on the morning of Christmas Eve, 1919.

In spite of the fact that twenty people swore that they had seen Vanzetti in North Plymouth selling eels at that very time in the morning, he was promptly convicted and sentenced to fifteen years in the Charlestown penitentiary. The fact that so many people testified to having bought eels was considered very suspicious by the court that did not know that the eating of eels on the fast day before Christmas is an Italian custom of long standing. Later Vanzetti was associated with Sacco in the murder charge. On July 14, 1923, both men were found guilty of murder in the first degree on two counts by the Norfolk County jury, a hundred per cent American jury, consisting of two realestate men, two storekeepers, a mason, two machinists, a clothing salesman, a farmer, a millworker, a shoemaker and a lastmaker.

The Dedham jail is a handsome structure, set among lawns, screened by trees that wave new green leaves against the robins-egg sky of June. In the warden's office you can see your face in the light brown varnish, you could eat eggs off the floor it is so clean. Inside, the main reception hall is airy, full of sunlight. The bars are cheerfully painted green, a fresh peagreen. Through the bars you can see the waving trees and the June clouds roaming the sky like cattle in an unfenced pasture. It's a preposterous complicated canary cage. Why aren't the birds singing in this green aviary? The warden politely shows me to a seat and as I wait I notice a smell, not green and airy this smell, a jaded heavy greasy smell of slum, like the smell of army slum, but heavier, more hopeless.

At last Sacco has come out of his cell and sits beside me.

The faces of men who have been a long time in jail have a peculiar frozen look under the eyes. The face of a man who has been a long time in jail never loses that tightness under the eyes. Sacco has been six years in the county jail, always waiting, waiting for trial, waiting for new evidence, waiting for motions to be argued, waiting for sentence, waiting, waiting, waiting.

Two men sitting side by side on a bench in a green bird cage. When he feels like it one of them will get up and walk out, walk into the sunny June day. The other will go back to his cell to wait.

He looks younger than I had expected. His face has a waxy transparence like the face of a man who's been sick in bed for a long time; when he laughs his cheeks flush a little. At length we manage both of us to laugh.

It's such a preposterous position for a man to be in, like a man who doesn't know the game trying to play blindfold chess. The real world has gone. We have no more grasp of our world of rain and streets and trolleycars and cucumbervines and girls and gardenposts. This is a world of phrases, *prosecution, defense, evidence, motion, irrelevant, incompetent* and *immaterial.* For six years this man has lived in the law, tied tighter and tighter in the sticky filaments of law-words like a fly in a spider web. And the wrong set of words means the Chair.

All the moves in the game are made for him, all he can do is sit helpless and wait, fastening his hopes on one set of phrases after another. In all these lawbooks, in all this terminology of clerks of the court and counsel for the defense, there is one move that will save him, out of a million that will mean death.

If only they make the right move, use the right words.

But by this time the nagging torment of hope has almost stopped, not even the thought of his wife and children out there in the world, unreachable, can torture him now. He is numb now, can laugh and look quizzically at the ponderous machine that has caught and mangled him. Now it hardly matters to him if they do manage to pull him out from between the cogs. And the wrong set of words means the Chair.

Nicola Sacco came to this country when he was eighteen years old. He was born in Puglia in the mountains in the heel of Italy. Since then up to the time of his arrest he has had pretty good luck. He made good money, he was happily married, he had many friends, latterly he had a garden to hoe and rake mornings and evenings and Sundays. He was unusually powerfully built, able to do two men's work. In prison he was able to stand thirtyone days of hunger strike before he broke down and had to be taken to the hospital.

In jail he has learned to speak and write English, has read many books, for the first time in his life has been thrown with nativeborn Americans. They worry him, these nativeborn Americans. They are so hard and brittle. They don't fit into the bright clear heartfelt philosophy of Latin anarchism. These are people who coolly want him to die in the electric chair. He can't understand them. When his head was cool he's never wanted anyone to die. Judge Thayer and the prosecution he thinks of as instruments of a machine.

The warden comes up to take down my name.

"I hope your wife's better," says Sacco.

"Pretty poorly," says the warden.

Sacco shakes his head. "Maybe she'll get better soon, nice weather."

I have shaken his hand, my feet have carried me to the door. The warden looks into my face with a curious smile. "Leaving us?" he asks.

Outside in the neat streets the new green leaves are swaying in the sunlight, birds sing, klaxons grunt, a trolleycar screeches round a corner. Overhead the white June clouds wander in the unfenced sky.

Going to the Charlestown Penitentiary is more like going to Barnum and Bailey's. There's a great scurry of guards, groups of people waiting outside; inside a brass band is playing *Home Sweet Home*. When at length you get let into the Big Show, you find a great many things happening at once. There are rows of benches where pairs of people sit talking. Each pair is made up of a free man and a convict. In three directions there are gray bars and tiers of cells. The band inside plays bangingly: *Should auld acquaintance be forgot*.

A short broadshouldered man is sitting quiet through all the uproar, smiling a little under his big drooping mustache. He has a domed, pale forehead and black eyes surrounded by many little wrinkles. The serene modeling of his cheekbones and hollow cheeks makes you forget the prison look under his eyes. This is Vanzetti.

Bartolomeo Vanzetti was born in Villa Faletto, in a remote mountain valley in the Piedmont. At the age of thirteen his father apprenticed him to a pastrycook who worked him fifteen hours a day. After six years of grueling work in bakeries and restaurant kitchens he went back home to be nursed through pleurisy by his mother. Soon afterward his mother died and in despair he set out for America. When, after the usual kicking around by the Ellis Island officials, he was dumped on the pavement of Battery Park, he had very little money, knew not a word of the language and found that he had arrived in a time of general unemployment. He washed dishes at Mouquin's for five dollars a week and at last left for the country for fear that he was getting consumption. At length he got work in a brick kiln near Springfield. There he was thrown with Tuscans, first learned the Tuscan dialect and read Dante and the Italian classics. After that he worked for two years in the stone pits at Meriden, Connecticut. Then he went back to New York and worked for a while as a pastrycook again, and at last settled in Plymouth where he worked in various factories and at odd jobs, ditchdigging, clamdigging, icecutting, snowshoveling and a few months before his arrest, for the sake of being his own boss, bought a pushcart and peddled fish.

All this time he read a great deal nights sitting under the gasjet when everyone else was in bed, thought a great deal as he swung a pick or made caramels or stoked brick kilns, of the workmen he rubbed shoulders with, of their position in the world and his, of their hopes of happiness and of a less struggling less animallike existence. As a boy he had been an ardent Catholic. In Turin he fell in with a bunch of socialists under the influence of De Amicis. Once in America he read St. Augustine, Kropotkin, Gorki, Malatesta, Renan, and began to go under the label of anarchist-communist. His anarchism, though, is less a matter of labels than of feeling, of gentle philosophic brooding. He shares the hope that has grown up in Latin countries of the Mediterranean basin that somehow men's predatory instincts, incarnate in the capitalist system, can be canalized into other channels, leaving free communities of artisans and farmers and fishermen and cattlebreeders who would work for their livelihood with pleasure, because the work was itself enjoyable in the serene white light of a reasonable world.

And for seven years, three hundred and sixtyfive days a year, yesterday, today, tomorrow, Sacco and Vanzetti woke up on their prison pallets, ate prison food, had an hour of exercise and conversation a day, sat in their cells puzzling about this technicality and that technicality, pinning their hopes to their alibis, to the expert testimony about the character of the barrel of Sacco's gun, to Madeiros' confession and Weeks' corroboration, to action before the Supreme Court of the United States, and day by day the props were dashed from under their feet and they felt themselves being inexorably pushed toward the chair by the blind hatred of well-meaning citizens, by the superhuman involved stealthy soulless mechanism of the law.

[1956] The protest against the denial of a new trial to Sacco and Vanzetti became world wide. Since every legal path seemed barred the governor was implored to grant a pardon or at least to commute the sentences. The governor passed the buck by appointing a commission of prominent laymen who were presumed to be above the battle to advise him on the matter. Both the president of Harvard University and the president of the Massachusetts Institute of Technology were members. The commission sent the governor in a report which justified every feature of Judge Thayer's conduct of the trial and showed a surprising ignorance of the political background of the case into the bargain. In those days college presidents were not yet liberals by definition. The two men were electrocuted in Charlestown Jail in August 1927.

Vanzetti left a statement:"If it had not been for these things, I might have lived out my life talking at street corners to scorning men. I might have died unknown, a failure. This is our career and our triumph. Never in our full life can we hope to do such work for tolerance, for justice, for man's understanding of man as now we do by accident. Our words, our lives, our pains, nothing. The taking of our lives—the lives of a good shoemaker and a poor fish peddler, all. The last moment belongs to us. That agony is our triumph."

Sinclair Lewis

Babbitt

No writer caught the cult of the businessman in the '20s as did Sinclair Lewis. Born in Minnesota in 1885, he attended Yale College, worked at odd jobs, did a turn as a reporter on Fremont Older's San Francisco Bulletin, *and then began writing. The result was* Main Street, *published in 1920; it was an immediate success, selling 400,000 copies the first year. Two years later* Babbitt *came out, followed by three more novels before the decade ended:* Arrowsmith *(1925),* Elmer Gantry *(1927), and* Dodsworth *(1929). Each of these novels commented on and analyzed some aspect of the '20s.* Babbitt *focused on the businessman, satirizing the hustler and booster mentality, the worship of success, and the quest of money. George Follansbee Babbitt, "the shambling, serio-comic figure . . . with his cash-and-carry measurement of success," was the epitome of the period. Of* Babbitt, *H. G. Wells wrote, he is "the common American prosperous businessman. . . . He lives and breathes. . . . He moves about. His baseness, his vile gregariousness, his vulgarity, and—what is the hope of America—his suffering and struggling intimations of beauty, are all wonderfully done." [From* Babbitt *by Sinclair Lewis, Chapters I and II. Copyright 1922 by Harcourt, Brace & World, Inc.; renewed 1950 by Sinclair Lewis. Reprinted by permission of the publishers. British rights courtesy of The Executors of the Sinclair Lewis Estate and Jonathan Cape Limited, London.]*

The towers of Zenith aspired above the morning mist; austere towers of steel and cement and limestone, sturdy as cliffs and delicate as silver rods. They were neither citadels nor churches, but frankly and beautifully office-buildings.

The mist took pity on the fretted structures of earlier generations: the Post Office with its shingle-tortured mansard, the red brick minarets of hulking old houses, factories with stingy and sooted windows, wooden tenements colored like mud. The city was full of such grotesqueries, but the clean towers were thrusting them from the business center, and on the farther hills were shining new houses, homes—they seemed—for laughter and tranquillity.

Over a concrete bridge fled a limousine of long sleek hood and noise-less engine. These people in evening clothes were returning from an all-night rehearsal of a Little Theater play, an artistic adventure consider-ably illuminated by champagne. Below the bridge curved a railroad, a maze of green and crimson lights. The New York Flyer boomed past, and twenty lines of polished steel leaped into the glare.

In one of the skyscrapers the wires of the Associated Press were closing down. The telegraph operators wearily raised their celluloid eye-shades after a night of talking with Paris and Peking. Through the building crawled the scrubwomen, yawning, their old shoes slapping. The dawn mist spun away. Cues of men with lunch-boxes clumped toward the immensity of new factories, sheets of glass and hollow tile, glittering shops where five thousand men worked beneath one roof, pouring out the honest wares that would be sold up the Euphrates and across the veldt. The whistles rolled out in greeting a chorus cheerful as the April dawn; the song of labor in a city built—it seemed—for giants.

There was nothing of the giant in the aspect of the man who was beginning to awaken on the sleeping-porch of a Dutch Colonial house in that residential district of Zenith known as Floral Heights.

His name was George F. Babbitt. He was forty-six years old now, in April, 1920, and he made nothing in particular, neither butter nor shoes nor poetry, but he was nimble in the calling of selling houses for more than people could afford to pay.

His large head was pink, his brown hair thin and dry. His face was babyish in slumber, despite his wrinkles and the red spectacle-dents on the slopes of his nose. He was not fat but he was exceedingly well fed; his cheeks were pads, and the unroughened hand which lay helpless upon the khaki-colored blanket was slightly puffy. He seemed prosperous, extremely married and unromantic; and altogether unromantic appeared this sleeping-porch, which looked on one sizable elm, two respectable grass-plots, a cement driveway, and a corrugated iron garage. Yet Babbitt was again dreaming of the fairy child, a dream more romantic than scarlet pagodas by a silver sea.

For years the fairy child had come to him. Where others saw but Georgie Babbitt, she discerned gallant youth. She waited for him, in the darkness beyond mysterious groves. When at last he could slip away from the crowded house he darted to her. His wife, his clamoring friends, sought to follow, but he escaped, the girl fleet beside him, and they crouched together on a shadowy hillside. She was so slim, so white, so eager! She cried that he was gay and valiant, that she would wait for him, that they would sail—

Rumble and bang of the milk-truck.

Babbitt moaned, turned over, struggled back toward his dream. He could see only her face now, beyond misty waters. The furnace-man slammed the basement door. A dog barked in the next yard. As Babbitt sank blissfully into a dim warm tide, the paper-carrier went by whistling, and the rolled-up *Advocate* thumped the front door. Babbitt roused, his stomach constricted with alarm. As he relaxed, he was pierced by the familiar and irritating rattle of some one cranking a Ford: snap-ah-ah, snap-ah-ah, snap-ah-ah. Himself a pious motorist, Babbitt cranked with the unseen driver, with him waited through taut hours for the roar of the starting engine, with him agonized as the roar ceased and again began the infernal patient snap-ah-ah—a round, flat sound, a shivering cold-morning sound, a sound infuriating and inescapable. Not till the rising voice of the motor told him that the Ford was moving was he released from the panting tension. He glanced once at his favorite tree, elm twigs against the gold patina of sky, and fumbled for sleep as for a drug. He who had been a boy very credulous of life was no longer greatly interested in the possible and improbable adventures of each new day.

He escaped from reality till the alarm-clock rang, at seven-twenty.

It was the best of nationally advertised and quantitatively produced alarm-clocks, with all modern attachments, including cathedral chime, intermittent alarm, and a phosphorescent dial. Babbitt was proud of being awakened by such a rich device. Socially it was almost as creditable as buying expensive cord tires.

He sulkily admitted now that there was no more escape, but he lay and detested the grind of the real-estate business, and disliked his family, and disliked himself for disliking them. The evening before, he had played poker at Vergil Gunch's till midnight, and after such holidays he was irritable before breakfast. It may have been the tremendous home-brewed beer of the prohibition-era and the cigars to which that beer enticed him; it may have been resentment of return from this fine, bold man-world to a restricted region of wives and stenographers, and of suggestions not to smoke so much.

From the bedroom beside the sleeping-porch, his wife's detestably cheerful "Time to get up, Georgie boy," and the itchy sound, the brisk and scratchy sound, of combing hairs out of a stiff brush.

He grunted; he dragged his thick legs, in faded baby-blue pajamas, from under the khaki blanket; he sat on the edge of the cot, running his fingers through his wild hair, while his plump feet mechanically felt for his slippers. He looked regretfully at the blanket—forever a suggestion to him of freedom and heroism. He had bought it for a camping trip which had never come off. It symbolized gorgeous loafing, gorgeous cursing, virile flannel shirts.

He creaked to his feet, groaning at the waves of pain which passed behind his eyeballs. Though he waited for their scorching recurrence, he looked blurrily out at the yard. It delighted him, as always; it was the neat yard of a successful business man of Zenith, that is, it was perfection, and made him also perfect. He regarded the corrugated iron garage. For the three-hundred-and-sixty-fifth time in a year he reflected, "No class to that tin shack. Have to build me a frame garage. But by golly it's the only thing on the place that isn't up-to-date!" While he stared he thought of a community garage for his acreage development, Glen Oriole. He stopped puffing and jiggling. His arms were akimbo. His petulant, sleep-swollen face was set in harder lines. He suddenly seemed capable, an official, a man to contrive, to direct, to get things done.

On the vigor of his idea he was carried down the hard, clean, unused-looking hall into the bathroom.

Though the house was not large it had, like all houses on Floral Heights, an altogether royal bathroom of porcelain and glazed tile and metal sleek as silver. The towel-rack was a rod of clear glass set in nickel. The tub was long enough for a Prussian Guard, and above the set bowl was a sensational exhibit of tooth-brush holder, shaving-brush holder, soap-dish, sponge-dish, and medicine-cabinet, so glittering and so ingenious that they resembled an electrical instrument-board. But the Babbitt whose god was Modern Appliances was not pleased. The air of the bathroom was thick with the smell of a heathen toothpaste. "Verona been at it again! 'Stead of sticking to Lilidol, like I've re-peat-ed-ly asked her, she's gone and gotten some confounded stinkum stuff that makes you sick!"

The bath-mat was wrinkled and the floor was wet. (His daughter Verona eccentrically took baths in the morning, now and then.) He slipped on the mat, and slid against the tub. He said "Damn!" Furiously he snatched up his tube of shaving-cream, furiously he lathered, with a belligerent slapping of the unctuous brush, furiously he raked his plump cheeks with a safety-razor. It pulled. The blade was dull. He said, "Damn —oh—oh—damn it!"

He hunted through the medicine-cabinet for a packet of new razor-blades (reflecting, as invariably, "Be cheaper to buy one of these dinguses and strop your own blades,") and when he discovered the packet, behind the round box of bicarbonate of soda, he thought ill of his wife for putting it there and very well of himself for not saying "Damn." But he did say it, immediately afterward, when with wet and soap-slippery fingers he tried to remove the horrible little envelope and crisp clinging oiled paper from the new blade.

Then there was the problem, oft-pondered, never solved, of what to do with the old blade, which might imperil the fingers of his young. As usual, he tossed it on top of the medicine-cabinet, with a mental note that some day he must remove the fifty or sixty other blades that were also temporarily, piled up there. He finished his shaving in a growing testiness increased by his spinning headache and by the emptiness in his stomach. When he was done, his round face smooth and streamy and his eyes stinging from soapy water, he reached for a towel. The family towels were wet, wet and clammy and vile, all of them wet, he found, as he blindly snatched them—his own face-towel, his wife's, Verona's, Ted's, Tinka's, and the lone bath-towel with the huge welt of initial. Then George F. Babbitt did a dismaying thing. He wiped his face on the guest-towel! It was a pansy-embroidered trifle which always hung there to indicate that the Babbitts were in the best Floral Heights society. No one had ever used it. No guest had ever dared to. Guests secretively took a corner of the nearest regular towel.

He was raging, "By golly, here they go and use up all the towels, every doggone one of 'em, and they use 'em and get 'em all wet and sopping, and never put out a dry one for me—of course, I'm the goat!—and then I want one and— I'm the only person in the doggone house that's got the slightest doggone bit of consideration for other people and thoughtfulness and consider there may be others that may want to use the doggone bathroom after me and consider—"

He was pitching the chill abominations into the bath-tub, pleased by the vindictiveness of that desolate flapping sound; and in the midst his wife serenely trotted in, observed serenely, "Why Georgie dear, what are you doing? Are you going to wash out the towels? Why, you needn't wash out the towels. Oh, Georgie, you didn't go and use the guest-towel, did you?"

It is not recorded that he was able to answer.

For the first time in weeks he was sufficiently roused by his wife to look at her.

Myra Babbitt—Mrs. George F. Babbitt—was definitely mature. She had creases from the corners of her mouth to the bottom of her chin, and her plump neck bagged. But the thing that marked her as having passed the line was that she no longer had reticences before her husband, and no longer worried about not having reticences. She was in a petticoat now, and corsets which bulged, and unaware of being seen in bulgy corsets. She had become so dully habituated to married life that in her full matronliness she was as sexless as an anemic nun. She was a good woman, a kind woman, a diligent woman, but no one, save perhaps Tinka her ten-year-old, was at all interested in her or entirely aware that she was alive.

After a rather thorough discussion of all the domestic and social aspects of towels she apologized to Babbitt for his having an alcoholic headache; and he recovered enough to endure the search for a B.V.D. undershirt which had, he pointed out, malevolently been concealed among his clean pajamas.

He was fairly amiable in the conference on the brown suit.

"What do you think, Myra?" He pawed at the clothes hunched on a chair in their bedroom, while she moved about mysteriously adjusting and patting her petticoat and, to his jaundiced eye, never seeming to get on with her dressing. "How about it? Shall I wear the brown suit another day?"

"Well, it looks awfully nice on you."

"I know, but gosh, it needs pressing."

"That's so. Perhaps it does."

"It certainly could stand being pressed, all right."

"Yes, perhaps it wouldn't hurt it to be pressed."

"But gee, the coat doesn't need pressing. No sense in having the whole darn suit pressed, when the coat doesn't need it."

"That's so."

"But the pants certainly need it, all right. Look at them—look at those wrinkles—the pants certainly do need pressing."

"That's so. Oh, Georgie, why couldn't you wear the brown coat with the blue trousers we were wondering what we'd do with them?"

"Good Lord! Did you ever in all my life know me to wear the coat of one suit and the pants of another? What do you think I am? A busted bookkeeper?"

"Well, why don't you put on the dark gray suit to-day, and stop in at the tailor and leave the brown trousers?"

"Well, they certainly need— Now where the devil is that gray suit? Oh, yes, here we are."

He was able to get through the other crises of dressing with comparative resoluteness and calm.

His first adornment was the sleeveless dimity B.V.D. undershirt, in which he resembled a small boy humorlessly wearing a cheesecloth tabard at a civic pageant. He never put on B.V.D.'s without thanking the God of Progress that he didn't wear tight, long, old-fashioned undergarments, like his father-in-law and partner, Henry Thompson. His second embellishment was combing and slicking back his hair. It gave him a tremendous forehead, arching up two inches beyond the former hair-line. But most wonder-working of all was the donning of his spectacles.

There is character in spectacles—the pretentious tortoise-shell, the meek pince-nez of the school teacher, the twisted silver-framed glasses of the old villager. Babbitt's spectacles had huge, circular, frameless lenses of the very best glass; the ear-pieces were thin bars of gold. In them he was the modern business man; one who gave orders to clerks and drove a car and played occasional golf and was scholarly in regard to Salesmanship. His head suddenly appeared not babyish but weighty, and you noted his heavy, blunt nose, his straight mouth and thick, long upper lip, his chin overfleshy but strong; with respect you beheld him put on the rest of his uniform as a Solid Citizen.

The gray suit was well cut, well made, and completely undistinguished. It was a standard suit. White piping on the V of the vest added a flavor of law and learning. His shoes were black laced boots, good boots, honest boots, standard boots, extraordinarily uninteresting boots. The only frivolity was in his purple knitted scarf. With considerable comment on the matter to Mrs. Babbitt (who, acrobatically fastening the back of her blouse to her skirt with a safety-pin, did not hear a word he said), he chose between the purple scarf and a tapestry effect with stringless brown harps among blown palms, and into it he thrust a snake-head pin with opal eyes.

A sensational event was changing from the brown suit to the gray the contents of his pockets. He was earnest about these objects. They were of eternal importance, like baseball or the Republican Party. They included a fountain pen and a silver pencil (always lacking a supply of new leads) which belonged in the righthand upper vest pocket. Without them he would have felt naked. On his watch-chain were a gold penknife, silver cigar-cutter, seven keys (the use of two of which he had forgotten), and incidentally a good watch. Depending from the chain was a large, yellowish elk's-tooth—proclamation of his membership in the Brotherly and Protective Order of Elks. Most significant of all was his loose-leaf pocket note-book, that modern and efficient note-book which contained the addresses of people whom he had forgotten, prudent memoranda of postal money-orders which had reached their destinations months ago, stamps which had lost their mucilage, clippings of verses by T. Cholmondeley Frink and of the newspaper editorials from which Babbitt got his opinions and his polysyllables, notes to be sure and do things which he did not intend to do, and one curious inscription—D.S.S.D.M.Y. P.D.F.

But he had no cigarette-case. No one had ever happened to give him one, so he hadn't the habit, and people who carried cigarette-cases he regarded as effeminate.

Last, he stuck in his lapel the Boosters' Club button. With the conciseness of great art the button displayed two words: "Boosters—Pep!" It made Babbitt feel loyal and important. It associated him with Good Fellows, with men who were nice and human, and important in business circles. It was his V.C., his Legion of Honor ribbon, his Phi Beta Kappa key.

With the subtleties of dressing ran other complex worries. "I feel kind of punk this morning," he said. "I think I had too much dinner last evening. You oughtn't to serve those heavy banana fritters."

"But you asked me to have some."

"I know, but— I tell you, when a fellow gets past forty he has to look after his digestion. There's a lot of fellows that don't take proper care of themselves. I tell you at forty a man's a fool or his doctor—I mean, his own doctor. Folks don't give enough attention to this matter of dieting. Now I think— Course a man ought to have a good meal after the day's work, but it would be a good thing for both of us if we took lighter lunches."

"But Georgie, here at home I always do have a light lunch."

"Mean to imply I make a hog of myself, eating down-town? Yes, sure! You'd have a swell time if you had to eat the truck that new steward hands out to us at the Athletic Club! But I certainly do feel out of sorts, this morning. Funny, got a pain down here on the left side—but no, that wouldn't be appendicitis, would it? Last night, when I was driving over to Verg Gunch's, I felt a pain in my stomach, too. Right here it was— kind of a sharp shooting pain. I— Where'd that dime go to? Why don't you serve more prunes at breakfast? Of course I eat an apple every evening—an apple a day keeps the doctor away—but still, you ought to have more prunes, and not all these fancy doodads."

"The last time I had prunes you didn't eat them."

"Well, I didn't feel like eating 'em, I suppose. Matter of fact, I think I did eat some of 'em. Anyway— I tell you it's mighty important to— I was saying to Verg Gunch, just last evening, most people don't take sufficient care of their diges—"

"Shall we have the Gunches for our dinner, next week?"

"Why sure; you bet."

"Now see here, George: I want you to put on your nice dinner-jacket that evening."

"Rats! The rest of 'em won't want to dress."

"Of course they will. You remember when you didn't dress for the Littlefields' supper-party, and all the rest did, and how embarrassed you were."

"Embarrassed, hell! I wasn't embarrassed. Everybody knows I can put on as expensive a Tux. as anybody else, and I should worry if I don't happen to have it on sometimes. All a darn nuisance, anyway. All right for a woman, that stays around the house all the time, but when a fellow's worked like the dickens all day, he doesn't want to go and hustle his head off getting into the soup-and-fish for a lot of folks that he's seen in just reg'lar ordinary clothes that same day."

"You know you enjoy being seen in one. The other evening you admitted you were glad I'd insisted on your dressing. You said you felt a lot better for it. And oh, Georgie, I do wish you wouldn't say 'Tux.' It's 'dinner-jacket.' "

"Rats, what's the odds?"

"Well, it's what all the nice folks say. Suppose Lucile McKelvey heard you calling it a 'Tux.' "

"Well, that's all right now! Lucile McKelvey can't pull anything on me! Her folks are common as mud, even if her husband and her dad are millionaires! I suppose you're trying to rub in *your* exalted social position! Well, let me tell you that your revered paternal ancestor, Henry T., doesn't even call it a 'Tux.'! He calls it a 'bobtail jacket for a ringtail monkey,' and you couldn't get him into one unless you chloroformed him!"

"Now don't be horrid, George."

"Well, I don't want to be horrid, but Lord! you're getting as fussy as Verona. Ever since she got out of college she's been too rambunctious to live with—doesn't know what she wants—well, I know what she wants!— all she wants is to marry a millionaire, and live in Europe, and hold some preacher's hand, and simultaneously at the same time stay right here in Zenith and be some blooming kind of a socialist agitator or boss charity-worker or some damn thing! Lord, and Ted is just as bad! He wants to go to college, and he doesn't want to go to college. Only one of the three that knows her own mind is Tinka. Simply can't understand how I ever came to have a pair of shillyshallying children like Rone and Ted. I may not be any Rockefeller or James J. Shakespeare, but I certainly do know my own mind, and I do keep right on plugging along in the office and— Do you know the latest? Far as I can figure out, Ted's new bee is he'd like to be a movie actor and— And here I've told him a hundred times, if he'll go to college and law-school and make good, I'll set him up in business and— Verona just exactly as bad. Doesn't know what she wants. Well, well, come on! Aren't you ready yet? The girl rang the bell three minutes ago."

Before he followed his wife, Babbitt stood at the western-most window of their room. This residential settlement, Floral Heights, was on a rise; and though the center of the city was three miles away—Zenith had between three and four hundred thousand inhabitants now—he could see the top of the Second National Tower, an Indiana limestone building of thirty-five stories.

Its shining walls rose against April sky to a simple cornice like a streak of white fire. Integrity was in the tower, and decision. It bore its strength lightly as a tall soldier. As Babbitt stared, the nervousness was soothed from his face, his slack chin lifted in reverence. All he articulated was "That's one lovely sight!" but he was inspired by the rhythm of the city; his love of it renewed. He beheld the tower as a temple-spire of the religion of business, a faith passionate, exalted, surpassing common men; and as he clumped down to breakfast he whistled the ballad "Oh, by gee, by gosh, by jingo" as though it were a hymn melancholy and noble.

Relieved of Babbitt's bumbling and the soft grunts with which his wife expressed the sympathy she was too experienced to feel and much too experienced not to show, their bedroom settled instantly into impersonality.

It gave on the sleeping-porch. It served both of them as dressing-room, and on the coldest nights Babbitt luxuriously gave up the duty of being manly and retreated to the bed inside, to curl his toes in the warmth and laugh at the January gale.

The room displayed a modest and pleasant color-scheme, after one of the best standard designs of the decorator who "did the interiors" for most of the speculative-builders' houses in Zenith. The walls were gray, the woodwork white, the rug a serene blue; and very much like mahogany was the furniture—the bureau with its great clear mirror, Mrs. Babbitt's dressing-table with toilet-articles of almost solid silver, the plain twin beds, between them a small table holding a standard electric bedside lamp, a glass for water, and a standard bed-side book with colored illustrations—what particular book it was cannot be ascertained, since no one had ever opened it. The mattresses were firm but not hard, triumphant modern mattresses which had cost a great deal of money; the hot-water radiator was of exactly the proper scientific surface for the cubic contents of the room. The windows were large and easily opened, with the best catches and cords, and Holland roller-shades guaranteed not to crack. It was a masterpiece among bedrooms, right out of Cheerful Modern Houses for Medium Incomes. Only it had nothing to do with the Babbitts, nor with any one else. If people had ever lived and loved here, read thrillers at midnight and lain in beautiful indolence on a Sunday morning, there were no signs of it. It had the air of being a very good room in a very good hotel. One expected the chambermaid to come in and make it ready for people who would stay but one night, go without looking back, and never think of it again.

Every second house in Floral Heights had a bedroom precisely like this.

The Babbitts' house was five years old. It was all as competent and glossy as this bedroom. It had the best of taste, the best of inexpensive rugs, a simple and laudable architecture, and the latest conveniences. Throughout, electricity took the place of candles and slatternly hearth-fires. Along the bedroom baseboard were three plugs for electric lamps, concealed by little brass doors. In the halls were plugs for the vacuum cleaner, and in the living-room plugs for the piano lamp, for the electric fan. The trim dining-room (with its admirable oak buffet, its leaded-glass cupboard, its creamy plaster walls, its modest scene of a salmon expiring upon a pile of oysters) had plugs which suppled the electric percolator and the electric toaster.

In fact there was but one thing wrong with the Babbitt house: It was not a home.

Often of a morning Babbitt came bouncing and jesting in to breakfast. But things were mysteriously awry to-day. As he pontifically tread the upper hall he looked into Verona's bedroom and protested, "What's the use of giving the family a high-class house when they don't appreciate it and tend to business and get down to brass tacks?"

He marched upon them: Verona, a dumpy brown-haired girl of twenty-two, just out of Bryn Mawr, given to solicitudes about duty and sex and God and the unconquerable bagginess of the gray sports-suit she was now wearing. Ted—Theodore Roosevelt Babbitt—a decorative boy of seventeen. Tinka—Katherine—still a baby at ten, with radiant red hair and a thin skin which hinted of too much candy and too many ice cream sodas. Babbitt did not show his vague irritation as he tramped in. He really disliked being a family tyrant, and his nagging was as meaningless as it was frequent. He shouted at Tinka, "Well, kittiedoolie!" It was the only pet name in his vocabulary, except the "dear" and "hon." with which he recognized his wife, and he flung it at Tinka every morning.

He gulped a cup of coffee in the hope of pacifying his stomach and his soul. His stomach ceased to feel as though it did not belong to him, but Verona began to be conscientious and annoying, and abruptly there returned to Babbitt the doubts regarding life and families and business which had clawed at him when his dream-life and the slim fairy girl had fled.

Verona had for six months been filing-clerk at the Gruensberg Leather Company offices, with a prospect of becoming secretary to Mr. Gruensberg and thus, as Babbitt defined it, "getting some good out of your expensive college education till you're ready to marry and settle down."

But now said Verona: "Father! I was talking to a classmate of mine that's working for the Associated Charities—oh, Dad, there's the sweetest little babies that come to the milkstation there!—and I feel as though I ought to be doing something worth while like that."

"What do you mean 'worth while'? If you get to be Gruensberg's secretary—and maybe you would, if you kept up your shorthand and didn't go sneaking off to concerts and talkfests every evening—I guess you'll find thirty-five or forty bones a week worth while!"

"I know, but—oh, I want to—contribute— I wish I were working in a settlement-house. I wonder if I could get one of the department-stores to let me put in a welfare-department with a nice rest-room and chintzes and wicker chairs and so on and so forth. Or I could—"

"Now you look here! The first thing you got to understand is that all this uplift and flipflop and settlement-work and recreation is nothing in God's world but the entering wedge for socialism. The sooner a man learns he isn't going to be coddled, and he needn't expect a lot of free grub and, uh, all these free classes and flipflop and doodads for his kids unless he earns 'em, why, the sooner he'll get on the job and produce—produce—produce! That's what the country needs, and not all this fancy stuff that just enfeebles the will-power of the working man and gives his kids a lot of notions above their class. And you—if you'd tend to business instead of fooling and fussing— All the time! When I was a young man I made up my mind what I wanted to do, and stuck to it through thick and thin, and that's why I'm where I am to-day, and—Myra! What do you let the girl chop the toast up into these dinky little chunks for? Can't get your fist onto 'em. Half cold, anyway!"

Ted Babbitt, junior in the great East Side High School, had been making hiccup-like sounds of interruption. He blurted now, "Say, Rone, you going to—"

Verona whirled. "Ted! Will you kindly not interrupt us when we're talking about serious matters!"

"Aw punk," said Ted judicially. "Ever since somebody slipped up and let you out of college, Ammonia, you been pulling these nut conversations about what-nots and so-on-and-so-forths. Are you going to— I want to use the car tonight."

Babbitt snorted, "Oh, you do! May want it myself!" Verona protested, "Oh, you do, Mr. Smarty! I'm going to take it myself!" Tinka wailed, "Oh, papa, you said maybe you'd drive us down to Rosedale!" and Mrs. Babbitt, "Careful, Tinka, your sleeve is in the butter." They glared, and Verona hurled, "Ted, you're a perfect pig about the car!"

"Course you're not! Not a-tall!" Ted could be maddeningly bland. "You just want to grab it off, right after dinner, and leave it in front of some skirt's house all evening while you sit and gass about lite'ature and the highbrows you're going to marry—if they only propose!"

"Well, Dad oughtn't to *ever* let you have it! You and those beastly Jones boys drive like maniacs. The idea of your taking the turn on Chautauqua Place at forty miles an hour!"

"Aw, where do you get that stuff! You're so darn scared of the car that you drive up-hill with the emergency brake on!"

"I do not! And you— Always talking about how much you know about motors, and Eunice Littlefield told me you said the battery fed the generator!"

"You—why, my good woman, you don't know a generator from a differential." Not unreasonably was Ted lofty with her. He was a natural mechanic, a maker and tinkerer of machines; he lisped in blueprints for the blueprints came.

"That'll do now!" Babbitt flung in mechanically, as he lighted the gloriously satisfying first cigar of the day and tasted the exhilarating drug of the *Advocate-Times* headlines.

Ted negotiated: "Gee, honest, Rone, I don't want to take the old boat, but I promised couple o' girls in my class I'd drive 'em down to the rehearsal of the school chorus, and, gee, I don't want to, but a gentleman's got to keep his social engagements."

"Well, upon my word! You and your social engagements! In high school!"

"Oh, ain't we select since we went to that hen college! Let me tell you there isn't a private school in the state that's got as swell a bunch as we got in Gamma Digamma this year. There's two fellows that their dads are millionaires. Say, gee, I ought to have a car of my own, like lots of the fellows."

Babbitt almost rose. "A car of your own! Don't you want a yacht, and a house and lot? That pretty nearly takes the cake! A boy that can't pass his Latin examinations, like any other boy ought to, and he expects me to give him a motor-car, and I suppose a chauffeur, and an aeroplane maybe, as a reward for the hard work he puts in going to the movies with Eunice Littlefield! Well, when you see me giving you—"

Somewhat later, after diplomacies, Ted persuaded Verona to admit that she was merely going to the Armory, that evening, to see the dog and cat show. She was then, Ted planned, to park the car in front of the candy-store across from the Armory and he would pick it up. There were masterly arrangements regarding leaving the key, and having the gasoline tank filled; and passionately, devotees of the Great God Motor, they hymned the patch on the spare inner-tube, and the lost jack-handle.

Their truce dissolving, Ted observed that her friends were "a scream of a bunch—stuck-up gabby four-flushers." His friends, she indicated, were "disgusting imitation sports, and horrid little shrieking ignorant girls." Further: "It's disgusting of you to smoke cigarettes, and so on and so forth, and those clothes you've got on this morning, they're too utterly ridiculous—honestly, simply disgusting."

Ted balanced over to the low beveled mirror in the buffet, regarded his charms, and smirked. His suit, the latest thing in Old Eli Togs, was skin-tight, with skimpy trousers to the tops of his glaring tan boots, a chorus-man waistline, pattern of an agitated check, and across the back a belt which belted nothing. His scarf was an enormous black silk wad. His flaxen hair was ice-smooth, pasted back without parting. When he went to school he would add a cap with a long vizor like a shovel-blade.

Proudest of all was his waistcoat, saved for, begged for, plotted for; a real Fancy Vest of fawn with polka dots of a decayed red, the points astoundingly long. On the lower edge of it he wore a high-school button, a class button, and a fraternity pin.

And none of it mattered. He was supple and swift and flushed; his eyes (which he believed to be cynical) were candidly eager. But he was not over-gentle. He waved his hand at poor dumpy Verona and drawled: "Yes, I guess we're pretty ridiculous and disgusticulus, and I rather guess our new necktie is some smear!"

Babbitt barked: "It is! And while you're admiring yourself, let me tell you it might add to your manly beauty if you wiped some of that egg off your mouth!"

Verona giggled, momentary victor in the greatest of Great Wars, which is the family war. Ted looked at her hopelessly, then shrieked at Tinka: "For the love o' Pete, quit pouring the whole sugar bowl on your corn flakes!"

When Verona and Ted were gone and Tinka upstairs, Babbitt groaned to his wife: "Nice family, I must say! I don't pretend to be any baa-lamb, and maybe I'm a little cross-grained at breakfast sometimes, but the way they go on jab-jab-jabbering, I simply can't stand it. I swear, I feel like going off some place where I can get a little peace. I do think after a man's spent his lifetime trying to give his kids a chance and a decent education, it's pretty discouraging to hear them all the time scrapping like a bunch of hyenas and never—and never— Curious; here in the paper it says—Never silent for one mom— Seen the morning paper yet?"

"No, dear." In twenty-three years of married life, Mrs. Babbitt had seen the paper before her husband just sixty-seven times.

"Lots of news. Terrible big tornado in the South. Hard luck, all right. But this, say, this is corking! Beginning of the end for those fellows! New York Assembly has passed some bills that ought to completely outlaw the socialists! And there's an elevator-runners' strike in New York and a lot of college boys are taking their places. That's the stuff! And a mass-meeting in Birmingham's demanded that this Mick agitator, this fellow De Valera, be deported. Dead right, by golly! All these agitators paid with German gold anyway. And we got no business interfering with the Irish or any other foreign government. Keep our hands strictly off. And there's another well-authenticated rumor from Russia that Lenin is dead. That's fine. It's beyond me why we don't just step in there and kick those Bolshevik cusses out."

"That's so," said Mrs. Babbitt.

"And it says here a fellow was inaugurated mayor in overalls—a preacher, too! What do you think of that!"

"Humph! Well!"

He searched for an attitude, but neither as a Republican, a Presbyterian, an Elk, nor a real-estate broker did he have any doctrine about preacher-mayors laid down for him, so he grunted and went on. She looked sympathetic and did not hear a word. Later she would read the headlines, the society columns, and the department-store advertisements.

"What do you know about this! Charley McKelvey still doing the sassiety stunt as heavy as ever. Here's what the gushy woman reporter says about last night:

> Never is Society with the big, big S more flattered than when they are bidden to partake of good cheer at the distinguished and hospitable residence of Mr. and Mrs. Charles L. McKelvey as they were last night. Set in its spacious lawns and landscaping, one of the notable sights crowning Royal Ridge, but merry and homelike despite its mighty stone walls and its vast rooms famed for their decoration, their home was thrown open last night for a dance in honor of Mrs. McKelvey's notable guest, Miss J. Sneeth of Washington. The wide hall is so generous in its proportions that it made a perfect ballroom, its hardwood floor reflecting the charming pageant above its polished surface. Even the delights of dancing paled before the alluring opportunities for tête-à-têtes that invited the soul to loaf in the long library before the baronial fireplace, or in the drawing-room with its deep comfy armchairs, its shaded lamps just made for a sly whisper of pretty nothings all a deux; or even in the billiard room where one could take a cue and show a prowess at still another game than that sponsored by Cupid and Terpsichore.

There was more, a great deal more, in the best urban journalistic style of Miss Elnora Pearl Bates, the popular society editor of the *Advocate-Times*. But Babbitt could not abide it. He grunted. He wrinkled the newspaper. He protested: "Can you beat it! I'm willing to hand a lot of credit to Charley McKelvey. When we were in college together, he was just as hard up as any of us, and he's made a million good bucks out of contracting and hasn't been any dishonester or bought any more city councils than was necessary. And that's a good house of his—though it ain't any 'mighty stone walls' and it ain't worth the ninety thousand it cost him. But when it comes to talking as though Charley McKelvey and all that booze-hoisting set of his are any blooming bunch of of, of Vanderbilts, why, it makes me tired!"

Timidly from Mrs. Babbitt: "I would like to see the inside of their house though. It must be lovely. I've never been inside."

"Well, I have! Lots of—couple of times. To see Chaz about business deals, in the evening. It's not so much. I wouldn't *want* to go there to dinner with that gang of, of high-binders. And I'll bet I make a whole lot more money than some of those tin-horns that spend all they got on dress-suits and haven't got a decent suit of underwear to their name! Hey! What do you think of this!"

Mrs. Babbitt was strangely unmoved by the tidings from the Real Estate and Building column of the *Advocate-Times:*

> Ashtabula Street, 496—J. K. Dawson to
> Thomas Mullally, April 17, 15.7 x 112.2,
> mtg. $4000 .... Nom.

And this morning Babbitt was too disquieted to entertain her with items from Mechanics' Liens, Mortgages Recorded, and Contracts Awarded. He rose. As he looked at her his eyebrows seemed shaggier than usual. Suddenly:

"Yes, maybe—Kind of shame to not keep in touch with folks like the McKelveys. We might try inviting them to dinner, some evening. Oh, thunder, let's not waste our good time thinking about 'em! Our little bunch has a lot liver times than all those plutes. Just compare a real human like you with these neurotic birds like Lucile McKelvey—all highbrow talk and dressed up like a plush horse! You're a great old girl, hon.!"

He covered his betrayal of softness with a complaining: "Say, don't let Tinka go and eat any more of that poison nutfudge. For Heaven's sake, try to keep her from ruining her digestion. I tell you, most folks don't appreciate how important it is to have a good digestion and regular habits. Be back 'bout usual time, I guess."

He kissed her—he didn't quite kiss her—he laid unmoving lips against her unflushing cheek. He hurried out to the garage, muttering: "Lord, what a family! And now Myra is going to get pathetic on me because we don't train with this millionaire outfit. Oh, Lord, sometimes I'd like to quit the whole game. And the office worry and detail just as bad. And I act cranky and— I don't mean to, but I get— So darn tired!"

F. Scott Fitzgerald

Echoes of the

Jazz Age

F. Scott Fitzgerald and the Jazz Age are indissolubly linked. He is, as Alfred Kazin noted, the laureate of the age. Born in Minnesota in 1896, Fitzgerald attended Princeton, but left in 1917 to join the army. Assigned to duty in the United States, he spent the war years writing his first novel, This Side of Paradise, *in military camp. In that novel (published in 1920), and in* The Beautiful and Damned *(1922), he depicted the war generation "of bright young creatures, consciously adrift from the ancestral ethical moorings, compact of disillusionment and cleverness, and passionately intent on escaping from boredom through inebriation and preoccupation with love affairs." In* The Great Gatsby *(1925), his major work, Fitzgerald represented the era superbly; "the people were right, the talk was right, the clothes, the cars were real." It is at the end of* This Side of Paradise *that he most sharply states the theme—"all gods dead, all wars fought, all faiths in man shaken." That first novel heralded the Jazz Age. It is fitting that Fitzgerald, who was the symbol of the age, should also have written its obituary eleven years later. His essay "Echoes of the Jazz Age" appeared in* Scribner's Magazine *for November 1931. [From* The Crack-Up *by F. Scott Fitzgerald. Edited by Edmund Wilson. Copyright 1945 by New Directions. Reprinted by permission of New Directions, Publishers.]*

It is too soon to write about the Jazz Age with perspective, and without being suspected of premature arteriosclerosis. Many people still succumb to violent retching when they happen upon any of its characteristic words—words which have since yielded in vividness to the coinages of the underworld. It is as dead as were the Yellow Nineties in 1902. Yet the present writer already looks back to it with nostalgia. It bore him up, flattered him and gave him more money than he had dreamed of, simply for telling people that he felt as they did, that something had to be done with all the nervous energy stored up and unexpended in the War.

The ten-year period that, as if reluctant to die outmoded in its bed, leaped to a spectacular death in October, 1929, began about the time of the May Day riots in 1919. When the police rode down the demobilized country boys gaping at the orators in Madison Square, it was the sort of measure bound to alienate the more intelligent young men from the prevailing order. We didn't remember anything about the Bill of Rights until Mencken began plugging it, but we did know that such tyranny belonged in the jittery little countries of South Europe. If goose-livered business men had this effect on the government, then maybe we had gone to war for J. P. Morgan's loans after all. But, because we were tired of Great Causes, there was no more than a short outbreak of moral indignation, typified by Dos Passos' "Three Soldiers." Presently we began to have slices of the national cake and our idealism only flared up when the newspapers made melodrama out of such stories as Harding and the Ohio Gang or Sacco and Vanzetti. The events of 1919 left us cynical rather than revolutionary, in spite of the fact that now we are all rummaging around in our trunks wondering where in hell we left the liberty cap—"I know I *had* it"—and the moujik blouse. It was characteristic of the Jazz Age that it had no interest in politics at all.

It was an age of miracles, it was an age of art, it was an age of excess, and it was an age of satire. A Stuffed Shirt, squirming to blackmail in a lifelike way, sat upon the throne of the United States; a stylish young man hurried over to represent to us the throne of England. A world of girls yearned for the young Englishman; the old American groaned in his sleep as he waited to be poisoned by his wife, upon the advice of the female Rasputin who then made the ultimate decision in our national affairs. But such matters apart, we had things our way at last. With Americans ordering suits by the gross in London, the Bond Street tailors perforce agreed to moderate their cut to the American long-waisted figure and loose-fitting taste, something subtle passed to America, the style of man. During the Renaissance, Francis the First looked to Florence to trim his leg. Seventeenth-century England aped the court of France, and fifty years ago the German Guards officer bought his civilian clothes in London. Gentleman's clothes—symbol of "the power that man must hold and that passes from race to race."

We were the most powerful nation. Who could tell us any longer what was fashionable and what was fun? Isolated during the European War, we had begun combing the unknown South and West for folkways and pastimes and there were more ready to hand.

The first social revelation created a sensation out of all proportion to its novelty. As far back as 1915 the unchaperoned young people of the smaller cities had discovered the mobile privacy of that automobile given to young Bill at sixteen to make him "self-reliant." At first petting was a desperate adventure even under such favorable conditions, but presently confidences were exchanged and the old commandment broke down. As early as 1917 there were references to such sweet and casual dalliance in any number of the *Yale Record* or the *Princeton Tiger.*

But petting in its more audacious manifestations was confined to the wealthier classes—among other young people the old standards prevailed until after the War, and a kiss meant that a proposal was expected, as young officers in strange cities sometimes discovered to their dismay. Only in 1920 did the veil finally fall—the Jazz Age was in flower.

Scarcely had the staider citizens of the republic caught their breaths when the wildest of all generations, the generation which had been adolescent during the confusion of the War, brusquely shouldered my contemporaries out of the way and danced into the limelight. This was the generation whose girls dramatized themselves as flappers, the generation that corrupted its elders and eventually overreached itself less through lack of morals than through lack of taste. May one offer in exhibit the year 1922! That was the peak of the younger generation, for though the Jazz Age continued, it became less and less an affair of youth.

The sequel was like a children's party taken over by the elders, leaving the children puzzled and rather neglected and rather taken aback. By 1923 their elders, tired of watching the carnival with ill-concealed envy, had discovered that young liquor will take the place of young blood, and with a whoop the orgy began. The younger generation was starred no longer.

A whole race going hedonistic, deciding on pleasure. The precocious intimacies of the younger generation would have come about with or without prohibition—they were implicit in the attempt to adapt English customs to American conditions. (Our South, for example, is tropical and early maturing—it has never been part of the wisdom of France and Spain to let young girls go unchaperoned at sixteen and seventeen.) But the general decision to be amused that began with the cocktail parties of 1921 had more complicated origins.

The word jazz in its progress toward respectability has meant first sex, then dancing, then music. It is associated with a state of nervous stimulation, not unlike that of big cities behind the lines of a war. To many English the War still goes on because all the forces that menace them are still active—Wherefore eat, drink and be merry, for to-morrow we die. But different causes had now brought about a corresponding state in America—though there were entire classes (people over fifty, for example) who spent a whole decade denying its existence even when its puckish face peered into the family circle. Never did they dream that they had contributed to it. The honest citizens of every class, who believed in a strict public morality and were powerful enough to enforce the necessary legislation, did not know that they would necessarily be served by criminals and quacks, and do not really believe it to-day. Rich righteousness had always been able to buy honest and intelligent servants to free the slaves or the Cubans, so when this attempt collapsed our elders stood firm with all the stubbornness of people involved in a weak case, preserving their righteousness and losing their children. Silver-haired women and men with fine old faces, people who never did a consciously dishonest thing in their lives, still assure each other in the apartment hotels of New York and Boston and Washington that "There's a whole generation growing up that will never know the taste of liquor." Meanwhile their granddaughters pass the well-thumbed copy of "Lady Chatterley's Lover" around the boarding-school and, if they get about at all, know the taste of gin or corn at sixteen. But the generation who reached maturity between 1875 and 1895 continue to believe what they want to believe.

Even the intervening generations were incredulous. In 1920 Heywood Broun announced that all this hubbub was nonsense, that young men didn't kiss but told anyhow. But very shortly people over twenty-five came in for an intensive education. Let me trace some of the revelations vouchsafed them by reference to a dozen works written for various types of mentality during the decade. We begin with the suggestion that Don Juan leads an interesting life ("Jurgen," 1919); then we learn that there's a lot of sex around if we only knew it ("Winesburg, Ohio," 1920), that adolescents lead very amorous lives ("This Side of Paradise," 1920), that there are a lot of neglected Anglo-Saxon words ("Ulysses," 1921), that older people don't always resist sudden temptations ("Cytherea," 1922), that girls are sometimes seduced without being ruined ("Flaming Youth," 1922), that even rape often turns out well ("The Sheik," 1922), that glamorous English ladies are often promiscuous ("The Green Hat," 1924), that in fact they devote most of their time to it ("The Vortex," 1926), that it's a damn good thing too ("Lady Chatterley's Lover," 1928), and finally that there are abnormal variations ("The Well of Loneliness," 1928, and "Sodome and Gomorrhe," 1929).

In my opinion the erotic element in these works, even "The Sheik" written for children in the key of "Peter Rabbit," did not one particle of harm. Everything they described, and much more, was familiar in our contemporary life. The majority of the theses were honest and elucidating—their effect was to restore some dignity to the male as opposed to the he-man in American life. ("And what is a 'He-man'?" demanded Gertrude Stein one day. "Isn't it a large enough order to fill out to the dimensions of all that 'a man' has meant in the past? A '*He*-man'!") The married woman can now discover whether she is being cheated, or whether sex is just something to be endured, and her compensation should be to establish a tyranny of the spirit, as her mother may have hinted. Perhaps many women found that love was meant to be fun. Anyhow the objectors lost their tawdry little case, which is one reason why our literature is now the most living in the world.

Contrary to popular opinion the movies of the Jazz Age had no effect upon its morals. The social attitude of the producers was timid, behind the times and banal—for example no picture mirrored even faintly the younger generation until 1923, when magazines had already been started to celebrate it and it had long ceased to be news. There were a few feeble splutters and then Clara Bow in "Flaming Youth"; promptly the Hollywood hacks ran the theme into its cinematographic grave. Throughout the Jazz Age the movies got no farther than Mrs. Jiggs, keeping up with its most blatant superficialities. This was no doubt due to the censorship as well as to innate conditions in the industry. In any case the Jazz Age now raced along under its own power, served by great filling stations full of money.

The people over thirty, the people all the way up to fifty, had joined the dance. We graybeards (to tread down F.P.A.) remember the uproar when in 1912 grandmothers of forty tossed away their crutches and took lessons in the Tango and the Castle-Walk. A dozen years later a woman might pack the Green Hat with her other affairs as she set off for Europe or New York, but Savonarola was too busy flogging dead horses in Augean stables of his own creation to notice. Society, even in small cities, now dined in separate chambers, and the sober table learned about the gay table only from hearsay. There were very few people left at the sober table. One of its former glories, the less sought-after girls who had become resigned to sublimating a probable celibacy, came across Freud and Jung in seeking their intellectual recompense and came tearing back into the fray.

By 1926 the universal preoccupation with sex had become a nuisance. (I remember a perfectly mated, contented young mother asking my wife's advice about "having an affair right away," though she had no one especially in mind, "because don't you think it's sort of undignified when you get much over thirty?") For a while bootleg negro records with their phallic euphemisms made everything suggestive, and simultaneously came a wave of erotic plays—young girls from finishing-schools packed the galleries to hear about the romance of being a Lesbian and George Jean Nathan protested. Then one young producer lost his head entirely, drank a beauty's alcoholic bath-water and went to the penitentiary. Somehow his pathetic attempt at romance belongs to the Jazz Age, while his contemporary in prison, Ruth Snyder, had to be hoisted into it by the tabloids—she was, as *The Daily News,* hinted deliciously to gourmets, about "to cook, *and sizzle, AND FRY!"* in the electric chair.

The gay elements of society had divided into two main streams, one flowing toward Palm Beach and Deauville, and the other, much smaller, toward the summer Riviera. One could get away with more on the summer Riviera, and whatever happened seemed to have something to do with art. From 1926 to 1929, the great years of the Cap d'Antibes, this corner of France was dominated by a group quite distinct from that American society which is dominated by Europeans. Pretty much of anything went at Antibes—by 1929 at the most gorgeous paradise for swimmers on the Mediterranean no one swam any more save for a short hangover dip at noon. There was a picturesque graduation of steep rocks over the sea and somebody's valet and an occasional English girl used to dive from them but the Americans were content to discuss each other in the bar. This was indicative of something that was taking place in the homeland—Americans were getting soft. There were signs everywhere: we still won the Olympic games but with champions whose names had few vowels in them—teams composed, like the fighting Irish combination of Notre Dame, of fresh overseas blood. Once the French became really interested the Davis Cup gravitated automatically to their intensity in competition. The vacant lots of the Middle-Western cities were built up now—except for a short period in school we were not turning out to be an athletic people like the British after all. The hare and the tortoise. Of course if we wanted to we could be in a minute; we still had all those reserves of ancestral vitality, but one day in 1926 we looked down and found we had flabby arms and a fat pot and couldn't say boop-boop-a-doop to a Sicilian. Shades of Van Bibber!—no utopian ideal, God knows. Even golf, once considered an effeminate game, had seemed very strenuous of late—an emasculated form appeared and proved just right.

By 1927 a wide-spread neurosis began to be evident, faintly signalled, like a nervous beating of the feet, by the popularity of cross-word puzzles. I remember a fellow expatriate opening a letter from a mutual friend of ours, urging him to come home and be revitalized by the hardy, bracing qualities of the native soil. It was a strong letter and it affected us both deeply, until we noticed that it was headed from a nerve sanitarium in Pennsylvania.

By this time contemporaries of mine had begun to disappear into the dark maw of violence. A classmate killed his wife and himself on Long Island, another tumbled "accidentally" from a skyscraper in Philadelphia, another purposely from a skyscraper in New York. One was killed in a speak-easy in Chicago; another was beaten to death in a speak-easy in New York and crawled home to the Princeton Club to die; still another had his skull crushed by a maniac's axe in an insane asylum where he was confined. These are not catastrophes that I went out of my way to look for—these were my friends; moreover, these things happened not during the depression but during the boom.

In the spring of '27, something bright and alien flashed across the sky. A young Minnesotan who seemed to have had nothing to do with his generation did a heroic thing, and for a moment people set down their glasses in country clubs and speak-easies and thought of their old best dreams. Maybe there was a way out by flying, maybe our restless blood could find frontiers in the illimitable air. But by that time we were all pretty well committed; and the Jazz Age continued; we would all have one more.

Nevertheless, Americans were wandering ever more widely—friends seemed eternally bound for Russia, Persia, Abyssinia and Central Africa. And by 1928 Paris had grown suffocating. With each new shipment of Americans spewed up by the boom the quality fell off, until toward the end there was something sinister about the crazy boatloads. They were no longer the simple pa and ma and son and daughter, infinitely superior in their qualities of kindness and curiosity to the corresponding class in Europe, but fantastic neanderthals who believed something, something vague, that you remembered from a very cheap novel. I remember an Italian on a steamer who promenaded the deck in an American Reserve Officer's uniform picking quarrels in broken English with Americans who criticised their own institutions in the bar. I remember a fat Jewess, inlaid with diamonds, who sat behind us at the Russian ballet and said as the curtain rose, "Thad's luffly, dey ought to baint a bicture of it." This was low comedy but it was evident that money and power were falling into the hands of people in comparison with whom the leader of a village Soviet would be a gold-mine of judgment and culture. There were citizens travelling in luxury in 1928 and 1929 who, in the distortion of their new condition, had the human value of pekinese bivalves, cretins, goats. I remember the Judge from some New York district who had taken his daughter to see the Bayeux Tapestries and made a scene in the papers advocating their segregation because one scene was immoral. But in those days life was like the race in "Alice in Wonderland," there was a prize for every one.

The Jazz Age had had a wild youth and a heady middle age. There was the phase of the necking parties, the Leopold-Loeb murder (I remember the time my wife was arrested on Queensborough Bridge on the suspicion of being the "Bob-haired Bandit") and the John Held Clothes. In the second phase such phenomena as sex and murder became more mature, if much more conventional. Middle age must be served and pajamas came to the beach to save fat thighs and flabby calves from competition with the one-piece bathing-suit. Finally skirts came down and everything was concealed. Everybody was at scratch now. Let's go—

But it was not to be. Somebody had blundered and the most expensive orgy in history was over.

It ended two years ago, because the utter confidence which was its essential prop received an enormous jolt and it didn't take long for the flimsy structure to settle earthward. And after two years the Jazz Age seems as far away as the days before the War. It was borrowed time anyhow—the whole upper tenth of a nation living with the insouciance of grand ducs and the casualness of chorus girls. But moralizing is easy now and it was pleasant to be in one's twenties in such a certain and unworried time. Even when you were broke you didn't worry about money, because it was in such profusion around you. Toward the end one had a struggle to pay one's share; it was almost a favor to accept hospitality that required any travelling. Charm, notoriety, mere good manners, weighed more than money as a social asset. This was rather splendid but things were getting thinner and thinner as the eternal necessary human values tried to spread over all that expansion. Writers were geniuses on the strength of one respectable book or play; just as during the War officers of four months' experience commanded hundreds of men, so there were now many little fish lording it over great big bowls. In the theatrical world extravagant productions were carried by a few second-rate stars, and so on up the scale into politics where it was difficult to interest good men in positions of the highest importance and responsibility, importance and responsibility far exceeding that of business executives but which paid only five or six thousand a year.

Now once more the belt is tight and we summon the proper expression of horror as we look back at our wasted youth. Sometimes, though, there is a ghostly rumble among the drums, an asthmatic whisper in the trombones that swings me back into the early twenties when we drank wood alcohol and every day in every way grew better and better, and there was a first abortive shortening of the skirts, and girls all looked alike in sweater dresses, and people you didn't want to know said "Yes, we have no bananas," and it seemed only a question of a few years before the older people would step aside and let the world be run by those who saw things as they were—and it all seems rosy and romantic to us who were young then, because we will never feel quite so intensely about our surroundings any more.

On October 24, 1929—"Black Thursday"—the stock market crashed. On that day about 13 million shares changed hands and prices collapsed. Although some of the leading bankers and financiers bought heavily that same afternoon to bolster the market, it could not be saved, and hundreds of thousands of investors faced ruin. Five days later, prices again dropped drastically, with 16½ million shares being traded. In November, trading continued active with further losses in value. By the end of the year the value of stocks had decreased by about $35 billion.

The crash was not immediately viewed by the business community or by the Administration as the harbinger of depression. Andrew Mellon, the Secretary of the Treasury and himself a financier, expressed confidence in the nation's economy, while President Herbert Hoover, on October 25, 1929, noted that "the fundamental business of the country—that is, production and distribution—is on a sound and prosperous basis." But within one month of the President's optimistic statement, officials of the federal reserve system informed him privately that the economy was weak. Hoover was then prepared to accept the debacle as no ordinary crash. Although he assured the people, in his annual message in December 1929, that all was well, it soon became perfectly clear to everyone that a depression had started. Production fell off, banks and factories closed, foreign trade diminished, wages dropped, and unemployment rose.

Business conditions continued to grow worse as the year turned. A slight recovery in the summer of 1930 was only a transitory affair, and the observance of Business Confidence Week, decreed for October 19–25, 1930, did not alter the trend. By the winter of 1930, the depression had deepened and appeared to have staying power. Nothing short of extraordinary measures could be expected to be effective in rescuing the national economy.

This was the worst depression in American history. By 1932, when the lowest point was reached, nearly 17 million were unemployed; national income had dropped from 68 billion in 1930 to 41 billion; stocks had sunk to an incredibly low point—General Electric from 396¼ to 8½ and United States Steel from 261¾ to 21¾, with the total value having gone from $87 billion to $15.6 billion; about 4700 banks, with a total of $3½ billion in deposit had closed their doors; over 100,000 commercial firms had failed with $3 billion in liabilities; and most of the railroads, including the biggest, were in receivership. Bread lines were everywhere, the homeless wandered about the country, and suffering was widespread.

What had caused the depression? As in almost every historical event, no single cause can be held responsible; nor, for that matter, can any one of a number of causes be assigned as the primary one. The stock market crash played some part in bringing it on, but only, as Broadus Mitchell

10

THE GREAT

DEPRESSION

has noted, as the "exciting force." The causes lie deeper. John K. Galbraith, in a chapter of his *The Great Crash, 1929,* isolates five weaknesses in the economy, and these may well provide the most reasonable explanation: (1) poor distribution of income; (2) bad corporate structure (holding companies, grafters and crooks in the corporations); (3) weak banking structure (too many independent banks); (4) the state of the foreign balance, involving the relation of imports to exports and American loans to countries that were bad credit risks; and (5) faulty economic intelligence (unwise advice by economists who should have known better). To these fundamental weaknesses may be added other causes, such as agricultural and industrial overexpansion (more was produced than could be consumed, huge surpluses were created, prices dropped, and farmers' purchasing power was reduced), much too high capital surpluses, and overexpansion of credit. Intimately connected with the American economy, of course, was the European situation. The failure of one of Europe's greatest banking institutions, the Kredit Anstalt in Vienna on May 11, 1931, followed by financial crises in other countries, had the deepest effect on the United States. Europe withdrew large quantities of gold from this country, causing American banks to call in loans and to unload securities, which in turn caused sags in the market.

President Hoover approached the problems of the depression in a cautious manner. As an admirer of the American character and economy, he blamed Europe for the continuance of the unfortunate conditions at home. In his annual message in December 1931, he declared, "Although some of the causes of our depression are due to speculation, inflation of securities and real estate, unsound financial investments, and mismanagement of financial institutions, yet our self-contained national economy, with its matchless strength and resources, would have enabled us to recover long since but for the continued dislocations, shocks, and setbacks from abroad." By instinct a conservative and devoted to free enterprise, he refused, at the outset, to permit the government to intervene directly in the economic processes. The administration's role was to act as organizer and instigator of private measures to speed recovery. Late in 1929, he called conferences of leaders of business, labor, and agriculture to urge them to take steps to fight the depression by spreading employment, maintaining hours and wages, and, wherever possible, conducting business as usual. It soon became apparent, nevertheless, that government action would be necessary. Distasteful as this was to the President, contrary though it was to his whole philosophy, he supported legislation designed to provide government leadership in improving conditions: the Agricultural Marketing Act of 1929, the creation of home loan banks, the establishment of the Reconstruction Finance Corporation, and the expansion of public works.

He refused consistently, however, to provide direct relief to the people or to permit the government to enter into competition with private industry. Nor would he countenance any federal controls. Nonetheless, the

President must be given credit for stepping beyond any of his predecessors in treating a depression. He may be criticized for doing too little too late and for excessive caution, but it should be recalled that Van Buren, Hayes, and Cleveland had disclaimed any responsibility for the dislocation of the economy.

The depression may be considered a watershed in American history. Lippmann, in fact, viewed it as "one of the great upheavals and readjustments of modern history." Momentous changes flowed from it in every part of the civilized world. For the United States, one of the most significant effects was the demand for government action to prevent the recurrence of so stagnating a crisis. A reform of economic institutions became a necessity. Private enterprise independent of controls went out with the Republican regime in 1933.

John K. Galbraith

Vision and Boundless

Hope and Optimism

Prosperity during the 1920s seemed to most people unending. On every hand, economists, politicians, and businessmen—conservative ones at that —exuded confidence. A report on Recent Economic Changes, *prepared by a special committee appointed by President Hoover and published early in 1929, declared the nation's economy to be in a healthy state. In an introduction to the report, Harvard Professor Edwin F. Gay, a distinguished economist, reflected confidence in the business community. Investors were urged to put more money into the stock market, and producers were enjoined to increase their output. Meanwhile, the market rose higher and higher, with production exceeding previous records.*

There were some, however, who sounded warnings and suggested caution. They saw danger ahead if a brake were not applied to the blind speculation. Early in 1929, a New York bank expressed misgivings "if the rate of credit increase rises above the rate of business growth." Others feared the unevenness of prosperity and the buying on borrowed funds. For example, at the end of 1928, James Truslow Adams—one of America's notable historians and a member of a Wall Street firm before abandoning business for scholarship—wrote a long analysis of business conditions in which he raised the gravest questions about the state of the economy. Noting that prosperity was an illusion and a state of mind, he predicted a crash unless drastic reforms were effected. After pointing out that numerous industries were suffering and that even among the prosperous ones only a few companies were healthy, he attacked a prevailing economic concept—the existence of a perfect circle capable of un-

limited expansion and based on the fact that high wages increased consuming power, thus making for increased production.

A perceptive and charming description of the sense of euphoria that pervaded the American people and the economic danger signals that they ignored is in Chapter Two of John K. Galbraith's The Great Crash, 1929. *Galbraith, most widely known for his study of* The Affluent Society, *has been professor of economics at Harvard for many years and has also served as Ambassador to India. [John K. Galbraith,* The Great Crash, 1929 *(Boston: Houghton Mifflin Company, 1961). Reprinted by permission of Houghton Mifflin Company. British rights by permission of Hamish Hamilton Ltd., London.]*

On December 4, 1928, President Coolidge sent his last message on the state of the Union to the reconvening Congress. Even the most melancholy congressman must have found reassurance in his words. "No Congress of the United States ever assembled, on surveying the state of the Union, has met with a more pleasing prospect than that which appears at the present time. In the domestic field there is tranquility and contentment . . . and the highest record of years of prosperity. In the foreign field there is peace, the goodwill which comes from mutual understanding . . ." He told the legislators that they and the country might "regard the present with satisfaction and anticipate the future with optimism." And breaking sharply with the most ancient of our political conventions, he omitted to attribute this well-being to the excellence of the administration which he headed. "The main source of these unexampled blessings lies in the integrity and character of the American people."

A whole generation of historians has assailed Coolidge for the superficial optimism which kept him from seeing that a great storm was brewing at home and also more distantly abroad. This is grossly unfair. It requires neither courage nor prescience to predict disaster. Courage is required of the man who, when things are good, says so. Historians rejoice in crucifying the false prophet of the millennium. They never dwell on the mistake of the man who wrongly predicted Armageddon.

There was much that was good about the world of which Coolidge spoke. True, as liberal misanthropes have insisted, the rich were getting richer much faster than the poor were getting less poor. The farmers were unhappy and had been ever since the depression of 1920–21 had cut farm prices sharply but left costs high. Black people in the South and white people in the southern Appalachians continued to dwell in hopeless poverty. Fine old-English houses with high gables, leaded glass, and well-simulated half-timbering were rising in the country club district, while farther in town one encountered the most noisome slums outside the Orient.

All this notwithstanding, the twenties in America were a very good time. Production and employment were high and rising. Wages were not going up much, but prices were stable. Although many people were still very poor, more people were comfortably well-off, well-to-do, or rich than ever before. Finally, American capitalism was undoubtedly in a lively phase. Between 1925 and 1929, the number of manufacturing establishments increased from 183,900 to 206,700; the value of their output rose from $60.8 billions to $68.0 billions. The Federal Reserve index of industrial production which had averaged only 67 in 1921 (1923–25 = 100) had risen to 110 by July 1928, and it reached 126 in June 1929. In 1926, 4,301,000 automobiles were produced. Three years later, in 1929, production had increased by over a million to 5,358,000, a figure which compares very decently with the 5,700,000 new car registrations of the opulent year of 1953. Business earnings were rising rapidly, and it was a good time to be in business. Indeed, even the most jaundiced histories of the era concede, tacitly, that times were good, for they nearly all join in taxing Coolidge for his failure to see that they were too good to last.

This notion of an iron law of compensation—the notion that the ten good years of the twenties had to be paid for by the ten bad ones of the thirties—is one to which it will be worthwhile to return.

One thing in the twenties should have been visible even to Coolidge. It concerned the American people of whose character he had spoken so well. Along with the sterling qualities he praised, they were also displaying an inordinate desire to get rich quickly with a minimum of physical effort. The first striking manifestation of this personality trait was in Florida. There, in the mid-twenties, Miami, Miami Beach, Coral Gables, the East Coast as far north as Palm Beach, and the cities over on the Gulf had been struck by the great Florida real estate boom. The Florida boom contained all of the elements of the classic speculative bubble. There was the indispensable element of substance. Florida had a better winter climate than New York, Chicago, or Minneapolis. Higher incomes and better transportation were making it increasingly accessible to the frost-bound North. The time indeed was coming when the annual flight to the South would be as regular and impressive as the migrations of the Canada Goose.

On that indispensable element of fact men and women had proceeded to build a world of speculative make-believe. This is a world inhabited not by people who have to be persuaded to believe but by people who want an excuse to believe. In the case of Florida, they wanted to believe that the whole peninsula would soon be populated by the holiday-makers and the sun-worshippers of a new and remarkably indolent era. So great would be the crush that beaches, bogs, swamps, and common scrubland would all have value. The Florida climate obviously did not insure that this would happen. But it did enable people who wanted to believe it would happen so to believe.

However, speculation does not depend entirely on the capacity for self-delusion. In Florida land was divided into building lots and sold for a 10 per cent down payment. Palpably, much of the unlovely terrain that thus changed hands was as repugnant to the people who bought it as to the passer-by. The buyers did not expect to live on it; it was not easy to suppose that anyone ever would. But these were academic considerations. The reality was that this dubious asset was gaining in value by the day and could be sold at a handsome profit in a fortnight. It is another feature of the speculative mood that, as time passes, the tendency to look beyond the simple fact of increasing values to the reasons on which it depends greatly diminishes. And there is no reason why anyone should do so as long as the supply of people who buy with the expectation of selling at a profit continues to be augmented at a sufficiently rapid rate to keep prices rising.

Through 1925 the pursuit of effortless riches brought people to Florida in satisfactorily increasing numbers. More land was subdivided each week. What was loosely called seashore became five, ten, or fifteen miles from the nearest brine. Suburbs became an astonishing distance from town. As the speculation spread northward, an enterprising Bostonian, Mr. Charles Ponzi, developed a subdivision "near Jacksonville." It was approximately sixty-five miles west of the city. (In other respects Ponzi believed in good, compact neighborhoods; he sold twenty-three lots to the acre.) In instances where the subdivision was close to town, as in the case of Manhattan Estates, which were "not more than three fourths of a mile from the prosperous and fast-growing city of Nettie," the city, as was so of Nettie, did not exist. The congestion of traffic into the state became so severe that in the autumn of 1925 the railroads were forced to proclaim an embargo on less essential freight, which included building materials for developing the subdivisions. Values rose wonderfully. Within forty miles of Miami "inside" lots sold at from $8000 to $20,000; waterfront lots brought from $15,000 to $25,000, and more or less bona fide seashore sites brought $20,000 to $75,000.

However, in the spring of 1926, the supply of new buyers, so essential to the reality of increasing prices, began to fail. As 1928 and 1929 were to show, the momentum built up by a good boom is not dissipated in a moment. For a while in 1926 the increasing eloquence of the promoters offset the diminishing supply of prospects. (Even the cathedral voice of Williams Jennings Bryan, which once had thundered against the cross of gold, had been for a time enlisted in the sorry task of selling swampland.) But this boom was not left to collapse of its own weight. In the autumn of 1926, two hurricanes showed, in the words of Frederick Lewis Allen, "what a Soothing Tropic Wind could do when it got a running start from the West Indies." The worst of these winds, on September 18, 1926, killed four hundred people, tore the roofs from thousands of houses, and piled tons of water and a number of elegant yachts into the streets of Miami. There was agreement that the storm had caused a healthy breathing spell in the boom, although its resumption was predicted daily. In the

Wall Street Journal of October 8, 1926, one Peter O. Knight, an official of the Seaboard Air Line and a sincere believer in the future of Florida, acknowledged that some seventeen or eighteen thousand people were in need of assistance. But he added: "The same Florida is still there with its magnificent resources, its wonderful climate, and its geographical position. It is the Riviera of America." He expressed concern that the solicitation of Red Cross funds for hurricane relief would "do more damage permanently to Florida than would be offset by the funds received."

This reluctance to concede that the end has come is also in accordance with the classic pattern. The end had come in Florida. In 1925 bank clearings in Miami were $1,066,528,000; by 1928 they were down to $143,364,000. Farmers who had sold their land at a handsome price and had condemned themselves as it later sold for double, treble, quadruple the original price, now on occasion got it back through a whole chain of subsequent defaults. Sometimes it was equipped with eloquently named streets and with sidewalks, street lamps, and taxes and assessments amounting to several time its current value.

The Florida boom was the first indication of the mood of the twenties and the conviction that God intended the American middle class to be rich. But that this mood survived the Florida collapse is still more remarkable. It was widely understood that things had gone to pieces in Florida. While the number of speculators was almost certainly small compared with the subsequent participation in the stock market, nearly every community contained a man who was known to have taken "quite a beating" in Florida. For a century after the collapse of the South Sea Bubble, Englishmen regarded the most reputable joint stock companies with some suspicion. Even as the Florida boom collapsed, the faith of Americans in quick, effortless enrichment in the stock market was becoming every day more evident.

It is hard to say when the stock market boom of the nineteen-twenties began. There were sound reasons why, during these years, the prices of common stocks should rise. Corporate earnings were good and growing. The prospect seemed benign. In the early twenties stock prices were low and yields favorable.

In the last six months of 1924, the prices of securities began to rise, and the increase was continued and extended through 1925. Thus at the end of May 1924, the *New York Times* average of the prices of twenty-five industrial stocks was 106; by the end of the year it was 134. By December 31, 1925, it had gained very nearly another 50 points and stood at 181. The advance through 1925 was remarkably steady; there were only a couple of months when values did not show a net gain.

During 1926 there was something of a setback. Business was off a little in the early part of that year; it was thought by many that values the year before had risen unreasonably. February brought a sharp fall in the market, and March a rather abrupt collapse. The *Times* industrials went down from 181 at the beginning of the year to 172 at the end of February, and then dropped by nearly 30 points to 143 at the end of March. However, in April the market steadied and renewed its advance. Another mild setback occurred in October, just after the hurricane blew away the vestiges of the Florida boom, but again recovery was prompt. At the end of the year values were about where they had been at the beginning.

In 1927 the increase began in earnest. Day after day and month after month the price of stocks went up. The gains by later standards were not large, but they had an aspect of great reliability. Again in only two months in 1927 did the averages fail to show an increase. On May 20, when Lindbergh took off from Roosevelt Field and headed for Paris, a fair number of citizens were unaware of the event. The market, which that day was registering another of its small but solid gains, had by then acquired a faithful band of devotees who spared no attention for more celestial matters.

In the summer of 1927 Henry Ford rang down the curtain on the immortal Model T and closed his plant to prepare for Model A. The Federal Reserve index of industrial production receded, presumably as a result of the Ford shutdown, and there was general talk of depression. The effect on the market was imperceptible. At the end of the year, by which time production had also turned up again, the *Times* industrials had reached 245, a net gain of 69 points for the year.

The year 1927 is historic from another point of view in the lore of the stock market. According to a long accepted doctrine, it was in this year that the seeds of the eventual disaster were sown. The responsibility rests with an act of generous but ill-advised internationalism. Some—including Mr. Hoover—have thought it almost disloyal, although in those days accusations of treason were still made with some caution.

In 1925, under the aegis of the then Chancellor of the Exchequer, Mr. Winston Churchill, Britain returned to the gold standard at the old or pre-World War I relationship between gold, dollars, and the pound. There is no doubt that Churchill was more impressed by the grandeur of the traditional, or $4.86, pound than by the more subtle consequences of overvaluation, which he is widely assumed not to have understood. The consequences, nonetheless, were real and severe. Customers of Britain had now to use these costly pounds to buy goods at prices that still reflected wartime inflation. Britain was, accordingly, an unattractive place for foreigners to buy. For the same reason it was an easy place in which to sell. In 1925 began the long series of exchange crises which, like the lions in Trafalgar Square and the street walkers in Piccadilly, are now an established part of the British scene. There were also unpleasant domestic consequences; the bad market for coal and the effort to reduce costs and prices to meet world competition led to the general strike in 1926.

Then, as since, gold when it escaped from Britain or Europe came to the United States. This might be discouraged if prices of goods were high and interest rates were low in this country. (The United States would be a poor place in which to buy and invest.) In the spring of 1927, three august pilgrims—Montagu Norman, the Governor of the Bank of England, the durable Hjalmar Schacht, then Governor of the Reichsbank, and Charles Rist, the Deputy Governor of the Bank of France—came to the United States to urge an easy money policy. (They had previously pled with success for a roughly similar policy in 1925.) The Federal Reserve obliged. The rediscount rate of the New York Federal Reserve Bank was cut from 4 to 3.5 per cent. Government securities were purchased in considerable volume with the mathematical consequence of leaving the banks and individuals who had sold them with money to spare. Adolph C. Miller, a dissenting member of the Federal Reserve Board, subsequently described this as "the greatest and boldest operation ever undertaken by the Federal Reserve System, and . . . [it] resulted in one of the most costly errors committed by it or any other banking system in the last 75 years!" The funds that the Federal Reserve made available were either invested in common stocks or (and more important) they became available to help finance the purchase of common stocks by others. So provided with funds, people rushed into the market. Perhaps the most widely read of all the interpretations of the period, that of Professor Lionel Robbins of the London School of Economics, concludes: "From that date, according to all the evidence, the situation got completely out of control."

This view that the action of the Federal Reserve authorities in 1927 was responsible for the speculation and collapse which followed has never been seriously shaken. There are reasons why it is attractive. It is simple, and it exonerates both the American people and their economic system from any substantial blame. The danger of being guided by foreigners is well known, and Norman and Schacht had some special reputation for sinister motives.

Yet the explanation obviously assumes that people will always speculate if only they can get the money to finance it. Nothing could be farther from the case. There were times before and there have been long periods since when credit was plentiful and cheap—far cheaper than in 1927–29 —and when speculation was negligible. Nor, as we shall see later, was speculation out of control after 1927, except that it was beyond the reach of men who did not want in the least to control it. The explanation is a tribute only to a recurrent preference, in economic matters, for formidable nonsense.

Until the beginning of 1928, even a man of conservative mind could believe that the prices of common stock were catching up with the increase in corporation earnings, the prospect for further increases, the peace and tranquility of the times, and the certainty that the Administration then firmly in power in Washington would take no more than necessary of any earnings in taxes. Early in 1928, the nature of the boom changed. The mass escape into make-believe, so much a part of the true speculative orgy, started in earnest. It was still necessary to reassure those who required some tie, however tenuous, to reality. And, as will be seen presently, this process of reassurance—of inventing the industrial equivalents of the Florida climate—eventually achieved the status of a profession. However, the time had come, as in all periods of speculation, when men sought not to be persuaded of the reality of things but to find excuses for escaping into the new world of fantasy.

There were many indications by 1928 that this phase had come. Most obvious was the behavior of the market. While the winter months of 1928 were rather quiet, thereafter the market began to rise, not by slow, steady steps, but by great vaulting leaps. On occasion it also came down the same way, only to recover and go higher again. In March 1928 the industrial average rose nearly 25 points. News of the boiling market was frequently on the front page. Individual issues sometimes made gains of 10, 15, and 20 points in a single day's trading. On March 12, Radio, in many respects the speculative symbol of the time, gained 18 points. On the following day it opened 22 points above the previous close. Then it lost 20 points on the announcement that the behavior of the trading in the stock was being investigated by the Exchange, gained 15 points, and fell off 9. A few days later, on a strong market, it made another 18-point gain.

The March boom also celebrated, beyond anything theretofore, the operations of the big professional traders. The lore of competitive markets pictures the stock exchange as the most impersonal of markets. No doctrine is more jealously guarded by the prophets and defenders of the Stock Exchange. "The Exchange is a market place where prices reflect the basic law of supply and demand," the New York Stock Exchange says firmly of itself. Yet even the most devout Wall Streeter allows himself on occasion to believe that more personal influences have a hand in his destiny. Somewhere around there are big men who put stocks up and put them down.

As the boom developed, the big men became more and more omnipotent in the popular or at least in the speculative view. In March, according to this view, the big men decided to put the market up, and even some serious scholars have been inclined to think that a concerted move catalyzed this upsurge. If so, the important figure was John J. Raskob. Raskob had impressive associations. He was a director of General Motors, an ally of the Du Ponts and soon to be Chairman of the Democratic National Committee by choice of Al Smith. A contemporary student of the market, Professor Charles Amos Dice of the Ohio State University, thought this latter appointment a particular indication of the new prestige of Wall Street and the esteem in which it was held by the American people. "Today," he observed, "the shrewd, worldly-wise candidate of one of the great political parties chooses one of the outstanding operators in the stock market . . . as a goodwill creator and popular vote getter."

On March 23, 1928, on taking ship for Europe, Raskob spoke favorably of prospects for automobile sales for the rest of the year and of the share in the business that General Motors would have. He may also have suggested—the evidence is not entirely clear—that G.M. stock should be selling at not less than twelves times earnings. This would have meant a price of 225 as compared with a current quotation of about 187. Such, as the *Times* put it, was "the magic of his name" that Mr. Raskob's "temperate bit of optimism" sent the market into a boiling fury. On March 24, a Saturday, General Motors gained nearly 5 points, and the Monday following it went to 199. The surge in General Motors, meanwhile, set off a great burst of trading elsewhere in the list.

Among the others who were assumed to have put their strength behind the market that spring was William Crapo Durant. Durant was the organizer of General Motors, whom Raskob and the Du Ponts had thrown out of the company in 1920. After a further adventure in the auto business, he had turned to full-time speculation in the stock market. The seven Fisher brothers were also believed to be influential. They too were General Motors alumni and had come to Wall Street with the great fortune they had realized from the sale of the Fisher-body plants. Still another was Arthur W. Cutten, the Canadian-born grain speculator who had recently shifted his market operations to Wall Street from the Chicago Board of Trade. As a market operator, Cutten surmounted substantial personal handicaps. He was very hard of hearing, and some years later, before a congressional committee, even his own counsel conceded that his memory was very defective.

Observing this group as a whole Professor Dice was especially struck by their "vision for the future and boundless hope and optimism." He noted that "they did not come into the market hampered by the heavy armor of tradition." In recounting their effect on the market, Professor Dice obviously found the English language verging on inadequacy. "Led by these mighty knights of the automobile industry, the steel industry, the radio industry . . ." he said, "and finally joined, in despair, by many professional traders who, after much sack-cloth and ashes, had caught the vision of progress, the Coolidge market had gone forward like the phalanxes of Cyrus, parasang upon parasang and again parasang upon parasang . . ."

In June of 1928 the market retreated a parasang or two—in fact, the losses during the first three weeks were almost as great as the March gains. June 12, a day of particularly heavy losses, was a landmark. For a year or more, men of vision had been saying that the day might come when five million shares would be traded on the New York Stock Exchange. Once this had been only a wild conversational gambit, but for some time it had shown signs of being overtaken by the reality. On March 12, the volume of trading had reached 3,875,910 shares, an all-time high. By the end of the month such a volume had become commonplace. On March 27,

4,790,270 shares were traded. Then on June 12, 5,052,790 shares changed hands. The ticker also fell nearly two hours behind the market; Radio dropped 23 points, and a New York paper began its accounts of the day's events, "Wall Street's bull market collapsed yesterday with a detonation heard round the world."

The announcement of the death of the bull market was as premature as any since that of the death of Mark Twain. In July there was a small net gain, and in August a strong upsurge. Thereafter not even the approach of the election caused serious hesitation. People remained unperturbed when, on September 17, Roger W. Babson told an audience in Wellesley, Massachusetts, that "if Smith should be elected with a Democratic Congress we are almost certain to have a resulting business depression in 1929." He also said that "the election of Hoover and a Republican Congress should result in continued prosperity for 1929," and it may have been that the public knew it would be Hoover. In any case, during the same month reassurance came from still higher authority. Andrew W. Mellon said, "There is no cause for worry. The high tide of prosperity will continue."

Mr. Mellon did not know. Neither did any of the other public figures who then, as since, made similar statements. These are not forecasts; it is not to be supposed that the men who make them are privileged to look farther into the future than the rest. Mr. Mellon was participating in a ritual which, in our society, is thought to be of great value for influencing the course of the business cycle. By affirming solemnly that prosperity will continue, it is believed, one can help insure that prosperity will in fact continue. Especially among businessmen the faith in the efficiency of such incantation is very great.

Hoover was elected in a landslide. This, were the speculators privy to Mr. Hoover's mind, should have caused a heavy fall in the market. In his memoirs Mr. Hoover states that as early as 1925 he became concerned over the "growing tide of speculation." During the months and years that followed this concern gradually changed to alarm, and then to something only slightly less than a premonition of total disaster. "There are crimes," Mr. Hoover said of speculation, "far worse than murder for which men should be reviled and punished." As Secretary of Commerce he had sought nothing so much as to get the market under control.

Mr. Hoover's attitude toward the market was, however, an exceptionally well-kept secret. People did not know of his efforts, uniformly frustrated by Coolidge and the Federal Reserve Board, to translate his thoughts into action. The news of his election, so far from causing a panic, set off the greatest increase in buying to date. On November 7, the day after the election, there was a "victory boom," and the market leaders climbed 5 to 15 points. Volume reached 4,894,670 shares, or only a little less than the all-time record of June 12, and this new level was reached on a rising, not a falling market. On November 16, a further wave of buying hit the market. An astonishing 6,641,250 shares changed hands—far above the previous record. The *Times* industrial averages made a net gain of 4½ points on the day's trading—then considered an impressive advance. Apart from the afterglow of the election, there was nothing particular to incite this enthusiasm. The headlines of the day told only of the sinking of the steamship *Vestris* and the epic achievements of the officers and crew in shouldering aside the women and children and saving their own lives. November 20 was another huge day. Trading—6,503,230 shares—was fractionally smaller than on the sixteenth, but by common agreement it was much more frantic. The following morning the *Times* observed that "for cyclonic violence yesterday's stock market has never been exceeded in the history of Wall Street."

December was not so good. Early in the month there was a bad break, and, on December 8, Radio fell a ghastly 72 points in one day. However, the market steadied and then came back. Over the whole year of 1928 the *Times* industrial average gained 86 points, or from 245 to 331. During the year Radio went from 85 to 420 (it had never paid a dividend); Du Pont went from 310 to 525; Montgomery Ward from 117 to 440; Wright Aeronautic from 69 to 289. During the year 920,550,032 shares were traded on the New York Stock Exchange, as compared with a record-breaking 576,990,875 in 1927. But there was still another and even more significant index of what was happening in the market. That was the phenomenal increase in trading on margin.

As noted, at some point in the growth of a boom all aspects of property ownership become irrelevant except the prospect for an early rise in price. Income from the property, or enjoyment of its use, or even its long-run worth are now academic. As in the case of the more repulsive Florida lots, these usufructs may be non-existent or even negative. What is important is that tomorrow or next week market values will rise—as they did yesterday or last week—and a profit can be realized.

It follows that the only reward to ownership in which the boomtime owner has an interest is the increase in values. Could the right to the increased value be somehow divorced from the other and now unimportant fruits of possession and also from as many as possible of the burdens of ownership, this would be much welcomed by the speculator. Such an arrangement would enable him to concentrate on speculation which, after all, is the business of a speculator.

Such is the genius of capitalism that where a real demand exists it does not go long unfilled. In all great speculative orgies devices have appeared to enable the speculator so to concentrate on his business. In the Florida boom the trading was in "binders." Not the land itself but the right to buy the land at a stated price was traded. This right to buy—which was obtained by a down payment of 10 per cent of the purchase price—could be sold. It thus conferred on the speculators the full benefit of the increase in values. After the value of the lot had risen he could resell the binder for what he had paid plus the full amount of the increase in price.

The worst of the burdens of ownership, whether of land or any other asset, is the need to put up the cash represented by the purchase price. The use of the binder cut this burden by 90 per cent—or it multiplied tenfold the amount of acreage from which the speculator could harvest an increase in value. The buyer happily gave up the other advantages of ownership. These included the current income of which, invariably, there was none and the prospect of permanent use in which he had not the slightest interest.

The stock market also has its design for concentrating the speculative energies of the speculator, and, as might be expected, it improves substantially on the crudities of the real estate market. In the stock market the buyer of securities on margin gets full title to his property in an unconditional sale. But he rids himself of the most grievous burden of ownership—that of putting up the purchase price—by leaving his securities with his broker as collateral for the loan that paid for them. The buyer again gets the full benefit of any increase in value—the price of the securities goes up, but the loan that bought them does not. In the stock market the speculative buyer also gets the earnings of the securities he purchased. However, in the days of this history the earnings were almost invariably less than the interest that was paid on the loan. Often they were much less. Yields on securities regularly ranged from nothing to 1 or 2 per cent. Interest on the loans that carried them was often 8, 10, or more per cent. The speculator was willing to pay to divest himself of all of the usufructs of security ownership except the chance for a capital gain.

The machinery by which Wall Street separates the opportunity to speculate from the unwanted returns and burdens of ownership is ingenious, precise, and almost beautiful. Banks supply funds to brokers, brokers to customers, and the collateral goes back to banks in a smooth and all but automatic flow. Margins—the cash which the speculator must supply in addition to the securities to protect the loan and which he must augment if the value of the collateral securities should fall and so lower the protection they provide—are effortlessly calculated and watched. The interest rate moves quickly and easily to keep the supply of funds adjusted to the demand. Wall Street, however, has never been able to express its pride in these arrangements. They are admirable and even wonderful only in relation to the purpose they serve. The purpose is to accommodate the speculator and facilitate speculation. But the purposes cannot be admitted. If Wall Street confessed this purpose, many thousands of moral men and women would have no choice but to condemn it for nurturing an evil thing and call for reform. Margin trading must be defended not on the grounds that it efficiently and ingeniously assists the speculator, but that it encourages the extra trading which changes a thin and anemic market into a thick and healthy one. At best this is a dull by-product and a dubious one. Wall Street, in these matters, is like a lovely and accomplished woman who must wear black cotton stockings, heavy woolen underwear, and parade her knowledge as a cook because, unhappily, her supreme accomplishment is as a harlot.

However, even the most circumspect friend of the market would concede that the volume of brokers' loans—of loans collateraled by the securities purchased on margin—is a good index of the volume of speculation. Measured by this index, the amount of speculation was rising very fast in 1928. Early in the twenties the volume of brokers' loans—because of their liquidity they are often referred to as call loans or loans in the call market—varied from a billion to a billion and a half dollars. By early 1926 they had increased to two and a half billions and remained at about that level for most of the year. During 1927 there was another increase of about a billion dollars, and at the end of the year they reached $3,480,780,000. This was an incredible sum, but it was only the beginning. In the two dull winter months of 1928 there was a small decline and then expansion began in earnest. Brokers' loans reached four billion on the first of June 1928, five billion on the first of November, and by the end of the year they were well along to six billion. Never had there been anything like it before.

People were swarming to buy stocks on margin—in other words, to have the increase in price without the costs of ownership. This cost was being assumed, in the first instance, by the New York banks, but they, in turn, were rapidly becoming the agents for lenders the country over and even the world around. There is no mystery as to why so many wished to lend so much in New York. One of the paradoxes of speculation in securities is that the loans that underwrite it are among the safest of all investments. They are protected by stocks which under all ordinary circumstances are instantly salable, and by a cash margin as well. The money, as noted, can be retrieved on demand. At the beginning of 1928 this admirably liquid and exceptionally secure outlet for non-risk capital was paying around 5 per cent. While 5 per cent is an excellent gilt-edged return, the rate rose steadily through 1928, and during the last week of the year it reached 12 per cent. This was still with complete safety.

In Montreal, London, Shanghai, and Hong Kong there was talk of these rates. Everywhere men of means told themselves that 12 per cent was 12 per cent. A great river of gold began to converge on Wall Street, all of it to help Americans hold common stock on margin. Corporations also found these rates attractive. At 12 per cent Wall Street might even provide a more profitable use for the working capital of a company than additional production. A few firms made this decision: instead of trying to produce goods with its manifold headaches and inconveniences, they confined themselves to financing speculation. Many more companies started lending their surplus funds on Wall Street.

There were still better ways of making money. In principle, New York banks could borrow money from the Federal Reserve Bank for 5 per cent and re-lend it in the call market for 12. In practice they did. This was, possibly, the most profitable arbitrage operation of all time.

However, there were many ways of making money in 1928. Never had there been a better time to get rich, and people knew it. 1928, indeed, was the last year in which Americans were buoyant, uninhibited, and utterly happy. It wasn't that 1928 was too good to last; it was only that it didn't last.

In the January issue of *World's Work,* Will Payne, after reflecting on the wonders of the year just over, went on to explain the difference between a gambler and an investor. A gambler, he pointed out, wins only because someone else loses. Where it is investment all gain. One investor, he explained, buys General Motors at $100, sells it to another at $150, who sells it to a third at $200. Everyone makes money. As Walter Bagehot once observed: "All people are most credulous when they are most happy."

Reed Smoot

Our Tariff and

the Depression

The question of the tariff has always been in the forefront of American issues. It has generated intense partisanship, and on one occasion, at least, had to be resolved by a threat of force. Scholars and statesmen have differed sharply on the wisdom of having high or low tariffs, and millions of words, polemical and scholarly, have been written on the subject. In the decade of the '20s, the American tariff was raised to the highest point in the nation's history through passage of the Fordney-McCumber bill in 1922 and the Smoot-Hawley bill in 1930. Every other nation similarly raised import duties. Between 1925 and 1929 there were 33 general revisions or changes in tariff schedules by the nations of Europe and Latin America—all increases. In assessing the causes of the depression, it was inevitable that the tariff—a central feature of international and domestic economic life—would be considered. As might be expected, there was a division of opinion on the matter. Reed Smoot, Senator from Utah for almost 30 years, powerful chairman of the Senate Finance Committee, and co-author of the tariff of 1930, quite naturally argued in favor of a high tariff as a desirable national policy. The tariff, in his view, not only did not cause the depression but saved the nation from the worst effects of it. [*Reed Smoot, "Our Tariff and the Depression,"* Current History, *November 1931. Reprinted by permission of* Current History, Inc.]

No event in recent history has emphasized the importance of the American tariff so much as has the current economic depression. Abnormal conditions throughout the world have made protective duties the key to industrial stability. In times of prosperity a tariff is essential to equalize costs of production here and abroad, but in this hour of national distress protection is imperative to save American industry from what might otherwise become the most serious upheaval it has ever experienced.

In attempting to elucidate the influence of the tariff on international trade we encounter a labyrinth of economic forces that affect every commercial nation. Tariff barricades that have been thrown up recently on nearly every international boundary are a result and not the cause of those forces. Inordinate production and maldistribution have made customs duties necessary to re-establish the economic balance.

Purchasing power has been reduced on every continent. In countries that produce mostly raw materials incomes have been drastically cut, and purchases in the world market have been consequently reduced. Economic law thus operates to curtail international commerce in direct relation to the slump in domestic business.

One remarkable aspect of this economic derangement is the plethora of commodities on the market. In those years of feverish activity before 1929 vast surpluses of goods were accumulated in nearly every country. When the undertow of fear and pessimism turned the consuming public from normal buying to abnormal saving, and unemployment further weakened purchasing power, the world markets became glutted with commodities of every kind. Each country sought outlets abroad, while most governments took steps to protect their home producers from inundation by this flood of cheap goods.

It is quite natural that every country should give preference to its own industries and its own working men, especially in economic crises. A similar surplus of commodities induced most countries to strengthen their tariff barriers after the World War. France, Germany, Italy and Great Britain had increased their customs duties even before Congress revised the American tariff in 1922. Since that time some European countries have built several elaborate additions to their protective barricades. In the two years since the depression began forty-five nations have made important changes in their tariff rates. Secretary Hyde's remark that beside many foreign tariff mountains American duties amount to nothing but a cluster of molehills was not exaggerated.

In our present stage of industrial development production is easy. We have no difficulty in turning out more food, more clothing, houses, automobiles and other necessities than the consuming public can buy. For this reason the theory that goods should be purchased where they can be produced most cheaply has undergone an ignominious collapse. The great problem today is to find employment for all our people; and, since we live at a higher standard than the rest of the world, this cannot be done unless we allow ample protection to American enterprise.

What would have happened to the United States if Congress had failed to keep pace with this world-wide protective movement? America would have become a dumping ground for all the surplus products of the world, as is Great Britain. Every month that country becomes more dependent upon industries in other lands, while an appalling number of her own working men subsist on doles supplied largely through taxation. Imports into the United Kingdom are valued at about 16 per cent less than they were a year ago. But exports are worth 30 per cent less. The pitiful position of British industry is an inevitable result of trying to fight the battles of modern commerce from a poorly barricaded position, while competitors are intrenched behind domestic protective policies.

Once before the days of quantity production Congress tried to cure an economic slump by lowering customs duties. Clouds of depression spread over the country in 1893. Critics demanded that international trade be unfettered. In 1894 Congress proceeded to remodel the tariff in the direction of free trade. Instead of stimulating foreign commerce and lifting the country out of its slough of despond, this act merely left the government with a huge deficit and the people with more acute economic distress. Even imports fell off sharply in spite of the lower rates of duty. In the last year under the Wilson low-tariff act exports decreased to $1,050,-000,000 as compared with $1,730,000,000 for the year before its enactment.

Not until after President McKinley had been elected and called Congress into extra session in 1897 was this era of hard times brought to an end. A new protective tariff was enacted. Prosperity gradually returned, with both imports and exports growing to larger volumes than had ever been known before. Since that time the United States has never been without protection for its domestic industries. Although the tariff rates were lowered in 1913, their effect was not felt, for when the war came and swept all America's chief competitors into a struggle for existence our industries enjoyed complete protection. War acts as a general embargo; not only does it relieve neutral countries of foreign competition in their own markets, but it affords opportunity to multiply exports to the combatant nations.

It is difficult to understand why any one should try to fasten responsibility for the general movement toward higher protective duties upon the United States. Many nations revised their tariffs before Congress passed the Smoot-Hawley bill in June, 1930, and many have increased their duties since. Each country has been prompted by economic considerations of its own. Only the purblind egotist can suggest that the world turned to protection in retaliation against the American tariff. What chiefly distinguishes the Smoot-Hawley act from foreign tariffs adopted since the depression began is its moderation.

Though the tariff of one country cannot be accurately compared with that of another, for a variety of reasons, duties on specific items can be studied with precision and the average height of tariff barriers can be estimated from the amount of duties collected in relation to the total volume of imports. Thus a recent test made by the Department of Agriculture showed that fourteen leading commodities exported from the United States, constituting 28 per cent of our agricultural sales abroad, were taxed in a dozen leading countries at rates double and quadruple any that may be found in our tariff act. Wheat is a good example. In less than a year and a half Germany increased her wheat tariff six times, beginning at 49 cents per bushel and ending at $1.62. The Italian duty has risen from 37 to 87 cents; the French, from 20 to 85 cents; the Mexican, from 66 to 90 cents. The American duty is 42 cents. Foreign tariffs on meats are still more drastic. The United States taxes hams and shoulders at $3.25 per hundred pounds, but Soviet Russia imposes a duty of $70; Bulgaria, Chile and Argentina, from $20 to $25; Brazil, Yugoslavia, Uruguay, Norway, Portugal and Rumania, from $10 to $20.

It is a prevalent but false belief that American duties are the highest in the world. Almost any test will prove that this is not so. How does the total amount of duties collected compare with the value of all imports for the various nations? The United States Tariff Commission has worked out such a calculation, using the average ad valorem equivalents for duties collected in 1930. The Japanese tariff, spread over all Japan's imports, both dutiable and free, amounts to 7.3 per cent; that of France, 8.7; Norway, 10.1; Germany, 11.7; the United Kingdom, 12.6; Spain, 12.9; the United States, 14.8; Italy, 15.4; Argentina, 16.5, and Chile, 23.5 per cent.

It should be noted that the percentage of duty to total imports during the first six months of the new tariff was only 13.7 per cent. This is not, of course, an exact calculation, because the effect of rates that are so high as greatly to restrict goods or exclude them entirely is not felt in this comparison. But it is apparent that European and South American Legislatures are quite as adept at imposing restrictive duties as is Congress. American automobiles, for example, are virtually excluded from many European markets.

There is nothing in the picture to indicate that Uncle Sam is the tariff Shylock. No other nation in the world is so well adapted to a protective policy as the United States; yet several have higher tariffs. If we were dependent upon the outside world for half our food and raw materials, a tariff might be less useful; but our country, with its vast and varied resources and its highly developed market, is almost an economic unit in itself. For this reason, the United States cannot be compared with Great Britain, Italy, Japan or other political units that do not enjoy economic self-sufficiency. Yet, in spite of these ideal conditions for application of the protective principle, America imports more free goods than any other country with the possible exception of the United Kingdom, which lives on trade.

Any attempt to measure the effect of the tariff on foreign trade must take into consideration current economic conditions; that is, we must talk about our foreign commerce in terms of 1931 values. The first question is, not how much the dollar value of exports and imports has diminished, but how America has fared in commerce as compared with the rest of the world. In 1913 American exports amounted to 12.3 per cent of the world's total; from 1921 to 1925, 16.5 per cent; in 1928, 15.6 per cent. Then the boom year of 1929 brought a new spurt and the United States furnished 16.8 per cent of the exports from sixty-seven chief commercial nations. In 1930 the ratio was again equal to that of 1928. For the period since the Smoot-Hawley act was passed statistics are available for only the fifty-six foremost commercial nations, but they are sufficiently clear to indicate the trend. During the first six months under the new tariff the American export ratio was 16.2, compared with 16.9 for the previous six months. This slight decline was less than that during the half year immediately before the new rates came into effect.

Turning attention now to the ratio of America's foreign purchases to imports throughout the world, we find a similar trend. In 1913 only 8.3 per cent of the world imports were absorbed in the United States; from 1921 to 1925, 12.5 per cent; in 1928, 11.7 per cent. Although the figures for the recent years are not exactly comparable, as they do not include the lesser commercial nations, they indicate that our imports were in excess in the first part of 1929 and that our proportion has since been declining. In the first half year under the new tariff our share was 11.1 per cent, compared with 12.6 per cent for the last half year under the old law. It is interesting to note that the percentage of all imports absorbed by the United States fell from 14.1 to 12.6 during the year before the Smoot-Hawley act took effect.

These calculations represent value and not physical quantity. Obviously, a country which chiefly exports raw materials will appear to have lost its relative position because of the drastic reduction in the prices of such products. Since prices of finished manufactures have been maintained more firmly, the countries of Western Europe, which manufacture many luxuries and specialties, assume a relatively more significant place in world commerce. America's share of international commerce appears to have shrunk partly because agricultural produce and raw materials still bulk large in our foreign shipments. During the last four years agricultural crops have constituted 36 per cent of our exports and semimanufactures an additional 14 per cent. Low prices of such commodities as cotton and copper have contributed largely to fixing the ratio of American foreign trade at a slightly smaller figure.

One conclusion from a study of America's share of international commerce is inevitable, and that is that nothing calamitous has happened.

Though trade overseas and across border lines has fallen off throughout the world, our portion of world exports remains about the same as in normal years before the depression. Our share of imports is slightly lower, as Congress intended it should be. The Smoot-Hawley tariff has proved to be a shock absorber against world-wide dumping.

To estimate our loss of trade with the losses of all other countries is only one way of calculating the effect of the tariff law. The relationship between domestic production and foreign commerce is even more significant. Some people who wish to attribute as much disaster as possible to the tariff talk as if foreign trade were one of our greatest industries, but it is not an industry at all. International commerce is merely an extension of domestic trade. Most industries produce primarily for the domestic market and sell their surplus abroad. International trade is thus subject to the laws of supply and demand and cannot be measured precisely from the height of customs barriers. An honest analysis must, therefore, discount the effect of domestic business on foreign trade before attributing the shrinkage to tariff changes.

How has business within the United States fared since the depression began? The most reliable data available show that industrial production began to decline about the middle of 1929 and continued with some variations until the first months of 1931. A reliable commercial index, which is based on production as well as distribution, shows a falling off of 40 per cent from the abnormal high peak of industrial activity two years ago. The extent of that decline is almost equally divided between the last two fiscal years, measuring 22 per cent from June, 1929, to June, 1930, and about 23 per cent from that time to the beginning of the Summer of 1931.

Another index of industrial production prepared by the Federal Reserve Board shows a decrease of 20 per cent during approximately the twelve months in which the 1930 tariff rates have been in effect. The index number for that year is 88, as compared with 110 for the previous year and 100 for 1923–25. Charts prepared by the Department of Commerce likewise show a decline of 20 per cent in wholesale prices during the last year, based on a combined index of 550 commodities and price quotations.

When domestic industry and business demonstrate such symptoms of maladjustment a similar condition may be expected in foreign trade. That is exactly what the records indicate. In the first quarter after the Smoot-Hawley bill became law exports fell off 19 per cent in quantity; in the second quarter, 22 per cent, and in the third quarter (from January to March, 1931), 24 per cent, each quarter being compared with the corresponding period of the previous year.

Imports held up much better in spite of the higher duties. In the first quarter under the Smoot-Hawley act the ebb of imports was quite pronounced. Shipments were 23 per cent lower than in the previous corresponding quarter. That can be accounted for by the rush in the last days of the Fordney-McCumber act to ship in large quantities of goods on which the duty was to be raised. In the next quarter imports were only 13 per cent lower. A decline of 16 per cent is registered for the third quarter.

This tendency for imports to hold their place better than exports is seen throughout the calendar year of 1930. While exports diminished 19 per cent in volume, the quantity of imports shrunk only 15 per cent as compared with 1929. Does this mean that the countries with which we deal have adopted more effectively restrictive tariffs than ours or that the Smoot-Hawley act affords inadequate protection for American enterprise? Many nations have certainly raised their customs duties far above those of the United States, but that has not been the primary factor in determining our ratio of imports and exports.

Purchasing power is undoubtedly the most important influence. Americans live much further above the margin of want than do the people of any other country. Wage scales were maintained here much longer and to a greater extent than in other countries. In time of depression, as in prosperity, the American people have more money to spend than their neighbors. The United States offers the world a better market than the world offers us.

Another factor is the decline in commodity prices. The unit value of exports for the first quarter of 1931 was 17 per cent below that of 1930, but the value of imports fell 25 per cent. Three-quarters of our purchases from abroad consist of raw materials, food-stuffs and semi-manufactures. Prices of those commodities have shrunk to a fraction of what they were when the depression began. Rubber, raw silk and wool, for example, are worth about 45 per cent less than a year ago. The world demand for such commodities has been curtailed, but they still flow into the most available market. Since the United States absorbs more imports than any other country except possibly Great Britain, and since 67 per cent of those imports come in without paying duty, it is not surprising that the volume of our foreign purchases has fallen off less than either exports or domestic production.

The unmistakable conclusion is that the decline in American business abroad is on a par with that in domestic industry. The proportion of our national output that is being exported has not diminished. Roughly calculated, both domestic industry and foreign commerce are a little more than 20 per cent below the level of last year. Equally evident is it that foreign interests have improved their position in the American market. Importers have about a 5 per cent advantage over domestic producers so far as the volume of goods moved in the last year is concerned.

The public often fails to understand this conclusion because it is confused by a maze of figures representing the dollar value of trade. In times like the present, statistics based on prices are extremely misleading. Changes in commodity prices in various countries upset almost any comparison of the dollar value of our trade. Indices worked out by the

Department of Commerce show that since the depression began agricultural prices have decreased 37.6 per cent, food prices 29.4 per cent, and other commodity prices, mostly of manufacturers, 21.6 per cent. A combined index for the United States places prices 27.2 per cent lower than the apex in 1929. Similar indices show a decline of 25.8 in Canada, 25.3 in the United Kingdom, 21.2 in France, 19.1 in Germany and 32.7 in Italy. In some countries the articles entering into international trade have maintained relatively stable prices. On the other hand, the bottom seems to have fallen out of prices for many raw materials.

Although shipments of copper abroad during the first three months of 1931 were 20 per cent lower in value, 41 per cent more copper was actually exported than in the corresponding period of 1930. Coffee became a leading import in the same period. Measured in dollar value it was worth 33 per cent less than the five-year average, but in actual quantity it amounted to 21 per cent more than the five-year average. The price of unmanufactured cotton fell lower than it has been since 1914. The United States exported 841,000,000 pounds in three months, 3 per cent less than during corresponding months of 1930, but the return to farmers in actual money was 40 per cent less. Such fluctuations in price make comparisons of total values very dubious.

Americans are inclined to lose sight of the relationship between this country's capacity to supply human wants and its sales abroad. Exports are more easily measured than goods which pass into domestic consumption. Hence we marvel at the rise of our foreign trade without stopping to ask if its relative importance has grown. Enormous figures dazzle us; achievements in foreign commerce are paraded before us; the effects of tariffs are distorted and our business with foreign nations comes to be regarded as more important than ever before. The United States has undoubtedly assumed a more imposing rôle in world commerce. The gains in our percentage of world trade have already been noted, while no one can fail to be impressed by the growth in both volume and total value of our trade with foreign countries in the last quarter century. But in appraising these gains let us not forget the extent to which American industry and the American market also have developed.

At the beginning of the century the United States was selling 12.8 per cent of all its output abroad. When the World War broke out the percentage stood at 9.7 The demands from the belligerent nations in the subsequent five years resulted in the shipment abroad of 15.7 per cent of all American output by 1919. Since that time the American market has been absorbing a greater portion of what we produce. In 1929, when our foreign commerce reached its highest point in history, only 9.8 per cent of movable goods produced was exported.

How then can it be said that the United States is more dependent than formerly upon foreign trade? The most striking feature of America's rise to the position of foremost industrial nation in the world is the creation of our immense domestic market. American inventive genius, American

capital and labor and agriculture have been utilized to such an extent
that the United States is becoming increasingly self-sufficient. Foreign
trade is relatively a less significant factor in our economic life than it was
before the days of quantity production. One authority has calculated that
96 per cent of our industrial production is absorbed in the United States.
With such an opulent market of our own, and such diversified resources
as we find within our confines, the United States is economically the most
self-contained nation on earth. Yet the exports which spill over the edges
of our vast home market exceed those of any other country.

The greatest free trade area in the world is the forty-eight States which
comprise the American Union. Because of that every commercial nation
clamors for the admittance of its products without duty. Obviously the
United States could temporarily extend its import trade by lowering
tariff barriers; and if other governments could be induced to do likewise,
some gains might be made in exports. But would that possibility justify
us in sharing our $50,000,000,000 domestic market to a greater extent with
foreign producers in the hope of increasing our $5,000,000,000 market
abroad?

Another unanswerable question confronts the economists who would
have the United States turn toward a free trade policy. How could American buying power be sustained and preserved if the industries which
create that buying power through high wages and dividends were submerged under foreign competition? Formerly it was argued that the
United States would divert its energies to those industries for which it is
especially adapted. But even with the preservation of all industries under
the protective system millions of men are out of work. What would
happen if part of our enterprises succumbed to foreign competition? Jobs
are now far more important than cheap goods. Production has become so
easy that the problem is to find work for the masses, to enable our people
to supply their own wants, so far as is practical, and to maintain living
standards commensurate with their productive capacity.

How the tariff is operating is indicated by a consideration of free and
dutiable imports. More than two-thirds of our imports are not in any
way affected by our protective policy, so that, if the tariff is responsible
for the upset in our foreign business, it ought to be confined to dutiable
commodities. But what do we find? In 1930 the variation between the
shrinkage of free and dutiable imports was so slight as to be negligible.
That comparison is, of course, unsatisfactory because the new duties were
applied during only half the year. Matching the first nine months under
the Smoot-Hawley act with the corresponding period one year earlier, we
find a falling off of 35 per cent in the free column and 43 per cent in the
dutiable column. But again we are handicapped by having to deal with
values rather than quantities. Most of our free imports are raw materials,
the prices of which have been dropping for at least a year. Nevertheless,
there has been a considerable demand for such imports because most of

them are not produced in the United States. We must have rubber, raw silk, coffee, &c., whether there is a depression or not.

After allowing for price changes part of the declines in dutiable imports may be attributed to the 1930 tariff act, which was devised to give a slightly higher margin of protection to American industry and to reserve so far as possible the agricultural market for our own farmers.

American industry as a whole does not enjoy greater protection than it did before the Smoot-Hawley act was passed. This does not mean that the new tariff has been ineffective, but that competition has increased. The quest for new markets by foreign countries to supplement failing markets at home has been frantic and persistent. Goods that in normal times would not have come in over the tariff wall have in this congestion of trade been dumped upon the American market. The tariff increases were thus not sufficient to give American enterprise a greater hold on the domestic market. The act of 1930 merely served to save industry from far worse consequences if duties had not been revised. In drafting the new tariff Congress did not entirely anticipate the intensified struggle for markets resulting from the world-wide economic derangement.

Congress was far more generous to farmers than to other producers. Ad valorem rates or their equivalent on agricultural raw materials rose from 38.1 per cent under the 1922 tariff to 48.92 under the 1930 tariff. Products manufactured from agricultural materials were allowed an increase from 36.15 to 48.87 per cent by way of compensation for the higher rates on raw materials. But industrial rates in which there was no compensatory element were raised only from 31.02 to 34.31. The Smoot-Hawley act was pre-eminently agricultural.

The value of protective duties to agriculture is frequently underestimated. Yet 90 per cent of all American crops come directly into competition with similar foreign products. In recent years the American market has been absorbing enormous quantities of foodstuffs from abroad, while our own farmers have been in distress because the tariff was not high enough to equalize costs of production. In the last year before the Smoot-Hawley act became effective our agricultural imports were valued at about $300,000,000 more than our agricultural exports. In the first nine months under the new tariff exports were worth more than imports, and at the close of the fiscal year, June 30, 1931, American farmers were close to a favorable trade balance for the first time in many years. This improved position is due to the tariff. The Department of Agriculture has prepared a table showing the relative volume of imports received during the first eleven months under the Smoot-Hawley act as compared with the same months of the previous year. It includes 44 chief commodities and groups of commodities, comprising 87 per cent of all agricultural imports. Free imports gained slightly in physical volume under the new tariff, indicating greater pressure from foreign countries upon our market, as a result of the depression. But agricultural imports that are dutiable decreased nearly 12 per cent. This difference may be regarded as further protection to agriculture.

The bottom has fallen out of agricultural prices because of fewer demands throughout the world. Excess production has brought distress to cotton and wheat growers. Although no tariff can remedy that, our protective system has saved our farmers from a deluge of foreign crops produced at lower costs by farmers with lower standards of living than ours.

In general, however, tariffs modify the world demand for goods in a rather minor degree. It is often said that countries against which the United States has raised its protective barriers are as a result refusing to buy American goods. But there is more theory than fact in the assertion. Other peoples buy our commodities not because of any policy adopted by Congress but because they need them. So long as we produce what the world wants and is able to buy we shall have markets regardless of tariff policies.

The trend of our foreign commerce since the depression began illustrates how little our customs duties actually interfere with our export trade. Most American tariffs are levied against the industrial products of Europe. In 1930 only 42.4 per cent of our imports from Europe were duty free. From the world as a whole 67 per cent were free. If it were true that the slump in our exports has been caused by retaliations against the Smoot-Hawley act, Europe should be taking less of what we sell abroad. But this is not so. In 1930 the value of our exports to Europe decreased 21 per cent as compared with 31 per cent for the rest of the world. Nearly 48 per cent of our foreign shipments went to Europe last year. In 1929, when no cause existed for retaliation against a new American tariff, Europe took only 44.7 per cent of our exports.

South American trade offers a remarkable contrast. Nearly 84 per cent of everything we import from South America comes in free, and the ratio of free and dutiable goods remains almost the same under the new tariff law. In 1929 South America took 10.3 per cent of our exports; in 1930, 8.8 per cent. Similar results may be noted in Asia, which sends 80 per cent of its imports to the United States free, in Oceania, with 69 per cent free and in Canada and Newfoundland, with about 70 per cent free.

Such comparisons are valuable only in that they illustrate how little influence a nation's import duties have on its export trade. European customers bought a larger percentage of our products because their purchasing power was better maintained. Prices of their finished products were more stable than the prices of raw materials and foodstuffs which determine the purchasing power of non-industrial regions.

In view of the world-wide economic and political upheavals it is remarkable that our commercial intercourse with other nations has not been more seriously interrupted. Today every nation is struggling to turn international trade to its own advantage. The United States must participate in this competition, using every aid that the tariff can give, or be overwhelmed by it. Yet when costs of production have been equalized and the domestic market protected, the exchange of goods with other nations continues. Neither the tariff nor any other force has destroyed or can destroy our international trade.

To sum up, the United States has not lost its relative position in world trade; the percentage of our total production exported has not changed; the volume of imports compared with domestic production has increased somewhat since the new tariff act became law; nations which live under the shadow of our tariff wall have purchased more from us since the depression than those countries that are only remotely affected by our protective policy, and finally, our enormous extension of productive power has been made possible not by selling greater portions of the output abroad, but by intensive cultivation of the home market.

How can we escape the conclusion that the tariff has been a stabilizing influence? In the scramble of all nations to dispose of surpluses it has saved American producers from a deluge of cheap foreign goods. It has served to maintain the balance between domestic and international trade. A flow of imports equal to that of 1929 at a time when American enterprise was prostrate would have been a greater calamity than the temporary decline in our foreign trade.

The United States has demonstrated that foreign trade can be developed without opening the domestic market to unrestricted exploitation. Much of our trade will continue to be independent of all customs duties. No country will allow foreigners to supply those wants which can just as well be supplied by labor at home. There is no prospect of abandonment of the protective systems which now reach throughout the world. In the future, therefore, we can look for continuous development of international commerce, but it will flow chiefly in non-competitive channels or over tariff walls that tend to equalize costs of production.

Sumner Slichter

Is the Tariff a Cause of Depression?

Sumner Slichter was for many years a professor of business economics in the Harvard Graduate School of Business Administration. The author of Modern Economic Society, *he was a distinguished and respected economist both in this country and abroad. His answer to Senator Reed Smoot, which appeared in the same journal two months later, pictures the tariff as a cause for the nation's and the world's ills, and a barrier to recovery. [Sumner Slichter, "Is the Tariff a Cause of Depression?"* Current History, *January 1932. Reprinted by permission of* Current History, Inc.]

When the Wiggin Committee of the Bank for International Settlements on Aug. 19 told the world that tariffs should be lowered, it was simply repeating advice which had been given many times during recent years. On April 21, 1931, a similar recommendation was made by General W. W. Atterbury, the former Republican National Committeeman from the protectionist stronghold of Pennsylvania. But the advice has been little heeded, in part because the man in the street does not clearly understand how and why rising tariffs have been undermining his prosperity. Tariffs, of course, are not the only reason why a large part of the world during the last two years was driven off the gold standard, why the harbors of Germany were congested during the Summer of 1931 with vessels that could not be unloaded because there was no means of payment or why wheat sold for the lowest price in several centuries. Nevertheless, the trade barriers that have been raised during recent years have had much to do with all these matters. They have been a major influence in making the world vulnerable to depression and in intensifying the slump when it came. Prosperity, it is safe to say, will not be established on a reasonably solid foundation until there have been substantial reductions in many tariffs.

In few periods in the world's history were tariff barriers raised more rapidly than in the years immediately preceding the present depression. Between 1925 and 1929, there were thirty-three general revisions or substantial tariff changes, nearly all increases, among the twenty-six countries of Europe, and seventeen among the twenty republics of Latin America. In 1927 and 1928 Australia, Canada and New Zealand made broad tariff revisions, generally upward. Several Asiatic countries achieved the right to make their own tariffs and promptly raised their duties—Siam in 1927, China and Persia in 1928. When prosperity collapsed, the increase in duties continued at an accelerated rate. The advance in the American tariff in June, 1930, was followed during the next eleven months by more or less general upward tariff revisions in twenty-five countries. In two principal ways these rising tariffs have undermined the world's prosperity—first, by misdirecting the investment of capital and thus prolonging and aggravating many maladjustments which had grown up during the war between the supply of commodities and the demand for them; second, by preventing trade from adjusting itself to the new international debtor-creditor relationships created by the war and the peace treaties.

It is easy to see why rising tariffs have prolonged and accentuated many of the war-time maladjustments between supply and demand. When the world is divided by trade barriers, a new duty or an increase in an old one may lead an industry to expand behind the tariff, despite the fact that the demand for its output at a profitable price does not equal the productive capacity already in existence, but located in other countries. Maladjustments thus aggravated by tariffs did not directly precipitate the collapse of prosperity but they did weaken the economic position of many countries and reduce their ability to resist depression. Moreover, when the slump came, the prices of the over-produced commodities fell more precipitously than most prices, diminishing the purchasing power of many countries and causing the depression to go from bad to worse.

Sugar, cotton textiles and wheat furnish three conspicuous illustrations of these maladjustments. Before the war, Europe was an important producer of sugar. During the war her production fell by half, but this loss was offset by the expansion of output in Cuba, Java and elsewhere. Cuba almost doubled its production, as did Java and several South American countries. Nevertheless, at the end of the war, many European nations sought by high tariffs to restore the sugar-beet industry. The result was that Europe by 1927–28 was producing more sugar than before 1914. Even the United States, which had raised the duty in 1922, was producing nearly 40 per cent more than in 1913. It is not surprising that the industry was in difficulty several years before the depression and that recently the price of Cuban raw sugar sank to 1 cent a pound.

Because the supply of British and German textiles was limited during the war, a rapid growth of the industry resulted, particularly the cotton branch, in the United States, Japan, India and South America. Although the end of the war found cotton manufacturing seriously overdeveloped, Bulgaria, Brazil, Czechoslovakia, Hungary, India, Rumania, Yugoslavia and other nations sought by tariffs to enlarge their production of cotton goods. In all these countries the industry has expanded rapidly. At the same time that this forced growth was taking place, cotton goods were experiencing severe competition from rayon and silk. Long before the general depression it was well known that the industry was in trouble. Even in the boom year of 1929 Great Britain's exports of cotton piece goods were scarcely half the pre-war volume, a decline which directly affected the British balance of trade. That fact, and the severe unemployment among the Lancashire cotton operatives and the resulting burden on the budget, have been among the many grave weaknesses in the British economic situation—weaknesses which eventually culminated in forcing Great Britain from the gold standard.

War and revolution eliminated Russian exports of wheat, stimulating wheat raising in the Argentine, Australia, Canada and the United States, with the result that the output of these countries between 1925 and 1929 averaged nearly 50 per cent above 1909–13. Furthermore, the output has been increased by power plowing and the combine harvester—a technological revolution scarcely less momentous than the McCormick reaper of the last century. In the face of the ever greater overproduction of wheat, some of the largest consumers, especially France, Italy and Germany, have been raising their duties. In November, 1927, France raised her duty to 37.4 cents a bushel; Italy, in July, 1925, imposed a rate of 39.4 cents, and in September, 1928, raised it to 57.7 cents; Germany, in 1925, restored a duty of 32.4 cents, and in July, 1929, raised it to 42.1 cents. Because tariffs, and export-control schemes also, stimulated the production of wheat but retarded its movement into consumption, the amount in storage more than doubled between July, 1926, and July, 1929, until it attained the highest figure on record. During 1930 the price of wheat declined, but as it did so the duties in many countries were increased. By June, 1930, the duty in France, Italy and Germany was more than 80 cents a bushel. The extreme protection given to wheat by several important consuming countries meant that in the midst of a large and ever-growing supply these countries were encouraging their farmers to raise more wheat and were refusing to buy it, except in small quantities, from the rest of the world. Is it surprising that in December, 1930, in the face of large exports from Russia and of a bumper crop in the Argentine, the price in Liverpool broke to the lowest point in over three centuries? In the Summer of 1931 even this record was broken. The collapse in the price of wheat greatly accentuated the financial difficulties of Argentina, Australia, Canada, Eastern Europe and the United States and indirectly intensified the depression in other countries.

Few people realize how violent were the shifts in international debtor-creditor relationships produced by the war and the peace treaties. Within less than ten years the United States was changed from the largest debtor nation in the world to the second largest creditor nation and Germany from the second largest creditor nation to the largest debtor nation. In addition, there were great increases in the foreign obligations and great decreases in the foreign holdings of many European countries and substantial increases in the foreign debts throughout Latin America and Australasia.

Every one knows that in the long run interest and dividends on international investments must be paid in goods. Consequently, the new debtor-creditor relationships required extensive changes in the flow of goods between nations. For example, they required that Germany, which for many years had an excess of imports, suddenly develop a large excess of exports, and that the United States, which for fifty years had had an excess of exports, promptly develop a large excess of imports. But in a world of steadily rising trade barriers Germany has been unable to build up a large surplus of exports. Failure to obtain sufficient exchange from the sale of goods to pay reparations and interest on the foreign debt has kept credit in Germany scarce and interest rates high. High interest rates attracted enough money to Germany until 1931 to enable her to meet her old obligations by incurring new ones. Unfortunately, however, a large part of Germany's new credits were short-term funds. Naturally, this large short-term indebtedness placed Germany in an exceedingly vulnerable position. Any condition which threatened withdrawal of foreign funds produced a recession in German business, because it limited the ability of German enterprises to obtain credit with which to buy goods. Once a recession started, it was likely to go from bad to worse, because its very existence provoked further withdrawals of foreign funds and prevented the sale abroad of long-term German securities. This weakness in the German situation manifested itself in the Spring of 1929, when fear of the failure of the Young Plan negotiations created a flight from the mark; again, in the Fall of 1930, when the results of the elections caused another flight, and, finally, in the Summer of 1931, when even the moratorium failed to avert an acute financial crisis which paralyzed German business. Certainly the inability of Germany to develop a large export surplus must be regarded as a major factor in precipitating the depression in 1929 and in intensifying the depression in the Fall of 1930 and the Summer of 1931.

The high and ever-rising American tariff has prevented us from developing an excess of imports. Indeed, so high have been our duties that for many years over 95 per cent of the manufactured articles consumed in the United States have been domestic products. Not only were rates raised in 1921 and again in 1922, but whenever a commodity began to flow over the tariff wall in appreciable quantities the Tariff Commission was disposed to recommend that the President use his authority under the so-called "flexible" clause to increase the duty. Of the thirty-seven changes made in the rates of 1922 under this provision, thirty-two were increases. As a result, our excess of exports over imports, instead of shrinking, as our new position of a creditor nation required, actually grew from $719,000,000 in 1922 to nearly $842,000,000 in 1929.

This failure to develop an excess of imports caused no acute difficulty while loans abroad continued in sufficient volume. But the export surplus was bound to draw gold to the United States in large quantities if, for any reason, the purchase of foreign securities should be seriously curtailed. Trouble started in 1929, when speculation in stocks destroyed the American market for foreign bonds. Gold began to enter the United States in great volume—our net imports of gold in 1929 were about $120,000,000—causing in other countries a credit stringency which was a major factor in precipitating the depression. The depression itself and the political unrest which accompanied it in many countries made American investors still more averse to foreign bonds and reduced the net American export of long-term capital in 1930 to one-third that of 1928. Consequently, when in 1930 one country after another was being forced off the gold standard, the United States, which already possessed a huge surplus of gold, drew about $278,000,000 more from the rest of the world. The high tariff was not the only reason why by the end of 1930 Australia and most of the South American countries had definitely abandoned the gold standard. There were other important causes—excessive and unwise borrowing during the boom period, the inability of these countries to raise new loans, the collapse in the prices of wheat, wool, coffee, tin and other commodities. But the American tariff, by restricting the ability of the world to pay us with goods instead of gold, was a major factor in forcing a large part of the world off the gold standard and in accentuating the depreciation of many foreign currencies.

The depreciation of foreign currencies, in turn, has been a principal reason why the depression has been so much longer and more severe than any one anticipated. Depreciated currencies have made exports cheap in terms of foreign currencies and thus have increased the downward trend of world prices; in addition, foreign goods have become expensive to countries with depreciated currencies, and thus their ability to buy from the rest of the world has been reduced.

Especial attention should be given to the American tariff of June, 1930—an act of almost incredible economic folly. Unlike some recent foreign tariff changes, revision of our tariff was not needed either to protect our exchanges from depreciation or to guard our gold supplies from depletion. On the contrary, the tariff law was passed when we possessed approximately 40 per cent of the world's monetary gold and when, as has been said, we were attracting large additional amounts. During the boom which preceded the depression, many countries borrowed abroad on a large and even reckless scale. When prices collapsed, these countries experienced great difficulty in meeting their foreign obligations and were compelled, in order to conserve their gold supply and to limit the depreciation of their currencies, to restrict their imports and to control the export of gold. Even six months before our tariff became law, Argentina, Australia and Brazil took extraordinary steps to control the export of gold. The desperate plight of many debtor countries plainly required that every possible aid should be given them to preserve their credit and to meet their obligations by selling goods rather than by exporting gold. This was desirable not only on account of the debtors themselves but of the world as a whole, since depreciation in some currencies tended to pull down the general price level and to intensify the depression throughout the world.

In the face of these facts Congress passed the Smoot-Hawley tariff. Duties were raised or new ones imposed on commodities whose import value in 1928 was $1,133,000,000, while duties were removed or reduced on articles of import whose total value in 1928 was $214,000,000. This amounted to a demand on our part that the world pay us less in goods and more in gold—despite the huge hoard which we already possessed, the weakness in many currencies and the dire need of debtor nations for a better opportunity to sell goods. Although the United States, after working for years to re-establish the gold standard throughout the world, did not deliberately seek to undo its work and to accentuate the depreciation of many currencies, such was the net result of our tariff. If the drastic decline in interest rates here and the premium on dollar exchange had not produced during 1930 a record-breaking export of short-term funds from the United States, our pull upon the world's gold supply would have been far more disastrous.

If prosperity is to be fully restored one of the things to be done is to stimulate the demand for labor and goods by reviving investment on a large scale. This, in turn, requires not only political stability in the countries which seek capital but also moderation in tariffs—particularly those of the lending countries—in order that the flow of trade may adjust itself to the distribution of international investments and that nations may borrow without jeopardizing the stability of their currencies. Of particular importance is moderation in our own tariff policy.

Time was when the United States could practice extreme protection with no disastrous consequences to itself or the rest of the world. This is no longer possible. We are now the second largest creditor nation in the world; adherence to our traditional policy means that we shall attract gold in great volume and jeopardize the gold standard in many countries whenever we fail to lend abroad on a large scale. A few people mistakenly believe that our recent heavy gold losses indicate that our pull upon the world's gold supply has ceased. But these losses are only temporary and have been largely due to the conversion of foreign bank balances and bill holdings here into gold. The effect is to strengthen rather than to weaken our creditor position, which is the basis of our pull on the world's gold. Consequently, we must either develop an import balance or exert a disastrous attraction upon the world's gold supply whenever we fail to lend abroad on a large scale. Every depression is bound temporarily to diminish our lending; a continuation of our present tariff policy will mean that we shall intensify future depressions, as we have the present one, by attracting gold which the rest of the world can ill afford to lose and by menacing the stability of many weak currencies. In addition, we shall retard the revival of business, because the countries which have been forced off the gold standard or which have had the stability of their currencies seriously threatened, will, even after the revival is under way, not easily obtain credit to buy goods from the rest of the world.

The outlook for a general reduction in tariffs, either our own or of other countries, is not bright. The League of Nations has failed to effect even a temporary tariff truce. The best hope appears to lie in the method of reciprocal agreements—either bilateral, as in the case of the recent agreement between Australia and Canada, or possibly multilateral—by which reductions are given in exchange for reductions. The method is not without its difficulties and dangers. Duties may possibly be raised for bargaining purposes, while some concessions may be prevented because the most-favored-nation treaties require that a concession to one country be extended to all countries enjoying most-favored-nation treatment. The method, however, has the important advantage of offering nations which are willing to open their doors an opportunity to have doors opened to them in return. On at least two occasions—after the Cobden-Chevalier treaty in 1860 and the Caprivi treaties in the early '90s—reciprocal agreements have led to substantial reductions in the world's tariffs.

Of the three leading industrial nations the United States is best able to initiate a movement to reduce tariffs by agreement. Great Britain, absorbed by her present emergency, is turning, for the time being at least, in the direction of protection. Germany can do little, because France more than once has made it plain that she will use her political and financial power to veto attempts by Germany to secure markets through lower tariffs. Is there any prospect that the United States will abandon its philosophy of extreme protectionism? Perhaps it is unreasonable to expect most voters to see the connection between commercial policies and their pocketbooks. Our tariff policy, however, has been molded, in the main, not by the masses of the voters but by a relatively small number of business leaders. Is it unreasonable to expect these men to perceive that extreme protection practiced by a large creditor nation works very differently from the same policy pursued by a debtor nation? Sooner or later are they not bound to see that prosperity for the United States and the rest of the world will not be promoted by our hoarding gold and threatening our debtors with ruin whenever there is a general depression? If and when business men understand this, we may expect many of our politicians to abandon their support of extreme protection and become the champions of moderate duties.

How long will business men require to discover the effects of our present policy? This is a question of great practical importance. Will the experience of the present depression be sufficient? Or must we have another object lesson in the interdependence of nations, must we go through another depression, intensified and prolonged by our pull on the world's gold supply, before our business leaders realize that we cannot add to the world's disaster without inflicting injury upon ourselves?

Arthur M. Schlesinger, Jr.

The Valley of Darkness

During the depression, innumerable remedies and panaceas for recovery were suggested. From every side schemes and plans appeared in books, articles and speeches. Each fit into one of two frameworks: controlled economy or free enterprise. There were intelligent and sincere proponents on each side. The leading exponent of the free-enterprise view was the President of the United States. Devoted to individualism and abhorring the intervention of the federal government in private affairs and the competition of government with business, Herbert Hoover urged the American people to accept no planned economy and no bureaucracy lest they eventually destroy liberty. In a notable speech delivered at Indianapolis on June 15, 1931—a speech widely viewed as a bid for renomination—he warned the nation to avoid regimentation and pledged to use the power of the state only to protect the people and to provide them with equality of opportunity.

In the first volume of his multi-volumed study of The Age of Roosevelt, *Arthur M. Schlesinger, Jr., a professor of history at Harvard who served as special adviser to President Kennedy, analyzes Hoover's approach to the problems of the depression. Despite Schlesinger's obvious partisanship for Roosevelt and the New Deal, he assesses Hoover's policies sympathetically. His principal criticism is concerned with the Republican President's lack of boldness and initiative, as contrasted with Roosevelt. [Arthur M. Schlesinger, Jr.,* The Crisis of the Old Order, *1919–1933 (Boston: Houghton Mifflin Company, 1957). Reprinted by permission of Houghton Mifflin Company. British rights by permission of William Heinemann Ltd., London.]*

But the President was somewhat more apprehensive. He feared that the crash might induce a general wave of contraction and panic; and he conceived it his duty to assume leadership in checking downward tendencies. "Liquidate labor, liquidate stocks, liquidate the farmers, liquidate real estate," the Secretary of the Treasury had said; his only cure was to let economic forces run their downward course as they had in '73. But Hoover, convinced that the economy was basically sound, saw no reason for bringing misery to every sector of society. Where laissez-faire policy would call for putting the whole structure of prices and costs through the wringer, the New Era philosophy called for the maintenance of price levels and of spending. If this could be done, Hoover reasoned, then the stock market crash could be contained.

He unfolded his program in a series of conferences with business and community leaders in the next weeks. Through voluntary pledges from industry, he hoped to maintain wage rates and stabilize industrial prices. Through understandings with industry and local governments, he hoped to continue capital expansion and public building at a normal pace. Through Federal Reserve policy, he planned to make credit abundant for business borrowers. Through the Federal Farm Board, he aimed to prop up the agricultural sector. Through an upward revision of the tariff, he could protect American industry against foreign competition. And, with these policies under way, he hoped through persuasive exhortation and wise counsel to restore business confidence.

Of these policies, only tariff revision required new legislation. The special session of 1929 having failed on the tariff, the preparation of a new bill became the main business of Congress in the months immediately after the crash. The task was in the charge of two fervent protectionists, Senator Reed Smoot of Utah and Congressman Willis C. Hawley of Oregon, determined to attain for the United States "a high degree of self-sufficiency" (Smoot), to make the nation "self-contained and self-sustaining" (Hawley). In many respects, it was an audacious effort. When Paul Douglas drafted a statement denouncing the bill, he was able to obtain the signatures of a thousand members of the American Economic Association in ten days. But academic disapproval could not embarrass the protectionist faith. "If this bill is passed," said the Republican leader of the Senate, Jim Watson of Indiana, "this nation will be on the up-grade, financially, economically and commercially within thirty days, and within a year from this date we shall have regained the peak of prosperity." When Congress enacted the Smoot-Hawley law, President Hoover signed it with six gold pens, saying that "nothing" would so retard business recovery as continued agitation over the tariff.

As the first months passed after the crash, the administration viewed the future without visible alarm. At the turn of the year Secretary Mellon observed, "I see nothing in the present situation that is either menacing or warrants pessimism." In late January President Hoover announced that the unemployment trend had already been reversed; and early in February Secretary Lamont said that production and distribution were at normal levels; "there is nothing in the situation to be disturbed about." At the same time the Employment Service declared that "within the next sixty or ninety days the country will be on a normal employment basis," and Dr. Julius Klein exulted in the *American Magazine,* "It's Great To Be a Young Man Today." On March 4 Lamont, in a meteorological mood, was certain that "as weather conditions moderate, we are likely to find the country as a whole enjoying its wonted state of prosperity." On March 7, in his most detailed statement on the economic situation, the President declared that unemployment, such as it was, was concentrated in twelve states; that "employment had been slowly increasing" since the low point in December; that business and the state governments were spending more for construction even than in 1929. *"All* the evidences," he said, "indicate that the worst effects of the crash upon unemployment will have been passed during the next sixty days."

Hoover's position was not an easy one. He had rightly decided he could not indulge in a public pessimism that would only feed the panic. His fault lay not in taking an optimistic line, but in bending the facts to sustain his optimism, and then in believing his own conclusions. For, despite the presidential exhortations, private spending was simply not maintaining 1929 levels. Despite the presidential cheer, unemployment was increasing. The leaders of business, for all their pledges, were finding it impossible to collaborate in pegging the economy. The solemn meetings of the fall, with their professions of common purpose, had turned out to be exercises in ceremonial—"no-business meetings," in J. K. Galbraith's phrase. "There has been more 'optimism' talked and less practiced," said Will Rogers, "than at any time during our history." Some Republican leaders even began to scent conspiracy in business reactions. "Every time an administration official gives out an optimistic statement about business conditions," complained Senator Simeon Fess of Ohio, chairman of the Republican National Committee, "the market immediately drops."

The crucial period when a small amount of spending might have checked the cumulative forces of breakdown had already slipped by. But Hoover found in pledges an acceptable substitute for actions; assurances given took the place of dollars spent. "Our joint undertaking," he said, on May 1, 1930, before the United States Chamber of Commerce, "has succeeded to a remarkable degree." The intensity of the slump "has been greatly diminished." "I am convinced," Hoover said, "we have now passed the worst and with continued unity of effort we shall rapidly recover." . . .

This was 1930; it was, in Elmer Davis's phrase, the Second Year of the Abolition of Poverty. And it introduced thousands of Americans to a new and humiliating mode of existence—life on the relief rolls. Most of the unemployed held out as long as they could. But, with savings gone, credit exhausted, work unobtainable, there seemed no alternative save to subdue pride and face reality.

The system was, in the main, one of local poor relief, supplemented by the resources of private welfare agencies. Even in 1929 public funds paid three-quarters of the nation's relief bill; by 1932, the proportion rose to four-fifths. In larger cities, the social workers had had some success in improving standards of relief care, replacing the old "overseers of the poor" by public welfare departments. But in smaller communities, there was often no alternative to the poorhouse. And the whole patchwork system had an underlying futility: it was addressed to the care of un-employables—those who could not work in any condition—and not at all to the relief of mass unemployment.

No other modern nation had in 1930 such feeble and confused provisions for the jobless. But the President had no doubt about the adequacy of the system for the winter of 1930–31. He told the American Federation of Labor in October that his antidepression policies had had astonishing success, and that workingmen should find inspiration in the devotion "of our great manufacturers, our railways, utilities, business houses, and public officials." Later in the month, rebuking those who were demanding a special session of Congress, the President reaffirmed his confidence that the nation's "sense of voluntary organization and community service" could take care of the unemployed.

Yet, a week before, he had appointed an Emergency Committee for Employment under the direction of Colonel Arthur Woods, who had been active in the relief field during the depression of 1921. Hoover was reluctant to do even this, fearing that such action would magnify the emergency; and he informed the Committee that unemployment was strictly a local responsibility. The Committee's function in consequence became that of advice and exhortation. Colonel Woods, a man of vigor, wanted to do more. He submitted to the President a draft message to Congress calling for a public works program, including slum clearance, low-cost housing, and rural electrification. Woods and his Committee also favored Senator Robert F. Wagner's bills proposing the advance planning of public works and setting up a national employment service. But the President, rejecting the Woods program, addressed Congress with his usual optimism. Getting nowhere, Woods saw the Committee through the winter and resigned in April 1931.

Other events began to define the President's position. In the summer of 1930 a prolonged drought killed cattle and crops throughout the Southwest. This was Hoover's sort of problem—Belgium all over again, so much more concrete than the irritating and intangible issues of depression. "To overcoming the drought," reported Mark Sullivan, Hoover's intimate among the newspapermen, "President Hoover turned with something like a sense of relief, almost of pleasure." With echoes of his old confidence, he organized a program of assistance and asked Congress to appropriate money for government loans to enable farmers to buy seed, fertilizer, and cattle feed.

Democratic senators promptly sought to apply the Hoover program to human beings as well as livestock. Thus the old Wilsonian, William G. McAdoo, now senator from California, suggested that wheat purchased by the Farm Board be distributed to the unemployed. But Hoover reaffirmed his unwavering opposition to such proposals. The opposition, fighting back, taunted the President without mercy. He considered it wise to feed starving cattle, they said, but wicked to feed starving men, women, and children. He had fed the Belgians and the Germans, but would not feed his own countrymen. Hurt and distressed, the President, in February 1931, issued a deeply felt statement. If America meant anything, he suggested, it meant the principles of individual and local responsibility and mutual self-help. If we break down these principles, we "have struck at the roots of self-government." Should federal aid be the only alternative to starvation, then federal aid we must have; but "I have faith in the American people that such a day shall not come."

And so the nation staggered into the second winter of the depression, and unemployment began to settle into a way of life. The weather was glorious much of the winter—clear, light air, brilliant sunlight, dry, frosty snow. But the cold was bitter in unheated tenements, in the flophouses smelling of sweat and Lysol, in the parks, in empty freight cars, along the windy waterfronts. With no money left for rent, unemployed men and their entire families began to build shacks where they could find unoccupied land. Along the railroad embankment, beside the garbage incinerator, in the city dumps, there appeared towns of tarpaper and tin, old packing boxes and old car bodies. Some shanties were neat and scrubbed; cleanliness at least was free; but others were squalid beyond belief, with the smell of decay and surrender. Symbols of the New

Era, these communities quickly received their sardonic name: they were called Hoovervilles. And, indeed, it was in many cases only the fortunate who could find Hoovervilles. The unfortunate spent their nights huddled together in doorways, in empty packing cases, in boxcars.

At the breadlines and soup kitchens, hours of waiting would produce a bowl of mush, often without milk or sugar, and a tin cup of coffee. The vapors from the huge steam cookers mingling with the stench of wet clothes and sweating bodies made the air foul. But waiting in the soup kitchen was better than the scavenging in the dump. Citizens of Chicago, in this second winter, could be seen digging into heaps of refuse with sticks and hands as soon as the garbage trucks pulled out. On June 30, 1931, the Pennsylvania Department of Labor and Industry reported that nearly one-quarter of the labor force of the state was out of work. Clarence Pickett of the Friends found schools where 85, 90, even 99 per cent of the children were underweight, and, in consequence, drowsy and lethargic. "Have you ever heard a hungry child cry?" asked Lillian Wald of Henry Street. "Have you seen the uncontrollable trembling of parents who have gone half starved for weeks so that the children may have food?"

And still unemployment grew—from 4,000,000 in March 1930 to 8,000,000 in March 1931. And, more and more, the community found the relief problem beyond its capacity to handle. Local fiscal sources were drying up; local credit was vanishing; towns and counties found they could tax or borrow less and less. Some states had constitutional prohibitions against the use of state funds for home relief. And states too were on the verge of exhausting their tax possibilities; the general property tax had almost reached its limit, and, as income fell, the income tax, for the few states that had it, brought in declining amounts.

The burdens of private charity were meanwhile falling ever more heavily on the poor themselves. Emergency relief committees talked virtuously of the staggering of work and the "sharing" of jobs. But men working a day less a week to provide jobs for other workers were obviously contributing a portion of their own meager wages to relief while their employers contributed nothing. And, even when employers joined in company campaigns of voluntary donations, it was too often under the principle used in the Insull group, by which all, whether top executives or unskilled workers, threw in one day's pay a month. The real recipients of the dole, wrote Professor Sumner H. Slichter of Harvard, were not the men lining up to receive a nickel from the Franciscan Fathers, but "the great industries of America," paying part of their labor overhead by taxing the wages of their employees.

As the number of unemployed grew, the standards of relief care declined. More and more it seemed as if the burden was too great for individual communities to carry longer. In the fall of 1931 Governor Franklin D. Roosevelt of New York established a state emergency relief administration; other states followed this example. Effective relief, said

William Allen White in September 1931, would be "the only way to keep down barricades in the streets this winter and the use of force which will brutalize labor and impregnate it with revolution in America for a generation."

But President Hoover announced that a nation-wide survey had convinced him that state and local organizations could meet relief needs in the coming winter. Giving ground slightly, he then appointed a new committee to supersede the old Woods committee. This was the President's Organization on Unemployment Relief, headed by Walter S. Gifford, president of the American Telephone and Telegraph Company. Gifford accepted the thesis of local responsibility with far more enthusiasm than Woods; and his main contribution was an advertising campaign designed to stimulate private charity. "Between October 18 and November 25," said Gifford and Owen D. Young in a joint statement, "America will feel the thrill of a great spiritual experience." Charity, the campaign hopefully suggested, could even inspire a new love between husband and wife.

On matters which might have fallen more directly within his responsibility, Gifford displayed indifference. Early in January 1932, after nearly five months in office, Gifford appeared before a committee of the Senate. There, under the incredulous questions of Robert M. La Follette, Jr., of Wisconsin and Edward P. Costigan of Colorado, Gifford disclosed imperturbably that he did not know how many people were idle, that he did not know how many were receiving aid, that he did not know what the standards of assistance were in the various states, that he did not know how much money had been raised in his own campaign, that he knew nothing of the ability of local communities to raise relief funds either through borrowing or taxation, that he did not know what relief needs were either in urban or rural areas, that he did not consider most of this information as of much importance to his job; but that, just the same, he had no question in his mind as to the capacity of the communities to meet the relief problem. "I hope you are not criticizing me for looking at life optimistically," he said plaintively. And, when Costigan asked him to supply the committee with the reports on which his optimism was based, Gifford replied, "I have none, Senator."

But on one question Gifford was clear: he was against federal aid. Should we not be concerned, asked La Follette, if the people in Philadelphia were receiving inadequate aid? As human beings, yes, said Gifford, adding incoherently, "but whether we should be concerned in the Federal Government officially with it, unless it is so bad it is obviously scandalous, and even then we would not be obliged to be concerned. I think there is grave danger in taking the determination of these things into the Federal Government." Federal aid, he said, would lessen the sense of local responsibility; it would reduce the size of private charity. His "sober and considered judgment" was that federal aid would be a "disservice" to the jobless; "the net result might well be that the unemployed who are in need would be worse instead of better off."

And so, through the winter of 1931–32, the third winter of the depression, relief resources, public and private, dwindled toward the vanishing point. In few cities was there any longer pretense of meeting minimum budgetary standards. Little money was available for shoes or clothing, for medical or dental care, for gas or electricity. In New York City entire families were getting an average of $2.39 a week for relief. In Toledo the municipal commissary could allow only 2.14 cents per meal per person per day. In vast rural areas there was no relief coverage at all. "I don't want to steal," a Pennsylvania man wrote Governor Pinchot, "but I won't let my wife and boy cry for something to eat. . . . How long is this going to keep up? I cannot stand it any longer. . . . O, if God would only open a way."

The shadow fell over the cities and towns; it fell as heavily over the countryside. Farmers had already drawn extensively on their savings before 1929. The Wall Street explosion only made their situation worse by diminishing even more the demand for farm products. And, where industry could protect its price structure by meeting reduced demand with reduced output, farmers, unable to control output, saw no way to maintain income except to increase planting. Total crop acreage actually rose in 1930 and showed no significant decline in 1931.

The burden of agricultural adjustment thus fell not on production but on price. The figures were dramatic. Between 1929 and 1934 agricultural production declined 15 per cent in volume, 40 per cent in price; industrial production 42 per cent in volume, 15 per cent in price. The relative stability of industrial prices worsened the farmers' terms of trade; the ratio of the prices the farmer received to the prices he paid plunged from 109 in 1919 (in terms of 1910–14 prices) and 89 in 1929 to 64 in 1931. Corn slid down to 15 cents, cotton and wool to 5 cents, hogs and sugar to 3 cents, and beef to 2.5 cents. A farmer who chewed one thick plug of Drummond a day required almost a bushel of wheat a day to keep him in chewing tobacco. It took 16 bushels of wheat—more than the average yield of a whole acre—to buy one of his children a pair of $4 shoes. Net farm income in 1932 was $1.8 billion—less than one-third what it had been three years earlier. So appalling a slump left many farm families with little income, and many with no income at all.

The farmer's obligations—his taxes and his debts—had been calculated in terms of the much higher price levels of the twenties. A cotton farmer who borrowed $800 when cotton was 16 cents a pound borrowed the equivalent of 5000 pounds of cotton; now, with cotton moving toward 5 cents, he must pay back the debt with over 15,000 pounds of cotton. And, while the farmer's income fell by 64 per cent, his burden of indebtedness fell a mere 7 per cent. In the meantime, fences were standing in disrepair, crops were rotting, livestock was not worth the freight to market, farm machinery was wearing out. Some found it cheaper to burn their corn than to sell it and buy coal. On every side, notices of mortgage foreclosures and tax sales were going up on gate posts and in county courthouses. William Allen White summed it up: "Every farmer, whether his farm is under mortgage or not, knows that with farm products priced as they are today, sooner or later he must go down."

The southwestern drought only intensified the sense of grievance. In January 1931, several hundred tenant farmers presented themselves at the Red Cross in England, Arkansas, and asked for food. They included whites and Negroes, and some carried rifles. When the Red Cross administrator said that his supply of requisition blanks had been exhausted, the mob marched on the stores and seized their own flour and lard. "Paul Revere just woke up Concord," said Will Rogers, "these birds woke up America." (A New York Communist wrote a short story based on newspaper reports of the incident. Lincoln Steffens, reading Whittaker Chambers's "Can You Hear Their Voices?" wrote the young author, "Whenever I hear people talking about 'proletarian art and literature,' I'm going to ask them to . . . look at you.") . . .

The American system remained essentially a presidential system: in the end, all things came to the man in the White House. "His is the vital place of action in the system, whether he accept it or not," Woodrow Wilson once wrote, "and the office is the measure of the man—of his wisdom as well as of his force." And Herbert Hoover, as President, had far more definite ideas than most members of Congress about the cause and the cure of the economic crisis.

The depression was caused, Hoover said repeatedly in 1929 and 1930, by uncontrolled speculation in the securities market leading to an "inevitable crash." Still, if the crash was inevitable, the securities speculation, in Hoover's view, was not. It had been a gratuitous indulgence by an economy of whose "fundamental correctness" Hoover remained as convinced as on the day of his acceptance address in 1928. If the system of production and distribution was sound, then there was obviously no point in basic reform. The need, as he first saw it, was simply to seal off the rest of the economy from the shock effects of the Wall Street crash. The problem was, not to reorganize a defective structure, but to protect a healthy one.

Hence his program of 1929: the support of purchasing power through attempts to peg wage rates and farm prices; the stimulus of credit through Federal Reserve open-market operations and the reduction of the discount rate; and, most important of all, the expansion of private and public construction. This, the President said, was the "greatest tool which our economic system affords for the establishment of stability"; and he placed the responsibility for its use on government at all levels, as well as on private industry. Appealing in late 1929 to governors to increase state programs, Hoover pledged that "the Federal Government will exert itself to the utmost within its own province."

For months the verbal encouragement of public works remained Hoover's chief weapon. In January 1930, he said that total construction spending for the year would be larger than in the boom year of 1929. In May he said that the acceleration of the construction program had been "successful beyond our hopes." But, while the President and other officials were making their cheerful forecasts, private outlays for construction actually fell off in 1930 by over $2 billion, and public outlays rose by a bare $400 million. In 1931 private outlays declined another $2 billion; by 1932, they were down almost to one-quarter of what they had been in 1926. And, while the federal contribution to construction expenditures steadily increased, reaching half a billion dollars in 1932, the total of public construction steadily declined, as state and local governments ran out of money. In 1932 total public construction was nearly a billion dollars less than it had been in 1930.

There were several reasons for the collapse of the public works effort. Despite all the talk about the "construction reserve" ever since the Unemployment Conference of 1922, nothing had been done, in Hoover's Department of Commerce or elsewhere, to establish a reserve fund or to work out a shelf of projects. Nor was there now the executive energy in the administration to push a public works program through. Mellon had always scoffed at the idea, and Hoover himself became at crucial moments a victim of his own optimism. In June 1930, a delegation headed by Dr. John A. Ryan of the National Catholic Welfare Council and Amos Pinchot urged on the President immediate expansion of federal public works. Hoover, listening with the exasperation of a man who knew the situation far better than his visitors, told the group that the interview was unnecessary. The tide had turned. Unemployment was declining. Business was expanding its activities. The government had the situation fully under control. Public works? "Gentlemen," the President said, "you have come sixty days too late. The depression is over."

Most important, the public works theory was fighting a losing battle in Hoover's mind against his mounting concern for the budget. For a time, this internal debate led to a dizzying alternation between presidential statements calling for more public works and presidential statements warning against more public expenditures. But as national income continued to sink through 1930, so did tax collections. Though the Treasury could still report a surplus of nearly $200 million for 1930, it was evident that the nation was headed for a deficit in 1931. As the deficit came nearer, Hoover became increasingly preoccupied with what he actually defined as "the primary duty of the Government, that is, to hold expenditures within our income." More and more, the growing federal debt seemed the primary threat to recovery. "For the Government to finance by bond issues," Hoover declared in December 1930, "deprives industry and agriculture of just that much capital for its own use and for employment. Prosperity cannot be restored by raids upon the public Treasury."

Tax revenues continued to fall in 1931; and the federal deficit that year was almost a billion dollars—the largest peacetime deficit in American history. With national income still going down, the prospect for 1932 was even more dismal; the deficit might well end up three times as great. Hoover now redoubled his efforts. He demanded the most rigid retrenchment in government. He called for an increase in taxes. He denounced proposals for public spending. "Nothing," he said flatly in November 1931, "will contribute more to the return of prosperity than to maintain the sound fiscal position of the Federal Government." In December 1931 he formally repudiated the contention, once his own, that further expansion of public works would aid recovery.

Fear of the deficit became an obsession in 1932. When Wagner and Garner urged Congress to increase public spending, Hoover harshly questioned their motives and assailed their programs—"the most gigantic pork barrel ever proposed to the American Congress," "an unexampled raid on the public Treasury." Vetoing the Garner-Wagner relief bill, he wrote, "Never before has so dangerous a suggestion been seriously made to our country." Others pointed out that his own policy of raising taxes and cutting government spending could only reduce purchasing power still further; but the President replied in a crescendo of statements—twenty of them from December to May alone—reiterating what was becoming his single theme. "The absolute necessity of a balanced budget" (March 25) was "the most essential factor to economic recovery" (May 5), "the imperative and immediate step" (May 13), "indispensable" (May 21), "the first necessity of the Nation" (August 11), "the foundation of all public and private financial stability" (August 11).

The infatuation with the balanced budget thus destroyed the major plank of Hoover's first antidepression program—the expansion of public works. In the meantime, the President was moving toward a radically new diagnosis of the depression. The theory of 1929—that the breakdown was the inevitable result of uncontrolled domestic speculation—was perhaps coming to seem irksome, possibly because it fixed responsibility too squarely on the American business community. In October 1930, Hoover suddenly discovered that the roots of the depression lay "only partly in the United States." The major cause, he now felt, had been the overproduction of raw materials abroad, leading to lower prices and reduced buying power in foreign countries and thus to reduced foreign purchases in America. The actual decline of the foreign trade balance in 1930 was less than $60 million, a sum which hardly explained the collapse of the American economy; but, despite statistics, the President grew rapidly more confident of his new thesis. In December he said that "the major forces of the depression now lie outside of the United States," and by

June 1931, that "the main causes . . . came not from within but from outside the United States."

Events in Europe soon gave a touch of plausibility to the new Hoover line. The failure of the Kreditanstalt in Vienna in June 1931 put the international gold standard under intense strain. Hoover's debt moratorium that summer was no more than a palliative, and in September it became evident that the City of London could no longer defend the pound. By January 1932 about forty nations—though not America or France—had gone off gold. The world financial crisis increased the pressure on the American economy.

For Hoover the restoration of the gold standard now became almost as indispensable as balancing the budget. Gold, he said, was a metal "enshrined in human instincts for over 10,000 years," and he did not mean to abandon it. John Maynard Keynes predicted that the curse of Midas would fall on the countries which clung to gold—that they would suffer the disadvantages of costs fixed in terms of gold, while their competitors in the world market could enjoy the benefits of devaluation. The United States, said Keynes, was setting "the rest of us the problem of finding some way to do without her wheat, her copper, her cotton and her motorcars"; it was willing the destruction of its own export industries. But Hoover identified America's economic future with gold. Indeed, he later claimed that the nation had been within two weeks of being driven off the gold standard early in 1932 when it was saved from incalculable disaster by the swift action of his administration. "Never," he subsequently recalled—perhaps a strong word for a century and a half of American history—"was our nation in greater peril."

There remained crucial contradictions in Hoover's new internationalism. His attitude toward foreign debts and convertibility showed a genuine concern for the world financial community. But the world financial community seemed to him somehow separate from the world trading community. He never quite put the two ideas together. Even when he spoke, in the same sentence, of the American economy both as "self-contained" and as vulnerable to "shocks and setbacks from abroad," he apparently saw no inconsistencies. The result was that his gold and tariff policies worked at cross-purposes. While with one hand he tried to maintain convertibility, with the other he raised American tariffs, evidently not understandng that exchange depreciation and import duties might be alternative means of achieving the same end.

The gold standard which Hoover sought so earnestly to protect in 1932 he had in fact already gravely wounded when he signed the tariff of 1930. Denied the opportunity to earn dollars in the American market, many nations had no choice but to protect themselves against American exports. Thus Italy, Spain, France, Britain, Canada were quick to raise barriers against American goods. The drift toward economic nationalism threatened not only the world trading community but the world financial community as well. Yet 1932 found Hoover combining his international theory of depression with a stout defense of protective tariffs. The suggestion of reciprocal trade agreements he rejected as "a violation of American principles."

By 1932 Hoover had moved from the New Era philosophy, with its emphasis on maintaining purchasing power in the American economy, toward something much closer to old-fashioned laissez faire, where faith in a balanced budget and the gold standard was tempered only by a commitment to protectionism. This evolution was assisted by the growing influence of the Undersecretary of the Treasury, Ogden L. Mills of New York, who became Secretary in February 1932, when Hoover finally induced Mellon to go to London as Ambassador. But it was evident to Hoover and Mills that the balanced budget and the gold standard, while primary, were not enough by themselves. Something also had to be done to protect the business of the nation against threatening bankruptcy and liquidation.

One possible approach was that suggested by Gerard Swope and H. I. Harriman. There were reasons for supposing that the President might look with favor on industrial planning. After all, no one had done more in the twenties to foster the trade association and to advocate self-government in industry than Hoover, and few men had seemed to care less about the Sherman Act. Even as President, he had questioned "destructive competition," suggested the revision of the antitrust laws, and called for "the development of cooperative spirit and responsibility in the American business world . . . such that the business of the country itself could and should assume the responsibility for the mobilization of the industrial and commercial agencies." "Self-government outside of political government," he told the American Banking Association in 1930, "is the truest form of self-government." But perhaps the Swope and Harriman proposals implied too much in the way of reorganizing the fundamentally sound economic system. In any case, he dismissed the Swope plan as "the most gigantic proposal of monopoly ever made in history" and the Chamber of Commerce plan as "sheer fascism." Evidently self-government outside of political government could be carried too far.

If the structure of business was not to be reorganized, the alternative was to guarantee the existing structure. The President was disappointed in his early hope that the New York banking community might bolster the credit system on its own, as it had in previous crises. Only twice during the depression, as he saw it, had the New York bankers come together for organized cooperation in an important way—once to save the reichsmark, once to save the pound. Counting on similar action in support of American business, Hoover summoned leading bankers to secret meetings in the fall of 1931, and invited them to pool their funds in order to provide a credit reserve for their weaker brethren. To his chagrin, most of the group insisted that this was the government's responsibility. "I returned to the White House after midnight," Hoover later wrote, "more depressed than ever before." After consideration, the bankers did agree to try the National Credit Association idea. But their hearts were not in it; and a few weeks later the project was an evident failure.

In the meantime, Eugene Meyer, whom Hoover had appointed governor of the Federal Reserve Board in 1930, had been advocating a new plan. Meyer wanted to revive his old War Finance Corporation in the guise of a Reconstruction Finance Corporation, empowered to make loans to banks, railroads, and insurance companies. With the National Credit Association fiasco behind him, Hoover now reluctantly accepted the Meyer proposal. He still objected to an ambitious lending program, but he hoped that the passage of the legislation would by itself reassure the credit system and restore confidence. "I look upon it," Ogden Mills said of the RFC, "as an insurance measure more than anything else. I think its very existence will have a great effect psychologically, and the sooner it is created, the less use we will have to make of it."

The RFC thus became in 1932 the administration's new weapon against the depression. It faced an increasingly critical situation. Banks were closing their doors—nearly 2300 suspended in 1931 alone, and anxious depositors were beginning to withdraw their savings from banks that were still open. In the meantime, the flight of gold from the country, as foreign investors threw their American securities on the market and took gold in exchange, drew further on the metallic reserve. When the RFC went into operation in February 1932, the total reserves of the Federal Reserve member banks had fallen to within $50 million of the lowest amount allowed by law.

But the RFC leadership—Eugene Meyer as chairman, Charles G. Dawes as president—were not ready for vigorous action. During the year, the agency succeeded in disbursing only about $1.5 billion of its $2 billion, and the great bulk of this money went to banks and trust companies. Even this transfusion was not as effective as it should have been; for the RFC was authorized only to make loans to banks, not to purchase their stock; and the great need for banks was not more indebtedness but more capital. "For a fatal year and a half," Russell Leffingwell of Morgan's later observed, "the Reconstruction Finance Corporation continued to lend money to the banks on adequate collateral security and gradually bankrupted them in the effort to save them."

For the first five months, RFC operations were kept secret—to some extent, even from the Democrats whom the RFC law required to be appointed to the board of directors. "Several months passed," Jesse Jones of Texas, the dominant Democrat in RFC, wrote later, "before Chairman Meyer and Secretary Mills seemed to think it necessary to regard the Democratic directors as their equals. . . . Apparently they expected us blindly to do their bidding." And, if it was bad to tell things to the Democratic directors, it was even worse to tell them to the people. In particular, Hoover objected to the publication of RFC loans on the ground that publicity might invite the very disasters—the run on the bank, for example—which the loans were intended to prevent. Jones, however, received this argument with skepticism. And the President did not strengthen his case by using secrecy to obscure the character of RFC loan policy.

In signing the bill, Hoover had declared that RFC was "not created for the aid of big industries or big banks." Statements issued in the first months of operation conveyed the impression that the agency was concentrating on help for the little fellow. But in July 1932, John Garner secured the passage of an amendment compelling the RFC to report its loans to Congress. An analysis of the loans outstanding now put a different face on the official statements. Thus Hoover's claim in April that the RFC had loaned $126 million to banks in 45 states took on a less virtuous aspect when it was discovered that over half this sum had gone to three large banks.

Charges of favoritism in the distribution of loans increased criticism of the RFC. In June Dawes suddenly resigned, announcing that he must return to Chicago to take charge of the affairs of the Central Republic Bank. A few weeks later the RFC loaned Dawes's bank $90 million; this was at a time when its total deposits amounted to only $95 million. Even this loan could not save the bank, which soon was forced into reorganization, though in time, and after litigation, the loan was repaid to the RFC. The circumstances by which Dawes's bank received prompt assistance from the agency he had just left while the unemployed were denied federal aid roused natural speculation. So too did the disclosure that Atlee Pomerene, Dawes's successor, had authorized a loan of $12 million to a Cleveland bank of which he was director. When John T. Flynn published these facts early in 1933, President Hoover's secrecy policy seemed to many wholly disreputable. And, to support this impression, the loans to big banks were tapered off as soon as the secrecy provisions were ended.

The administration's special concern for business was natural enough. "The sole function of government," Hoover said in the fall of 1931, "is to bring about a condition of affairs favorable to the beneficial development of private enterprise." Let business recover, Hoover believed, and recovery for the rest of the nation—the worker, the farmer, the unemployed—would come in due course.

Thus the plight of labor received little direct attention. By September 1931 the President was forced to abandon his early effort to maintain wage rates. When the Norris–La Guardia bill outlawing yellow-dog contracts came up in 1932, the administration greeted it without enthusiasm. Republicans denounced it in Congress; and Hoover's Secretary of Labor, in a meeting with the counsel of the National Association of Manufacturers, even offered Donald Richberg a federal judgeship if he would abandon support of the measure. Richberg spurned the suggestion, and Congress finally passed the bill, Hoover appending a glum signature. In August 1932, when Hoover called together Business and Industrial Committees from the twelve Federal Reserve Districts to organize "a concerted program of action along the whole economic front," he did not think to ask labor representatives.

At the start, the farmers received somewhat more attention. Depression suddenly brought into prominence what had been a peripheral part of the original Farm Board program—that is, the stabilization corporations, designed to support farm prices by holding temporary crop surpluses off the market. This stabilization system, however, had been intended as a means of ironing out minor crop variations, not of dealing with major surpluses. Any effect the Board's purchases of wheat and cotton had in maintaining prices in 1930 was quickly offset by the encouragement stiffening prices offered to new production, as well as by the continuing decline in demand. It became rapidly clear that price support could not work without production control.

In January 1930 the Board began to warn that it could not "protect farmers when they deliberately over-plant." By mid-summer Alex Legge, president of International Harvester, whom Hoover had made chairman of the Board, and Secretary of Agriculture Arthur Hyde launched a campaign for voluntary acreage reduction. To cotton farmers, the Board suggested that they plow up every third row. To wheat farmers, it urged reduced sowing. But most farmers, having no assurance that their neighbors would reduce their planting, or perhaps thinking that they would, went on producing in the hope of cashing in on prospective higher prices.

"I believe," said Hyde, "in controlled production." But, he hastily added, "such control, in my judgment, must come about by voluntary action of the farmers themselves, and not by mandate of law." Yet in a few months the Board itself conceded that voluntary methods would not work because of the "individualistic character" of the American farmer. "While there are still a few of the agricultural leaders who lower their voices when they speak of production control," Legge told Hoover, "yet practically all of them have accepted the principle as essential."

But the President hated the idea of federal surplus control. He disliked almost as much the tentative experiments in stabilization permitted under his act of 1929. "Even indirect purchase and sale of commodities," he said, "is absolutely opposed to my theory of government." And so the Hoover farm policy declined into self-inflicted impotence. By mid-1931, the Board abandoned its price support efforts and devoted itself to the task of disposing of its holdings. Thereafter the administration watched farm prices fall with helpless defeatism.

The same belief that government should concentrate on aid to business led the President to continue to resist proposals for federal action on behalf of the unemployed. As the third winter of the depression approached, Hoover's principle began to receive new challenges. "We shall help the railroad; we shall help the financial institutions; and I agree that we should," said Senator Wagner. "But is there any reason why we should not likewise extend a helping hand to that forlorn American, in every village and every city of the United States, who has been without wages since 1929? Must he alone carry the cross of individual responsibility?" Nor was the argument that relief was a local problem as persuasive as it had been in 1929 or 1930. The administration did not tell General Dawes, noted Edith Abbott, the social worker, that he should seek assistance for his bank from the Chicago city council.

The La Follette–Costigan bill, with its provisions for federal grants to states for relief purposes, was beaten in February 1932. But Senator Wagner and Congressman Henry T. Rainey, the Democratic leader in the House, began a new fight in the spring for alternative forms of federal aid. When Joseph T. Robinson of Arkansas, the Democratic leader in the Senate, proposed in May a federal bond issue of over $2 billion to subsidize self-liquidating public works, and Al Smith, Bernard Baruch, and Owen D. Young promptly backed the project, Hoover, his hand forced, came up with a counterproposal of his own, making the RFC the instrumentality of federal assistance.

The first result of the jockeying between the Democrats and White House was the passage of the Wagner-Garner bill, which added to its spending proposals a provision enlarging the lending authority of the RFC by $300 million for loans to supplement local relief in needy states. Though Hoover favored this provision, as well as a provision enabling the RFC to undertake a program of self-liquidating loans, he objected to other aspects of the bill and vetoed it. When these provisions were enacted in a slightly different form a week later, the President accepted them, thereby approving the Emergency Relief Act of 1932. The use of loans, repayable with interest in July 1935, maintained to his satisfaction the pretense of local responsibility. It was evident in any case that the administration proposed to construe its new powers as narrowly as possible.

"These loans," the President said, "are to be based upon absolute need and evidence of financial exhaustion. I do not expect any state to resort to it except as a last extremity." From the White House viewpoint, the RFC was to discharge a banking function. When Governor Pinchot of Pennsylvania, pointing out that the expenditure of $60 million among the more than one million jobless in his state would give each of them only 13 cents worth of food per day for a year, applied for the sum of $45 million, the RFC, after due deliberation, made about $11 million available. By the end of the year, only $30 million of the $300 million was allotted for relief, and even less for public works.

The President stood manfully by his principles. But it remains unclear both from his statements at the time and from his subsequent recollections what his actual picture was of the state of his nation. Years later he wrote, "Many persons left their jobs for the more profitable one of selling apples." This sentence perhaps epitomized the presidential incredulity before the depression. If people sold apples on the street corners, it must have been because they could make more money doing that than doing something else. What jobs there were which offered even less security than apple-selling did not rouse his curiosity.

From time to time, the President produced letters from his Surgeon-General affecting to show that the state of public health was better in depression than it had been in prosperity; "no greater proof could be adduced," he liked to say, "that our people have been protected from hunger and cold." When the United Hospital Fund of New York City replied with statistics showing an "abnormal and progressive" increase in sickness, when the Pennsylvania Secretary of Public Health reported alarming increases in malnutrition and tuberculosis, when the daily newspaper contained items demonstrating the effects of privation, the President brusquely rejected them. "Nobody is actually starving," he told newspapermen. "The hoboes, for example, are better fed than they have ever been. One hobo in New York got ten meals in one day."

As there could be nothing basically wrong with conditions, so there could be nothing basically wrong with the economic mechanism. The problems thus lay in the area of psychology, not economics. As Ogden Mills put it, "There is more to fear from frozen minds than from frozen assets." Something of this feeling undoubtedly lay behind the optimistic exhortations of 1930. When the economy failed to respond to pep talks, the President looked for other stimulants. "What the country needs," he told Raymond Clapper in February 1931, "is a good, big laugh. There seems to be a condition of hysteria. If someone could get off a good joke every ten days, I think our troubles would be over." He said the same thing to Weber and Fields. In 1932 he asked Will Rogers to think up a joke that would stop hoarding. To Rudy Vallee, the crooner, he said, "If you can sing a song that would make people forget their troubles and the Depression, I'll give you a medal." And to Christopher Morley: "Perhaps what this country needs is a great poem. . . . I keep looking for it, but I don't see it. Sometimes a great poem can do more than legislation."

No President ever worked harder. Up at six, he threw on old clothes for his only bout of exercise—his seven-o'clock session with his "medicine ball cabinet." For thirty or forty minutes he fired the ball hard back and forth with a group of friends; then breakfast; and he was in his office by eight-thirty. It was characteristic that he was the first President to have a phone on his desk. From breakfast until bedtime at eleven, he labored without stint, smoking long, thick cigars as worry etched new lines into his gray face and his eyes became strained and bloodshot. "I am so tired," he sometimes said, "that every bone in my body aches." His manner grew increasingly preoccupied and dour. As he walked about the White House, he rarely spoke to the servants; "never a good-morning or even **a** nod of the head," said Ike Hoover, the White House usher. If someone addressed him, a low murmur came in reply, almost as if dragged out by force. He rarely looked at people in conversation, instead shuffling papers on his desk and doodling on blank sheets. He had no capacity for relaxation and was irritated by interruption. "There was always a frown on his face and a look of worry," said Ike Hoover; he "never laughed aloud." One of his secretaries remonstrated with him over his lack of small talk. Said the President sternly, "I have other things to do when a nation is on fire."

Hoover was, as William Allen White said, "constitutionally gloomy, a congenital pessimist who always saw the doleful side of any situation." "He worried more than any President," said Ike Hoover. The Secretary of State, Henry L. Stimson, regretted his chief's fatal preference for "seeing the dark side first." Stimson, noting "the ever present feeling of gloom that pervades everything connected with the administration," could not remember a single joke cracked in a year and a half of Cabinet meetings. One private session with the President seemed to the Secretary of State "like sitting in a bath of ink."

Friends urged him to be more of a public leader. "I can't be a Theodore Roosevelt," the President would say with sadness; or, "I have no Wilsonian qualities." And the strain of maintaining his principles in the face of the accumulating evidences of human need doubtless led both to anxiety and to self-righteousness. Said Esmé Howard, the genial British Ambassador, "I found him, without exception, the most difficult American to know whom I have ever met." "Of all the administrations," said Ike Hoover, who served for forty-two years at the White House, "the hardest one to work for was that of President Hoover," adding that whenever the Hoovers left the White House, the employees were "glad when they were gone." H. G. Wells had visited the White House twice before when he came to call on Hoover. In the days of Theodore Roosevelt, it had been like any comfortable, free-talking country house. Calling on Harding had been like attending a politician's reception, all loud geniality and handshaking. But his visit with Hoover, Wells felt, had been an intrusion on a "sickly, overworked and overwhelmed" man, with distraught officials appearing and disappearing through unexpected doors. Hoover could not converse, but delivered a discourse on American economic self-sufficiency, intended, Wells felt, for Pierre Laval, who had left Washington a few days before. "I did not find it interesting."

All the official optimism could not conceal the underlying strain. The newspapermen were perhaps first to sense the situation. There was much about the Hoover regime they had disliked—the evident pleasure in ceremonial trappings, the company of Marines on guard at the summer camp, the buglers at official dinners, the Secret Service men stationed in odd corners of the White House. But the President's attitude in press conferences aroused more serious concern. He played favorites (Mark

Sullivan and William Hard, for example, were in the medicine-ball group) and complained to publishers of reporters whose stories he did not like. Gradually he began to cancel his press conferences. In his last two years, he held hardly more than one a month. The conferences themselves consisted increasingly of official handouts. Bumbling attempts by White House secretaries to withhold news and to control the writing of stories only aggravated the situation. The President's relations with the press, Paul Y. Anderson of the St. Louis *Post-Dispatch* reported in 1931, had reached "a stage of unpleasantness without parallel during the present century. They are characterized by mutual dislike, unconcealed suspicion, and downright bitterness."

The gloom and insecurity communicated itself to the nation. A people looking for leadership could not but respond with resentment. Hoover became the butt of a thousand bitter jokes. One told of Hoover's request to Mellon for the loan of a nickel to call up a friend, and of the Mellon reply: "Here's a dime, call up all your friends." Another asserted that there was no question about Hoover's being the world's greatest engineer: "in a little more than two years, he has drained, ditched and damned the United States." Vaudeville comedians, on being told that business was turning up, asked, "Is Hoover dead?"

Furtive books began to appear, investigating Hoover's years in the Far East and in high finance, accusing him of crimes ranging from British citizenship to cheating the Chinese government, oppressing coolie labor, engaging in the slave trade, making money out of Belgian relief, and even bringing about the execution of Edith Cavell. The very word "Hoover" became a prefix charged with hate: not only "Hoovervilles," but "Hoover blankets" (newspapers wrapped around for warmth), "Hoover wagons" (brokendown automobiles hauled by mules), "Hoover flags" (empty pockets turned inside out), "Hoover hogs" (jackrabbits).

The sense of popular hatred wounded the President. "It is a cruel world," he remarked at one point; and, again, "My men are dropping around me." And it also, perhaps, helped confirm his intellectual rigidities. The White House usher noted that, where Theodore Roosevelt and Wilson liked to send for people who took views different from their own, Hoover preferred to discuss matters with people whom he knew in advance would agree with him. Looking back twenty years later in his *Memoirs,* Hoover himself could see no mistakes committed during his presidency, no opportunities missed, no wrong guesses, nothing to regret. And at the time, criticism began to seem to him, not just the give-and-take of politics, but a dangerous threat to the American way of life. "He regarded some of it," Theodore Joslin, his faithful secretary, said, "as unpatriotic." He felt himself fighting, not just for the established order, but for the survival of American institutions.

The ideological issue emerged with increasing clarity in the second half of his administration. He felt, no doubt, genuine indignation at the behavior of leading businessmen. William Allen White reported that in private he grumbled at their perfidy and complained of their greed. "But also," White added, "because he had worked for thirty years with men of wealth, he could not publicly scold a million dollars, much less a hundred million." This was the America he respected, whatever its faults, and this America had to be preserved. His anger was directed rather at those who threatened to change this America, especially by enlarging the power of the federal government.

Hoover had, he admitted, "no taste" for emergency powers. To avoid the drift toward a superstate, he wanted "to solve great problems outside of Government action." Victory over depression must be won "by the resolution of our people to fight their own battles in their own communities." For the federal government to assume what had been local obligations would be to undermine "the very basis of self-government." The question for the future, he believed, was whether history should be written in terms of individual responsibility or of the "futile attempt to cure poverty by the enactment of law." Depression, he said, could not be ended "by legislative action or executive pronouncement. Economic wounds must be healed by the action of the cells of the economic body."

Yet the same man who could invoke the healing processes of nature and warn with passion against centralization could also, in another mood, boast of "the most gigantic program of economic defense and counterattack ever evolved in the history of the Republic." For all his faith in individualism, he brought great areas of the economy—the banks, the railroads, the insurance companies, the farmers, even, toward the end, the unemployed—into the orbit of national action. No doubt, he entered on these programs grudgingly, and did as little as he could to develop their possibilities. Yet he breached the walls of local responsibility as had no President in American history.

How could he be so certain where the exact line of demarcation was drawn between beneficent intervention and limitless evil? Senator Norris's project for the government ownership and operation of Muscle Shoals seemed to him, for example, "the negation of the ideals upon which our civilization has been based." Yet his own projects seemed equally Bolshevistic, for example, to James M. Beck. In the end, Hoover, dragged despairingly along by events, decided that wherever he finally dug in constituted the limits of the permissible. Doctrinaire by temperament, he tended to make every difference in degree a difference in kind and to transform questions of tactics into questions of principles.

As his term wore on, the ideological obsession grew. He had himself done unprecedented things to show the potentialities of national action; but anyone who went a step beyond transgressed the invisible line and menaced the American way of life. His was the tragedy of a man of high ideals whose intelligence froze into inflexibility and whose dedication was smitten by self-righteousness.

President Roosevelt entered office on March 4, 1933, with an overwhelming victory at the polls behind him. A popular vote of over 22 million (to Hoover's 15 million), a whopping 472 to 59 edge in the electoral college (only six states went Republican), and a safe Democratic majority in both houses of Congress provided him with the strength to meet the problems of the depression, great and frightening though they were. The problems were not insurmountable, he told the people. It was his "firm belief that the only thing we have to fear is fear itself— nameless, unreasoning, unjustified terror. . . . Our distress comes from no failure of substance. We are stricken by no plague of locusts. . . . Nature still offers her bounty. . . . Plenty is at our doorstep." The trouble lay only in the failure by the preceding administration to take the proper measures and

11

THE NEW DEAL

in the insistence by its leaders to work "in the pattern of an outworn tradition." Given swiftness, boldness, and courage, the country would be saved, and the President was determined to save it. One way or another, he would carry out his program. If the Congress would not support his measures, he said, he "would not evade the clear course of duty that will then confront me. I shall ask the Congress for the one remaining instrument to meet the crisis—broad executive power to wage a war against the emergency as the power that would be given me if we were in fact invaded by a foreign foe."

The President moved at once. The first hundred days constituted a period of rapid action unparalleled in our history. He did more in that period than any preceding President had ever dreamed of doing. As Arthur M. Schlesinger, Jr., noted, he had "sent 15 messages to Congress, guided 15 major laws to enactment, delivered ten speeches, held press conferences and cabinet meetings twice a week, conducted talks with foreign heads of state, sponsored an international conference, made all the major decisions in domestic and foreign policy . . . " Legislation so drastic and far-reaching in its effects had never before been enacted in a comparable period of time. Schlesinger lists the achievements: the Emergency Banking Act, the Economy Act, the creation of the Civilian Conservation Corps, leaving the gold standard, the Federal Emergency Relief Act, the Agricultural Adjustment Act, the Emergency Farm Mortgage Act, the Tennessee Valley Authority, the Truth-in-Securities Act, the abrogation of the gold clause in contracts, the Home Owners' Loan Act, the National Industrial Recovery Act, the Glass-Steagall Banking Act, the Farm Credit Act, the Railroad Co-ordination Act. Nothing like such geometric acceleration in government action had ever occurred before.

The New Deal continued, at not so hectic a pace to be sure, but still moving ahead firmly into other areas that required action to erase the disastrous consequences of the depression and to provide safeguards against a recurrence. The Social Security Act, the Wagner-Connery Act, and the Fair Labor Standards Act, among others, stand out as landmarks in the New Deal program.

Because of its swiftness, boldness, adventurous spirit, and absence of inhibitions, and because of its lack of consistency, numerous contradictions, experimental nature, and failure to articulate a philosophy, the New Deal led to a feeling of bewilderment and confusion for many Americans. They questioned its direction and purpose, its goals and objectives. How American were the measures taken? Did they break with the past or did they have roots in the nation's history? What lasting good was the New Deal achieving? And what of the President—was he autocrat or Democrat? These were some of the important questions contemporary observers and later historians sought to answer. Their speculations and analyses form the substance of the readings in this chapter.

By 1938 the New Deal had run its course. As the President said on January 4, 1939, "We have now passed the period of internal conflict in the launching of our program of social reform. Our full energies may now be released to invigorate the processes of recovery in order to preserve our reforms." As a matter of fact, the President was turning his attention more and more to foreign affairs and away from domestic matters. Even so, the New Deal had done its work. True, it had not promoted complete recovery; the war economy took care of that. It had, however, brought the nation a long way on the road to recovery from the depths of despair of 1933. It had suffered reverses and setbacks, as in the Supreme Court fight, the invalidation of the NRA and the AAA, and the recession of 1937; but it had enjoyed great victories, too, particularly at the polls. It had violent opposition from many quarters and contended with threats from people like Francis Townsend, Father Coughlin, and Huey Long. At the same time it had mighty support from the American people, who returned the President to office three times.

The greatest achievement of the New Deal lay in providing security for millions of Americans without destroying their liberties, and in demonstrating that a democracy operating within constitutional limitations (although slightly stretched) can cure a nation's ills. It was not necessary to stray from the middle path nor to use un-American remedies. What the New Deal did could not be undone. Republicans as well as Democrats were committed to government intervention in periods of prosperity as well as depression. As a result, it seemed perfectly natural and reasonable for a Republican Secretary of Labor in 1953 to pledge that his administration "stands ready to step in with public works and other measures to help maintain high employment if the nation's economy falters. The Administration is committed to every useful measure both public and private to foster economic stability."

Richard Hofstadter

The Age

of Reform

Did the New Deal break sharply with the American past or did it follow in the American tradition? This question, which has troubled contemporary observers and later historians, prompted many Republicans to cry "revolution," indicting all of Roosevelt's acts as un-American. Democratic idolizers of the President similarly labeled the New Deal acts revolutionary but in the most laudatory sense, hailing them as bold and noble innovations. Roosevelt himself, in a victory speech on March 4, 1937, accepted the concept of revolution when he characterized his accession to office in 1933 as "the death of one era and the birth of another." More recently, Richard Hofstadter—the Columbia University historian—has argued persuasively that the New Deal was a "drastic departure in the history of American reform." In the selection that follows, he sees the New Deal as a political "revolution." [Copyright 1955 by Richard Hofstadter. Condensed from The Age of Reform *by Richard Hofstadter, by permission of Alfred A. Knopf, Inc.]*

The New Departure. The Great Depression, which broke the mood of the twenties almost as suddenly as the postwar reaction had killed the Progressive fervor, rendered obsolete most of the antagonisms that had flavored the politics of the postwar era. Once again the demand for reform became irresistible, and out of the chaotic and often mutually contradictory schemes for salvation that arose from all corners of the country the New Deal took form. In the years 1933–8 the New Deal sponsored a series of legislative changes that made the enactments of the Progressive era seem timid by comparison, changes that, in their totality, carried the politics and administration of the United States farther from the conditions of 1914 than those had been from the conditions of 1880.

It is tempting, out of a desire for symmetry and historical continuity, to see in the New Deal a return to the preoccupations of Progressivism, a resumption of the work of reform that had begun under Theodore Roosevelt and Woodrow Wilson, and a consummation of the changes that were proposed in the half-dozen years before the first World War. Much reason can be found for yielding to this temptation. Above all, the New Dealers shared with the Progressives a far greater willingness than had been seen in previous American history to make use of the machinery of government to meet the needs of the people and supplement the workings of the national economy. There are many occasions in its history when the New Deal, especially in its demand for organization, administration, and management from a central focus, seems to stand squarely in the tradition of the New Nationalism for which such Progressives as Herbert Croly had argued. Since it is hardly possible for any society to carve out a completely new vocabulary for every new problem it faces, there is also much in the New Deal rhetoric that is strongly reminiscent of Progressivism. Like the Progressives, the New Dealers invoked a larger democracy; and where the Progressives had their "plutocrats," the New Dealers had their "economic royalists." F. D. R., asserting in his first inaugural address that "The money changers have fled from their high seats in the temple of our civilization. We may now restore that temple to the ancient truths," sounds very much like almost any inspirational writer for *McClure's* in the old days. On a number of particular issues, moreover, like the holding-company question, monopoly, and public power, one feels as though one is treating again, in the New Deal, with familiar problems—just as, in the crucial early days of 1933, the formation of a strong bloc of inflationist Senators from the West seemed to hark back to the populist movement.

Still, granting that absolute discontinuities do not occur in history, and viewing the history of the New Deal as a whole, what seems outstanding about it is the drastic new departure that it marks in the history of American reformism. The New Deal was different from anything that had yet happened in the United States: different because its central problem was unlike the problems of Progressivism; different in its ideas and its spirit and its techniques. Many men who had lived through Progressivism and had thought of its characteristic proposals as being in the main line of American traditions, even as being restoratives of those traditions, found in the New Deal an outrageous departure from everything they had known and valued, and so could interpret it only as an effort at subversion or as the result of overpowering alien influences. Their opposition was all too often hysterical, but in their sense that something new had come into American political and economic life they were quite right.

Consider, to begin, the fundamental problem that the New Dealers faced, as compared with the problems of the Progressives. When Theodore Roosevelt took office in 1901, the country was well over three years past a severe depression and in the midst of a period of healthy economic development. Its farmers were more prosperous than they had been for about forty years, its working class was employed and gaining in living standards, and even its middle class was far busier counting the moral costs of success than it was worrying about any urgent problems of family finance. When F. D. R. took his oath of office, the entire working apparatus of American economic life had gone to smash. The customary masters and leaders of the social order were themselves in a state of near panic. Millions were unemployed, and discontent had reached a dangerous pitch on the farms and in the cities.

Indeed, the New Deal episode marks the first in the history of reform movements when a leader of the reform party took the reins of a government confronted above all by the problems of a sick economy. To be sure, the whole nineteenth-century tradition of reform in American politics was influenced by experience with periodic economic breakdowns; but its political leaders had never had to bear responsibility for curing them. Jefferson in 1801, Jackson in 1829, and after them T. R. and Wilson—all took over at moments when the economy was in good shape. While each of them had experience with economic relapse—Jefferson in 1807 as the consequence of his embargo policies, the Jacksonians briefly in 1834 and again after 1837, T. R. briefly during the "bankers' panic" of 1907, and Wilson with a momentary recession just before the wartime boom—their thinking, and the thinking of the movements they represented, was centered upon sharing an existing prosperity among the various social classes rather than upon restoring a lost prosperity or preventing recurrent slumps.

The earlier American tradition of political protest had been a response to the needs of entrepreneurial classes or of those who were on the verge of entrepreneurship—the farmers, small businessmen, professionals, and occasionally the upper caste of the artisans or the working class. The goal of such classes had generally been to clear the way for new enterprises and new men, break up privileged business, big businesses, and monopolies, and give the small man better access to credit. The ideas of this Progressive tradition, as one might expect, were founded not merely upon acceptance but even upon glorification of the competitive order. The Jeffersonians, the Jacksonians, and after them most of the Progressives had believed in the market economy, and the only major qualification of this belief they cared to make stemmed from their realization that the market needed to be policed and moralized by a government responsive to the needs of the economic beginner and the small entrepreneur. Occasionally, very occasionally, they had argued for the exercise of a few positive functions on the part of the national government, but chiefly they preferred to keep the positive functions of government minimal, and, where these were necessary, to keep them on the state rather than put them on the national level. Their conceptions of the role of the national government were at first largely negative and then largely preventive. In the Jeffersonian and Jacksonian days it was to avoid excessive expenditure and excessive taxation, to refrain from giving privileged charters. Later, in the corporate era, it was to prevent abuses by the railroads and the monopolists, to check and to regulate unsound and immoral practices. It is of course true that some of the more "advanced" thinkers of the Populist and Progressive movements began to think tentatively of more positive functions for government, but it was just such proposals—the subtreasury scheme for agricultural credits and the various public-ownership proposals—that provoked the greatest opposition when attempts were made to apply them on a national scale.

The whole reformist tradition, then, displayed a mentality founded on the existence of an essentially healthy society; it was chiefly concerned not with managing an economy to meet the problems of collapse but simply with democratizing an economy in sound working order. Managing an economy in such a way as to restore prosperity is above all a problem of organization, while democratizing a well-organized economy had been, as we have seen, in some important respects an attempt to find ways of attacking or limiting organization. Hence the Progressive mind was hardly more prepared than the conservative mind for what came in 1929. Herbert Hoover, an old Bull Mooser, while more disposed to lead the country than any president had been in any previous depression, was unprepared for it, and was prevented from adjusting to it by a doctrinaire adherence to inherited principles. F. D. R.—a fairly typical product of Progressivism who had first won office in 1910—was also unprepared for it in his economic thinking, as anyone will see who examines his career in the 1920's; but he was sufficiently opportunistic and flexible to cope with it somewhat more successfully.

Hoover, an engineer born in Iowa, represented the moral traditions of native Protestant politics. An amateur in politics who had never run for office before he was elected President in 1928, he had no patience with the politician's willingness to accommodate, and he hung on, as inflexibly as the situation would permit, to the private and voluntary methods that had always worked well in his administrative career. F. D. R., a seasoned professional politician who had learned his trade straddling the terrible antagonisms of the 1920's, was throughly at home in the realities of machine politics and a master of the machine techniques of accommodation. Unlike Hoover, he had few hard and fast notions about economic principles, but he knew that it would be necessary to experiment and improvise. "It is common sense," he said in 1932, "to take a method and try it. If it fails, admit it frankly and try another. But above all, try something."

To describe the resulting flood of legislation as economic planning would be to confuse planning with interventionism. Planning was not quite the word for the New Deal: considered as an economic movement, it was a chaos of experimentation. Genuine planners like Rexford Guy Tugwell found themselves floundering amid the cross-currents of the New Deal, and ended in disillusionment. But if, from an economic standpoint, the New Deal was altogether lacking in that rationality or consistency which is implied in the concept of planning, from a political standpoint it represented a masterly shifting equipoise of interests. And little wonder that some of the old Republican insurgents shuddered at its methods. If the state was believed neutral in the days of T. R. because its leaders claimed to sanction favors for no one, the state under F. D. R. could be called neutral only in the sense that it offered favors to everyone.

Even before F. D. R. took office a silent revolution had taken place in public opinion, the essential character of which can be seen when we recall how little opposition there was in the country, at the beginning, to the assumption of the New Dealers that henceforth, for the purposes of recovery, the federal government was to be responsible for the condition of the labor market as a part of its concern with the industrial problem as a whole. Nothing revolutionary was intended—but simply as a matter of politics it was necessary for the federal government to assume primary responsibility for the relief of the unemployed. And, simply as a matter of politics, if the industrialists were to be given the power to write enforceable codes of fair practice, labor must at least be given some formal recognition of its right of collective bargaining. Certainly no one foresaw, in the first year or two of the New Deal, that the immense infusions of purchasing power into the economy through federal unemployment relief would be as lasting or as vital a part of the economy of the next several years as they proved in fact to be. Nor did anyone foresee how great and powerful a labor movement would be called into being by the spirit and the promise of the New Deal and by the partial recovery of its first few years. But by the end of 1937 it was clear that something had been added to the social base of reformism. The demands of a large and powerful labor movement, coupled with the interests of the unemployed, gave the later New Deal a social-democratic tinge that had never before been present in American reform movements. Hitherto concerned very largely with reforms of an essentially entrepreneurial sort and only marginally with social legislation, American political reformism was fated henceforth to take responsibility on a large scale for social security, unemployment insurance, wages and hours, and housing.

Still more imposing was the new fiscal role of the federal government. Again, none of this was premeditated. Large-scale spending and unbalanced budgets were, in the beginning, a response to imperative needs. While other schemes for recovery seemed to fall short of expectations, spending kept the economy going; and it was only when F. D. R. tried in 1937 to cut back expenditures that he learned that he had become the prisoner of his spending policies, and turned about and made a necessity into a virtue. His spending policy never represented, at any time before the outbreak of the war, an unambiguous or wholehearted commitment to Keynesian economics. Here only the war itself could consummate the fiscal revolution that the New Deal began. In 1940 Lord Keynes published in the United States an article in which he somewhat disconsolately reviewed the American experience with deficit spending during the previous decade. "It seems politically impossible," he concluded, "for a capitalistic democracy to organize expenditure on the scale necessary to make the grand experiment which would prove my case—except in war conditions." He then added that preparations for war and the production of armaments might teach Americans so much about the potentialities of their economy that it would be "the stimulus, which neither the victory nor the defeat of the New Deal could give you, to greater individual consumption and a higher standard of life." How remarkably prophetic this was we can now see. There had been under peacetime conditions an immense weeping and wailing over the budgets of F. D. R. —which at their peak ran to seven billion dollars. Now we contemplate budgets of over eighty billion dollars with somewhat less anguish, because we know that most of this expenditure will be used for defense and will not be put to uses that are politically more controversial. But, above all, we have learned things about the possibilities of our economy that were not dreamed of in 1933, much less in 1903. While men still grow angry over federal fiscal and tax policies, hardly anyone doubts that in the calculable future it will be the fiscal role of the government that more than anything else determines the course of the economy.

And what of the old Progressive issues? They were bypassed, side-stepped, outgrown—anything but solved. To realize how true this was, one need only look at the New Deal approach to those two *bêtes noires* of the Progressive mind, the machines and the trusts.

Where the Progressives spent much of their energy, as we have seen, trying to defeat the bosses and the machines and to make such changes in the political machinery of the country as would bring about direct popular democracy and "restore government to the people," the New Deal was almost completely free of such crusading. To the discomfort of the old-fashioned, principled liberals who were otherwise enthusiastic about his reforms, F. D. R. made no effort to put an end to bossism and corruption, but simply ignored the entire problem. In the interest of larger national goals and more urgent needs, he worked with the bosses wherever they would work with him—and did not scruple to include one of the worst machines of all, the authoritarian Hague machine in New Jersey. As for the restoration of democracy, he seemed well satisfied with his feeling that the broadest public needs were at least being served by the state and that there was such an excellent rapport between the people and their executive leadership.

The chief apparent exception to this opportune and managerial spirit in the field of political reform—namely, the attempt to enlarge the Supreme Court—proves on examination to be no exception at all. F. D. R.'s fight over the Supreme Court was begun, after all, not in the interest of some large "democratic" principle or out of a desire to reform the Constitutional machinery as such, but because the Court's decisions had made it seem impossible to achieve the managerial reorganization of society that was so urgently needed. His first concern was not that judicial review was "undemocratic" but that the federal government had been stripped, as he thought, of its power to deal effectively with economic problems. Nor was this fight waged in the true Progressive spirit. The Progressives, too, had had their difficulties with the judiciary, and had responded with the characteristically principled but practically difficult proposal for the recall of judicial decisions. In short, they raised for reconsideration, as one might expect of principled men, the entire question of judicial review. F. D. R. chose no such method. To reopen the entire question of the propriety of judicial review of the acts of Congress under a representative democracy would have been a high-minded approach to what he felt was a Constitutional impasse, but it would have ended perhaps even more disastrously than the tactic he employed.

F. D. R. avoided such an approach, which would have involved a cumbersome effort to amend the Constitution, and devised a "gimmick" to achieve his ends—the pretense that the age of the judges prevented them from remaining abreast of their calendar, and the demand for the right to supplement the judiciary, to the number of six, with an additional judge for each incumbent who reached the age of seventy without retiring.

Students of the Court fight are fond of remarking that Roosevelt won his case because the direction of the court's decisions began to change while the fight was in progress and because Justice Van Devanter's retirement enabled the President to appoint a liberal justice and decisively change the composition of the Court. It seems important, however, to point out that a very heavy price had to be paid for even this pragmatic attempt to alter a great and sacrosanct conservative institution. The Court fight alienated many principled liberals and enabled many of F. D. R's. conservative opponents to portray him to the public more convincingly as a man who aspired to personal dictatorship and aimed at the subversion of the Republic.

If we look at the second of the two great foes of Progressivism, big business and monopoly, we find that by the time of the New Deal public sentiment had changed materially. To be sure, the coming of the depression and the revelation of some of the less palatable business practices of the 1920's brought about a climate of opinion in which the leadership of business, and particularly of big business, was profoundly distrusted and bitterly resented. Its position certainly was, in these respects, considerably weaker than it had been twenty-five years before. Still, by 1933 the American public had lived with the great corporation for so long that it was felt to be domesticated, and there was far more concern with getting business life on such a footing as would enable it to provide jobs than there was with breaking up the larger units. The New Deal never developed a clear or consistent line on business consolidation, and New Dealers fought over the subject in terms that were at times reminiscent of the old battles between the trust-busters and the trust-regulators. What can be said, however, is that the subject of bigness and monopoly was subordinated in the New Deal era to that restless groping for a means to bring recovery that was so characteristic of Roosevelt's efforts. The New Deal began not with a flourish of trust-busting but rather, in the NRA, with an attempt to solve the problems of the business order through a gigantic system of governmentally underwritten codes that would ratify the trustification of society. One of the first political setbacks suffered by the New Deal arose from just this—for it had put the formation of its codes of fair practice so completely in the hands of the big-business interests that both small businessmen and organized labor were seriously resentful. Only five years from the date of its passage, after the NRA had failed to produce a sustained recovery and had been declared unconstitutional by the Supreme Court, did the administration turn off and take the opposite tack with its call for an inquiry into corporate consolidation and business power that led to the Temporary National Economic Committee's memorable investigation. Although at the time many observers thought that the old Progressive trust-busting charade was about to be resumed, the New Deal never became committed to a categorical "dissection" of the business order of the sort Wilson had talked of in 1912, nor to the "demonstration" prosecutions with which T. R. had both excited and reassured the country. The New Deal was not trying to re-establish the competitive order that Wilson had nostalgically invoked and that T. R. had sternly insisted was no longer possible. Its approach, as it turned out, was severely managerial, and distinctly subordinated to those economic considerations that would promote purchasing power and hence recovery. It was, in short, a concerted effort to discipline the pricing policies of businesses, not with the problem of size in mind, nor out of consideration for smaller competitors, but with the purpose of eliminating that private power to tax which is the prerogative of monopoly, and of leaving in the hands of consumers vital purchasing power.

History cannot quite repeat itself, if only because the participants in the second round of any experience are aware of the outcome of the first. The anti-trust philosophers of the closing years of the New Deal were quite aware that previous efforts to enforce the Sherman Act had been ceremonial demonstrations rather than serious assaults upon big business. Thurman Arnold, who was put in charge of the anti-trust program, was well known for his belief that earlier interpretations of the Sherman Act had actually concealed and encouraged business consolidation. In his account of the contemporary function of anti-trust prosecution Arnold put his emphasis upon benefits for the consumer and repudiated the earlier use of the Sherman Act: "Since the consumers' interest was not emphasized, such enforcement efforts as existed were directed at the punishment of offenses rather than the achievement of economic objectives. Indeed, in very few antitrust prosecutions was any practical economic objective defined or argued with respect to the distribution of any particular product. In this way the moral aspects of the offense, and that will-o'-the-wisp, corporate intent, became more important considerations than economic results. Antitrust enforcement, not being geared to the idea of consumers' interests, became a hunt for offenders instead of an effort to test the validity of organized power by its performance in aiding or preventing the flow of goods in commerce. The result was that although the economic ideal of a free competitive market as the cornerstone of our economy was kept alive, no adequate enforcement staff was ever provided to make the ideal a reality. Such, broadly speaking, was the state of the Sherman Act from 1890 down to the great depression."

But if such a position as Thurman Arnold's can be legitimately distinguished from the Progressive type of anti-trust, as I think it can, there are men today whose political thinking was forged in the service of the New Deal who go beyond him in repudiating anti-trust action as a

mere attack upon size, and who take, on the whole, an acquiescent attitude toward big business. A few years ago John Kenneth Galbraith made
quite a stir with his book *American Capitalism*, whose central thesis was
that the process of business consolidation creates within itself a "coun-
tervailing power"—that is, that it brings about the organization not
merely of strong sellers but of strong buyers as well, who distribute
through large sectors of the economy their ability to save through organization. In Galbraith's book, as in most recent literature in defense of
bigness, it is not the effort at disorganization but the effects of counter-
organization, in labor, agriculture, and government and within business
itself, that are counted upon to minimize the evils of consolidation. More
recently David Lilienthal, another graduate of the New Deal administrative agencies, has written a strong apologia for big business that
followed Galbraith in stressing the technologically progressive character
of large-scale industry in language that would have horrified Brandeis
and Wilson. It is not clear whether the attitudes of men like Galbraith
and Lilienthal represent dominant liberal sentiment today—though it
may be pertinent to say that their books brought no outpouring of protest from other liberal writers. The spectacle of liberals defending, with
whatever qualifications, bigness and concentration in industry suggests
that that anti-monopoly sentiment which was so long at the heart of
Progressive thinking is no longer its central theme. The generation for
which Wilson and Brandeis spoke looked to economic life as a field for
the expression of character; modern liberals seem to think of it quite
exclusively as a field in which certain results are to be expected. It is this
change in the moral stance that seems most worthy of remark. A generation ago, and more, the average American was taught to expect that a
career in business would and should be in some sense a testing and
proving ground for character and manhood, and it was in these terms
that the competitive order was often made most appealing. Contrariwise,
those who criticized the economic order very commonly formed their
appeals within the same mold of moral suasion: the economic order
failed to bring out or reward the desired qualities of character, to reward
virtue and penalize vice; it was a source of inequities and injustices.
During the last fifteen or twenty years, however, as Galbraith observes,
"the American radical has ceased to talk about inequality or exploitation
under capitalism or even its 'inherent contradictions.' He has stressed,
instead, the unreliability of its performance."

The New Opportunism. The New Deal, and the thinking it engendered, represented the triumph of economic emergency and human
needs over inherited notions and inhibitions. It was conceived and executed above all in the spirit of what Roosevelt called "bold, persistent
experimentation," and what those more critical of the whole enterprise
considered crass opportunism. In discussing Progressivism I emphasized
its traffic in moral absolutes, its exalted moral tone. While something

akin to this was by no means entirely absent from the New Deal, the later movement showed a strong and candid awareness that what was happening was not so much moral reformation as economic experimentation. Much of this experimentation seemed to the conservative opponents of the New Deal as not only dangerous but immoral.

The high moral indignation of the critics of the New Deal sheds light on another facet of the period—the relative reversal of the ideological roles of conservatives and reformers. Naturally in all ideologies, conservative or radical, there is a dual appeal to ultimate moral principles and to the practical necessities of institutional life. Classically, however, it has been the strength of conservatives that their appeal to institutional continuities, hard facts, and the limits of possibility is better founded; while it has usually been the strength of reformers that they arouse moral sentiments, denounce injustices, and rally the indignation of the community against intolerable abuses. Such had been the alignment of arguments during the Progressive era. During the New Deal, however, it was the reformers whose appeal to the urgent practical realities was most impressive—to the farmers without markets, to the unemployed without bread or hope, to those concerned over the condition of the banks, the investment market, and the like. It was the conservatives, on the other hand, who represented the greater moral indignation and rallied behind themselves the inspirational literature of American life; and this not merely because the conservatives were now the party of the opposition, but because things were being done of such drastic novelty that they seemed to breach all the inherited rules, not merely of practicality but of morality itself. Hence, if one wishes to look for utopianism in the 1930's for an exalted faith in the intangibles of morals and character, and for moral indignation of the kind that had once been chiefly the prerogative of the reformers, one will find it far more readily in the editorials of the great conservative newspapers than in the literature of the New Deal. If one seeks for the latter-day equivalent of the first George Kennan, warning the people of San Francisco that it would do them no good to have a prosperous town if in gaining it they lost their souls, one will find it most readily in the 1930's among those who opposed federal relief for the unemployed because it would destroy their characters or who were shocked by the devaluation of the dollar, not because they always had a clear conception of its consequences, but above all because it smacked to them of dirtiness and dishonesty. In the past it had been the conservatives who controlled the settlement of the country, set up its great industrial and communications plant, and founded the fabulous system of production and distribution upon which the country prided itself, while the reformers pointed to the human costs, the sacrifice of principles, and drew blueprints to show how the job could be better done. Now, however, it was the reformers who fed the jobless or found them jobs, saved the banks, humanized industry, built houses and schools and public buildings, rescued farmers from bankruptcy, and restored hope—while the conservatives, expropriated at once from their customary control of affairs and from their practical role, invoked sound principles, worried about the Constitution, boggled over details, pleaded for better morals, and warned against tyranny.

Lamentably, most of the conservative thinking of the New Deal era was hollow and cliché-ridden. What seems most striking about the New Deal itself, however, was that all its ferment of practical change produced a very slight literature of political criticism. While the changes of the Progressive era had produced many significant books of pamphleteering or thoughtful analyses of society—the writings of such men as Croly, Lippmann, Weyl, Brooks Adams, Brandeis, the muckrakers, Socialist critics like W. J. Ghent and William English Walling—the New Deal produced no comparable body of political writing that would survive the day's headlines. In part this was simply a matter of time: the Progressive era lasted over a dozen years, and most of the significant writing it engendered came during its later phases, particularly after 1910; whereas the dynamic phase of the New Deal was concentrated in the six hectic years from 1933 to 1938. Perhaps still more important is the fact that the New Deal brought with it such a rapid bureaucratic expansion and such a complex multitude of problems that it created an immense market for the skills of reform-minded Americans from law, journalism, politics, and the professoriat. The men who might otherwise have been busy analyzing the meaning of events were caught up in the huge expanding bureaucracy and put to work drafting laws that would pass the courts, lobbying with refractory Congressmen, or relocating sharecroppers.

To this generalization there is one noteworthy exception: in his two books, *The Symbols of Government* and *The Folklore of Capitalism*, Thurman Arnold wrote works of great brilliance and wit and considerable permanent significance—better books, I believe, than any of the political criticism of the Progressive era. But what do we find in these works, the most advanced of the New Deal camp? We find a sharp and sustained attack upon ideologies, rational principles, and moralism in politics. We find, in short, the theoretical equivalent of F. D. R.'s opportunistic virtuosity in practical politics—a theory that attacks theories. For Arnold's books, which were of course directed largely against the ritualistic thinking of the conservatives of the 1930's, might stand equally well as an attack upon that moralism which we found so insistent in the thinking of Progressivism.

Arnold's chief concern was with the disparities between the way society actually works and the mythology through which the sound lawyers, economists, and moralists attempt to understand it. His books are an explanation of the ritualistic and functionally irrational character of most of the superficially rational principles by which society lives. At the time his books were written, the necessity of coping with a breakdown in the actual workings of the economy had suddenly confronted men with the operational uselessness of a great many accepted words and ideas.

The language of politics, economics, and law had itself become so uncertain that there was a new vogue of books on semantics and of works
attempting to break "the tyranny of words," a literature of which Arnold's books were by far the most important. The greater part of Arnold's task was to examine, and to satirize, the orthodox conservative
thinking of the moment. This is not our main concern, but what is of
primary interest here is the extent to which Arnold's thinking departs
from, and indeed on occasion attacks, earlier Progressivism. The deviation of Arnold's system of values from the classic values of American
Progressivism was clear from his very terminology. I noted, in discussing
the Progressive climate of opinion, the existence of a prevailing vocabulary of civic morals that reflected the disinterested thinking and the
selfless action that was expected of the good citizen. The key words of
Progressivism were terms like *patriotism, citizen, democracy, law, character, conscience, soul, morals, service, duty, shame, disgrace, sin,* and
selfishness—terms redolent of the sturdy Protestant Anglo-Saxon moral
and intellectual roots of the Progressive uprising. A search for the key
words of Arnold's books yields: *needs, organization, humanitarian, results, technique, institution, realistic, discipline, morale, skill, expert,
habits, practical, leadership*—a vocabulary revealing a very different constellation of values arising from economic emergency and the imperatives
of a bureaucracy.

Although primarily concerned with the conservatives of the present,
Arnold paid his respects to the reformers of the past often enough to
render a New Dealer's portrait of earlier Progressivism. He saw the reformers of the past as having occupied themselves with verbal and moral
battles that left the great working organizations of society largely untouched. "Wherever the reformers are successful—whenever they see their
direct primaries, their antitrust laws, or whatever else they base their
hopes on, in actual operation—the great temporal institutions adapt
themselves, leaving the older reformers disillusioned, like Lincoln
Steffens, and a newer set carrying on the banner." Respectable people
with humanitarian values, Arnold thought, had characteristically made
the mistake of ignoring the fact that "it is not logic but organizations
which rule an organized society"; therefore they selected logical principles, rather than organizations, as the objects of their loyalties. Most
liberal reform movements attempt to make institutions practice what
they preach, in situations where, if this injunction were followed, the
functions of the institutions could not be performed. Where the Progressives had been troubled about the development of institutions and organizations, Arnold's argument often appeared to be an apotheosis of
them.

At one point or another, Arnold had critical observations to make on
most of the staple ideas of Progressive thinking. *The Folklore of Capitalism* opened with a satire on "the thinking man," to whom most of the
discourse of rational politics was directed; and the thinking man was

hardly more than a caricatured version of the good citizen who was taken as the central figure in most Progressive thinking. While Progressive publicists had devoted much of their time to preachments against what they called "lawlessness," one of the central themes of Arnold's books was an analysis of law and legal thinking showing that law and respectability were so defined that a good many of the real and necessary functions of society had to go on outside the legal framework. Similarly anti-Progressive was his attack on the anti-trust laws—a source of some amusement when he was later put in charge of the enforcement of these laws. But Arnold did not deny that the laws, as they had been interpreted by reformers, had had some use. Their chief use, as he saw it, had been that they permitted the organization of industry to go on while offering comfort to those who were made unhappy by the process. They had, then, a practical significance, but a far different one from that which the reformers had tried to give them. The reformers, however, had had no real strategy with which to oppose the great trusts: "The reason why these attacks [against industrial organizations] always ended with a ceremony of atonement, but few practical results, lay in the fact that there were no new organizations growing up to take over the functions of those under attack. The opposition was never able to build up its own commissary and its service of supply. It was well supplied with orators and economists, but it lacked practical organizers. A great cooperative movement in America might have changed the power of the industrial empire. Preaching against it, however, simply resulted in counterpreaching. And the reason for this was that the reformers themselves were caught in the same creeds which supported the institutions they were trying to reform. Obsessed with a moral attitude toward society, they thought in Utopias. They were interested in systems of government. Philosophy was for them more important than opportunism and so they achieved in the end philosophy rather than opportunity."

Arnold professed more admiration for the tycoons who had organized American industry and against whom the Progressives had grown indignant than he did for the reformers themselves. He spoke with much indulgence of Rockefeller, Carnegie, and Ford, and compared John L. Lewis with such men as examples of skillful organizers who had had to sidestep recognized scruples. "Actual observation of human society . . . indicates that great constructive achievements in human organization have been accomplished by unscrupulous men who violated most of the principles which we cherish." The leaders of industrial organization ignored legal, humanitarian, and economic principles. "They built on their mistakes, their action was opportunistic, they experimented with human material and with little regard for social justice. Yet they raised the level of productive capacity beyond the dreams of their fathers."

Not surprisingly Arnold also had a good word for the politicians, who, for all their lack of social values and for all the imperfections in their aims and vision, are "the only persons who understand the techniques of government." One would prefer a government in the hands of disinterested men, to be sure, but such men are so devoted to and satisfied with the development of good principles that they fail to develop skills, and hence fail to constitute "a competent governing class." Hence society is too often left with a choice between demagogues and psychopaths on one side, or, on the other, "kindly but uneducated Irishmen whose human sympathies give them an instinctive understanding of what people like." Several pages of *The Folklore of Capitalism* were given to a defense of the political machines for the common sense with which they attack the task of government and for the humanitarian spirit in which their work is conducted.

Taken by itself, Arnold's work, with its skepticism about the right-thinking citizen, its rejection of fixed moral principles and disinterested rationality in politics, its pragmatic temper, its worship of accomplishment, its apotheosis of organization and institutional discipline, and its defense of the political machines, may exaggerate the extent of the difference between the New Deal and pre-war Progressivism, but it does point sharply to the character of that difference.

To emphasize, as I have done, the pragmatic and "hard" side of the New Deal is not to forget that it had its "soft" side. Not all its spokesmen shared Arnold's need to pose as hard-boiled. No movement of such scope and power could exist without having its ideals and its ideologies, even its sentimentalities. The New Deal had its literature of inspiration and indignation, its idealistic fervor, its heroes and villains. The difference I hope to establish is that its indignation was directed far more against callousness and waste, far less against corruption or monopoly, than the indignation of the Progressives, and that its inspiration was much more informed by engineering, administration, and economics, considerably less by morals and uplift. For the New Deal not only brought with it a heartening rediscovery of the humane instincts of the country; it also revived the old American interest in practical achievement, in doing things with the physical world, in the ideal that had inspired the great tycoons and industry-builders of the Gilded Age but that afterwards had commonly been dismissed by sensitive men as the sphere only of philistines and money-grubbers.

At the core of the New Deal, then, was not a philosophy (F. D. R. could identify himself philosophically only as a Christian and a democrat), but an attitude, suitable for practical politicians, administrators, and technicians, but uncongenial to the moralism that the Progressives had for the most part shared with their opponents. At some distance from the center of the New Deal, but vital to its public support, were other types of feeling. In some quarters there was a revival of populistic sentiment and the old popular demonology, which F. D. R. and men like Harold Ickes occasionally played up to, chiefly in campaign years, and which Harry Truman later reflected in his baiting of Wall Street. Along with this came another New Deal phenomenon, a kind of pervasive tenderness for the underdog, for the Okies, the sharecroppers, the characters in John Steinbeck's novels, the subjects who posed for the FSA photographers, for what were called, until a revulsion set in, "the little people." With this there came, too, a kind of folkish nationalism, quickened no doubt by federal patronage of letters and the arts, but inspired at bottom by a real rediscovery of hope in America and its people and institutions. For after the concentration camps, the Nuremberg Laws, Guernica, and (though not everyone saw this so readily) the Moscow trials, everything in America seemed fresh and hopeful, Main Street seemed innocent beyond all expectation, and in time Babbitt became almost lovable. Where Progressivism had capitalized on a growing sense of the ugliness under the successful surface of American life, the New Deal flourished on a sense of the human warmth and the technological potentialities that could be found under the surface of its inequities and its post-depression poverty. On the far fringe there was also a small number of real ideologues, aroused not only by the battle over domestic reform but by the rise of world fascism. Although many of them were fellow travelers and Communists, we stand in serious danger of misunderstanding the character of the New Deal if we overemphasize the influence of this fringe either upon the New Deal core or upon the American people at large. It has now become both fashionable and, for some, convenient to exaggerate the impact of the extreme left upon the thinking of the country in the 1930's. No doubt it will always be possible to do so, for Marxism had a strong if ephemeral impact upon many intellectuals; but the amateur Marxism of the period had only a marginal effect upon the thought and action of either the administrative core of the New Deal or the great masses of Americans. For the people at large—that is, for those who needed it most—the strength of the New Deal was based above all upon its ability to get results.

The New Deal developed from the beginning under the shadow of totalitarianism, left and right. F. D. R. and Hitler took office within a few months of each other, and from that time down to the last phases of the New Deal reforms, not a year went by without some premonition of the ultimate horror to come. In the earliest days of the Roosevelt administration a great many of its critics, influenced by such models of catastrophe as they could find abroad, saw in it the beginnings of fascism or Communism. Critics from the left thought, for instance, that the NRA was a clear imitation of Mussolini's corporate state. And—though this is now all but forgotten—critics from the right at first thought they saw fascist tendencies in the "violations" of fundamental liberties with which they regularly charged the architects of the New Deal. Only later did they find it more congenial to accuse the New Deal of fostering Communism.

To a sober mind all of this rings false today, for it is easier to see now that Roosevelt and his supporters were attempting to deal with the problems of the American economy within the distinctive framework of American political methods—that in a certain sense they were trying to continue to repudiate the European world of ideology. Between the London Economic Conference and Roosevelt's "quarantine" speech of 1937, the New Deal, for all its tariff-reduction agreements, was essentially isolationist. What it could not escape was the reality of what even some of the Republican leaders later began to characterize as "one world." After 1939 that reality was the dominant force in American life. The beginning of the war meant that Americans, with terrible finality, had been at last torn from that habitual security in which their domestic life was merely interrupted by crises in the foreign world, and thrust into a situation in which their domestic life is largely determined by the demands of foreign policy and national defense. With this change came the final involvement of the nation in all the realities it had sought to avoid, for now it was not only mechanized and urbanized and bureaucratized but internationalized as well. Much of America still longs for—indeed, expects again to see—a return of the older individualism and the older isolation, and grows frantic when it finds that even our conservative leaders are unable to restore such conditions. In truth we may well sympathize with the Populists and with those who have shared their need to believe that somewhere in the American past there was a golden age whose life was far better than our own. But actually to live in that world, actually to enjoy its cherished promise and its imagined innocence, is no longer within our power.

Eric Goldman

Rendezvous

with Destiny

On the other hand, many people saw the New Deal as the direct descendant of earlier reform movements, particularly the New Nationalism and the New Freedom. They considered Theodore Roosevelt and Woodrow Wilson precursors of Franklin D. Roosevelt. Henry Steele Commager has pointed out the foreshadowing of New Deal legislation in Granger, Populist, and Progressive laws, and Eric Goldman, a professor of history at Princeton University, has noted, ". . . in a very real sense the New Dealers were right when they insisted that what they were doing hitched on to long-running American ideas." In the selection that follows, Goldman explains why he thinks the New Deal was the result of "evolution" rather than "revolution." [Copyright 1952 by Alfred A. Knopf, Inc. Reprinted from Rendezvous with Destiny *by Eric Goldman, by permission of the publisher.]*

The day after the Inaugural the new President proclaimed a four-day bank holiday, summoned Congress into special session, and started day-

and-night White House conferences on emergency banking legislation. The bill was ready seventy-two hours later. The House of Representatives debated it thirty-eight minutes. The Senate debated it three hours. That night the President signed it. The Hundred Days were under way, the most controlled, directed, overpowered period in all the history of Congress.

Many of the bills whisked through Congress bespoke the central idea common to both principal reform traditions, the New Freedom and the New Nationalism—the belief that the best solution for economic and social ills was action by the federal government under strong executive leadership. The powerful leadership of Franklin Roosevelt set up federal protections for bank depositors and for all investors in stocks. Federal credit eased the burden of debt on farmers and householders, and federal guidance reorganized the railroads. A variety of federal devices made phony bankruptcy proceedings more difficult, imposed excess-profit and dividend taxes, created the Civilian Conservation Corps for the youthful unemployed, and raised prices by taking the country off the haloed gold standard. "Liberal" measures, the country called them, and quite clearly liberalism had come to mean not the Mencken-type emphasis of the Twenties but a full-blown revival of economic and social reformism. Talk of liberty in reform circles now was likely to produce a yawn, if not a scowl; opportunity, at least opportunity for the millions to have jobs, was the point.

The New Deal handling of the desperate unemployment problem produced the most sweeping reaffirmation of general progressive doctrine. For three years Herbert Hoover and the conservative press had been arguing that the use of large-scale federal funds for unemployment relief would bring about a dangerous political centralization, tear down the character of the recipients, and violate the economic law that the national debt cannot go beyond a fixed point without bankrupting the government. To these arguments, liberals of a dozen schools of thought made substantially one set of replies. Unemployment on its 1933 scale was too big a problem for the states and cities; environment shaped human character, and federal relief funds, by helping to remove squalor, would build character rather than injure it. The conservative appeal to economic laws was met by a barrage of Reform Darwinism, even by a fresh Reform Darwinian formulation of economics. Well before the depression began, a number of economists had been developing theories which brushed aside the alleged economic law standing in the way of large-scale public spending. During the Thirties the long-time leader in world reform thinking, John Maynard Keynes, was rapidly developing these ideas into a persuasive system. The supposed economic law, Keynes argued in the authentic manner of Reform Darwinism, was simply the rationalization of upper-income groups who did not want to pay heavy taxes. There was nothing dangerous about running up a government debt. On the contrary, when private expenditures of money fell off, a sensible government would start "compensatory spending."

Franklin Roosevelt, together with a large segment of the liberal movement, distrusted the Keynes-type argument in the early New Deal days. At heart they hankered for a balanced budget. Yet the idea of large-scale federal spending on relief, with its implied contempt for rigid economics, its assignment of a key role to the national government, and its promise of quick alleviation of human distress, was a natural for the President and his following. Amid the roar of the Hundred Days, Congress passed a half-billion-dollar relief bill, and the President gave the administration of the money to a *de facto* Keynesian whose economics consisted largely of an urge "to feed the hungry and Goddamn fast."

Harry Hopkins had always been in a hurry. He was already in a hurry when his father, a convivial jack-of-all-trades, finally settled the family in Grinnell, Iowa, and the homely youngster hustled his way to the title of "Big Man of the Class" at Grinnell College. On graduation, Hopkins almost took a job on a Montana newspaper; he almost did a dozen things; and somewhere in the middle of it all, a professor urged him to sign up as counselor in a boys' camp in New Jersey. A charitable boys' camp sat well with the son of a pious Methodist mother, who had bundled her five children off to church every Sunday and made them repeat the minister's points afterward. A boys' camp sponsored by influential people and near New York City had special attractions for the ne'er-do-well's son who was determined to find a place for himself in the exciting world of power. The professor did not have to urge long.

Nor did Hopkins remain long in the camp organization. Quickly he was off to a series of successes in the social-work profession. By 1933 Hopkins had attained the number-one social worker's position in the nation, director of emergency relief in New York State, and a striking if somewhat mixed reputation. Associates knew him as a man who thought more swiftly than anyone working for, with, or against him, a first-class administrator with a habit of cutting through red tape like so much confetti, a wraith of quick cigarettes, frayed suits, curt sarcasms, and a highly developed ability to confuse advancing mankind with advancing Harry Hopkins.

Transferred to Washington to direct the New Deal relief program, Hopkins sat down at his desk before the workmen had moved it out of the hallway and in two hours spent more than five million dollars. During the ensuing months Hopkins's shabby little office in the old Walker-Johnson Building, with the faded paint and the water pipes up and down the walls, became the most swift-acting agency in all frenzied Washington. When somebody brought in a plan that "will work out in the long run," Hopkins snapped: "People don't eat in the long run—they eat every day." When inspectors from the Budget Bureau came around to see the "organizational chart," they heard that Hopkins had ordered: "I don't want anybody around here to waste any time drawing boxes. You'll always find that the person who drew the chart has his own name in the middle box." Out of the fury came striking new practices of unemployment relief, a devil for conservatives to flay, and an application of liberal doctrine so personal that its effects sank deep into the national mind.

The level-headed businessman, Frank Walker, discovered just how personal the application was when Roosevelt sent him on a tour to inspect the workings of the relief program. In his home state of Montana, Walker found former businessmen laying sewer pipes in their old business clothes because they had no money to buy overalls. And one of the ditch-diggers spoke for millions when he told Walker: "I hate to think what would have happened if this work hadn't come. . . . I'd sold or hocked everything I could. And my kids were hungry. I stood in front of the window of the bake-shop down the street and wondered just how long it would be before I got desperate enough to pick up a rock and heave it through that window and grab some bread to take home."

In the White House the lights burned late six or seven nights a week. Wearing out assistants by his energies, amazing intimates by his ability to toss off worries, Roosevelt kept prodding, brain-picking, quipping, politicking the Hundred Days ahead. Federal relief would alleviate distress; it could hardly cure a depression.

There was no lack of advice on the cure. The president of the Chamber of Commerce, a charwoman from Butte, the head of the AFL, Harvard classmates of Roosevelt, the third vice-president of Kiwanis, and some five thousand other people all brought or sent the President sure-fire remedies. Immediately around the President was the group of brilliant and contentious minds that the country had been calling the Brain Trust since the campaign of 1932. Yet amid all the babble, the proposals from informed and responsible people revealed a striking fact. Many business leaders and labor officials, Farm Bureau men and liberals, Brain-Trusters and Kiwanians, agreed on certain fundamentals of a recovery program.

Some concurrence from supposed ideological opposites was not surprising. Although the New Nationalism and the Associational Activities outlook had important differences, they agreed on encouraging the formation of large economic units and on an important role for government in economic life. The depression of 1929, by presenting free enterprise in its most chaotic and inhumane form, brought an onrush of converts to the general idea of national planning of national economic units. New Freedomite reformers, who had so long battled any program that accepted the concentration of industry, now forgot their old battle in their concern with getting government controls over the existing situation. Businessmen who had railed at any system restricting their independence besought the government to tell them how to avoid bankruptcy. As the banks closed and the abyss seemed near in March 1933, free enterprise virtually abdicated. "There was hardly an industrial, economic, financial, commercial, reform, or agricultural leader who did not advance some idea of governmental intervention," the Washington insider Hugh Johnson has recalled. "A snowfall of paper plans drifted about the Capitol, and there was not one of them that would not, in some measure, have modified the Anti-Trust Acts."

The merger of Associational Activities ideas and New Nationalist thinking in a demand for national planning was plain in the Brain Trust. Raymond Moley, chief of the group, perfectly represented the coalescence in his own amiable, hardheaded self. As a boy in Berea, Ohio, Moley wept at the 1896 defeat of Williams Jennings Bryan, and as a young man he made a hero of Tom Johnson. Then, while the trust-busters kept on thundering and the trusts kept on growing, Moley began to wonder whether moralistic anti-big-business agitation was not trying to change the tides of economic development. As a professor of political science, first in the Midwest and then at Columbia, Moley sought solutions of the nation's ills that assumed the necessity of a battle against "ignorance" rather then against "sin." The nature of the proper enlightenment was not always clear. But the Moley who became important in the Roosevelt circle was a man who talked easily with people of an Associational Activities persuasion and who cited approvingly the Cro-lyite book that Theodore Roosevelt had quoted to the Bull Moose convention, Van Hise's *Concentration and Control*. The essential, Moley was sure, was to end "the thoughtlessness and aimlessness" of free competition.

The merger of the New Nationalism and Associational Activities was no less striking in the relations of two important figures who gathered around Moley in the Brain Trust. No human beings could have seemed more different than Hugh Johnson and Rexford Tugwell. Johnson learned to spell to the whinnying of cavalry horses and the bawling of top sergeants at Fort Scott, Kansas, yelling to anyone who would listen to him: "Everybody in the world is a rink-stink but Hughie Johnson and he's all right!" Tugwell, the son of a prosperous farmer and cannery-owner in Sinclairville, New York, was raised to a genteel tradition of concern with community problems, almost to a Rooseveltian *noblesse oblige*. West Point remembered Johnson as the most talented hazer and the possessor of the biggest nose in the history of the school. The University of Pennsylvania recalled Tugwell as a handsome, smartly dressed ideologue, a gourmet with a special pride in his elaborate salads, who was given to practicing his sharp wit on bourgeois America and was more than likely to steer his date to a reform soirée. While Johnson was doing a hellroaring border patrol along the Rio Grande, Tugwell was showing intimates a poem that included the lines:

> *I am sick of a Nation's stenches*
> *I am sick of propertied Czars. . . .*
> *I shall roll up my sleeves—make America over!*

The mature careers of the two men showed no more similarities. Johnson swashbuckled his way to a brigadier general's star, interrupting his military life only for tossing off children's books that were chock-full of carnage and last-minute touchdowns. Somewhere along the line, the Army discovered that its leathery-faced cavalryman, a perfect Captain Flagg in his tough talk and his sentimentality, also had a mind, a quick, perceptive instrument that expressed itself in curiously effective off-beat phrases. The Army sent Johnson to law school, then made him its principal representative on the War Industries Board of World War I. After the Armistice, Johnson resigned from the Army and entered business, first as an officer of the Moline Plow Company, later as one of the men who helped Bernard Baruch manage his web of interests. Still clattering across any room in a roar of Army attitudes, deeply involved with large-scale business, Johnson in 1933 seemed a caricature of the traditional reform type. Tugwell was close to being a typecase of the liberal professor. Settled at Columbia, he was entrancing classes by his iconoclasm and making a national reputation as a heretical agricultural economist. It was hardly surprising that at early Brain Trust sessions the relations between Tugwell and Johnson were a study in hostility, Tugwell holding Johnson off with witticisms, Johnson snapping and snarling at his debonair torturer.

Yet with the passage of a few months, Tugwell and Johnson were soon bending happily over the same charts and memoranda. Johnson had emerged from his service with the War Industries Board and his work with Baruch an ardent advocate of Associational Activities, though he added to Hoover's reliance on co-operation between government and economic units the belief that some degree of governmental compulsion should be used. Tugwell had emerged from his books and his indignation a highly involved economic thinker but fundamentally a New Nationalist. The line between Johnson's planning by partial co-operation and Tugwell's planning by over-all compulsion was a wavering one, much too wavering not to be pushed aside by the impact of depression. The common denominator of their thinking in 1933, and of his own, was described by Moley when he wrote of the Brain Trust's "rejection of the traditional Wilson-Brandeis philosophy. . . . We believed that any attempt to atomize big business must destroy America's greatest contribution to a higher standard of living for the body of its citizenry—the development of mass production. . . . We recognized that competition, as such, was not inherently virtuous; that competition . . . created as many abuses as it prevented." So the Brain-Trusters, Moley summarized, turned "from the nostalgic philosophy of the 'trust busters,'" turned to national economic planning.

This was the kind of thinking swirling around the President during the Hundred Days, and it did not disturb him. In the period immediately preceding his election Roosevelt had begun to submerge the New Freedom element in his own thinking; he too could find little in trust-busting liberalism that seemed to apply to the emergency at hand. The real question for him, the real quarrel among his advisers, was not national planning versus free competition. The issue was: should the planning hew closer to the Associational Activities pattern, with its emphasis on noncompulsory relations between the government and economic life, or should it follow more the New Nationalist pattern of powerful federal controls? . . .

In the White House, testiness had long since disappeared. Only a short while after the invalidation of the NRA, Roosevelt was musing to Secretary of Labor Frances Perkins: "You know the whole thing is a mess . . . [and] we have got the best out of it anyhow. Industry got a shot in the arm. Everything has started up. . . . I think perhaps NRA has done all it can do. . . . I don't want to impose a system on this country that will set aside the anti-trust laws on any permanent basis." The President was back to his old self, impatient at the thought of permanence for the New Nationalism or any other ism, happily playing by ear.

Roosevelt could hardly improvise on the keyboard of American reform thought without hitting one chord constantly. Use the power of the federal government to smash concentrated wealth and to restore free enterprise; use it simultaneously to lift the standard of living of the country's less favored groups; and, by both these moves, make opportunity more abundant—in short, the reform program conceived in the depression of 1873, erected into a powerful political force by decades of agitation, given effectiveness and respectability by the early Theodore Roosevelt and by Woodrow Wilson, kept alive even during the complacent Twenties. When Uncle Ted's New Nationalism failed, there was always Jeffersonian New Freedom of the Chief.

Even in the middle of Roosevelt's New Nationalist period, two quite different facts had been reopening his mind to the New Freedom. The Roosevelt of the early Thirties had considerable sympathy for big business, and thought of government controls less as a crackdown than as a partnership between government and business. But during the NRA period the President discovered that corporation executives could prove highly unsatisfactory partners. Many openly flouted or skirted around all provisions of the NRA which were not entirely favorable to them, assailed most of the other New Deal measures, and spent millions of dollars trying to convince the country that Roosevelt was an egomaniacal Communist. By the time the President had to consider substitutes for the NRA, his irritation with big-business men had reached the point where he was remarking to intimates: "I get more and more convinced that most of them can't see farther than the next dividend."

Simultaneously, the President's mind was being moved in an anti-bigbusiness direction by a push from the left. The shrewd, unscrupulous Senator Huey Long, clawing his way toward the Presidency, was not asking his audiences to wait for the workings of elaborate reforms, or to understand that there might be some point in co-operating with trust magnates. He was flailing his arms, pointing to his pockmarked face as evidence of the way the rich ground the poor, and announcing that after the election of 1936 "your Kingfish, Huey, asittin' in the White House, will know how to handle them moguls." By late 1935 the Kingfish had demagogued himself to a political strength which, if it could not move him into the White House, might possibly move Roosevelt out. A secret poll taken by the Democratic National Committee indicated that Long at the head of a third-party ticket would poll three to four million votes. This strength was not confined to the area around Louisiana but reached into pivotal Northern states—including a potential one hundred thousand votes in New York State, which could swing that big group of electors to the Republicans. Before the election an assassin's bullet ended the Long threat. But Roosevelt had learned to worry about what could happen to a reform President who did not reckon sufficiently with the anti-big-business feeling rooted in decades of American agitation. From the demagogic left and from the uncooperative right, the Jeffersonian reformer in Roosevelt was being pushed to the fore.

The New Deal never did pass over to a strict New Freedom pattern. The Social Security Act, one of the most important bills passed after the invalidation of NRA, was no more Jeffersonian than it was New Nationalist; if it belonged to either pattern, it probably fitted better the Crolyan conception of the protective state. Nor did any one date or action mark the transition from the New Nationalism to the New Freedom. The shift came, in a blurred gradualism, after the invalidation of the NRA and the Triple A in 1935.

The change was marked by a slow turnover in the President's Brain-Trusters. By 1938 Washington was saying: "Moley is in opposition; Tugwell is in the city-planning business; and Hugh Johnson is in a rage," and the place of the early Brain-Trusters was being filled by a much larger group who shared an enthusiasm for New Freedom liberalism. Some of these men had been in the Administration almost from its start —most importantly, Harold Ickes and Harry Hopkins—and were now moving into the inner circle. Others were new figures, working together in shifting combinations, rising and falling in importance, men like Robert H. Jackson, Leon Henderson, Isador Lubin, and a half-dozen or more brilliant young graduates of Harvard Law School who had been placed in New Deal posts through the influence of the day's leading Jeffersonian legalist, Felix Frankfurter.

Early in the Hundred Days, one of these young lawyers showed up at a White House reception, maneuvered a friend into asking him to perform, and enchanted the President for two hours by singing Irish ballads, sea chanteys, and mountain laments. "You certainly stole the show, Tommy," the friend congratulated him. "I always steal the show," said Tommy Corcoran, and he always did. Springing somehow from a humdrum Rhode Island merchant family, Corcoran left Brown University loaded with prizes and then proceeded to equal Brandeis's record at Harvard Law School, a record that had seemed about as vulnerable as Babe Ruth's sixty home runs. The Hundred Days were not over before Corcoran was the unquestioned leader of Frankfurter's protégés, ranging airily through the government bureaus, making droves of friends and bringing the friends together for a session of songs and denunciations of big business, calling them all "my kids" from the senescence of his thirty-three years.

By 1934 Corcoran began admitting that one of his kids was his full equal, and at first friends were amazed at the choice. The anointed of the handsome, ebullient Tommy was a pale, shy ascetic, completely oblivious of pleasure or even comfort, who was shepherded around by Corcoran like a child at his first visit to an Automat. But Ben Cohen, Corcoran kept telling everyone, was something special, and everyone soon agreed. Cohen's legal powers aroused an admiration akin to worshipfulness, and his selfless absorption in public service won for the Corcoran-Cohen team a respect that Corcoran's pyrotechnics could never have achieved alone.

The team enjoyed a moment of importance in early New Deal days when, through Frankfurter's recommendation, Corcoran and Cohen were called on to draft the Securities and Exchange Act and the Securities Tax Bill. The President was impressed with their skill but these were not the days for militant Wilsonians. Corcoran and Cohen gained their real admission to the inner circle in 1935, when Roosevelt made one of the first important moves of his New Freedom period, the attack on holding companies in the power utilities field. The President asked the long-time trust-buster, Secretary of the Interior Harold Ickes, to supervise the working out of a bill, and, through Ickes's office, Corcoran and Cohen were assigned the detailed work.

The pair went at the task in a manner that was soon to be famous—all-night furies of work, with endless cups of sticky-sweet black coffee—and the bill that went to Congress would have delighted the heart of any trust-hating Populist. All holding companies in the power field, the "death sentence" clause provided, had to prove their social usefulness within five years or dissolve. When the provision provoked a savage battle in Congress, Corcoran bobbed up in the middle of the fight, artfully explaining and defending, dangling patronage before the eyes of reluctant Congressmen, rushing back and forth to the White House for reports and instructions. The holding companies were partially reprieved before Congress passed the bill, but the Corcoran-Cohen team was made. From then on, few important White House conferences did not include one or both of the men, at least four key laws were products of their legal wizardry, and "Tommy the Cork," as the President was soon affectionately calling the front man of the team, emerged as one of the two or three most inside New Deal insiders.

Shortly after the Holding Company Act went to Congress, Roosevelt sent to Congress a tax bill that was truculently anti-corporation. The President's "State of the Union" address of January 1936 bristled with phrases about the men of "entrenched greed" who sought "the restoration of their selfish power." All suggestions to revive the New Nationalist aspects of the NRA and the Triple A were brushed aside. Instead, the Administration pressed ahead with key legislation that bore the unmistakable New Freedom stamp. It went along with the Wagner-Connery Labor Act, probably the most bluntly anti-corporation legislation the United States has ever accepted, and pressed the Fair Labor Standards Act, with its ironclad provisions of minimum wages and maximum hours. A modified Triple A and other agricultural legislation, dropping much of the national-planning aspect of the original Triple A, aimed directly to improve the economic position of farmers and took especial care to promote the interests of the lowest-income group.

Amid this churn of legislation the most symbolic of all New Freedom moves was made. In October 1937 a recession declared itself to the roar of crashing stocks, and the Corcoran group, attributing the recession to greedy price-fixing by monopolistic combines, urged on the President a series of bold steps, among them a general trust-busting campaign. Roosevelt was a willing listener, but the New Nationalist in him had not entirely disappeared. For the moment, the President decided, he would ask for a new housing act, hoping that this would stimulate employment. Beyond that, he would sit tight.

But Tommy Corcoran had no intention of sitting tight. The Administration was now being assailed on all sides, by conservatives for having caused the recession and by liberals for not ending it. To Corcoran it seemed as if the whole New Deal was on the run and something had to be done quickly. In a council of war instigated by Corcoran, a group of the new Brain-Trusters decided to gamble. They would go ahead on their own trust-busting campaign, hoping to stir the President into joining them but leaving him free to repudiate them at any time.

Assistant Attorney General Robert Jackson opened the campaign. In a radio speech written by Corcoran and Cohen, Jackson charged: "By profiteering, the monopolists and those so near monopoly as to control their prices have simply priced themselves out of the market, and priced themselves into the slump." In the excitement that followed, Corcoran asked Harold Ickes to speak and the Secretary responded with two blistering assaults on big capital. Washington was in a tumult. Conservative Senators demanded that Roosevelt immediately repudiate Jackson and Ickes. Ickes told his friends he slept with his hat hanging ready on the bedpost.

But the business indices were fighting on the side of the New Freedom trust-busters. As the recession worsened in the spring of 1938, Uncle Ted's New Nationalist nephew was overwhelmed by the Chief's disciple; Roosevelt, too, became convinced that the whole New Deal was threatened by selfish and shortsighted big capital. In March he reinvigorated the antitrust division of the Justice Department, naming as its chief the able, combative Thurman Arnold. The next month the President sent to Congress a srong message urging "a thorough study of the concentration of economic power in American industry and the effect of that concentration upon the decline of competition."

The New Nationalism and then the New Freedom—in a very real sense the New Dealers were right when they insisted that what they were doing hitched on to longrunning American ideas. Yet there was something more to New Deal liberalism in both its New Nationalist and New Freedom phases, and the something more, as always, was connected with the climate of national opinion.

The New Deal, though it had given the country a way of coping with fear, had not entirely conquered it, and the common attitude was to go along with the New Deal enthusiastically but warily. If it could produce, fine; but there was always the reservation, accentuated by the recession of 1937, that the New Deal might not solve the problem. "Here we come, WPA!" the college boys wisecracked, and millions beyond college age smiled understandingly.

The depression not only created a continuing uneasiness that another crash was round the corner; it brought into frightening focus a number of long-time trends that also spelled insecurity. Every year of increased urbanization and mechanization left thousands of individuals feeling more like an easily replaceable cog in the wheel, more alone in the impersonal crowd. By the late Thirties students of American society were also writing of "the specter of insecurity" raised by the steadily mounting percentage of the population who depended on someone else for a job, the growing proportion of women supporting themselves or contributing a vital portion to the family income, the ineluctable decline in independent farming. At the same time, the average age of the population was rapidly changing, with the age curve moving ever farther beyond the confidence of youth. It was the 1930's that, poignantly, kept Walter Pitkin's *Life Begins at Forty* at or near the top of the best-seller list for two solid years.

The general sense of insecurity was accompanied by a special restiveness among America's minority groups. They were not only, in fact, the least secure—the "last hired, the first fired," as the Negroes put it. By the 1930's the Negroes were more than half a century from slavery, and thousands of the newer immigrant families were raising a second or third generation on American soil. Often these later products of minority origins had the education and the manner to compete successfully for higher prestige positions and to move in higher-status circles, and the general liberal atmosphere of the Thirties encouraged their aspirations. Just because of this encouragement and the increased adaptation to the ways of the dominant groups, the enormous obstacles still standing in the way were the more frustrating.

Despite these developments, there is little evidence that any consider-able part of the population gave up the faith in America as the land of opportunity. Too many generations had rooted their whole way of life in the belief; too many facts still proclaimed that the United States, more than any other country, did actually throw open the road for ambition. What happened was that millions of Americans were supplementing the credo of opportunity with a demand for laws that would guarantee them greater economic security and more equality in the pursuit of eco-nomic and social status. In case—just in case—economic opportunity did not knock, they wanted to be sure that the mailman would be around with a social-security check. In case—just in case—the social ladder proved too steep, they wanted laws which would guarantee that they would not be left on too humiliating a rung.

These trends showed themselves plainly in liberal thinking. Previous generations of reformers had been little concerned with security or equal-ity brought about by law. The emphasis had been simply on creating a situation in which men could compete on reasonably even terms. Now, during both the New Nationalist and the New Freedom phases of the New Deal and increasing in intensity, a drive was being made to bring about greater security by legislation. The President himself laid down the line in 1934 when he placed "the security of the men, women and children of the Nation" first among the objectives of his Administration. The Social Security Act of 1935, of course, was the keystone of the Ad-ministration's security legislation, but a similar purpose marked a variety of New Deal legislation, ranging from the creation of the Home Owner's Loan Corporation in 1933 to the establishment of the Farm Security Administration in 1937. How far New Deal liberalism was ready to go in guaranteeing security was far from clear. Conservatives could only gloom-ily note the portents. The President spoke of a security program "which because of many lost years will take many future years to fulfill"; both the Farm Security and Resettlement Administrations were bringing group security ideas even into that sanctuary of individual relations, the medical field; and many powerful New Dealers were ready to agree with Eleanor Roosevelt when she declared: "In the nineteenth century . . . there was no recognition that the government owed an individual certain things as a right. . . . Now it is accepted that the government has an obligation to guard the rights of an individual so carefully that he never reaches a point at which he needs charity."

The New Deal made no concrete moves toward enforced equality, unless it was in its none too vigorous steps against segregation in public housing and against discrimination in employment on government con-tracts, but it smiled sympathetically on a liberal movement that was hurrying in that direction. The very tone of the New Deal was far more aggressively equalitarian than that of either Populism or progressivism. It was the New Dealer's President who told the Daughters of the American Revolution: "Remember, remember always that all of us, and you and I especially, are descended from immigrants." It was his wife who gladly permitted herself to be photographed while escorted by two Negro R.O.T.C. cadets.

Over much of previous progressivism had hung an air of patronizing the unfortunate, of helping the group that reformers often called "the little people." The attitude of the new liberalism was spoken with classic tartness when Joseph Mitchell presented his stories of "McSorley's Wonderful Saloon." The phrase "little people," Mitchell declared, was "repulsive. . . . There are no little people in this book. They are as big as you are, whoever you are." The point was carried to its further significance by a discerning, upper-income liberal, who added: "For quite a while I have lived in a commuter community that is rabidly anti-Roosevelt and I am convinced that the heart of their hatred is not economic. The real source of the venom is that Rooseveltism challenged their feeling that they were superior people, occupying by right a privileged position in the world. I am convinced that a lot of them would even have backed many of his economic measures if they had been permitted to believe the laws represented the fulfillment of their responsibility as 'superior people.' They were not permitted that belief. Instead, as the New Deal went on, it chipped away more and more at their sense of superiority. By the second term, it was pressing hard on a vital spot and the conservatives were screaming."

To many liberals, it was just these variations in reform that gave the New Deal its great strength. "This isn't a do-gooder tea club, patching things up here and there," one of the President's close associates exulted. "This is a real people's movement getting at the heart of the great modern problem, insecurity—insecurity in jobs and insecurity in feelings." Other liberals were not so confident. Even with the new concerns over economic security and social equality, American liberalism of the late Thirties was still fundamentally the New Freedom, and once it was tested over any considerable period of time, it could easily develop all the serious difficulties inherent in the New Freedom.

The New Deal was to have time only to begin the test of its variety of the New Freedom. For just as it was really swinging into its new phase, frenetic men across the oceans, whose interest in liberalism had always been minimal, decided to shove a different issue to the fore.

Henry Steele Commager

Twelve Years

of Roosevelt

The New Deal was subjected to critical evaluation from the moment it began. Its accomplishments, its place in American history, its contributions have been the subject of countless words both ephemeral and permanent. Opinions, of course, varied greatly; both praise and criticism have been leveled at it. Henry Steele Commager, a professor of history at Amherst College and a prolific writer on American history, wrote an evaluation of the New Deal the same month the President died. His article is reprinted below. It is a sympathetic and favorable assessment, in keeping with Commager's general view of the excellence of the President's programs and policies. Listing its achievements, Commager considers the New Deal to be one of the most important periods in our history. He credits it with restoring confidence and hope in a desperate period, for helping the underprivileged, and for providing for welfare and security—all this while safeguarding liberty. [Henry Steele Commager, "Twelve Years of Roosevelt," American Mercury, April 1945. Reprinted by permission.]

Now that the bitter controversies over New Deal policies have been drowned out by the clamor of war, it is possible to evaluate those policies in some historical perspective. And now that the outcome of this war which is to determine the future of democracy and of America's rôle in world affairs, is certain, it is possible to interpret something of the significance of the foreign policy, or program, of the Roosevelt administrations. Those policies, domestic and foreign, have been four times decisively endorsed by large popular majorities: so fully have they been translated into accomplished and irrevocable facts that controversy about them is almost irrelevant. It should be possible to fix, if not with finality, at least with some degree of accuracy, the place occupied by Roosevelt in American history. . . .

All this may be in the realm of the intangible. If we look to the more tangible things, what does the record show? Of primary importance has been the physical rehabilitation of the country. Notwithstanding the splendid achievements of the Theodore Roosevelt administrations, it became clear, during the twenties and thirties, that the natural resources of the country—its soil, forests, water power—were being destroyed at a dangerous rate. The development of the Dust Bowl, and the migration of the Okies to the Promised Land of California, the tragic floods on the Mississippi and the Ohio, dramatized to the American people the urgency of this problem.

Roosevelt tackled it with energy and boldness. The Civilian Conservation Corps enlisted almost three million young men who planted seventeen million acres in new forests, built over six million check dams to halt soil erosion, fought forest fires and plant and animal diseases. To check erosion the government organized a co-operative program which enlisted the help of over one-fourth the farmers of the country and embraced 270 million acres of land, provided for the construction of a series of huge dams and reservoirs, and planned the creation of a hundred-mile-wide shelter belt of trees on the high plains. The Resettlement Administration moved farmers off marginal lands and undertook to restore these to usefulness. More important than all this, was the TVA, a gigantic laboratory for regional reconstruction. Though much of this program owes its inspiration to the past, the contrast between the New Deal and what immediately preceded it cannot be better illustrated than by reference to Hoover's characterization of the Muscle Shoals bill of 1931 as not "liberalism" but "degeneration."

Equally important has been the New Deal achievement in the realm of human rehabilitation. Coming into office at a time when unemployment had reached perhaps fourteen million, and when private panaceas had ostentatiously failed, it was perhaps inevitable that Roosevelt should have sponsored a broad program of government aid. More important than bare relief, was the acceptance of the principle of the responsibility of the state for the welfare and security of its people—for employment, health and general welfare.

That this principle was aggressively and bitterly opposed now seems hard to believe: its establishment must stand as one of the cardinal achievements of the New Deal. Beginning with emergency legislation for relief, the Roosevelt program in the end embraced the whole field of social security—unemployment assistance, old age pensions, aid to women and children, and public health. Nor did it stop with formal "social security" legislation. It entered the domains of agriculture and labor, embraced elaborate programs of rural rehabilitation, the establishment of maximum hours and minimum wages, the prohibition of child labor; housing reform, and, eventually, enlarged aid to education. Under the New Deal the noble term "commonwealth" was given a more realistic meaning than ever before in our history.

That to Roosevelt the preservation of democracy was closely associated with this program for social and economic security is inescapably clear. He had learned well the moral of recent continental European history: that given a choice between liberty and bread, men are sorely tempted to choose bread. The task of democracy, as he conceived it, was to assure both. In a fireside chat of 1938 he said:

Democracy has disappeared in several other great nations, not because the people of those nations disliked democracy, but because they had grown tired of unemployment and insecurity, of seeing their children hungry while they sat helpless in the face of government confusion and government weakness through lack of leadership in government. Finally, in desperation, they chose to sacrifice liberty in the hope of getting something to eat. We in America know that our democratic institutions can be preserved and made to work. But in order to preserve them we need . . . to prove that the practical operation of democratic government is equal to the task of protecting the security of the people. . . . The people of America are in agreement in defending their liberties at any cost, and the first line of that defense lies in the protection of economic security.

In the political realm the achievements of the New Deal were equally notable. First we must note the steady trend towards the strengthening of government and the expansion of government activities—whether for weal or for woe only the future can tell. As yet no better method of dealing with the crowding problems of modern economy and society has revealed itself, and it can be said that though government today has, quantitatively, far greater responsibilities than it had a generation or even a decade ago, it has, qualitatively, no greater power. For our Constitutional system is intact, and all power still resides in the people and their representatives in Congress, who can at any moment deprive their government of any power.

But we seem to have solved, in this country, the ancient problem of the reconciliation of liberty and order; we seem to have overcome our traditional distrust of the state and come to a realization that a strong state could be used to benefit and advance the commonwealth. That is by no means a New Deal achievement, but it is a development which has gained much from the experience of the American people with their government during the Roosevelt administrations.

It has meant, of course, a marked acceleration of the tendency towards Federal centralization. This tendency had been under way for a long time before Roosevelt came to office: a century ago liberals were deploring the decline of the states and the growth of the power of the national government. That under the impact first of depression and then of war it has proceeded at a rapid rate since 1933 cannot be denied. It is apparent in the administrative field, with the growth of bureaus and departments and civil servants—and of the budget! It is apparent in the legislative field, with the striking extension of Federal authority into the fields of labor, agriculture, banking, health, education and the arts. It is apparent in the executive field with the immense increase in the power of the President. And it has been ratified by the judiciary with the acceptance and application of a broad construction of the Constitution.

Yet it cannot be said that this Federal centralization has weakened the states or local communities. What we are witnessing is a general increase in governmental activities—an increase in which the states share—witness any state budget at present. And it can be argued, too, that political centralization strengthens rather than weakens local government and the health of local communities. For if we look below forms to realities we can see that during the last decade Federal aid to farmers, to homeowners, to labor, Federal assistance in road-building, education and public health, has acutally restored many communities to financial

and economic health. It is by no means certain that community sentiment is weaker today than it was a generation ago.

Along with Federal centralization has gone a great increase in the
power of the executive. The charge that Roosevelt has been a dictator can
be dismissed, along with those hoary charges that Jefferson, Jackson, Lincoln, Theodore Roosevelt, and Wilson were dictators. American politics
simply doesn't run to dictators. But Roosevelt has been a "strong" executive—as every great democratic President has been a strong executive.
There is little doubt that the growing complexity of government plays
into the hands of the executive; there is little doubt that Roosevelt accepted his situation cheerfully. Today Roosevelt exercises powers far
vaster than those contemplated by the Fathers of the Constitution, as vast,
indeed, as those exercised by the head of any democratic state in the
world. Yet it cannot fairly be asserted that any of these powers has been
exercised arbitrarily, or that the liberties of Americans are not so safe
today as at any other time.

Two other political developments under the New Deal should be
noted. The first is the revitalization of political parties; the second the
return of the Supreme Court to the great tradition of Marshall, Story,
Miller and Holmes. Four observations about political parties during the
last decade are in order. First, the danger that our parties might come to
represent a particular class or section or interest was avoided: both major
parties retained—after the election of 1936—a broad national basis. Second, minor parties all but disappeared: in the elections of 1940 and 1944
the minor parties cast less than 1 per cent of the total vote—the first time
this happened since 1872. Third, legislation such as the Hatch Act diminished the possibility that any party might come to be controlled by
powerful vested interests or by patronage. And finally, with the organization of the PAC in the campaign of 1944, labor for the first time in
our history became an important factor in elections; and labor chose
to work within the framework of existing parties rather than, as elsewhere, to organize its own party.

The New Deal, as far as can be foreseen, is here to stay: there seems no
likelihood of a reversal of any of the major developments in politics in
the last twelve years. This was recognized by the Republicans in 1940 and
again in 1944. For both platforms endorsed all the essentials of the
New Deal and confined criticism to details and administration. How
far the reforms and experiments of the Roosevelt era will be carried
is a hazardous question. That the program of conservation will be
continued and enlarged seems obvious. A recent Congress, to be sure,
cavalierly ended the life of the National Resources Planning Board,
but the present Congress seems disposed to undertake a Missouri Valley
development along the lines of the TVA, and doubtless other "little
TVA's" are ahead. Social Security, too, will be maintained and possibly
enlarged: whether it will come to embrace socialized medicine or a
broad rehousing program is more dubious.

There may be a reaction against some of the labor legislation of the New Deal, but labor's newly discovered political power would seem to make that unlikely. It is improbable that there will be any relaxation of governmental peacetime controls over business, banking, securities, power, though here a change in taxation policies may do much to stimulate private enterprise and create an appearance of a shift away from New Deal practices. Federal centralization, which has been under way so long, is doubtless here to stay; planning, imperatively required by war, will in all probability wear off its faintly pink tinge, and flourish as a peacetime technique. And, finally, it seems probable that the restoration of the dignity of politics and statecraft, which came with 1933, will survive.

Today it is foreign affairs rather than domestic policy that commands our most agitated attention. Here, too, the large outlines of the Roosevelt achievements are clear, though the details are blurred and the future projection uncertain.

The problem of America's rôle in world affairs has been with us in one form or another since Colonial days. Then, we are sometimes inclined to forget, we were heavily involved in the affairs of the Western world—but as victims, one might say, rather than as independent participants. Our War for Independence was a world war; our War of 1812 was part of another world war. Between 1815 and the 1890's we achieved, or fancied that we achieved, some degree of isolation, but for two out of three centuries of our history we have been inextricably entangled in world affairs. In the 1890's we aggressively assumed a position as a world power, and the roots of our present involvement trace back to that decade. It is unnecessary to rehearse the details of that emergence as a world power: the Spanish War, the acquisition of Hawaii and of the Philippines, the Open Door policy, the reassertion of the Monroe Doctrine and the addition of corollaries; the construction of a powerful navy, indirect participation in the Algeciras Conference and intervention to end the Russo-Japanese War. All these and other indications dramatized the fact that the United States was a world power, with world-wide interests.

Since that time isolation has been a delusion. How futile that delusion was, was revealed by our participation in the first World War; how profound and widespread it was, was confessed in the retreat of the twenties—the refusal to join the League or the World Court, the withdrawal from the Far East, the gestures towards economic self-sufficiency, the adolescent disillusionment with the world.

Reflected on the background of a half-century of experience, Roosevelt's understanding of the responsibility of America as a world power seems logical and obvious; contrasted with the half-baked and half-witted isolationism of the twenties it becomes not only creditable but impressive. The international problems of the thirties were at once more complex and more urgent than those of any previous decade.

Future generations may indeed wonder that Americans of the thirties could have been paralyzed by hesitation and doubt, and may find in the neutrality legislation of 1935–37 one of the most intriguing enigmas of history; the historian can but record that opinion was divided, that the majority seemed to approve of this legislation, and that this majority included its share of the intelligent and the sincere.

We know now that from the time Japan struck in Manchuria and Hitler entered the Rhineland the issue confronting the United States was one of ultimate survival. It is to the credit of President Roosevelt that he sensed this from the beginning, that his record of hostility to what Hitler represented is clear and consistent, and that from 1937 on he sought ceaselessly to rally American opinion against totalitarianism and to prepare America for the test that finally came. Campaign orators have lamented that he was not more outspoken than he was, that he did not take more aggressive steps, make more energetic preparations.

These critics conveniently forgot that Roosevelt was consistently ahead of public opinion—witness the reaction to the Quarantine speech of 1937—and that in a democracy public opinion is the ultimate tribunal to which even a President must bow. And those who think that America was inexcusably unready for war in December 1941 should compare our readiness then with our pitiful state of unreadiness in April 1917—after almost three years of warning.

Roosevelt's foreign policy has, indeed, over a period of twelve years, a remarkable consistency—a consistency sometimes concealed from us by specific and minor aberrations. From the beginning he worked within the framework of the American system and respected the limitations of American politics. He did not attempt to reopen the issue of the League; he conceded defeat on the issue of the World Court; he accepted—though as we now know reluctantly—neutrality legislation. With reference to the European and Pacific problem he did what he could. He kept the record straight, insisted upon the validity of the principles involved, educated the American people to the underlying issues, set our domestic house in order, and pushed forward a naval building program. When the test came, there was much still to be done; there was nothing to retract.

From 1939 on, both the material and the moral achievements were of inestimable importance. On the material side the achievement was spectacular. There was the destroyer-bases deal which at once strengthened Britain in her heroic struggle against the Nazis and America in her self-defense. There was the Lend-Lease program which made America a veritable arsenal of democracy and which may eventually be regarded as the decisive turning point of the war. There was the acquisition of bases in Greenland and Iceland, and the "shoot on sight" order against German U-boats. There was the first peacetime conscription—the continuation of which was saved by a single vote in the lower House. There was the development of a vast and marvelously organized program of industrial mobilization—shipbuilding, munitions manufacture, airplane production. Without all this, it is safe to say, the war would have been lost.

The moral achievement will probably be better appreciated by future generations than by our own. Like Wilson, Roosevelt put the issues at once upon a moral plane, and kept them there: without Wilson's eloquence, Roosevelt had fundamentally the same philosophy—a philosophy fundamentally religious and moral. If the Atlantic Charter seems tarnished at the moment, we must remember that the Fourteen Points, too, came to seem tarnished. The tarnish rubs off. Roosevelt made clear, from the beginning, that this was more than a war for self-defense, a task which the Germans and Japanese made relatively easy for him. In a war message reminiscent of Wilson's he declared that

The true goal we seek is far above and beyond the ugly field of battle. When we resort to force, as now we must, we are determined that this force shall be directed toward ultimate good as well as against immediate evil. We Americans are not destroyers—we are builders. . . .

And in the dark hours of this day—and through dark days that may be yet to come—we will know that the vast majority of the members of the human race are on our side. Many of them are fighting with us. All of them are praying for us. For, in representing our case, we represent theirs as well—our hope and their hope for liberty under God.

When war finally came, the nation was united—united as it had never been for any previous war. That the war has been fought with effectiveness and efficiency cannot be doubted: compared with any previous war in which our unmilitary people have been involved, compared even with World War I, this has been a very miracle of efficiency. The details need not detain us; the results are sufficient.

Yet one more observation needs to be made with respect to Roosevelt's foreign policy, and that has to do with his comprehension of the problems of the future. Like Wilson, Roosevelt has envisioned a postwar international organization empowered to maintain peace. He has, so far, managed to avoid most of the errors which helped defeat Wilson's plans. Instead of keeping aloof from our Allies, he has associated with them, thus laying the groundwork now for a group of united nations. Instead of postponing the practical details of international co-operation, he has sponsored a series of conferences—relief, currency, aviation, Dumbarton Oaks—looking to the creation, now, of machinery competent to the solution of the most pressing problems. Instead of regarding Russia as a menace or a broken reed, he has actively and enthusiastically co-operated with her. Instead of antagonizing the Senate, he has taken the Senate and the American people into his confidence. Many problems still confront us and plague us, but that the outlook for an effective international order is more auspicious now than at any previous time in our history can scarcely be denied.

And what, finally, of Roosevelt himself? It may seem too early to fix his position in our history, yet that position is reasonably clear. He takes his place in the great tradition of American liberalism, along with Jefferson, Jackson, Lincoln, Theodore Roosevelt and Wilson. Coming to office at a time when the very foundations of the republic seemed threatened and when men were beginning to despair of the ability of a constitutional democracy to meet a crisis, he restored confidence and proved that democracy could act as effectively in crisis as could totalitarian governments. A liberal, he put government clearly at the service of the people; a conservative, he pushed through reforms designed to strengthen the natural and human resources of the nation, restore agriculture and business to its former prosperity, and save capitalism. He saw that problems of government were primarily political, not economic; that politics should control economy—not economy, politics; and that politics was an art as well as a science. He repudiated isolationism, demanded for America once more her proper station and responsibility in world affairs, and, after unifying the American people on the major issues of aid to the democracies and war, furnished a war leadership bold, energetic and successful.

In all this Roosevelt was an opportunist—but an opportunist with a philosophy. He was the same kind of opportunist that Jefferson—that earlier "traitor to his class"—had been. The close view of Roosevelt has discovered numerous inconsistencies. But if we look back over Roosevelt's long career in politics—beginning with his fight on the Tammany machine in 1910, we can see that amidst the hurly-burly of politics he has been unfalteringly consistent in his fundamental social and political philosophy. He has sought ends, and cheerfully adopted the "quarterback" technique with respect to means. And as the bitterness of particular controversies dies away, the larger outlines of his achievements during the past twelve years emerge with striking clarity. We can see that the promises of the New Deal platform of 1932 were carried out, more fully perhaps than those of any party platform since that of Polk a century ago. We can see that the democratic philosophy which Roosevelt asserted was applied and implemented. Under his leadership the American people withstood the buffetings of depression and the fearful trial of war, and emerged strong and respected, refreshed in their faith in democracy and in the ultimate triumph of justice in human affairs.

"The only sure bulwark of continuing liberty," Roosevelt said, "is a government strong enough to protect the interests of the people, and a people strong enough and well enough informed to maintain its sovereign control over its government."

The Roosevelt administration proved once more that it was possible for such a government to exist and such a people to flourish, and restored to the United States its position as "the hope of the human race."

John T. Flynn

The Roosevelt

Myth

Far to the other side is John T. Flynn's conclusions on the accomplishments of the New Deal. Once an ardent liberal, a leading Progressive, and a member of the staff of the New Republic, *Flynn went conservative with a vengeance. In books and articles beginning in 1940 he leveled diatribes at every liberal cause. Franklin Roosevelt and the New Dealers became his bête-noir. To him, the New Deal was a catastrophe, leaving a legacy of evil and a heritage of debt and waste. [Quoted from* The Roosevelt Myth *by John T. Flynn, published 1948 by* The Devin-Adair Co., *New York; revised edition published 1956. Copyright 1948 by John T. Flynn. Reprinted by permission of The Devin-Adair Co.]*

When the war drums rolled a great golden veil came down upon the American scene through which its actors would be viewed. Behind it they postured—statesmen and generals and admirals—in the role of heroes. And lifted above them all, posing in the full glory of the stage lights, decorated by propaganda with the virtues of a national god, was the figure of the Leader. When the battlefield is so far away, war is the greatest of all shows. It is the greatest of all booms. The money flows in rushing streams and for millions it becomes and remains the dizziest and most abundant memory of their lives. The lights have been going out, the bands have ceased playing, the propaganda machines are being slowly silenced and little by little life, scenery and actors are assuming their normal dimensions. Despite all this, many good people in America still cherish the illusion that Roosevelt performed some amazing feat of regeneration for this country. They believe he took our economic system when it was in utter disrepair and restored it again to vitality; that he took over our political system when it was at its lowest estate and restored it again to its full strength. He put himself on the side of the underprivileged masses. He transferred power from the great corporate barons to the simple working people of America. He curbed the adventurers of Wall Street, and gave security to the humble men and women of the country. And above all he led us through a great war for democracy and freedom and saved the civilization of Europe.

But not one of these claims can be sustained. He did not restore our economic system to vitality. He changed it. The system he blundered us into is more like the managed and bureaucratized, state-supported system of Germany before World War I than our own traditional order. Before his regime we lived in a system which depended for its expansion upon private investment in private enterprise. Today we live in a system which depends for its expansion and vitality upon the government. This is a prewar European importation—imported at the moment when it had fallen into complete disintegration in Europe. In America today every fourth person depends for his livelihood upon employment either directly by the government or indirectly in some industry supported by government funds. In this substituted system the government confiscates by taxes or borrowings the savings of all the citizens and invests them in non-wealth-producing enterprises in order to create work. Behold the picture of American economy today: taxes which confiscate the savings of every citizen, a public debt of 250 billion dollars as against a pre-Roosevelt debt of 19 billions, a government budget of 40 billions instead of four before Roosevelt, inflation doubling the prices and reducing the lower-bracket employed workers to a state of pauperism as bad as that of the unemployed in the depression, more people on various kinds of government relief than when we had 11 million unemployed, Americans trapped in the economic disasters and the political quarrels of every nation on earth and a system of permanent militarism closely resembling that which we beheld with horror in Europe for decades, bureaucrats swarming over every field of life and the President calling for more power, more price-fixing, more regulation and more billions. Does this look like the traditional American scene? Or does it not look rather like the system built by Bismarck in Germany in the last century and imitated by all the lesser Bismarcks in Europe?

No, Roosevelt did not restore our economic system. He did not construct a new one. He substituted an old one which lives upon permanent crises and an armament economy. And he did this not by a process of orderly architecture and building, but by a succession of blunders, moving one step at a time, in flight from one problem to another, until we are now arrived at that kind of state-supported economic system that will continue to devour a little at a time the private system until it disappears altogether.

He did not restore our political system to its full strength. One may like the shape into which he battered it, but it cannot be called a repair job. He changed our political system with two weapons—blank-check congressional appropriations and blank-check congressional legislation. In 1933, Congress abdicated much of its power when it put billions into his hands by a blanket appropriation to be spent at his sweet will and when it passed general laws, leaving it to him, through great government bureaus of his appointment, to fill in the details of legislation.

These two baleful mistakes gave him a power which he used ruthlessly. He used it to break down the power of the states and to move that power to Washington and to break down the power of Congress and concentrate it in the hands of the executive. The end of these two betrayals—the smashing of our economic system and the twisting of our political system—can only be the Planned Economic State, which, either in the form of Communism or Fascism, dominates the entire continent of Europe today. The capitalist system cannot live under these conditions. Free representative government cannot survive a Planned Economy. Such an economy can be managed only by a dictatorial government capable of enforcing the directives it issues. The only result of our present system—unless we reverse the drift—must be the gradual extension of the fascist sector and the gradual disappearance of the system of free enterprise under a free representative government.

There are men who honestly defend this transformation. They at least are honest. They believe in the Planned Economy. They believe in the highly centralized government operated by a powerful executive. They do not say Roosevelt saved our system. They say he has given us a new one. That is logical. But no one can praise Roosevelt for doing this and then insist that he restored our traditional political and economic systems to their former vitality.

The most tragic illusion about this man is that built up by the ceaseless repetition of the false statement that he gave us a system of security.

Security for whom? For the aged? An old-age security bill was passed during his first administration which provides for workers who reach the age of 65 a pension of $8 a week at most. And even this meager and still very badly constructed plan had to be pushed through against a strange inertness on his part. Roosevelt's mind ran in curious circles. People have forgotten his procrastination about putting through the social security bill until in the 1934 congressional elections the Republicans denounced him for his tardiness. It is difficult to believe this now after all the propaganda that has washed over people's minds. And when he did finally consent to a bill, like so many good ideas that went into his mind, it came out badly twisted. It contained a plan for building a huge reserve fund that would have amounted to nothing more than a scheme to extract billions from the workers' payrolls without any adequate return. Over the protest of the President, the Congress finally took that incredible joker out of the law. But it is in every respect a pathetically inadequate law. Does anyone imagine that $8 a week is security for anyone, particularly since Roosevelt's inflation has cut the value of that in half?

But what of the millions of people who through long years of thrift and saving have been providing their own security? What of the millions who have been scratching for years to pay for their life insurance and annuities, putting money in savings banks, commercial banks, buying government and corporation bonds to protect themselves in their old age? What of the millions of teachers, police, firemen, civil employees of states and cities and the government, of the armed services and the army of men and women entitled to retirement funds from private corporations—railroads, industrial and commercial? These thrifty people have seen one-half their retirement benefits wiped out by the Roosevelt inflation that has cut the purchasing power of the dollar in two. Roosevelt struck the most terrible blow at the security of the masses of the people while posing as the generous donor of "security for all." During the war boom and in the post-war boom created by spending 40 billion dollars a year the illusion of security is sustained. The full measure of Roosevelt's hopeless misunderstanding of this subject will come when security will be most needed—and most absent.

To say that Roosevelt roused in the people a social consciousness is absurd. There has always been a social consciousness in our people. And when Roosevelt as governor in New York took his first steps in this field, he was merely following in the footsteps of Al Smith, who made him governor. Of course when the depression arrived, its grave necessities stirred the minds of our people to social measures upon a greater scale. Roosevelt had never given the subject a thought until he was elected governor. However, has anyone ever bothered to consult those fruitful studies in social problems which Herbert Hoover caused to be made while he was Secretary of Commerce and President before the onset of the crisis brought this subject to everyone's mind?

As for the great war for freedom and democracy, it would be well to get that clear in our minds. In one breath we are told that Roosevelt did not take us into that war—that we were dragged in by the dastardly attack by the Japs at Pearl Harbor, while Roosevelt was trying to keep out. In the next breath we are told he took us into that war for freedom and democracy. But how has it advanced the cause of democracy? We liberated Europe from Hitler and turned it over to the mercies of a far more terrible tyrant and actually tried to sell him to the people as a savior of civilization. Behold Europe! Does one refer to the wreckage there as liberation and salvation? Is anyone so naive as to suppose that democracy and free capitalism have been restored in Europe? Fascism has departed from Germany, but a hybrid system of socialism and capitalism in chains has come to England, which is called social democracy but is on its way to Fascism with all the controls without which such a system cannot exist. And in America the price of the war is that fatal deformity of our own economic and political system which Roosevelt effected under the impact of the war necessities.

Roosevelt's star was waning sadly in 1938 when he had 11 million unemployed and when Hitler made his first war moves in Europe. All his promises had been defaulted on. The cities were filling with idle workers. Taxes were rising. The debt was soaring. The war rescued him and he seized upon it like a drowning man. By leading his country into the fringes of the war at first and then deep into its center all over the world he was able to do the only things that could save him—spend incomprehensible billions, whip up spending in the hot flames of war hysteria, put every man and his wife and grandparents into the war mills, while under the pressure of patriotic inhibitions, he could silence criticism and work up the illusion of the war leader. Of course the war against Germany was won—America with her 140 million people, Russia with her 180 million, France, England and the Commonwealth with another 100 million, with practically all the naval power and with the choice of the earth's resources, against 70 million of the enemy—of course we won. But at what price to our institutions? And then, while the war was still raging and as victory appeared, Roosevelt disappeared from the scene. The staggering debts, the larcenous inflation, the insoluble division amongst the victors, the appalling consequences of his fantastic surrenders to Moscow—all this is left in the hands of his successors, after the ballyhoo is spent, the fireworks extinguished, the martial music silenced and the money nearly gone, leaving only the great spectacle of a disordered, divided and bankrupt world.

On the moral side, let me say that I have barely touched that subject. It will all yet be told. But go back through the years, read the speeches and platforms and judgments he made and consider them in the light of what he did. Look up the promises of thrift in public office, of balanced budgets and lower taxes, of disbanded bureaucrats, of honesty in government and of security for all. Read again the warnings he uttered to his own people against those wicked men who would seize upon a war in Europe to entangle them upon specious visions of false war abundance. Read the speeches he made never, never again to send our sons to fight in foreign wars. Look up the promises he made, not to our own people, but to the Chinese, to Poland, to Czechoslovakia, to the Baltic peoples in Lithuania and Latvia and Estonia, to the Jews out of one side of his mouth and to the Arabs out of the other side. He broke every promise. He betrayed all who trusted him. If any escaped it was the British and the Russians because they were represented by two strong men who, in dealing with Roosevelt, were inflexible realists who knew what they were about, who played the game with him upon the basis of solid realism, as they should, who remembered their own countries and held him with iron resolution to his incredible pledges.

The figure of Roosevelt exhibited before the eyes of our people is a fiction. There was no such being as that noble, selfless, hardheaded, wise and farseeing combination of philosopher, philanthropist and warrior which has been fabricated out of pure propaganda and which a small collection of dangerous cliques in this country are using to advance their own evil ends.

Marquis W. Childs

They Hate

Roosevelt

Few figures in history have generated as much controversy as did Franklin D. Roosevelt. He aroused passions as only great and dynamic leaders can. He was either loved or hated—no one seemed to be neutral about him, as people might be about the drab and the colorless. He either subverted the republic or saved it—he never merely led it. H. L. Mencken called him a quack and a fraud. Albert Jay Nock compared him to Woodrow Wilson in that both had megalomaniac delusions. Laurence Dennis considered him a master showman but not a master builder. Yet millions of people hailed him as a great humanitarian. In the article that follows, Marquis W. Childs— writing in 1936—examines the attitudes of those who were strongly opposed to the President. [Marquis W. Childs, "They Hate Roosevelt," Harper's Magazine, May 1936. © *1936 by Harper & Row, Publishers, Incorporated. Reprinted from Harper's Magazine by the author's permission.]*

A resident of Park Avenue in New York City was sentenced not long ago to a term of imprisonment for threatening violence to the person of President Roosevelt. This episode, with the conclusions as to the man's probable sanity, was recorded at length on the front pages of the newspapers of the land. In itself it was unimportant. Cranks with wild ideas are always to be found here and there in any large community. Yet it was significant as a dramatically extreme manifestation of one of the most extraordinary phenomena of our day, a phenomenon which social historians in the future will very likely record with perplexity if not with astonishment: the fanatical hatred of the President which to-day obsesses thousands of men and women among the American upper class.

No other word than hatred will do. It is a passion, a fury, that is wholly unreasoning. Here is no mere political opposition, no mere violent disagreement over financial policies, no mere distrust of a national leader who to these men and women appears to be a demagogue. Opposition, disagreement, distrust, however strong, are quite legitimate and defensible, whether or not one agrees that they are warranted. But the phenomenon to which I refer goes far beyond objection to policies or programs. It is a consuming personal hatred of President Roosevelt and, to an almost equal degree, of Mrs. Roosevelt.

It permeates, in greater or less degree, the whole upper stratum of American society. It has become with many persons an *idée fixe*. One encounters it over and over again in clubs, even in purely social clubs, in locker and card rooms. At luncheon parties, over dinner tables, it is an incessant theme. And frequently in conversation it takes a violent and unlawful form, the expression of desires and wishes that can be explained only, it would seem, in terms of abnormal psychology.

In history this hatred may well go down as the major irony of our time. For the extraordinary fact is that whereas the fanatic who went to prison had lost his fortune and, therefore, had a direct grievance, the majority of those who rail against the President have to a large extent had their incomes restored and their bank balances replenished since the low point of March, 1933.

That is what makes the phenomenon so incredible. It is difficult to find a rational cause for this hatred. I do not mean, of course, that it is difficult to find a rational cause for criticism, even passionately strong criticism, of the New Deal. One may quite reasonably be convinced that its policies are unsound, that its leaders are hypocritical, that its total influence is pernicious. But the venom to which I refer is of a sort seldom found among men and women who have not been personally hurt, and badly hurt, by those whom they excoriate.

Some members of this class have undoubted grounds for feeling personally hurt. Some, for example, have found themselves with income still depleted, and have warrant for attributing the still sorry state of their investments to various measures sponsored by the Administration. Yet others have prospered exceedingly since March, 1933; and certainly on the average they find their present circumstances much improved.

As the New Dealers themselves have been at pains to point out, taxes on the rich have not been materially increased. Secretary Ickes, speaking before the Union League Club in Chicago recently, developed this at length, showing that a man with a net income annually of $50,000 would pay no more to the Federal government in taxes this year than he paid last year; with $60,000 annually he would pay $90 additional; with $80,000 he would pay $775 more, and on an income of $1,000,000, an added $1,875. And although a new tax program is being drafted as this is written, probably no small proportion of the burden will be placed upon the mass of consumers through processing or excise taxes.

Surely the explanation does not lie in the trifling changes made thus far. Nor would the fear of inflation seem to account for it. In the first place, the rise in prices from 1933 to date has, by and large, helped these people more than it has hurt them. Witness the long advance in the stock market, which has doubled, tripled, or quadrupled the prices of stocks—and indeed has multiplied some of them by ten. In the second place, there is no denying that, conversely, the deflation of 1929–1933 did great damage to the fortunes of the rich. In the third place, fears of the future possibilities of the credit-inflation policy of the Administration, whether justified or not, are at any rate not fears of immediate or definitely predictable trouble. Finally—and still more important—the rich are seldom the victims of inflation. It is well known that most of the very wealthy profited from the German inflation. Long before the storm breaks large investments have been safeguarded by diversification in real property or in stocks adapted by their nature to adjust to swiftly changing price levels. Many wealthy persons have already begun to shift their holdings to such things as farm land.

That there is a widespread conviction among the wealthy that they are being butchered to make a Roman holiday for the less fortunate is undeniable. But it is certain that as a class the wealthy have suffered relatively less than any other from the economic events of the past three years; and in that single word *relatively* there is a world of meaning. As for their feeling that butchery has at least been intended by the Roosevelt Administration, let us glance for a moment at some opinions from the other side of the fence.

A great many liberals, and certainly all radicals, complain that President Roosevelt's chief mission has been to save the fortunes of the very rich. Economists for the American Federation of Labor estimated in the annual report for 1935 that in the course of that year corporate profits—dividends and so forth—had increased forty per cent, while real wages had increased slightly less than two per cent. What is more, the wage increase had been in part offset by a corresponding increase in the work-week of an hour and a half.

Surveying the present state of the nation—stock-market boom, crowded Florida resorts, thronged night clubs, the revival of luxury spending—one might almost imagine the fury of the rich to be part of a subtle plot to return Mr. Roosevelt to office. For surely such uncritical vituperation, such blind hostility, must contribute to that end. Is that it then? To throw the workers and the farmers off their guard, the American rich are simulating this rage against the man who—if one listens to the other side—has been their savior?

But such choler could not be simulated. Anyone who has seen it now and then at close range must be aware that it is too authentic for that.

While this phenomenon has gone virtually unrecorded, it is familiar to most middle-class people to-day. Indeed, it has had its influence upon the middle class. There are those who have been only too eager to pick up crumbs of emotion dropped from the rich man's table. In general, however, the violence of the hatred varies directly with the affluence of the social group. The larger the house, the more numerous the servants, the more resplendent the linen and silver, the more scathing is likely to be the indictment of the President.

It may be useful to record certain recent examples of the present temper of the two per cent, if only because the rapid shifting of events may leave slight evidence of it for the notebook of the social historian. In the following scenes I have altered names and circumstances just enough to prevent identification; but the episodes are not only in essence true, they are being duplicated daily wherever the very fortunate congregate.

The fortune of the Skeane family is in the manufacture of textile-weaving machines, a closely owned enterprise built upon the inventiveness of old Jeremiah Skeane. Jeremiah's widow (it was a late marriage for Jeremiah to his attractive young secretary) is, needless to say, very wealthy. The return on the family business dwindled in 1933 to less than two per cent and there was a panicky feeling among all the Skeanes; result, "economy"—the dismissal of gardeners, chauffeurs, the second girl upstairs. To-day the return on the family business is more than ten per cent.

The Skeane "seat," The Oaks, where the widow lives two or three months a year, is at Elkins Park, a suburb of Philadelphia. She is leaving, in the middle of February when slush and snow make Philadelphia so dreary, for Florida in a private car with two of her grandchildren and their governess. Mrs. Skeane is giving a luncheon for eighteen, in farewell.

The furs which the guests have left upstairs would make for any department store a costly, well-bred display. The dining room, the table, everything about the establishment has the impeccability, the perfection, that is achieved only on fifty thousand dollars (or more) a year. From the long windows at one side you look out on a well-tailored landscape and beyond, far enough beyond, the roofs of another English country house.

At the outset of the luncheon Mrs. Skeane has her butler pass on a silver tray copies of a radio talk given by Mr. Cameron of the Ford Motor Company. Mr. Cameron told his audience that wealth in America is really very widely distributed, that many people own their homes, that the equity in industry is largely dispersed through ownership of common stock. There is an appreciative glow about the table over this gift. But Mrs. Skeane says, deprecatingly, "I just wanted to start you thinking; it seemed to me so fine that I sent for as many copies as I could get. It answers so many things, you know."

The Cameron pamphlet serves at least to start the conversation going in a familiar channel. Al Smith's Liberty League speech was to these women an event of the most vital importance. They speak of him now, nearly a month after the address, as one would speak of a folk hero, with a mixture of reverence and warm familiarity. And this, incidentally, is true of the whole group; the Smith speech was treasured as though it had been wisdom handed down from on high on tablets of stone. Al's wisecracks are quoted verbatim and *in extenso* as final proof of the case against the President.

"Now don't you think that Al Smith would make a fine President for us?" says Mrs. Skeane ardently.

The table takes up this suggestion with enthusiasm until suddenly someone remembers Mrs. Smith and the things that these same people said of her in the presidential campaign of 1928. For a moment this is a little dampening.

"Oh, but don't you see," says Mrs. Robley, "Mrs. Smith knows that she doesn't know anything. She would employ an efficient social secretary and things would be decently run in the White House again. She wouldn't be like that terrible woman who thinks she knows everything about running the whole country."

Thus the 1928 specter of Mrs. Smith in the White House is exorcised. Thereupon Mrs. Derouen offers her contribution. Her husband was in New York at a business conference yesterday with Mr. Blank (naming one of the high officials of the Hoover Administration). And Mr. Blank told Mr. Derouen what the Republicans proposed to do when they came into office. They would stop all this nonsense about relief, all this foolish made-work especially, and they would enlarge the police force. Then if there was any trouble, let it come. Mrs. Derouen reports this very solemnly, and it is accepted as bearing the authority of the inner sanctum, as having come from the holy of holies.

Having discussed the issues of the day in relation to the high principles involved, Mrs. Skeane and her guests are free to come out with the real lowdown. That has to do with the personal conduct of the Roosevelt family. It is bad, very bad. There is, in fact, nothing good to be said for it. It runs a horrid gamut between divorce and dissipation. And these women air their familiarity with the shocking and manifold details. Creole broth, delicate sole, individual squab, and so on, are the dishes passed one after the other. Canards and rumored scandal are the intellectual fare. Faultlessly the luncheon proceeds to coffee and cigarettes and to farewells to Mrs. Skeane.

Mrs. Skeane is exceptional only in her ardor—her patriotism, her friends call it. She is a contributor to several organizations, including the American Liberty League, that are concerned with saving the Constitution. She has small red, white, and blue stickers, with the words "Save the Constitution," with which she seals her letters. Each of the five cars in her garage bears a plate above the license plate: "Save the Constitution."

Among the young in Mrs. Skeane's circle the hatred of Roosevelt takes a particularly brash and violent form. There is the post-debutante whose complete disapproval of the whole Roosevelt family is expressed in terms of the utmost contempt and scorn, as one would speak of a degraded order of beings. The diatribe she offers for the obvious approval of her elders concludes with what is apparently in her eyes the most damning sin of all: the President is a traitor to his class. And what has he ever done, she demands (forgetting that she herself is safely established in the bosom of a family that has had money for at least three generations), but live off his mother's income?

This is a frequent theme that may explain something of the rancor that the mere mention of the Roosevelt name is certain to evoke. It may well have its origin in a primitive source. It would seem that we can forgive, or at least understand, an act of hostility from our enemy, but not from one of our own kind. Certainly if there is an aristocracy in the United States, the Roosevelts are of it. They have owned landed estates in the neighborhood of Skaneateles and Poughkeepsie since early in the seventeenth century. They have always had sufficient money to enable them to lead cultivated, pleasant lives. And so there is no forgiveness for their seeming disloyalty. Mr. Roosevelt, say the members of his class, has insinuated himself into a position of supreme authority and now proceeds to snipe at his friends.

To attempt to make a reasonable answer, to point out a few stray facts, even to inquire whether the President of the United States should govern on behalf of a class, is soon seen to be futile in the face of this unrelenting hostility. Facts, unless they happen by chance to serve the purpose, have very little to do with the emotion in question.

Let me turn to another characteristic scene. This one is in Florida. James Hamilton is the head of a firm of commodity brokers in Chicago. During the Roosevelt Administration, the Hamilton firm has made a handsome profit handling various products for the Commodities Credit Corporation. And in other indirect ways Hamilton has profited from the great increase in governmental activity. He owns a considerable block of stock, inherited from his grandfather, in a flour milling company, and into the treasury of this closely owned firm the Supreme Court dumped a sum in impounded processing taxes greater than the net profits for 1928 and 1929.

But even the warm sun of Florida cannot moderate one degree James Hamilton's grim antipathy to the President and his every word and deed. At Miami Beach he sits on the porch of the cabana he has leased at one of the best beach clubs and vituperates. The President has deliberately tried to destroy the foreign market for our cotton, to the profit of Brazil. One may talk in vain about the decline in soil fertility in the cotton States, about the world movement toward national self-sufficiency, about trends and tendencies existing long before Mr. Roosevelt came into office. It is breath wasted. The President, says James Hamilton, is ruining the farmers of the middle-west by permitting the importation of corn. He will not hear you if you point out the exact number of bushels of corn that have been imported, a negligible number, or the fact that it is in considerable part corn unsuited for feeding to cattle, not to mention the graph that shows clearly how the farmers' purchasing power has mounted.

With James Hamilton is his son, James Hamilton III, also a partner in the firm. The younger Hamilton specializes in Roosevelt horror stories. He repeats with a knowing air, as having come from the inner councils, all the preposterous canards that have passed through the country by word of mouth during the past year. Many of these are built round the report that the President is insane. A number of versions of this story have become familiar. The commonest one has to do with the strange laughter with which the President greets his visitors, a laughter that—if one were to believe the story—continues foolishly and irrelevantly during most of the interview.

But James Hamilton III can improve upon these stories. He had it from a man who had dinner in the White House last week that . . . James Hamilton III becomes unprintable. He reveals with a kind of painstaking delight the horrible details of the intimate life of the first family of the land. And when this phase of the career of the Roosevelts has been exhausted, he will describe radical plots to undermine the Constitution, the church, and the state in all of which President Roosevelt has had a part.

This is not idle talk. It is for James Hamilton III the gospel, and only slightly less so for his father, who occasionally puts in a word of moderation by way of restraining young hotheads. The elder Hamilton wouldn't, in short, go so far as to say the President is insane now, but he might have been in 1933 when he seized power. For authority for the radical plots in which Mr. Roosevelt has had a hand, James Hamilton III will quote from a Hearst editorial article, from a speech by Governor Talmadge, or from any one of a half dozen weekly papers and pamphlet services that are feeding the fiercer anti-Roosevelt fires.

The social historian would do well to make a collection of these obscure papers and pamphlets, for they will one day be invaluable source material. Perhaps the noisiest of these sheets, and therefore the one that is most frequently passed about, is *The Awakener,* which is "For The Americanization Of The Right" and "Against The Socialism Of The Left." Its tone is not unlike that of the Communist *New Masses* prior to the shift in Communist policy toward co-operation with other social and economic groups, the united front. *The Awakener* goes in for headlines such as "Mrs. Roosevelt Approves Communist Youth Group." It delights in quoting George Bernard Shaw to prove that Mr. Roosevelt is a Communist. And having done this to his complete satisfaction, the columnist for *The Awakener* adds the following:

"Embarrassing item number two came to light during an investigation into the death of Joseph Shoemaker at Tampa, Florida, some weeks ago. Shoemaker, an avowed radical, and a group of friends, all members of the Workers Alliance, a Socialist organization, were busily engaged in two collateral endeavors. On the one hand they were organizing in the political field as 'Modern Democrats' while at the same time carrying on subversive agitation among the unemployed. A group of patriotic citizens resented their trouble-making activities and one night, unfortunately, they were set upon by vigilantes and flogged. Subsequently Shoemaker developed blood poisoning and died. At the time not even the most rabid anti-New Dealer offered to suggest that these 'reds,' in organizing the 'Modern Democrats,' had Franklin D. Roosevelt as an inspiration. A telltale letter, however, dated April 28, 1932, and bearing F.D.R.'s signature, found recently among Shoemaker's effects, brands the President as being in thorough accord with basic Socialistic principles. . . ."

This is enough to indicate the nature of *The Awakener.* And while it decants a stronger wine than the others, they all have a family resemblance. There has been a small boom in the business of issuing anti-Roosevelt publications. Although some are run for profit, others have financial backers proud to pay not only the printing bill but the cost of distribution too. "Confidential" news services that go out of Washington into Wall Street have recognized the value of the hate-Roosevelt theme.

We change the scene again—to New York. Joshua and Ellen Thornberry are giving a large cocktail party in their apartment in the east 'Sixties. The three floors of the Thornberry apartment are filled with things, things, things, a superfluity of things—a collection of jade, a collection of Persian enamels, enough Georgian silver to furnish a museum. The Thornberrys are about to leave for South Carolina for some shooting. Their large living room is filled with talk, cigarette smoke, expensive scent, and servants passing champagne cocktails. In one corner Joshua is telling three or four of his friends of a deal he had in the stock market last week that netted a neat profit. He is relating the story only to illustrate the awful kind of government we live under, with "that man" in Washington. "Why, just think of it," says Joshua, "I shall have to give sixty per cent of my profit to the government. Just think of that! That's the kind of system we live under."

I recall my own encounter, last fall, with the owner-manager of a handsome inn in New England. He had invested in the property in 1930 and had weathered three very lean years; 1934 was better, 1935 very good. But this man's snarling vindictiveness was turned on for the benefit of all his guests. It went, unfortunately. with one's view of the distant autumnal hills. And what gave it a touch of distinction was that it was broad enough in its scope to take in not only the Roosevelt family but certain members of his government, the supply of personal slime being sufficient to smear a few members of the cabinet, just in passing.

Ordinarily the almost complete concentration of the attack upon the President himself is remarkable. If reference is made to other members of the Administration it usually serves only as another stick with which to beat the dog. He is damned, on the one hand, for the "radicalism" of Messrs. Tugwell, Wallace, and Ickes, in the order named, and, on the other, for the political machinations of Messrs. Farley, Cummings, and Roper. It is taken for granted by those who hate the President that the men about him are mere puppets who do his bidding.

It is a disconcerting fact that when one is solemnly told across a well-appointed dinner-table that "everybody in Washington knows that the whole Roosevelt family is drunk most of the time," or that "of course it's no secret in Washington that the reason Mrs. Roosevelt is so all over the place is that she's planning to succeed her husband in the Presidency until it's time for the sons to take over," or that Roosevelt is out of his mind, or that other less printable things are matters of "common knowledge," the fantastic misinformation is as likely as not to come from someone whose educational advantages might be supposed to have included some training in the sifting of evidence and the suspension of judgment, and who professes a scorn for the gullibility of the common herd.

The hate-Roosevelt school of thought has no geographical limitations. Its restrictions are, in general, economic. (There are exceptions, of course, among the two per cent; there are many men and women whose opposition to the Administration is devoid of any taint of personal vindictiveness, and one may even—by combing the woods—find here and there a lonely defender of the President.) If a statistician were making one of those shaded maps on which geographical distribution is graphically indicated, whole areas in and about New York would be colored with the deepest dye. (Black the color would doubtless be.) Chicago's wealthy suburbs might be a shade lighter, but the difference would scarcely be perceptible to the untutored eye. New England's blackness would be broken only by a few gray patches, shading off to a faint oyster color in the neighborhood of regions especially blessed by the New Deal.

Prosperous Washington would be a notable exception, among cities on the eastern seaboard, and not alone because it is the seat of government. A goodly number of the wealthy men in Washington are corporation lawyers who hold that what has happened during the past three years does not differ essentially from what has gone on in Washington under previous Administrations. It makes a different noise but the grist is ground in the same old way in the same old mill. It is for this reason that those who go out from Washington into other parts of the country now and then are startled by the fearful anathemas breathed upon the name of Roosevelt. To a man who has watched the Washington wheels go round year after year the loud cursing of the gentlemen in the upper brackets appears to have little relation to anything the present occupant of the White House has thus far done.

Attempting to trace the rise of the current hate one falls into useless conjecture. If one might have a graph such as only an omniscient statistician could produce, showing the development of this animosity year by year, it would be interesting to superimpose upon it a graph representing the rise that has occurred since 1933 in every index of price and production. My guess is that there would be a fairly close correspondence. To be sure the animosity was a little slow in developing. In the spring and summer of 1933, when prices were rising fast from the panic levels of the banking crisis, there was among the rich a great deal of resentment at the tendency in Washington to blame the bankers for all that had happened, there was uneasiness over the wholesale legislation introduced by the Administration, and over the President's inflationary tendencies, but there was little real denunciation of Roosevelt. That came later. Since the latter part of 1933, however, it has increased in volume and in unanimity—and never faster, apparently, than during the sustained advance of the stock market and the less uniform but, nevertheless, hopeful advance of business during 1935.

This phenomenon might be perplexing to the future historian. The usual evidence of history is that men and women whose fortunes are rising do not turn against the government in power. Yet apparently every ten-point rise in common stocks within the past year or two has but added to the confidence with which its major beneficiaries have conducted their attack, has but added to their anger at having to pay high taxes on their winnings. Here are some pertinent questions for the psychologist. Is the memory of fear, once we have recovered from that fear, an intolerable thing? No one can deny that there was panic in February and March of 1933 among those who stood to lose most by a sharp break with the past. And does gratitude toward the hero of the hour turn upon itself in proportion as the crisis is left behind? It cannot be doubted that there was almost universal gratitude for the warm, reassuring voice that came over the radio in March, 1933.

What one returns to—the incredible, the amazing fact—is that most of these people seem to have no realization whatever of the present plight of the world. The events that occurred between the autumn of 1929 and the spring of 1933 have apparently left no mark upon their memories. The fact that there are in the United States still some twelve million unemployed is seemingly without significance to them. The fact that when Mrs. Skeane dismissed her gardeners and chauffeurs in 1933 the dismissal was more disastrous to them than to her does not lodge in her mind. The fact that in a time when millions are destitute through no fault of their own James Hamilton is very fortunate to have a cabana on the warm sands of Florida has not dawned upon him. Nor does it seem to have occurred to Joshua Thornberry that the plight of hundreds of thousands of families in his own city, who without governmental relief would speedily starve or freeze to death in the zero weather from which he can so readily flee, may have some logical connection with the taxing of the money which he has cleaned up in a quick and easy stock-market deal.

If you were so rude as to remind Mr. Thornberry of this connection he simply would not believe that it was real. He thinks that most of the present unemployed could find jobs if they tried, and that the rest would quickly find them if he and his like were permitted to do just as they pleased with their takings. He thinks—while he sips his champagne cocktail and looks forward to his leisure hours in the South—that the unemployed are wasters living lavishly on funds expropriated from the hard-working and the thrifty. (As he talks, through one's mind run the words of the Ghost in *A Christmas Carol*—"Oh God! to hear the Insect on the leaf pronouncing on the too much life among his hungry brothers in the dust!") Not that Mr. Thornberry is not, among his peers, a good fellow, kindly and generous. He simply is not aware of the gravity of the unemployment problem, has not bothered to look into it closely. His ignorance of what goes on outside his little insulated and padded world is abysmal.

Even more disturbing is the fact that this ignorance does not shame him. He does not think of the unemployment problem as *his* problem as an American citizen. He and others of his class who share his views appear to think that they have discharged their full responsibilities when they have touched off a string of adjectives, peppered by a few sulphurous epithets. If they cannot have at Washington an Administration of their own choosing, they in effect resign from the United States. They could hardly regard with greater hostility an alien government set over them by a foreign power. (One recalls that dinner of New Jersey public utility men at which a toast to the President of the United States was greeted by a roar of laughter.) The only department of the government which they regard with anything but contempt is the Supreme Court, and the reason, stripped of its idealized protective coloring, is not far to seek: the Supreme Court has recently appeared to aid their own interests. One listens despairingly at some of their gatherings for any word which will suggest a sense that the government is a continuing instrument for the benefit of all, in the direction and support of which they expect as citizens to share, regardless of the policy or the personality which for the time being is in the ascendant.

It is precisely this sense of identification with the government which distinguishes the wealthy British conservatives, whatever may be their shortcomings in other respects, from the American variety. One wonders how many of our two per cent would follow the example of Stanley Baldwin, who shortly after the War wrote to the *Times* an anonymous letter stating his belief that the national debt was too high and that, therefore, he was presenting one-fifth of his fortune to the government in order to ease the burden to that extent. The early part of Baldwin's letter struck a note which one often hears in the conversation of well-to-do Americans. "It is so easy," he wrote, referring not only to individuals but to governments, "to live on borrowed money; so difficult to realize that you are doing so." But he continued his argument with words which one hears less often. "They (the wealthy classes) know the danger of the present debt; they know the weight of it in years to come. They know the practical difficulties of a universal statutory capital levy. Let them impose upon themselves, each as he is able, a voluntary levy."

The debt, be it remembered, was not the creation of Baldwin's party nor the outgrowth of anything that he had personally advocated, but, quite regardless, he felt a responsibility that he could not deny. Nor was this letter, it should be added for the cynical, a gesture to gain immediate goodwill or political esteem. The identity of the author of the letter to the *Times* was not, as I recall, discovered for some years.

In part, of course, Mr. Roosevelt's lot has been that of other Presidents, and particularly Democratic Presidents. Grover Cleveland came in for much sheer abuse. Theodore Roosevelt, Republican though he was, was cordially hated by big business in his trust-busting days. It is ironic that the memory of both Cleveland and Theodore Roosevelt is now invoked to shame the present President Roosevelt. Woodrow Wilson also brought down the wrath of the gods by his program of reforms; the masters of finance and industry forgave him only under the exigencies of war.

Most observers are agreed, however, that those earlier rages cannot compare with the present chant of hate. The lines to-day are more sharply drawn and there is no sign of any truce. A major war would serve of course, as it did for Wilson, to dissolve the fury. But nothing less than that would reconcile Mr. Roosevelt's enemies to his presence in the White House.

There is a much earlier historical figure with whom Mr. Roosevelt would appear to have something in common. That, as has been pointed out, is the wise Turgot who tried briefly to restore some order and reason to the France of Louis XVI. As comptroller general, he favored restricting the monopoly privileges enjoyed by certain powerful corporations. He wanted to reform the royal household and restrain the more fantastic and flagrant extravagances of the court. He succeeded in abolishing many of the artificial impediments that had been put in the way of free trade. At the same time he proposed to ameliorate the lot of the petit bourgeois and the long-suffering peasants by removing the tax on salt and other burdensome levies.

For all his wisdom, M. Turgot lasted only a little more than two years. The rich and the powerful were outraged at what this radical proposed to do. Why, he struck at the very foundation of orderly government. The arguments of the time could almost be taken from current newspaper headlines. At any rate M. Turgot was removed as comptroller general, his reforms swept into the wastebasket.

And here, perhaps, is a happy exemplar for Mr. Roosevelt. Turgot retired to his country estate where he devoted himself to peaceful study and the pleasant pursuits of leisure. He died in 1781, quietly in his bed; which was not the lot, if one recalls correctly, of those who sent him into exile.

Richard L. Neuberger

They Love

Roosevelt

Richard L. Neuberger, writing near the end of Roosevelt's second term, looked at the other extreme of the emotions Roosevelt aroused. Using the same approach as did Childs in the preceding selection— an examination of attitudes through personal interviews and quotations—Neuberger wrote of Roosevelt's overwhelming popularity among ordinary Americans rather than among the wealthy ones whom Childs discussed. He found that the President's policies were almost totally divorced in the minds of most Americans from his personal qualities and attitudes. [Richard L. Neuberger, "They Love Roosevelt," Forum, January 1939. Reprinted by permission of Current History, Inc.]

A vanquished Democratic candidate for the United States Senate looked over my shoulder as an Associated Press teletype machine jerkily recorded the Republican triumphs of the recent election. "Gosh!" moaned he, "if only the President's popularity could have carried us through!"

This remark, muttered in the bitter disappointment of defeat, describes the major political phenomenon of our time—the spectacle of a president beloved by his people, yet who is almost completely disassociated in the public mind from the candidates of his party and the policies of his administration. Although many of Mr. Roosevelt's advisers and theories of government are thoroughly unpopular, the same men and women who scoff at them admire him, with an admiration that is fervent and intense.

There seems little relationship between the standing of New Deal policies and the standing of the chief sponsor of those policies. The same straw polls that, last spring, showed government spending in high disfavor revealed an identically opposite verdict on the man who had just proposed a new spending program. There also is scant connection between the President's popularity and that of his party's candidates.

Just after the crushing "purge" setback in Maryland, a staff correspondent of the *New York Times* wrote: "Yet President Roosevelt, should he be running tomorrow for re-election, would carry the state."

A *Times* correspondent in Georgia said the President himself could sweep the State "hands down" despite the fact that his chosen candidate finished a wobbly third in a three-way contest.

It is significant that, all during the disastrous purge, the Gallup poll detected no harshening in the public attitude toward Mr. Roosevelt.

Two weeks before the November election, Dr. Gallup announced a rise in the President's standing. He was found to have the support of 59.6 per cent of the electorate, not far below the 62.5 per cent he polled in the overwhelming victory of 1936.

The *Fortune* survey, released nearly simultaneously, discovered the President at "his all-time height of public applause." The country, declared *Fortune*, is devoted to Mr. Roosevelt personally.

But these same polls indicated that numerous New Deal policies and most New Deal strategists were as unpopular as the President himself was popular—and not many days later the Republicans made substantial gains in the House and Senate and took over the capitals of eleven States.

The election left no doubt about the general estimate of many New Deal innovations. The farm program is discredited in the Middle West. The National Labor Relations Board has failed to settle the violent labor wars along the Pacific Coast. The spending spree has not restored prosperity to the industrial East. All over the nation the WPA politics of Harry Hopkins are in disrepute. Republican candidates hammered away at these policies but not at the man most responsible for them. Charles A. Sprague, the successful Republican aspirant for Oregon's governorship, minced no words about the racketeering and coercion rife in the labor situation, yet he had only kind phrases for "the great humanitarian in the White House." Even the incredible Congressman Dies, with his blanket attacks on practically every individual prominently associated with the New Deal save one, was mild to that solitary exception. "The President," said the usually raucous Mr. Dies, "has been misinformed."

This is the new strategy of Republicans and conservative Democrats alike. The politicians have sensed a tendency among the people to detach Mr. Roosevelt from any objectionable New Deal features. Ickes, Hopkins, Corcoran, Jackson, Douglas—all are fair game, but not their boss.

Even as he was in the process of being "purged" from the Democratic Party, Governor Martin of Oregon carefully distinguished between the noble leader and such "incompetent federal officials" as Miss Perkins and Secretary Ickes.

While his name was on the White House black list, Senator George of Georgia stumped his state hailing "that great and good man, Franklin D. Roosevelt." And, a few hours after the President had endorsed one of his opponents, the Senator said that the peerless chief executive had been misinformed by rascally advisers. The names of these advisers he did not want his listeners to think he was "mentioning in the same breath with that of the President."

Senator Herring of Iowa helped his colleague, Senator Gillette, decisively conquer a White House candidate and then announced that Mr. Roosevelt was more personally popular than ever in the Corn Belt.

Even the indomitable Borah, after labeling the Supreme Court "reform" plan an "evasion of the Constitution," introduced the promoter of that plan in Idaho as "our great President."

The political small talk of average Americans is conclusive proof that the country exonerates the President himself from responsibility for New Deal bungling. A few days after the recent elections, Drew Pearson and Robert S. Allen of the "Washington Merry-Go-Round" made a quick trip through six or seven States in which the Republicans had won decisive triumphs. They found the people indignantly opposed to many New Deal policies. Yet they also found that the people "blame everything on the brain trust or the cabinet or the politicians, but they still speak of Mr. Roosevelt as a man who is trying, who may make mistakes, but by and large is doing his best for the country."

This remarkable state of public opinion has so impressed itself on Frank E. Gannett, one of the President's most persistent newspaper critics, that not many weeks ago he predicted that Mr. Roosevelt would run for a third term and be re-elected. He said the President had such personal strength with the people that only he could carry the New Deal standard to another victory.

Mr. Roosevelt's vast following, it seems to me, is attributable to personal faith rather than political agreement. This explains many things. It reveals why in States where he is tremendously popular the President cannot transfer that popularity to others of his political outlook.

He went through Texas in what Robert S. Allen of the *New York Post* described as "a triumphal procession." Senator Tom Connally too, another foe of the Court plan, called him " our great President." But the

President's endorsement failed utterly to re-elect the left-wing New Dealers, Maverick and McFarlane.

To the people the New Deal appears to mean trust in a man, not a legislative program to be enacted by sympathetic congressional members. Just as the voters mentally isolate the President from his unpopular advisers, so do they isolate him from senators and representatives. That is why many Democrats elected in the sweep of 1936 have been men out of line with the New Deal; it also is why the President could carry Massachusetts by 174,103 votes at the same time that the State gave a senator hostile to the New Deal an almost identical majority; it is why the country could tell Dr. Gallup that it is 57 per cent against regulating farm prices, 58 per cent against government spending, 62 per cent for the Ludlow war referendum, 64 per cent no better off economically—and 59.6 per cent for Franklin D. Roosevelt!

To the voters with whom I have talked, the President is not the responsible head of a co-ordinated government and political party. He is simply Mr. Roosevelt, "our great President."

How else account for the fact that Pennsylvania and Ohio have just elected Republican governors, only a few short months after tumultuous welcomes from their people impelled Thomas L. Stokes, the Scripps-Howard reporter who wrote the articles indicting WPA politics in Kentucky, to say, "If the President went out deliberately to find the answer to the question, 'How'm I doing?' he should be pleased"? What else explains *Fortune's* discovery that the voters are devoted to Mr. Roosevelt—and extremely skeptical of his policies. Is there another explanation why Oregon balloted nearly three to one for the President in 1936, still supports him by 70 per cent in the Gallup poll, and yet has just rejected emphatically two referendums calling for State collaboration in New Deal power and housing programs?

When else in our history a condition parallel to this? The sins of past administrations were also the sins of presidents. But today the same people who condemn and distrust the New Deal call the man in the White House "our great President." What is the background of this political paradox?

Much has been written and said about the attitude of many wealthy Americans toward Mr. Roosevelt. Their hatred of him is a common topic. The lack of objectivity with which they view the New Deal has been widely discussed. Cartoons and jokes poke fun at the situation.

Considerably less attention has been paid to the outlook of the masses of the people. Aside from conceding their sympathy with the President, few have attempted to estimate the real nature of that sympathy. Does it stem from a general understanding of the New Deal? Is it because of the President's impressive personality? How readily can it be jolted? Will it endure if Mr. Roosevelt runs a third time?

Scarcely any president since George Washington has maintained so high a pitch of personal popularity as long as has Mr. Roosevelt. No president has survived as many prophecies of political disaster.

"The New Deal is nearly 20 months old and has shown slim results," wrote the President's future son-in-law, John Boettiger, in the *Chicago Tribune* in the autumn of 1934. "The *Literary Digest* poll announced a few days ago has shown the administration policies now receiving endorsement by only the barest majority."

That was four full years back, at the twilight of the temporary armistice between the New Deal and the conservatives. The interim has been packed with predictions of impending political doom for the President.

The bitter struggle in Congress over holding-company legislation, the threats of Dr. Townsend and Father Coughlin, the collapse of the NRA, the long succession of Supreme Court rulings hostile to the Administration, the nomination of Landon, the plan to revise the judiciary, the sit-down strikes, the charges involving Mr. Justice Black and the Klan, the "recession" in business, the defeat of the reorganization bill, the break with the Vice President, the ill-fated intrusion into the Democratic primaries, the recent Republican conquests—these and a dozen other happenings of the last four years have been hailed successively by the opposition as marking the beginning of the end for Mr. Roosevelt.

Yet he still travels on. After almost six years in the White House, his personal popularity is so great that a third term is not regarded as beyond the realm of possibility. What is the bond between President and people that has withstood political failure and economic adversity?

Out at the end of a trolley line in Cleveland, a tall motorman with graying temples told me: "I'm not much better off than I was back in thirty-three. But that's not our President's fault. He's trying to do all the good he can. He's doing his best."

And, nearly a continent away, in the hills of California, a ruddy stump-rancher assured me: "The New Deal hasn't helped me very much, but our President is for the little fellow, and I'll string along with him."

Practically the width of the country and an era in civilization separate the places where I jotted down those remarks. One was uttered by a man who runs a streetcar through a crowded metropolis; the other came from a backwoodsman far in the Western hinterlands. But both expressed the same sort of faith in the President: a belief in his sincerity and his devotion to the people and no tendency to put on him any blame for mistakes and failures. And both referred to him as "our President."

To men and women in twenty-two States—States all the way from frontier Washington to industrial Connecticut—I have put, in the past seven months, the question I asked the motorman in Cleveland and the stump-rancher in California. I have inquired not whether they are for or against the President but *how they feel about him*. In the great majority of instances, I have found the replies astonishingly similar.

The bulk of the people are for the President. They are not certain of what he is doing. About much of his program they have only vague and indefinite ideas. Confusion and misinformation are legion. But they are for him.

Scarcely one person in ten seems to have the slightest notion how the money for the PWA and WPA has been raised. Nevertheless there are plenty of complaints about such specific New Deal policies as are understood. All except outright labor partisans seem resentful of the Wagner act. The huge public debt causes almost universal fear. Interference in State elections is not approved.

But subordinating all this is the general feeling that the President's heart is in the right place, that whatever he does is with the best of intentions. Bruce Barton has thus described this feeling:

> Those men and women who have been most neglected in our American life believe they have found a friend. They say to themselves: "He cares. He is trying to do something about it."

This kind of adherence is more significant than that based on studied agreement with principles and proposals. The latter sort of support might prove to be ephemeral and easily lost on a single issue. Leadership founded on faith and trust is different. It endures many crises. And, all the way across America, only an occasional individual is found who is for Mr. Roosevelt because he has done this or done that. The others do not give specific reasons. They are for him because of a conviction that he is *their* President and will not let them down. It is a belief that will survive a lot of punishment.

Ersel Gibson, a dairy farmer in the basin of the Columbia River, says:

> Our President has made a lot of mistakes. The farm program is not working out very well for me. But I think he is doing what he honestly thinks is best for the people. That is the most important thing right now.

Rollie House is a portly Shrine potentate who pilots the Union Pacific streamliners over the Wyoming hills. Hear what he says as he looks at his watch to see if he has the *City of San Francisco* in Rawlins on time:

> Hoover rode up here in the cab the other day. He's a nice man, but Roosevelt is the President for me. I don't always think he's right, but he's doing his level best. It's not his fault things haven't picked up with the railroads.

Let Ray Morse talk for a minute. He sells insurance in Michigan, once captained his football team at college. He believes too much attention has been paid to industrial labor and not enough to the so-called white-collar worker. But for this Ray does not blame the President:

> He's fair to everybody. It's only natural for him to make some mistakes when he's trying to do so much for so many people. You can bet your last dollar he's not neglecting anyone deliberately.

These are typical specimens of the American public opinion I sampled. The talk of "economic democracy" and "making capitalism work" comes from a small, politically conscious minority and not from such average people as Rollie House and Ray Morse. The voters whom I asked about the President appeared to be for him because of a hunch that they have his sympathy. This feeling is so firmly rooted that, when these people become disillusioned about a particular governmental policy or act, they mentally separate Mr. Roosevelt from that phase of his administration.

An Indian at Celilo Falls on the Columbia River was certain the federal dam at Bonneville had destroyed the Chinook salmon runs. He blamed the army engineers. "If White Chief know, he fix."

A taxi driver in Baltimore contended the Labor Board had turned over the country to the C.I.O. "They've even double-crossed the President," he assured me, at exactly the time the newspapers were reporting that Mr. Roosevelt would reappoint one of the three Board members to another term.

The master of the Washington State Grange said the new farm bill was disastrous to the ranchers of his State. He held Secretary Wallace responsible "for deceiving the President"—and yet the President signed the bill.

A shopgirl in New York wondered why so many loafers were kept on the WPA. "Our President would do something if he ever saw those bums leaning on their shovels."

Harry Hopkins came into a State and completely messed up the Democratic political situation. A precinct captain of the Democratic Party told me he was sure Hopkins was a communist. The man wore a red, white, and blue button that blared *I Want Roosevelt Again*. I wondered if he knew that Harry Hopkins was supposed to have a standing invitation to dinner at the White House.

That these are not isolated instances is shown by the Gallup poll, which announced that only 30 per cent of the people blame Mr. Roosevelt for the business recession.

I have talked politics with some of the war veterans attacking Miss Perkins because she will not deport Harry Bridges and other radical labor leaders. Many of these veterans are strongly for the President.

Farm spokesmen disgusted with the agricultural program are still zealous Roosevelt followers.

Consider the American Federation of Labor, for example. Its executive council has unequivocally condemned Administration policies. William Green has blessed many candidates on the roster of White House enemies. But an Institute of Public Opinion survey reveals the rank and file of the A.F. of L. almost as solidly in favor of the President personally as are the members of the C.I.O.

Is this a salutary condition?

It has shocked me to talk with people who think the labor unions full of communists and who fear inflation is just around the corner, yet worship at the shrine of "our great President." It seems to indicate a complete lack of political direction when grown men and women who are militantly for Mr. Roosevelt complain that cabinet officers are deceiving him or that he is in the clutches of irresponsible advisers.

What has caused this confused thinking? The opposition to the Administration must bear much of the onus. Its hysteria over the reorganization bill was not designed to make people study issues through. Nor are Mohawk Valley formulas drafted to promote intelligent political thinking.

A country editor in Montana remarked:

No wonder the people are so blindly and personally devoted to Roosevelt. The Republicans and most of the press try so hard to bewilder them there is nothing else they can do.

But the President must shoulder some of the responsibility. Many of his economic trails have been so meandering that even learned economists lose them in the undergrowth.

From the people I have chatted with and questioned, I think Mr. Roosevelt might win a third term. In the first place, these enthusiastic adherents will be reluctant to let him retire. Secondly, theirs is the sort of faith and devotion not shaken by precedent or tradition.

One of my friends, a successful insurance man with a humble background, said to me not long ago:

My mother looks upon the President as someone so immediately concerned with her problems and difficulties that she would not be greatly surprised were he to come to her house some evening and stay to dinner. She almost regards him as one of the family.

Fidelity of this type is slow to assess blame. Jibes at Secretary Mellon used to strike President Hoover at the same time. But the arrows aimed at the machine politics of Jim Farley and the primary-election tactics of Harry Hopkins have yet to graze Mr. Roosevelt. He and his advisers move in different spheres, so far as vast sections of the people are concerned.

In a speech delivered last year the President said he had to keep faith—"faith with those who have faith in me." The extent and exclusively personal nature of that faith may result in the first attempt of an American president to win a third consecutive full term in office.

A merican policy in relation to the Second World War can be examined through three major issues: (1) intervention in Europe's affairs both before the outbreak of war in 1939 and between 1939 and 1941; (2) responsibility for our involvement in 1941; and (3) the nature of America's post-war participation in maintaining the peace.

As conditions deteriorated in Europe in the mid-1930s, a deep uneasiness possessed the American people. The world was collapsing, some nations were going berserk, brute force was replacing the rule of law. What should America's role be in the face of the irrational acts of the fascist dictators? On this question the nation split and debated. Many people believed that the United States had a duty to halt Germany and Italy before the democracies went down to destruction. As the *New York Times* put it in 1937: "We have an inescapable interest in the future of other nations. We are certain to be affected by the decisions they may

12

THE SECOND
WORLD WAR

make between democracy and dictatorship, between peace and war. We have a rich stake in their markets, in their science, in their culture. And in the long run it seems probable that we shall recognize the necessary limitations of a policy of isolation and come to accept, however gradually, the share of responsibility which falls naturally to a great world power."

The majority of Americans, however, were convinced that the fight was not theirs and that the United States must not get involved in the political affairs of the Old World. America must not repeat 1917 when, as Walter Millis wrote in 1935, "a peace-loving democracy, muddled but excited, misinformed and whipped to frenzy, embarked upon its greatest foreign war. . . ." The nation had at that time rushed in to save the Old World from the clutches of another warlord—only to find at the war's end, that the great crusade had been in vain. The New York *Nation,* in 1935, rather soberly and sadly summed up the prevailing attitude: "As a people, we have little sympathy for the inhumanity of Italian Fascism. We are shocked and indignant at Mussolini's brazen invasion of Ethiopia. But the experience of one war for what we believed to be the highest of idealistic principles has convinced us, rightly or wrongly, that the harm resulting from Il Duce's mad adventure will be slight compared with the havoc that would be wrought by another world conflict."

Inevitably, this majority view led to legislation designed to keep America out of a European war. The first law, passed in 1935, sought to prevent the United States from becoming involved by eliminating points of contact between its citizens and the belligerents. To this end, Americans were, in the event of an outbreak of war, prohibited from traveling on belligerent merchant ships, lending money to the warring nations, selling them arms and munitions, or sending their vessels into combat zones. Applauding this legislative wisdom, the New York *Nation* wrote, "The speed with which temporary neutrality legislation was rushed through Congress dramatizes the American people's abhorrence of war." On the other hand, the *New York Herald-Tribune* caustically labeled a modified version of this law passed in 1937 "an act to preserve the United States from intervention in the war of 1917–1918."

President Roosevelt himself came strongly to believe, as the '30s mounted, that America had no choice but to aid the democracies. He took every opportunity to warn the people that their security was interwoven with that of Europe and that the Western Hemisphere was not immune from the diseases infecting the Old World. In his famous "quarantine speech" in Chicago on October 5, 1937, he warned, "Let no one imagine America will escape." He then urged that the aggressor nations be quarantined to preserve the health of the international community.

The American people seemed unwilling to heed the President's admonitions. They ignored his entreaties to provide him the authority to aid the democracies. He found it extremely difficult to persuade the Congress to amend or repeal the neutrality laws so as to permit aid to be sent abroad. After the lightning German victory in Poland in September 1939, American complacency was somewhat shaken. Congress lifted the arms embargo but stipulated that the belligerents must carry the munitions away in their own vessels only after title to the cargo had passed to the buyers. It was only after the shooting war began in November 1941 that Congress did away with the neutrality statute. Similarly, after the fall of Denmark, Norway, the lowland countries, and France, in the spring and summer of 1940, Americans wished to give more aid to Britain and to the other allies. Congress approved the Lend-Lease Act in 1941, authorizing the government to furnish supplies but prohibiting American vessels from convoying the goods. This ambivalence and reluctance on the part of the American people to realize the full implications of the European war prompted the President to take steps—by executive order or executive agreement—that violated American neutrality and took the nation closer to the war. Seizing Axis merchant ships in American ports, occupying Greenland and Iceland, freezing Axis assets, convoying lend-lease goods, ordering the Navy to shoot "rattlesnakes of the sea," embargoing shipments of petroleum to Japan, standing in the path of that power's advance in Asia—these and other acts seemingly made inevitable America's participation in the war against Germany and Japan.

Whether the President was justified in taking those steps without the consent of the representatives of the people in Congress, whether he deliberately deceived the American people by planning to take them into war even while pledging to avoid war, or whether he should have kept us out of war altogether constitutes one of the most controversial issues in American history. Not nearly so controversial, but more important, was the great debate on the nature of American participation in the post-war world—if, indeed, there was to be participation. Once the war got underway and the rancor of the pre-war period was obliterated by the attack on Pearl Harbor, Americans began the discussion of the country's role in the peace that was to follow victory. It was an intense debate engaged in by the country's leading statesmen, publicists, and scholars. On the outcome of the debate hinged nothing less than the fate of the world.

Henry L. Stimson

The Illusion

of Neutrality

Of the distinguished men who joined in the great debate on America's role in the international relations of the 1930s, Walter Lippmann, Hamilton Fish Armstrong, Lewis Mumford, Sumner Welles, Cordell Hull, and William A. White were among those who believed America must act. On the other side were ranged equally sincere men: Edwin M. Borchard, William E. Borah, Charles A. Lindbergh, Burton K. Wheeler, and a host of others involved in the America-First Committee. The debate was on two levels: on the specific provisions of the neutrality laws and on a more theoretical and general plane. On the latter plane, the question boiled down to this: Is the struggle our business or is it not? Many people argued that it did not concern us, that it was a fight for power and not for democracy. Sentimental, emotional, and ideological affinities must not blind us to the true nature of the conflict. Others believed we had a duty to defend Western civilization from the barbarism of Adolf Hitler and to protect democracy from totalitarianism; they believed that if Britain went down we would be next in line. In 1935, on the eve of the outbreak of the Italo-Ethiopian War and the passage of the first neutrality act, Henry L. Stimson urged that the United States take sides. Stimson had a lengthy career of public service behind him, including four years as Secretary of State, and he was soon to enter upon another important career as Secretary of War [Henry L. Stimson, "The Illusion of Neutrality," Forum, November 1935. Reprinted by permission of Current History, Inc.]

Approaching the subject of neutrality, as I do, from the standpoint of the layman rather than the expert in international law, I find that there is a great deal of confusion and misunderstanding among our people as to its true meaning and scope.

In the first place, when the average man speaks of neutrality he often confuses it with impartiality. Of course a greater mistake could hardly be made. Effective neutrality does not mean effective impartiality. It may mean just the opposite. If the war involves a power which has control of the sea, it may mean that by remaining neutral we are in effect taking sides with that power against its opponents who do not control the sea.

Again, many people think that the doctrine of neutrality means entire isolation from the nations which are fighting. They do not realize that, on the contrary, traditional neutrality involves taking active steps to protect trade with the combatants on both sides.

Only once in our history has our government attempted to convert neutrality into isolation. Although this was done at a time when the world was a very much simpler place than now and by Thomas Jefferson, who was one of our most popular presidents and who had to a very strong degree the confidence of his people, his attempt to isolate this country from the rest of the world speedily proved unsuccessful. It produced such a violent domestic reaction as to almost disrupt our federal union, and the bitter feeling excited was ultimately in part the cause of getting us into the War of 1812.

So, when we say that the great mass of our people wishes to remain neutral, speaking with exactness we do not mean that at all. We mean only that it wishes to keep out of war—which is a very different thing. Such a statement does not solve our real problem. It is a platitude which does not get us anywhere. The real problem is to decide what methods of action will best keep us out of war. Will the method of traditional neutrality do so? If not, should something better be substituted for it?

Traditional neutrality has a powerful sentiment behind it in the hearts of our race. In Europe during medieval times, when war was a regular and customary implement for carrying out dynastic policy, the growth of the doctrine of neutrality measured the progress of humanity toward peace. Originally there had been no neutrals. "He who is not for me is against me" was a maxim customarily enforced in the Old World by anyone strong enough to do so. Gradually the doctrine of neutrality produced oases of security and peace in a world pretty generally devoted to war.

Moreover, this development of neutrality was accompanied by a development of the rules of war in the direction of humanity—such as the preservation of the lives of prisoners who originally had been regularly put to death, the protection of women and children and other noncombatants, as well as a rather rudimentary recognition of the rights of private property on land and sea. All of these changes represented steps in the direction of peace and humanity in a warlike world, and they were predicated upon the assumption that war was one of the natural and inevitable features of that world.

An important result of the doctrine of neutrality as thus developed was the assumption that war was solely the business of the two combatants. Neutral nations were not supposed to pass judgment upon the rights and wrongs of the controversy which was being fought out. If they did so, it was likely to be held that they had taken sides and thus lost their neutral rights. The idea that the rest of the world had any right to pass a judgment on the issue of an armed controversy was strongly discouraged by the very history of the neutral doctrine. And, since neutrality had been so important a factor in the restriction of war and in the development of humanitarian rights, nations were very shy about exhibiting a judicial attitude toward war which might tend to impair the value of the doctrine they so cherished.

There was another reason peculiar to our own country for our historical devotion to the doctrine of neutrality. This lay in the fact that we began our history as an infant nation during a very troubled period of the outside world. We found that our safest and manifestly wisest course lay in maintaining a strict neutrality towards the nations in Europe, in the long wars which were going on. Not only were we then very much smaller than any of the fighting nations of Europe but also by remaining neutral we were able to maintain a profitable commerce with both sides. Nevertheless, even in a world so simple in its organization as that world was then, we found great difficulty in preserving our neutrality and had to exchange vigorous blows in our effort to do so. The patriotic sentiments associated with those efforts and that time lingered on to create an additional halo around neutrality, long after the situation which gave them birth had completely changed.

Since that period of our early history there has now come the mightiest and most sudden economic and social revolution which has visited the earth during all the millions of years of man's life upon this planet. The reservoirs of power stored up in the earth during those millions of years have suddenly been tapped by man's technical skill and invention. The age of steam and electricity has arrived, and the world has suddenly become interconnected and interdependent. In this process it has developed large urban and industrial populations entirely dependent upon distant sources of food and other supplies. Civilized life has suddenly become extremely complex and extremely fragile. Industrial Europe and to a lesser extent industrial North America suddenly have been filled with huge, complicated habitations of men, women, and children, all of whom are supported by a delicate economic mechanism of life, the stoppage or impairment of which would bring millions to discomfort and poverty or even starvation.

With equal suddenness war has become immensely more destructive. Within my adult lifetime I have watched the development of the long-range, rapid-fire rifle, with its smokeless powder; the infinitely longer range, quick-firing artillery, shooting projectiles filled with an explosive so much more terrible than anything theretofore known that, when it was first invented there was a strong movement to prohibit its use in war; the bombing airplane; the commerce-destroying submarine; and the various forms of poison gas. What is worse, we have seen all these used against civil and noncombatant populations. We have seen practically an entire continent, peopled with the most advanced civilization on the earth, brought by a blockade to the very verge of starvation. War has no longer even the semblance of a joyous adventure—the sport of kings. As it was described to me in 1918 by a British officer on the grim battle-field opposite Cambrai: "War has no longer any romance. It is merely methodical homicide."

It is this revolutionary change in the fragility of our present civiliza-tion and revolutionary increase in the destructiveness of war that are changing the attitude of the world toward neutrality. In August, 1932, when in a speech before the Council on Foreign Relations, on the subject of the Pact of Paris, I first mentioned this change of attitude toward neutrality, I was taken sharply to task by some eminent international lawyers who thought I was attributing far too much potency to the new multilateral peace treaties which they believed would be of short dura-tion and effect. Those gentlemen quite misunderstood my argument. It is not the treaties which have produced the change. It is the change which is producing the treaties.

For the treaties were the result of the conviction that war had become too dangerous a thing to be dealt with by old methods. War is no longer a contest between two nations which the rest of the world can stand by and watch. War has become like a prairie fire which will spread with great rapidity and become immeasurably destructive. Therefore it is the business of the whole world to unite for the purpose, if possible, of preventing it from starting and, if it starts, of stamping it out at once. That is the attitude of the realists. The people who think they can stand aside and look at war from a distance without ultimately becoming in-volved in it are not realists but dreamers. The several multilateral treaties which followed the war; the Covenant of the League of Nations; the Nine Power Treaty relating to the Far East; the Pact of Paris; the Geneva Protocol; the Locarno treaties of 1925; the treaties to which at various times France, Poland, the Little Entente, the Balkan States, and other nations have become signatories; the Four Power Treaty; the recent conference at Stresa each represents in a different way the groping efforts of nations in Europe to secure protection by co-operation against the dangers of modern war.

At the same time it is becoming increasingly recognized that the adop-tion of any such collective action necessitates also the adoption of ma-chinery for solving peaceably situations of injustice and oppression which may exist in the world as at present organized. And so we find that, amid these gropings for collective action, there have been laid also the founda-tions for a peaceful and judicial readjustment of differences and inequal-ities. The various arbitration treaties, the World Court, the provisions in Article XIX of the League Covenant for voluntary revision and readjust-ment of agreements and treaties are the safety valves of the collective movement. Otherwise a collective system might try the impossible task of freezing into permanence a very imperfect *status quo*.

These groping efforts to establish a new and more effective resistance to war depend for their success upon the ability of mankind to learn from experience and, in this case, to learn very much more rapidly than he has been accustomed to learn. Technical skill has so rapidly outstripped wisdom and self-control that it has created an emergency in man's development which is very likely to involve him in disaster. The success of these new experiments depends upon man's powers of enlightened realism, his power to interpret developing facts, and his constructive ability to devise appropriate machinery to meet new situations. Above all, it depends upon the development in the world of an intelligent public opinion which will give to mankind the will to peace.

History shows clearly that our traditional policy of neutrality is no insurance against being drawn into a major war, especially where one of the great sea powers of the world, either in Europe or Asia, is involved. Twice in our brief national history we have been drawn into such a war. To assert our traditional neutral rights not only is not a help but is an actual threat to our peace. The profits to be enjoyed by successful neutral trade can be relied upon to tempt adventurous Americans to embark upon that trade and thereafter to seek the assistance of their government to protect them in their adventures.

But to recognize this fact is merely to scratch the surface of the problem. The real nub of that problem lies in the fact that in the modern world a nation does not have actually to be drawn into war at all in order to suffer from that war. The suffering of our farmers today arises in large part directly out of economic dislocations of the trade in foodstuffs which took place long before we entered the war. The overdevelopment of American wheat fields began as soon as the European farmers stopped farming and started fighting, and the same is true of our industrial dislocations all the way down the scale. If in 1917 we had stood aside and allowed the cause of individual freedom on the earth to go down, we should still have suffered to almost the same degree from the dislocations that now plague us and we should also have been on the way to suffer from much worse dangers from which we are now free. The world has been tied together, and, the sooner we face that fact and stop talking about self-sufficiency, the sooner we shall be ready to make intelligent progress upon this question of war.

The result of this is to indicate that it is more important to prevent war anywhere than to steer our own course after war has come. When a serious war breaks out in the world, we are likely to be gravely hurt, whatever we do. Whether we shall allow ourselves to be drawn into the actual fighting or not is then of comparatively minor importance. All we can do is consider whether the additional injury which will be done us by entering the war will offset the evils which will be done to us by some of the combatants if we do not step forward and defend ourselves against them. The theory that we can save ourselves entirely by isolation is today an economic fantasy worthy of the ostrich.

Of first importance in approaching this problem of neutrality today is to realize that it is only a subordinate problem; that the real problem is to prevent war from arising—not how to act after it has arisen. The first duty for us today is to get that central fact into the heads of our countrymen and to prevent them from relying solely upon subsequent steps which at best can do them very little good. As a medicine, our main effort should be for preventive hygiene, not subsequent surgery; war prevention, not subsequently keeping out of war. And anyone who realizes the amount of false, selfish, and misleading doctrine which is being preached in this country today on that central and fundamental fact can estimate without further argument the work which lies before us.

It is not within my province to discuss in detail the various steps which might helpfully be taken by our government, in order to co-operate with a group of our neighbor nations who were trying to restrict and terminate a war. But there are two principles of action on our attitude to which I strongly believe we should reassure the world even before such an emergency has actually arisen.

We should formally let the world know at once that, in the event of any crisis which affects or threatens the peace of the world, we shall be ready to consult with the other nations as to steps for preserving peace. Secondly, we should now make it clear to those other nations that, if in the exercise of our own independent judgment we then concur with them as to the responsibility for any breach of the peace which they may hereafter seek to terminate by collective action, we will at least refrain from any steps in protecting our neutral trade which would tend to defeat their efforts to restore peace.

Both of these steps are matters which lie wholly within the constitutional power of the American executive. Although these principles may seem to be modest in their scope, yet the world's prior knowledge that in an emergency the United States could be counted upon to act according to such principles would be at all times a powerful reassurance to the cause of peace. There is no phase of human activities where the maxim, "An ounce of prevention is worth a pound of cure," is so true as in international relations, and here our country can exercise a most effective influence toward the stabilization of an unsteady world.

At the present moment, the issues between Italy and Ethiopia are tense: troops are being moved by Italy to the borders of Ethiopia, and reports indicate that war between the two nations may be imminent. Strenuous efforts are being made by many of the nations of the world to prevent such a catastrophe. The Assembly of the League of Nations is in session. Various measures for war prevention are being discussed, and the press of the world is reporting that in these discussions sanctions are being proposed and that, in case of an actual aggressive movement by one of these countries against the other, some form of economic pressure upon the aggressor may be adopted by the nations of the League.

In the face of this situation the Congress of the United States on August 31 adopted a joint resolution attempting to provide for the neutrality of this nation in case the crisis in Ethiopia should ripen into war. This resolution provides that, upon the outbreak of war between two or more foreign states, the President shall proclaim such fact, and

it shall thereafter be unlawful to export arms, ammunition, or implements of war from any place in the United States . . . to any port of such belligerent states or to any neutral port for transshipment to, or for the use of, a belligerent country.

This provision is effective only until February 29, 1936. The resolution allows the President no power of discretion between the various belligerents, and it applies only to "arms, ammunition, or implements of war." President Roosevelt had asked Congress for broader and more flexible powers in dealing with the traffic in arms to belligerent countries. President Hoover had made the same request in 1932, when the subject was placed before the preceding Congress. Both presidents asked that the same discretion be vested in the American executive in dealing with a war between nations as for many years has been given to him in dealing with a domestic rebellion against the government of a foreign power, by the joint resolutions of March 14, 1912, and January 31, 1922. Such a domestic rebellion may often involve questions of the utmost delicacy and even present a case where, after a recognition of the belligerency of the rebels, the rules of neutrality under international law may apply; yet the President has been for over twenty years empowered by these earlier statutes with complete discretion as to whether an embargo shall be applied and a very broad discretion as to the commodities which such an embargo shall cover.

Nevertheless Congress has refused this request of President Roosevelt and has insisted instead that the prohibition shall apply to all belligerents, without any discrimination between them, and shall cover only "arms, ammunition," and "implements of war." Its action is in marked contrast to the general attitude of the American Constitution in providing for the conduct of our foreign relations. The problems which arise on the outbreak of war in the world are not uniform or static, and their details and intricacies cannot be anticipated beforehand. The American Constitution left the hands of the President very free in such matters, evidently in a wise appreciation of their complexity and constantly changing character.

Thus under the neutrality resolution of last August, not only is the President given no power to act in concert with the other nations of the world in seeking to prevent a war by putting brakes upon the aggressor who may be starting it, but the action which is provided for may be entirely ineffective in accomplishing its main purpose of keeping us from being embroiled in animosities with other nations.

Let us examine the situation and see what may be quite likely to occur: The class of supplies which under this resolution will be prevented from reaching the belligerents is comparatively narrow. It apparently does not apply to many kinds of supplies which are quite as indispensable as are arms and ammunition. The number and nature of raw materials which are essential to the manufacture of weapons, as well as to the clothing, feeding, and transport of troops, are constantly growing with each development of modern warfare. If the other nations of the world, through the League, should impose sanctions upon either Italy or Ethiopia, their prohibitions may very possibly be much broader in scope than those covered by our resolution.

What would be the result? There would at once be a great demand from the country affected for imports of supplies and material which are not forbidden by our resolution but which are forbidden by those of the other nations. The door would then be opened to a profitable trade in such supplies, and many of our citizens, anxious for the high profits thus obtainable, would try to embark in such trade. In such a case our government could be put in a most unenviable position. On the one hand the United States will be regarded by the other nations of the world as supporting the war which they are endeavoring to terminate in the interest of all mankind; on the other hand our government will be besieged by our citizens for protection in their discreditable trade. Not only may our nation come to be regarded as seeking the sordid gains to be derived from a traffic in blood, but she may get into a position somewhat similar to that of one who interferes with the action of a police force against a lawbreaker. I do not think that the great majority of our citizens want their government in any such position.

Thus the action of Congress does not bid fair to be of much help to the government in dealing with the impending crisis. In case of war it would clamp down the bars on the supply of any arms and ammunition to Italy and Ethiopia. Italy is said to be already well supplied with such arms and ammunition and would therefore not be affected or checked in case she were the aggressor. In such a case the resolution would give us no power to render any real aid in preventing the war or in checking it after it comes. And, what is ultimately even more important, if the war should prove to be an act of flagrant aggression involving a breach not only of the Covenant of the League but of our own Kellogg-Briand Treaty, it would give our government no power to join in any judgment of condemnation which might be determined upon by the nations of the rest of the world. On the contrary, it is expressly designed to prevent any such thing. In the face of the needs of the modern interdependent and war-vulnerable world which I have sought to analyze, this resolution is essentially a backward step.

There will remain, however, for our government, the powers which the executive already has under the Constitution. He can promptly use the leadership of his office to make clear to his countrymen the issue of right and wrong, if it arises, and to urge sympathy on their part with the efforts of the other nations to curb a war which has been brought upon the world by a nation in violation of its solemn pledges to us. He can refuse to use the naval force of the United States to interfere with the efforts of the other peace-seeking nations. He can announce (and, if the situation which I have pointed out arises, he should in my opinion promptly announce) that Americans who seek to trade with the aggressor nation under such conditions will do so at their own risk.

Charles A. Beard

Complicated

Moves

Of all the books written on the subject of America's entry into the Second World War, Charles A. Beard's President Roosevelt and the Coming of the War, 1941, *published in 1948, received the widest circulation and achieved the greatest immediate prominence. His thesis, in brief, was that the President deliberately led the nation to war after promising to keep it out. He plotted with Churchill to get the United States involved with Germany, and, failing that, he provoked Japan into attacking the naval base at Pearl Harbor. The book emphasizes the diabolical, the mean, the underhanded. The publicity that greeted Beard's work was prompted not only by the simplicity of the viewpoint but also by the fact that Beard was one of the best known of American historians, the author of dozens of significant works, and a trail blazer in new interpretations of important events in our history. [Reprinted by permission of Yale University Press from* President Roosevelt and the Coming of the War, 1941 *by Charles A. Beard. Copyright 1948 by Yale University Press.]*

On December 14, 1940, the American Ambassador in Tokyo, Joseph Grew, wrote a long letter to President Roosevelt on American-Japanese relations, in the course of which he said that, unless the United States was prepared to withdraw bag and baggage from the entire sphere of Greater East Asia and the South Seas, "(which God forbid), we are bound eventually to come to a head-on clash with Japan." President Roosevelt replied, January 21, 1941, "I find myself in decided agreement with your conclusions"; and went on to say that "our strategy of self-defense must be a global strategy which takes account of every front and takes advantage of every opportunity to contribute to our total security." In other words, in January, 1941, President Roosevelt envisaged a head-on clash with Japan as a phase of assistance to Great Britain in a world of inseparable spheres of interest. This conclusion squared with the conviction he had expressed to Admiral Richardson on October 8, 1940: Japan will make a mistake and we will enter the war.

Concerning the course of specific transactions in official relations between the United States and Japan from the opening at the Atlantic Conference until December 7, 1941, the American people knew little at the time. Those who read the newspapers learned from reports of the President's meetings with representatives of the press that, at the Atlantic Conference, no new commitments had been made, that the country was no closer to war, that arrangements for operations under the Lend-Lease Act had been developed, that a list of grand principles, soon known as the Atlantic Charter, expressing hopes for a better world, had been promulgated over the names of the President and the Prime Minister, and that relations with Japan were dangerously strained. From the President's quip that he and Mr. Churchill had discussed affairs in all the continents of the earth, newspaper readers possessed of the slightest imagination could conclude that affairs in the Far East had in some manner been reviewed at the Atlantic Conference.

But the American people had no official information until 1945 that Japanese affairs had come up first in the proceedings of the Atlantic Conference, that there the President made a definite commitment to Mr. Churchill's proposal for joint action in respect of Japan. It is true that after the United States had been involved in war for several months, two journalists, Forrest Davis and Ernest K. Lindley, permitted to make a "scoop" from secret information which had been conveyed to them by the White House and the State Department, published a story that approached a correct, if in many respects inadequate, account of the transactions relative to Japan at the Atlantic Conference. Yet, after all, Davis and Lindley were simply journalists whose report could be repudiated as unofficial or unreliable by any defender of the Roosevelt Administration, if their allegations made trouble for its high officials. Hence, it is proper to say that nothing like the real truth about the discussions of Japanese affairs at the Atlantic Conference in August, 1941, was revealed to the American people until December, 1945, when an official record of certain proceedings at the conference made by the Undersecretary of State, Sumner Welles, was placed among the exhibits in the documentation of the Congressional Committee on Pearl Harbor. What does the record show?

Japanese affairs, it was learned from the Welles' memoranda, were taken up by the principal parties to the Atlantic Conference on the evening of August 9, and they received close attention subsequently until agreement was reached on a program of parallel warnings to Japan. President Roosevelt rejected Mr. Churchill's proposal that he strengthen his warning to the Japanese Government by adding a declaration of his intention to seek authority from Congress to aid any power attacked by Japan in the Southwestern Pacific. But the President agreed to send a stiff note to Japan—a note in the nature of an ultimatum—after he had returned to Washington.

Although Mr. Churchill said that, as a result of the warning agreed upon, there was a reasonable chance of avoiding war in the Pacific, President Roosevelt expressed no such hope. On the contrary, he remarked that by taking this course "any further move of aggression on the part of Japan which might result in war could be held off for at least thirty days." Hence, it now appears, President Roosevelt did not think, on August 11, 1941, that the warning he was about to give to Japan would go very far in the direction of the "maintenance of peace in the Pacific."

On August 17, 1941, after his return from the Atlantic Conference, President Roosevelt called the Japanese Ambassador to the White House and told him point-blank, among other things:

> . . . this Government now finds it necessary to say to the Government of Japan that if the Japanese Government takes any further steps in pursuance of a policy or program of military domination by force or threat of force of neighboring countries, the Government of the United States will be compelled to take immediately any and all steps which it may deem necessary toward safeguarding the legitimate rights and interests of the United States and American nationals and toward insuring the safety and security of the United States.

Such was the formula of the President's warning as recorded in the State Department's *Peace and War,* published in July 1943 (p. 714).

To the Japanese Ambassador, familiar with the language of diplomacy, the statement could have had only one meaning. Although the President did not even hint that he would appeal to Congress for a declaration of war if the Japanese Government failed to heed his warning, he did indicate that if that government took any further steps in the direction of dominating neighboring countries, by force or threat of force, the United States would do something besides send another diplomatic memorandum to Tokyo.

Long historical practice justified this interpretation of his note on August 17. When on July 31, 1914, for instance, the German Ambassador in Paris asked the French Foreign Minister what France would do in case of a war between Germany and Russia, the latter replied: "France will have regard to her interests"; and that meant France would fight. When President Roosevelt informed Japan on August 17, 1941, that, in case of any more aggressive moves on her part against her neighbors, the United States would safeguard its interest, he meant that the United States would, sooner or later, take effective action to stop such moves. This interpretation of the President's intention is supported by evidence produced by the Congressional Committee on Pearl Harbor.

At a hearing of the Congressional Committee on November 23, 1945, when the former Undersecretary Welles appeared as a witness, the Assistant Counsel, Mr. Gesell, first offered as Exhibit 22, two telegrams and a draft of a proposed communication to the Japanese Ambassador brought to the State Department by Mr. Welles after the Atlantic Conference. After the documents had been put on record, Mr. Gesell asked Mr. Welles to indicate briefly his position in the State Department during the years 1940 and 1941. The following dialogue ensued:

MR. WELLES. During those years my time and attention were primarily given to relations between the United States and the other American republics and, to a considerable extent, to our relations with European governments. I had no participation in the diplomatic discussions which went on between Secretary Hull and the Japanese Government representatives and only at certain times, when the Secretary was away on a much needed vacation or was not in the Department and I had to act as Acting Secretary of State did I take any active part.

MR. GESELL. You were present, were you not, during the meeting in the Atlantic between President Roosevelt and Prime Minister Churchill?

MR. WELLES. I was.

MR. GESELL. *Did you at that time participate in any discussions between President Roosevelt and Prime Minister Churchill concerning Japan or developments in the Far East?*

MR. WELLES. *No. During the meeting at Argentia the President delegated to me the work which had to do with the drafting of the Atlantic Charter. My conversations were almost entirely taken up with talks with the British Under Secretary of State for Foreign Affairs, Alexander Cadogan, and those conversations related solely to the drafting of the Atlantic Charter text* and to one of the diplomatic negotiations, *none of which had to do with Japan.* (Italics supplied.)

MR. GESELL. Did you receive any information at that meeting as to any agreement or arrangement or understanding that had been arrived at, if there was any, between President Roosevelt and Prime Minister Churchill concerning joint action of the United States and Great Britain in the Pacific?

MR. WELLES. When I left the President, since he was due to return to Washington before myself, he told me that he had had a conversation, or several conversations, with Mr. Churchill with regard to the Japanese situation and the increasing dangers in the Far East; that Mr. Churchill had suggested to him that the two Governments, as a means which might be of some effect, should take parallel action in issuing a warning to the government of Japan.

As I recall it, the President stated that what Mr. Churchill had suggested was that the Government of the United States should state to the Government of Japan that if Japan persisted in her policy of conquest and aggression the United States, in the protection of its legitimate interests and in order to provide for its own security, would have to take such acts as were necessary in its own judgment.

The President also asked me to tell Secretary Hull that he wished to see the Japanese Ambassador immediately upon his return and that warning which had been suggested as a parallel action by Mr. Churchill was communicated to the Japanese Ambassador by the President on August 17 of that year.

MR. GESELL. Were you present at the meeting?

MR. WELLES. I was not. You mean the meeting between the President and the Japanese Ambassador?

MR. GESELL. Yes.

MR. WELLES. No.

MR. GESELL. Now, the Exhibit 22 which has just been introduced includes as the first document a document dated August 10, 1941, reading as follows:

Declaration by United States Government that:
"1. Any further encroachment by Japan in the South West Pacific would produce a situation in which the United States Government would be compelled to take counter measures even though these might lead to war between the United States and Japan.

"2. If any third Power becomes the object of aggression by Japan in consequence of such counter measures or of their support of them, the President would have the intention to seek authority from Congress to give aid to such Power."

Declaration by H. M. G.
"Same as above, mutatis mutandis, the last phrase reading:
'. . . their support of them H. M. G. would give all possible aid to such Power.'"

Declaration by Dutch Government.
"Same as that by H. M. G.
"Keep the Soviet Government informed. It will be for consideration whether they should be pressed to make a parallel declaration."

Do you recall ever having seen this document?

MR. WELLES. I do not remember having seen that document. I remember seeing the draft, however, which I took from Argentia to Washington and which is one of the exhibits itself in this collection.

MR. GESELL. Well, now, did you prepare that draft or do you know who prepared it?

MR. WELLES. As I recall it that was prepared after discussions between the President and myself the last day of the Argentia meeting.

MR. GESELL. The last paragraph of that draft reads:

"The Government of the United States, therefore, finds it necessary to state to the Government of Japan that if the Japanese Government undertakes any further steps in pursuance of the policy of military domination through force or conquest in the Pacific region upon which it has apparently embarked, the United States Government will be forced to take immediately any and all steps of whatsoever character it deems necessary in its own security notwithstanding the possibility that such further steps on its part may result in conflict between the two countries."

Was that, in essence, your understanding of the agreement between President Roosevelt and Prime Minister Churchill concerning the notice or threat which should be given to the Japanese?

MR. WELLES. That is correct.

MR. GESELL. Now, referring to Volume 2, Foreign Relations of the United States with Japan 1931–1941, where the conversations between President Roosevelt and the Japanese Ambassador on August 17, 1941 is reported.

At page 556 I find in the paragraph beginning at said page what appears to be a somewhat different statement. This is the oral statement handed by the President to the Japanese Ambassador. It reads:

"Such being the case, this Government now finds it necessary to say to the Government of Japan that if the Japanese Government takes any further steps in pursuance of a policy or program of military domination by force or threat of force of neighboring countries, the Government of the United States will be compelled to take immediately any and all steps which it may deem necessary toward safe-guarding the legitimate rights and interests of the United States and American nationals and toward insuring the safety and security of the United States."

That statement that I have just read is a somewhat watered down version of the one you brought back, is it not, Mr. Welles?

MR. WELLES. That is correct.

MR. GESELL. Is it your opinion that the statement that I have just read from Volume II is, in fact, the statement which was made at this meeting rather than the statement that you brought back?

MR. WELLES. The statement was handed by the President, I understood, to the Japanese Ambassador in writing, as an aide-mémoire, and that is the statement to which you refer.

MR. GESELL. Have you any information as to what accounted for the watering down process?

MR. WELLES. I am not informed on that point, beyond the fact that the papers I brought back were given to Secretary Hull and he discussed them with the President before the President handed them to the Ambassador.

So much for Mr. Welles' accounting to the Congressional Committee on what happened at the Atlantic Conference with regard to the warning message handed to the Japanese Ambassador on August 17, 1941. At its hearing on December 18, 1945, about three weeks after the examination of Mr. Welles, Mr. Gesell placed in the records of the Congressional Committee three documents which had been secured from the State Department. These documents, entered as Exhibits 22-B, 22-C, and 22-D, were memoranda, dated August 10–11, 1941, of conversations at the Atlantic Conference. These memoranda set down by Mr. Welles' own hand put in a curious perspective his sworn statements to the Congressional Committee in November. Either Mr. Welles' memory had been faulty on November 23, 1945, or his understanding of the English language differed from that which generally prevails among persons less experienced in diplomatic usages.

Mr. Welles, on November 23, 1945, had said "No," when asked whether he had participated in any discussions between President Roosevelt and Mr. Churchill concerning Japan or developments in the Far East. But, according to Mr Welles' memorandum for August 10, 1941, a conversation on the subject of a warning to Japan actually was held by President Roosevelt, Mr. Churchill, Sir Alexander Cadogan, and Sumner Welles at dinner on the evening of August 9. Sir Alexander made tentative drafts of proposed parallel and simultaneous declarations by the British and the United States Governments relating to Japanese policy in the Pacific, to be presented to Japan by the President and the Prime Minister at the close of the Atlantic meeting. The next day, August 10, Sir Alexander handed drafts of the proposed declarations to Mr. Welles; and on August

11, the subject was taken up at a meeting attended by the President, Mr. Churchill, Sir Alexander, Harry Hopkins, and Sumner Welles, and discussed. As a result, a general formula was agreed upon, to be finally shaped up by Sir Alexander and Mr. Welles.

Out of the conversations and arrangements at the Atlantic Conference, with Mr. Welles acting as the President's agent in draftsmanship, emerged a text or draft of a warning note to Japan. This text or draft Mr. Welles took to the State Department on his return. It represented in substance the formula upon which the President and the Prime Minister had agreed at the conference. That formula as outlined by the President at the conference had met the approval of Mr. Churchill, who said that "it had in it an element of 'face saving' for the Japanese and yet, at the same time would constitute a flat United States warning to Japan of the consequences involved in a continuation by Japan of her present course." The text or draft dated August 15, 1941, taken by Mr. Welles to the State Department was sharper than the note of August 17 delivered to the Japanese Ambassador by the President. The draft of August 15 read:

The Government of the United States, therefore, finds it necessary to state to the Government of Japan, that if the Japanese Government undertakes any further steps in pursuance of the policy of military domination through force or conquest in the Pacific region upon which it has apparently embarked, the United States Government will be forced to take immediately any and all steps of whatsoever character it deems necessary in its own security notwithstanding the possibility that such further steps on its part *may result in conflict between the two countries.*

In the memoranda made by Mr. Welles on the meetings at the Atlantic Conference it is patent that the notice given by President Roosevelt to the Japanese Ambassador on August 17, 1941, was intended to be in the nature of a war warning. It is true that in the final form given to the notice, two points brought up at the Atlantic Conference had been eliminated or softened. Mr. Churchill's suggestion that the President inform Japan that he intended to seek authority from Congress to implement his notice was rejected. Also eliminated from the draft dated August 15, 1941, were the words: "notwithstanding the possibility that such further steps on its [Japan's] part may result in conflict between the two countries"; for these words were substituted a formula more veiled, but scarcely any less meaningful to Ambassador Nomura and the Government of Japan.

Nevertheless, Secretary Hull, who was present when President Roosevelt delivered this warning to the Japanese Ambassador on August 17, 1941, refused to concede in 1946 that the President's statement implied warlike action if Japan refused to heed. In May, 1946, Senator Ferguson, as a member of the Congressional Committee on Pearl Harbor, directed a written question to Secretary Hull, inquiring whether the Japanese warlike movements between November 30 and December 6, 1941, in the Southeastern Pacific, constituted a challenge to the United States to implement the position it had taken in its note of August 17, 1941, to Japan. Secretary Hull replied in a statement that looks queer when put beside Undersecretary Welles' account of the agreement concerning action against Japan reached by President Roosevelt and Mr. Churchill at the Atlantic Conference.

Secretary Hull's statement of May, 1946, read:

The purpose of the United States in making the statement of August 17 under reference was to tell Japan *in a friendly* way that if she kept encroaching upon *our rights and interests, we would defend ourselves*. This Government at that time was acutely concerned over Japan's refusal to agree to our proposal for the neutralization of Indochina, to abandon her jumping-off place there, and otherwise to desist from the menace she was creating to us and other peace-minded nations. It *wholly misrepresents the attitude of the United States* in the period after August 17 *to allege that this Government was planning any step other than that of pure defense in the event the Japanese should attack. Other aspects* of this question, for example, where, when, and how we would resist the Japanese, *were essentially a military matter.*

While the Japanese Government was considering President Roosevelt's stern warning of August 17, with a diplomatic postulate of implementation, it was seeking to develop a proposal to the President, which, at least on its surface, looked in the direction of maintaining peace in the Pacific. Indeed, the very day that Ambassador Nomura called at the White House and received his warning, he drew from his pocket an instruction from his Government to the effect that the Prime Minister, Prince Konoye, felt strongly and earnestly about preserving peaceful relations with the United States and would be disposed to meet the President somewhere in the Pacific for the purpose of talking the matter out "in a peaceful spirit."

Subsequently, the Japanese project for a Pacific Conference was explored by exchanges of views between the two governments, over the merits of which students of diplomatic history will probably differ for years to come. These diplomatic exchanges continued for nearly two months—until the fall of the Konoye Cabinet in Tokyo on October 16, 1941. Whatever the justification for the position finally taken by President Roosevelt and Secretary Hull on the Japanese proposal, the methods they employed during this period were dilatory, and from start to finish they pursued the usual policy of secrecy. Numerous "leaks" in Washington, noncommittal releases from the Department of State, and rumors kept the American public in expectancy—and confusion. In fact, at one time, when it was openly said in newspaper circles that arrangements had been made for a meeting of President Roosevelt and Premier Konoye, this "rumor" was brushed aside humorously by the President's Secretary, Stephen Early, at the White House.

Although, during the tortuous exchanges of notes on the proposed conference in the Pacific, the American public remained in the dark with regard to the nature of the various offers and counteroffers, documents made available since December 7, 1941, have partly disclosed the nature of the tactics employed by President Roosevelt and Secretary Hull in conducting those exchanges. For example, in July, 1943, the State Department published *Peace and War, 1931–1941,* which contained many papers on relations with Japan; and in the same year it issued two bulky volumes, *Foreign Relations with Japan 1931–1941,* with a prefatory note to the effect that additional documents were to come. In 1944, Joseph Grew, former American Ambassador at Tokyo, published his *Ten Years in Japan,* which illuminated the official documents released by the State Department. Additional evidence unearthed by the Congressional Committee on Pearl Harbor amplified the accounts of the Department and Ambassador Grew.

The strategy pursued by the President and the Secretary of State during these conversations on the Japanese Premier's proposal for a peace conference in the Pacific was, in brief, as follows. The President and the Secretary expressed to Japan a willingness to consider favorably the idea of a Pacific Conference, but insisted that the Premier should first agree upon certain principles in advance, with a view to assuring the success of the conference.

The Premier of Japan, on September 6, 1941, informed the American Ambassador in Tokyo that he subscribed fully to the four great principles of American policy laid down in Washington. Then President Roosevelt and Secretary Hull declared that this was not enough, that agreement on more principles and formulas was necessary, that the replies of the Japanese Government were still unsatisfactory; but they refrained from saying in precise language just what it was they demanded in detail as fixed conditions for accepting the Japanese invitation to a conference in the Pacific. To meet their obvious distrust of Japanese authorities and especially the Japanese militarists, Premier Konoye assured them that he had authority for bringing with him to the conference high army and naval officers as evidence that his commitments would have the support of the Army and the Navy of Japan. Still the President and the Secretary continued adamant in their tactics of prolonging the conversations as if they were merely playing for time, "babying the Japanese along."

It may be said that President Roosevelt and Secretary Hull thus chose a course well within their discretion, and demonstrated wisdom in so doing. That militarists in the Japanese Government and outside had been engaged in barbaric practices in China for many years and were rattling the sabers in the autumn of 1941, was a matter of general knowledge in the United States. That the Roosevelt Administration had long been opposed to Japan's policies and measures was, at least, equally well known. Still, if keeping out of war in the Pacific was a serious issue for the United States, then the primary question for President Roosevelt and Secretary Hull was: Did the Japanese proposal offer an opportunity to effect a settlement in the Pacific and were the decisions they made in relation to it actually "looking" in the direction of peace?

Immediately pertinent to this question, and necessary to an informed judgment on it, is a report by Ambassador Grew to Secretary Hull and thus to the President, dated Tokyo, September 29, 1941, after discussions of the Japanese Conference proposal had been dragging along for more than a month. Mr. Grew had been the American Ambassador in Japan for about ten years. He was well acquainted with Japanese institutions, politics, party interests, and the bitter struggle between conciliatory citizens of Japan and the bellicose militarists. He and his secretaries were in intimate and constant touch with the Japanese Premier and Foreign Office from the beginning of the controversy over the proposed peace conference in the Pacific. To say that Mr. Grew had more first-hand knowledge about the possibilities of these negotiations looking in the direction of peace in the Pacific and about the probable outcome of a conference, if held, than did President Roosevelt and Secretary Hull is scarcely an overstatement. Hence, the advice given to them by their representative in the Japanese capital has an immediate bearing on how war came.

In his report to Washington, September 29, Ambassador Grew laid stress on the growing eagerness of the Japanese Government to bring about a peace conference with the President. He expressed the hope that "so propitious a period" be not permitted to slip by without laying a new foundation for a better order in Japan and her relations to the United States. Japan, he said, had joined the Italo-German Axis to obtain security against Russia and avoid the peril of being caught between the Soviet Union and the United States and was now attempting to get out of this dangerous position. The Ambassador considered that the time had arrived for the liberal elements to come to the top in Japan. He saw a good chance that Japan might fall into line if a program of world reconstruction could be followed as forecast by the joint declaration of President Roosevelt and Mr. Churchill at the Atlantic Conference. The United States, Mr. Grew thought, could choose one of two methods in dealing with Japan: progressive economic strangulation or constructive conciliation, "not so-called appeasement." If conciliation failed, he reasoned, the other method—coercion and war—would always be available. He believed that a failure of the United States to use the present opportunity in the interest of conciliation would result in adding to the chances of an armed conflict.

While admitting that there were risks in any course of dealings with Japan, Ambassador Grew offered "his carefully studied belief" that there would be substantial hope of preventing the Far Eastern situation from becoming worse, and perhaps of insuring "definitely constructive results, if an agreement along the lines of the preliminary discussions were brought to a head by the proposed meeting of the heads of the two Governments." The Ambassador then raised "the question whether the

United States is not now given the opportunity to halt Japan's program without war, or an immediate risk of war, and further whether, through failure to use the present opportunity, the United States will not face a greatly increased risk of war. The Ambassador stated his firm belief in an affirmative answer to these two questions." Mr. Grew conceded that certain elements in Japan or the United States might so tend to inflame public opinion in the other country as to make war unavoidable; and he recalled the cases of the *Maine* and the *Panay*. But he solicitously advised President Roosevelt and Secretary Hull to accept the offer of the Japanese Premier to discuss the situation directly, especially since the Premier had taken important steps in showing evidences of good faith.

Aware that in negotiations with the Japanese Ambassador in Washington, President Roosevelt and Secretary Hull were insisting upon further explorations of the Japanese proposal and that more than a month had passed in these "exploratory" operations, Mr. Grew warned them against this procedure. He told them that if the United States expected or awaited "clear-cut commitments" which would satisfy the United States "both as to principle and as to concrete detail," the conversations would be drawn out indefinitely and unproductively "until the Konoye cabinet and its supporting elements desiring rapprochement with the United States will come to the conclusion that the outlook for an agreement is hopeless and that the United States Government is only playing for time." In this case, the Ambassador continued, the Konoye Government would be discredited. "The logical outcome of this will be the downfall of the Konoye cabinet and the formation of a military dictatorship which will lack either the disposition or the temperament to avoid colliding head-on with the United States."

If Premier Konoye was sincere in his intentions why could he not give President Roosevelt and Secretary Hull clear-cut commitments as to details before the conference? To this central question Ambassador Grew gave serious attention and provided for the President and the Secretary an answer based on his knowledge of the critical situation in Tokyo. Mr. Grew knew that a "liberal" government in Japan, or indeed any government inclined to keep peace with the United States, was beset by the militarist and chauvinist press, always engaged in frightening and inflaming the Japanese public by warmongering. He knew also, what had recently been demonstrated many times, that the head and members of any such government were likely to be assassinated in cold blood by desperate agents of "patriotic" societies. He knew and so did Premier Konoye that Axis secret agents and Japanese enemies of peace with the United States were boring within the Konoye Government and watching with Argus eyes every message or communication sent from Tokyo to Washington. In other words, Premier Konoye could not be sure that any note he dispatched to Washington, no matter how guardedly, would escape the vigilance of his enemies on every side in Japan.

This situation Ambassador Grew went into at length in his report of

September 29, 1941, to Secretary Hull and President Roosevelt. He had been in close and confidential communication with Premier Konoye. On the basis of very intimate knowledge, he informed them that the Japanese Government was ready to undertake commitments other than those set down in the communications which had already passed. He reported, if in cautious language as befitted a diplomat, that he had been told that "Prince Konoye is in a position in direct negotiations with President Roosevelt to offer him assurances which, because of their far-reaching character, will not fail to satisfy the United States." Mr. Grew added that he could not determine the truth of this statement, but he said definitely that while the Japanese Government could not overtly renounce its relations with the Axis Powers, it "actually has shown a readiness to reduce Japan's alliance adherence to a dead letter by its indication of willingness to enter formally into negotiations with the United States."

Thereupon Mr. Grew presented the alternatives as he saw them from his point of vantage in Tokyo. The Japanese military machine and army could be discredited by wholesale military defeat. That was one alternative. On the other hand the United States could place a "reasonable amount of confidence" in

the professed sincerity of intention and good faith of Prince Konoye and his supporters to mold Japan's future policy upon the basic principles they are ready to accept and then to adopt measures which gradually but loyally implement those principles, with it understood that the United States will implement its own commitments *pari passu* with the steps which Japan takes.

This was the alternative which the American Ambassador commended to President Roosevelt and Secretary Hull as "an attempt to produce a regeneration of Japanese thought and outlook through constructive conciliation, along the lines of American efforts at present."

As to the alternatives, Mr. Grew closed his plea by inquiring "whether the better part of wisdom and of statesmanship is not to bring such efforts to a head before the force of their initial impetus is lost, leaving it impossible to overcome an opposition which the Ambassador thinks will mount inevitably and steadily in Japan." In Mr. Grew's opinion it was evidently a question of now or never, though he ended by paying deference to "the much broader field of view of President Roosevelt and Secretary Hull" as compared with "the viewpoint of the American Embassy in Tokyo."

While the negotiations over the proposed meeting between President Roosevelt and Premier Konoye were still dragging along, the Japanese Foreign Minister, Toyoda, discussed with the British Ambassador in Tokyo, Sir Robert Craigie, various problems in the then delicate relations between Japan and the United States. At the same time, he asked Ambassador Grew to speak to Ambassador Craigie and later he learned that the British and American Ambassadors had held a conference on these questions. On October 3, 1941, Minister Toyoda sent to Ambassador Nomura in Washington information respecting the Japanese-British-

American transactions in Tokyo and said to Ambassador Nomura: "Subsequently, according to absolutely unimpeachable sources, Ambassador Craigie cabled Foreign Secretary Eden and Ambassador Halifax, explaining the importance of having the United States and Japan come to an immediate agreement to hold a conference."

In a supplementary message to Ambassador Nomura, Tokyo furnished him with "the gist of Craigie's opinions" expressed in messages to Anthony Eden and Lord Halifax, with a warning to keep the information strictly secret. According to Minister Toyoda's summation, Ambassador Craigie presented the following views to his government in London and his colleague, Lord Halifax, in Washington. First, with the resignation of former Foreign Minister Yosuke Matsuoka "the chances of turning away from the Axis policy and toward the democracies, has been considerably enhanced." Second, to Japan the speeding up of the conference between President Roosevelt and Premier Konoye is important for the reason that undue delay would place the Konoye Cabinet in a precarious position owing to the opposition in Japan to a reversal of relations with the Axis. Third,

by pursuing a policy of stalling, the United States is arguing about every word and every phrase on the grounds that it is an essential preliminary to any kind of an agreement. It seems apparent that the United States does not comprehend the fact that by the nature of the Japanese and also on account of the domestic conditions in Japan, no delays can be countenanced. It would be very regrettable indeed if the best opportunity for the settlement of the Far Eastern problems since I assumed my post here, were to be lost in such a manner. . . . Both the U.S. Ambassador in Japan and I are firmly of the opinion that it would be a foolish policy if this superb opportunity is permitted to slip by assuming an unduly suspicious attitude.

Fourth, British retaliatory economic measures should be continued until "the Konoye principles actually materialize."

Nevertheless, President Roosevelt and Secretary Hull rejected the advice of their Ambassador in Japan and prolonged the "explorations" until the Konoye Cabinet fell about two weeks later, October 16, 1941. Why? Records now available provide no answer. As far as the President was concerned, the question remains open, save for such inferences as may be drawn from collateral documents. Secretary Hull's answer is to be sought in many words spread over many pages, and, owing to the fact that he was the President's agent in the conduct of foreign affairs, his answer, by inference, may be treated as that of the Administration. When Secretary Hull's prolix and involved explanations as yet presented to the American public are all analyzed, compared, and tabulated, they amount to this: The Japanese had a long record of barbaric deeds; Prince Konoye was not much better, if any, than the bloodthirsty militarists; the promises and proposals of the Konoye Government were not to be trusted as offering any hope of peace to the "peace-loving nations of the world," as represented by the United States.

If this summation is regarded as too simple, then resort may be had to Secretary Hull's own summation. Although the state of Secretary Hull's health did not permit him to undergo a cross examination by any Republican members of the Congressional Committee on Pearl Harbor during its proceedings of 1945–46, he answered in his own way certain questions formulated by Senator Ferguson and submitted to him in writing on April 5, 1946.

In Questions 71 and 72, Senator Ferguson dealt with conversations relative to the Japanese proposal for negotiations looking to the maintenance of peace in the Pacific. Senator Ferguson referred to the message of the Japanese Foreign Minister on the resumption of conversations in mid-August transmitted to Washington with a covering note by Ambassador Grew. He quoted from the Ambassador's covering note in which he urged "with all the force at his command, for the sake of avoiding the obviously growing possibility of an utterly futile war between Japan and the United States, that this Japanese proposal be not turned aside without every prayerful consideration." Senator Ferguson also reminded Secretary Hull of Ambassador Grew's words that the proposal was "unprecedented" in Japanese history, and had been made with the approval of the Emperor and the highest authority of Japan. "That is correct, is it not?" the Senator asked.

Secretary Hull replied that there was no controversy about the contents of the documents in question and then said:

The President and I, together with our Far Eastern advisors, were looking at the situation with the benefit of all the worldwide information available to us in Washington. We judged that the Japanese Government had no serious expectation of reaching an understanding at the proposed meeting [in the Pacific] unless the American Government surrendered its basic position while Japan rigidly adhered to and went forward with its policy of aggression and conquest. We had fully tested out the Japanese Government by preliminary inquiries and found it adamant in its position.

In other words, the President and Secretary Hull regarded the Japanese proposal for a Pacific Conference as essentially dishonest, as if a kind of subterfuge to deceive the Government of the United States while Japan went on with aggression and conquest.

It is at present impossible to determine the parts played by President Roosevelt and Secretary Hull respectively in the final decision to reject the Konoye proposal, as it is in the case of their action on the memorandum of November 26, 1941 (see below, p. 559). According to Premier Konoye's Memoirs (CJC, Part 20, Exhibit 173), the President was at first enthusiastic about the idea of a conference in the Pacific but Secretary Hull was at the outset cool and at length resolute in pursuing the course which, as Ambassador Grew had warned him in effect, would end in failure and war.

Nor is it possible now to discover whether, if the Pacific conference had been held, Premier Konoye could have carried out his intentions as communicated to the President and Secretary Hull. It is easy, of course, to take passages from Premier Konoye's Memoirs, and other fragmentary documents at present available, for the purpose of making an argument for or against American acceptance of his proposal; but, as Ambassador Grew informed the President and Secretary Hull at the time, the alternative of war would remain open to the United States if the conference had not fulfilled expectations. The "solution" of this insoluble "problem," however, lies outside the purposes and limitations of my inquiry (see above, p.484).

Though the Konoye Cabinet in Tokyo had been succeeded by what was regarded as a "strong" government headed by General Hideki Tojo, supposed to be an irreconcilable militarist, the Japanese did not break off conversations "looking to the maintenance of peace in the Pacific." On the contrary, the Japanese Government early in November dispatched to Ambassador Nomura two proposals for new discussions to be taken up with President Roosevelt and Secretary Hull and sent a special agent, Saburo Kurusu, to assist the Ambassador in further explorations. The first of these proposals, called proposal "A," was plainly a document for bargaining; the second, proposal "B," was more conciliatory and had the signs of being the last offer the Japanese Government might make to the United States—"a last effort to prevent something happening." Was this move on the part of Japan just another evidence of what Secretary Hull called Japanese trickery, a desire to prolong negotiations and to deceive the Government of the United States?

On their face the two proposals, as finally presented to the State Department, might have been so regarded by Secretary Hull. But as a matter of fact, having previously broken the Japanese code, American Navy and Army Intelligence had intercepted, translated, and made available to the Administration, before either of the projects had been laid before Secretary Hull, the substance of the two documents as sent in code from Tokyo to Ambassador Nomura. It had done more. It had intercepted accompanying messages from Tokyo to the Ambassador which indicated, in the first place, that the Tojo Cabinet was anxious to reach some kind of settlement with the United States; and, in the next place, that the second proposal was, to use the language of the Japanese dispatch containing it, "advanced with the idea of making a last effort to prevent something from happening." If the opinion often expressed by Secretary Hull to the effect that the Japanese were chronic liars be accepted as correct, still it is hardly to be presumed that the Japanese Government was lying to its Ambassador when, in secret messages intended for his eyes alone, it informed him that a settlement was urgently desired in Tokyo and that proposal "B" was to be offered in a last effort to prevent something from happening—that is, doubtless, an open break and war.

In short, Secretary Hull knew in advance, on November 4, 1941, that the Japanese proposals were coming to him, that the Tokyo Government had expressed to Ambassador Nomura anxiety to reach some settlement with the United States, that it had fixed November 25 as a dead line, that failure to achieve a settlement or truce meant drastic action, if not war, on the part of the Japanese Government. On November 1, Secretary Hull had asked the Army and Navy whether they were ready to give support to new warnings to Japan, and expressed the opinion that there was no use to issue any additional warnings "if we can't back them up." On November 5, General Marshall and Admiral Stark addressed to President Roosevelt a memorandum in which they strongly objected to military action against Japan at the moment and urged the postponement of hostilities in order to allow the Army and Navy as much time as possible to effect better preparations for war. It was in this state of affairs that Secretary Hull undertook to deal with Ambassador Nomura when he presented a sketch of proposal "A," November 7, 1941.

As history long ago recorded, explorations of the Japanese proposal "A" came to nothing. On the afternoon of November 7, the day Ambassador Nomura laid the proposal before Secretary Hull, the President, at a meeting of his Cabinet, took a poll on the question "whether the people would back us up in case we struck at Japan down there and what the tactics should be." The vote was a solid yea. Such are the facts as recorded by Secretary Stimson in his *Diary* for his own eyes. He also added that Secretary Hull made a good presentation of the general situation and that he narrowed it down, following steps already taken to show "what needed to be done in the future." Secretary Stimson likewise noted that "the thing would have been much stronger if the Cabinet had known—and they did not know except in the case of Hull and the President—what the Army is doing with the big bombers and *how ready we are to pitch in.*"

With reference to the conduct of foreign affairs, it is enlightening to compare the record of this Cabinet meeting as entered in Secretary Stimson's secret *Diary* with Secretary Hull's public statement describing the meeting to the Congressional Committee on Pearl Harbor in November, 1945. Mr. Hull then said that the President at the outset asked him whether he had anything on his mind and that he thereupon took about fifteen minutes in describing the dangers of the international situation. Mr. Hull stated that relations were extremely critical and that "we should be on the lookout for a military attack anywhere by Japan at any time." When he had finished, Mr. Hull continued, "the President went around the Cabinet. All concurred in my estimate of the dangers." The Cabinet agreed that some speeches should be delivered in order that "the country would, if possible, be better prepared for such a development." Four days later, November 11, 1941, Secretary Knox and Undersecretary Welles carried out the mandate. They served notice on the people of the United States. Secretary Knox called their attention to the dangers in the

Pacific; and Mr. Welles informed them that "at any moment war may be forced upon us."

It was with this matured conviction secretly maintained in the Cabinet and the notice given to the public by Secretary Knox and Mr. Welles in circulation, that Secretary Hull began to explore proposition "B" with the Japanese Ambassador and Mr. Kurusu. This Japanese proposal, slightly modified as they presented it on November 20, embraced five principal points as follows:

1. Both the Governments of Japan and the United States undertake not to make any armed advancement into any of the regions in the Southeastern Asia and the Southern Pacific area excepting the part of French Indochina where the Japanese troops are stationed at present.

2. The Japanese Government undertakes to withdraw its troops now stationed in French Indochina upon either the restoration of peace between Japan and China or the establishment of an equitable peace in the Pacific Area.

In the meantime the Government of Japan declares that it is prepared to remove its troops now stationed in the southern part of French Indochina to the northern part of the said territory upon the conclusion of the present arrangement which shall later be embodied in the final agreement.

3. The Government of Japan and the United States shall cooperate with a view to securing the acquisition of those goods and commodities which the two countries need in Netherlands East Indies.

4. The Governments of Japan and the United States mutually undertake to restore their commercial relations to those prevailing prior to the freezing of the assets.

The Government of the United States shall supply Japan a required quantity of oil.

5. The Government of the United States undertakes to refrain from such measures and actions as will be prejudicial to the endeavors for the restoration of general peace between Japan and China.

When President Roosevelt and Secretary Hull were called upon to make decisions with regard to the Japanese program for a kind of modus vivendi looking to a general settlement in the Pacific, they confronted a fateful choice and they knew it. From secret Japanese messages intercepted by the Army and Navy Intelligence, they had learned that this proposal was the final offering from the Japanese Government. They confronted the urgent appeal from General Marshall and Admiral Stark to postpone hostilities with Japan on the ground that the Army and Navy were not ready for war. Should at least a truce of some form be attempted if only to give the United States more time to prepare for war? The idea of a truce had been taken up by the President with Secretary Stimson as early as November 6, two days after the secret Japanese message on the negotiations had been intercepted. And Mr. Stimson had strongly objected to the idea.

Despite Secretary Stimson's objections, however, the President apparently decided that a truce or modus vivendi might and should be attempted; for he sent an undated note to Secretary Hull, giving his suggestions for the terms of such a temporary or preliminary adjustment with Japan. The President's note contained the following points:

6 Months

1. United States to resume economic relations—some oil and rice now—more later.
2. Japan to send no more troops to Indo-China or Manchurian border or any place South (Dutch, Brit. or Siam).
3. Japan to agree not to invoke tripartite pact even if the U.S. gets into European war.
4. U.S. to introduce Japs to Chinese to talk things over but U.S. to take no part in their conversation.

Later in Pacific agreements.

In addition to President Roosevelt's suggestions for a modus vivendi, Secretary Hull had for his consideration, in arriving at a decision, a long memorandum on the subject from his experts in the Far Eastern Division of the State Department. This document, dated November 11, 1941, contained a draft of principles and details to be applied in efforts to arrive at some kind of middle course in handling the now tense relations with Japan. The authors of the memorandum called Mr. Hull's attention to the difficulties involved in an attempt at the moment to reach a comprehensive settlement "covering the entire Pacific area," and then stated:

Such a prospect prompts the question whether it might not be possible to propose some tentative or transitional arrangement the very discussion of which might serve not only to continue the conversations pending the event of a more favorable situation, even if the proposal is not eventually agreed to, but also to provide the entering wedge toward a comprehensive settlement of the nature sought providing the proposal is accepted by Japan and provided further that China is able to obtain satisfactory terms from Japan.

While working at his reply to the "last effort" of Tokyo to reach an adjustment, Secretary Hull had, besides the President's proposals and the memorandum from the Far Eastern Division, a strong recommendation from the senior officers of the Far Eastern Division relative to a project for a Pacific settlement, not a mere truce. This recommendation from his specialists in Far Eastern affairs, dated November 19, grew out of an outline for "a proposed basis for agreement between the United States and Japan," prepared by the Secretary of the Treasury, Henry Morgenthau, Jr. It took the form of a covering note to Secretary Hull initialed by Maxwell Hamilton, Chief of the Division. Mr. Hamilton pronounced the proposal offered by the Secretary of the Treasury "the most constructive I have seen," and added that all the senior officers in his Division concurred in his judgment. Therefore, he urged Secretary Hull to give it prompt and careful consideration and suggested a conference with General Marshall and Admiral Stark on the proposal.

During this period, as the testimony, documents, and exhibits procured by the Congressional Committee on Pearl Harbor abundantly demonstrate, hectic negotiations and conversations went on in Washington, with foreign ambassadors, ministers, and special agents, as well as American citizens and members of the Cabinet bringing pressures to bear on the President and Secretary Hull—some for war and others for peace. Insiders knew that the die was about to be cast, and some outsiders knew it too. If newspapers reflected the state of popular opinion, thousands of American citizens, utterly uninformed as to the nature of the inner transactions of the Administration, were aware of an approaching crisis. If they believed Undersecretary Welles' speech of November 11, they feared that war might at any moment be "forced upon us." Those who recalled the President's peace pledges of 1940, which still stood in the record, may have hoped that he could or would, in spite of the crisis, keep the country out of war.

It was amid complicated circumstances that Secretary Hull worked at the problem raised by the Japanese proposal for a truce or modus vivendi. He knew from intercepts of secret Japanese messages, that this was regarded in Tokyo as the "last effort" on the part of the Japanese Government. Should he make a blunt reply or resort to supreme diplomatic ingenuity in an attempt to keep conversations going in the hope of peace in the Pacific or at least postponing war for a time until the American Army and Navy were better equipped to fight it? He knew that on August 17, 1941, President Roosevelt had served a warning notice on Tokyo to the effect that in case of any further Japanese encroachments on their neighbors, the United States would take steps that meant war. He knew that during all the explorations since August, the position then taken had been firmly maintained, that the war plans for coöperation with Great Britain, the Netherlands, and Australia were all predicated upon joint action against Japan if she moved southward beyond definite boundary lines. Secretary Hull was well aware that General Marshall and Admiral Stark had been and were pressing for more time in which to prepare the Army and Navy for war. Was it not for him a matter of supreme statesmanship to prevent, if humanly possible, a two-front war for the United States—a war in the Pacific as well as the "shooting war" in the Atlantic?

As far as the documentary record goes, Secretary Hull for a few days at least considered a modus vivendi with Japan desirable and feasible. From November 22 to November 26, the Secretary, in consultation with the President and the highest military authorities, worked over proposals and plans for some kind of adjustment with Japan on the basis of the Japanese note of November 20. In this connection the project was discussed with representatives of Great Britain, Australia, the Netherlands, and China. The principles of the final draft were approved by Secretary Stimson, who declared that it adequately safeguarded "American interests."

Alarmed lest the Government of the United States make something like a truce or temporary standstill with Japan, with a view to further negotiation actually looking to the maintenance of peace in the Pacific,

Chinese diplomatic and special agents, supported by powerful American interests, made a storm over the proposed modus vivendi with Japan. In this operation, they were ably led by the Chinese Ambassador, Dr. Hu Shih, a liberal, wise in the ways of the West and the East, once well marked by the dread police of the Chiang Kai-shek Government, now serving it in the United States where "liberalism" was an asset. From day to day, hour to hour, the Chinese and their agents bombarded Secretary Hull so heavily with protests against any truce with Japan that the situation in Washington became almost hysterical.

This state of affairs was later described by Secretary Hull himself. The Secretary, in a subsequent statement relative to the pressures then brought to bear on him by the Chinese, declared that Chiang Kai-shek "has sent numerous hysterical cable messages to different cabinet officers and high officials in the Government other than the State Department, and sometimes even ignoring the President, intruding into a delicate and serious situation with no real idea of what the facts are." Secretary Hull further said that "Chiang Kai-shek had his brother-in-law, located here in Washington, disseminate damaging reports at times to the press and others, apparently with no particular purpose in mind." Besieged by Chinese agents in London, Prime Minister Churchill, instead of support-ing his Ambassador in Washington, Lord Halifax, who was eager for a truce in the Pacific, intervened by sending a confusing message as if trying to support the Chinese side of the dispute with the Government of the United States.

Disturbed by the vacillations introduced by Mr. Churchill's intrusion into American affairs, Secretary Hull exclaimed that

it would have been better if, when Churchill received Chiang Kai-shek's loud protest about our negotiations here with Japan, instead of passing the protest on to us without objection on his part, thereby qualifying and virtually killing what we knew were the individual views of the British Government toward these negotiations, he had sent a strong cable back to Chiang Kai-shek telling him to brace up and fight with the same zeal as the Japanese and the Germans are displaying instead of weakening and telling the Chinese people that all of the friendly countries were now striving primarily to protect themselves and to force an agreement between China and Japan, every Chinese should understand from such a procedure that the best possible course was being pursued and that this calls for resolute fighting until the undertaking is consummated by peace negotiations which Japan in due course would be obliged to enter into with China.

In other words, while the negotiations over the Japanese proposal for a modus vivendi were proceeding, Secretary Hull was disgusted with the operations of Chinese agents. He was convinced that the tentatives of the proposal should be explored and efforts be made to reach some kind of basis for further explorations in the direction of a settlement in the Far East. He was likewise convinced that in the proceedings along this line the real interests of China could be protected by the United States, indeed advanced, until, at least, the willingness of Japan to come to decent terms could be probed to the bottom. So, at least, it seems.

But for reasons which are nowhere explicit, despite the thousands of words on the subject that appear in the Pearl Harbor documents and testimony, Secretary Hull, after consulting President Roosevelt, suddenly and completely abandoned the project and on November 26, 1941, handed the Japanese Ambassador and Mr. Kurusu, the historic memorandum which the Japanese Government treated as an ultimatum. When the Japanese representatives in Washington read the document, Mr. Kurusu assured the Secretary that the Japanese Government, after examining it, would be likely to throw up its hands. When, the next morning, Secretary Stimson asked Secretary Hull what had been done about the modus vivendi project, the Secretary replied that "he had broken the whole matter off." He then added: "I have washed my hands of it and it is now in the hands of you and Knox—the Army and the Navy."

Samuel Eliot Morison

History through

a Beard

Charles A. Beard's judgments on the events leading up to our intervention were seriously questioned by many competent historians, who replied in articles and reviews. One of the most cogent retorts was by Samuel Eliot Morison, eminent Harvard historian, biographer of Columbus, and author of many books, including a monumental multi-volumned history of the U.S. Navy in World War II. Morison dissected Beard's book not only by exposing its "error, innuendo, and misconception," but also by attacking the author's methods and frame of reference. The review is, indeed, a tour de force, *and is itself a notable contribution to the literature of the Second World War as well as to historical method. It first appeared in the August 1948 issue of* Atlantic Monthly, *in somewhat reduced form. [Copyright 1953 by Priscilla B. Morison. Reprinted from* By Land and By Sea *by Samuel Eliot Morison, by permission of Alfred A. Knopf, Inc.]*

History by Innuendo. About twenty years ago Oliver Wendell Holmes in a letter to his friend Sir Frederick Pollock had something to say about Charles A. Beard's *Economic Interpretation of the Constitution.* Beard, said Holmes, argued "that the Constitution primarily represents the triumph of the money power over democratic agrarianism and individualism. Beard . . . went into rather ignoble though most painstaking investigation of the investments of the leaders, with an innuendo even if

disclaimed. I shall believe until compelled to think otherwise that they
wanted to make a nation and invested (bet) on the belief that they would
make one, not that they wanted a powerful government because they had
invested. Belittling arguments always have a force of their own, but you
and I believe that high-mindedness is not impossible to man."

That famous book came out in 1913. The "innuendo" that Holmes
alluded to has been disclaimed by the author more than once, and his
penultimate work, *The Enduring Federalist* (1948), might have pleased
Alexander Hamilton. But his latest, *President Roosevelt and the Coming
of the War* (1948), may also be characterized as a "rather ignoble though
most painstaking investigation." It is a coldly passionate argument, posing
as objective history, to prove that Franklin D. Roosevelt planned to pull
his country into World War II shortly after it commenced, deceived the
American people into re-electing him a second time by swearing to keep
them out, plotted with Winston Churchill to provoke some incident
which he could call an "attack" by Germany; and, when Hitler refused
to fall into the trap, "maneuvered" Japan into hitting the Pacific Fleet at
Pearl Harbor. All this, it seems, for personal power. Beard could see no
menace to the United States if Hitler conquered all Europe, and Japan
took the other half of the world, suppressing liberty as they proceeded.
He had taken care of that in an earlier book, *A Foreign Policy for America* (1940).

Nobody can laugh Beard off. He is, by any standards, an important
historian and a fine man. Born in Indiana seventy-three years ago, he
went through the regular mill for professional historians, rose to be full
professor at Columbia, and taught students effectively for several years.
His *Rise of American Civilization*, which appeared twenty-odd years ago,
is still, in my opinion, the most brilliant historical survey of the American scene ever written; a delight to read; stimulating, witty, and revealing. He has been president of the American Historical Association. His
American Government and Politics has been a standard text for almost
forty years.

As a man, Beard is and should be an object of admiration. His resignation from Columbia University in 1917, as a protest against the dismissal of Professors Cattell and Dana, was a noble and a courageous
gesture. No American since John Fiske had been able to earn a living by
writing history, apart from an academic milch cow. But Charles and
Mary Beard, the forthright lady whom he had married in 1900, preferred
four-legged cows to the academic variety. They established themselves on
a hilltop farm in New Milford, Connecticut, created a successful dairy
farm, and continued to write books which have been no less profitable.
Farmer Beard has been a good neighbor and a power in his community,
while Dr. Beard has performed countless acts of kindness and encouragement to younger students, including myself. I won't pretend that I hate
to write what follows, for I enjoy controversy quite as much as does the

Sage of New Milford; but my esteem for Beard the man far outweighs my indignation with Beard the historian.

No more rugged individualist exists than Charles Austin Beard. Since his salad days he has belonged to no party and joined no sect. He takes a puckish delight in shocking the smug and the complacent; but he also enjoys letting down with a thump any group of liberals who claim him as their own. At the present moment he is the darling of the McCormick-Patterson Axis, but I doubt whether he enjoys their patronage. Beard is no joiner, his name never appears on those long letterheads that spill down the margins, and he is always one jump ahead of the professional patrioteers. On rare occasions when a Legonnaire goes after Charles, or a D.A.R. after Mary, the assailant retires howling from the scene, like a jackal that attacks a lion; for Beard keeps a blunderbuss loaded with facts and figures at his barn door.

One of the amusing if unamiable devices of Beard's historical method is an effective use of innuendo, as Holmes observed. A typical one, in *The Rise of American Civilization* (II, 83), describes how "on one occasion" during the American Civil War, "Gladstone, whose family fortune contained profits from the slave trade . . . virtually acknowledged southern Independence." Admiral Mahan, anathema to Beard, makes his bow in *A Foreign Policy for America* (p. 39) as "the son of a professor and swivel-chair tactician at West Point," who "served respectably, but without distinction, for a time in the navy," and "found an easy berth at the Naval War College." In the Roosevelt book (p. 254), referring to a constitutional opinion that he dislikes, written by the Assistant Solicitor General, Beard remarks: "Mr. Cox, with a B.A. acquired at Christ Church, Oxford, England, whose knowledge of the American Constitution may have been slighter than his knowledge of the English Constitution. . . ." Mr. Cox spent three years at Oxford as a Rhodes Scholar, after graduating from the University of Nebraska, and, for several years before his government appointment, practiced law in New York. With equal unfairness I might write: "Mr. Beard, whose favorable reception in Japan many years ago predisposed him to favor that country rather than his own in 1941."

Beard's New Jerusalem. Another trait that runs through Beard's writings is a disbelief in the Great Man. One looks in vain for any appreciation of Washington, Hamilton, Jefferson, Jackson, Clay, Webster, Lee, or Cleveland as men. Their intellectual qualities may be praised, not their moral stature. Some are treated with subtle disparagement; others appear as wan products of economic forces. In all his work I can remember but three clear, well-rounded pictures of eminent personalities: Lincoln in the *Basic History*, Theodore Roosevelt and Jonathan Edwards in the *Rise*; and even T.R. is described as a natural product of a bourgeois background. Jonathan Edwards appears to be one of Beard's few objects of admiration, and an instructive parallel might be drawn between his theology and Beard's historiography. If Charles could only have moved to Connecticut two centuries earlier, how he and Jonathan would have lambasted each other from rival pulpits!

A third constant in Beard's work is his attitude toward war and those who fight and direct wars. Since his youth, when he tried to get into the summer frolic of 1898, Beard has detested war. Consistently in his works he has ignored war, minimized its results, and derided military men. He would probably say, in defense of ignoring war, that his writings are largely on political subjects or on cultural history, in which war has a slight part; but Albert J. Beveridge could find place for the impact of the War of Independence on the federal debates of 1787–8, and could point out that some of the differences between the doctrines of Marshall and those of Jefferson were due to the fact that Marshall had been a soldier.

Now, one may share Beard's detestation of war as a barbarous survival; but one must admit that American liberty, union, and civilization would never have been unless men had been willing to fight for them. Whether well directed or not, an immense amount of American effort has gone into preparation for war, making war, and paying for war; and to leave war out of any general history of the United States, whether it be called Basic, Political, Constitutional, or Cultural, is an invasion of essential truth. Beard, aloof on his Connecticut hilltop, was unofficial high priest for the thousands of churchmen, teachers, and publicists who promoted disarmament in a world where aggressive nations were arming, and who prepared the younger generation for everything but the war that they had to fight.

The clue to Beard's inconsistencies and tergiversations is furnished by the historical method he has consciously adopted and consistently preached. This method, spread at large in several articles and books, is well known to the profession but hardly to the public, who have no reason to suspect that his standards of truth and objectivity differ from those of any other professional historian. He starts with a negative, the denial of Ranke's classic dictum to write history "as it actually happened" (*wie es eigentlich gewesen ist*). Nobody, says Beard, can do that, since history, conceived as the sum total of human activity, is so multifarious and multitudinous that nobody could possibly put it all down in writing; and if he did, nobody would read it. (Of course that is not what Ranke meant, but never mind.) The historian therefore tries to make sense out of the totality of history by selecting facts that to him are significant. Consciously or not, he selects and arranges these facts according to some "frame of reference" as to what is socially desirable for the time, place, and circumstances in which he writes. "The historian who writes history . . . performs an act of faith, as to order and movement. . . . He is thus in the position of a statesman dealing with public affairs; in writing he acts and in acting he makes choices, large or small, timid or bold, with respect to some conception of the nature of things, and the degree of his influence and immortality will depend upon the length and correctness of his forecast."

G. M. Trevelyan reminds us that "the object of history is to know and understand the past on all its sides"; but Beard will not have it so. The object of history, according to him, is to influence the present and future, in a direction that the historian considers socially desirable. The ordinary, dumb, as-it-really-happened historian admits he has some frame of reference; but he does not consciously go about polishing one up before he starts writing, nor does he reject facts that do not fit the frame. He believes that he has an obligation to keep himself on the alert for facts that will alter any tentative conclusions with which he starts. Moreover, an historian conceives it to be his main business to illuminate the past in the light of his acquired knowledge and skill; not to use the past to project the future. He may wish to influence the future, but that should not be his main preoccupation. I naturally hope, through my naval history, to help persuade the American people not to scrap their navy; but that is incidental. My real task is to tell what the navy did in World War II, mistakes and all.

History fitted to a consciously set frame, with the historian's sights set for the future, not the past, is really a kind of preaching. However noble or generous the objective set by such a writer may be, his end product could only by exception be history in any modern or reputable meaning of that word. It would ordinarily be in a class with the violent sectarian histories of past centuries, or with those in which Communist historians throw the "party line."

When Beard set himself up as preacher and prophet, he was lost as an historian. One may quote against him the lines that James Russell Lowell wrote on himself:

> *There is Lowell, who's striving Parnassus to climb*
> *With a whole bale of* isms *tied together with rhyme;*
>
> .   .   .   .   .   .
>
> *His lyre has some chords that would ring pretty well,*
> *But he'd rather by half make a drum of the shell,*
> *And rattle away till he's old as Methusalem,*
> *At the head of a march to the last new Jerusalem.*

Beard's last new Jerusalem is a socialized, collectivist state in isolation. "Does the world move, and if so, in what direction?" he asked in 1933, after both Hitler and Roosevelt were in power. "Does it move forward to some other arrangement which can be only dimly divined—a capitalist dictatorship, a proletarian dictatorship, or a collectivist democracy? The last of these is my own guess. . . ." And in an article, "The World as I Want It," which he wrote for the *Forum* in June 1934, he showed clearly that by "collectivist democracy" he meant a "workers' republic" without poverty or luxury; "a beautiful country . . . labor requited and carried on in conditions conducive to virtue." A fair vision indeed, such as his Fabian friends had dreamed of at the turn of the century.

Within two years, however, there appeared a disturbing shadow, the threat of war. While Beard was not a pacifist in the strict meaning of the term, he felt he had been sold by Woodrow Wilson and the Treaty of Versailles. Although he had time and again urged students to get behind the documents and discover the reality behind the phrase, warning them to be skeptical of "the next grand committee on public mystification," he swallowed the famous Nye Committee report complete. During the interval between world wars he actively supported disarmament and cast ridicule on the generals and admirals who opposed stripping the national defense.

"Continental Americanism." Beard realized, however, that negative criticism was not enough. Hating war, yet faced with a world where Japan and Germany were arming feverishly, he conscientiously sought a way out. And in a series of publications he presented a positive program which he believed would let America live in peace and prosperity even if the rest of the world went to hell. The United States should evacuate the Philippines, renounce all "engines of war and diplomacy," and apply its entire political thought and energy to a super New Deal directed by a super TVA, the "Standard of Life Authority." Foreign trade would be controlled by a National Trade Authority with an eventual purpose of attaining complete economic isolation. Immigration must cease, except for students and tourists; the merchant marine must be allowed to sink, and the navy be reduced to a submarine or coast-defense force.

"Continental Americanism," as Beard called this blueprint for the future, made no headway. It looked too much like that which the Chinese Empire had followed for some five hundred years, the end product of which was not alluring. It also had a disquieting resemblance to the economic autarchy practiced by Hitler. His friends wondered how a scholar of Beard's knowledge and experience could propose anything so extravagant. Perhaps the answer is that isolation breeds isolationism. In a university there is an intellectual rough-and-tumble that one lacks on a hilltop. You get more back talk even from freshmen than from milch cows.

This pacifistic super-isolationism has apparently become Beard's frame of reference for recent history. In a thoughtful letter to the *Saturday Review of Literature* (August 17, 1935), answering an article by Julian Huxley, he declared that there was an objective test for every system of economics or sociology; namely, "its continuing appropriateness for life and thought amid the remorseless changes of human affairs in time—which is the subject of historical inquiry." In other words, did the prophet make good? One would suppose that if Hitler and Tojo had not convinced Beard that a Chinese policy was inappropriate for America, the atomic bomb would. On the contrary, the whole Roosevelt book falls within that same frame. Beard is trying to show that Roosevelt dragged the nation into an unnecessary war. He is trying to revive the same masochistic state of public opinion into which he and most of the American people fell at the end of World War I. Wilson then, Roosevelt again, sold us down the river; watch out that Truman does not pick a quarrel with Russia.

Indeed, Beard is so firmly and emotionally enmeshed in this new frame of reference that he has smashed his earlier ones. Time was when history through a Beard moved with the sweep of relentless, dynamic forces. The American Revolution and the Civil War were foreordained by economics; the concept of the former as a quarrel caused by George III and his ministers "shrinks into a trifling joke"; the latter "was merely the culmination of the deep-running transformation that shifted the center of gravity in American Society. . . ." In a little book of 1936, entitled *The Devil Theory of War,* he again stressed dynamic economic-social forces, and reserved his most devastating sarcasm for the "childish" theory that "wicked politicians, perhaps shoved along by wicked bankers," marshaled innocent people into war; that the politician "is a kind of *deus ex machina* . . . making the people do things they would never think of doing otherwise."

Yet, note how the *deus* (or rather *diabolus*) *ex machina* emerges ten years later. Franklin D. Roosevelt, personally, without dynamic forces or economic interests behind him, is accused of changing the orientation of his country in *American Foreign Policy in the Making, 1932–1940* (1946) and now appears in full diabolic array, with Stimson, Hull, Knox, Stark, and Marshall as attendant imps, in *President Roosevelt and the Coming of the War* (1948).

The premise of both books is stated in the opening sentence of the second: "President Roosevelt entered the year 1941 carrying moral responsibility for his covenants with the American people to keep this nation out of war–so to conduct foreign affairs as to avoid war. Those covenants, made in the election campaign of 1940, were of two kinds. The first were the pledges of the Democratic Party. . . . The second were his personal promises. . . .

"The anti-war covenants of the Democratic Party . . . were clearcut: 'We will not participate in foreign wars, and we will not send our Army, naval or air forces to fight in foreign lands outside the Americas, except in case of attack. . . . The direction and aim of our foreign policy has been, and will continue to be, the security and defense of our own land and the maintenance of its peace.' "

This is the first time, to the writer's knowledge, that any historian has honored a party platform with the old Puritan name of "covenant." As Beard is a great stickler for semantics, the use of so solemn a word for flimsies like party platforms and campaign promises is astonishing. Yet, even if we concede that a party platform is a promise binding the candidate, all promises have implied predicates. If Farmer Beard promises to sell twenty heifers on a certain date for a certain price, it is understood that if in the meantime the heifers die or the other party goes bankrupt,

or if he dies and his widow needs the heifers for her support, the promise
no longer binds. So, political promises imply no important change of
conditions that will make their implementation contrary to the public
interest. A party platform is a party platform, not the supreme law of the
land. The presidential oath of office—that the President will, to the best
of his ability, "preserve, protect and defend the Constitution of the
United States"—must override any campaign promise. Moreover, that
platform had the saving clause: "except in case of attack." Not that that
daunts Beard! Off he goes, like Don Quixote, to prove that the Japanese
did not attack us at Pearl Harbor; F.D.R. attacked them.

Roosevelt's Foreign Policy. The main object of foreign policy is not
peace at any price, but the defense of the freedom and security to the
nation. It is clear that Beard still firmly believes that nothing that the
European Axis or Japan did or could do endangered the freedom or
security of the United States, which he holds no less dear than does any
other citizen. His argument for the faithlessness of President Roosevelt to
his "covenant" is carried out in a sort of dialectic isolationism, as if the
issue of peace or war, the most momentous the nation had to face since
1861, was merely a matter of debate and negotiation between the two ends
of Pennsylvania Avenue, Washington, D.C., with Charles A. Beard of New
Milford, Connecticut, in the role of God Almighty delivering the last
judgment. If all books on the war before 1942 but Beard's should perish
from the earth, the curious reader in the far future would have to infer
that a dim figure named Hitler was engaged in a limited sort of war to
redress the lost balance of Versailles; that Japan was a virtuous nation
pursuing its legitimate interests in Asia; and that neither threatened or
even wished to interfere with any legitimate American interest.

.Beard would answer, maybe the Nazis and Japs were devils too, but
what the hell? Adopt my Chinese foreign policy and American is safe.
Those responsible for American foreign policy naturally did not see it
that way. Unlike the Sage of New Milford they lacked the imagination to
suppose that American freedom could be defended if Japan was allowed
to bring half the world's population under her hegemony, and Hitler
controlled most of the other half.

Even his stoutest supporters will not deny that President Roosevelt
failed to take the American people into his complete confidence or that
he attempted to build up national defense without clearly indicating
what the dangers were. Secretary Stimson was evidently troubled by this
and still believes that Theodore Roosevelt by sounding the trumpet earlier and more frequently would better have prepared the people psychologically for war. Robert E. Sherwood in his book based on the Harry
Hopkins papers regrets that the President had to utter soothing phrases
in 1940 in order to be re-elected. No one can be certain whether they are
right or not. Let the reader, however, cast his mind back to 1940, or read
a few newspapers or magazines of that year, and he will recall or ascer-

tain a climate of opinion which compelled the President to do good by
stealth. The American people were still bogged down in the most pacifistic or anti-war phase of their history since 1806. Disillusion with the
results of World War I, the Nye Report, the appeasement of Hitler by
Neville Chamberlain, the Communist propaganda against an "imperialist war," and the speeches and writings of hundreds of able men, of
whom Beard was one of the best, had brought about a state of opinion
that regarded American entry into World War II as unthinkable. During
the first half of 1940 men of good will, leaders in business and the professions, journalists and crossroads philosophers, were virtually united in
the belief that the European war was "no concern of ours," that to stop
Hitler was not worth the life of one American, that the oceans were a
sure defense of the United States, and that if Hitler tried any monkey
business in South America, the American nations could stop him without
aid from anyone. The fall of France and of the Low Countries and the
expected attack on Britain shook this complacency but failed to break it.

Thus, the essential problem of the administration was to support Great
Britain (and after June 1941, Russia) as much and as far as Congress and
public opinion would permit, to build up American armed strength, and
to keep Japan quiet by diplomacy; hoping by measures "short of war" to
prevent an Axis victory or, if that did not suffice, to come into the war
prepared to win it. There is no distinction of kind, in a world at war,
between measures that a neutral takes to prevent being involved, and
measures taken to win if finally involved; only a difference of degree.
James Madison, Beard's great hero among the founding fathers, once
wrote: "The means of security can only be regulated by the means and
the danger of attack. They will, in fact, be ever determined by these rules
and by no others."

Exactly when President Roosevelt and his advisers decided that "short
of war" would not suffice may never be known. It is improbable that they
knew, themselves. As the fortunes of war fluctuated in Europe, it seemed
one day that with Lend-Lease and indirect aid Britain and Russia would
win; then would come a sudden blitz in North Africa or Crete or elsewhere that dashed Allied hopes. Under those circumstances, inconsistency
appeared between the administration's words and its deeds. It is an easy
matter to draw a brief of Rooseveltian "hypocrisy." Other great men
under similar circumstances, puzzled and baffled under myriad pressures,
have been subject to the same accusation. James Monroe published in
1797 a furious diatribe against Washington's inconsistent conduct of foreign affairs; Lincoln was accused of vacillating over the issue of secession;
Sir Edward Grey lay under the same charge in 1914; even Winston
Churchill was not so firm and consistent as he makes out in *The Second
World War.*

Appearances and Realities. Now for a few sordid details on *President
Roosevelt and the Coming of the War,* a book so full of *suppressio veri*

and *suggestio falsi* that it would take one of almost equal length to expose every error, innuendo, or misconception. The book is divided into three parts, "Appearances," "Unveiling Realities," and "Realities as Described by the Pearl Harbor Documents"; but there is a rather confusing interplay of the three, as Beard's principles of division are subjective or polemical. "Appearances" includes a good many genuine realities, and "Realities" includes the conjectures of Washington gossip columnists, articles by *Chicago Tribune* writers, and odd scraps from any sources that support Beard's thesis.

Thus, Beard taunts Roosevelt with doing nothing to help Britain until he was re-elected; but the destroyer-naval bases deal, the first "short of war" aid, was consummated on September 2, 1940. An entire chapter, "Patrols as Appearances," is vitiated by Beard's confusion of the Neutrality Patrol, set up as early as September 5, 1939, and approved by the Act of Panama on October 2, with escort-of-convoy operations; nor does he distinguish between escorting ships to occupied Iceland and escorting ships to belligerent Britain. The first Lend-Lease Act was passed by Congress March 11, 1941; Iceland was occupied by United States forces on July 7; and the navy was ordered to escort convoys to Iceland only a few days later. The first transatlantic convoy to be assisted by the U.S. Navy sailed from Halifax September 16; and until war was formally declared by Germany on the United States, the American escort dropped such convoys at a mid-ocean meeting point. The President's denials in April that the navy was escorting British ships to Britain were true and not false, as Beard contends; and the reference Beard gives on page 98, note 16, to prove the contrary proves only that the Atlantic Patrol was being augmented at the expense of the Pacific Fleet. For a neutral nation to provide armed escorts to protect ships against submarine attack was illegal according to pre-1914 conceptions of neutrality. But the elaborate structure of neutral rights and duties erected at the Hague Conventions had completely broken down by 1940. Hitler's Germany flouted the Kellogg-Briand Pact, broke the treaty against unrestricted submarine warfare on the very first day of the European war, and showed no respect for the most scrupulous neutrality observed by Denmark, Norway, and the Netherlands. Consequently the legal advisers of the Roosevelt administration very properly regarded the United States as no longer bound by pre-1914 conceptions of neutral duties.

Part II, "Unveiling Realities," affords Beard a marvelous opportunity, by quoting all manner of guesses, editorials, speeches and the like, to build up in the reader's mind an impression of frightful iniquity on the part of the administration. For instance, David Lawrence is quoted on pages 289–90 as asking a number of rhetorical questions, such as: "Why were all our battleships in harbor in Hawaii on December 7, 1941, instead of out at sea, and who in Washington gave the orders to keep them there?" But Beard never gives the answer: that they were there by Admiral Kimmel's order, in accordance with normal peacetime routine, after he had received the "war warning" message of November 27.

Again, Lawrence is quoted to the effect that Admiral Richardson protested in 1940 against concentration of ships in Pearl Harbor on the ground that it "was dangerous and offered the Japanese a chance to destroy much of the Navy at a single blow." But Beard, after combing through the Richardson testimony before the Joint Congressional Committee, is not candid enough to state that the Admiral expressly disclaimed danger as motive for his protest, which was based entirely on logistic grounds—the difficulty of supply and the deprivation of leave and liberty to naval personnel.

The "Realities as Described by the Pearl Harbor Documents" are "realities" only in the Beardian sense; namely, such selections from the multitude of available facts as fit his conscious frame of reference, to the effect that President Roosevelt was a villain and the war was unnecessary.

An important insinuation against "the management of the Congressional Committee" (probably meaning its counsel, Seth Richardson) appears in a note on page 420. The "management" is accused of leaving out of the printed record, "for reasons of its own," a letter of Admiral Stark, dated April 3, 1941, to the commanders in chief of the three United States fleets, in which Stark says: "The question of our entry into the war now seems to be *when* and not *whether.*" "Students of history" are pompously warned by Beard to be "on guard" against such omissions. The Committee, however, did print this letter, but in another place in its voluminous report: Part 33, Exhibit No. 73, p. 1357. And it also printed Stark's private letter to Kimmel on April 4, in which he says: "Something may be forced on us at any moment which would precipitate action, though I don't look for it as I can see no advantage to Mr. Hitler in forcing us into the war. . . . On the surface, at least, the Japanese situation looks a trifle easier, but just what the Oriental *really* plans, none of us can be sure." This does not, of course, fit the Beard frame of reference.

Beard concludes his handling of Stark with another unjustified sneer. "Perhaps it was for this 'indiscretion,'" he says—said indiscretion being the generous submission of his private correspondence file to the Congressional Committee—"that Admiral Stark, after services in the war for which he was awarded high honors, was cashiered by Secretary Forrestal . . ." (p. 585). Admiral Stark was never "cashiered"; the reproof by Admiral King and Secretary Forrestal, to which Beard refers, was dated almost two years prior to the Joint Congressional Committee's Report; and after that report was submitted, Admiral King withdrew his reproof. In other words, the real story is the exact converse of Beard's "reality."

As part of the case for Japanese innocence and Rooseveltian guilt, Beard adduces the American-Dutch-British staff conversations at Singapore in March 1941. It is suggested (pp. 450–1) though not directly stated, that a military agreement of the three nations to go to each other's defense if any one were attacked was an "encirclement" that justified aggression on the part of Japan. One is reminded of Buffon's *cet animal est méchant*—"this animal is wicked, he defends himself when attacked." However, the ADB Plan of the Singapore Conference was rejected by Admiral Stark and General Marshall on July 3, 1941. Whatever co-operation existed between the three powers in the disastrous Southwest Pacific campaign was improvised.

By harping on a rather unfortunate use of the word "maneuver" in the diary of Secretary Stimson (who, unlike Beard, is no expert in semantics), the author tries to prove that Japan was prodded and pushed into the attack on Pearl Harbor. Stimson, recording the Cabinet meeting of November 25, 1941, noted (p. 516) that the President predicted "we were likely to be attacked perhaps next Monday. . . . The question was how we should maneuver them into the position of firing the first shot without allowing too much danger to ourselves." Why should this caution be regarded as iniquitous? Throughout modern history Western nations in danger of war have chosen to await the first blow rather than give it. If Beard is right, American history will have to be rewritten; Captain Parker who at Lexington Green said: "Stand your ground. Don't fire unless fired upon, but if they mean to have a war let it begin here," must be called a warmonger.

Although Beard gives the chronology of the approach of war well enough, and makes accurate summaries of the voluminous notes that were exchanged, he relates so little of what the Japanese were doing as to make a distorted picture. And it is strange that an historian so identified with economic influences should almost wholly ignore the significance of oil. The assets-freezing order of July 26, 1941, which included complete stoppage of oil exports to Japan, is mentioned as a provocation without observing that it was an answer to the Japanese occupation of French Indo-China.

Again (p. 496), Roosevelt is attacked for his secrecy as to Prince Konoye's proposed personal conference in September; but Beard fails to inform his readers that the secrecy was urgently requested by the Prince Premier, because he knew that if the proposal leaked, the Tojo crowd would throw him out—which is exactly what happened. We now know from Japanese sources, published by the Joint Committee, that Konoye promised us one thing and Tojo another. That is just what Hull suspected, and that is why he urged the President not to meet Konoye, as he had originally intended to do.

Beard gives the Japanese a break by describing their proposals of November 20 as a *modus vivendi* (pp. 506 ff.). They were not that, but (as the Japanese Foreign Minister said) an ultimatum: Japan's last alternative to making war on us and the British and the Dutch. They required the United States to cease reinforcing the Philippines and to stop sending naval vessels into the South Pacific; but Japan was to be free to pour more troops into French Indo-China. The United States must unfreeze Japanese assets, restore the flow of oil and other strategic materials, and stop all aid to Chiang Kai-shek. The only thing Japan offered to do in return for these concessions, appropriate for a nation already defeated in war, was to move troops from southern Indo-China into northern Indo-China (whence she was planning to cut the Burma Road) and to evacuate that French colony after forcing China to conclude peace. Such is the proposed Japanese settlement which Beard considers fair and equitable, and the rejection of which by Hull and Roosevelt "proves" that they were bent on war at any price.

There then came the episode of the proposed *modus vivendi* which the administration decided not to present because it smelt too strongly of Munich; and the "Outline of Proposed Basis of Agreement" of November 26, 1941. This, again, is misrepresented as a deliberate stepping-up of demands to provoke Japan. Actually, as Tojo admitted at his trial, the "Outline" contained nothing more than was in the Nine-Power Treaty on China, to which Japan was a party. It was not an ultimatum, but a penultimate attempt—the final one being the President's personal appeal to the Emperor—to make a peaceful settlement. An ultimatum means a last alternative to war; but war was neither threatened nor suggested by Secretary Hull if Japan should reject this "Outline." In order to avoid war with the United States, Japan merely had to keep what she already had taken, and conquer nothing more. That is what Prince Konoye wished the Tojo government to do; but the Konoye memoirs prove that Tojo was bent on war unless the United States gave in completely.

Pearl Harbor. As for Pearl Harbor, Beard carries over from the minority report of the Joint Congressional Committee the insinuation that Washington knew all along that Japan was going to strike, and where. What Washington knew, as early as November 25, was that Japanese forces were moving southward and that something unpleasant was going to happen soon. But everyone made two grave errors in evaluating the information at hand. They believed the Japanese to be incapable of more than one major operation at a time; and they assumed Tojo's government had more sense than to arouse America by a sneak attack. Nobody in authority at Washington, civil or military, anticipated the assault on Pearl Harbor.

Perhaps the most indecent of Beard's numerous innuendoes in this book are those respecting the Roberts Commission. Secretary Stimson suggested Justice Roberts to head the Pearl Harbor Commission, not only because of his personal integrity, but because he was an experienced lawyer who had investigated the Teapot Dome scandal, and had been appointed by President Hoover. Nevertheless, Beard insinuates (p. 380) that Justice Roberts's appointment was part of a triple play to put Kimmel and Short "out," and conceal the iniquities of F.D.R. and Stimson in a cloud of dust. He creates suspicion by declaring (p. 378) that the appointment of a Justice of the Supreme Court to head an investigating commission was improper, unprecedented, and unconstitutional. That is pure nonsense. In *Hayburn's Case,* to which Beard refers, the Supreme

Court under Chief Justice Jay refused as a Court to accept the additional duty of passing on pension claims, but at the same time declared that individual justices might do it. Chief Justice Hughes served as chairman of President Taft's committee to determine postal rates to be paid by newspapers; Justice Reed and others have recently served on civil service commissions. Even if Justice Roberts were the man to accept the dishonorable role imputed to him, how could he have played it, with two generals and two admirals, one a former commander in chief of the fleet, as colleagues?

Since the discrediting of the Roberts Report is necessary for Beard's case, the Justice's testimony in the congressional investigation is also attacked. Beard's three charges against him on page 362—that he had been uninformed on vital matters, that Senator Brewster forced him to concede error on a "crucial point," and that he showed "unbecoming levity"—are not supported by the record. The point was trivial and not crucial, and the "vital matter" was not relevant to the scope of his inquiry. Justice Roberts did keep his balance and sense of humor under the badgering to which he was subjected by Senators Ferguson and Brewster, frustrating those who hoped to trap him; that seems to be what Beard regards as "unbecoming."

After all, the Roberts Commission was only concerned with the question whether the military authorities in Hawaii had shown "derelictions of duty or errors of judgment" on the basis of the information they then had; it had no competence or means to investigate the political aspects.

Beard's statement (page 604) that Admiral Kimmel was "exonerated by the Navy Board" is incorrect. Admiral King's endorsement on the report of that board, dated November 6, 1944, and without which the report is incomplete, brackets Stark with Kimmel as committing "derelictions" which were "faults of omission rather than faults of commission," indicating a "lack of superior judgment." The Roberts Commission said no more as to Kimmel, and the conduct of Stark did not come under its jurisdiction. The final report of the Joint Congressional Committee, after consuming months of time, examining hundreds of witnesses and tens of thousands of documents, found few significant facts relating to the conduct of the armed forces at Oahu that were not disclosed by the brief investigation of Justice Roberts and his four military colleagues; nor did it reach any different conclusion as to the responsibility of Kimmel and Short. The "official thesis," as Beard calls the Roberts Report, never has been "undermined," except by partisan Congressmen or so-called historians who are unwilling to face the facts fairly.

So one might continue through the book, demonstrating page after page how cleverly facts and opinions have been slected to fit the Beard "frame of reference." For it is by selection and rejection that Beard makes his effect. He never misquotes or garbles a document or quotation, he never invents (though he often insinuates) something false; he merely jumbles the multitudinous facts, opinions, surmises, and events of a very crowded and recent era into the pattern that he believes to be socially desirable. He is desperately trying to prove to the American people that they were "sold down the river" by Roosevelt, and anxious to prevent them from being tricked by Truman into a war with Russia.

In concluding, I wish long life and much happiness to Charles the Prophet and to Mary his wife, who have done so much in the past to illuminate American history. May they rise above the bitterness that has come from brooding over their lost horizon of a happy, peaceful, collectivist democracy insulated from a bad world. May Dr. Beard recast his frame of reference once again, raise his sights a little higher than the Connecticut hills, and apply his erudition, wit, and craftsmanship to writing history without innuendo, history tolerant of mistakes that men make under great stress; may he try to understand rather than to blame and to sneer, and even discover before he dies "that high-mindedness is not impossible to man."

Robert A. Taft

A Program

for Peace

Although Pearl Harbor did not destroy completely the isolationist sentiment in the United States, it was no longer a possible course of action for America after the war. The isolationist voices of the pre-war period were raised during the war only to warn that exaggerated internationalism could be as dangerous as narrow nationalism. Active participation in international affairs after the peace was accepted as inevitable.

Senator Robert A. Taft's "Program for Peace" was an important statement by a leading spokesman of the Republican Party. Long an isolationist and a powerful voice in opposing America's entry into the war, Taft reflected the degree to which isolationist sentiment diminished. It is noteworthy, however, that his support of American involvement with other nations did not go beyond safeguarding America's security and preserving the peace. [Robert A. Taft, "A Program for Peace," The New York Times Magazine, February 6, 1944. © 1944 by The New York Times Company. Reprinted by permission.]

What is the ultimate purpose of American foreign policy? Until that question is clearly thought out and fixed in our minds it is impossible to explain our past policy in time of peace, the reasons why we should go to war, or the purpose of an organization of nations after the war. To me it is clear that the purpose of foreign policy is to insure freedom for the people of the United States, and prevent invasion of this country and foreign wars which might bring destruction to our people and prevent their working out here at home the destiny of the American Republic.

The ultimate purpose of our foreign policy is not to benefit other nations by spreading democracy or the Four Freedoms throughout the world or otherwise. We desire to be good neighbors with the world. We are anxious to help other peoples, but only to the extent that this can be done without involving us in unnecessary wars or endangering the future welfare of our own people. We did not enter the present war in order to crusade throughout the world for the Atlantic Charter or the Four Freedoms. There is no intention on our part to insist on the freedom of India or, apparently, even the freedom of the Baltic states or eastern Poland. We are not fighting for democracy except for our own.

As a matter of fact, if we admit that a military crusade for an ideal, or a way of life, or a form of government, is justified against other nations, the world would be involved in perpetual turmoil. We pursued a warlike course against Germany because our people were convinced, whether rightly or wrongly, that a German victory would threaten the peace and security of the United States. Our interest in the British Empire is not in maintaining the empire, but because we feel that war between us is inconceivable and the existence of Britain as a great sea power is a strong element in preventing any attack on this country across the seas. The Good Neighbor policy and assistance to other nations throughout the world are sufficiently justified by the desirability of creating a friendly feeling for the United States among other peoples and preventing the development of hostile alliances, which, if stimulated by poverty and hardships, may lead to the development of aggressive military dictators.

Our commentators and columnists are constantly belaboring a supposed policy of isolationism, which they picture to the people as the desire of some one to withdraw entirely from any interest in world affairs. There has never been such a policy under any Administration. The traditional policy of the United States has always interested itself in international affairs: witness the Monroe Doctrine, the disarmament treaties, the Kellogg-Briand Treaty.

It is true that we have always refused to commit ourselves in advance to any nation, as an ally or otherwise, to make war under any specified circumstances. Our past policy has insisted on maintaining a free hand to deal with each international emergency as it might arise. We refused to interfere with other peoples, and particularly with their internal affairs, on the very correct ground that this was more likely to produce war than to prevent it. The refusal to enter the League of Nations was based on the theory that our association with the quarrels of Europe would be more likely to produce war than to prevent it. I never agreed that such an argument justified a refusal to join in an attempt to outlaw war.

The question we have to face today is whether conditions in the world have so changed, or may so change during the next decade, that the policy of the free hand is no longer the best method of preventing aggression against the United States. In my opinion the conditions which we face after the war are substantially different, and do require a departure from our traditional policy. I myself believe that those conditions had changed twenty-five years ago. It had become apparent then that any major war between great nations was likely to involve the rest of the world, and grow into a war which might threaten the peace and freedom of the United States. We had, therefore, acquired an interest in preventing the development of a major war. If by agreeing to join with other nations in preventing aggression we could discourage the beginning of war, or if by joining in a minor war we could prevent a world conflagration, I always thought we should have been prepared to make definite commitments in advance.

It may be pointed out that this was not the question with which we were faced in 1940 and 1941. By that time there was no way in which a world war could be prevented. We had in no way promoted or been responsible for the beginning of that war. We were asked to participate at once in the very kind of war the prevention of which is the whole purpose of a league of nations. The only question we had to face was whether a German victory or an inconclusive peace would bring about a successful attack on the United States. I myself thought that it would not; certainly not after Hitler attacked Russia. The country and the Senate were kept in ignorance of the real situation in Japan, so that I always felt that the policy of bluff which the Administration pursued in the Pacific might be successful in preventing war in that part of the world.

However, after this war the necessity of preventing the development of future wars is even more manifest. The development of air power creates two definite threats. In the first place, a sudden air attack may be made with such surprise that it conceivably may be successful as an invasion. In the second place, even if we can still defend this country successfully against invasion, air power is becoming so destructive, and will become so much more destructive, that all our cities and public works may be wiped out even while we defend a blackened land. In the third place, modern war is so expensive as to threaten our economic structure and way of life, and destroy within the freedom for which we battle throughout the world. We should not hesitate to assume any international obligations, even to use military force against aggressors, to prevent the result.

However, there have been plenty of plans in the past for preventing war, and none has been successful. It is not the will to establish perpetual peace which has been lacking. It has been the inability to devise an effective method. The attempt to impose restrictions on other peoples creates new reasons for disputes between nations and new causes for war. The form of organization must be such as to minimize these causes and make the attempt to preserve peace hopeful of success.

I am convinced that the effort to set up a single world state is utterly impractical, that it would destroy in America the very freedom which is the purpose of our foreign policy. I am further convinced that a military alliance with England, or with England and Russia, would inevitably produce a counter-alliance which in the end would make war more likely.

In effect it would destroy freedom throughout the rest of the world, and we could not destroy that freedom without in the end threatening that of the people of the United States. I do believe that a league of sovereign nations, agreeing upon a rule of law and order throughout the world has today a real chance of success. The utter destruction produced by modern war is so obvious to every people that the determination to keep the peace will be overwhelming if it can be properly organized.

The first step in any league is to write an international law by which the nations shall agree to be governed. It should prohibit any nation from making war without international sanction. It should provide a set of laws dealing with relations between nations, and provide for the submission of all disputes involving such laws to a world court. It should provide for the submission of other disputes to arbitration. The nations should agree to abide by the decisions rendered.

Most of the argument of the theorists has been on the method by which this international law shall be enforced, but the first step is to determine what the law shall be, and with what international relations it shall deal. It must be written clearly, and in accord with principles generally accepted by civilized peoples. Force will never succeed unless it is backed up by the public opinion of the world, and it is only possible to mobilize that opinion behind a law or court decision which is clear and obviously just. In the case of the prohibition amendment we saw that even within a nation laws may be so unpopular or so incapable of enforcement as to bring about violence and lawbreaking.

If we attempt to prescribe laws dealing with the internal affairs of the member nations or others, I believe it is more likely to cause wars than to prevent them. Furthermore, we must not impose on any nation obligations which seem unreasonable to those people, or obligations which we ourselves are unwilling to assume, nor should we force them to take part in disputes where they cannot see any interest whatsoever.

I suggest, therefore, that the permanent law which we write deal only with the action of nations outside of their territorial boundaries, with one exception as to limitation of armament. Temporary internal restraints may have to be imposed upon the Axis nations, but it should be understood that the time will come when they will be removed. I would prefer to build the association on the old League of Nations, although the covenant will require such extensive revisions that it may be simpler as an administrative matter to begin over again.

There should be subordinate organizations, such as a Council of Europe, a Council of America, and a Council of the Far East, with courts to consider the questions which involve those areas alone. Special laws may be written, applicable to any given area, but not applicable throughout the world. When the law has been defined, I believe all nations should enter into an obligation to join, and use economic sanctions and force if necessary, to prevent law violation which is defined as aggression and found to be aggression by an international council.

This is the respect in which we are asked to depart from our traditional policy. We will no longer have a free hand because we will have agreed to make war under circumstances found to exist by an international body in which we do not have a majority voice. I see no infringement of sovereignty in undertaking that obligation. However, I think the obligation should be carefully defined. The types of law violation constituting aggression should be clear and definite, and the method of finding the action of any nation to be aggression should be equally clear.

I do not believe a nation in one area should be called upon to furnish forces to prevent aggression in another area until the nations of that area have made every effort to settle their own problems. We certainly should not go into Europe unless we are invited to do so by a substantial majority of the people of that continent who have shown their willingness to cooperate with us when we do so. Otherwise we will not only make ourselves exceedingly unpopular but we shall probably fail in our objective.

Under the regional plan, our forces could be compared to a suburban fire department, called in only on a three-alarm fire. It would be necessary for us to maintain an army, navy and air force specially trained for operations in all parts of the world. I believe such a force need not be extraordinarily large or expensive, probably no greater than the American people will insist on maintaining in any event after the war. It will require no conscription. If adequate pay is given the men, it should be an attractive profession.

I would be inclined to oppose an international police force. If such a force were large enough to overcome the forces of every other nation, it would subject the entire world to the rule of some international body and would have the same dangers as an international state. Someone would have to be chief of police, and the executive or council which directed him, or he himself, would rule the world. If the force were a small one, merely designed to interfere with small nations, it would still be controlled predominantly by one or two powerful nations, and would always be a threat to the freedom of all smaller nations.

It would be necessary to prescribe a definite limitation of armaments for each nation, and the covenants between them must provide that they shall not exceed this limitation, and must permit inspection by the council to determine from time to time whether they are complying with their covenant. A violation of this covenant would be defined as aggression. In this one field of arms limitation it seems to me necessary for the league to interfere with action going on within the boundaries of individual nations, for I see no other way in which to prevent the competitive growth of armaments, which would certainly destroy the hope of peace.

Can such an organization as I have described succeed? Frankly, no one can be certain. Every detail must be worked out to eliminate as much friction as possible. The machinery must operate smoothly without offense to the reasonable desire of all peoples to be free and determine their own future. A league is not likely to succeed if it contains in its basic law, or in the structure of nations on which it is built, any fundamental wrong. It is not likely to succeed if peoples earnestly desiring freedom are subjected to the arbitrary rule of other nations. It is not likely to succeed unless economic arrangements are made so that every nation shall have means available to obtain necessary raw materials and pay for them.

There has been too much emphasis on the question whether we are willing to agree to use force, and too little on the basic nature of the league and the law which it is attempting to impose upon the world. There should be no rushing into a new organization. Plenty of time ought to be taken after hostilities cease to build up the foundations of peace before we attempt to place upon them a permanent structure. If we finally complete a league of nations three years after the end of the war, there will be more chance of success than if we rush into it the day after the armistice under the pressure of some emotional propaganda.

No peace organization will be a success unless the people of this country, including the men who have served abroad, are persuaded in their hearts that the organization is necessary and appropriate to maintain future freedom and peace. Those who try to force the people into an organization now, on the theory that later they may not be so agreeable to the idea, endanger the success of the whole project. I am confident that the people can be permanently persuaded. I am determined that some such effort as I have outlined shall be made.

During the Second World War, there was reason to believe that after the defeat of the Axis powers the world could look forward to a long period of peace and repose. The Grand Alliance, consisting of the United States, Great Britain, and Russia, had reached agreement in a series of notable conferences at Moscow, Teheran, and Yalta on the future of Europe and Asia. Josef Stalin, the Soviet dictator, had pledged Russia's cooperation in the post-war settlements, had renounced territorial ambitions, and had promised no interference in the domestic affairs of the nations liberated from the Nazi yoke. Most encouraging was his dissolution of the Comintern, or Communist International, in May of 1943, signaling the abandonment of this militant and aggressive Moscow-centered movement. There were, to be sure, those who were suspicious of Russia's intentions "to do as she pleases, take what she pleases, and confer with nobody," but their views were submerged in the fervor of wartime unity and the promise of a rosy future.

13

THE COLD WAR

The meeting of the three leaders of the Grand Coalition in February 1945 at Yalta, in the Russian Crimea—at which they laid final plans for the destruction of Germany and Japan and for the liberation and governance of Europe—augured well for the future. Robert Sherwood described the mood of the American delegates as "one of high exultation as they left Yalta. . . . The Russians had proved that they could be reasonable and farseeing and there wasn't any doubt in the mind of the President or of any of us that we could live with them peacefully for as far into the future as any of us could imagine."

Within a few weeks after Yalta, the Soviet Union began a course of action that was to destroy any American hopes for post-war peace and cooperation. Stalin set up a communist government in Poland in violation of his pledge at Yalta to support a broadly based democratic government, and he cast covetous eyes on other territory eastward and westward. The conference at Potsdam in the summer of 1945—designed to fix in detail the occupation of Germany—was labeled by Secretary of State Byrnes "the success that failed." It did result in substantial agreement, but Stalin and his lieutenants had revealed a disturbing disposition to unilateral action, recalcitrance, and petulance. At the meeting of the Council of Foreign Ministers in London in September, the evidence mounted that the Soviets did not wish to cooperate in Europe to maintain the peace but sought rather to achieve a position of supremacy, particularly in Eastern Europe and in the Balkans.

Americans were reluctant to accept the fact of Russian waywardness. After four years of sacrifice and bloodshed, they were not willing to face strife again so soon. Yet they could not ignore the threat to their own security that Soviet hegemony on the continent implied. Therefore, in mid-1946, when Stalin made demands on Turkey for a share in the control of the Straits and unleashed communist guerilla forces on Greece to add to the confusion of civil war in that country, the United States acted. Warships were dispatched to the eastern Mediterranean to encourage the Greek Royal government, and Turkey was urged to refuse Russia's demands.

Early in 1947, President Harry S. Truman asked Congress to go beyond moral support and do more than make a naval demonstration. He requested an appropriation of $400,000,000 to aid both nations to resist Soviet domination. Said the President, "No peace is possible unless we are willing to help free peoples to maintain their free institutions and their national integrity against aggressive movements that seek to impose upon them totalitarian regimes. I believe that it must be the policy of the United States to support free peoples who are resisting attempted subjugation by armed minorities and outside pressure."

This statement, which came to be called the Truman Doctrine, marked the beginning of the policy of containment. The logical development of this policy of containing Russia within her existing boundaries and preventing her expansion into Western Europe led to the Marshall Plan and the North Atlantic Treaty. The former was designed to bolster the economy of Europe to enable it to resist Communist ideology; the latter was calculated to enhance the military capabilities of the West to permit it to thwart Russian military penetration. As an extension of the North Atlantic Treaty idea, the United States entered into various bilateral and multilateral treaties and agreements with Asiatic nations in the early 1950s. Large-scale economic assistance was also supplied to them in the spirit of the Marshall Plan.

The overwhelming and bipartisan approval given by Congress to all these measures to contain the Soviet Union reflected the widespread support of the American people. There was, however, a sizable body of opposition to containment, and the policy came under attack from diverse sources. Some maintained that it was provocative and would lead to a war more horrible than the previous one; some considered it useless either because Europe was not worth defending or was indefensible; some believed it unrealistic because Europe really lay within Russia's sphere of influence; some viewed it as negative and lacking in dynamism.

Critics were quick to supply alternatives, and, in the decade following the enunciation of the containment policy, two other courses of action were suggested: (1) liberation and massive retaliation, and (2) disengagement. Each of these received considerable backing in the nation and was widely discussed in Congress, in the press, and in the public forum. Among the spokesmen for each cause were distinguished and respected Americans. The readings in this chapter illustrate the original idea of containment as well as the other two courses of action proposed.

None of the proposed alternatives to containment were put into practice. Massive retaliation became official policy under President Dwight D.

Eisenhower, but it was never seriously considered as a basis for action. Indeed, within a few months of the announcement, it came under attack from several leading, high-ranking military and naval officers. They claimed it put American policy in a straitjacket and prevented flexibility—that it deprived the United States of the choice of replying to a Soviet thrust by means more suitable than large-scale retaliation. Secretary Dulles himself so modified the doctrine in an article in the April 1954 issue of *Foreign Affairs* (reprinted in this chapter) that it was virtually nullified and soon lay dormant. As for the "Fortress America" concept—meaning an isolated America armed only as a protection against invasion—it was never more than a wishful dream to return to a bygone era when Washington's advice in his valedictory address could be followed without endangering the nation's existence. A few conservative Republicans and Democrats continued to pursue the will-o'-the-wisp of isolationism in new garb, but they did not make an appreciable imprint on the country. The idea of disengagement, too, fell quickly from the public view. The fear of the Soviets eventually filling the vacuum created by the removal of American troops from Germany was enough to crowd the ranks of its opponents.

Containment alone remained the policy of the United States. To ring the western boundary of the Soviet sphere with steel and be prepared to exert counterpressure at points of Soviet pressure was the course followed by both Republican President Eisenhower and his successor, Democratic President John F. Kennedy. Kennedy's first full budget presented to the second session of the Eighty-seventh Congress, in which he requested funds to cover the increase in America's military might and to provide the capability for meeting a Soviet thrust, conventional or nuclear, reflected clearly the Administration's commitment to containment.

George F. Kennan

The Sources of

Soviet Conduct

The philosopher of the policy of containment was a career diplomat in the Foreign Service of the United States, George F. Kennan. Born in 1904, he entered the Foreign Service in 1927 shortly after graduating from Princeton University. He served in various posts in Europe, including a tour as a Russian-language student in Berlin. When the United States extended diplomatic recognition to the Soviet Union in 1933, Kennan accompanied Ambassador William C. Bullitt to Moscow to open the Embassy. He served again in Moscow in 1935–1937, 1945–1946, and 1952—the latter year as ambassador. With the advent of the Republican administration in 1953, Kennan retired from the Foreign Service to devote himself to lecturing and to recording diploma-

*tic history while in residence as a professor at the Institute for Advanced
Study in Princeton, New Jersey. The product of his scholarship is
encompassed in three fine studies of the diplomatic history of the United
States:* Russia Leaves the War *(1956),* The Decision to Intervene *(1958),
and* Russia and the West Under Lenin and Stalin *(1961). These works
have won for Kennan coveted literary awards in America and recognition as a leading authority in the field. He returned to active service in
1961 when he was appointed Ambassador to Yugoslavia, but two years
later resigned to resume his career of scholarship at Princeton.*

*It was while a member of the Policy Planning Staff of the Department
of State that Kennan wrote his influential analysis of Soviet conduct and
the American response, the heart of which lies in a single sentence:
"Soviet pressure against free institutions of the Western world is something that can be contained by the adroit and vigilant application of
counterforce at a series of constantly shifting geographical and political
points." The article, reprinted below, was written early in 1947, and
appeared in* Foreign Affairs *for July of that year under the authorship of
"X." It was widely and correctly believed to be, if not an official statement of policy, at least an officially inspired one. Before very long the
author was identified as George F. Kennan.*

*The views expressed created worldwide interest. Europeans, militarily
and economically defenseless and at the mercy of the Soviet Union, accepted the statement as clear indication of America's determination to
throw her power and might halfway across the world to succor the threatened nations. For the United States, the containment policy took on the
highest significance as an expression of the maturity of a people in rising
to meet a crisis. Unlike the policy of a decade earlier, when Adolf Hitler
picked off the democracies one by one while America refused to inter-
cede, the United States now served notice on Russia that counterpressure
would be heavily exerted. [*"The Sources of Soviet Conduct" *by* "X," Foreign Affairs, *July 1947. Copyright by the Council on Foreign Relations Inc., New York.*]

The political personality of Soviet power as we know it today is the
product of ideology and circumstances: ideology inherited by the present
Soviet leaders from the movement in which they had their political
origin, and circumstances of the power which they now have exercised for
nearly three decades in Russia. There can be few tasks of psychological
analysis more difficult than to try to trace the interaction of these two
forces and the relative rôle of each in the determination of official Soviet
conduct. Yet the attempt must be made if that conduct is to be understood and effectively countered.

It is difficult to summarize the set of ideological concepts with which
the Soviet leaders came into power. Marxian ideology, in its Russian-
Communist projection, has always been in process of subtle evolution.
The materials on which it bases itself are extensive and complex. But the

outstanding features of Communist thought as it existed in 1916 may perhaps be summarized as follows: (a) that the central factor in the life of man, the factor which determines the character of public life and the "physiognomy of society," is the system by which material goods are produced and exchanged; (b) that the capitalist system of production is a nefarious one which inevitably leads to the exploitation of the working class by the capital-owning class and is incapable of developing adequately the economic resources of society or of distributing fairly the material goods produced by human labor; (c) that capitalism contains the seeds of its own destruction and must, in view of the inability of the capital-owning class to adjust itself to economic change, result eventually and inescapably in a revolutionary transfer of power to the working class; and (d) that imperialism, the final phase of capitalism, leads directly to war and revolution.

The rest may be outlined in Lenin's own words: "Unevenness of economic and political development is the inflexible law of capitalism. It follows from this that the victory of Socialism may come originally in a few capitalist countries or even in a single capitalist country. The victorious proletariat of that country, having expropriated the capitalists and having organized Socialist production at home, would rise against the remaining capitalist world, drawing to itself in the process the oppressed classes of other countries." It must be noted that there was no assumption that capitalism would perish without proletarian revolution. A final push was needed from a revolutionary proletariat movement in order to tip over the tottering structure. But it was regarded as inevitable that sooner or later that push be given.

For 50 years prior to the outbreak of the Revolution, this pattern of thought had exercised great fascination for the members of the Russian revolutionary movement. Frustrated, discontented, hopeless of finding self-expression—or too impatient to seek it—in the confining limits of the Tsarist political system, yet lacking wide popular support for their choice of bloody revolution as a means of social betterment, these revolutionists found in Marxist theory a highly convenient rationalization for their own instinctive desires. It afforded pseudo-scientific justification for their impatience, for their categoric denial of all value in the Tsarist system, for their yearning for power and revenge and for their inclination to cut corners in the pursuit of it. It is therefore no wonder that they had come to believe implicitly in the truth and soundness of the Marxian-Leninist teachings, so congenial to their own impulses and emotions. Their sincerity need not be impugned. This is a phenomenon as old as human nature itself. It has never been more aptly described than by Edward Gibbon, who wrote in "The Decline and Fall of the Roman Empire": "From enthusiasm to imposture the step is perilous and slippery; the demon of Socrates affords a memorable instance how a wise man may deceive himself, how a good man may deceive others, how the conscience may slumber in a mixed and middle state between self-illusion and voluntary fraud." And it was with this set of conceptions that the members of the Bolshevik Party entered into power.

Now it must be noted that through all the years of preparation for revolution, the attention of these men, as indeed of Marx himself, had been centered less on the future form which Socialism would take than on the necessary overthrow of rival power which, in their view, had to precede the introduction of Socialism. Their views, therefore, on the positive program to be put into effect, once power was attained, were for the most part nebulous, visionary and impractical. Beyond the national- ization of industry and the expropriation of large private capital hold- ings there was no agreed program. The treatment of the peasantry, which according to the Marxist formulation was not of the proletariat, had always been a vague spot in the pattern of Communist thought; and it remained an object of controversy and vacillation for the first ten years of Communist power.

The circumstances of the immediate post-revolution period—the ex- istence in Russia of civil war and foreign intervention, together with the obvious fact that the Communists represented only a tiny minority of the Russian people—made the establishment of dictatorial power a necessity. The experiment with "war Communism" and the abrupt attempt to eliminate private production and trade had unfortunate economic con- sequences and caused further bitterness against the new revolutionary régime. While the temporary relaxation of the effort to communize Russia, represented by the New Economic Policy, alleviated some of this economic distress and thereby served its purpose, it also made it evident that the "capitalistic sector of society" was still prepared to profit at once from any relaxation of governmental pressure, and would, if permitted to continue to exist, always constitute a powerful opposing element to the Soviet régime and a serious rival for influence in the country. Somewhat the same situation prevailed with respect to the individual peasant who, in his own small way, was also a private producer.

Lenin, had he lived, might have proved a great enough man to recon- cile these conflicting forces to the ultimate benefit of Russian society, though this is questionable. But be that as it may, Stalin, and those whom he led in the struggle for succession to Lenin's position of leader- ship, were not the men to tolerate rival political forces in the sphere of power which they coveted. Their sense of insecurity was too great. Their particular brand of fanaticism, unmodified by any of the Anglo-Saxon traditions of compromise, was too fierce and too jealous to envisage any permanent sharing of power. From the Russian-Asiatic world out of which they had emerged they carried with them a skepticism as to the possibilities of permanent and peaceful coexistence of rival forces. Easily persuaded of their own doctrinaire "rightness," they insisted on the sub- mission or destruction of all competing power. Outside of the Communist Party, Russian society was to have no rigidity. There were to be no forms of collective human activity or association which would not be dominated by the Party. No other force in Russian society was to be permitted to achieve vitality or integrity. Only the Party was to have structure. All else was to be an amorphous mass.

And within the Party the same principle was to apply. The mass of Party members might go through the motions of election, deliberation, decision and action; but in these motions they were to be animated not by their own individual wills but by the awesome breath of the Party leadership and the overbrooding presence of "the word."

Let it be stressed again that subjectively these men probably did not seek absolutism for its own sake. They doubtless believed—and found it easy to believe—that they alone knew what was good for society and that they would accomplish that good once their power was secure and un-challengeable. But in seeking that security of their own rule they were prepared to recognize no restrictions, either of God or man, on the char-acter of their methods. And until such time as that security might be achieved, they placed far down on their scale of operational priorities the comforts and happiness of the peoples entrusted to their care.

Now the outstanding circumstance concerning the Soviet régime is that down to the present day this process of political consolidation has never been completed and the men in the Kremlin have continued to be pre-dominantly absorbed with the struggle to secure and make absolute the power which they seized in November 1917. They have endeavored to secure it primarily against forces at home, within Soviet society itself. But they have also endeavored to secure it against the outside world. For ideology, as we have seen, taught them that the outside world was hostile and that it was their duty eventually to overthrow the political forces beyond their borders. The powerful hands of Russian history and tradi-tion reached up to sustain them in this feeling. Finally, their own ag-gressive intransigence with respect to the outside world began to find its own reaction; and they were soon forced, to use another Gibbonesque phrase, "to chastise the contumacy" which they themselves had provoked. It is an undeniable privilege of every man to prove himself right in the thesis that the world is his enemy; for if he reiterates it frequently enough and makes it the background of his conduct he is bound eventu-ally to be right.

Now it lies in the nature of the mental world of the Soviet leaders, as well as in the character of their ideology, that no opposition to them can be officially recognized as having any merit or justification whatsoever. Such opposition can flow, in theory, only from the hostile and incorri-gible forces of dying capitalism. As long as remnants of capitalism were officially recognized as existing in Russia, it was possible to place on them, as an internal element, part of the blame for the maintenance of a dictatorial form of society. But as these remnants were liquidated, little by little, this justification fell away; and when it was indicated officially that they had been finally destroyed, it disappeared altogether. And this fact created one of the most basic of the compulsions which came to act upon the Soviet régime: since capitalism no longer existed in Russia and since it could not be admitted that there could be serious or widespread opposition to the Kremlin springing spontaneously from the liberated masses under its authority, it became necessary to justify the retention of the dictatorship by stressing the menace of capitalism abroad.

This began at an early date. In 1924 Stalin specifically defended the retention of the "organs of suppression," meaning, among others, the army and the secret police, on the ground that "as long as there is a capitalist encirclement there will be danger of intervention with all the consequences that flow from that danger." In accordance with that theory, and from that time on, all internal opposition forces in Russia have consistently been portrayed as the agents of foreign forces of reaction antagonistic to Soviet power.

By the same token, tremendous emphasis has been placed on the original Communist thesis of a basic antagonism between the capitalist and Socialist worlds. It is clear, from many indications, that this emphasis is not founded in reality. The real facts concerning it have been confused by the existence abroad of genuine resentment provoked by Soviet philosophy and tactics and occasionally by the existence of great centers of military power, notably the Nazi régime in Germany and the Japanese Government of the late 1930's, which did indeed have aggressive designs against the Soviet Union. But there is ample evidence that the stress laid in Moscow on the menace confronting Soviet society from the world outside its borders is founded not in the realities of foreign antagonism but in the necessity of explaining away the maintenance of dictatorial authority at home.

Now the maintenance of this pattern of Soviet power, namely, the pursuit of unlimited authority domestically, accompanied by the cultivation of the semi-myth of implacable foreign hostility, has gone far to shape the actual machinery of Soviet power as we know it today. Internal organs of administration which did not serve this purpose withered on the vine. Organs which did serve this purpose became vastly swollen. The security of Soviet power came to rest on the iron discipline of the Party, on the severity and ubiquity of the secret police, and on the uncompromising economic monopolism of the state. The "organs of suppression," in which the Soviet leaders had sought security from rival forces, became in large measure the masters of those whom they were designed to serve. Today the major part of the structure of Soviet power is committed to the perfection of the dictatorship and to the maintenance of the concept of Russia as in a state of siege, with the enemy lowering beyond the walls. And the millions of human beings who form that part of the structure of power must defend at all costs this concept of Russia's position, for without it they are themselves superfluous.

As things stand today, the rulers can no longer dream of parting with these organs of suppression. The quest for absolute power, pursued now for nearly three decades with a ruthlessness unparalleled (in scope at least) in modern times, has again produced internally, as it did externally, its own reaction. The excesses of the police apparatus have fanned the potential opposition to the régime into something far greater and more dangerous than it could have been before those excesses began.

But least of all can the rulers dispense with the fiction by which the maintenance of dictatorial power has been defended. For this fiction has been canonized in Soviet philosophy by the excesses already committed in its name; and it is now anchored in the Soviet structure of thought by bonds far greater than those of mere ideology.

So much for the historical background. What does it spell in terms of the political personality of Soviet power as we know it today?

Of the original ideology, nothing has been officially junked. Belief is maintained in the basic badness of capitalism, in the inevitability of its destruction, in the obligation of the proletariat to assist in that destruction and to take power into its own hands. But stress has come to be laid primarily on those concepts which relate most specifically to the Soviet régime itself: to its position as the sole truly Socialist régime in a dark and misguided world, and to the relationships of power within it.

The first of these concepts is that of the innate antagonism between capitalism and Socialism. We have seen how deeply that concept has become imbedded in foundations of Soviet power. It has profound implications for Russia's conduct as a member of international society. It means that there can never be on Moscow's side any sincere assumption of a community of aims between the Soviet Union and powers which are regarded as capitalist. It must invariably be assumed in Moscow that the aims of the capitalist world are antagonistic to the Soviet régime, and therefore to the interests of the peoples it controls. If the Soviet Government occasionally sets its signature to documents which would indicate the contrary, this is to be regarded as a tactical manoeuvre permissible in dealing with the enemy (who is without honor) and should be taken in the spirit of *caveat emptor*. Basically, the antagonism remains. It is postulated. And from it flow many of the phenomena which we find disturbing in the Kremlin's conduct of foreign policy: the secretiveness, the lack of frankness, the duplicity, the wary suspiciousness, and the basic unfriendliness of purpose. These phenomena are there to stay, for the foreseeable future. There can be variations of degree and of emphasis. When there is something the Russians want from us, one or the other of these features of their policy may be thrust temporarily into the background; and when that happens there will always be Americans who will leap forward with gleeful announcements that "the Russians have changed," and some who will even try to take credit for having brought about such "changes." But we should not be misled by tactical manoeuvres. These characteristics of Soviet policy, like the postulate from which they flow, are basic to the internal nature of Soviet power, and will be with us, whether in the foreground or the background, until the internal nature of Soviet power is changed.

This means that we are going to continue for a long time to find the Russians difficult to deal with. It does not mean that they should be considered as embarked upon a do-or-die program to overthrow our society by a given date. The theory of the inevitability of the eventual fall of capitalism has the fortunate connotation that there is no hurry about it. The forces of progress can take their time in preparing the final *coup de grâce*. Meanwhile, what is vital is that the "Socialist fatherland"—that oasis of power which has been already won for Socialism in the person of the Soviet Union—should be cherished and defended by all good Communists at home and abroad, its fortunes promoted, its enemies badgered and confounded. The promotion of premature, "adventuristic" revolutionary projects abroad which might embarrass Soviet power in any way would be an inexcusable, even a counter-revolutionary act. The cause of Socialism is the support and promotion of Soviet power, as defined in Moscow.

This brings us to the second of the concepts important to contemporary Soviet outlook. That is the infallibility of the Kremlin. The Soviet concept of power, which permits no focal points of organization outside the Party itself, requires that the Party leadership remain in theory the sole repository of truth. For if truth were to be found elsewhere, there would be justification for its expression in organized activity. But it is precisely that which the Kremlin cannot and will not permit.

The leadership of the Communist Party is therefore always right, and has been always right ever since in 1929 Stalin formalized his personal power by announcing that decisions of the Politburo were being taken unanimously.

On the principle of infallibility there rests the iron discipline of the Communist Party. In fact, the two concepts are mutually self-supporting. Perfect discipline requires recognition of infallibility. Infallibility requires the observance of discipline. And the two together go far to determine the behaviorism of the entire Soviet apparatus of power. But their effect cannot be understood unless a third factor be taken into account: namely, the fact that the leadership is at liberty to put forward for tactical purposes any particular thesis which it finds useful to the cause at any particular moment and to require the faithful and unquestioning acceptance of that thesis by the members of the movement as a whole. This means that truth is not a constant but is actually created, for all intents and purposes, by the Soviet leaders themselves. It may vary from week to week, from month to month. It is nothing absolute and immutable—nothing which flows from objective reality. It is only the most recent manifestation of the wisdom of those in whom the ultimate wisdom is supposed to reside, because they represent the logic of history. The accumulative effect of these factors is to give to the whole subordinate apparatus of Soviet power an unshakeable stubbornness and steadfastness in its orientation. This orientation can be changed at will by the Kremlin but by no other power. Once a given party line has been laid down on a given issue of current policy, the whole Soviet governmental machine, including the mechanism of diplomacy, moves inexorably along the prescribed path, like a persistent toy automobile wound up and headed in a given direction, stopping only when it meets with some unanswerable force. The individuals who are the components of this machine are unamenable to argument or reason which comes to them from outside sources. Their whole training has taught them to mistrust and discount the glib persuasiveness of the outside world. Like the white dog before the phonograph, they hear only the "master's voice." And if they are to be called off from the purposes last dictated to them, it is the master who must call them off. Thus the foreign representative cannot hope that his words will make any impression on them. The most that he can hope is that they will be transmitted to those at the top, who are capable of changing the party line. But even those are not likely to be swayed by any normal logic in the words of the bourgeois representative. Since there can be no appeal to common purposes, there can be no appeal to common mental approaches. For this reason, facts speak louder than words to the ears of the Kremlin; and words carry the greatest weight when they have the ring of reflecting, or being backed up by, facts of unchallengeable validity.

But we have seen that the Kremlin is under no ideological compulsion to accomplish its purposes in a hurry. Like the Church, it is dealing in ideological concepts which are of long-term validity, and it can afford to be patient. It has no right to risk the existing achievements of the revolution for the sake of vain baubles of the future. The very teachings of Lenin himself require great caution and flexibility in the pursuit of Communist purposes. Again, these precepts are fortified by the lessons of Russian history: of centuries of obscure battles between nomadic forces over the stretches of a vast unfortified plain. Here caution, circumspection, flexibility and deception are the valuable qualities; and their value finds natural appreciation in the Russian or the oriental mind. Thus the Kremlin has no compunction about retreating in the face of superior force. And being under the compulsion of no timetable, it does not get panicky under the necessity for such retreat. Its political action is a fluid stream which moves constantly, wherever it is permitted to move, toward a given goal. Its main concern is to make sure that it has filled every nook and cranny available to it in the basin of world power. But if it finds unassailable barriers in its path, it accepts these philosophically and accommodates itself to them. The main thing is that there should always be pressure, unceasing constant pressure, toward the desired goal. There is no trace of any feeling in Soviet psychology that that goal must be reached at any given time.

These considerations make Soviet diplomacy at once easier and more difficult to deal with than the diplomacy of individual aggressive leaders like Napoleon and Hitler. On the one hand it is more sensitive to contrary force, more ready to yield on individual sectors of the diplomatic front when that force is felt to be too strong, and thus more rational in the logic and rhetoric of power. On the other hand it cannot be easily defeated or discouraged by a single victory on the part of its opponents. And the patient persistence by which it is animated means that it can be effectively countered not by sporadic acts which represent the momentary whims of democratic opinion but only by intelligent long-range policies on the part of Russia's adversaries—policies no less steady in their purpose, and no less variegated and resourceful in their application, than those of the Soviet Union itself.

In these circumstances it is clear that the main element of any United States policy toward the Soviet Union must be that of a long-term, patient but firm and vigilant containment of Russian expansive tendencies. It is important to note, however, that such a policy has nothing to do with outward histrionics: with threats or blustering or superfluous gestures of outward "toughness." While the Kremlin is basically flexible in its reaction to political realities, it is by no means unamenable to considerations of prestige. Like almost any other government, it can be placed by tactless and threatening gestures in a position where it cannot afford to yield even though this might be dictated by its sense of realism. The Russian leaders are keen judges of human psychology, and as such they are highly conscious that loss of temper and of self-control is never a source of strength in political affairs. They are quick to exploit such evidences of weakness. For these reasons, it is a *sine qua non* of successful dealing with Russia that the foreign government in question should remain at all times cool and collected and that its demands on Russian policy should be put forward in such a manner as to leave the way open for a compliance not too detrimental to Russian prestige.

In the light of the above, it will be clearly seen that the Soviet pressure against the free institutions of the western world is something that can be contained by the adroit and vigilant application of counter-force at a series of constantly shifting geographical and political points, corresponding to the shifts and manoeuvres of Soviet policy, but which cannot be charmed or talked out of existence. The Russians look forward to a duel of infinite duration, and they see that already they have scored great successes. It must be borne in mind that there was a time when the Communist Party represented far more of a minority in the sphere of Russian national life than Soviet power today represents in the world community.

But if ideology convinces the rulers of Russia that truth is on their side and that they can therefore afford to wait, those of us on whom that ideology has no claim are free to examine objectively the validity of that premise. The Soviet thesis not only implies complete lack of control by the west over its own economic destiny, it likewise assumes Russian unity, discipline and patience over an infinite period. Let us bring this apocalyptic vision down to earth, and suppose that the western world finds the strength and resourcefulness to contain Soviet power over a period of ten to fifteen years. What does that spell for Russia itself?

The Soviet leaders, taking advantage of the contributions of modern technique to the arts of despotism, have solved the question of obedience within the confines of their power. Few challenge their authority; and even those who do are unable to make that challenge valid as against the organs of suppression of the state.

The Kremlin has also proved able to accomplish its purpose of building up in Russia, regardless of the interests of the inhabitants, an industrial foundation of heavy metallurgy, which is, to be sure, not yet complete but which is nevertheless continuing to grow and is approaching those of the other major industrial countries. All of this, however, both the maintenance of internal political security and the building of heavy industry, has been carried out at a terrible cost in human life and in human hopes and energies. It has necessitated the use of forced labor on a scale unprecedented in modern times under conditions of peace. It has involved the neglect or abuse of other phases of Soviet economic life, particularly agriculture, consumers' goods production, housing and transportation.

To all that, the war has added its tremendous toll of destruction, death and human exhaustion. In consequence of this, we have in Russia today a population which is physically and spiritually tired. The mass of the people are disillusioned, skeptical and no longer as accessible as they once were to the magical attraction which Soviet power still radiates to its followers abroad. The avidity with which people seized upon the slight respite accorded to the Church for tactical reasons during the war as eloquent testimony to the fact that their capacity for faith and devotion found little expression in the purposes of the régime.

In these circumstances, there are limits to the physical and nervous strength of people themselves. These limits are absolute ones, and are binding even for the cruelest dictators, because beyond them people cannot be driven. The forced labor camps and the other agencies of constraint provide temporary means of compelling people to work longer hours than their own volition or mere economic pressure would dictate; but if people survive them at all they become old before their time and must be considered as human casualties to the demands of dictatorship. In either case their best powers are no longer available to society and can no longer be enlisted in the service of the state.

Here only the younger generation can help. The younger generation, despite all vicissitudes and sufferings, is numerous and vigorous; and the Russians are a talented people. But it still remains to be seen what will be the effects on mature performance of the abnormal emotional strains of childhood which Soviet dictatorship created and which were enormously increased by the war. Such things as normal security and placidity of home environment have practically ceased to exist in the Soviet Union outside of the most remote farms and villages. And observers are not yet sure whether that is not going to leave its mark on the over-all capacity of the generation now coming into maturity.

In addition to this, we have the fact that Soviet economic development, while it can list certain formidable achievements, has been precariously spotty and uneven. Russian Communists who speak of the "uneven development of capitalism" should blush at the contemplation of their own national economy. Here certain branches of economic life, such as the metallurgical and machine industries, have been pushed out of all proportion to other sectors of economy. Here is a nation striving to become in a short period one of the great industrial nations of the world while it still has no highway network worthy of the name and only a relatively primitive network of railways. Much has been done to increase efficiency of labor and to teach primitive peasants something about the operation of machines. But maintenance is still a crying deficiency of all Soviet economy. Construction is hasty and poor in quality. Depreciation must be enormous. And in vast sectors of economic life it has not yet been possible to instill into labor anything like that general culture of production and technical self-respect which characterizes the skilled worker of the west.

It is difficult to see how these deficiencies can be corrected at an early date by a tired and dispirited population working largely under the shadow of fear and compulsion. And as long as they are not overcome, Russia will remain economically a vulnerable, and in a certain sense an impotent, nation, capable of exporting its enthusiasms and of radiating the strange charm of its primitive political vitality but unable to back up those articles of export by the real evidences of material power and prosperity.

Meanwhile, a great uncertainty hangs over the political life of the Soviet Union. That is the uncertainty involved in the transfer of power from one individual or group of individuals to others.

This is, of course, outstandingly the problem of the personal position of Stalin. We must remember that his succession to Lenin's pinnacle of preëminence in the Communist movement was the only such transfer of individual authority which the Soviet Union has experienced. That transfer took 12 years to consolidate. It cost the lives of millions of people and shook the state to its foundations. The attendant tremors were felt all through the international revolutionary movement, to the disadvantage of the Kremlin itself.

It is always possible that another transfer of preëminent power may take place quietly and inconspicuously, with no repercussions anywhere. But again, it is possible that the questions involved may unleash, to use some of Lenin's words, one of those "incredibly swift transitions" from "delicate deceit" to "wild violence" which characterize Russian history, and may shake Soviet power to its foundations.

But this is not only a question of Stalin himself. There has been, since 1938, a dangerous congealment of political life in the higher circles of Soviet power. The All-Union Congress of Soviets, in theory the supreme body of the Party, is supposed to meet not less often than once in three years. It will soon be eight full years since its last meeting. During this period membership in the Party has numerically doubled. Party mortality during the war was enormous; and today well over half of the Party members are persons who have entered since the last Party congress was held. Meanwhile, the same small group of men has carried on at the top through an amazing series of national vicissitudes. Surely there is some reason why the experiences of the war brought basic political changes to every one of the great governments of the west. Surely the causes of that phenomenon are basic enough to be present somewhere in the obscurity of Soviet political life, as well. And yet no recognition has been given to these causes in Russia.

It must be surmised from this that even within so highly disciplined an organization as the Communist Party there must be a growing divergence in age, outlook and interest between the great mass of Party members, only so recently recruited into the movement, and the little self-perpetuating clique of men at the top, whom most of these Party members have never met, with whom they have never conversed, and with whom they can have no political intimacy.

Who can say whether, in these circumstances, the eventual rejuvenation of the higher spheres of authority (which can only be a matter of time) can take place smoothly and peacefully, or whether rivals in the quest for higher power will not eventually reach down into these politically immature and inexperienced masses in order to find support for their respective claims? If this were ever to happen, strange consequences could flow for the Communist Party: for the membership at large has been exercised only in the practices of iron discipline and obedience and not in the arts of compromise and accommodation. And if disunity were ever to seize and paralyze the Party, the chaos and weakness of Russian society would be revealed in forms beyond description. For we have seen that Soviet power is only a crust concealing an amorphous mass of human beings among whom no independent organizational structure is tolerated. In Russia there is not even such a thing as local government. The present generation of Russians have never known spontaneity of collective action. If, consequently, anything were ever to occur to disrupt the unity and efficacy of the Party as a political instrument, Soviet Russia might be changed overnight from one of the strongest to one of the weakest and most pitiable of national societies.

Thus the future of Soviet power may not be by any means as secure as Russian capacity for self-delusion would make it appear to the men in the Kremlin. That they can keep power themselves, they have demonstrated. That they can quietly and easily turn it over to others remains to be proved. Meanwhile, the hardships of their rule and the vicissitudes of international life have taken a heavy toll of the strength and hopes of the great people on whom their power rests. It is curious to note that the ideological power of Soviet authority is strongest today in areas beyond the frontiers of Russia, beyond the reach of its police power. This phenomenon brings to mind a comparison used by Thomas Mann in his great novel "Buddenbrooks." Observing that human institutions often show the greatest outward brilliance at a moment when inner decay is in reality farthest advanced, he compared the Buddenbrook family, in the days of its greatest glamour, to one of those stars whose light shines most brightly on this world when in reality it has long since ceased to exist. And who can say with assurance that the strong light still cast by the Kremlin on the dissatisfied peoples of the western world is not the powerful afterglow of a constellation which is in actuality on the wane? This cannot be proved. And it cannot be disproved. But the possibility remains (and in the opinion of this writer it is a strong one) that Soviet power, like the capitalist world of its conception, bears within it the seeds of its own decay, and that the sprouting of these seeds is well advanced.

It is clear that the United States cannot expect in the foreseeable future to enjoy political intimacy with the Soviet régime. It must continue to regard the Soviet Union as a rival, not a partner, in the political arena. It must continue to expect that Soviet policies will reflect no abstract love of peace and stability, no real faith in the possibility of a permanent happy coexistence of the Socialist and capitalist worlds, but rather a cautious, persistent pressure toward the disruption and weakening of all rival influence and rival power.

Balanced against this are the facts that Russia, as opposed to the western world in general, is still by far the weaker party, that Soviet policy is highly flexible, and that Soviet society may well contain deficiencies which will eventually weaken its own total potential. This would of itself warrant the United States entering with reasonable confidence upon a policy of firm containment, designed to confront the Russians with unalterable counter-force at every point where they show signs of encroaching upon the interests of a peaceful and stable world.

But in actuality the possibilities for American policy are by no means limited to holding the line and hoping for the best. It is entirely possible for the United States to influence by its actions the internal developments, both within Russia and throughout the international Communist movement, by which Russian policy is largely determined. This is not only a question of the modest measure of informational activity which this government can conduct in the Soviet Union and elsewhere, although that, too, is important. It is rather a question of the degree to which the United States can create among the peoples of the world generally the impression of a country which knows what it wants, which is coping successfully with the problems of its internal life and with the responsibilities of a World Power, and which has a spiritual vitality capable of holding its own among the major ideological currents of the time. To the extent that such an impression can be created and maintained, the aims of Russian Communism must appear sterile and quixotic, the hopes and enthusiasm of Moscow's supporters must wane, and added strain must be imposed on the Kremlin's foreign policies. For the palsied decrepitude of the capitalist world is the keystone of Communist philosophy. Even the failure of the United States to experience the early economic depression which the ravens of the Red Square have been predicting with such complacent confidence since hostilities ceased would have deep and important repercussions throughout the Communist world.

By the same token, exhibitions of indecision, disunity and internal disintegration within this country have an exhilarating effect on the whole Communist movement. At each evidence of these tendencies, a thrill of hope and excitement goes through the Communist world; a new jauntiness can be noted in the Moscow tread; new groups of foreign supporters climb on to what they can only view as the band wagon of international politics; and Russian pressure increases all along the line in international affairs.

It would be an exaggeration to say that American behavior unassisted and alone could exercise a power of life and death over the Communist movement and bring about the early fall of Soviet power in Russia. But the United States has it in its power to increase enormously the strains under which Soviet policy must operate, to force upon the Kremlin a far greater degree of moderation and circumspection than it has had to observe in recent years, and in this way to promote tendencies which must eventually find their outlet in either the break-up or the gradual mellowing of Soviet power. For no mystical, Messianic movement—and particularly not that of the Kremlin—can face frustration indefinitely without eventually adjusting itself in one way or another to the logic of that state of affairs.

Thus the decision will really fall in large measure in this country itself. The issue of Soviet-American relations is in essence a test of the over-all worth of the United States as a nation among nations. To avoid destruction the United States need only measure up to its own best traditions and prove itself worthy of preservation as a great nation.

Surely, there was never a fairer test of national quality than this. In the light of these circumstances, the thoughtful observer of Russian-American relations will find no cause for complaint in the Kremlin's challenge to American society. He will rather experience a certain gratitude to a Providence which, by providing the American people with this implacable challenge, has made their entire security as a nation dependent on their pulling themselves together and accepting the responsibilities of moral and political leadership that history plainly intended them to bear.

John Foster Dulles

Policy for

Security and Peace

The Republican Party's hopes for an election victory in 1952 lay in a foreign policy that was radically different from that of the Democrats. Consequently, the Republican platform promised numerous changes. The principal change was to be in the approach to the Soviet Union. The new policy would be bold, positive, and vigorous. Whereas the Democrats had been content to contain the Russians within the boundaries of their sphere of influence, which included the Eastern European satellites, the Republicans pledged to roll back those boundaries and liberate the enslaved nations. Liberation, indeed, was one of the slogans of the presidential campaign. Similarly, while the Democrats had been willing to stay on the defensive and exert counterpressure at the points the Soviets might choose as targets, the Republicans served notice they they would build a "great capacity to retaliate instantly, by means and places of our own choosing." The warning was clear; a strike at the heart of the Soviet Union, rather than a local defensive counterthrust, would be the American retort to a Russian move.

The architect of the "new look" was John Foster Dulles, author of the foreign-policy plank in the Republican platform and Secretary of State from 1953 until his death in 1959. Grandson of one Secretary of State and nephew of another, Dulles first served his country abroad in 1907 when at the age of nineteen he acted as a secretary to the American delegation at the Second Hague Peace Conference. Thereafter, he divided his time and talents between a private law practice and government service. A Republican, he served Democratic Presidents as well—after World War I as counsel to the American Commission to Negotiate the Peace and after World War II as principal negotiator of the treaty of peace with Japan. Perhaps his most famous address was the one to the Council on Foreign Relations in New York on January 12, 1954, in which he announced his doctrine of massive retaliation. The speech aroused great interest and consternation, the latter chiefly because it was feared that any Communist aggression, however small, would elicit "massive retaliation" and inaugurate an all-out atomic war. To allay these fears, Dulles wrote the article reprinted below. The piece was an effort to clarify his January speech. [John Foster Dulles, "Policy for Security and Peace," Foreign Affairs, April 1954. Copyright by the Council on Foreign Relations Inc., New York.]

Since World War II, the United States has faced the difficult task of finding policies which would be adequate for security and peace and at the same time compatible with its traditions. Never before has a great nation been called upon to adjust its thinking and its action so radically in so short a period.

During the nineteenth century the maintenance of peace and order depended largely on Great Britain, with its Navy and the system of naval bases which enabled it to operate with mobility and flexibility throughout the world. By suitable commercial, investment and monetary policies, Great Britain and other nations with surplus capital stimulated economic growth in underdeveloped areas. The French Revolution had aroused men to respect and promote human rights and fundamental freedoms. The United States also made its contribution. Our people devoted their energies largely to domestic matters, not because they lacked concern for others but believing that what our founders called "the conduct and example" of freedom would exert a liberating influence everywhere. In fact, it did so. The "great American experiment" was a source of hope and inspiration to men everywhere, and especially to those living under despotism. Our dynamic example of freedom drew many to our shores and inspired others, in the old world and the new, to emulate our course.

All of these influences contributed to giving the world relative peace and security for the 100 years between the ending of the Napoleonic wars and the beginning of the First World War. During this period there were many advances in the practice of political liberty, and generally throughout the world there was a great advance in material and social well-being.

The events of the twentieth century, and especially the two World Wars and their aftermaths, have created an entirely new situation. In large measure the United States has inherited a responsibility for leadership which, in the past, has been shared by several nations. Today there rests upon us, to a unique degree, the threefold task of providing insurance against another world war; of demonstrating the good fruits of freedom which undermine the rule of despots by contrast; and of providing a major part of the effort required for the healthy growth of underdeveloped areas.

The Eisenhower Administration inherited security policies that had much worth. Many of these policies were bipartisan in character. They reflected a national recognition of the peril facing the civilized world, a united determination to meet it, and an acceptance of the rôle of leadership thrust on us by events. We had helped to reëstablish the economies of other countries shattered by the war. We had taken a major part in resisting the aggression in Korea. In the face of the Soviet threat we were engaged in rebuilding our military strength and that of other free countries.

These and like measures were costly. But they were necessary to our security. However, they partook much of an emergency character. By 1953 there was need to review our security planning and to adjust our continuing military effort to the other requirements of a well-rounded, permanent policy.

Under the conditions in which we live, it is not easy to strike a perfect balance between military and non-military efforts and to choose the type of military effort which serves us best. The essential is to recognize that there is an imperative need for a balance which holds military expenditures to a minimum consistent with safety, so that a maximum of liberty may operate as a dynamic force against despotism. That is the goal of our policy.

The Nature of the Threat. The threat we face is not one that can be adequately dealt with on an emergency basis. It is a threat that may long persist. Our policies must be adapted to this basic fact.

The Soviet menace does not reflect the ambitions of a single ruler, and cannot be measured by his life expectancy. There is no evidence that basic Soviet policies have been changed with the passing of Stalin. Indeed, the Berlin Conference of last February gave positive evidence to the contrary. The Soviet Communists have always professed that they are planning for what they call "an entire historical era."

The assets behind this threat are vast. The Soviet bloc of Communist-controlled countries—a new form of imperialist colonialism—represents a vast central land mass with a population of 800,000,000. About 10,000,-000 men are regularly under arms, with many more trained millions in reserve. This land force occupies a central position which permits striking at any one of about 20 countries along a perimeter of some 20,000 miles. It is supplemented by increasing air power, equipped with atomic weapons, able to strike through northern Arctic routes which bring our industrial areas in range of quick attack.

The threat is not merely military. The Soviet rulers dispose throughout the world of the apparatus of international Communism. It operates with trained agitators and a powerful propaganda organization. It exploits every area of discontent, whether it be political discontent against "colonialism" or social discontent against economic conditions. It seeks to harass the existing order and pave the way for political coups which will install Communist-controlled régimes.

By the use of many types of manœuvres and threats, military and political, the Soviet rulers seek gradually to divide and weaken the free nations and to make their policies appear as bankrupt by overextending them in efforts which, as Lenin put it, are "beyond their strength." Then, said Lenin, "our victory is assured." Then, said Stalin, will be the "moment for the decisive blow."

It is not easy to devise policies which will counter a danger so centralized and so fast, so varied and so sustained. It is no answer to substitute the glitter of steel for the torch of freedom.

An answer can be found by drawing on those basic concepts which have come to be regularly practised within our civic communities. There we have almost wholly given up the idea of relying primarily on house-by-house defense. Instead, primary reliance is placed upon the combining of two concepts, namely, the creation of power on a community basis and the use of that power so as to deter aggression by making it costly to an aggressor. The free nations must apply these same principles in international sphere.

Community Defense. The cornerstone of security for the free nations must be a collective system of defense. They clearly cannot achieve security separately. No single nation can develop for itself defensive power of adequate scope and flexibility. In seeking to do so, each would become a garrison state and none would achieve security.

This is true of the United States. Without the coöperation of allies, we would not even be in a position to retaliate massively against the war industries of an attacking nation. That requires international facilities. Without them, our air striking power loses much of its deterrent power. With them, strategic air power becomes what Sir Winston Churchill called the "supreme deterrent." He credited to it the safety of Europe during recent years. But such power, while now a dominant factor, may not have the same significance forever. Furthermore, massive atomic and thermonuclear retaliation is not the kind of power which could most usefully be evoked under all circumstances.

Security for the free world depends, therefore, upon the development of collective security and community power rather than upon purely national potentials. Each nation which shares the security should contribute in accordance with its capabilities and facilities. The Inter-American Treaty of Reciprocal Assistance (Rio Pact) of 1947 set a postwar example in establishing the principle that an armed attack against one would be considered as an attack against all. The North Atlantic Treaty is based on the same principle. Its members have gone much further in organizing joint forces and facilities as a part of the integrated security system. NATO provides essential air and naval bases, to which its various members can contribute—each according to its means and capabilities. It provides the planes and ships and weapons which can use these bases. It provides so many points from which an aggressor could be harassed, in so many different ways, that he cannot prudently concentrate his forces for offense against a single victim.

While NATO best exemplifies this collective security concept, there are other areas where the same concept is evolving, although as yet in a more rudimentary form. An example is the Western Pacific, where the United States has a series of collective security treaties which now embrace Australia, New Zealand, the Philippines, Japan and Korea. Collective arrangements are now in the making in the Middle East, with Turkey-Pakistan as the nucleus. These developments show the growing acceptance of the collective security concept we describe.

The United Nations is striving to make collective security effective on a basis broader than regionalism. The central principle of the Charter is that any armed attack is of universal concern and calls for collective measures of resistance. The Soviet Union, by its veto power, has made it impractical, as yet, to make available to the Security Council the "armed forces, assistance, and facilities" contemplated by Article 43 of the Charter. When aggression occurred in Korea, however, the principle of collective action was invoked by the United Nations and acted on by more than a majority of the members, including 16 which sent armed forces to Korea to repel the aggression. The "Uniting for Peace" Resolution, adopted by the General Assembly in November 1950, grew out of that experience. That resolution will enable members of the United Nations to join in carrying out similar collective measures against any future aggression without being blocked by a Soviet veto.

The free world system of bases is an integral part of its collective security. At the recent Four-Power Conference in Berlin, Mr. Molotov repeatedly attacked these bases as evidence of aggressive purpose. Actually these bases on the territory of other sovereign countries are merely a physical expression of the collective security system. They were constructed only at the request of the host nation and their availability depends upon its consent, usually as a legal condition and always as a practical one. The requisite consent to the use of these bases would never be accorded unless it was clear that their use was in response to open aggression, and reasonably related to its scope and nature. This gives assurance of their community function.

Thus the free world has practical means for achieving collective security both through the United Nations and the various regional arrangements already referred to.

The Strategy to Deter Aggression. The question remains: How should collective defense be organized by the free world for maximum protection at minimum cost? The heart of the problem is how to deter attack. This, we believe, requires that a potential aggressor be left in no doubt that he would be certain to suffer damage outweighing any possible gains from aggression.

This result would not be assured, even by collective measures, if the free world sought to match the potential Communist forces, man for man and tank for tank, at every point where they might attack. The Soviet-Chinese bloc does not lack manpower and spends it as something that is cheap. If an aggressor knew he could always prescribe the battle conditions that suited him and engage us in struggles mainly involving manpower, aggression might be encouraged. He would be tempted to attack in places and by means where his manpower superiority was decisive and where at little cost he could impose upon us great burdens. If the free world adopted that strategy, it could bankrupt itself and not achieve security over a sustained period.

The free world must devise a better strategy for its defense, based on its own special assets. Its assets include, especially, air and naval power and atomic weapons which are now available in a wide range, suitable not only for strategic bombing but also for extensive tactical use. The free world must make imaginative use of the deterrent capabilities of these new weapons and mobilities and exploit the full potential of collective security. Properly used, they can produce defensive power able to retaliate at once and effectively against any aggression.

To deter aggression, it is important to have the flexibility and the facilities which make various responses available. In many cases, any open assault by Communist forces could only result in starting a general war. But the free world must have the means for responding effectively on a selective basis when it chooses. It must not put itself in the position where the only response open to it is general war. The essential thing is that a potential aggressor should know in advance that he can and will be made to suffer for his aggression more than he can possibly gain by it. This calls for a system in which local defensive strength is reinforced by more mobile deterrent power. The method of doing so will vary according to the character of the various areas.

Some areas are so vital that a special guard should and can be put around them. Western Europe is such an area. Its industrial plant represents so nearly the balance of industrial power in the world that an aggressor might feel that it was a good gamble to seize it—even at the risk of considerable hurt to himself. In this respect, Western Europe is exceptional. Fortunately, the West European countries have both a military tradition and a large military potential, so that through a European Defense Community, and with support by the United States and Britain, they can create an adequate defense of the Continent.

Most areas within the reach of an aggressor offer less value to him than the loss he would suffer from well-conceived retaliatory measures. Even in such areas, however, local defense will always be important. In every endangered area there should be a sufficient military establishment to maintain order against subversion and to resist other forms of indirect aggression and minor satellite aggressions. This serves the indispensable need to demonstrate a purpose to resist, and to compel any aggressor to expose his real intent by such serious fighting as will brand him before all the world and promptly bring collective measures into operation. Potential aggressors have little respect for peoples who have no will to fight for their own protection or to make the sacrifices needed to make that fighting significant. Also, they know that such peoples do not attract allies to fight for their cause. For all of these reasons, local defense is important. But in such areas the main reliance must be on the power of the free community to retaliate with great force by mobile means at places of its own choice.

A would-be aggressor will hesitate to commit aggression if he knows in advance that he thereby not only exposes those particular forces which he chooses to use for his aggression, but also deprives his other assets of "sanctuary" status. That does not mean turning every local war into a world war. It does not mean that if there is a Communist attack somewhere in Asia, atom or hydrogen bombs will necessarily be dropped on the great industrial centers of China or Russia. It does mean that the free world must maintain the collective means and be willing to use them in the way which most effectively makes aggression too risky and expensive to be tempting.

It is sometimes said that this system is inadequate because it assures an invaded country only that it will eventually be liberated and the invader punished. That observation misses the point. The point is that a prospective attacker is not likely to invade if he believes the probable hurt will outbalance the probable gain. A system which compels potential aggressors to face up to that fact indispensably supplements a local defensive system.

Practical Applications. We can already begin to see applications of these policies.

In Korea the forces fighting aggression had been so closely limited that they were forbidden even to apply the doctrine of "hot pursuit" in relation to enemy planes that were based across the Yalu. The airfields from which attacks were mounted were immune, as were the lines and sources of their supply. The fighting there was finally stopped last July on terms which had been proposed many months before. That result was achieved, at least in part, because the aggressor, already denied territorial gains, was faced with the possibility that the fighting might, to his own great peril, soon spread beyond the limits and methods which he had selected, to areas and methods that we would select. In other words, the principle of using methods of our choice was ready to be invoked, and it helped to stop the war which the enemy had begun and had pursued on the theory that it would be a limited war, at places and by means of its choosing.

The 16 members of the United Nations who fought in Korea have invoked the same principle. They have given public notice that if the Communists were to violate the armistice and renew the aggression, the response of the United Nations Command would not necessarily be confined to Korea. Today, if aggression were resumed, the United Nations Command would certainly feel free to inflict heavy damage upon the aggressor beyond the immediate area which he chose for his aggression. That need not mean indulging in atomic warfare throughout Asia. It should not be stated in advance precisely what would be the scope of military action if new aggression occurred. That is a matter as to which the aggressor had best remain ignorant. But he can know and does know, in the light of present policies, that the choice in this respect is ours and not his.

In relation to Indo-China, the United States has publicly stated that if there were open Red Chinese Army aggression there, that would have "grave consequences which might not be confined to Indo-China."

On December 26, 1953, President Eisenhower made an important statement which clearly reflected our present policy as applied to Asia. He announced a progressive reduction of United States ground forces in Korea. However, he went on to point out that United States military forces in the Far East will now feature "highly mobile naval, air and amphibious units;" and he added that in this way, despite some withdrawal of land forces, the United States will have a capacity to oppose aggression "with even greater effect than heretofore." In the same month the United States reaffirmed its intent to maintain in Okinawa the rights made available to us by the Japanese Peace Treaty. This location is needed to ensure striking power to implement the collective security concept.

In Europe, our intentions are primarily expressed by the North Atlantic Treaty. Following the aggression in Korea of June 1950, the Treaty members proceeded to an emergency buildup of military strength in Western Europe. The strength built between 1950 and 1953 has served well the cause of peace. But by 1953, it did not seem necessary to go on at the original pace.

At the April 1953 meeting of the NATO Council, the United States put forward a new concept, now known as that of the "long haul." It meant a steady development of defensive strength at a rate which would preserve and not exhaust the economic strength of our allies and ourselves. This would be reinforced by the availability of new weapons of vastly increased destructive power and by the striking power of an air force based on internationally agreed positions. President Eisenhower is now seeking an amendment of the present law to permit a freer exchange of atomic information with our NATO allies.

When we went back to the NATO Council meeting of last December, we found that there was general acceptance of the "long haul" concept. The result is that most of our NATO allies are now able to achieve budgetary and economic stability, without large dependence on our economic aid.

The growing free-world defensive system, supported by community facilities and coupled with adequate policies for their use, reflects the nearest approach that the world has yet made to a means to achieve effective defense, at minimum cost.

The Current Military Program. One of the basic tasks of the new Administration has been to review our military program in the light of the foregoing policies.

In the years 1945–53, our military programs went through wide fluctuations which hindered orderly and efficient administration. During the first part of this period, the policy was to reduce the military establishment drastically. During the latter part of the period, the policy was to increase the military establishment rapidly. During both the decrease and the increase the military budget reflected the so-called "balance of forces" concept. In practical terms, this meant splitting the available funds into three roughly equal slices for the Army, Navy and Air Force.

When the Eisenhower Administration took office, our national security programs, at home and abroad, were costing over 50 billion dollars a year, and were planned at about 55 billion dollars for the next year. Budgetary deficits were of the order of 10 billion dollars, despite taxes comparable to wartime taxes. Inflation was depreciating the purchasing power of the dollar. Our allies were similarly burdened.

The American people have repeatedly shown that they are prepared to make whatever sacrifices are really necessary to insure our national safety. They would no doubt support military expenses at the levels which their government told them were required for security, even at the cost of budget deficits, resultant inflationary pressures and tax-levels which would impair incentives. But the patriotic will to sacrifice is not something to be drawn upon needlessly. Government has the high duty to seek resourcefully and inventively the ways which will provide security without sacrificing economic and social welfare. The security policies we here describe make possible more selective and more efficient programs in terms of the composition of forces and of procurement.

The new Administration has sought to readjust, in an orderly way, the program for the military forces. Before this could be done, it was necessary to clarify the extent of our reliance on collective security; to define more clearly our basic strategy both in Europe and the Far East; to reassert our freedom of action in repelling future aggression; to assess the impact of newer types of weapons; and to relate the composition and size of our ready and potential forces to all these factors.

Inevitably this has taken time. It has required a series of difficult basic decisions by the President with the advice of the National Security Council and with supporting decisions by the Department of State, the Department of Defense and the Treasury Department. It has been necessary to exchange views with Congressional leaders and our principal allies and to inform world opinion so that neither our friends nor our enemies abroad would misinterpret what we were doing. By now, however, the new course is charted and is guiding our military planning. As a result, it is now possible to get, and share, more basic security at less cost. That is reflected in the budget which the President has submitted for the 1955 fiscal year. In this budget, national security expenditures for fiscal year 1955 will amount to 45 billion dollars as compared with 50 billion dollars for 1953 and 49 billion dollars for 1954.

Initially this reshaping of the military program was misconstrued in various respects. Some suggested that the United States intended to rely wholly on large-scale strategic bombing as the sole means to deter and counter aggression. What has already been said should dispose of this erroneous idea. The potential of massive attack will always be kept in a state of instant readiness, but our program will retain a wide variety in the means and scope for responding to aggression. Others interpreted the program as a move away from collective security. The exact opposite is the case, as has been shown. Our policies are based squarely on a collective security system and depend for their success on its continuing vitality. Still others feared that we intended to withdraw our forces from abroad in the interest of mobility. Now that the fighting is ended in Korea, our forces in the Far East will be reduced in numbers, as has previously been announced, but the kind of force that remains will have great striking power. Moreover, the program does not mean that we intend to pull our forces out of Europe. It is, of course, essential that the continental nations themselves provide a harmonious nucleus of integrated defense. If they do so, the United States would expect to maintain substantial forces of its own in Europe, both in support of the forward strategy of defense and for political reasons.

Another consequence of our new policies is that it has become practicable to reduce our economic aid to our allies. The Technical Assistance Program will go on and economic aid is not wholly excluded. There are still some places near the Soviet orbit where the national governments cannot maintain adequate armed forces without help from us. That is notably so in the Middle and Far East. We have contributed largely, ungrudgingly, and I hope constructively, to end aggression and advance freedom in Indo-China. The stakes there are so high that it would be culpable not to contribute to the forces struggling to resist Communist oppression.

But broadly speaking, economic aid in the form of grants is on its way out as a major element of our foreign policy. This is highly desirable from many standpoints. It helps to make our own budget more manageable and it promotes more self-respecting international relationships. That is what our allies want. Trade, broader markets and a flow of investment are far more healthy than intergovernmental grants-in-aid. It is, of course, important that we do actually develop these mutually advantageous substitutes for "aid." To do so is one of the major objectives of the Eisenhower Administration. It is an essential component of the over-all policies already described.

In the ways outlined, the United States and its allies gather strength for the long-term defense of freedom.

Our National Purpose. We do not, of course, claim to have found some magic formula that ensures against all forms of Communist successes. Despotism is entrenched as never before. It remains aggressive, particularly in Asia. In Europe, its purposes remain expansive, as shown by Mr. Molotov's plans at the Berlin Conference for Germany, Austria and all Europe. However, time and fundamentals will work for us, if only we will let them.

The dictators face an impossible task when they set themselves to suppress, over a vast area and for a long time, the opportunities which flow from freedom. We can be sure that there is going on, even within the Soviet empire, a silent test of strength between the powerful rulers and the multitudes of human beings. Each individual seems by himself to be helpless in this struggle. But their aspirations in the aggregate make up a mighty force. There are some signs that the Soviet rulers are, in terms of domestic policy, bending to some of the human desires of their people. There are promises of more food, more household goods, more economic freedom. This does not prove that the dictators have themselves been converted. It is rather that they may be dimly perceiving that there are limits to their power indefinitely to suppress the human spirit.

That is a truth which should not be lost sight of as we determine our own policies. Our national purpose is not merely to survive in a world fraught with appalling danger. We want to end this era of danger. We shall not achieve that result merely by developing a vast military establishment. That serves indispensably to defend us and to deter attack. But the sword of Damocles remains suspended. The way to end the peril peacefully is to demonstrate that freedom produces not merely guns, but the spiritual, intellectual and material richness that all men want.

Such are the guiding principles we invoke. We have confidence that if our nation perseveres in applying them, freedom will again win the upper hand in its age-long struggle with despotism, and that the danger of war will steadily recede.

Dean Acheson

The Illusion of Disengagement

One of the principal objections to containment lay in the possibility of a clash between the two opposing armies as they faced each other in central Europe. Such a clash might set off a new world war. A shot fired in anger or in error by some obscure soldier, a hasty command by a lowly subaltern at an isolated spot on the border might invite local retaliation and lead to setting the whole frontier ablaze. A solution to this dangerous proximity seemed to be in establishing a neutral zone between the two contending forces; such a zone would minimize, if not eliminate, the possibility of hostile contact.

In the fall of 1957, proposals emanated from both sides for the creation of a neutral buffer zone comprising East and West Germany, Czechoslovakia, and Poland. Troops of both blocs, except local national armies, would be withdrawn from the area, and nuclear weapons would be neither manufactured nor stockpiled there. Not only would such a plan end the danger of a clash, it was believed, but it would also lead to a relaxation of tension, make easier a political settlement, and leave to the Germans the solution of their own problem of unification.

Adam Rapacki, the Polish Foreign Minister, advanced such a proposal in October 1957 at the United Nations. At about the same time, George F. Kennan voiced similar views in the Reith Lectures over the radio network of the British Broadcasting Corporation. The impact of the two suggestions was great, particularly Kennan's, which appeared in book form in 1958 and in two articles in Harper's *(February and March 1958). Support came from both sides of the Iron Curtain. Nikita S. Khrushchev, the Soviet Premier at that time, endorsed the plan in March 1958 in his call for a summit conference. Senators Mike Mansfield and William J. Fulbright spoke in its favor, and Prime Minister Macmillan and Hugh Gaitskell, the Labor Party leader, also came out for it. But many Americans and Europeans opposed the scheme on the grounds that it would create a vacuum that the Soviets would easily and quickly fill. They feared that once American troops began a withdrawal from West Germany they would continue westward until they reached the United States, thus leaving the continent to Russia. If they did not leave Europe, their training capability and maneuverability would be greatly constricted by the loss of West Germany.*

The most effective retort to the Kennan disengagement thesis came from Dean Acheson, who had served as Undersecretary and as Secretary of State at the time containment was being formulated and implemented. His dissent is reprinted below. A graduate of Yale College and Harvard Law School, Acheson had been secretary to Supreme Court Justice Louis D. Brandeis before embarking on a successful career as a lawyer. He served briefly as Undersecretary of the Treasury in Franklin D. Roosevelt's first cabinet. [Dean Acheson, "The Illusion of Disengagement," Foreign Affairs, *April 1958. Copyright by the Council on Foreign Relations Inc., New York.]*

The other day I was re-reading Clarence Day's wise and delightful book, "This Simian World," and came across the paragraph remarking on what unpromising entrants in the struggle for supremacy on this planet the lemurs might have seemed many millions of years ago. "Those frowzy, unlovely hordes of apes and monkeys," he wrote, "were so completely lacking in signs of kingship; they were so flighty, too, in their ways, and had so little purpose, and so much love for absurd and idle chatter, that they would have struck us . . . as unlikely material. Such traits, we should have reminded ourselves, persist. They are not easily left behind, even after long stages; and they form a terrible obstacle to all high advancement."

It does seem to be true that, in our day, only in a sort of cyclical way do free societies retain an understanding of their own experience, and hold to the purposes which it has inspired. Is this because some echo of those early traits still persists, or because the inevitable hardening of the arteries of each generation brings on some failure of memory, or for still other reasons?

Certainly moods change as memories, once fearful, become dimmed, as new anxieties arise, and as present exertions become increasingly distasteful. The bitter teachings of 1914–1918, and the determination they fired, had quite disappeared by 1938, to be replaced by ideas of neutralism, withdrawal from conflict, "America First." After these, in turn, were swept away by the devastation of another world war and by a display of world leadership entailing vast national effort, another 20 years has ended by bringing back the old yearnings and errors under a new name. "Disengagement," it is called now; but it is the same futile—and lethal—attempt to crawl back into the cocoon of history. For us there is only one disengagement possible—the final one, the disengagement from life, which is death.

Soon after we had awakened from the daze of the Second World War, it became clear to us that our protected adolescence as a great Power was over. The empires which had spawned us, whose capital had developed us, whose balance of power had given us security, either disappeared in the two world wars or passed to more minor rôles. We were face to face with the responsibility of adult national life in the most critical situation imaginable. A world which for a century had had an integral life of sorts was split into three segments. One—the Soviet-Communist segment, militarily unequalled, except in nuclear power in which it was weak, was held together by an ideological and economic system supported by force. Another—containing the vast populations of Asia, the Middle East, and North and West Africa—was left in confusion and turmoil at the end of the war; and, in addition, either had newly gained national independence or was demanding it from rulers gravely weakened. To these people had come also expectations of an improving life to a degree never before imagined and, perhaps, unfulfillable.

The third segment was what was left of the old world order—roughly Europe and the Western Hemisphere. The second and third segments had certain important common characteristics. They were not in the Soviet power system. But various and large parts of them could, under some conditions, be added to it.

In this situation, as it appeared not long after the end of the Second World War, the task of what has since come to be called the Atlantic Community, that is, the states of Western Europe and the Western Hemisphere, was to bring about and maintain with increasing strength and vitality a non-Communist world system. Within this system, not only the states mentioned, but those in the second segment as well, should, if the system was workable and working, be able to pursue their national ends in their own way.

This effort required, at the beginning, a great deal of reconstruction, particularly in Europe. The only state strong enough to furnish the leadership in this effort was the United States. Both its government and its people responded vigorously to the press of necessity. The steps which were taken are well known and need not be recalled here. The important thing is that they were successful in bringing about a common sense of purpose, certainly in Western Europe and the Western Hemisphere, and to a large extent were effective in giving opportunity to those nations in Asia and Africa which were just coming to the point where they were free to pursue their national destinies undirected from the outside.

Since the war, therefore, the foreign policy of the United States has become, by necessity, a positive and activist one. It has been one of attempting to draw together, through various groupings, that Western area which must be the center of a free and open world system, and of taking the leading part in providing it with military security, and with a developing economy in which trade could grow and industrial productivity could be developed, both in areas which were already industrially advanced and those which were at the threshold. At the same time it was an essential part of this policy to produce the maximum degree of cohesion throughout the whole non-Communist area, through political policies which would make for integration and strength rather than for exploitation.

Various aspects of this effort—the military, the economic, the political—I have attempted to describe in some detail elsewhere. I have there pointed out the interdependence of the Western Hemisphere and Western Europe; how the power factors involved make it essential that this part of the world shall stand firmly united; how, without the American connection, it is impossible to maintain independent national life in Western Europe; and how, without Western Europe, the power factors would turn disastrously against the United States.

Broadly speaking, these conceptions have for the past decade or more had wide acceptance both in this country and throughout the Western world. They have been successful beyond the dream of those who first advocated them. They are beginning to bear the most valuable fruit.

Recently, efforts have been relaxed. Our military security and much of our prestige resting upon it have been impaired, though not so far that vigorous action cannot make the necessary repair. But, throughout the world, as I indicated at the beginning of this article, voices are being raised to ask whether it is necessary to continue facing the hazards of the military situation, to continue bearing the expense of making vital and progressive the economic life of the whole free world; whether coexistence with the Communist system cannot be bought at a cheaper price and with less effort. And so, when people are told, as they have been by Mr. George Kennan, a man of the highest character and reputation and justly entitled to a respectful hearing, that this is possible, his words have a powerful impact.

Mr. Kennan's views are not new to him. They do not spring from a fresh analysis of the current situation. He has held and expressed these views for at least a decade. The effect which they have had currently makes us realize anew that the reception given to the expression of ideas depends upon the mood of the hearers. This reception may have little to do with the truth of the ideas expressed; it has a great deal to do with their power. Mr. Kennan has told people what they want to hear, though not because they want to hear it. What is it that he has said?

The ideas are almost as vague as the style is seductive. The thoughts are expressed as musings, wonderings, questionings, suggestions. But what comes out of it is about this: First, there is the idea of disengagement in Europe. By this is meant mutual withdrawal of American, British and Canadian, as well as Russian, forces from somewhere. This somewhere first appears to be East and West Germany; then the "heart of Europe;" again, the Continent; and sometimes, from the general ethos of the discussion, it appears to be all overseas areas.

The second idea is the neutralization of Germany. The third is that there should be no nuclear weapons in Europe. And the fourth is that throughout Asia and Africa, in what are called the "uncommitted areas," there is little "to be done . . . except to relax;" that "It is perfectly natural that Russia . . . should have her place and her voice there too;" that "our generation in the West" has no "obligation vis-à-vis the underdeveloped parts of the world," and, anyway, there is no "absolute value attached to rapid economic development. Why all the urgency?" If any sound schemes for development are presented, we should support them, "when they arise;" but, only on the condition that they tell us first "how you propose to assure that if we give you this aid it will not be interpreted among your people as a sign of weakness and fear on our part, or of a desire to dominate you." If Asian and African states should find in this grudging, meager and humiliating policy no opportunity to push their economic development within the non-Communist system, and should turn to Communist methods and Communist help, we should accept their action without concern and with good nature.

One sees at once that these conceptions are the very opposite of those which the West has been following for the past ten years or more. It is an assertion that the struggle naught availeth; that it is dangerous, unwise and unproductive. It is a withdrawal from positive and active leadership in the creation of a workable system of states. It is a conception, blended of monasticism and the diplomacy of earlier centuries, by which the United States would artfully manœuvre its way between and around forces without attempting to direct or control them.

If we attempt to analyze these suggestions, the problems which they create promptly emerge. First, let us consider the idea that something called disengagement can be brought about by removing American, British, Canadian and Russian troops from some area in Europe. What disengagement does this bring about? Very little, as one sees if one pauses to consider the realities. Compare the confrontation which takes place between the United States and the Soviet Union in Germany with that which occurs along the DEW line—that system of early warning stations which stretches from Alaska, across the Arctic regions and far out into the Atlantic. Here there are daily contacts on a thousand radarscopes, and doubtless the same is true on the other side of the screen. Some of these blips on the radar are actual aircraft; sometimes atmospheric conditions produce them. But they represent a contact which no action in Germany can disengage. There is confrontation in every part of the world where the area of the open and free world system may be reduced by Soviet military, economic or political penetration. No action in Germany will produce disengagement here. The word is a mere conception, which confuses and does not represent any reality.

So, let us turn from it to consider something more capable of delineation. For instance, exactly what is the extent of the mutual withdrawal about which we are asked to negotiate? The answer to this question does not depend upon penetrating the vagueness of Mr. Kennan's language. For there can be little doubt, I believe, that, once a withdrawal begins, it will be complete, so far as United States, British and Canadian troops are concerned. All the forces, foreign and domestic, will combine to bring this about. As the withdrawal makes the military position weaker, our forces will be less desired wherever they may remain. If withdrawal is represented as advantageous for Germans, it would seem equally advantageous to Frenchmen. Icelanders, Moroccans, Saudi Arabians and the rest would quickly follow. And, once the idea caught hold, Americans would, of course, join in the general demand. The *New Statesman* shows us how the matter is now being presented to a small section of British opinion and how it could bemuse a still larger one in that country:

> Yet the missile agreement is one of the most extraordinary and complete surrenders of sovereignty ever to be made by one country for the exclusive benefit of another. For the missiles are not intended to defend Britain; on the contrary, they decisively increase its vulnerability. Their prime purpose is to reduce the likelihood of a Soviet ICBM onslaught on America during the crucial three-year period which must elapse before America possesses ICBMs herself. The sole beneficiary will be America.

We should not deceive ourselves. After disengagement, we would soon find ourselves discussing complete withdrawal from all European areas and, very possibly, from bases in the Far East and Near East as well. Indeed, Mr. Khrushchev has twice served warning, once in Berlin in 1957 and again in January of 1958, that the sort of withdrawal which he is talking about is withdrawal from all overseas bases. This would cut the striking power of the free world by at least a half, and, perhaps, until our missile program accelerates, by much more.

We must think of what we purchase for this vast price. What would Russian withdrawal from Germany or the heart of Europe amount to? Is it possible to believe that the Soviet Government, whatever it may say or whatever agreement it may sign, would, or could, contemplate withdrawing its forces behind, say, the River Bug, and keeping them there? And, by forces, I mean effective Russian physical power, by whatever name called. It is hard to see, after the events in Poland and Hungary, whatever the Russian Government might wish, how it could possibly undertake so hazardous a course. For, if its physical force were permanently removed from Eastern Europe, who can believe that even one of the Communist régimes would survive? Therefore, wherever Soviet forces might be garrisoned, the expectation and threat of their return must continue to be ever present (at most it would require from 12 to 18 hours) if Russia is to maintain the power which it has insisted upon as recently as the Hungarian uprising.

At this point in our discussion we must examine the conception of the neutralization of Germany; and then bring together the consequences of withdrawal and neutralization. It is necessary, we are told, that Germany should not be allowed to be free to choose its own course after unification. It must accept limitations upon its military forces and its military alignment. In other words, its national life will be conducted under far greater limitations than those in which other sovereign people live. The possibility that any such situation could endure seems to me quite fantastic.

Whatever Germans might initially think they would be willing to do, there is no precedent in history for, nor does there seem to me to be any possibility of, the successful insulation of a large and vital country situated, as Germany is, between two power systems and with ambitions and purposes of its own. Constant strain would undermine the sanctions of neutralization. The final result would be determined by the relative strength of the pressures from the two sides. As I have already suggested, the pressure would all be from the Russian side. For, there would be no Power in Europe capable of opposing Russian will after the departure of the United States from the Continent and the acceptance of a broad missile-free area. Then, it would not be long, I fear, before there would be an accommodation of some sort or another between an abandoned Germany and the great Power to the East. Under this accommodation, a sort of new Ribbentrop-Molotov agreement, the rest of the free world would be faced with what has twice been so intolerable as to provoke world war—the unification of the European land mass (this time the Eurasian land mass) under a Power hostile to national independence and individual freedom.

But, without this withdrawal of forces and the neutralization of Germany, Mr. Kennan sees "little hope for any removal of the division of Germany at all—nor, by the same token, of the removal of the division of Europe." Naturally enough, these words have found a strong echo in Germany. But it is a fading one, as Germans ponder the conditions which would flow from unification by withdrawal and neutralization, and see the end of the best hopes of the German people. Two weak states—East and West Germany—jockeying for position in a sort of no-man's land, could raise the East-West "tensions" to a point compared to which anything we have yet experienced would seem mild indeed. In all this West

Berlin would, of course, be the first victim. It would be a wholly inadequate judgment upon those whose naïveté and weakness produced this result that they should share the guilt of those Western politicians whose preaching of "liberation" encouraged the uprisings in East Berlin and Hungary, and, like them, should sit in supine impotence while more gallant men suffered. The best hope for German unification I shall mention shortly.

Turning to Eastern Europe, Mr. Kennan sees those countries, without the withdrawal of Russian troops, caught between the dilemma of constant revolutions, bloodily suppressed, and the acknowledgment of Soviet domination. This view seems to me founded on nothing but its assertion. I cannot for the life of me see how the movement toward a greater degree of national identity in Eastern Europe is furthered by removing from the Continent the only Power capable of opposing the Soviet Union.

Nor do I see that the facts bear out Mr. Kennan's gloomy predictions. For instance, if the experience of 1956 had produced only the development in Poland or if the Hungarians had acted with as much restraint, it would have been plain to all that the attraction of the power of the West, of the possibilities which its system opens to all, was proving very strong indeed—stronger even than the secret police and Soviet occupation troops. The fact that in Hungary the reaction was pushed to the point where the Russians felt it necessary to suppress it with force proves only that it was handled unwisely.

So, as we think about the matter, we must wonder whether there is anything we can purchase "one-half so precious as the goods" we sell. We are told not to worry about this; that, even though it seems quite unlikely that the Russians would carry out any withdrawal, nevertheless, it is good propaganda to make the offer and cause them to refuse it. This seems to me profoundly false. In the first place, it treats international negotiations as though all the figures on the chessboard were made of wood or ivory; whereas, in fact, we are dealing with living people, subject to all the emotions of mankind. If I were a European and had to live through two or three years of American negotiations about withdrawing from the Continent, I think that very early in the game I would discount America's remaining and would prepare to face a new situation. Furthermore, to believe that the Russians can be put in the position of refusing to evacuate Europe underrates their skill in negotiation. They would simply, as they have already done, continue to raise the price. And it would be we and not they who would do the refusing.

The evils of a timid and defeatist policy of retreat are far deeper than its ineptness as a move in the propaganda battle. It would abandon the efforts of a decade, which are bringing closer to realization the hopes of Western Europe, of Germany, and of Eastern Europe as well. From the low point of 1946–1947 the economic, social and political health and strength of Western Europe—of which West Germany has become an integral and vital part—have grown greatly. Their pull on Eastern Europe continues to mount. To continue this the American connection is essential. The success of the movement toward unity in the west of Europe is no longer in doubt. Only the rate of progress is undecided. The Coal and Steel Community, Euratom, the Common Market have been accepted. A common currency and political community are on the way.

All of this is threatened by the call to retreat. It will not do to say that a united Germany, made militarily impotent and neutralized, can play an effective part in bringing to fruition a united and vigorous European community. The slightest puff of reality blows this wishful fancy away. The jockeyings and tensions of the two parts of Germany, the unopposable threat of Russian power, the bribes which can be dangled before Germany by the Soviet Union in the form of boundary rectifications and economic opportunities—these alone are enough to put an end to hope of a united and strong Europe, invigorated by Germany.

For those who believe that Eastern Europe would welcome American and Russian troop withdrawals as the beginning of liberation, I suggest a quiet sampling of candid Polish opinion. I venture to predict that what they would find is a horror at being abandoned by the West and left between the Soviet Union and a Germany similarly abandoned, to which the offer of another partition of Poland might be irresistible.

But, if one looks at the other side of the medal, what a different face it bears! A strong, united Europe could have the men and the resources—along with British and United States contingents—to deal by conventional forces with invasion by conventional forces, particularly as the Eastern European satellites are becoming a danger, and not an asset, to Soviet military power. This, if pressed, gives real mutuality of benefit to a negotiated reduction in forces. It makes possible, too, a time when nuclear forces would no longer have to be relied on as a substitute for conventional forces, and with it a real opportunity to negotiate this threat further and further into the background.

Finally, a thriving Western Europe would continue its irresistible pull upon East Germany and Eastern Europe. This would, in turn, have its effect upon the demands of the Russian people on their government. With a rise in the standards of living in the Soviet Union, and as some broader participation in the direction of affairs was made essential by their very magnitude and complexity, the Russian need for the forced communization and iron control of Eastern Europe would diminish. Then negotiations looking toward a united Germany, under honorable and healing conditions, and toward the return of real national identity to the countries of Eastern Europe, while preserving also the interests of the Russian people in their own security and welfare, could for the first time be meaningful and show the buds of hope. This has been the goal of Western policy for the past decade.

It would be self-delusion to close our eyes to the difficulties which lie before us along this road. Some we have created ourselves. Our military strategy, with its sole reliance on massive retaliation, and a budgetary

policy which has neglected even that, have caused us a loss of relative
military power and of prestige. Some of our political policies have weakened our alliances. Our allies, too, are having their troubles. In what are
perhaps the two closest of them, we could wish (as they undoubtedly do,
too) that both the present and the immediate future held greater promise
for the development of strength and popular attitudes more attuned to
reality. We all share together the common problem of devising a military
policy for NATO which will avoid making the proposed defense seem as
fearsome as the potential enemy's threat, and which will be a real deterrent because it is a credible one.

I have suggested elsewhere that this is possible. Briefly, the way is to
create a situation in fact which equals the political purpose of the North
Atlantic Treaty—that is, a situation where in order for the Soviet Union
to attack, or coerce, Europe it would have to attack, or coerce, the United
States as well. This, if we all use a fair degree of intelligence about our
defenses, the Soviet Union could be deterred from doing. What is required
is a short-range effort which does not preclude a sustained effort toward a
wiser long-range goal. The short-range effort would be to provide NATO
with such effective nuclear power that the Soviet Union could not have its
way without destroying that power; and an attempt to destroy it would
be impractical apart from a simultaneous attempt to disable the United
States, which could be made too dangerous. The longer-range purpose
would be to develop adequate conventional forces in Europe, with British
and American participation, to make mutually desirable a real reduction
and equalization of both Soviet and NATO forces and a controlled
elimination of nuclear material for military use.

I quite understand that all of this is difficult. But I believe also that
"the mode by which the inevitable comes to pass is effort."

Finally, Mr. Kennan's discussion of the uncommitted countries of Asia
and Africa seems to me to disclose a complete lack of understanding of
the forces which are at work there. In the first place, he would like to tell
them, as Thoreau would have done, that the whole march of industrial
civilization since the beginning of the nineteenth century has been a
mistake; that they must be patient about increasing their standard of
living; that they must curb the mad rate at which they reproduce; that
we have no sense of guilt or obligation to them because we are in a
position to help their economic development as our own was helped. But
when they have any sound plans, we will consider them on terms which
they cannot accept. This means that we find nothing to our interest in
their industrialization; and that they are in reality ward heelers who
threaten one political side with desertion to the other unless they receive
a handout or a sinecure.

Nothing could be further from the truth. These governments are faced
with a demand, just as are the Government of the United States and the
Government of the Soviet Union, that conditions shall exist under which
a rising standard of living is possible. The conditions in these countries

vary from those which are still deep in an agricultural stage to those which have begun industrialization and are ready, once capital is available, to push it speedily forward. Governments cannot stay in power unless they respond to the demands of those who will keep them there. Even the oligarchs in the Kremlin are under pressure, which they cannot altogether refuse, to expand the standard of living in Russia.

There are two ways in which the governments of the undeveloped countries can bring about conditions which their peoples demand. Both of these involve acquiring capital, but under very different conditions. One involves the adoption of totalitarian authority, a temporary depression of the standard of living, forced savings, and industrial equipment from Russia, paid for by the export of raw materials. The other involves the maintenance, and perhaps a steady expansion, of the standard of living, the maintenance of systems of government in which there is a considerable area of freedom, the import of capital from Western Europe and North America, and the repayment of these loans over a considerable period of time by participation in the expanding trade of an open economic system. To say that economic development has nothing whatever to do with political alignment is a fallacy of the gravest sort. It is, of course, true that economic aid cannot force, cannot ensure, a political alignment from any country. But it is certain that, without it, a different alignment will take place.

May I conclude by repeating that the new isolationism which we have been discussing, and the reception it has received, is gravely disturbing, not only because it is utterly fallacious, but because the harder course which it calls on us to forego has been so successful. If one compares the non-Communist segments of the world today with what they were 12 years ago, one sees enormous progress. If one compares, as we have tried to do here, the pull of a vigorous free system, held together by the joint efforts of at least some of its members to provide military security, economic power and political leadership, one sees how strong it is and what effect it has had. If one considers the changes which have already occurred within the Soviet Union, one can see the time approaching when adjustments in Eastern Europe are possible, when military forces can be reduced, and when the menace of nuclear destruction will be greatly diminished, if not removed. Surely, there are dangers, and great dangers, but with good sense we can live through these. We will not make them less by weakening ourselves, destroying the confidence of our allies, and refusing to help those people who are willing to work to some extent, at least within the system which we and our allies, together, have created and can make ever more vigorous and appealing.

The United States at midcentury was prosperous. Corporate profits were on the rise; the stock market was climbing. Most important, the nation's well-being was spread among the masses; salesman and executive, factory worker and manager were enjoying much the same luxuries, living in much the same split-levels or Cape Cods, and sending their children to much the same schools. Prosperity had reached down to levels hitherto untouched, and the good things of life were had by more people than ever before in the history of the nation or, for that matter, of the world. Refrigerators, washing machines, radios, and all the other symbols of a high standard of living were everywhere in evidence in the United States. O. Henry's Four Hundred had grown into several millions. Those who could not support themselves because of infirmities of age, sickness, or lack of skills were provided for by a socially conscious government. Few people starved, almost everyone watched television, and most people punctuated their ever decreasing hours of labor with vacations at seashore or mountains, driving their own automobiles and, frequently, their own small boats. To many observers the good life was finally achieved. Of all the nations of the world, the United States alone had been able to provide for a more nearly equitable distribution of the nation's wealth and resources.

14

MIDCENTURY

To many others, however, the rosy economic situation could not hide a discouraging malady. In a letter to Adlai Stevenson in 1959, John Steinbeck expressed his deep concern over the state of his country. Americans were too prosperous, too comfortable; they had too many of the good things of life. "If I wanted to destroy a nation," Steinbeck said, "I would give it too much, and I would have it on its knees, miserable, greedy and sick."

There were, indeed, evidences of a sickness. Americans were spending millions of dollars and thousands of hours searching for purpose and direction. They jammed psychiatrists' offices, frequented spiritualists' seances, and bought untold numbers of pills and tranquilizers.

A more distressing sickness was what Steinbeck called "the cynical immorality of my country. . . . What we have beaten in nature, we cannot conquer in ourselves." There were indications that Americans had succumbed to the base instincts of mankind. Expense-account padding, "payola," dishonesty in advertising, and what Joseph Wood Krutch called "the replacement of personal morality and integrity by socially desirable conduct" seemed to be on the rise.

A meeting of the Catholic hierarchy in America in 1960 noted yet another feature, "the loss of individual responsibility and initiative." The Catholic leaders regretted the "uniformity of thought and supine loyalty to the organization" as a significant aspect of American life. The manifestations of this loss of personal responsibility could be seen in the decline of the family, the increased rate of divorce, the broken homes, the demand for welfare benefits and the weakening of religious convictions. The conformity also accounted for the absence of a sense of personal obligation.

There is no reason to believe, however, that the prosperity of mid-century America and the presence of certain evils in society need result in the downfall of the American republic. Analogies to the last days of the Roman Empire are plentiful but not altogether accurate. Americans in midcentury, while concentrating on material well-being and on enjoying the benefits of the country's great resources, did not shirk their responsibilities; they were not oblivious of the role they had to play in international affairs; they lived not alone in hedonistic search for pleasures. In the '20s, after another world war and during another period of opulence, Americans did indeed retreat from fulfilling their obligations to help maintain the peace of the world. Not so in the 1950s. Shortly after the end of the Second World War, the United States undertook the leadership of the free world in its struggle with communism. American arms, money, and technical skills were spread around the world to bolster defenses, increase productivity in underdeveloped countries, and restore the economic well-being of countries devastated by the war. The Truman Doctrine, the Marshall Plan, the North Atlantic Treaty Organization, and the Point Four Program are not indications of a selfish, decadent people. Taxing oneself heavily to aid distant, suffering peoples is a sign of great maturity. Deep concern for peace on the other side of the world, even in one's self-interest, reflects a certain amount of nobility that no amount of disparagement can shatter.

The readings that follow illustrate three of the important problems facing Americans at midcentury: the movement away from the cities; automation; and civil rights.

Daniel Seligman

The New Masses

Two revolutions in midcentury America were the movement to the suburbs and the leveling of the classes. "We are almost all middle classes as to income and expectations," wrote Herbert Gold in an article in the Atlantic. *No longer could there be said to exist three separate and distinct groups—workers, middle class, and upper class. A transformation of American society resulted in the creation of what Daniel Seligman has called "the new masses—those who share in all the amenities hitherto reserved for one single, narrowly based class. In the article reprinted below, Seligman explores the whys, hows, and implications of the change. [Daniel Seligman, "The New*

Masses." *Reprinted from the May 1959 issue of* Fortune Magazine *by special permission;* © *1959 Time Inc.*]

Only ten years ago, the following description of an American family's style of life would have enabled one to form some fairly firm impressions about the father's occupation and the general social "rank" of the family:

> The parents, who are about forty, live with their two boys in a comfortable six-room suburban house outfitted with a full line of appliances, a television set that is in more or less constant use, and a car in which the father drives to work. The car is also used for camping trips during the summer. The mother shops at a local supermarket and at several local department stores; the boys attend the good local public schools; and on weekends the family often goes swimming at a local beach, although recently the father and mother and their older son have begun to take an interest in golf.

Given these facts in 1949, one might have inferred, quite reasonably, that the head of the house was a lower or middle-echelon executive, or salesman, or the proprietor or part owner of some small business, or a professional man, and that the family's position in society was solidly middle class.

Given these same facts in 1959, one could deduce practically nothing about the family's social rank or the father's occupation. For the fact is that in the past few years the broad style of life described above has become available, not only to an identifiable "middle class," but to a great mass of Americans, perhaps even a majority. The family head today might be a truck driver earning $5,500, a college professor earning $7,000, a life-insurance salesman earning $8,000, a skilled production worker earning $9,000, an airline pilot earning $15,000, or an executive earning $18,000. In the new American society, it is increasingly difficult to tell the players apart without subpoenaing their tax returns. . . .

Diamonds and Pyramids. Many otherwise alert Americans continue to think and talk of their countrymen as though all of them could be sorted out into three clear-cut classes. The biggest of these, of course, would be a low-income *working class,* or simply *workers* ("lower class" has never come easily to American lips), symbolized most aptly by the "blue collars" in manufacturing but also including farmers. Then there would be the middle-income *middle class,* whose prototype is the small proprietor, or the professional or white-collar employee. And at the top there would be a small layer of important businessmen, prominent professionals, government officials, etc. Europeans would forthrightly call this the American *upper class*; Americans themselves are more likely to speak of *rich people, society people, big shots,* etc., and of course nobody is more reluctant to say "upper class" than a qualified member.

These traditional class concepts still have a kind of shorthand utility in connoting various styles of life, but when they are used to denote a neatly layered social pyramid they are today simply a source of confusion. For one thing, the shape is all wrong: by income standards, at least, what we have in the U.S. today more nearly resembles a diamond than a pyramid—i.e., there are more people in the middle than there are at the top or bottom.

Aside from the shape of the income structure, it is increasingly difficult to "layer" a society of such great flux and diversity. It was never easy to diagram the "class structure" of the U.S. as a matter of fact, and most sociologists have usually been obliged to limit their descriptive efforts to relatively small, self-contained communities like Weirton, West Virginia, or like Newburyport, Massachusetts (whose inhabitants were divided, by W. Lloyd Warner and Paul S. Lunt in a study starting in the 1930's, into *six* classes, ranging from upper-upper to lower-lower). But in the 1950's it is increasingly difficult to find even small communities in which classes are clearly separable.

Russell Lynes, a witty amateur sociologist who is an editor of *Harper's* magazine, has suggested that we visualize the new U.S. society as a series of independent pyramids, each with its own interest, hierarchies, and rewards. That is, one pyramid for business executives, and others for scientists, labor-union officials, the military, sports figures, etc.—even one for criminals (An ex-convict named Lewis Dent has described the criminal pyramid in some detail: in prison, the professionals who live entirely by the criminal code are held in highest regard, then come the gifted amateurs who can show some genuine antisocial accomplishments, e.g., rapists, and at the bottom are the "creeps" who are ostracized because they reject the mores of the underworld.) But the pyramids also present difficulties when one tries to relate them to the realities of American life. There are too many pyramids, and all have different shapes. Some of them, in fact, are not really pyramids—e.g., among professional baseball players there are more men in the major leagues than in class B. Furthermore, too many Americans have different positions on several pyramids, and on any one pyramid there is the problem that insiders and outsiders often evaluate individuals differently; the young "comer" may have more prestige within a corporation than many of the executives who apparently outrank him.

But the basic reason for the increased confusion about class in the U.S. is the steady growth in the number of Americans who can afford at least some of the amenities once associated with the highest positions in our society. If most "workers" still cannot afford $110 suits, boats, Thunderbirds, *and* trips to Florida, they have at least enough discretionary income so that they can have some of these things some of the time. As much as five years ago *Fortune* noted that 43 per cent of all nonfarm families had become concentrated in the middle-income range—i.e., they had cash income after taxes of $4,000 to $7,500 (in 1953 dollars); and it also noted that almost 60 per cent of these families were actually headed by blue-collar workers (see "The Rich Middle-Income Class," May,

1954). This bunching-around-the-middle has persisted in the years since 1954, with the noteworthy difference that the "middle" keeps moving higher up on the money scale. Now about 43 per cent of all nonfarm families have after-tax cash incomes between $5,000 and $10,000 (in current dollars).

The Modern Maggies. The most conspicuous breakdown of class lines is the one that has taken place just in the past five years as the ex-"proletarians" who are now the heart of the middle-income class began finally to adopt a middle-class style of life. This phenomenon, portentous in its implications for the markets of the 1960's, is hard to express statistically, but there can no longer be any doubt about the broad facts of the case. Nelson Foote, a distinguished sociologist who recently left academic life to work for General Electric, says that he has observed the change even in Detroit, a city where class consciousness dies hard. "During the war," Foote says, "you could sit on a streetcar and tell at a glance who were the defense workers and who were the white collars. Then, while the war was still on, the companies did something which has had a profound effect on our society: they installed cafeterias and lockers in the plants. After a while, you stopped seeing lunch boxes and work clothes on the streetcars, and today you just can't tell who's who. The city is full of auto workers whose wives shop at Hudson's—who wouldn't be caught dead buying a pair of shoes at Sears."

Foote is convinced, in fact, that it is the wives of the blue-collar workers who are instrumental in changing their families' style of life, and he has observed at least some blue-collar families in which the familiar old American saga of Jiggs and Maggie is being re-enacted—though in the modern version Maggie is more concerned with "bringing up father" to be an active P.T.A. member than to be a society swell. In some respects, of course, the blue-collar husbands accept middle-class ways with enthusiasm; many suburban shopping-center proprietors argue that the husband is an easier prospect than the wife when a couple are pondering something of a splurge, especially when the splurge promises greater comfort or just plain fun. The wives, however, are closer to the children, hence closer to the real or fancied social pressures the children are under in the suburban schools. Moreover, many of the wives of blue-collar workers have themselves held white-collar jobs in offices, which brought them into contact with longer-established members of the middle class and their style of life.

A Foothold in Levittown. How many blue-collar families have arrived in the suburbs? Even if no sociologists had observed the phenomenon, it can be inferred from available government data that a sizable number of blue collars *have to be* in suburban, or semi-suburban, areas. Families headed by blue collars comprise about 60 per cent of nonfarm families today. It is manifest that they cannot all be in the metropolitan areas' inner cities (which have about 25 per cent of the nonfarm population) and in the smaller cities and towns (which have about 30 per cent).

In an effort to gauge more precisely the impact of the blue-collar families on suburbia, and vice versa, *Fortune* recently surveyed real-estate agents and developers, bankers, school officials, as well as some sociologists, in the suburbs of seven major metropolitan areas. There was almost unanimous agreement among these observers that the blue collars have moved increasingly into suburban homes, especially those in the $10,000-to-$15,000 price range—though there are sizable numbers of sales all the way up to $21,000. An agent in northeastern Philadelphia guessed that about half the $15,000-to-$20,000 homes he sold last year went to skilled blue-collar workers; and near Dallas there is a new development of some 200 homes in the same price range that are almost entirely occupied by production workers for Texas Instruments. On the other hand, an agent near Atlanta who has also sold many homes to skilled workers—especially to airline mechanics and Ford assembly-plant employees—finds that not many of them break through the $10,000 price barrier. An estimate by Charles M. Fink, an attorney and realtor who has been directly involved in the sale or rental of some 4,000 homes in the Levittown, Pennsylvania, suburban development, offers this picture of the blue-collar foothold there:

Price	Number of houses	Proportion of blue-collar occupancy
Over $17,500	1,200	Under 5 per cent
About $15,000	750	About 5–10 per cent
$10,000–$12,500	12,500	About 50 per cent
Under $10,000	2,700	About 65 per cent

This breakdown corresponds closely to the figures and impressions obtained from the other suburban areas. In 1954, *Fortune* estimated that about 30 million Americans lived in communities that were "strictly suburban" in character (see "The Lush New Suburban Market," August, 1954). The figure is in the neighborhood of 40 million today, and comprises about one-quarter of all nonfarm families. *Fortune*'s survey suggests that perhaps a quarter of these are now blue-collar families, and in the newer suburban developments the proportion may be over a third.

Blue and White Values. In several interesting respects the blue and white collars still play different roles in the suburbs, and still have different reasons for moving there. There have always been some blue-collar families in suburbia, of course, but until recently they tended to be the local service and construction workers who, in middle-class communities, lived on the other side of the tracks. The newer blue-collar suburbanites are characteristically the skilled production workers who man the new industrial plants on the outskirts of metropolitan areas. (Between 1952 and 1957, the suburbs accounted for 80 per cent of all new jobs in the New York metropolitan area.) Unlike the white-collar man, who characteristically moves *away* from his job when he migrates to the suburbs, the blue-collar man is usually moving closer to his job, and is much preoccupied with traffic conditions and driving time between his suburban home and his suburban factory.

The white collar is often acutely conscious of the prestige thought to attach to some particular suburban town or neighborhood. He may load an extra commuting burden on himself to live in such a place—indeed, he may feel that commuting itself is invested with a kind of upper-middle-class prestige value. The blue collar, however, tends to see commuting time simply as an extension of his working day.

The young white collar usually regards his first suburban home as a temporary lodgment on the way to a better one. The blue collar sees it as security for his old age, and for this reason, perhaps, is much more concerned with getting a durable physical property than the white collar is.

But the significant fact is that, while these differences persist, the living habits of the blue and white collars have been converging in many respects; indeed, one might regard the suburbs today as the new American melting pot. A community leader in Royal Oak, a Detroit suburb, notes that the auto workers who followed the plants out of town were "swallowed up" when they lived in Detroit. "When they come out here, they seem hungry for community affairs." Indeed, the fact that they regard their first suburban homes as permanent living places often gives the blue collars a stake in local government that the more transient white collars do not feel they have. A real-estate developer who built a community of $16,000-to-$17,000 houses northwest of Chicago says that about half the community is blue collar, and that he has been "amazed and pleased to see how they've taken hold and run the community. I've sat in on some committees they have, and I'll tell you they make a hell of a lot more sense than some of the junior-executive types I've seen." Even in Park Forest, the Chicago suburb that has been much discussed (in *Fortune* and elsewhere) as a prototypical junior-executive community, there is now a blue-collar minority verging on 10 per cent, and in two recent years the Little League baseball chairmen have been blue collars. With a few exceptions, the people surveyed by *Fortune* reported that the new blue-collar suburbanites are *not* segregated socially.

The breakdown of the older class distinctions can be seen in an extreme form in southern California, especially in and around Los Angeles —an area that is not exactly suburban in character, but not exactly urban either. Nathan Glazer, a young Bennington College sociologist who has recently spent a year in California, is still marveling at Los Angeles. "First of all, so many of the people have come from somewhere else that 'backgrounds' have less meaning; nobody cares about your family, or your religion, or the schools you went to. Then the outdoor living tends to make everyone live alike. Everyone uses the same communal facilities, especially the national parks and beaches. In the East, you feel it's kind of immoral to go swimming at four o'clock Wednesday afternoon, but out there you get used to it pretty fast—and the people there on the beach with you are aircraft workers, bellhops, pensioners, intellectuals, and even businessmen. We're used to defining people in terms of their jobs, but around Los Angeles there's a strange lack of emphasis on jobs. There's no central business district, and working hours tend to be quite irregular, principally because there are so many part-time workers, so many service employees who work odd hours, and so many professionals—and pensioners—who are able to keep their own hours. The traffic into and out of the city is heavy morning and evening, but it is always going both ways, and you can never be sure who is going to the beach, to the supermarket, to Disneyland, or to work. The result of it all is that you don't identify people with their occupations, as you naturally do in the East, and class distinctions become further blurred."

What the Difference Is. While the older class lines are losing their meaning, it would be wildly unrealistic to argue that the U.S. is developing into a society of equals. Instead of having a fairly clear position in an oversimplified but still identifiable "class," the American of 1959 and the 1960's is seen by the sociologists as a man with a "status." There are dozens of shadings of status—of a man's standing in the eyes of others. Status is more easily changed, obviously, than class. A family's status may jump a notch not only with the father's promotion at the office, but with the mother's election to the chairmanship of a suburban charity drive, or the son's enrollment at the state university.

Spending and status are still intimately related, of course, but in such diverse and sometimes paradoxical ways that novel opportunities and hazards are continually cropping up in the consumer markets. On the one hand, as more and more Americans have been enabled to adopt some form of the middle-class style of life, they have also become increasingly aware of, and more finely attuned to, the nuances that can disclose "the difference"—the difference between those with more and with less income and responsibility. In an age when millions of Americans live in superficially similar suburban developments, the flagstone walk the developer has given his more expensive houses is attentively noted.

The nuances involve much more than displays of income and raw purchasing power, however, since status is importantly bound up with education—which implies, among other things, the exercise of good taste in consumption. In an age when millions can travel abroad, the difference between a three-week economy trip to London-Paris-Rome and a six-week trip taking in Athens and Istanbul is not just the difference in cost but also in sophistication of the itinerary. Then there is the "keeping-down-with-the-Joneses" phenomenon so often seen in modern suburbia, which is not so much a pressure against heavy spending as a pressure to spend money as educated men are supposed to spend it—i.e., on fine high-fidelity sets and good wines rather than expensive fur coats and cars. And yet—just to complicate things still more—there has been such a proliferation of interesting, sophisticated, or chic things to spend money on that it is increasingly difficult to say that any two or three of these things are *the* badges of status.

The preoccupation with status is a phenomenon whose origins are interesting—especially, perhaps, to marketing and advertising men who are increasingly obliged to think of products as status symbols. The preoccupation is related in part to the fact that since 1940 over 20 million adult Americans have spent a good deal of time in the armed forces, where one is obliged constantly to think about "rank." It is also related to the fact that more and more Americans work for large organizations: at present, something like 38 per cent of the labor force is employed in organizations that have over 500 employees. The figure (which includes all government employees) was only 28 per cent in 1940. In the nature of the case, large organizations are status-ridden: titles and responsibilities are carefully defined in job descriptions, and relationships are carefully plotted on organization charts.

Of all corporate employees, the blue collars have been traditionally the least concerned about status, because their status seemed quite unambiguous. Their wages, job descriptions, even their vacation privileges and other fringes have generally been matters of public record (in a union contract). And whatever his dreams for his son, the future of the blue-collar man himself has been fairly predictable, for he moves up in accordance with seniority rosters that are posted publicly; he has no important opportunities to advance by pulling wires or gaining favor with his superiors. Hence he has taken his job position as something "fixed"; he has not dwelt on the social implications of his job, but has seen it as a means to make money.

The New Strivers. There are some signs, however, that the blue collars are becoming more preoccupied with status: in part because they are now living with white collars in the suburbs, and having their first prolonged exposure to the latter's values; and in part because of the changing nature of blue-collar work. Next month's article will explore the change in detail, but it may be said at this point that the blue-collar labor force is becoming much more skilled—which means it is becoming more mobile—and at its higher reaches, as the technology of U.S. production becomes more and more advanced, the labor force is becoming "professionalized," a phenomenon already noted in a previous *Fortune* article in this series (see "How the U.S. Can Become 50 Per Cent Richer," March). To some extent, the skilled blue-collar worker, eating now in the same company cafeteria as the white collar, working now in shirtsleeves instead of "work clothes," driving home from work to a middle-class suburban community, is beginning to feel the first twinges of concern about his status in society. Nelson Foote, commenting recently on these changes, said that "it would be a shame, in a way, if the old hardheaded blue-collar values disappeared, and nothing were left in this country except success-strivers."

The corporate white-collar workers, especially the men in the middle and higher reaches of the corporation, have a more ambiguous and volatile status position, and they are prone to develop what the sociologists call "status anxieties." (A number of sociologists have demonstrated that "upwardly mobile" families have a disproportionately high incidence of psychosomatic diseases.) Their preoccupation with status symbols—e.g., with the size and physical trappings of their offices—has been a recurrent theme in business fiction and satire in recent years. (There is a scene in the movie *A Face in the Crowd* in which an advertising-agency executive suffers a heart attack after realizing he will lose a crucial account. He gasps out to the entertainer who is taking the account away from him: "You've seen my office. A corner office with four windows. Do you know how long it takes at Browning, Schlagel & McNally to get a corner office?" And then he slumps to the floor.)

In the years ahead, status will almost certainly hinge on education more than it has in the past. Indeed, the U.S. may now be moving into a period in which education will make and break men in a totally new fashion. It is a well-publicized fact that college enrollments, now running around 3,200,000, will almost double by 1970. What is not so well appreciated is the fact that the number of living Americans who *have been to college* will also grow furiously during the 1960's—probably by about a third. Right now, something like 16,500,000 Americans have attended college for at least a year. By 1970, the figure will be in the vicinity of 22 million, of whom about 11 million will have graduated. (A rule of thumb that has held up pretty well in recent years is that of all those who go to college about half graduate.) At that point there are likely to be serious difficulties in finding enough "top jobs" for the college-trained.

Room at the Top? The problem can be seen in sharp focus if we limit it to men in their twenties and early thirties. In 1950 there were 2,200,000 men between twenty-five and thirty-four who had completed at least a year of college. Today, the figure is about 2,800,000, and by 1970, the Census Bureau estimates, it will be about 3,800,000, and will represent almost a third of all the men in this age band (vs. less than a fifth in 1950). What kinds of job opportunities are these growing numbers of college men encountering?

It would appear that their opportunities to move toward the top jobs have already been narrowed considerably. At present, the number of men between twenty-five and thirty-four who are employed (in Census Bureau terminology) as "professional, technical, and kindred workers," or as "managers, officials, and proprietors," or as "sales workers," is three million—i.e., it is only a little higher than the number of college men in this age band. Virtually all the jobs that are at the top, or that can lead to the top, are in these three Census categories; but it should be noted that the categories also include a lot of "bottom jobs" we do not normally link with college education—e.g., the proprietors include marginal news dealers, and the sales workers include clerks in the five-and-dime stores as well as high-paid life-insurance salesmen. Hence it is obvious that a fair number of college-trained men must already be working at jobs to which no high status attaches.

The trend can be seen in a study prepared by the Bureau of Applied Social Research at Columbia University, working in cooperation with *Time*, and also in a study of U.S. consumers conducted for *Life* by the Alfred Politz research organization. Though the data in the two studies are not exactly comparable, they suggest that college training is increasingly unlikely to lead automatically to top jobs. The *Time* study, based on 1947 data, showed that 5 per cent of male college graduates were holding blue-collar jobs. The *Life* study, based on 1955–56 data, showed that almost 20 per cent of employed "household heads" (mostly male, of course) who had any college training were blue collars.

One partial solution to the job problems of the "educated many" would be to give professional or managerial status to the broad band of corporate and government employees who at present hover uneasily between the clerical and executive layers or, in manufacturing, between the skilled workers and the technical staff. In an age preoccupied with status, a lot can be done simply by changing titles. A lot is being done already, in fact, and at all levels. The janitors in schools are often designated "custodial engineers," though in some industries the term "sanitors" is preferred. Girls who type letters for $70 a week are billed as "Gal Fridays"—there are usually a hundred-odd listings under this heading in the help-wanted section of the Sunday *New York Times*—and thereby gain a kind of executive-assistant status. The U.S. Labor Department ruled recently that any "executive" who earned less than $80 a week had to be paid time and a half for overtime. A part of the recent and prospective increase in the ranks of the professional and managerial groups represents not a true increase in the number of such jobs, but an inflation of titles. This depreciation of managerial status has contributed further to the blurring of the old class lines, and to the preoccupation with the symbols that help one to determine a man's real status.

The Ups and Downs. One fairly certain consequence of the great proliferation of college graduates will be an increase in social and occupational mobility. Education has always been the principal path by which sons gained higher positions than their fathers had; and though the Horatio Alger legend dies hard, numerous studies of the American "business elite" make it plain that the top jobs have *always* gone to the relatively well educated. A recent study by S. M. Lipset and Reinhard Bendix shows that even in the first half of the nineteenth century, when only about 5 per cent of Americans went to high school, 22 per cent of the "elite" had graduated from college, another 10 per cent had attended college, 51 per cent had attended some kind of high school, and only 17 per cent had not gone beyond elementary school. The same authors show that in a more recent generation of elite businessmen (those born between 1891 and 1920) 84 per cent had gone to college and only 5 per cent had not gone beyond elementary school.

It is possible that the value of college degrees will undergo some depreciation, as more and more Americans get them. But at the same time, the degree is becoming an almost universal requirement for admission to the managerial group, and the fact that corporate managers are no longer divided into men with and men without a college education makes for greater mobility within the group. This mobility is fostered by the increasing tendency of corporations to select their managers "scientifically," e.g., with the aid of aptitude and personality tests. The test may represent invasions of privacy, they may be based on misconceptions about managerial qualities, and they may not even be successful in finding the qualities they are set up to detect, but they attempt at least to put promotions on a more *objective* basis, and make the candidate's background (his college, national origins, religion, father's occupation, etc.) much less relevant. In short, they make it easier for a clerk's son to become a vice president—and vice versa. (Talk about social mobility often seems to proceed on the assumption that mobility is only upward, but in any generation there is always a substantial minority of sons whose positions are lower than their fathers'. Data collected by the Michigan Survey Research Center suggested that, in 1952, of all employed persons whose fathers were "managers, officials, and proprietors," 25 per cent were skilled or semiskilled workers, and 8 per cent were actually laborers.)

The Homogeneous Life. The increased bunching of Americans around the middle-income levels, the increased blurring of occupational distinctions, and the increased adoption of middle-class living styles by families of diverse occupational background, have all tended to make the U.S. a much more homogeneous society. At this point it may be interesting to observe that we have been "homogenized" in several other respects as well.

National backgrounds have less meaning than they used to. About 95 per cent of all Americans today are native-born (vs. 87 per cent in 1920), and about 80 per cent of them are at least "third generation" Americans (vs. 65 per cent in 1920)—i.e., both their parents were also native-born. With immigration averaging only about 250,000 a year, about 85 per cent of the U.S. population will be at least third generation by 1970. And though the point cannot be verified statistically, it is nonetheless clear that Americans are less prone than they once were to think of other Americans as "Swedes," or "Irishmen," or "Italians"—in part because the old-country ways and languages are largely unknown to the third and fourth generations, and in part because these generations so often have hopelessly *mixed* national backgrounds.

Religious differences are also less meaningful. A number of theologians have remarked, with some bitterness, that while Americans are more interested than they used to be in having a religion, they are much less interested in the *content* of religion, or in religious differences. Americans are increasingly being admonished, on television, for example, to "attend your place of worship this weekend"—and the inference is plain that it doesn't matter which one you attend. In *Religion and the Free Society*, a pamphlet published recently by the Fund for the Republic, William Lee Miller of the Yale Divinity School complained of "the drive toward a shallow and implicitly compulsory common creed. . . . The kind of religion that results from this common civic faith is a religion-in-general, superficial and syncretistic, destructive of the profounder elements of faith." William Clancy, educational director of the Church Peace Union, commented in the same pamphlet, "The 'religion' that is accepted as a part of our public life is largely a matter of good fellowship and good works." Where religion once divided Americans on strongly felt sectarian lines, the new good fellowship and good works tend to emphasize nonsectarian activities (e.g., running nursery schools open to children of all religious backgrounds).

Political differences are also becoming blurred: American political debate is increasingly conducted in a bland, even-tempered atmosphere, and extremists of any kind are becoming rarer. The political expression of the new society, in which more and more families are bunched around the middle-income levels and adapting to middle-class ways, is a Congress in which more and more politicians are bunched around the middle of the road, in which both parties are increasingly dominated by "reasonable" liberals who were called, in a recent article in *Commentary* by Karl E. Meyer, the "Smooth Dealers." Many of them—e.g., Nelson Rockefeller, John F. Kennedy—could fit plausibly into either the Republican or the Democratic party; and as their numbers have grown, American voters increasingly cross party lines to vote for them. In short, the old party divisions are less meaningful.

The New Ivy Leaguer. The net of these "homogenizing" trends is that we all seem to live alike—or, at least, a great many of us live and think and dress more nearly alike than we used to. Many Americans appear to be disturbed by this trend, and to detect in it a threat to their own sense of individuality; they are endlessly complaining about all the "conformity" and "togetherness" in American life.

But the complaints seem to miss a crucial point about the new society—a point that most marketing men have *not* missed. The point is that while our society is more homogeneous, the individual's own opportunities to live in diverse fashions have been expanded considerably. The man in the Ivy League suit may be a millionaire or a skilled machinist, and so may the man at the wheel of the sports car and the man on the beach in Miami. To the spectator, this may look like a new uniformity; to the machinist, it involves a new diversity—a diversity that, it may safely be presumed, he is enjoying immensely.

Walter A. Reuther

Automation and

Technical Change

The replacement of the worker by the machine has been, ever since the earliest days of the Industrial Revolution, one of society's principal concerns. But not until the mid-twentieth century did automation threaten so drastically the position of the working classes. The manifold consequences—social as well as economic—were outlined to a Joint Committee of Congress by Walter A. Reuther, who represented the industry that seemed most affected by automation. Born in 1907 in West Virginia, Reuther entered the labor movement while still in his twenties. In 1935 he organized the automobile workers and became president of Local 174, United Automobile Workers, CIO. When the AFL and CIO merged in 1955, he became president of the CIO division. [Walter A. Reuther, "Automation and Technical Change," Hearings before the Sub-Committee on Economic Stabilization of the Joint Committee on the Economic Report, 84th Congress, 1st session, October 17, 1955, pp. 98–107.]

We have been told so often that automation is going to bring on the second industrial revolution that there is, perhaps, a danger we may dismiss the warning as a catch-phrase, and lose sight of the fact that, not only the technique, but the philosophy of automation is revolutionary, in the truest sense of the word. Automation does not only produce changes in the methods of manufacturing, distribution, many clerical operations, and in the structure of business organization, but the impact of those changes on our economy and our whole society bids fair to prove quite as revolutionary as were those of the first industrial revolution.

Through the application of mechanical power to machinery, and the development of new machinery to use this power, the first industrial revolution made possible a vast increase in the volume of goods produced for each man-hour of work. Succeeding technological improvements—such as the development of interchangeable parts and the creation of the assembly line which were essential to the growth of mass production industries—have led to continuous increases in labor productivity. But however much these machines were improved, they still required workers to operate and control them. In some operations, the worker's function was little more than to feed the material in, set the machine in operation and remove the finished product. In others, proper control of the machine required the exercise of the highest conceivable skills. But whether the required skill was little or great, the presence of a human being, using human judgment, was essential to the operation of the machine.

The revolutionary change produced by automation is its tendency to displace the worker entirely from the direct operation of the machine, through the use of automatic control devices. No one, as far as I know, has yet produced a fully satisfactory definition of automation, but I think John Diebold came close to expressing its essential quality when he described automation as "the integration of machines with each other into fully automatic, and, in some cases, self-regulating systems."

In other words, automation is a technique by which whole batteries of machines, in some cases almost whole factories and offices, can be operated according to predetermined automatic controls. The raw material is automatically fed in, the machine automatically processes it, the product is automatically taken away, often to be fed automatically into still another machine that carries it automatically through a further process. In some cases the machine is self-regulating—that is, it is set to turn out a product within certain tolerances as to size or other factors, and if those tolerances are exceeded, the machine itself detects the variation and automatically adjusts itself to correct it.

The revolutionary implications of this new technology can best be understood by looking at a few examples of what is actually being done through automation today, in scattered parts of the economy.

The Lathe That Replaces Its Own Tools. The application of automation ranges all the way from individual automatic machines to virtually automatic factories.

An example of the first is an automatic lathe, produced by the Sundstrand Machine Tool Co., described in American Machinist, March 14, 1955, page 117, which gages each part as it is produced and automatically resets the cutting tools to compensate for tool wear. In addition, when the cutting tools have been worn down to a certain predetermined limit, the machine automatically replaces them with sharp tools. The parts are automatically loaded onto the machine and are automatically unloaded as they are finished. These lathes can be operated for 5 to 8 hours without attention, except for an occasional check to make sure that parts are being delivered to the loading mechanism.

An Automatic Plant. A completely automatic plant is now producing mixed and ready-to-use concrete for the Cleveland Builders Supply Co. (Business Week, Apr. 16, 1955, p. 80). Operated from an electronic control panel, the plant can produce and load into ready-mix trucks any one of some 1,500 different mixing formulas that may be demanded. This plant uses no manual labor at any point in the process.

By a combination of teletype and radio, the control operator is informed as to the particular formula to be loaded into each truck as it arrives. He gets out a punched card, coded for that formula, and the automatic mechanisms take over. Specified amounts of the required materials are delivered by conveyors, in precisely the right quantities, to a mixing bin where they are automatically mixed and then loaded into the waiting truck. The control mechanisms even measure and compensate for any deficiency or excess of water in the aggregate (sand, coarse rock, slag, etc.) which goes into the mixer, and if the order calls for a dry mix, the materials are automatically routed through a dry spout.

This automatic plant has a capacity of 200 cubic yards of concrete per hour, as against 100 cubic yards per hour in the company's conventional plants.

The Automatic Broaching Machine Cuts Direct Labor Costs Drastically. An automatic two-way horizontal broaching machine for machining automobile cylinder heads has cut direct labor costs between 1949 and 1954 by more than all the technological improvements made in this process during the previous 35 years—and with an actual decline in the investment required (Instruments & Automation, January 1955, p. 111).

In 1914 the Cincinnati Milling Machine Co. would have used 162 machines, representing an investment of $243,000, to machine 108 cylinder heads per hour at a direct labor cost of 40 cents per piece. By 1949 it took six machines, representing an investment of $240,000, to turn out the same volume of production at a direct labor cost of 20 cents per piece. (The saving in man-hour requirements is much greater than indicated by these figures, when the increase in wage rates between 1914 and 1949 is taken into account.)

By 1954, however, those six machines had been replaced by a single automatic machine, representing an investment of only $230,000, for the same volume of production, and direct labor costs had been cut from 20 cents a piece in 1949 to 4 cents a piece in 1954—a reduction of 80 percent in 5 years.

Merely Change the Tape to Change the Job Run. One of the important features of automation is that it can be applied not only to long runs of identical operations, but to fairly short-run jobs where instructions given to the machines have to be changed at the end of each job. This is made possible through the use of printed tape, punch cards, etc., on which the instructions are coded, and the machine is given a new set of instructions simply by changing the tape or card.

Minneapolis-Honeywell Regulator Co., for example, reports (Wall Street Journal, April 22, 1955) the development of a precision boring machine, used in aircraft equipment production, which can bore holes with an accuracy of one-thousandth of an inch. Electronic signals from a tape move the blank metal back or forward, rotate it into position, and then turn on the boring mechanism to cut the hole exactly where it is desired. The machine is specially suited for medium-size production in lots of several hundred parts.

Running a Bank with an Electronic Computer. The use of automation is not restricted to manufacturing plants. Increasingly, so-called electronic brains are taking over the functions of office clerks, accountants, and other white-collar workers.

Stanford Research Institute has produced for the Bank of America (*Fortune*, October 1955, p. 131) an electronic computer which will do the jobs of many employees. When a check comes to the bank, an operator merely punches into the machine the amount on the face of the check. The check itself carries a code, printed in magnetic ink, which identifies the account number. The machine scans this code to identify the account. It then refers to its "memory bank," which contains information on 32,000 separate accounts, makes sure there is enough in the account to meet the check (if there is not a warning "over-draft" light is blinked at the operator's desk), and deducts the amount of the withdrawal from the account. The machine also checks up to make sure that there is no stop-payment order against the account. The whole operation takes approximately 1 second.

The transaction is recorded, first in a "temporary memory" bank, and is transferred later to a "permanent memory" bank. At the end of the month, the computer automatically calculates the service charge and then, connected to a high-speed printer which can print 800 characters a second, it prints the customer's complete monthly statement in less than 5 seconds. It is claimed that 9 operators and 1 such machine can replace up to 50 bookkeepers.

Similar computers are being used to make up payrolls, to prepare insurance premium notices and record payments, to prepare telephone bills, to take inventory, to control the operation of electric power generating plants, and for many similar purposes. One central computer to be installed by the Ohio Edison Co., for example, will simultaneously control the operations of 35 generators in 9 plants scattered over an area of 9,000 square miles (*New York Times*, August 18, 1955).

Even automation itself is being automated. One of the bottlenecks in the use of computers to which data is punched cards has been the time required to have the information punched on the cards by trained operators. Now the Burroughs Corp. has produced for the First National City Bank of New York (*Wall Street Journal*, June 17, 1955) an electronic device which "reads" the serial numbers on travelers' checks and reproduces them on punched cards at a rate of 7,200 checks per hour, doing the work of 10 highly skilled operators.

The great variety of applications shown in these few examples illustrates one of the most significant features of the new technology—its wide applicability. That is the real quality that makes automation a genuinely revolutionary force in our economy, rather than just another technological improvement.

It is technically possible to apply the feedback principle of automation, and the servomechanisms which implement it, to virtually every situation where human control of industrial processes is now used. The growing flood of new uses of automation indicates how quickly the economics of its application are being worked out.

Even Routine Technology Is Accelerating. One of the factors which has been responsible for the steadily increasing rate of productivity since World War II has been the enormous increase in research expenditures both by industry and by Government. Alfred North Whitehead, the British philosopher, once said, "The greatest invention of the 19th century was the invention of the art of inventing." We might add that one of the great developments of the 20th century has been to change inventing from an art to a standard business procedure. The research department is now a fixture in every important corporation, while the needs of government, especially in national defense, have added to the numbers of research workers, many of whose discoveries are readily applied to industry.

As a result, the flow of what may be considered routine technological innovations—new production methods, new materials and machines applicable only to specific processes or industries, and improvements in work flow—has been greatly accelerated. Harlow Curtice, president of General Motors, noted recently that "new products, new processes are coming off the drawing boards of the engineers and out of the laboratories of the scientists at ever faster pace."

This great expansion of industrial research, and the flood of routine technological innovations it produces, have been sufficient, alone, in recent years, to boost the rate of rising productivity to the extent that past notions of what were normal productivity increases are already obsolete. Technological improvements of this sort, and on an increasing scale, can be expected to continue. By themselves, they would pose serious problems of adjusting our economy so as to provide sufficient purchasing power to absorb the steadily accelerating flow of goods which can be produced with every man-hour of labor.

"We Are Merely on the Threshold of the Technological Age." Beyond these routine technological improvements, however, we are now confronted with the potentially explosive impact of automation, and we can be sure that this new technology, too, will grow by leaps and bounds.

In discussing the rapid advances of technology, David Sarnoff, chairman of the Radio Corporation of America, stated in a pamphlet entitled "The Fabulous Future":

"The quantity of new powers and products and processes at man's disposal is important; but even more important is the increasing speed at which these things have come. It is not a case of continued increase but of continued acceleration of increase. We need only project the trend into the future to realize that we are merely on the threshold of the technological age."

Summing up the potential impact of the new technologies, Mr. Sarnoff says:

"The very fact that electronics and atomics are unfolding simultaneously is a portent of amazing changes ahead. Never before have two such mighty forces been unleashed at the same time. Together they are certain to dwarf the industrial revolutions brought about by steam and electricity."

Organized Labor Welcomes Automation. What is the attitude of the trade-union movement, and specifically of the CIO, to this new technology of automation?

First of all, we fully realize that the potential benefits of automation are great, if properly handled. If only a fraction of what technologists promise for the future is true, within a very few years automation can and should make possible a 4-day workweek, longer vacation periods, opportunities for earlier retirement, as well as a vast increase in our material standards of living.

At the same time, automation can bring freedom from the monotonous drudgery of many jobs in which the worker today is no more than a servant of the machine. It can free workers from routine, repetitious tasks which the new machines can be taught to do, and can give to the workers who toil at those tasks the opportunity of developing higher skills.

But We Cannot Sidestep Its Problems. But in looking ahead to the many benefits which automation can produce, we must not overlook or minimize the many problems which will inevitably arise in making the adjustment to the new technology—problems for individual workers and individual companies, problems for entire communities and regions, problems for the economy as a whole.

What should be done to help the worker who will be displaced from his job, or the worker who will find that his highly specialized skill has been taken over by a machine? What about the businessman who lacks sufficient capital to automate his plant, yet has to face the competition of firms whose resources enable them to build whole new automatic factories? Will automation mean the creation of whole new communities in some areas, while others are turned into ghost towns? How can we increase the market for goods and services sufficiently, and quickly enough, to match greatly accelerated increases in productivity?

Finding the answers to these questions, and many others like them, will not be an easy process, and certainly not an automatic one. Even if the greatest care is taken to foresee and meet these problems, adjustments for many people will prove difficult and even painful. If there is no care and no foresight, if we subscribe to the laissez-faire belief that "these things will work themselves out," untold harm can be done to millions of innocent people and to the whole structure of our economy and our free society.

The CIO insists that we must recognize these problems and face up to them. But our recognition that there will be problems, and serious problems, to be solved, does not mean that we are opposed to automation. We are not. We fully recognize the desirability, as well as the inevitability of technological progress. But we oppose those who would introduce automation blindly and irresponsibly, with no concern for any result except the achievement of the largest possible quick profit for themselves.

When the first industrial revolution took place, no effort was made to curb or control greedy, ruthless employers. Businessmen took advantage of unemployment to force workers to labor 12 and 14 hours a day for a pittance so small that not only wives, but children scarcely out of infancy, had to enter the factories to contribute their mite to the family earnings. The benefits which we today can so readily recognize as the fruits of the first industrial revolution were achieved only after decades of privation, misery, and ruthless exploitation for millions of working people.

Most of us find it difficult to believe that the second industrial revolution—the automation revolution—can possibly produce similar results. But if vast social dislocations are prevented this time it will be only because the combined social wisdom of private groups and government will be used to prevent them.

We now know that the greatest good of society is not served by permitting economic forces to operate blindly, regardless of consequences. We now know that economic forces are manmade and subject to controls, that the economic and social consequences of economic decisions can be foreseen, and when the consequences threaten to be harmful, preventive action can be taken. That philosophy is expressed, however imperfectly, in the Employment Act of 1946. We recognize today that it is not only possible, but necessary, for the Government to analyze, to foresee and to give direction to the economic forces that determine whether we shall have prosperity or depression.

Unfortunately, there are those who refuse to admit that automation poses any problems for individuals and for society as a whole. More unfortunately still, they are the very people who should be in the best position to foresee the difficulties that will have to be met, and in cooperation with Government and the trade unions, to take action to meet them. Their spokesman is the National Association of Manufacturers. Their attitude has been all too clearly expressed in a pamphlet issued by the NAM entitled "Calling All Jobs." This pamphlet recognizes, and indeed elaborates on, the parallel between the first industrial revolution which ushered in the machine age and the second industrial revolution which today is ushering in the age of automation. But with almost inconceivable blindness to the facts of history, the NAM completely disregards the misery and suffering that accompanied the introduction of the machine age, and dismisses all the protests of workers of that day as unfounded complaints.

The workers of 150 years ago who tried to smash the machines that had taken away their jobs had ample foundation for their complaints. They were wrong only in their methods. Their real complaint was not against the machines, but against the blindness of society which allowed the machines to be used as a means of ruthless exploitation.

Magic Carpet Economics Are Not Good Enough. We, in the labor movement today, have no complaint against the new technology of auto-mation. We do not intend to let ourselves be misrepresented as oppo-nents of automation. What we do oppose is the spirit of the NAM and those of like mind, whose views are expressed in the closing sentences of the pamphlet previously referred to:

"Guided by electronics, powered by atomic energy, geared to the smooth, effortless workings of automation, the magic carpet of our free economy heads for distant and undreamed of horizons. Just going along for the ride will be the biggest thrill on earth."

We do not believe that any thinking person is prepared to accept the NAM's magic-carpet theory of economics. Automation holds the promise of a future of new abundance, new leisure, and new freedoms, but before that future can be achieved there will be many serious and difficult problems to be solved. We do not believe that the American people or the Congress are prepared to just go along for the ride.

Many Problems Can Be Foreseen. Let us consider some of the specific problems that will have to be met. One of the major problems is that no one as yet has made a thorough study of what has been done in the field of automation, what is being planned for the near future, or what impact it has had or will have on our lives. As a result, an exhaustive list of the problems that automation will pose does not yet exist.

There are some problems, however, which can be foreseen. Obviously, there will be problems for the workers who are displaced from their jobs by automation. This is not merely a problem of finding a new job. One point on which most of the writers on automation seem agreed is that, by its very nature, automation will tend to eliminate unskilled and semi-skilled jobs, while the new jobs it creates will be at a much higher level of skill. As one spokesman for the Ford Motor Co. has put it: "The hand trucker of today replaced by a conveyor belt might become tomorrow's electronic engineer."

That sounds very nice, but it immediately poses the problem: How does the hand trucker become an electronics engineer—or a skilled tech-nician? If automation destroys unskilled jobs and creates skilled jobs, means must be found to train large numbers of unskilled workers in the needed skills.

Another aspect of the same problem is that of the worker with a special-ized skill who finds that his skill has been made valueless because a machine has taken over his job—such as the skilled machine operator displaced by a self-operating lathe or the bookkeeper whose job is taken over by an electronic "brain."

You can easily see that if automation is going to displace any substan-tial number of workers in either or these two ways, we will need a carefully organized retraining program to give them the opportunity of acquiring the skills they will need. Such a program must take into ac-count the needs of the workers, the fact that most of them will be mature men and women to whom the learning of new skills may not come easily, and that they have to live and support their families while they are acquiring these skills. The program will require not merely training facilities and expert vocational guidance. It will have to include provision for training allowances to replace lost wages during the training period.

Without such a program, there may be a job as an electronics engineer for the hand trucker's son, but the hand trucker himself may have to join the ranks of the unemployed—one of a "lost generation" of workers who will have been scrapped as ruthlessly as so many items of obsolete equipment.

"He Couldn't Keep Up." An alternative solution will have to be found in the case of older workers, not old enough for normal retirement, but too old to learn new skills or to adjust to the demands of the new technology. A single instance will be enough to point up the problem. This is from a report in the New York Post:

"Then there are workers who can't keep up with automation. Such as Stanley Tylak. Tylak, 61 and for 27 years a job setter at Ford, was shifted from the River Rouge foundry machine shop to the new automated engine plant. He was given a chance to work at a big new automatic machine.

"Simply, straightforwardly, he told his story: 'The machine had about 80 drills and 22 blocks going through. You had to watch all the time. Every few minutes you had to watch to see everything was all right. And the machines had so many lights and switches—about 90 lights. It sure is hard on your mind.

"If there's a break in the machine the whole line breaks down. But sometimes you make a little mistake, and it's no good for you, no good for the foreman, no good for the company, no good for the union.'"

"And so Stanley Tylak, baffled by the machine he couldn't keep up with, had to take another job—at lower pay."

This was a case where automation resulted in downgrading—not the upgrading so widely heralded by industry spokesmen as one of the fruits of automation. Yet in one sense Stanley Tylak was lucky. He at least was able to take another job. In many cases there will be no other jobs available for a man in his sixties or even younger. Perhaps if Stanley Tylak had been given more than just a chance to work at the new machine, perhaps if he had been given careful training for the job, taking into account the difficulties of adjustment to a new job at his age, he could have learned to do it even at 61. But for those older workers who cannot adjust, I think we must be prepared to offer the opportunity of early retirement with the assurance of an adequate pension.

In some of our collective bargaining agreements we have already laid the foundations for a system of early retirement which could help to meet such situations. But in the very nature of most private pension plans the problem cannot be solved through collective bargaining alone. Industrial pension plans are based on the assumption that the worker, when he retires, will also be eligible for social-security benefits. Much as we have improved the level of private pensions in recent years, a worker who is forced to retire before the age of 65 would find it impossible to maintain a decent standard of living on his industrial pension alone. I would strongly urge this committee to consider, in formulating its recommendations, the need for earlier social security payments to workers who are forced into retirement before the age of 65 because technological changes have taken their jobs from them and their age makes it impossible for them to find other work.

Community Dislocations. The growth of automated factories can create problems of dislocation not only for individual workers but for whole communities. It is often cheaper to build a new plant from the ground up, so that the whole design of the buildings can be related to the industrial processes, than to attempt to remodel an existing plant. In addition, corporations frequently seem to prefer to employ on automated processes workers who have had no experience with older methods. Thus an employer whose only concern is his own profit may decide that it is to his advantage to build a new plant in a new location, perhaps hundreds of miles away—without any consideration for the old community.

Automation is not the only technological change which may produce such shifts in industry. The large-scale conversion of atomic energy into electric power in quantities sufficient to supply the needs of industry is now an assured possibility which will become a reality within relatively few years. A more far-reaching possibility exists in the direct conversion of energy from the sun, which has already been developed to the point of successful use in applications requiring small amounts of power. Such developments can provide limitless new sources of power for industry, but they can also produce severe dislocations and shifts in the geographical distribution of industries.

Many of the large industrial centers in our country today owe their location to ease of access to coal or other power sources. With the advent of new power sources the advantages of such locations may disappear and large-scale movements of industry to new areas may well take place.

Let me make it clear that we are not opposed to such changes when they are based on sound economic and social considerations. Such changes are part of the long-run dynamic economic growth, upon which the advance of prosperity depends. But it would be foolish to deny that changes of this sort will produce their own problems.

Special assistance will be needed to prevent the spread of distressed communities and there will be innumerable questions to be answered. When important industries move out of town, for example, what can be done to replace them with others? Should workers be encouraged to move to a new community, and if so, what help will they need in relocating themselves? When the movement of industry means a sudden burst of expansion for some communities, or perhaps the creation of brand new towns and cities, what help will they need in the way of housing programs and the building of schools, hospitals, and other community facilities?

Even today, there are scores of distressed communities in our Nation, where hundreds of thousands of workers have been left stranded by shutdown plants, industry migration, closed coal mines, and curtailed operations of railroad repair shops. The impact of automation will possibly create additional pockets of substantial unemployment, even if high-employment levels are maintained nationally.

Government assistance is required to aid in solving the pressing problems of such communities at present; Government assistance has not yet been forthcoming, despite campaign promises that were made in the fall of 1952. Additional Government aid will be needed in the future, as the new technology becomes widespread.

These are existing problems that result from the accumulation of routine technological change. Are we going to permit their multiplication and aggravation during the period of the widespread introduction of automation?

Long-Run Mobility Is Not Good Enough. There is a tendency among management spokesmen, including some management-oriented economists, to dismiss these problems with the phrase "mobility of labor." Workers who are displaced from their jobs in one community, so the argument runs, will simply move to another community where workers are needed and jobs are plentiful. Some have even suggested that proposals like the guaranteed annual wage, or other measures designed to cushion the shock of readjustment, are harmful because they interfere with the mobility of labor.

As any study of real life situations, like Professor Miernyk's Inter-Industry Labor Mobility, will show, for a substantial proportion of workers no real mobility exists. Because of financial obligations, family responsibilities, strong community ties, or simply because they are too old to hope to find new jobs, they continue to cling to their home communities.

In the long run, of course, the labor market will show a high degree of mobility, because in a stranded community, the older workers will eventually give up the search for nonexistent jobs and retire from the labor market, and few younger workers will move in to take their place. But that concept of mobility represents merely the use of statistics to camouflage the reality of a myriad of individual tragedies.

Even to the extent that labor is mobile, we know that such mobility can be achieved only at a price—the cost of retraining, the cost of moving and rehousing, etc. Those who consider that all of management's responsibilities can be made to disappear by invoking the term "mobility of labor" take it for granted that working people should be prepared to bear all the risks and pay all the costs of economic changes which destroy their jobs. Such an attitude is both irrational and irresponsible. As Prof. Walter S. Buckingham of Georgia Institute of Technology has said:

"There is no reason why labor should be more mobile, flexible and willing to assume the enormous risks of economic dislocation than the other components of production—capital, management and natural resources—which are to varying degrees organized, concentrated and immobilized. Indeed sacrifices made by other factors of production in participating in a competitive market are ordinarily much less than those made by labor. . . . The worker has not his, or someone else's, money at stake, but his life, and his children's lives, on the auction block of the commercial market."

The Employer's Responsibility. Although most of the needed help will have to come from governmental agencies, we should also give serious thought to the responsibility of business itself in attempting to solve these problems.

I have said that we welcome dynamic growth in our economy, even while we recognize the problems that such growth may bring. But we must not permit business to excuse irresponsible actions with the claim that, "this is part of the process of dynamic growth." The shutting down of a plant, the displacement of thousands of workers, the dislocation of whole communities, cannot be justified simply because a corporation accountant can show that the potential profits to the corporation are greater than the direct costs reflected in the corporation's books.

In the program for a guaranteed annual wage, toward which the trade union movement has taken a long first step this year, one of our objectives has been to curb irresponsible action on the part of employers by requiring them to pay some of the social costs of policies which result in unemployment. In the same way, consideration should be given as to whether the costs of helping individual workers to adjust to the changes produced by automation should be borne by society as a whole, or whether some means should be sought to insure that the employers will bear a share of the burden.

For example, if the result of automation is that a large number of workers in a plant have to learn new skills, I believe it is just as reasonable to expect the employer to pay the cost of retraining, including the payment of wages during the retraining period, as it is that he should pay the cost of building the new plant or installing the new equipment. When a plant is moved to a new locality, I believe the employer has a responsibility, not merely to retrain those workers who wish to move with the plant, but also to bear at least part of their cost of moving and new housing. These are just as much costs arising out of the employer's business decision, as the business costs he now takes for granted.

This is primarily a matter for collective bargaining, but I feel the committee should be aware of it. In our experience with employers—and it has been considerable—the one sure way of making them socially responsible is to make them financially responsible for the social results of what they do or fail to do.

Automation and Educational Needs. The transition to the new technology will require a great expansion in our education system. As I have already noted, there seems to be general agreement that one of the results of automation will be a substantial raising of the level of skills required in automated factories and offices. That will require, in turn, a vastly improved program of vocational education to train young people in the new required skills, as well as to retrain the present working force for the responsibilities in automated operations.

I want to emphasize, however, that it is not enough to provide merely the physical facilities—the schools, the teachers, the teaching equipment. It is equally necessary that students should have the economic means to delay their entry into the labor market so as to pursue their studies and training. Even today there are far too many young people dropping out of school before they should, simply because they and their families are not in a position to make the financial sacrifices that would be involved in their continuing at school. We need a greatly expanded program of financial aid to students through scholarships, and as the level of skill required in the factories of tomorrow rises, that need will be greatly intensified.

With the spread of automation, there will be a growing need for specialized semiprofessional technicians, as well as for professional engineers and skilled workers. The education system of the Nation should be preparing now to meet these requirements.

I have made particular reference to the need for an improved program of vocational education because it ties in directly with the needs of automated factories and offices for workers with new skills. But we should not stop there. One of the benefits we should expect to gain from the great increases in productivity that automation makes possible is not only a reduction in hours of work—and I shall return to that subject in a few moments—but a reduction in the years of work. That reduction can be partly achieved by making it possible for more young people to continue their education in whatever field they choose and are fitted for. To meet the needs of our people, we require today far more teachers, doctors, nurses, and members of other professions than are now entering our schools to train for those professions.

We are dangerously short of engineers, especially at a time when in Russia the school system is being deliberately oriented toward the education of vast numbers of engineers as a necessary basis of further industrial expansion. Professional training apart, we should make it one of the major goals of our society that every young person will have not only the physical opportunity but the economic means to gain the fullest education of which he or she is capable.

Automation and the National Economy. So far I have been dealing primarily with the impact of automation on individuals and on local communities. But even more serious consideration must be given to its possible impact on the economy of the Nation as a whole.

From the viewpoint of the national economy, the greatest problem posed by automation is the threat of violent fluctuations in employment and production during the period of adjustment to the new technology. With the widespread introduction of automation speeding up the potential output of goods and services, there is the possibility that markets may not grow fast enough to sustain high employment levels.

I am not reassured by those who tell us that all will work out well in the long run because we have managed to live through radical technological changes in the past. Human beings do not live long enough for us to be satisfied with assurances about the long-run adaptation of society to automation. And while it is true that radical technological improvements have been introduced in the past, it is well to remember that they were accompanied by vast social dislocations, recurring depressions, and human suffering.

Most of us remember the depression of the 1930's only too well, when the American people paid a heavy price for the economy's failure to adjust to the introduction of mass production after World War I. We should now be thinking about and planning for the transition period—the next 10 years or so—when the spread of automation may result in dislocations of our society and in distress for countless individuals and communities.

Our economic needs will be rising in the years ahead. The population, it is expected, will increase from approximately 165 million at present to about 190 million 10 years from now. The number of households will rise from about 48 million now to an estimated 56 million in 1965. But the increase of economic needs does not mean that these needs will be filled automatically, adjust market demands to the rising output of goods and services, made possible by the new technology. We are compelled to rely, instead, on our own wisdom or lack of it, and upon our private and public policies.

If the national economy expands with sufficient rapidity in the coming decade or two, along with the widespread introduction of automation, the problems posed by the new technology will be minimized and localized. But economic expansion does not arise simply because we desire it. Economic growth is the product of expanding markets that make possible the profitable utilization and further expansion of productive capacity.

Even under normal conditions, the national economy is compelled to expand on a continuing basis if high levels of production and employment are to be maintained. In a year when the civilian labor force is some 62 to 64 million, as in the recent past, the economy is burdened with the responsibility of providing over 3 million new job opportunities, when productivity rises 4 percent and the labor force increases by some 700,000. In other words, we have to increase our purchases of goods and services by an amount equal to the output of over 3 million workers to absorb the increase in the labor force, as well as the displacement effect of rising productivity. The answer to such a burden is economic growth—a 5-percent expansion of the Nation's total output and consumption of goods and services, equal to the combined percentage increases in productivity and labor force.

It was substantial economic growth of that approximate magnitude—achieved through expanding markets—that gave us high levels of employment in much of the post-World War II period. But in 1949 and in 1953–54, we saw how easily our economy can be shoved off balance—when markets fail to expand fast enough to absorb the rising output of an increasingly efficient economy.

These problems of attempting to maintain high levels of employment in the recent past will probably appear small by comparison with those that will demand our attention in the period ahead. One of the great challenges of automation is that it continues present difficulties in much more serious form.

A. Philip Randolph

Civil Rights

There is no more significant movement in midcentury America than the struggle by the Negroes to achieve complete equality in every aspect of American life. In this effort, the name of A. Philip Randolph is prominent. Born in 1889 in Florida, Randolph organized the Brotherhood of Sleeping Car Porters, of which he became president. He is also a vice president of the AFL-CIO. It was Randolph who headed a march on Washington in 1941 which led to the establishment of the Fair Employment Practices Commission, and it was Randolph who guided the demands of the Negroes which culminated in the eradication of segregation in the armed services in 1948. During the 1950s, he directed three marches on Washington in support of school desegregation.

In August, 1963, 200,000 Negroes walked from the Washington monument to the Lincoln memorial in a mammoth one-day civil rights demonstration designed to put pressure on Congress to pass the pending Civil Rights Bill. It was the most widely publicized and effective element in the whole chain of acts in support of the Bill. On the day before the march, Randolph, who directed it, stated its purposes in a speech to the National Press Club in Washington. There is no better statement of the hopes and aspirations of the civil rights movement.

In periods of popular upheavals, tumult, fermentation, profound social change and the advancement of the frontiers of freedom, equality and human dignity can be made.

Out of the revolutionary struggle for independence came the Declaration of Independence, the Federal Constitution of the United States.

Then, in the middle of the nineteenth century, during the Jacksonian era, we had great ferment. Then the workingmen's parties appeared, the abolitionists' forces came into view, transcendentalism was the vogue among the intellectuals.

This was a time when the forces of creative literature were active, colleges came into existence, and the seeds of secessionism were sown.

Out of these periods of upheaval, profound change inevitably follows.

During the period around the Civil War, and as a result of the Civil War, the Proclamation of Emancipation was issued, slavery was abolished, and the Reconstruction democracy came into being.

And, of course, in 1890, we had the rise of Populism, the voice of the small farmers complaining against the railroads and the banks.

Then the Sherman Antitrust Law was enacted, the Interstate Commerce Commission was founded—in other words, out of these upheavals, profound and creative change has come.

During the period of the Wilson era we had the progress of organized labor, especially in the railroad area, and also the advancement of social legislation. Hundreds of thousands of people migrated north looking for work, especially Negroes.

And then followed the era of the New Deal, under Franklin Delano Roosevelt. Out of that era came the Wagner Labor Disputes Act, social-service legislation in the form of the Social Security Act, fair-employment-practice legislation.

Therefore, we are now in the era of the New Frontier, under President Kennedy. And there is tumult. We have social upheavals. There is fermentation. And there will be profound social change.

Now is the opportunity to advance the frontiers of freedom, the frontiers of human dignity, equality and social justice. This is the reason for the march-on-Washington movement and all of the demonstrations throughout the nation, in whatever form they take. This is the reason for the civil-rights revolution—a full-dress revolution.

In our pluralistic democratic society, causes must gain acceptance and approval and support. They can only gain acceptance, approval and support if they can get attention, and in order to get attention—with numerous causes seeking the focus of public opinion—it is necessary for dramatization to be developed of a given cause—especially in these times when you have Sputniks, when you have various struggles to reach the moon, when you have the science of space moving at an accelerated pace. Therefore, the march-on-Washington movement is designed to effect the dramatization of the civil-rights revolution.

The march-on-Washington movement will serve as a witness of commitment on the part of Negroes all over America, as well as our white brothers and sisters, in a great moral protest against racial bias.

The march-on-Washington movement will provide an opportunity for the ordinary man to have participation in a great demonstration for his own liberation, will give him a sense of his importance and responsibility to do something about the problem of abolishing racial bias.

Moreover, the march-on-Washington movement will bring into focus— world focus—the struggle of peoples of color in America for first-class citizenship. It will have the value of giving the peoples of the world some concept of this problem, because it will highlight the idea of the struggle of Negroes in America to achieve the transition from second-class citizenship to first-class citizenship, and it will serve to bring world pressure upon the United States of America to step up the struggle to wipe out race bias, because in the cold war—in the conflict of the free world with the totalitarian world—the free world is seeking the alliance of the Afro-Asian world, and, in order that the free world may win the alliance of the Afro-Asian world, the free world must show that we are not only making promises to Africa and promises to Asia to help them advance their cause, but we are going to keep our promises, fulfill our promises with our own citizens at home—especially Negroes of African descent.

Africa will not trust the United States in its promise to the peoples of Africa unless they realize and understand that the Negroes here in America are giving and evincing basic trust in the promises that have been made by our own country to them.

So, the march on Washington is an expression, a great step forward of the confrontation between the civil-rights revolution and our American society.

Why is it necessary to have the march on Washington? Why is it that we have the civil-rights revolution?

The reason for the existence of the civil-rights revolution is that Negroes are not yet fully free. Negroes are not free to secure the jobs they desire. The unemployment rate among Negroes is $2\frac{1}{2}$ times that among whites.

Young Negro teen-agers have greater difficulty in finding placement than any other group of teen-agers. It is estimated that 16 per cent of teen-agers are unemployed, and, if the same ratio between white and black teen-agers obtains as we have between the white unemployed and the black unemployed, then 40 percent of black teen-agers are unemployed. And not only are black teen-agers unemployed, but they're out of school. They have fallen out of school, dropped out of school. The reason for this is the inadequate income of the home—the inadequate income of the main earner—the main wage earner of the home.

As a matter of fact, the Negro home finds it necessary not only to permit the youngsters to go to work at an early age, but the wife, too, must help subsidize the inadequate income. The median average wage of the Negro wage earner is just a little over 50 per cent that of the white wage earner.

Consequently, the question of jobs is a major one, and the Negro struggle upward requires that they have the opportunity to go into the national job market and sell their labor on a basis of equality with other workers. But wherever there is racial bias, then you do not have a basically sound, free labor market. It is only free to workers who are not handicapped by any other unusual condition.

Then there is the problem of schools. Negroes are not free to attend the schools they desire. They are, as a rule, segregated in schools that are always situated in the slum areas. And they have not been able to have access to schools of higher learning in certain areas of the country—especially the South.

Then there is the matter of housing. It is utterly impossible to desegregate schools until housing is desegregated. Negroes, though they may possess the money, can't secure housing in areas that are desirable.

And, of course, there is voting. A hundred years after the issuance of the Proclamation of Emancipation, Negroes can't register and vote in certain areas of the country.

In addition to that, we have the problem of public accommodations. Negroes with their families who drive throughout the country find it impossible to secure adequate and proper public accommodations. They always meet up with intense humiliation or agony of soul, especially when their little children and their wives are with them and they are rebuffed and turned away. Youngsters want to know, "Why is this, father? Why is it you can't go into places other citizens are permitted to enter?" And consequently you have this intense humiliation on the part of Negro citizens in the nation.

This is why Negroes are insisting upon a broad public-accommodations act with no limitations whatsoever, but a broad public-accommodations act.

Now, why are not Negroes fully free? Well, Negroes are not fully free because the Civil War revolution was never fully completed. The Civil War revolution was responsible for the abolition of the Confederate governmental system. It was responsible for the emancipation of the slaves, but the Civil War revolution never transformed the former slaves into free workers.

Following the Civil War, the Confederate governmental apparatus was abolished. But no public-school system was established for the freedmen—no sound public-school system. Then, they never got free suffrage. When they were emancipated, they were turned out moneyless, landless, voteless and friendless—and, hence, the Civil War revolution, so far as the freedmen were concerned, was never fully developed.

And why was that? Well, the rising industrial and financial interests of the North, and the Republican forces, no longer had any interest in completing the revolution, because they had effected the centralization of political power in a strong federal system. They had effected the economic unification of the country when they saved the union.

The rising Northern industrial and financial interests were concerned about saving the union in order to maintain a national free market, and this was done. Following that, there was little concern about the freedman, although the freedmen had fought to the numbers of 200,000 for the triumph of the Union forces; and, without the service of the freedmen—the slaves in the armies of the Union forces—victory might not have come.

Abraham Lincoln seemed to have been conscious of that fact.

Now, we have also the problem following the Civil War of building up some kind of protection for the freedmen. The Thirteenth Amendment of 1865, the Fourteenth Amendment of 1868, the Fifteenth Amendment of 1870 were enacted. However, it was not long before the forces of a counterrevolution set in.

Now, Thaddeus Stevens in the House—the great commoner—Charles Sumner in the Senate fought vigorously for a congressional reconstruction program. They achieved one. A Freedmen's Bureau was established. But Andrew Johnson, the President, issued proclamations of amnesty, not only restoring citizenship to the Confederate men, the ex-slaveholding masters, but also gave them back their plantations. Of course, the plantations were the basis of slavery, and, if the plantations were not broken up, then the foundation for some re-enslavement of the freedmen still existed.

So the problem of developing a sound reconstruction program was carried out so long as Thaddeus Stevens lived and Charles Sumner was able to carry on. But when they passed away, the Reconstruction acts and the Thirteenth, Fourteenth and Fifteenth Amendments were nullified. Following the nullification of those acts, the civil-rights bill of 1875 was declared unconstitutional by the United States Supreme Court in 1883. Then, in 1896, the Plessy v. Ferguson decision was handed down, known for its "separate but equal" doctrine.

This constituted the foundation of segregation, and not only was segregation consolidated, but the Negro freedmen were gradually being driven back on the plantation, and they were being driven back as sharecroppers and tenant farmers and farm laborers under a debt system that practically reduced them to slaves.

The Ku Klux Klan arose. Terror spread out through the nation, and Negroes were driven from the ballot box by the shotgun, and hence they were undoubtedly, practically reduced to a condition not much different from that of a slave before the Civil War took place. And around that time the movements for civil rights began to stir.

W. E. Burghardt Du Bois, the great scholar, with Oswald Garrison Villard and Mary White Ovington—dedicated white liberals—got together and started the National Association for the Advancement of Colored People. The National Association for the Advancement of Colored People went into the courts and successfully carried on a campaign that resulted in declaring racial discrimination illegal as a general thing in various areas of the nation.

However, the problem became increasingly acute and lynching began to spread, mob action was general throughout the nation, designed to break the spirit of the freedmen. Thus we have come now to this period, when the work of the National Association for the Advancement of Colored People is being supplemented by new civil-rights organizations.

Dr. Martin Luther King, in his Southern Christian Leadership Conference; the Non-Violent Coordinating Committee of Students in the South; the Congress of Racial Equality, and the National Urban League—these organizations are carrying the banner in the interest of the creation of first-class citizenship to peoples of color in the country at this time.

They are making headway, but the problems ahead are still grave, and hence we see manifestations in the form of demonstrations spreading all over the nation.

We have all sorts of demonstrations. And, of course, some of our friends are a bit concerned about this. But let me tell you that demonstrations are the hallmark of every revolution since the birth of civilization. As a matter of fact, you had demonstrations during the days of Jesus Christ, when he was building the Christian movement.

These are the outbursts, these are the manifestations of deep convictions about the evils that people suffer. While they sometimes take the form of some irrational upsurge of emotionalism, they come from the fact that the peoples are the victims of long-accumulated wrongs and deprivations. Therefore, these are an outburst and an outcry for justice, for freedom. And there is no way—there is no way to stem these demonstrations until the cause is removed, and the cause is racial bias, the cause is exploitation and oppression, the cause is a second-class citizen in a first-class nation. This is the reason for the march-on-Washington movement. This is the reason for the civil-rights revolution.

A revolution seeks to bring about a complete overturn, so far as the peoples involved are concerned, with their relation to the community.

The civil-rights revolution is not trying to tear down a democratic Government, it is not trying to overthrow the Government, because a civil-rights revolution is a bourgeois revolution. It is concerned about what it says—civil rights—and civil rights certainly will not upset our economic structure, not by any means.

However, Negroes want the same things that white citizens possess—all their rights. They want no reservations. They want complete equality—social, economic and political—and no force under the sun can stem and block and stop this civil-rights revolution which is now under way. It will have a tremendously creative influence in American life.

As a matter of fact, its value now is quite evident in the fact that it is bringing together our white brothers in the church, in the labor movement, where black and white workers and black and white Christians, black and white Jews—we march together. What for? For evidence and witness of our commitment to the great ideal of human dignity.

In other words, this is the doctrine and the philosophy of the Judaeo-Christian tradition, the doctrine that every human being has worth, every individual has value, and he has value because he is a son and one of the children of God.

If we're all children of God, then we're all equal. If we're all equal, then we're all entitled to equal treatment. And if we're all entitled to equal treatment, race bias is a sin. It's a sin against God, and it's a sin against man.

Therefore, we are seeking to implement our human rights. Civil rights represent forces that are designed to implement human rights. We already possess our human rights. Why? Because we are human. And no individual and no State has the right to take from me my life, my liberty, and my right to the pursuit of happiness. These are natural rights. These are rights I was born with. But individuals and States may intervene and prevent one from exercising and enjoying his human rights.

This is the reason, then, for this great struggle for civil-rights legislation, because civil-rights legislation will serve as the implementation of our human rights.

In conclusion, may I say that the march-on-Washington movement, which is just a day or so away, will represent one of America's great human experiences.

We do not expect that there is going to be any violence. As a matter of fact, we have taken the utmost precautions to prevent any eruptions of violence.

Of course, I wouldn't stand up here and tell you that I know nothing is going to occur. People are human beings, and human beings are fallible. But we have provided all of the discipline measures. We have, for instance, 2,000 guardians, disciplined Negro policemen of New York who are paying their own way to Washington for the purpose of helping to maintain a peaceful and orderly demonstration.

We have had demonstrations before. We have had marches before. We had a march on Washington for integrated schools in 1957. We had one in 1958. Then we had a prayer pilgrimage here in 1959. There wasn't any trouble. There was no incident, no eruptions of conflict or anything of that sort. And, consequently, we know the organizations and the places from which the people are coming. They're coming from the churches. They're coming from the fraternal societies. They're coming from the labor unions. They're coming from various civic organizations. Certainly they are not coming here to provoke or develop any conditions that would discredit their own movement, because we are primarily concerned about the building of free life for the Negroes in a free society, in our American free society.

It is our purpose to have the march exercise influence in the interest of the enactment of the package of proposals for civil rights that President Kennedy has presented to the Congress.

In addition to the proposals of President Kennedy, we have some proposals of our own. We want to stress, for instance, a federal law for fair-employment practice. This law has already been developed—that is, the bill has been developed—in the Committee on Education and Labor under the leadership of Congressmen Powell [Adam Clayton Powell, of New York] and James Roosevelt [of California] and it is our hope that this bill may be enacted into law, because it is fundamental.

Now we had, for instance, a march proposed in 1941, and I recall when President Roosevelt told me—he said: "Now, Phil Randolph, Phil, what do you want me to do?"

I said: "Well, we want you to do something that will enable Negro workers to go into the defense plants and work. They are being turned away from the plants. Yet they are supposed to go abroad and fight in order to carry on the program of the nation, the foreign policies of the nation. Why can't they work?"

And he said: "Why, surely I want them to work, too, and I'll call up the heads of the various departments and have them see to it that Negroes are given the same opportunity to work in the defense plants as any other citizen in the country."

And I said: "Well, Mr. President, we want you to do more than calling up the heads of these departments. We want something concrete. We want something that is tangible, definite and positive, affirmative."

He said: "What do you mean?"

I said: "We want you to issue an executive order making it mandatory that Negroes be permitted to work in the defense plants."

And he said: "Well, now, I can't do that, because if I issue an executive order in this instance, I will be beset by groups from time to time to issue comparable executive orders." And he said: "However, now, Phil, I want you to call off this march."

I said: "Well now, Mr. President, I can't call off this march unless you issue an executive order."

He said: "Well, Stimson"—Henry L. Stimson [Secretary of War] was there; he had a full-dress Cabinet meeting—he said: "I want you to take this group into one of my rooms and see what can be done to bring about a solution of this problem."

That was done. However, they wanted to follow the line of the President—that is, not issue an executive order or anything of that sort, but to use a hortatory system of calling up people and trying to get them to agree to carry out a certain policy.

Mayor La Guardia [of New York City] was in it, and he said to the group—he said: "Well, now, let us not waste any time. Suppose we have a committee of about five, and have that committee sit down and work out something that is going to be effective in meeting this grave question." Mayor La Guardia—whom I knew very well, and who wanted to do whatever he could do in order to meet this issue—said: "Now, let me tell you, friends, you are not going to get Phil Randolph to call off this march unless an executive order is written and signed by President Roosevelt."

In the next day or two such an order was written, and it was signed by the President. That executive order helped to get Negroes in jobs they had never entered before. It was a landmark, it was historic. I talked to the President following the issuance of that executive order, and he told me that he was proud that the order was issued during his Administration.

So now, today, President Kennedy certainly has displayed a very fine and fundamental and constructive interest in this whole civil-rights struggle, and has presented this package of proposals to the Congress. But, in addition to presenting the package of proposals to the Congress, these proposals have got to be enacted into law. And after they are enacted into law, they've got to be implemented.

Therefore, these proposals perhaps never would have been presented to the Congress had it not been for the demonstrations in Birmingham, Ala., the demonstrations throughout the nation, because there was no intention on the part of the President to issue a package of proposals such as he did, and present them to the Congress.

Just as demonstrations were responsible for the presentation of these proposals to Congress for civil-rights legislation, demonstrations are necessary in order to see to it that these proposals are enacted into law.

Not only that: In order that we might be able to mold a better social and moral order in our nation, whereby all of the forces of racism may be eliminated, and that people will recognize that there is no such thing as inferior beings and superior beings—that all people are equal fundamentally and that all people have comparable capacities for achievement.

A black boy on the banks of the Congo is just the same as a baby in Buckingham Palace—no basic difference. Both are children of God, and both are human beings, and both are entitled to all of the privileges and rights enjoyed by any other human being.

Thus, let me say: May I hope that the day is not far distant when all forms of race bias will be banished from our land, and may God grant that we may have the courage and the will and the strength to move forward on the basis of the unity of the human family and the dignity of the personality of every individual regardless or race, creed, color, national origin or ancestry.